Writer's INC

Written and Compiled by

Patrick Sebranek, *Former English Chairman, Union High School,*
Union Grove, Wisconsin
Verne Meyer, *Associate Professor, Dordt College,*
Sioux Center, Iowa
Dave Kemper, *Parkview Junior High, Mukwonago, Wisconsin*

Illustrated by **Chris Krenzke**

WRITE SOURCE EDUCATIONAL PUBLISHING HOUSE
Box J, Burlington, WI 53105

Acknowledgments

Writers INC is a reality because of the help, advice, and understanding given by our families: Judy, Julie, and Janae; Gidge, Nathaniel, and Benjamin; Yvonne, Todd, and Tim; Lois and Katie. Also, several of our students allowed us to use their papers as samples in the handbook: Monica, John, Ann, Kris, Lisa, Amy, Lynn, and Susie.

We are especially grateful for the help and advice of a number of people, among them Lois Krenzke, Sherry Gordon, and Mary Anne Hoff. And a special thank you as well to the rest of the crew at the Write Source: John, Jane, Ellen, Judy, and Myrna.

Carl Vandermuelen, best known for his *Photography for Student Publications*, contributed to "The News Story" section. The sections on poetry, the short story, and thinking were written by Randall VanderMey.

Contributing Editor, Randall VanderMey,
Iowa State University

2nd Edition   **2nd Printing**
ISBN 0-939045-48-6 (Soft Cover)   ISBN 0-939045-49-4 (Hard Cover)

(For additional information or to place an order, write to The Write Source, Box J, Burlington, WI 53105, or call 1-800-445-8613.)

Using the Handbook

Your **Writers INC** emphasizes writing, a challenge for individuals of all ages. But, the handbook does not stop with writing. It is also a handy reference book that provides information on reading techniques, vocabulary building, study skills, note taking, using the library, speech skills, and thinking skills. In addition, the **Appendix** at the back of the book provides many extras like eight full-color maps, a table of decimal equivalents of common fractions, the traffic signs, the periodic table of the elements, and a copy of the Constitution of the United States.

The **Table of Contents** near the front of the handbook gives you a list of the major sections and the chapters found under those sections. It also tells you the page number on which each unit begins.

The **Index** at the back of *Writers INC* is one of its most useful parts. It is arranged in alphabetical order and includes every specific topic discussed in the handbook. The numbers after each word in the index are **topic numbers**, not page numbers. (The topic numbers are the numbers which appear to the left of each new topic in the handbook.) Since there are often many topics on one page, these topic numbers will help you find information more quickly.

Using Topic Numbers: Let's say, for example, you were asked to find information on *collective nouns.* If the index listed only page numbers, you would be directed to page 294. Go to page 294 and look for information on collective nouns. Did it take you a while to find it?

Now look at the sample index to the right and locate *collective nouns.* In addition to topic number 844 (which you found on page 294), you will also find a second topic number listed. Go to that number and locate this additional information. Was it easier and quicker this time? It should have been. That is the advantage of using topic numbers in an index rather than page numbers. It saves time.

Look through your handbook and notice the wide variety of material. Notice in particular the material which will be most useful to you. Like a dictionary, thesaurus, or any other reference book, *Writers INC* won't do you much good sitting on a bookshelf or lining the bottom of your locker. You must take the time to become familiar with it. If you do, you will find a number of explanations and guidelines which will help you improve your reading, writing, speaking, and study skills. Knowing how to use your handbook effectively will put you at a distinct advantage for years to come.

Table of
Contents

Reading & Learning

Speaking & Thinking

Final Re-Marks

Appendix

Personal Writing

Finding the Writer Within

Why We WRITE

I was going to be a father, and I wasn't so sure I was ready to become one. I liked my peaceful house. I liked my independence. I liked living free and easy. Being a father meant settling down, being responsible, being a role model. Me. Who changed jobs every three years. Me. Who hated yard work. I had this vision of my wife and me with the kids in the family station wagon off to visit Grandma. Strictly middle-aged stuff. No, I wasn't so sure that I was ready to be a father.

Then one day I wrote an autobiographical piece. I started my story in a bomb shelter . . . not literally, but that is where my parents would often meet in London during World War II air raids. I thought beginning in this way would surely draw a reader into my autobiography, and I was going to make my story a clever one.

The more I wrote, however, the more I was drawn to the ordinary things about my life. I began to recall life in our household when my sister and I were young. We weren't rich, but we always had good food and lots of it. We had nice clothes. We had our own rooms. We were secure.

And then it struck me. It was my turn to provide for someone else, and I owed it to my parents. It was my way of saying, "Look, Mom and Dad, I'm going to make sure that what you did for me won't be forgotten. I'm going to provide as best I can for my own child, someone who is a little bit of you."

What a wonderful way to thank them and their parents, and their parents before that. My child would be a gift to all of them. I probably would have realized this soon after my son was born. But making this discovery when I did gave new meaning to becoming a father.

Writing does that. It helps you make meaning out of your experiences. You may not always like what you discover when you write, but, if you give writing an honest chance, it will help you to better understand *you* and the people you care for. What could be more important than that? ***Maybe that's why we write.***

Wouldn't it be nice if each of your writing assignments meant something to you personally . . . if each one helped you make meaning out of your life and your experiences? But you know that is not the case. You are often asked to summarize facts, recall and interpret information, and explore topics in research papers. These assignments are important for obvious academic reasons. Yet they seldom get at your heartbeat—what makes you who you are, and you have little personal control over them. They are assigned, and you must deal with them as best you can.

There is a type of writing that you can control, a type of writing that will help you explore your cares and concerns. This writing (for lack of a better term) is called personal writing. All it takes is a commitment on your part, a notebook (journal) reserved for writing, and a ready supply of your favorite pens and pencils. Nothing more.

Write every day, preferably at a set time. Some writers do their personal writing early in the morning when they are fresh and alert. Others like to record their thoughts at the end of the day. Write when and where it feels comfortable for you— during your study hall, while taking a bath, or on the beach. The important thing is to get into a writing routine and stick to it.

Think of writing as a skill. You set aside time to improve your musical or athletic skills; do the same with writing. Exercise your mind as well as your body. Keep "sharp" as well as "in shape." Write nonstop for at least 10 minutes at a time. Explore your thoughts, your impressions, and your experiences. Don't worry about how your writing sounds or how it looks. You are writing for no one except yourself.

Meaning will come if you make an honest effort. If you stick to it, you'll enter the world of your inner thoughts and impressions; and in time, you'll feel a little different, a little sharper, as if your senses have been fine-tuned. A squeaky closet door will no longer go unnoticed. You'll begin to wonder how long it has been squeaky, why no one has fixed it, and what else is "squeaky" in your life.

But just writing a few emotional lines about an experience won't help you develop as a thinker or writer. If, for example, a friend treats you differently as soon as another person shows up, by all means express your displeasure, but don't dwell on this annoying action in your writing. Dig deeper. See if you can discover something meaningful about your friend, about your place among your friends, about friendship in general, or even about the fickle nature of people.

Writing is a lot like running or other forms of exercise. It is sometimes hard to get started, but once you do, you feel much better for it. If nothing personal moves you to write, pick up on the actions of a family member, on something you have read in the newspaper, or on anything that catches your eye. But please don't say that you have nothing to write about. There is always something to write about if you just get at it.

Once you get into personal writing, you'll soon realize that your experiences and thoughts are no more than points of departure. As you write, you will bend, stretch, and turn these initial ideas inside out and see them in new ways. You'll become more reflective; you'll want to think, wonder, and even write, before you react. This might sound like heady stuff, but it really isn't. Personal writing is simply an effective way to help you understand and marvel at your world.

Whenever you get into a writing rut, try something different. If you've been writing in the park, and it's not working anymore, try the far corner of the student cafeteria, your favorite hangout, a study hall, etc. Try writing with someone else, occasionally sharing ideas. Then keep writing. Also, vary the type of writing you are doing. Try listing, clustering, unfocused dialogues, or any other technique useful for generating and developing writing ideas.

Don't expect your personal writing to consist of an unlimited series of profound thoughts. Your mind does not work that way. Instead, you will discover hidden among all of the words you write a few interesting or revealing ideas—ideas that clarify something for you or pique your curiosity. As you review your personal writing, underline these ideas so that you don't forget them. And, by all means, keep writing, learning, and thinking about them. (*Note:* The best ideas in your personal writing will serve as a valuable resource of topics and details for school-related writing assignments.)

If you stick with it (and it won't take long), you will eventually feel the need to "go public" with some of your ideas. That is, you will feel the need to share some of the discoveries you have made. You might pick someone you trust and simply share with this person some of your raw personal writing. Or, you might develop the ideas you really like into more polished writing: personal narratives, poems, plays, letters, dialogues, etc. Write and rewrite until you feel you are ready to step out into the world with your very own ideas. What an exciting, yet scary undertaking! Write long enough and honestly enough, and it will happen.

Personal writing benefits you in more ways than one. Its main benefit, as you now know, is to help you make meaning out of your experiences. It also helps you gain confidence in your ability to write in general. If the only writing you do is the assigned writing in school, you can't expect to write as well as those people who regularly practice. No professional writers automatically start writing well. They have spent years sharpening this skill, and they are published because they are willing to practice and continue practicing.

Take charge. Start writing and learning; learn about yourself and the world around you. This, in turn, will help you prepare for your assigned writing. Your handbook will offer you valuable advice about developing your personal and academic writing.

"All glory comes from daring to begin."

– Eugene F. Ware

The Writing Process

"*Writing is mind traveling, destination unknown.*"

Read the bold statement above, read it again, repeat it after every meal, have it tattooed on your arm. And by all means remember it as you work on your writing assignments. Let this statement be a constant reminder that when you write, you are often engaged in uncharted thinking, mind traveling, so to speak, in which you stumble upon old memories, face realities of the present, and confront hidden thoughts and feelings about what is yet to be. You won't necessarily know where your writing will take you, at least not at the beginning. Your destination will only become clear as you travel further and further into your writing and make new discoveries and uncover new ideas.

This is why writing may frighten some of you. You feel you must know "where" you are going before you start your journey. That is, you feel your route must be mapped out before you travel, so that you don't wander off course and end up lost. But writing rarely works that way. Instead, most writing works best when it is the product of a detour, an unexpected thought burst, an ordinary idea gone haywire.

And this is how writing works best for all writers—even professionals. Do you think writers like Robert Frost or James Baldwin knew what they were going to say before they started a poem or novel? No. They began each work with a general idea in mind and started writing (searching, experimenting, playing) to see what would develop. They realized that somewhere in their journey a "destination" would appear, perhaps faintly at first, and that eventually a clearer focus and form would emerge. In other words, they fully realized that they must do some mind traveling if they hoped to discover something worth writing about.

> "*For me the initial delight is in the surprise of remembering something I didn't know I knew. . . . I have never started a poem yet whose end I knew. Writing a poem is a discovery.*"
>
> – **Robert Frost**

> *"You go into a book and you're in the dark, really. You go in with a certain fear and trembling. You know one thing. You know you will not be the same person when this voyage is over. But you don't know what's going to happen to you between getting on the boat and stepping off."*
>
> **– James Baldwin**

Remember: **Writing is mind traveling, destination unknown.** Make it your writing motto. Join mind travelers like Frost and Baldwin, and "step into" the writing process with the same sense of excitement and anticipation.

Understanding the Process

002   The writing process begins long before you actually put pen or pencil to paper. In fact, the writing process begins the day you think your first thought and never really stops. You are subconsciously involved in the writing process every day of your life. Each of life's experiences becomes part of what you know, what you think, and what you have to say. Your mind is a storehouse for these past experiences, as well as a creative processor for your thoughts of today and tomorrow. Writing is the process of getting those thoughts and experiences down on paper at the right time and place so that you can share them with others.

The four steps in the writing process discussed in your handbook address different segments of "mind traveling." **Prewriting** helps you search for potential starting points, experiment with them, and eventually focus on one idea for writing. **Writing the First Draft** helps you see what a particular idea has to offer. **Revising** helps you clarify and polish what it is you have discovered on your journey. **Editing** is the final stage where your writing is fine-tuned (proofread and inked) and made ready to share.

> *"A writer is not so much someone who has something to say as he is someone who has found a process that will bring about new things he would not have thought of if he had not started to say them."*
>
> **– William Stafford**

003   **Setting the Stage:**   You must understand several things about the writing process before you use this section to help you with your writing.

1. All four steps in the writing process require some type of writing. *Prewriting, revising,* and *editing* are as much writing activities as the actual composing of the first draft.

2. Writing is a backward as well as a forward activity, so don't expect to move neatly and efficiently through the steps in the writing process. In actual practice, you will often backtrack and sidestep as you write. Mind traveling by its very nature includes detours, wrong turns, and dead ends.

3. It is unlikely that you will approach any two writing assignments in the same way. For one composition, you might struggle with finding a writing subject. For another composition, you might have trouble finding a point of departure. For still another, you might be ready to write your first draft with very little prewriting or planning.

4. No two writers develop their writing in the same way. Some writers work more in their heads while others work more on paper. Some writers need to talk about their writing early on while others would rather keep their ideas to themselves. Some writers need to step away from their writing at times to let their thoughts incubate. Other writers can't stop until they produce at least a first draft. Your own writing personality will develop as you write more and more.

5. All the suggestions and guidelines offered in this section won't necessarily make you a better writer unless you practice writing. You wouldn't expect to play the piano well just by reading about it—you must practice. The same holds true for writing. Practice often and experiment with different forms of writing—journals, jokes, short stories, poems, plays, free writings, letters, songs, ads, cartoons, bumper stickers. . . . (See "Personal Writing," 001, for helpful guidelines.)

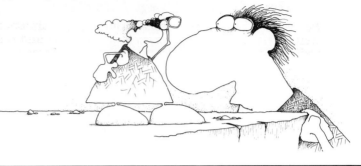

Prewriting

004   Your first conscious step into the writing process is called **prewriting.** It begins when you decide to write or when you are given a writing assignment. Let's say, for example, that your English teacher assigns a personal essay, and her only advice is that you write about someone or something you know from firsthand experience. Your initial prewriting task is to come up with a worthwhile idea to explore and develop. And if you already know what you would like to write about, you will next need to find an interesting way to approach your topic—head-on, sideways, or upside down.

Searching for a Subject

005   If you have done any personal or journal writing, review your entries for possible writing ideas. You should at least be able to find a general idea that could serve as a point of departure in your search for a specific writing subject. Suppose you are attracted to a particular line in a personal writing: *". . . and Ms. Judge just doesn't understand me,"* a reference to a teacher. You might use this line, a line which reminds you of several firsthand experiences, to begin your topic search:

1. You could start by free writing with this line as the initial focus of the writing.

2. You could try clustering with Ms. Judge as the center or nucleus of your cluster.

3. You could create an imaginary dialogue between Ms. Judge and yourself (or some other person).

4. Or you could talk (brainstorm) with friends, classmates, or family members about your relationship with her. Discover what they know or would like to know about this relationship.

Note: See "Free Writing," 035, and "Guidelines for Selecting a Subject," 031, for an explanation of activities for finding and expanding a topic.

Starting from Scratch: If you have no ideas to get you going, start your subject search by thinking of something that happened earlier that day, or yesterday, or last week. Maybe you've found an old photograph or favorite T-shirt. Or maybe you've come across someone you haven't seen for a while, or you've witnessed something that reminded you of another personal experience. All you're looking for is a spark, a nudge, a prompt to get you writing. Once you find that spark, then try free writing, clustering, or another prewriting activity. (See the "Sample Writing Topics," 034, for a list of ideas that might help you get started.)

Suppose you began free writing with "... and Ms. Judge just doesn't understand me" as your starting point. And also suppose that for some reason you dismiss her early in your writing and begin addressing a number of people who do understand you. (Ideas that don't deal directly with your first idea will often come up in free writing.) This turnabout in your free writing could lead you to a whole new set of experiences to explore.

Taking It One Step Further

> *"Bring ideas in and entertain them royally, for one of them may be the king."*
>
> *– Mark Van Doren*

006   Each new idea you have may indeed be the *king*. Let's say you develop an imaginary dialogue between two people who surfaced in your free writing, and their conversation turns into an argument about your strengths and weaknesses. This new idea should be entertained "royally" for if it is developed further, it could serve as the basis—the *king*— of a lively, personal essay. Or this dialogue might help you turn up a number of other interesting questions.

Where do I fall short?
Where do I excel?
Who am I like?
Where do I fit in?
Who knows me best?

Any of these questions could become the subject of a personal essay. Or they could lead to more prewriting if you have the time and inclination to do more. The point is that **if you give prewriting a chance—if you allow your mind to travel freely—you will discover something new and unexpected, something worth writing about.**

Still not sure? The writing process allows for mistakes and misstarts. If after working with a certain writing idea, you lose your enthusiasm for it, drop it and look for a new one. Nothing can be more tedious than writing a paper about a subject that doesn't interest you.

Searching for Specifics

007   Many of the same techniques you used to find a writing idea can be used to learn more about your subject. Free writing and clustering are again good starting points. Peter Elbow, a noted writer on writing, suggests that you approach free writing at this point as if it were an "instant version" of the finished product. This will give you a good feel for your subject. You might also experiment with activities such as cubing or offbeat questions to explore your subject. (See "Guidelines for Searching and Shaping a Subject," 033, for an explanation of these activities and others that will help you learn more about a subject.)

Note: For most academic writing (unless you are writing a strictly personal or creative piece), you will need to do some form of research. When you do gather facts and details from the experts, use their ideas to reinforce or reconsider your own thinking. Don't simply summarize what they have already said about your subject.

Taking Inventory of Your Thoughts

"I learn by going where I have to go."

– Theodore Roethke

008   Let's say you still don't feel comfortable with your subject after considerable prewriting. That is, you've done some searching and you've discovered some interesting things about your writing idea, but you still don't feel ready to write a first draft. This may be a good time to see how well you and your topic match up to the situation, audience, and other guidelines for this assignment. After carefully considering the questions which follow, you should be able to decide whether to move ahead or look for another approach— or even another topic.

Situation: Why am I writing? What are the specific requirements of this assignment?
Do I have enough time and material to do a good job with this topic? this approach?

Self: How committed am I to my writing subject?
Is it worth spending additional time on?
What can I learn/gain from continuing to write on this topic?

Subject: How much do I now know about this subject?
Is there additional information available?
Have I tried more than one of the searching activities?
Do I have a clear focus in mind?

Audience: Who is my "true" audience and what kind of response do I want from them?
How much do they care or already know about this subject?
How can I get my audience interested in my ideas?

Style: In what form could I present my ideas: story, essay, poem, personal narrative, parody, interview?
Can I think of an especially interesting way to lead into my paper?
What style/approach best fits me, my audience, my subject, and my situation?

Focusing Your Efforts

009   Sooner or later you will feel the urge to say to your readers exactly what you think and what you alone are best suited to say about a particular subject. This should be your focus. A focus is a meaningful and interesting way to write about your subject, one that hopefully develops from your prewriting.

Suppose you choose one of the questions you generated in an imaginary dialogue— *Where do I fall short?*—to develop in your essay. To find a focus, determine what is out of bounds and what is in bounds for you. For example, deciding on one or more areas in which you do fall short is obviously an issue that is in bounds. After studying this question and reviewing your prewriting, let's say you decide to address your unpredictable mood swings in your essay. And you also decide that you can't address this shortcoming without including your parents since they are the ones who are mainly affected by your emotions. Fine. You've drawn a circle around your subject and identified a potential focus for your writing.

> *"The two most engaging powers of an author are to make new things familiar and familiar things new."*
>
> **– Dr. Samuel Johnson**

In order to clarify your thinking, state your focus in a sentence that you feel effectively expresses what you want to explore in your essay. Write as many versions as it takes to come up with a sentence that establishes the right tone and direction for your writing. Let's assume you feel most comfortable with the following focus statement: "My parents know full well that my emotions can spin out of control."

Note: A focus statement is often called a **thesis statement** in a more formal composition. It is also similar to a **topic sentence** which is the controlling idea of a paragraph. (See 091.)

Testing the Waters: With a clear focus in mind, you might decide it's time to develop your first draft. Keep your focus statement in view when you write. If the direction or focus of your writing changes somewhat as it unfolds, you can either change with it or get back in line with your original thinking. Or, rather than diving headlong into a complete version, you may decide to get just your feet wet and write only the opening section or paragraph (see guidelines below). If you are able to write this opening with little trouble, perhaps you are ready to go on; if not, continue gathering information and planning until you feel ready to write your first draft.

Writing an Opening or Lead Paragraph

010   Writing your opening or lead paragraph should further clarify your thinking on your writing subject, and it should set a number of things in motion: It should 1) point the way into your essay, 2) spark your readers' interest as well as reveal who you expect your readers to be, 3) commit you to a certain language, and 4) establish a frame or form for your writing. The lead paragraph is one of the most important elements of each composition you write. Several possible angles or starting points are listed below.

You might

- *begin with a funny story to set a humorous tone.*
- *challenge or puzzle your readers with an unanswerable question.*
- *open with a thought-provoking and fitting quotation.*
- *offer a little "sip" of the conclusion and pique your readers' curiosity.*
- *list all your main points and treat your subject in a very serious, straightforward manner.*
- *describe your latest dream and relate it to the stark reality of your writing topic.*
- *come up with an angle that none of your readers have seen before.*

Whichever angle you use, it should be clear that the direction, tone, and your own personal style will be affected. This is why your opening, your angle, is so important.

011   **Sample Opening Paragraph:** The paragraph which follows could be used to open an essay on being a temperamental teenager. It begins with a question and quickly turns into a personal confession. You will note that the overall theme or focus of the essay has been implied rather than directly stated, and an entertaining tone has been established.

> *How do you handle a no-good, two-faced rat? Someone who snaps at her parents when they try to console her. Someone who will snarl just as loud if they don't give her the attention she wants when things aren't going so well. Just ask my parents. They've had plenty of practice . . . they've had to deal with me.*

If you have been successful in writing an opening paragraph, you should have a pretty good idea of how the rest of your first draft might develop. You might, for example, develop the sample essay idea by identifying several examples of your temperamental behavior and your parents' responses, or you might re-create in detail one particular experience that portrays you as "a no-good, two-faced rat." And, if you are an adventurous mind traveler, you might even consider something a bit out of the ordinary (a short play, an imaginary interview with your parents, a look back—ten years from now).

A form usually unfolds naturally as you write, so don't worry if you can't see too far into your first draft. Remember that your destination is often unknown in mind traveling. That's part of the fun of taking the trip in the first place.

Designing a Writing Plan

> *"I want to get the structural problems out of the way first, so I can get to what matters more."*
>
> **– John McPhee**

012   Once you've found a good idea and a good way to begin, you should be champing at the bit to continue writing. If so, have a nice trip. If, however, you are a careful mind traveler or your topic is quite complex, you might need to design a writing plan before you start your first draft. (Naturally, there is greater need to organize your ideas in a formal report or research paper than there is in a personal narrative or essay.) Your plan can be anything from a brief list of ideas to a detailed sentence outline. (See 110.) Use the guidelines which follow to help you plan and organize your writing:

1. Review all of the facts and details you have produced so far to see if an overall picture or pattern is emerging.
2. Consider the different methods for developing a composition. (See 013.)
3. Consider developing your writing using induction or deduction, the two classic patterns of organization. (See 014.)
4. Consider using a specific writing device (sensory details, anecdotes, quotations) as a way to help you structure your writing.
5. Organize your ideas in some kind of list, cluster, or outline.
6. If nothing seems to work, consider gathering more information, or consider writing your first draft to see what unfolds.

Note: Many writers decide how to organize their writing after they have written their first draft. They prefer to see where their mind traveling takes them first.

Selecting a Method of Development

013   Chris bought the first pair of shoes she tried on. The style, the color, and the fit were that good. Larry tried on five pairs of shoes before he found what he was looking for. Not unusual. Sometimes we know that the first thing we try on is right for us; other times we aren't so sure. The same holds true with the way you develop your thoughts in a piece of writing. At times, the first method that comes to mind will be the best approach for a particular piece of writing. (Narration or description, for example, is a logical choice for the sample essay idea.) At other times, you will have to do some comparison shopping before you feel comfortable with a method for developing your writing.

Several **methods of development** are listed here. Any one of them can help you shape your writing. You can choose to . . .

narrate: tell a story or re-create an incident or experience. (See 093 for an example.)

describe: tell in detail how something or someone appeared. (See 094 and 119 for an example and guidelines.)

define: distinguish what something is from what it is not. (See 095 and 122 for an example and guidelines.)

analyze: break down a thing or a process into its parts and subparts.

classify: divide a large and complex set of things into smaller groups and identify each group.

compare: measure one thing against something more or less like it, or explain one thing by using an analogy to something quite different.

evaluate: use some fitting criteria to decide how good something is or what it is worth.

argue: use reasoning or emotional appeal to prove that something is true, that something should be valued, or that something should be done. (See 544 for guidelines.)

Note: In a longer composition you might begin with one method of development, but utilize other methods once you get into the piece. In the sample essay, for example, you might begin by *re-creating* an incident that typifies your relationship with your parents. Then you might *describe* each of your parents and *analyze* their responses to your mood swings before you close your paper. Variety in the writer's approach to the subject usually makes for appealing reading.

Organizing Logically

014   If you want to share the details of your writing first and lead up to the main idea which is stated in the conclusion of the paper, you will be organizing **inductively**. In short stories, poems, and certain personal essays, the main idea is suggested rather than stated. The information leading up to the conclusion speaks for itself and offers the reader a subtle (or obvious) attitude.

If the main idea is stated early in your writing and details which follow define the idea, expand it, illustrate it, support it, or repeat it with a harder punch, you will be organizing **deductively**.

Most scientific writing, report writing, academic writing, and informative writing in general is organized deductively. The reason is not hard to understand. Deductive reasoning makes complicated material easy to understand by eliminating the guesswork. General statements come first; supporting details follow.

It's important to remember, however, that writers need not be locked into either inductive or deductive patterns of organization. A paragraph might be inductively arranged, yet the writing as a whole may be deductively arranged. Or vice versa. Some writers of personal essays do away with both patterns and create a pattern which better suits their needs.

Writing the First Draft

015   This is it. Your pen is scrawling. Your typewriter is clacking. Or your word processor is clicking. All of your searching and planning has led to this. You're into your first draft, your first look at the finished product. Write as much of your draft as possible in your first sitting while your thinking and prewriting is still fresh in your mind. Refer to your plan (if you have one), but be flexible. A more interesting path of travel might unfold as you write. Keep writing until you come to a logical stopping point.

Remember: **"First Draft" means just that.** It is your first look at a developing writing idea, your first at bat. You may have to step to the plate two or three times before you get a clean, solid hit.

Write naturally: Be yourself, they say.

But, you say, I don't like the way I "naturally" write. It never sounds natural, for one thing. Sometimes it sounds dumb or boring. And even if it sounds okay, I usually don't end up saying anything very interesting.

Don't worry. Your writing will seem natural and pleasing if you keep one thought above all others: **The writer is never alone.** Your writing is one-half of a conversation with a reader you invent. Talk to your "silent partner." Then your writing will sound natural.

1. **Write as you would speak; as a writer, you are never alone.**

    (There is always someone out there listening. Clustering and free writing can help you write in your true "voice.")

2. **Know your subject.**

    (Remember that it is hard to work with a stranger.)

3. **Be honest; don't try to fake it.**

    (Readers are drawn to writers who are honest and trustworthy, writers who talk to them like a friend.)

4. **Be personally involved in your writing.**

    (Create real-life images by using powerful moments from your past.)

5. **Be at ease; don't rush or nervously bounce around.**

    (Think about what you've already said—repeat it in your mind or on paper—and let that help you decide what you should say next.)

A style like this should appeal to most readers in most situations. It will also move you, as a developing writer, in the direction of a more mature personal style. (See 050 for additional suggestions on style.)

Revising

016   Think of your first draft as both an end product and the raw material for a product still in development. It is the end product of your searching and planning, and it is the raw material that you will work into shape as you revise. During revising you will need to proceed more carefully than you did earlier in the writing process. This is the point at which you should ask yourself a number of important questions about your writing:

- *Does my writing "work"? If not, am I committed to making it work?*
- *Is the content interesting and worth sharing?*
- *Have I met the requirements of the assignment and/or my personal goal?*
- *Is the style natural and effective in getting my message across?*
- *Are there any major gaps or soft spots in my writing?*
- *How can I improve what I have done so far?*

> *". . . the first task of revision is vision. The writer must stand back from the work the way any craftsman does to see what has been done."*
>
> **– Donald Murray**

Evaluate the results of your mind traveling by reading your first draft a number of times. (Step away from your writing for a day or two between readings if time permits.) Read carefully since you have two important decisions to make. First, decide if the main idea or focus of the draft is right for you. When you are personally committed to a writing idea, you will naturally put more effort into your work. Second, decide if this idea is appropriate for your audience. That is, do you have the potential with this particular idea to say something interesting and worthwhile to your readers?

Reviewing, Reworking, and Refining

> *". . . there are days when the result is so bad that no fewer than five revisions are required. In contrast, when I'm greatly inspired, only four revisions are needed."*
>
> **– John Kenneth Galbraith**

017   No writer gets it right the first time. Few writers get it right the second time. In fact, professional writers often have to write a handful of revisions before they are satisfied with their work. Don't be surprised if you have to do the same.

Once you've reviewed what you've written and decided more specifically what you want to say, your revisions may have to pass through a number of stages. You may have to **reorder** some of the material; reviewing and reordering may prove that you need to **add** some new material and **cut** some existing copy; and after making all of the necessary changes, you will need to **refine** the whole thing. As you work through your first draft, test yourself with questions like the following:

1. *Have I made all the important points?*
2. *Have I sufficiently supported the points?*
3. *Have I given enough information to answer my readers' most likely questions?*
4. *Do I answer those questions in the best places?*
5. *Have I placed ideas in a logical and interesting order?*

Note: Keep in mind that anecdotes, quotations, and comparisons often mean much more to a reader than lists of numbers or facts. Also, remember that the paragraph is the basic unit of information in nonfiction prose. Each paragraph should serve a necessary function, responding to all the paragraphs that come before it and preparing for the paragraphs that follow it.

Escaping the "Badlands" of Writing

018   This later stage of revising is one of the most important in the whole composing process. Why? Because here you can escape the "Badlands" of writing—those stretches of cliched, uninspired, or jumbled prose that can make writing seem boring and wasted. Here you can catch opportunities you missed the first time around. Six such examples follow:

1. *Is your topic worn-out?* ("What I Did on My Summer Vacation," for example?) With a new twist you can revive it: "The Week 'Old Faithful' Burned."

2. *Is your purpose stale?* If you have been writing merely to please the teacher or to get a good grade, start again. But this time try writing to learn something or to make your readers laugh. You might find your new purpose refreshing.

3. *Is your voice predictable or fake?* If it is ("A good time was had by all"), start again. This time, be honest. Be real.

4. *Is your essay organized around one of those tired old formulas?* The "Three-Part Essay" (Introduction, Body, Conclusion), or the "Five-Paragraph Essay" (Introduction, Three Main Points, Conclusion)? These work as formulas only when they don't sound like formulas. So read your draft again, and the first time your inner voice starts moaning "formula, formula," cross out some words and start blazing a more unpredictable trail.

5. *Does your first draft sound boring?* Maybe it's boring because it pays an equal amount of attention to everything. Shorten some passages by summarizing them; lengthen others by explaining. If you're telling a story, skim through the less significant parts by "telling" what happened; dwell on the more important parts by "showing" what happened. Summarize and explain. Tell and show. These powerful shaping tools let you control your readers' interest so that you can concentrate on your purpose.

6. *Do your sentences fall into a rut?* Do they all begin with "He," "It," or "There"? Do they all use "be" verbs (is, was, were, will be)? If so, you have probably missed many opportunities to use interesting detail, to show action, or to explain interesting relationships. Wherever you see two or more words or sentence structures repeated without reason, cross out the first repetition and right at that point search for a more striking detail, a more vivid action, or a more interesting relationship.

Remember: Don't let your writing become predictable. Cliches can be more than tired figures of speech; they can be worn-out topics, purposes, voices, tones, and structures as well. Each cliche is a missed opportunity for invention and discovery. When you rework the first draft, you have a second chance to escape the "Badlands." Try to see it as an opportunity, not a chore. Be unpredictable. Make your second draft come to life! If you need to refuel your thinking at any point during revising, consider using one of the prewriting activities.

Opening and Closing Paragraphs

*"Any writer overwhelmingly honest about pleasing himself
is almost sure to please others."*

– Marianne Moore

019   After making changes in the body of your writing, the opening paragraph might need to be altered as well (or written if you have not already done so). Make sure it draws your reader into the main part of your paper and that it accurately introduces the point or focus of your writing. (See 011 for an example.)

Also work on a closing for your paper. The closing usually ties any loose ends left in the body of the paper and helps the reader see the significance of what you have written. The sample which follows could serve as a closing for a personal essay on "that temperamental teenager."

> *There is hope. I'm at least aware of my temperament and its effect on my parents. This doesn't mean I'm suddenly going to change my ways. Someone as sensitive as I am will always have her tense moments—when I need an hour to cool off. That's just part of being me, and there is little I can do about it. And I suppose I'll eventually gain more and more control of my mood swings, at least I hope I will. I'd hate to be 25 and still making life difficult for people who are close to me.*

Special Note: It is not always necessary to write a special closing, especially if your writing ends naturally and effectively after the last important point is made.

Consider Your Reader
Angle of Vision: Up, Down, or Eye-to-Eye?

020   An important concern during revising is to check where you stand as a writer in relation to your readers. Generally your compositions should read as if you are talking *eye-to-eye* with your audience. There are times, however, that you might take a slightly different stance in your writing.

– For example, in a report to experts, you might show respect by **talking up** to your audience:

> *Is rap music perhaps much better poetry than some critics say?*

– Or, if you consider yourself older or more knowledgeable than your readers, you may **reach down** to them:

> *If you're through criticizing rap music, maybe you should listen closely to it for a change.*

– But in most of your writing, remember that an **eye-to-eye** stance is the best approach. It has an honest and sincere ring to it:

> *Some of the toughest-sounding rappers are actually pleading for a drug-free society and the end to violence that we all desire.*

Level of Diction: T-Shirts or Tuxedoes

021   As you revise, be sure your word choice sticks to an appropriate level of formality. Your choice of words should reflect and reinforce the purpose of a particular writing assignment. For example, you might write a story in which jazzy street language or **slang** will be appropriate:

> *Geez, I can't believe what a nerd I was.*

Or, you might write a composition in which the **informal English** (also known as colloquial English) used in relaxed conversation seems the best choice. Informal English is characterized by contractions, sentence fragments, popular expressions (you know, like, forget it), cliches (like a chicken with its head cut off), frequent references to oneself (I couldn't quite figure out. . .), and meaningless qualifying words (really, kind of, a lot, incredibly).

> *We weren't afraid to admit we were scared silly when the cops stopped us that time. Who wouldn't be?*

Or you might write an essay or research paper in which the word choice meets the standards of **semiformal English**. When writing is published, it usually is edited to meet such standards. In semiformal English, slang and colloquialisms are replaced by more carefully chosen words and phrases:

> *Semiformal English, such as you are reading in this sentence, is worded correctly and cautiously so that it can withstand repeated readings without seeming tiresome, sloppy, or cute.*

Note: For special purposes, like permanent documents or specialized instruction manuals, highly formal or technical diction may be required.

Choice of Words: Developing a Style

022   Don't worry too much about style as long as you still face major questions concerning the content, focus, and organization of your writing. All the reviewing, reworking, and refining that you do will naturally bear the stamp of your personal style.

But at some point, mature writers "graduate" to a genuine concern with style. They know that the real accuracy and the true "charm" of what they have to say can only come across in the most subtle word choices or the most graceful line of logic. They want their writing to have their unique personal blend of energy, restraint, emotion, precision, humor, delicacy, or power.

View the growth of your personal style as a lifetime challenge and each writing task as a new episode in your struggle to meet it. And why settle for the tired, the sloppy, or the haphazard? Set a high standard. If you want your style to "live," as writers say, you must always reach for something higher than before. (See 050 for a detailed explanation of style.)

Revising on the Run

023   When you have little time for anything else, Peter Elbow recommends "cut-and-paste revising." The five steps which follow describe this quick revising technique:

> *1. Don't add any new information.*
>
> *2. Remove unnecessary facts and details.*
>
> *3. Find the best possible information and go with it.*
>
> *4. Put the pieces in the best possible order.*
>
> *5. Do what little rewriting is necessary.*

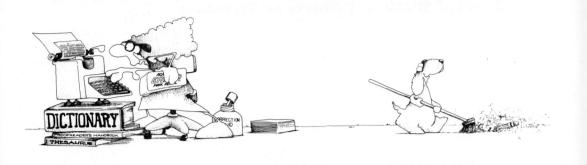

Editing and Proofreading

024   Once you feel comfortable with the content and style of your writing, you are ready to prepare it for publication. (Publication can be anything from sharing your writing with classmates to actually submitting something to a publisher.) This is when you clean, brush, and polish your work until it is clear and precise. During this final step in the writing process, you should

- *check your writing for usage, mechanics, and grammatical errors,*
- *write or type the final draft,*
- *and proofread the final draft for typing errors.*

It is sometimes hard to let go of your writing. But there comes a point when you must stop "coddling your baby" and see if it can stand on its own two feet. That point, as you well know, is usually a deadline or due date. Before you send a composition on its way, make sure you check it over carefully for errors.

Have a dictionary, thesaurus, and an English handbook nearby when you proofread. No one is a perfect speller, no one knows every rule of punctuation and capitalization, and no one always has just the right word at his pencil tip. Also, ask a friend, classmate, writing group, teacher, or parent to help you check your writing for errors.

Preparing the Final Draft: Follow all the rules and guidelines given to you regarding your final draft. Use the correct paper, margins, and spacing. Always write in ink or type your composition. Proofread the final draft against the edited version of your writing. And make every effort to meet your deadline.

Note: See 173 for writing and editing tips when preparing a paper with a computer.

Editing for Accuracy

Use the following checklist to help you with your editing and proofreading:

1.   Reread your entire piece of writing for accuracy after you have revised your writing for content and style. Make sure you have not left out any important words or phrases.

2.   Have a dictionary, thesaurus, and your English handbook close at hand.

3.   Check for errors in usage, punctuation, capitalization, spelling, and grammar. (Use "Re-marks," 600, as your guide.)

4.   Ask for help from a reliable editor—a friend, classmate, teacher, or parent who has a good grasp of the language—for those questions you cannot answer yourself.

5.   Write or type a neat final copy of your writing. Follow the established format or guidelines for a final draft or manuscript.

6.   Proofread the final draft at least once before submitting it for publication.

Group Advising and Revising

025   All writers can benefit from an attentive audience, especially one which offers constructive and honest criticism during a writing project in progress. And who could make a more attentive audience than your fellow writers? Some of you might work in writing groups, so you already know the value of writers sharing their work. Groups of three to five are usually the best size for group sessions.

How *exactly* can a writing group help you? Your fellow writers can tell you what does and doesn't work for them in your writing. You should seek their advice throughout the writing process. But it is especially helpful to seek their advice early in the process since they can tell you whether or not a potential writing idea is one they would be interested in reading about.

Some experts go so far as to say that talking about writing is the most critical step in understanding the process of writing. By sharing ideas and concerns, a community spirit will develop, a spirit that will help make writing a meaningful and exciting process of learning rather than "just another assignment." This enthusiasm is bound to have a positive effect on the final product.

Maintaining Good Relations

> *"At first, I thought, 'Why bother?' What did we know about writing? I resented the group discussions about my writing and offered very few suggestions for the others. It took me awhile to realize that in my small group we were talking about what we each really needed right now, for this paper. That was something even the teacher couldn't tell me."*
>
> *– Paul, a student*

026   To maintain good relations among group members, focus your critical comments as much as possible on elements that are observable in the piece of writing. For example, an observation such as "I noticed many 'There is' statements in your opening" will mean much more to a writer than a general, subjective comment such as "Your opening is really boring" or "Put some life into your opening." The observation helps the writer see a specific problem without hurting his or her confidence. The subjective comments attack the writer without offering any constructive advice. A writer's psyche is a fragile thing: do as little as possible to damage it.

Give praise when praise is due, but base it on something you observe or feel in the writing. Writing sessions should not be popularity contests. "The series of questions and answers was an effective way to organize your essay" is an example of a meaningful compliment based on a specific observation. "There is an enthusiasm and energy in this writing that I really like" is an example of an honest and praiseworthy reaction to a piece of writing.

Don't comment on grammar and mechanics unless you are helping someone with editing and proofreading. Comment on things you actually hear and feel in the writing. At first you might only be able to comment on the repetition of a certain word, the length or brevity of the writing, a point you don't understand, or the nice sound the writing has. Fine. As long as these comments are honest and sincere, offer them as observations. Your writer's vocabulary and ability to make a variety of observations will naturally increase with practice.

Note: Reviewing the guidelines for the writing process (030), writing style (050), and the special forms of writing in your handbook will help you prepare for group sessions.

Reacting to Writing

027   Peter Elbow, in *Writing Without Teachers,* offers four types of reactions group members might have to a piece of writing: pointing, summarizing, telling, and showing. **Pointing** refers to the words, phrases, or ideas in the writing that make a positive or negative impression on a reader or listener. **Summarizing** refers to a reader's general understanding of the writing in question. This shouldn't be a lengthy restatement of the piece, but rather a list of main ideas, a sentence, or maybe a word that gets at the heart of the writing as a reader sees it. These two types of reactions will be the most useful for group work.

   Telling refers to readers expressing what was happening as they read a piece: first this happened, then this happened, later this happened, and so on. Readers must make sure that their "stories" do not stray too far from the writing in question. **Showing** refers to those feelings about a piece that a reader cannot clearly express. Elbow suggests that readers share these feelings metaphorically. A reader might, for example, talk about something in the writing as if it were a voice quality, a manner of appearance (or type of clothing), a type of motion, a color, a shape, etc. ("Why do I feel like I've been lectured to in this essay?" or "Your writing has a neat, tailored quality to it.")

Writing Group Guidelines

028   ## The Author/Writer

1. Come prepared with a substantial piece of writing. (Prepare a copy for each group member if this is part of normal group procedure.)

2. Introduce your writing. Don't say too much, though; let your writing do the talking.

3. Read your copy out loud.

4. As the group reacts to your writing, listen carefully and take brief notes. Don't be defensive about your writing, since this will stop some members from commenting honestly about your work. Answer all of their questions.

5. If you have some special concerns or problems, share these with your fellow writers.

The Group Members

1. Listen carefully as the writer reads. Take notes if this is part of normal group procedure. However, make them brief because you might miss part of the reading as you jot down your ideas. Some groups find it more beneficial to listen to the entire work, and then do a mini free writing immediately after the reading. Still other groups use a critique sheet to evaluate a piece of writing. (See 029.)

2. Keep your comments positive and constructive.

3. Focus your comments as much as you can on specific things you observed in the writing.

4. Don't, however, be afraid to share your feelings about a particular piece of writing.

5. Ask questions of the author: "Why? How? What do you mean when you say . . .?" And answer questions the author might have of you.

6. Listen to other comments and add to them.

Critiquing a Paper

"Comment on what you like in the writing. . . . What you say must be honest, but you don't have to say everything you feel."

– Ken Macrorie

A Checklist for Critiquing a Paper

029 Use the checklist which follows to help you critique compositions during group writing sessions.

– Purpose . . . Does the writer have a clear purpose in mind? That is, is it clear what the writer is trying to accomplish: to entertain, to inform, to persuade, to arouse?

– Voice . . . Does the writing sound sincere and honest? That is, do you hear the writer when you read his or her paper?

– Audience . . . Does the writing address a specific audience? And will the readers understand and appreciate this subject?

– Content . . . Has the writer considered the subject from a number of angles? For example, has he or she tried to compare, classify, define, or analyze his or her writing idea?

– Form . . . Is the subject presented in an effective or appropriate form?

– Personal Thoughts and Comments . . . Has the writer included any personal thoughts or comments in his or her writing? Are they needed or desirable?

– Writing Devices . . . Does the writing include any figures of speech, anecdotes, effective detail, dialogue, specific examples, etc.? Which ones are most effective?

– Purpose Again . . . Does the writing succeed in making a person smile, nod, or react in some other way? What is especially good about the writing?

WRITING GUIDELINES

Using the Writing Process

030   The four steps in the writing process address different segments in the development of a composition. **Prewriting** helps you search for potential starting points, experiment with them, and eventually focus on one idea for writing. **Writing the First Draft** helps you see what a particular idea has to offer. **Revising** helps you clarify and polish what it is you have discovered. **Editing and Proofreading** is the final stage where your writing is fine-tuned (proofread and inked) and made ready to share. (See 002 for a more detailed look at the writing process.)

Prewriting

1. Your goal is to find a meaningful idea to write about—one that meets the requirements of the assignment and lends itself to worthwhile mind traveling.

2. Begin your subject search with free writing, clustering, or other prewriting activities. (See 031 and 035.)

3. Learn as much as you can about a potential subject. (See 033 for a list of searching activities.)

4. Take inventory of you and your subject after some initial prewriting to help you evaluate your progress. (See 008.) If one subject leads to a dead end, drop it and search for another one.

5. Once you have a topic, find an interesting way (a focus) to write about it.

6. Write your first draft at this point if you feel ready.

7. Or, consider writing only the opening section or paragraph to set the tone and direction of your writing. (You may also choose to continue gathering information on your topic.)

8. Think about an overall plan or design for organizing your writing. (This can be anything from a brief list to a detailed outline.)

Writing the First Draft

1. Write the first draft while your preliminary thinking and writing is still fresh in your mind; write as much as you can in your first sitting.

   Helpful Hint: Skip every other line; it will make revising much easier.

2. Refer to your plan or outline (if you have one), but be flexible. A more interesting route may unfold as you write.

3. Keep writing until you come to a natural stopping point. Concentrate on ideas, not mechanics.

4. Remember that looking back sometimes helps you move forward in your writing. Stop to reread and "listen" to what you have written from time to time.

5. Write naturally and honestly. "Talk" to your readers.

6. Remember that your first draft is your first look at a developing writing idea.

Revising

1. First, commit yourself to your writing idea. If you don't feel strongly about your writing, you will lack the necessary care and concern to revise effectively.

2. Review and revise the content of the first draft. This is the time to add, cut, reword, or rearrange information. Always keep your readers in mind. The content of your writing should answer any questions they might have. (See 017 for help.)

3. Review your writing for any opportunities you might have missed to make it as meaningful and lively as possible. (See 018 for help.)

4. Review (or write) the opening and closing paragraphs. They should accurately reflect the content of your paper. (See 011 and 019 for examples and explanations.)

5. Review and refine the style of your writing. That is, review your words, sentences, and paragraphs to make sure they read the way you want them to read. (See 050-082 for help.)

6. Ask a parent, friend, or teacher to read your revised writing and make suggestions for improvement.

Editing and Proofreading

1. Reread your entire piece of writing for accuracy after you have revised your writing for content and style. Make sure you have not left out any important words or phrases.

2. Have a dictionary, thesaurus, and your English handbook close at hand.

3. Check for errors in usage, punctuation, capitalization, spelling, and grammar. (Use "Re-marks," 600, as your guide.)

4. Ask for help from a reliable editor—a friend, classmate, teacher, or parent who has a good grasp of the language—for those questions you cannot answer yourself.

5. Write or type a neat final copy of your writing. Follow the established format or guidelines for a final draft or manuscript.

6. Proofread the final draft at least once before submitting it for publication.

Guidelines for Selecting a Subject

031   The following activities will help you find a worthwhile starting point for your writing. Read through the entire list before you choose an activity to begin your subject search. *Note:* The more activities you attempt, the more potential writing subjects you will discover.

1. **Journal Writing** Write on a regular basis in a journal. Explore your personal feelings, develop your thoughts, and record the happenings of each day. Underline ideas in your personal writing that you would like to explore in writing assignments. (See 001 for a detailed explanation of personal writing.)

2. **Free Writing** Write nonstop for ten minutes to discover possible writing ideas. Begin writing with a particular focus in mind; otherwise, pick up on something that has recently attracted your attention. (See 035 for a detailed explanation of free writing.)

3. **Clustering** Begin a cluster with a *nucleus word.* Select a word that is related to your writing topic or assignment. For example, suppose you were to write an essay on responsibility and what it means to you. *Responsibility* or *duty* would be an obvious nucleus word. Record words which come to mind when you think of this word. Don't pick and choose; record every word. Circle each word as you write it, and draw a line connecting it to the closest related word. (See the cluster example below.)

> "Clustering is that magic key. In fact, it is the master key to natural writing. It is the crucial first step . . . to touch the mental life of daydream, random thought, remembered image . . ."
> —Gabriele Rico

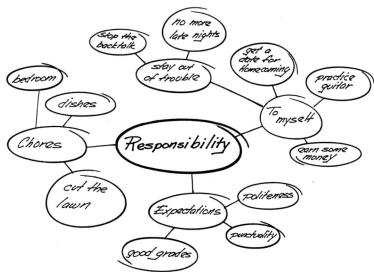

After three or four minutes of clustering, you will probably be ready to write. Scan your cluster for a word or idea that will get you going and write nonstop for about eight minutes. A writing subject should begin to develop from your clustering and writing.

4. **Listing** Freely listing ideas as they come to mind is another effective technique for searching for a writing subject. Begin with an idea or key word related to your assignment and simply start listing words.
    Note: **Brainstorming**—the gathering and listing of ideas in groups—can also be an effective and enjoyable way to search for writing ideas.

5. **Imaginary Dialogue** Create an imaginary dialogue between you and someone else or between two strangers. The subject of this dialogue should be an idea related somehow to your writing assignment if at all possible. Continue this dialogue as long as you can, or until a possible writing idea begins to unfold.
   Note: Give this method a chance. You'll be surprised at the number of unusual turns imaginary dialogues can take.

6. **Sentence Completion** Complete any open-ended sentence in as many ways as you can. Try to word your sentences so that they lead you to a subject you can use for a particular writing assignment. See the list below.

I wonder how...	I hope our school...	Our grading system...
Too many people...	I just learned...	Television is...
The good thing about...	One place I enjoy...	Cars can be...

   Note: Try alternating responses with a friend or classmate and work from each other's ideas.

7. **"Found" Writing Ideas** Be alert for writing ideas you find unexpectedly as you shop, drive, goof around, or walk home from school. Watch for unusual events, persons, objects, or conversations. For example, you might come across an obviously well-cared-for, healthy plant perched on the porch of a neglected, ramshackle home. A "flower-in-the-rough" scene such as this one could bring to mind a number of writing subjects.

8. **Experience** Experience as many different aspects of your community as you can. Visit museums, churches, neighborhoods, businesses, factories, farms, college campuses. As you expand the scope of your world, you will naturally build a supply of potential writing ideas.

9. **Reflect, Participate, and Listen** Think about possible writing ideas as you read, as you ride the school bus, as you wait in the cafeteria line. Participate in something related to a possible topic so that you have firsthand thoughts and feelings about the subject. Interview someone who is knowledgeable or experienced about a writing idea. An "expert's" insights might help you decide on a particular focus for your writing. Also talk with family members, friends, and classmates about possible subjects for writing assignments.

10. **Use a Checklist** Oftentimes, you can find lists of topics and categories in the library. These may be lists of articles kept in the vertical file or nonfiction titles recently added to the library. An issue of the *Readers' Guide to Periodical Literature* can be useful as a checklist of current topics. Even a magazine or newspaper can serve to remind you of the numerous topics being written about today. Below you will find a checklist of the major categories into which most things in our lives are divided. The checklist provides a variety of subject possibilities. You must then decide which subject you would like to write about and which specific subtopic would work best for your writing assignment.

    Example: *clothing* . . . fashionable clothing . . . the changing fashion in school clothing . . . The type of clothing students wear today varies with each group of students.

——Essentials of Life Checklist ——

032

clothing	love	work/occupation	natural resources
housing	measurement	community	personality/identity
food	senses	science	recreation/hobby
communication	machines	plants/vegetation	trade/money
exercise	intelligence	freedom/rights	literature/books
education	history/records	energy	entertainment
family	agriculture	rules/laws	health/medicine
friends	environment	tools/utensils	art/music
purpose/goals	land/property	heat/fuel	faith/religion

Guidelines
for Searching and Shaping a Subject

033   The following activities will help you learn more about your subjects and develop them for writing. If you already have a good "feel" for a particular writing subject, you might attempt only one of the activities. If you need to explore your subject in some detail and time permits, you might attempt two or more of the activities. Read through the entire list before you choose an activity.

1. **Free Writing**   At this point, you can approach free writing in two different ways. You can do a *focused* writing to see how many ideas come to mind about your subject as you write. Or you can approach your writing as if it were an *instant version* of the finished product. An instant version will give you a good feel for your subject, and also tell you how much you know or need to find out.

2. **Clustering**   Try clustering again, this time with your subject as the nucleus word. This clustering will naturally be more focused or structured than your earlier prewriting cluster since you now have a specific subject in mind. (See 031 for a model cluster.)

3. **5 W's of Writing**   Answer the 5 W's—*Who? What? Where? When?* and *Why?*—to identify basic information about your subject. (You can add *How?* to the list for even better coverage.)

4. **Cubing**   Do a variation of free writing by writing the following instructions (or your own) on each side of a cube (any small box or block will do):

   > **Describe it.** *What do you see, hear, feel, smell, taste . . . ?*
   > **Compare it.** *What is it like? What is it different from?*
   > **Associate it.** *What connections between this and something else come to mind?*
   > **Analyze it.** *What parts does it have? How do they work (or not work) together?*
   > **Apply it.** *What can you do with it? How can you use it?*
   > **Argue for or against it.** *(seriously or humorously)*

   Switch your cube at least four different times. Each time you switch write freely (three to five minutes), list, or cluster, and learn something new about your subject.

5. **Structured Questions**   Answering structured questions will help you understand what is important or unique about your writing idea in a systematic fashion.

   These questions will work with any type of writing subject: *persons, places, things, ideas,* or *events.*

   Note: Answer only those questions that will help you shape your subject. Consider writing your answers in the form of mini free writings (five minutes) to unlock valuable ideas.

   a. *What makes your subject different from others that are similar to it?*
   b. *How can your subject change without becoming someone (something) else?*
   c. *How can your subject be classified?*
   d. *How is your subject changing?*
   e. *How does your subject fit into her (its) world or realm?*
   f. *What larger group(s) is your subject a part of?*
   g. *What features make your subject part of this larger group?*
   h. *What features make your subject different from this group?*
   i. What other questions can *you* think of?

6. **Offbeat (Unstructured) Questions**   Creating and answering offbeat questions will help you see your writing idea in unexpected ways. The sample questions which follow suggest a number of offbeat ways to look at different types of writing subjects. ("Offbeat Questions" are an adaptation of Peter Elbow's "Metaphorical Questions" in *Writing with Power.*)

Note: Consider answering your questions in the form of mini free writings (five minutes) to unlock creative ideas. You might also consider answering your questions with the help of a friend, classmate, or writing group.

Writing About a Person

a. What type of clothing is he (she) like?
b. What type of light best shines on him?
c. What does his menu look like?

Writing About a Place

a. What is the place's best sense?
b. Where does this place go for advice?
c. What is its future?

Writing About an Object

a. What would make this object stand at attention?
b. What does it look like upside down?
c. What kind of shadow does it cast?

Writing About an Issue or Event

a. What is its class rank?
b. What machine does it most resemble?
c. What is in its refrigerator?

Writing to Persuade

a. What clubs or organizations would your argument or viewpoint join?
b. Would your argument take the stairs or the elevator?
c. Which viewpoint would win in a wrestling match? A game of Ping-Pong?

Writing to Explain a Process

a. What restaurant is this process like?
b. Where in a hardware store would this process feel most at home?
c. What would you find in its garbage can?

Writing a Narrative

a. What fruit does this story resemble?
b. What would a fortune teller say about this story?
c. What would your great-grandmother say about it?

7. **Imaginary Dialogue** Create an imaginary dialogue between two people in which your specific subject is the focus of the conversation. The two speakers should build on each other's comments, reinforce them, elaborate on them, or give them a new "spin."

8. **Twisted Version** Write a "twisted" version of your paper. You might write as if you were a different person or someone from a different time or place, or you might write an exaggerated or fairy-tale version of your paper.

9. **Precision Poetry** Write a poem about your subject (*cinquain, list, alphabet, name,* or *phrase* poetry, for starters).

10. **Audience Appeal** Select a specific audience to address in an exploratory writing. Consider a group of preschoolers, a live television audience, readers of a popular teen magazine, a panel of experts, the local school board . . .

Sample Writing Topics
Quotations

"Knowledge is of two kinds. We know a subject ourselves, or we know where we can find information upon it." —Samuel Johnson

"A lie can travel half way around the world while the truth is putting on its shoes." —Mark Twain

"A problem well stated is a problem half solved." —C.F. Kettering

"I'm a great believer in luck, and I find the harder I work the more I have of it." —Thomas Jefferson

"The man who does not read good books has no advantage over the man who can't read them." —Mark Twain

"What appears to be the end may really be a new beginning."

"The impossible is often the untried." — Jim Goodwin

"Too often we give children answers to remember rather than problems to solve." —Roger Lewin

"Civilization is a race between education and catastrophe." —H.G. Wells

"The best argument is that which seems merely an explanation." —Dale Carnegie

"The man who makes no mistakes does not usually make anything." —W.C. Magee

"You can always tell a true friend; when you've made a fool of yourself, he doesn't feel you've done a permanent job." — Laurence J. Peter

"When people are free to do as they please, they usually imitate each other." —Eric Hoffer

"Happiness is not a state to arrive at, but a manner of traveling." —M.L. Runbeck

"We can't all be heroes because someone has to sit on the curb and clap as they go by." —Will Rogers

"In every child who is born, under no matter what circumstances, and of no matter what parents, the potentiality of the human race is born again." —James Agee

"Everybody is ignorant, only on different subjects." —Will Rogers

Descriptive

Person: friend, teacher, relative, classmate, minister (priest, rabbi), co-worker, teammate, coach, neighbor, entertainer, politician, sister, brother, bus driver, an older person, a younger person, a baby, someone who taught you well, someone who spends time with you, someone you wish you were more like, someone who always bugs you

Place: school, neighborhood, old neighborhood, the beach, the park, the hangout, home, your room, your garage, your basement, the attic, a roof top, the alley, the bowling alley, a classroom, the theatre, the lockerroom, the store, a restaurant, the library, a church, a stadium, the office, the zoo, the study hall, the cafeteria, the hallway, the barn

Thing: a billboard, a bulletin board, a poster, a photograph, a camera, a machine, a computer, a video game, a music video, a musical instrument, a tool, a monkey wrench, a monkey, a pet, a pet peeve, a bus, a boat, a book . . . a car, a cat, a camp . . . a dog, a drawing, a diary . . . a model, a miniature, a muppet . . .

Narrative

stage fright, just last week, on the bus, learning a lesson, learning to drive, the trip, a kind act, homesick, Christmas, mysteries, a big mistake, field trips, studying, a reunion, a special party, getting lost, being late, asking for help, after school, Friday night, getting hurt, success, flirting, an embarrassing moment, staying overnight, moving, the big game, building a _____, the first day of _____, the last day of _____, a miserable time, all wet, running away, being alone, getting caught, a practical joke, cleaning it up, being punished, staying after, a special conference, the school play, being a friend

Expository

How to . . . wash a car, make a taco, improve your memory, get a job, make a legal petition, prevent accidents, care for a pet, entertain a child, impress your teacher, earn extra money, get in shape, study for a test, conserve energy, program a computer, take a good picture

How to operate . . . control . . . run . . .
How to choose . . . select . . . pick . . .
How to scrape . . . finish . . . paint . . .

How to store . . . stack . . . load . . .
How to build . . . grow . . . create . . .
How to fix . . . clean . . . wash . . .
How to protect . . . warn . . . save . . .

The causes of . . . acid rain, acne, hiccups, snoring, tornados, inflation, northern lights, shinsplints, dropouts, rust, birth defects, cheating, child abuse

Kinds of . . . music, crowds, friends, teachers, love, intelligence, rules, compliments, commercials, punishment, censorship, dreams, happiness, pain, neighbors, pollution, poetry, taxes, clouds, stereos, heroes, chores, homework, fads, adoption, vacations, calendars, clocks, communication, mothers

Definition of . . . rock 'n' roll, best friend, "class," poverty, generation gap, free agent, a good time, a disabled person, hassle, government, a radical, a conservative, SALT, Arab, metric system, dialect, bankruptcy, "soul," grandmother, school, brain, nerd, arthritis, antibiotic, loyalty, credit union, astrology, CPR, Kosher

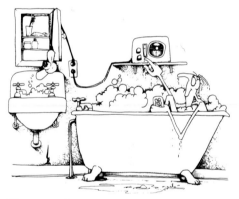

Persuasive

safety in the home, dieting, girls in all sports, organ transplants, sex education, homework, study halls, capital punishment, the speed limit, smoking in public places, shoplifting, seat belts, air bags, gun control, courtroom television, required courses, graduation requirements, final exams, tuition-free colleges, students on school boards, the drinking age, four-day work week, public housing, a career in the armed forces, teen centers, something that needs improving, something that deserves support, something that's unfair, something that everyone should have to see or do, something . . .

The Writing Process **29**

Guidelines
for Free Writing

"Free writing helps you think of topics to write about. Just keep writing, follow threads where they lead and you will get to ideas, experiences, feelings, and people that are just asking to be written about."

—Peter Elbow

035   **Reminders . . .**

1. Thoughts are constantly passing through your mind; you *never* have *nothing* on your mind.
2. Free writing helps you get these thoughts down on paper.
3. Free writing is also a way to develop these thoughts by adding details and making meaning out of them.
4. Many things seem awkward or difficult when you first try them; free writing will probably be no different.
5. Some days will be better than others; don't be discouraged.
6. To succeed at anything, you must give it an honest effort.

The Process . . .

1. Write nonstop and record whatever comes to mind. (Write for at least ten minutes if possible.)
2. If you have a particular focus or starting point in mind, begin writing about it. Otherwise, pick up on anything that comes to mind and begin writing.
3. Don't stop to judge, edit, or correct your writing; that will come later.
4. Keep writing even when you think you have exhausted all of your ideas. Switch to another mode of thought (sensory, memory, reflective) if necessary, but keep writing.
5. Continue to shift the focus of your thinking until ideas and details begin to flow.
6. When a particular topic seems to be working, stick with it and record as many specific details as possible.
7. Listen to and read the free writings of others; learn from them.
8. Carry your journal with you and write freely in it whenever you have an idea you don't want to forget, or even when you simply have nothing else to do; these free writings will help you become a better writer.

The Result . . .

1. Review your writings and underline ideas you like. The ideas will often serve as the basis for more formal writings.
2. Make sure a free writing idea meets the requirements of an assignment (if that's why you did it) and is also one you feel good about sharing.
3. Determine exactly what you plan (or are required) to write about and add specific details as necessary. (This may require a second, more selective free writing.)
4. If the subject seems to be working, keep writing; if your ideas dry up, look for a new idea in your free writing or begin a new nonstop writing. (See 031 and 033 for additional activities for developing a subject.)

A Survey of Writing Forms

036   The chart which follows classifies the different forms of writing according to **purpose, audience**, and other basic **characteristics**. You will note that all forms of writing can generally be classified in one of five ways: either as **personal** writing, **functional** writing, **creative** writing, **expository** writing, or **persuasive** writing. Experiment with all forms of writing, moving freely between "categories." An essay, for example, can (and should) be creative as well as informative.

Personal Writing

Characteristics	Forms	
Primary purpose—to explore private concerns **Audience**—primarily the writer Foundation for all writing Free flowing Exploratory Builds writing fluency Facilitates thinking	Journals Logs Diaries Free writing Clustering	Listing Informal essays and narratives Brainstorming Reminiscences

Functional Writing

Characteristics	Forms	
Primary purpose—to standardize communication **Audience**—others Highly Structured Follows prescribed forms Business and social writing	Business letters and memos Letters of application, appreciation, etc. Resumes Invitations	Contracts

Creative Writing

Characteristics	Forms	
Primary purpose—to satisfy need to invent and create **Audience**—the writer and others Expression of private feelings, beliefs Delights and inspires Leads to reflection Experimental Special attention to language	Poems Myths Plays Stories Anecdotes Sketches	Essays Letters Songs Jokes Parodies

Expository Writing

Characteristics	Forms	
Primary purpose—to explore and present information **Audience**—the writer and others Academic and business writing Straightforward Factual Follows patterns of organization Informs, describes, explains	Reports Reviews Letters Research papers Essays	News stories Interviews Instructions Manuals

Persuasive Writing

Characteristics	Forms	
Primary purpose—to influence and change opinion **Audience**—others Intellectual and/or emotional appeal Academic, business, and political writing May follow definite pattern of organization Real or imagined	Editorials Letters Cartoons Research papers Essays	Advertisements Slogans Pamphlets Petitions Commercials

Style
&
Form

"With every choice you make, you create a style. Your style, like your set of fingerprints, is yours, and only yours."

Think about your hair. This morning when you first yawned into the mirror, you had to choose: Shall I wash my hair? Shall I comb it? Shall I blow it dry? Shall I use mousse, gel, spritz, or some other glop? Shall I try something new? Shall I braid it, cornrow it, rubber band it, slick it, toss it, or just leave it? Do I want my football number shaved in back or shall I get a mohawk? Whatever you do—or don't do—that is *your style*.

Your writing style, similarly, comes from a series of choices that makes your writing yours. It is your words, your sentences, and your paragraphs and nobody else's. Fortunately, as a writer, you don't have to change your *'do* every month or two to be in fashion. Your writing will always be in style if it exhibits the traits of effective writing which follow.

Traits of an Effective Style

050   Evaluate your writing style in a particular piece of writing using the following guidelines:

Originality   To be original, writing must spring from your own fresh look at the subject matter, a new encounter with reality. Say what you think and feel, not what you assume others expect you to say.

Awareness   Aware writing shows sensitivity to the current events at the time of its composition. Notice what is going on around you—in your school, your neighborhood, your community, and the world in general. Then, if it applies, relate this information to your topic.

Vitality   Vital writing is lively. It crackles with energy and has a sense of purpose. Instead of a lazy, "just-get-it-done" feeling, it shows signs of conviction and life: growth, warmth, movement, interaction with the environment. The words and thoughts leap out at you instead of lying dead on the page. The use of vivid verbs, fresh images, and twisted phrases will lend vitality to your writing.

Variety   Variety in writing is the interplay of differences everywhere—among vowels and consonants, words and phrases, sound and meaning. Variety comes from connecting ideas in new and different ways. Do the unexpected: use negative definitions (what something is *not),* contrasts and contraries, dialogue and poetry. Also do the obvious: use synonyms instead of the same word over and over again and include different sentence types, lengths, and arrangements. Variety will keep the reader around long enough to get your message.

Simplicity (Conciseness) Simple, concise writing may have many complicated parts, but it unites them behind a single controlling purpose. Keep the focus (the main point) of your writing in mind. Then, use one word where one will do, one sentence where one will do. And remember that big words and flowery language only clutter and disguise your message.

Accuracy Accurate writing is precise and clear. It cites facts correctly. It observes the rules of grammar and uses correct punctuation, spelling, and capitalization. It uses words in their proper sense, never confusing "their" with "there" or "they're"; never confusing "affect" with "effect"; never confusing "eminent" with "imminent," and so forth.

Concreteness Concrete writing uses language that appeals to the five senses or brings sensory images to mind. Use nouns and modifiers that are precise and colorful. Instead of generic terms like *animal, sea creature, emotion,* or *Mexican sauce;* consider *schnauzer, bottlenose dolphin, corrosive envy,* or *tongue-numbing salsa.*

Honesty Honest writing conveys the writer's feelings or wishes without being artificial. Don't bother pretending to know more than you do. It never works. Honest writing conveys strong emotion without straining to do so.

Grace Graceful writing flows through difficult assignments, right through to the end. Be fluent. Keep your focus in mind, linking your phrases and sentences to move smoothly instead of bumping and rambling along. Get rid of the extra words and phrases that detract from your main point.

Adding Style to Your Writing

051 Showing versus Telling

Writer Donald Murray suggests that you put people in your writing whose actions communicate important ideas for you. Brief "slices of life" add spark to your writing. They allow you to **show** your readers something in a lively and interesting manner rather than **tell** them matter-of-factly.

Don't, for example, state in a paper that a commitment has been made to improve students' math scores when you can show this more vividly:

> The students were already seated when the instructor for first-hour trigonometry bustled into the room. She picked up today's assignments, passed back yesterday's work, and took her place behind the podium. Miss Shaw was ready to begin, well before the final bell. There was no time to waste. Like her math colleagues, she was committed to improving her students' math scores.

And don't state that a visitor helped you see your home in a new light when you can show your readers this in a much more dramatic fashion:

> His "bee-yoo-tee-ful" stopped me short. This lanky Mr. Sophisticate from "just outside Paris" was describing the North Dakota prairie. The wild grasses and big sky, the black-eyed Susan and sagebrush, the hum of dog days were new to him. Now all he could say as he lay exhausted in Mother's recliner was "bee-yoo-tee-ful."
> Two days later we all huddled around a book about Paris, every picture in full color. Suddenly our guest pointed to a photo and repeated "bee-yoo-tee-ful." It was the Champs Elysee at night. The Champs Elysee and the North Dakota prairie described with the same

word? My prairie and a Parisian street linked? That was when I knew I would always like him.

And don't state that a particular cross-country ski run was difficult when you can show this:

For intermediate skiers? No. This trail was for the young and the reckless. At some turns, the path became so narrow that the blur of trees seemed to be only a foot away. Fortunately, the thought that I might hit one of them or perhaps run into a fallen skier around the next bend never entered my mind until later. Just staying in the track and reacting to the contour of the trail demanded all of my attention. The smallest bump was nearly enough to send me tumbling. . . .

Note: Don't disrupt the development of your writing idea by "overpopulating" a composition with people and their stories. Occasionally work them into the main body of your writing to give it personality.

052 Writing Metaphorically

> *"Metaphors create tension and excitement by producing new connections, and in so doing reveal a truth about the world we had not previously recognized."*
>
> *– Gabriele Rico*

A **metaphor** can connect an idea or an image in your writing to something new and unexpected and create a powerful picture for your readers.

- Don't, for example, say that your speech was "uninspiring" when you can say that it was a real "choke sandwich, all peanut butter and no jelly."

- And don't describe your mother as a "wonderful, strong person" when you can say it much more powerfully as Alice Walker did when she spoke of her mother and other mothers of her generation as "Headragged Generals."

Essentially, you can express a metaphor directly or indirectly:

Direct comparisons:

> *"The crinkled shadows around his eyes were string beans."*   *– Annie Dillard*

> *"Television is, if not a formal system, at any rate a huge, cool authority . . . ."*
>
> *– Michael Arlen*

Indirect (implied) comparisons:

> *"[Casual dress] often contains what might be called 'slang words': blue jeans, sneakers, baseball caps . . . ."*   *– Alison Lurie*

> *". . . another roar as the pilot pushes the throttle up to full military power and another smear of rubber screams over the skillet . . . ."*   *– Tom Wolfe*

Caution: Make sure that your metaphors are original and clear.

The student who wrote, *"Meryl Streep's last movie sent me to the moon and elevated me to new heights"* has spent too much time stargazing and not enough time creating original images.

The student who wrote, *"Homelessness is a thorn in the city's image"* has created a confusing figure of speech. Homelessness may be a thorn in the city's side, but not in its image.

The reporter who wrote, *"In the final debate, Senator Jones dodged each of his opponent's accusations and eventually scored the winning shot"* has carelessly shifted from one comparison (boxing) to another (basketball) and created a mixed metaphor.

Common Ailments of Style

"With sixty staring me in the face, I have developed inflammation of the sentence structure and a definite hardening of the paragraphs."
—James Thurber, at 59

Review the list of common ailments in style which follows. If your writing falls prey to any of these "diseases," pay close attention to the suggested "cures."

053 Primer Style

The Disease: Here the writer breaks thoughts into short sentences without effective connections. The result is a style like that of a grade-school reading textbook or "primer":

> Our tardy policy is unfair. The teachers go strictly by the rules. They don't care if it's -10° F outdoors. They don't care if your bus breaks down. You get a detention if you walk in 10 seconds after the bell. Who will change this policy? It's so unfair.

The Cure: Do some careful sentence combining. First, figure out your major points and put them in the main clauses. Then, reduce the other thoughts to words, phrases, or dependent clauses and add them to your sentences. Unless special emphasis is needed, get rid of repeated subjects, verbs, and especially pronouns. Here's the same passage revised:

> When it comes to tardiness, our teachers go strictly by the rules. If you walk in 10 seconds after the bell, you're late and you get a detention. They don't care if it's -10° F outdoors or if your bus breaks down. This policy is unfair, and someone should change it.

054 Passive Voice

The Disease: For no good reason, the writer prefers passive verbs to active ones. With passive verbs, the subject of the sentence is the receiver of the action mentioned in the verb. The doer of the action is either not stated or is mentioned in a prepositional phrase beginning with "by." Here's an example:

> Our biology teacher was greatly loved by us. He was often asked for extra help, which was always given. He was visited by his students before and after school and often was the object of our personal jokes—and sincere praises! He was given compliments every year for a job well done.

The result is a sluggish and impersonal style which leaves a reader begging for a more direct picture of the actors and their actions.

The Cure: Test all your verbs, quite deliberately. If a verb is passive, judge whether a passive verb is needed. If not, first name the performer of the action (this will be your subject); then use a verb that describes the action, and follow through to complete the thought. Here is the previous passage in the active voice:

> We loved our biology teacher. He was always available for extra help or just to share a little time with us. We often dropped in before or after school to visit, study, or play a practical joke. He didn't mind. He always seemed happy to see us. We were lucky to have him as a teacher and a friend.

055 Wordiness

The Disease: Wordiness means multiplying words and phrases to express ideas that could be expressed much more simply. Here is an example:

> Despite repeated efforts and much experimentation, members of the scientific community who have worked on the problem for years have made

as yet no significant progress toward unraveling the biological mysteries obscuring from view the potential cures of the malady usually referred to in the vernacular as the "common cold."

The Cure: First, zero in on the main idea and try to express it in shorthand form. (Often, the main thought will focus on a single strong verb.) Then add necessary phrases to explain, elaborate, or qualify the idea. The wordy passage above says little more than this:

Scientists have not yet discovered a cure for the "common cold."

Note: Be especially alert for lengthy phrases that can be reduced to a simple noun or verb:

members of the scientific community = scientists

made . . . significant progress toward unraveling the biological mysteries obscuring from view = discovered

Special Caution! Be alert for a special type of wordiness that turns would-be verbs into nouns or phrases, creating longer, clumsier sentences. *Encourage* becomes *encouragement*. *Justify* becomes *justification* or *give a justification for*. *Agree* becomes *agreement* or *express agreement with*, and so on. Look for the verb hidden in these nouns and phrases, and rebuild the sentence around the verb. Here are a few examples:

Wordy: Mr. Peebles gave our petition his consideration.
Better: Mr. Peebles considered our petition.

Wordy: The convict's record did not show justification for his early release.
Better: The convict's record did not justify his early release.

056 Jargon

The Disease: The technical vocabularies of many different fields often creep into writing contexts where they don't belong, turning off and confusing the reader. While it may be necessary for doctors, computer programmers, bureaucrats, engineers, and the like to use specialized terms, the everyday writer must be wary of them. Here are a few examples: *infrastructure, systems analysis, hacker, prioritization, finalize, impact on,* etc.

That helmet should prevent *cranial lesions.*
The warehouse was packed with *surplus product inventory.*

The Cure: Get out your jargon-detector. Unless you are writing to an audience that knows the jargon and expects it from you, translate the fancy terms into more ordinary synonyms. As a writer, always aim for being an honest, plainspoken individual. Here are the previous sentences revised:

That helmet should prevent head injuries.
The warehouse was packed with leftover lawn mower parts.

057 Insecurity

The Disease: A lack of self-confidence makes some writers back off from their own statements even while they are making them: "Maybe I'm wrong, but . . . " The same insecurity may lead them to keep emphasizing a point even after they've successfully made it: "Our rotten vacation was so bad we never enjoyed a minute of it." Phrases such as *to be perfectly honest* or *to tell the truth*, besides being tired and overused, give the impression that the speaker does not expect to be believed. The constant use of needless intensifiers like *really, truly, definitely, completely, totally,* or *absolutely* gives the same shaky impression. Consider this example:

I totally and completely agree with Mr. Grim about changing our school's drug policy, but that's only my opinion.

The Cure: Review what you have to say. Remind yourself of its importance to you and your audience. Visualize yourself standing up boldly before an audience and saying exactly what you mean, without hedging or apologizing. Write as you would speak, and let clear statements stand, as in this revised example:

I agree with Mr. Grim about changing our school's drug policy.

Improving Sentence Style

"To err is human, but when the eraser wears out ahead of the pencil, you're overdoing it."

—J. Jenkins

Complete & Mature

With a few exceptions in special situations, you should use complete sentences when you write. By definition, a complete sentence expresses a complete thought. However, a sentence may actually contain several ideas, not just one. The trick is getting those ideas to work together to form mature, colorful sentences that are interesting to read.

Among the most common errors made when attempting to write complete (and effective) sentences are **fragments, comma splices, run-ons,** and **rambling** sentences.

058 A **fragment** is a group of words used as a sentence. It is not a sentence, though, since it lacks a subject, a verb, or some other essential part which causes it to be an incomplete thought. *Note:* Fragments are sometimes used in fiction, especially in dialogue.

Fragment:	Gradually, the delicate, lacy colors of spring. (This phrase lacks a verb.)
Sentence:	Gradually, the delicate, lacy colors of spring covered the hillside.
Fragment:	The minute she stepped into the barn. (This clause lacks a subject and a verb which are needed to complete the thought of what happened "The minute she stepped into the barn.")
Sentence:	The minute she stepped into the barn, cats darted in every direction.
Fragment:	She reached into her pocket. Searching from side to side for that last lump of sugar. (This is a sentence followed by a fragment. This error can be corrected by combining the fragment with the sentence.)
Sentence:	She reached into her pocket, searching from side to side for that last lump of sugar.

059 A **comma splice** is a mistake made when two independent clauses are *spliced* together with only a comma. (Also called a comma fault)

Splice:	The concert crowd had been waiting in the hot sun for two hours, many of the people were beginning to show their impatience by chanting and clapping.
Corrected:	The concert crowd had been waiting in the hot sun for two hours. Many of the people were beginning to show their impatience by chanting and clapping. (Comma has been changed to a period.)
Corrected:	The concert crowd had been waiting in the hot sun for two hours, and many of the people were beginning to show their impatience by chanting and clapping. (Coordinating conjunction *and* has been added.)
Corrected:	The concert crowd had been waiting in the hot sun for two hours; many of the people were beginning to show their impatience by chanting and clapping. (Comma has been changed to a semicolon. See 620.)

A comma splice can be corrected by rearranging the ideas in a sentence.

Splice:	One of the players stands in front of the net and tries to keep the puck from going in, he is called the goalie.
Corrected:	One of the players, called the goalie, stands in front of the net and tries to keep the puck from going in.

The problem can also be solved by adding a needed word(s).

> **Splice:** Everyone must leave the building when the fire alarm rings, you never know when the alarm is for a real fire.
>
> **Corrected:** Everyone must leave the building when the fire alarm rings *since* you never know when the alarm is for a real fire.

060 A **run-on sentence (fused sentence)** is the result of two sentences being joined without adequate punctuation or a connecting word.

> **Run-on:** I thought the ride would never end my eyes were crossed and my fingers were going numb.
>
> **Corrected:** I thought the ride would never end. My eyes were crossed and my fingers were going numb.

061 A **rambling sentence** is one which goes on and on. It is often brought about by the overuse of the word *and*.

> **And-and:** The intruder entered silently through the window and moved sideways down the corridor and under a stairwell and stood waiting in the shadows.
>
> **Corrected:** The intruder entered silently through the window. He moved sideways down the corridor and under a stairwell where he stood waiting in the shadows.

Clear & Exact

> *"If any man wishes to write a clear style, let him first be clear in his thoughts."*
>
> **—Johann Wolfgang von Goethe**

Writing is thinking. Before you can write clearly, you must think clearly and re-think (revise) carefully. Nothing is more frustrating for the reader than writing which is muddy or confusing, writing which must be reread or dissected just to discover its basic message.

Look carefully at the common errors (and corrections) which follow. Return to this section as you revise your writing. Keep track of other instances of vague, unclear writing which you come across and work to make your own writing as exact as possible.

062 An **incomplete comparison** is the result of leaving out a word(s) which is necessary to make the sentence clear and complete.

> **Incomplete:** I get along better with Rosa than my sister. (Are you saying that you get along better with Rosa than you do your sister …or that you get along better with Rosa than your sister does?)
>
> **Clear:** I get along better with Rosa than I do my sister.

063 **Ambiguous wording** is wording with two possible meanings.

> **Ambiguous:** Mike decided to take his new convertible to the drive-in movie, which turned out to be a real horror story. (What turned out to be a real horror story, Mike's taking his new convertible or the movie?)
>
> **Clear:** Mike decided to take his new convertible to the drive-in movie, a decision which turned out to be a real horror story.

064 An **indefinite reference** is a problem caused by careless use of pronouns. As a result, the reader is not sure what the pronoun(s) is referring to.

> **Indefinite:** *It* is an interesting story and *she* does a good job of telling about all of *their* problems.
>
> **Clear:** *To Kill a Mockingbird* is an interesting story in which the author, Harper Lee, tells of the many problems faced by Atticus Finch and his family.
>
> **Indefinite:** As he pulled his car up to the service window, *it* made a strange rattling sound. (Which *rattled,* the car or the window?)
>
> **Clear:** His car made a strange rattling sound as he pulled up to the service window.

065 **Misplaced modifiers** are modifiers which have been placed incorrectly; therefore, the meaning of the sentence is not clear.

> **Misplaced:** We have an assortment of combs for physically active people with unbreakable teeth. (*People* with *unbreakable teeth?*)
>
> **Corrected:** For physically active people, we have an assortment of combs with unbreakable teeth.

We have an assortment of combs for physically active people with unbreakable teeth.

066 **Dangling modifiers** are modifiers which appear to modify a word which isn't in the sentence. (Sometimes, they also appear to modify the wrong word *in* the sentence.)

Dangling:	Trying desperately to get the watermelon under the fence, Paul's mother called him. (There is nothing for the phrase *Trying desperately to get the watermelon under the fence* to modify.)
Corrected:	Trying desperately to get the watermelon under the fence, Paul heard his mother call him. (Here the phrase modifies *Paul.*)
Dangling:	After standing in line for five hours, the manager announced that all the tickets had been sold. (In this sentence, it appears as if the manager had been *standing in line for five hours.*)
Corrected:	After standing in line for five hours, Ian heard the manager announce that all the tickets had been sold. (Now the phrase clearly modifies the person who has been standing in line: *Ian.*)

Concise & Natural

"Read over your compositions and, when you meet a passage which you think is particularly fine, strike it out."
—**Samuel Johnson**

Samuel Johnson, a noted writer of the eighteenth century, was undoubtedly talking about the kind of writing which is lofty, artificial, overworked. One of the greatest temptations facing developing writers is to use lots of words—big words, clever words, fancy words. For some reason, we get into our heads that writing simply and concisely is not writing effectively. Nothing could be further from the truth.

The very best writing is straightforward, not fancy; natural, not artificial. That's why it is so important to master the art of free writing. It is your best chance at a personal style, a personal voice which will produce natural, honest passages you will not have to "strike out." The samples which follow are either wordy or artificial (or both). Learn from them.

067 **Wordiness** occurs when a word (or a synonym for that word) is repeated unnecessarily.

Redundant:	He had *a way* of keeping my attention by *the way* he raised and lowered his *voice* for *every single* word he *spoke.*
Concise:	He kept my attention by raising and lowering his voice when he spoke.
Double Subject:	Some *people they* don't use their voices as well as they could. (Drop *they*, since *people* is the only subject needed.)
Tautology:	*widow woman, descend down, audible to the ear, return back, unite together, final outcome* (Each phrase says the same thing twice.)

068 **Deadwood** is unnecessary wording.

Wordy:	At this point in time, I feel the study needs additional work before the subcommittee can recommend it be resubmitted for consideration.
Concise:	The study needs more work.

069 **Flowery language** is the result of using more or bigger words than needed. It is writing which often contains too many adjectives or adverbs.

Flowery:	The cool, fresh breeze, which came like a storm in the night, lifted me to the exhilarating heights from which I had been previously suppressed by the incandescent cloud in the learning center.
Concise:	The cool breeze was a surprising and refreshing change from the muggy classroom air.

070 A **trite expression** is one which is flat, emotionless; as a result, it is neither fresh nor natural. (Use vivid, specific words in your descriptive writing.)

Trite:	It gives me *a great deal of pleasure* to present to you this plaque as *a token of our appreciation.* Let me read it:
Natural:	The words on this plaque speak for all of us:

071 A **euphemism** is a word or phrase which is substituted for another because it is considered a less "offensive" way of saying something. (Avoid overusing euphemisms.)

Euphemism:	I am so *exasperated* that I could *expectorate.*
Natural:	I am so mad, I could spit.

072 **Jargon** is language used in a certain profession or by a particular group of people. It is usually very technical and not at all natural.

Jargon:	The storeroom is *maxed out* with last year's *surplus calendar inventory,* a problem which can be *resolved in-house via the circular file.*
Natural:	The storeroom is filled with last year's calendars which can simply be thrown out.

073 A **cliche** is an overused word or phrase, one which springs quickly to mind but just as quickly bores the user and the audience. A cliche gives the reader nothing new or original to think about—no new insight into the subject.

Cliche:	Her face was as red as a beet.
Natural:	Her face flushed, turning first a rosy pink, then a red too deep to hide.

Smooth & Graceful

"Interrupting someone who is writing is a minor infraction of the rules—a five-yard penalty; interrupting someone who is reading your writing is a flagrant foul—fifteen yards and a loss of down."

—**Patrick Ennis**

Once your reader begins his journey into your writing, he wants to stay on course, avoiding detours and distractions. Your job is to move your writing forward smoothly and gracefully, linking your words and sentences so that there are no unnecessary interruptions which force the reader to go back and re-read. Likewise, writing which contains too many short, choppy sentences takes away from the pleasure of reading and often leaves the reader a bit seasick from the constant stop and start, pitch and sway. Read over the samples below; then add smoothness to your growing list of writing goals.

074 **Period faults (Primer Style)** are sentences which are short and choppy, usually from an overreliance on periods. (To correct the problem, do some sentence combining. Put the major points in the main clauses and add the other thoughts *before, after,* and occasionally *within* the main clause.)

Choppy:	Bowling is a good winter sport. It is good exercise. It doesn't cost that much. It's also a game that requires some skill. I bowl a lot in the winter, but not so much in the summer.
Smoother:	I like bowling because it's an inexpensive sport which requires some skill and provides a good deal of exercise even in the winter.

075 **Awkward interruptions** or **split constructions** result when a word or phrase is placed in the middle of the main thought rather than before or after the main thought.

Awkward:	You can pick up whenever it's convenient the film you left for developing.
Smoother:	Whenever it's convenient, you can pick up the film you left for developing.

076 **Mixed construction** results when a writer begins a sentence with one plan of construction but switches to another approach midway through the sentence.

Mixed:	A folk guitar is when you have a guitar with a hollow body and no electrical pickup built in. (In this sentence, an object is being described as if it were a condition or event: *when*.)
Smoother:	A folk guitar has a hollow body and no electrical pickup.

Correct & Appropriate

"You can be a little ungrammatical if you come from the right part of the country."

—Robert Frost

What Robert Frost says is very true. Much of the color and charm of literature comes from the everyday habits, customs—and especially the speech—of its characters. Keep that in mind when you write fiction of any kind. However, also keep in mind, when you are writing essays, reports, and most other assignments, you must usually stick to language that is correct and appropriate.

077 **Substandard (nonstandard) language** is language which is often acceptable in everyday conversation, but seldom in formal writing (except fiction).

Colloquial:	Avoid the use of colloquial language such as *go with, wait up*. Can I *go with?* (Substandard) Can I *go with you?* (Standard)
Double preposition:	Avoid the use of certain double prepositions: *off of, off to, in on*. I am going to start *in on* my homework. (Substandard) I am going to start *on* my homework. (Standard)
Substitution:	Avoid substituting *and* for *to* in formal writing. Try *and* get here on time. (Substandard) Try *to* get here on time. (Standard) Avoid substituting *of* for *have* when combining with *could, would, should*, or *might*. I should *of* studied for that test. (Substandard) I *should have* studied for that test. (Standard)
Slang:	Avoid the use of slang or any *in* words. Hey, Dude, what's happenin'? (Substandard)

078 **Double negative** is a sentence which contains two negative words. Because two negatives make a positive, this type of sentence can take on a meaning opposite of what is intended. Usually, it just sounds bad.

Awkward:	I haven't got no money. (This actually says—after taking out the two negatives which are now a positive—*I have got money*.)
Corrected:	I haven't got any money *or* I have no money.

Do not use *hardly, barely,* or *scarcely* with a negative; the result is a double negative.

Awkward:	After doing a "one and one-quarter" off the high dive, Brad could *not hardly* breathe.
Corrected:	After doing a "one and one-quarter" off the high dive, Brad could hardly breathe.

Logical & Consistent

"Take care of the sense and the sounds will take care of themselves."

—Lewis Carroll

Sometimes it is necessary to write in a very logical, organized manner to prove a point or support an opinion. When this is true, it may well be necessary to take a refresher course in *logic*—the science of making sense. (See "Thinking Logically" in your handbook.) Other times it's not so much the logic of *what* you say as *how* you say it. In other words, are the ideas in your sentences arranged correctly, logically, so that the reader sees clearly and accurately what you are trying to show?

What follows is a sampler of common errors which in one way or another go against basic logic or grammar.

079 **Upside-down subordination** occurs when the main idea of a sentence is expressed in the dependent clause or phrase rather than in the independent clause.

Upside-down:	As the lightning struck, Joe was putting the aluminum ladder in the garage.
Logical:	As Joe was putting the aluminum ladder in the garage, the lightning struck.

080 **Anticlimax** is the term for a sentence which begins with the most important idea (climax) and continues with details which seem unimportant and out of place.

Anticlimax:	Anyone missing the passport-application deadline will not be allowed to go on the European tour nor will their two-dollar fee be refunded.
Logical:	Anyone missing the passport-application deadline will not be allowed to go on the European tour.

081 **Inconsistent (Unparallel) construction** occurs when the structure of the words being used is changed.

Inconsistent:	In my hometown, the people pass the time shooting bow, pitching horseshoes, and at softball games. (The change in word structure is from the *ing* words, *shooting* and *pitching,* to *at softball games.)*
Consistent:	In my hometown, the people pass the time shooting bow, pitching horseshoes, and playing softball. (Now all three things being discussed are *ing* words—they are now **consistent** or **parallel**.)

082 **Shift in construction** is a change in the structure or style midway through a sentence. (Also see 921-929, "Agreement of Subject and Verb.")

Shift in number:	When *a person* goes shopping for a used car, *he* or *she* (not *they*) must be careful not to get a lemon.
Shift in tense:	The trunk should be checked to see that it *contains* a jack and a spare tire which *are* (not *should be*) in good shape.
Shift in person:	*One* must be careful to watch for heavy, white exhaust or *one* (not *you*) can end up with real engine problems.
Shift in voice:	As you continue to look for the right car (active voice), many freshly painted ones are sure to be seen (passive voice).
Corrected:	As you continue to look for the right car, you are sure to see many freshly painted ones. (Both verbs are in the active voice. *Note:* Use the active rather than the passive voice in most writing.)

Writing
PARAGRAPHS

For many developing writers, the key to writing well is gaining control of the focus or topic of their writing. This is especially true of expository or academic writing. Learning to write solid paragraphs—paragraphs which make a clear statement—will help you gain the control you need. The section which follows discusses the paragraph and all that goes into writing and using it effectively.

What is a Paragraph?

090   The paragraph is a device for helping you keep your thoughts together on the page, making it easier for the reader to follow your thinking. By definition, a paragraph is a series of related sentences which work together to develop a specific topic or idea. Most paragraphs contain a sentence somewhere which states (or strongly suggests) the focus or topic of the paragraph. This sentence is sometimes called the *topic sentence* and is often found at or near the beginning of the paragraph.

In a tightly organized paragraph, every sentence is closely related to the topic sentence, bringing a sense of unity and clarity to your writing. To develop another thought, "simply" write another paragraph. The individual paragraphs can then be tied together into essays, reports, and other compositions which call for highly organized writing.

But is it necessary, you ask, to purposely compose a topic sentence for each paragraph you write? Obviously, *no.* If your thoughts are flowing logically, topic sentences (controlling ideas) will work their way naturally into the fabric of your writing. If, however, you are having trouble organizing or controlling your thoughts and very little is "flowing logically," the answer may well be *yes.* An effective topic sentence can help you focus on one idea at a time. It can help you clarify your feelings and impressions. It can help point you in the right direction and keep you on track by specifically defining your destination.

Another word of caution about paragraphs is that they can work against you if you aren't careful. If you write simply to fill your paper with "thought blocks," each dutifully following the other down the page, you may not be controlling your writing after all. The writing (or the form of it) may be controlling you. You must never allow your creativity or your natural voice to fall victim to the form of your writing. A paragraph, like any form of writing, should be a means to an end—a means of helping you express your thoughts in a fresh, efficient way.

The Topic Sentence

091   A **topic sentence** reveals what your subject is and what it is you plan to say about that subject. Below is a sample topic sentence and a simple formula to remember when writing topic sentences:

Music helps people relax.

Formula: A limited topic (*Music*) + a specific
impression (*helps people relax*) = a topic sentence.

With a clear topic sentence, you should be able to gather the appropriate specific details and arrange them in an order that is both clear and interesting. Continue to write as naturally and honestly as you can, so that you feel comfortable with both the words and the ideas you are using to support your topic sentence. Let your personality, feelings, and creativity be as much a guide as the topic sentence. Only then will you achieve the balance all writers strive for.

If the sentences which support your topic sentence (your main idea) flow naturally and work well together, the result will be a paragraph which is easy and enjoyable to read. Other times, however, your sentences will not go together as well as you would like. The ideas are there, but the sentences do not carry them effectively to the reader. Maybe they lack color or rhythm or balance. Or maybe they are too much alike—short and choppy, long and wordy, simple and predictable. Writing mature, colorful sentences and arranging them into an effective order is a basic goal of writing. (See 102.)

Once you have arranged all of your ideas into a sensible order, it is time to bring your paragraph to a logical stopping point. Often, your writing will find its own stopping point. Other times, you will need to think about how you can bring your writing to a close. You might, for example, add a final sentence (or two) which ties all of your thoughts together, drawing attention to the message or impression you are trying to make. In either case, your paragraph should end as naturally as possible.

092 Keeping It Together

Every sentence in a paragraph should be closely related to the topic sentence. This brings a sense of **unity** to the paragraph. Note how the boldfaced sentence in the paragraph below does not relate to the topic sentence and should *not,* therefore, be included in this paragraph. The topic sentence is italicized and does represent an acceptable topic sentence for that paragraph.

The announcement of the cancellation was all the rockfest crowd needed to turn into a frenzied mob. The entire audience of sun-baked fans rose out of disbelief and moved in the direction of the speaker. Those nearest the stage pushed forward and as if by instinct began tearing the canvas drapes from the side of the makeshift platform. The stage suddenly came alive as people poured on it from all directions. **The group scheduled to appear was the hottest name in the business.** It was soon a stage no longer, but a swarming mass of destruction. The curtains came ripping to the ground and the speaker stands fell like goalposts after a championship game. Those who had been sitting and watching were now drawn irresistibly into the chaos. No semblance of order remained.

Types of Paragraphs

There are four basic types of paragraphs: **narrative, descriptive, expository,** and **persuasive.**

093   A **narrative paragraph** tells a story of one kind or another. (See "Writing About an Event," 123.)

> In first grade I learned some of the harsh realities of life. I found out that circuses aren't all they're supposed to be. We were going to the circus for our class trip, and I was really excited about it because I had never been to one before. Our class worked for weeks on a circus train made of shoe boxes, and Carrie Kaske told me her mom had fainted once when she saw the lion trainer. The day of the trip finally came, and my wonderful circus turned out to be nothing but one disappointment after another. I couldn't see why Carrie's mom fainted when she saw the lion trainer; I couldn't even see the lion trainer. I couldn't see much of anything for that matter. I could just barely make out some tiny figures scurrying around in the three rings that seemed to be a hundred miles away from my seat. After the first half hour, all I wanted to do was buy a Pepsi and a monkey-on-a-stick and get out of there. Of course, nothing in life is that easy. We weren't allowed to buy anything; so I couldn't have my souvenir, and instead of a cold Pepsi to quench my thirst, I had warm, curdled milk that the room mothers had so thoughtfully brought along. I returned to school tired and a little wiser. I remember looking at our little circus train on the window ledge and thinking that I'd rather sit and watch it do nothing than go to another circus.

094   A **descriptive paragraph** is one in which the sentences work together to present a single, clear picture (description) of a person, place, thing, or idea. (See "Writing About a Person, . . . Place, . . . Object," 119-121.)

> My Uncle John is normally a likable and friendly man, but when there is a group of people and one of those instant cameras around, he becomes a real pest. No matter what the occasion, even something as uneventful as a few of our relatives getting together for a visit after work, Uncle John appoints himself official photographer. He spends the whole time with one eye looking through the lens and the other scoping out the potential subjects for his pictures. In most situations, taking pictures is a great way to spend some time and have a little fun, but when Uncle John is pushing the button, it's quite another story. He doesn't believe in candids. Instead, Uncle John insists upon interrupting all activity to persuade his prey to pose for his pictures. In return, he gets photographs of people arranged in neat rows smiling through clenched teeth. Although we have tried again and again to convince Uncle John that his old, traditional methods of photography aren't necessarily the best, he continues to insist that we, "Come over here, so I can take your picture." About the only solution is to convince Uncle John that he should be in some of these pictures and that you'd be happy to snap a few. Then once you get the camera in your hands don't stop shooting until all the film is gone.

095   An **expository** paragraph is one which presents facts, gives directions, defines terms, and so on. This type of writing can be used when you wish to present or explain facts or ideas. (See "Writing an Explanation," 124.)

> Braille is a system of communication used by the blind. It was developed by Louis Braille, a blind French student, in 1824. The code consists of an alphabet using combinations of small raised dots. The dots are imprinted on paper and can be felt, and thus read, by running the fingers across the page. The basic unit of the code is called a "cell" which is two dots wide and three dots high. Each letter is formed by different combinations of these dots. Numbers, punctuation marks, and even a system for writing music are also expressed by using different arrangements. These small dots, which may seem insignificant to the sighted, have opened up the entire world of books and reading for the blind.

096   A **persuasive** paragraph is one which presents information to support or prove a point. It expresses an opinion and tries to convince the reader that the opinion is correct or valid. (See "Writing to Persuade," 125, and "Thinking Logically," 543.)

> Capital punishment should be abolished for three major reasons. First, common sense tells me that two wrongs don't make a right. To kill someone convicted of murder contradicts the reasoning behind the law that taking another's life is wrong. The state is committing the same violent, dehumanizing act it is condemning. Second, the death penalty is not an effective deterrent. Numerous studies show that murder is usually the result of a complex psychological and sociological problem and that most murderers do not contemplate the consequences of their act; or if they do, any penalty is seen as a far-off possibility. The gain from the offense, on the other hand, brings immediate results. The third and most serious objection is that death is final and cannot be altered. Errors in deciding guilt or innocence will always be present in our system of trial by jury. There is too great a risk that innocent people will be put to death. Official records show that it has already happened in the past. For these reasons, I feel capital punishment should be replaced with a system that puts all doubt on the side of life—not death.

Types of Detail

097   When you are attempting to add specific details to your paragraphs, you can use sensory, memory, and reflective details (or a combination of the three). Most of the time you will not stop to think about what "type" of specific detail you are using. Other times, it will be helpful to think about which kind of detail would be most effective in your writing. The explanation which follows may help:

Sensory details are those which come to you through the senses (*smell, touch, taste, hearing,* and *sight*). Sensory details are especially important when you are attempting to describe something you are observing (or have observed) firsthand.

> I could feel the warmth of the kerosene stove and smell its penetrating odor even before I opened the squeaky door leading to his third-floor apartment.

Memory details are those which you recall from past experiences. Often, memory details will come to you in the form of mental pictures or images which you can use to build strong, colorful descriptions.

> I can remember as a kid walking the noisy, wooden stairway to his attic room and how he was always waiting at the half-opened door to take the newspaper from my shaking hand.

Reflective details are those which come to mind as you reflect on or wonder about something (*I wish, hope, dream, wonder, if only,* etc.). Reflective details bring a strong personal tone to your writing and allow you to write about the way things might have been or may yet be.

> I wonder if he ever knew how frightened I was then and how I imagined there to be all varieties of evil on the other side of that half-opened door—beyond the kerosene stove.

Methods of Organization

098   If your writing is flowing smoothly, it will most likely have an inner-logic or natural direction which holds it together for the reader. If you need to, however, you can purposely arrange the details in your paragraph or other forms of writing in any of several basic ways:

Chronological (*time*) **order** is effective for narrating personal experiences, summarizing steps, and explaining events. Details are arranged in the order in which they happen, as in the paragraph which follows:

> General Sherman and his men devised ingenious methods for the wrecking of the Southern railroad. They first used a portable rail-lifter which consisted of a chain with a hook on one end and a large iron ring on the other. The hook would be placed under the rail and a small pole put through the ring. By bracing the pole on the ground, a group of soldiers could lift the rail from the ties. The rails, which were made of a flimsy type of steel, could be heated and easily twisted into almost any shape. Initially, Sherman and his men took the heated rails and twisted them around nearby trees into what they called "Sherman's hairpins." After it was pointed out that the Confederates might be able to straighten these rails and use them again, Sherman's men devised a new system. They again heated the rails, but this time they used huge wrenches on either end and twisted in opposite directions. This left a useless, licorice-shaped rail.

Order of location is useful for many types of descriptions. It helps provide unity by arranging details left to right, right to left, top to bottom, edge to center, from the distant to the near, and so on.

Illustration (*deduction*: general to specific) is a method of arrangement in which you first state a general idea (topic sentence) and follow with specific reasons, examples, facts, and details to support the general idea. (See 014.)

Climax (*induction:* specific to general) is a method of arrangement in which you present specific details followed by a general statement or conclusion which can be drawn from the specific information provided. (If a topic sentence is used, it is placed at the end. See 014.)

Cause and effect arrangement helps you make connections between a result and the events that preceded it. A general statement (*a result or cause*) can be supported by specific effects—or the general statement (*an effect*) can be supported by specific causes. (See 116 and 117 for examples.)

Comparison is a method of arrangement in which you measure one subject against another subject which is often more familiar. State the main point of the comparison early and present the likenesses (details) in a clear, organized fashion. Readers should not have to jump back and forth between subjects. **Contrast** uses details to measure the differences between two subjects. (See 103.)

Definition or **classification** can be used when explaining a term or concept (a machine, theory, game, etc.). Begin by placing the subject in the appropriate species or class and then provide details which show how that term or concept is different from others in the same class. Do not include more than a few features or distinctions in one paragraph. (See 122 and 033 for help.)

Adding Coherence and Variety

099   Each sentence you write should fit together with those which come before and after it, giving a sense of oneness to whatever you are writing. Getting your writing to stick together (cohere) can sometimes be a challenge. You can achieve paragraph coherence using one or more of the following techniques.

- Use a logical method of organization. (See preceding section.)
- Use (but don't overuse) pronouns to refer to nouns in previous sentences.
- Use repetition of words, synonyms, or ideas. (See 101.)
- Use parallel structure. (See 116: paragraph three.)
- Use transitional words. (See 103.)

Variety

100   It is also important that your paragraphs contain a variety of sentences. You can achieve sentence variety in a number of ways, each of which can contribute to effective paragraph writing.

- Vary the length of your sentences to suit the topic and tone of your paragraph. Short, concise sentences, for example, are appropriate for explaining complex ideas or for adding feeling or dramatic effect. (See 102.)
- Vary your sentence beginnings. Rather than beginning each sentence with the subject, use modifiers, phrases, and clauses in that position.
- Vary the arrangement of the material within the sentence. There are three basic classifications of sentence arrangement; periodic, balanced, and loose. (See 920.)
- Vary the kinds of sentences you use. (See 919.)

> Of all the things a student needs to make it through a typical day, probably the most important, yet least appreciated, is paper. (*Complex*) Paper is used for academic, social, and personal purposes by nearly all students every day. (*Simple*) The most obvious use is for the academic or classroom assignment, whether it comes in the form of a test, an essay, or a summary of plant life on Easter Island. (*Complex*) The social uses of paper center around the "note," which any student can tell you is as important a part of a student's social life as Friday night ball games or the Junior Prom. (*Complex*) As for the personal applications, there is doodling for the nervous mind, and there is scrunching for the nervous hand. (*Compound*) The traditional paper airplanes and spit wads are still around, but they seem less popular than in days gone by—probably because it is easier for a student to move freely about the classroom today than it used to be. (*Compound-Complex*) In any case, there can be no doubt that paper is just as important as ever—Bryan, may I borrow a piece of paper to finish my paragraph?—to the high school student whose days would be a waste without it. (*Compound-Complex*)

101   Use synonyms to avoid using the same word or phrase over and over again. This tedious repetition can become annoying and make your writing sound immature and unreliable. A thesaurus can be helpful when you are stuck for a fresh word. Do not, however, overdo it! Too many "new" words will take away from the natural flow of your writing. Note the change in tone and maturity of the paragraph below after the redundant words (in italics) have been replaced or eliminated:

> January in Wisconsin can be bitter cold. The temperature often drops to 20 and 30 degrees below zero. If there is also a wind, the result can be a windchill of 70 to 80 degrees below. *That's cold!* (eliminate altogether) It is so *cold* (frigid) at times that you can't go outside for fear of *having some real problems with the cold hurting your hands or face* (frostbite). On these *really cold* (face-numbing) days, people are warned against traveling except for an emergency. If the *cold* (arctic-like weather) continues for more than a couple of days, almost all traffic stops since you cannot trust your car to run—even if it does start. Too often a car will stall in the middle of nowhere, leaving a traveler stranded in the *extreme cold* (frozen air). About the only way to beat the incredible *cold* (keep as it is to draw the paragraph together) of a Wisconsin winter is to huddle around the fireplace and dream of the warm, sunny days of summer.

Guidelines for Combining Sentences

Each sentence you write (if it is a complete sentence) contains at least one idea. Most sentences contain several basic ideas which work together to form a complete thought. For example, if you were to write a sentence about a tornado which struck a small town without warning, causing damage, injury, and death, you would actually be working with six different ideas in that sentence. Each of those ideas could be written as a separate sentence:

1. There was a tornado.
2. The tornado struck a small town.
3. The tornado struck without warning.
4. The tornado caused a great deal of damage.
5. The tornado caused a number of serious injuries.
6. The tornado caused several deaths.

As a writer, you must now decide how to arrange or combine these six ideas into one or more effective sentences. Ideally, this will happen naturally as you write; however, sometimes you have to consciously add, delete, and rearrange information as you write or revise. There are many possible ways to go about doing this.

1. Use a **series** to combine three or more similar ideas.
   The unexpected tornado struck the small town causing *much damage, numerous injuries,* and *several deaths.*

2. Use a **relative pronoun** (*who, whose, that, which*) to introduce the subordinate (less important) ideas.
   The tornado, *which was completely unexpected,* swept through the small town causing much damage, numerous injuries, and several deaths.

3. Use an **introductory phrase or clause** for the less important ideas.
   Because the tornado was completely unexpected, it caused a great deal of damage, numerous injuries, and several deaths.

4. Use a **participial phrase** (*-ing, -ed*) at the beginning or end of a sentence.
   The tornado swept through the small town without warning, *leaving behind a trail of death and destruction.*

5. Use a **semicolon.** (Use a conjunctive adverb with the semicolon when appropriate.)
   The tornado swept through the small town without warning; *as a result,* it caused a great deal of damage, numerous injuries, and several deaths.

6. Repeat a **key word** or phrase to emphasize an idea.
   The tornado left a permanent *scar* on the small town, a *scar* of destruction, injury, and death.

7. Use a **dash** to set off a key word(s) or phrase at the beginning or the end of the sentence.
   The tornado which unexpectedly struck the small town left behind a grim calling card—*death and destruction.*

8. Use a **correlative conjunction** (*either, or; not only, but also*) to compare or contrast two ideas in a sentence.
   The tornado *not only* inflicted much property damage, *but also* much human suffering.

9. Use a **colon** to emphasize an important idea.
   The destruction caused by the tornado was unusually high for one reason: *it came without warning.*

10. Use an **appositive** (a word or phrase which renames) to emphasize an idea.
    A single incident—*a tornado which came without warning*—changed the face of the small town forever.

Writing Paragraphs **51**

Useful Transitions

Transitions which can be used to **show location:**				
above	among	beneath	in front of	on top of
across	around	beside	inside	outside
against	away from	between	into	over
along	back of	beyond	near	throughout
alongside	behind	by	off	to the right
amid	below	down	onto	under

Transitions which can be used to **show time:**				
about	first	until	soon	then
after	second	meanwhile	later	next
at	third	today	afterward	in the meantime
before	prior to	tomorrow	immediately	as soon as
during	till	yesterday	finally	when
		next week		

Transitions which can be used to compare two things:

in the same way	likewise	as
also	like	similarly

Transitions which can be used to contrast things (show differences):

but	yet	on the other hand	although	otherwise
however	in the meantime	still	even though	counter to
even so	nevertheless	on the contrary	conversely	as opposed

Transitions which can be used to emphasize a point:

again	indeed	for this reason	truly
to repeat	with this in mind	in fact	to emphasize

Transitions which can be used to conclude or summarize:

as a result	consequently	accordingly	in short
finally	thus	due to	to sum up
in conclusion	therefore	in summary	all in all

Transitions which can be used to add information:

again	and	furthermore	next
also	besides	likewise	finally
additionally	equally important	moreover	as well
in addition	for example	further	together with
another	for instance	furthermore	along with

Transitions which can be used to clarify:

that is	put another way	to clarify
in other words	stated differently	for instance

> *"We live in a time that allows writers freedom to choose what they investigate, to follow their thoughts wherever they lead, and to use a variety of styles and strategies. Therefore, the essay thrives...."*
>
> **— Donald Hall**

Writing ESSAYS

Choosing an Approach

A good deal of your academic writing is essay writing. Themes are essays as are book reports or book reviews. You take essay tests; you write procedure (how-to) papers; some of you write editorials. All of these are essays—writing in which you explain, argue, describe, or interpret your thinking on a particular topic. The way you develop an essay depends on the guidelines established by your instructor and your own good judgment about a particular writing idea. For some essays, a straightforward, traditional approach might be best; for others, a more creative approach might be more effective.

No matter what approach you take when you write an essay, keep in mind that it is a demanding form of writing. You must understand your writing idea, have confidence in your position, and then develop it so that your readers can clearly share in your thinking.

Two Case Studies:

105 The Traditional Essay

Sarah wrote a paper about one of America's most important resources: oil. The fact that the U.S. is so dependent on foreign oil is what particularly interested her. Her paper specifically addresses the effects that the 1973 oil crisis had on America. This is the topic proposed in her opening paragraph. She develops it by describing how the oil crisis disrupted American life during that year.

Her first developmental paragraph describes the initial effects of the crisis that summer; her second paragraph describes the effects later that fall; her third paragraph describes the effects at the end of the year. Sarah's closing paragraph ties all of the important points together and draws a final conclusion for her readers. Her paper is clear, logical, and to the point—a classic five-paragraph composition. (See 116.)

106 The Creative Essay

Rudy wrote a paper about a critical international issue: world hunger. The fact that there are so many starving people in the world today particularly disturbs him. His paper specifically addresses the causes of hunger in Africa. This is his thesis, but it isn't proposed or developed in the traditional way.

Rudy decides that the most effective way to develop his thesis is to tell the story of a young boy named Kamal (not a real person) who is dying of starvation. He develops Kamal's story so that it eventually becomes the story of hunger in all of Africa. His closing ideas offer some alarming statistics followed by a question addressed to the readers. Rudy's paper is clear, logical, and dramatic—a creative and innovative composition. (See 117.)

At first glance these two papers seem to have little in common. But they are both essays, cause and effect essays as a matter of fact. They illustrate the wide range of writings that fall under the heading of the essay. Sarah's paper is a good example of the traditional essay (informative, straightforward, and tightly organized); whereas Rudy's paper is a good example of a creative essay (informative, organized, and original).

The Importance of Organization

107   Since an essay is often detailed and complex, many essay writers use an outline to help them organize their ideas. Some may use it before they write the rough draft; others may use it afterward to help reorganize their ideas. You, as a writer, are free to choose where in the writing process an outline will help. It is a good tool if used wisely. Don't allow the outline to inhibit the free flow of your ideas, but don't ignore its usefulness in revising a wandering, unclear essay.

Considering the length and complex nature of an essay—opening, developmental paragraphs (however many are needed for your topic), and closing—special attention must also be given to transitions and linking devices. This must be done to keep your reader on a clear path throughout your writing. (See 103.)

Below is a list of twelve steps which can be followed when planning and writing your essay. Follow them as they are, or adapt them to better suit your individual needs and your instructor's guidelines.

108 Steps in the Essay Writing Process

1.   Select a general subject area that interests you.

2.   List all of your initial thoughts or ideas about the subject. (See "Prewriting Techniques," 046, for help with generating initial ideas.)

3.   Use your list(s) to help you focus on a specific topic within the subject area.

4.   Do any reading, researching, or thinking necessary to expand your knowledge of the specific topic.

At this point you may continue planning, or you may write an early draft of your essay. Follow either column of steps, whichever is best for you. The column on the left describes a very systematic, traditional approach to developing an essay. The column on the right is a much more open approach.

109 Systematic Approach

5.   Determine what it is you would like to say about this topic and write a tentative statement which reflects this purpose. (This statement is sometimes called a thesis statement.)

Open Approach

5.   Many writers feel that they must write an early draft in order to discover the message of their essay. Write freely, allowing new opinions and directions to emerge as they occur to you.

Systematic Approach	Open Approach
6. Work up a list of details which can be used to support your thesis statement.	6. Read over your early draft and determine the controlling idea or specific focus of your essay. This statement of topic should appear in the opening to your essay.
7. Arrange this list of details into a well-ordered outline. (See 110.)	7. Try outlining the developmental paragraphs of your early draft. (A simple list of the topic sentences will do.) Is your statement of topic adequately supported by this list of main ideas? Add, delete, and rearrange ideas (details) as necessary.
8. If you need additional support for any area of your essay, do the reading, researching, or thinking necessary.	8. If you need additional support for any area of your essay, do the reading, researching, or thinking necessary.
9. Write the first draft of your paper.	9. Write the first revision of your paper, restructuring it as necessary to clearly support your thesis statement.

10. Revise the first draft of your essay. (If you wrote an early draft and have already written a revision, determine if you need another.) Rewrite at least once for content—pay special attention to the opening and closing paragraphs. Rewrite a second time for the style of your writing. (See 016 and 050 for help.)

11. Proofread your revised paper for spelling, punctuation, usage, and other mechanical errors.

12. Type or write (in ink) your final copy according to your instructor's guidelines.

The Outline

110 An **outline** is an orderly arrangement of related ideas. It is a *sketch* of what the final composition will look like; it is a *guide* which keeps the writer on the right path; it is a *blueprint* which makes clear where each piece of information belongs. An outline must be flexible in the planning stage so as to allow for needed changes; yet, it must also be rigid enough to keep the writer from wandering off the topic. In the planning stages, your outline should be a changing, *working outline*; in its final form, your outline should be a permanent guide to your completed composition.

The details in an outline should be listed from general to specific. (The following details are listed from general to more specific: *transportation, motor vehicle, car, Ford, Thunderbird.*) This means that the general topic of your writing (*thesis statement*) is listed first, followed by the major subtopics and the supporting details and examples. If, for instance, you were assigned to write a paper about the subject of "Trees," you might choose to write about "Trees used in landscaping" (**topic**). In the planning of your paper, you might decide to divide your topic into "Trees used for landscaping in cold climates" and "Trees used for landscaping in warm climates" (**subtopics**). You might then further divide your subtopics into the different kinds of trees suitable in each climate (supporting details). To complete your outline, you could list specific examples of each kind of tree (**specific examples**). It is important to remember that each additional division in an outline must contain information which is more specific than the division before it. (See the sample outline on the next page.)

111 Outlining Details — General to Specific

Subject: Trees

I. **Topic**

   A. **Subtopic**

      1. **Supporting detail**

         a. **Specific example**
         b. **Specific example**

      2. **Supporting detail**

         a. **Specific example**
         b. **Specific example**

   B. **Subtopic**

I. Many trees can be used for landscaping.

   A. Some trees are best suited for cold climates.

      1. Evergreens are hardy and provide year-round color.
         a. Norway pine...
         b. Scotch pine...

      2. Maples hold up well and provide brilliant seasonal color.
         a. Red maple...
         b. Silver maple...

   B. Some trees are better suited for warm climates.

112 The Topic Outline

    A **topic outline** is a listing of the *topics* to be covered in a piece of writing; it contains no specific details. Topics are stated in words and phrases rather than complete sentences. This makes the topic outline useful for short compositions, especially those for which little time is available as on an essay test. It is always a good idea to begin your outlining task by placing your *thesis statement* or controlling idea at the top of your paper. This will serve as a reminder of the specific topic you are going to be outlining and later writing about. Use the standard format shown below for labeling the lines of your outline. Do not attempt to outline your opening or closing unless specifically told to do so.

Thesis statement: America's supply of resources is vast, but not unlimited, as shown in the energy crisis of 1973.

Outline Format	I.
	  A.
	  B.
	    1.
	    2.
	      a.
	      b.
	        (1)
	        (2)
	          (a)
	          (b)
	II.
		Topic Outline
		
		Introduction
		  I. Gasoline shortage
		    A. Long lines
		    B. Gas "rationing"
		    C. Station closings
		  II. Voluntary energy conservation
		    A. Gasoline
		    B. Electricity
		    C. Home heating fuel
		  III. Forced energy conservation
		    A. Fuel allocation
		    B. Speed limit
		    C. Airline flights
		    D. Christmas lighting
		Conclusion

Note: No new subdivision should be started unless there are at least two points to be listed in that new division. This means that each *1* must have a *2*; each *a* must be followed by a *b*.	

113 **The Sentence Outline**

The **sentence outline** contains not only the major points to be covered, but also lists many of the important supporting details as well. It is used for longer, more formal writing assignments; each point should, therefore, be written as a complete sentence. The sentence outline is especially useful when you find yourself asking others for help with your composition. It will be much easier for them to understand an outline written in complete sentences than one written using single words and phrases. (See sample essay.)

Sentence Outline	I. In the summer of 1973, gasoline was in short supply.
	  A. Long lines of cars at the pumps became a familiar sight.
	  B. Some stations "rationed" their gasoline.
	  C. Other stations closed early.
	II. The Arab oil boycott forced additional cutbacks in energy use.
	  A. Many Americans turned down their home thermostats.
	  B. Some businesses shortened working hours to conserve.
	  C. Unnecessary lighting and driving were cut.
	III. Late in 1973, new laws were passed to assure energy savings.
	  A. The amount of fuel available for heating was reduced.
	  B. A fifty-mile-per-hour speed limit took effect for all states.
	  C. Airline flights were cut back.
	  D. Outdoor Christmas lighting was banned.

The Structure of the Traditional Essay

114 The traditional essay is quite highly structured; that is, it contains an opening paragraph, several developmental or body paragraphs, and a closing or summary paragraph. Your **opening paragraph** should state the topic of the essay (thesis statement), gain the attention of the reader, and allow for a smooth transition into the body of the essay. There are several techniques or devices which you can use to develop this paragraph:

- a series of questions about the topic
- an interesting story or anecdote about the subject
- a startling or unusual fact or figure
- a reference to a famous person or place associated with the topic
- a quotation from a well-known figure or literary work
- a definition of an important, topic-related term

The **developmental paragraphs** are the heart of the essay. They must be developed and arranged in a logical, yet interesting, way. If, for instance, you are going to explain the process of carving a figure from a bar of soap, you will most likely use a step-by-step explanation. Your developmental paragraphs will naturally follow one another from the beginning of the explanation through the last step in the carving process. At the same time, you cannot let the explanation become so matter-of-fact that the reader loses interest in it. You might call upon some additional sensory details to make the paragraphs vivid and colorful as well as accurate. (*Note:* The same methods of arrangement which are used for the single paragraph can also be used to arrange details in developmental paragraphs.)

A new paragraph is started whenever there is a shift or change in the essay. This change is called a paragraph shift and can take place for any of six basic reasons:

1) a change in emphasis or ideas	4) a change in speakers
2) a change in time	5) a change in place or setting
3) a change in action	6) to break up an exceptionally long paragraph

Each new paragraph should begin with a sentence which either serves as a transition or states a new or additional step in the development of the essay topic.

The **closing** or summary paragraph should tie all of the important points in the essay together and draw a final conclusion for the reader. It should leave the reader with a clear understanding of the meaning and the significance of the essay.

A Closer Look
Thinking Through Your Essay:

You have already done a lot to shape your thinking if you have read the sections on the writing process and writing the essay. But let us look more closely: How does an essay writer think?

Suppose you are assigned to write an essay about an event in your life which led you to an important realization or understanding. You decide to write about a recent ski trip with your father — your third time down the slopes, his first. You know that something important happened that day, but you're not sure what.

Thinking through what you want to say can improve your essay. But the reverse is also true: writing an essay can improve your thinking about that ski trip. The essay writer's first rule for thinking, therefore, is this: "Think to write; write to think."

Be a "Three-Eyed"
Writer

115 As you write your essay, open three "eyes" in your head: a **material eye** to study your subject, a **critical eye** to check the thinking process, and an **intuitive eye** to foresee what your writing has to offer you and your readers. Here is what those three "eyes" might see as you think through your ski essay.

The Material Eye

With the **material eye** you remember what your dad said on the chair lift, how prickly you felt under your thermal underwear, how musty the rented ski boots smelled, the fear in your dad's voice when he refused to jump a ramp. You compare his "safety-first" attitude with your own daredevil tactics. Remembering how you scraped your forehead in a bad fall, you discover that you really wanted him to fall, not so that he would be hurt but so that he could really live on the cutting edge, just for once. Finally, you realize that he was on the cutting edge, in his own terms, simply because in middle age he had dared to ski for the first time. You end feeling secretly proud and closer to him than you had felt before.

The Critical Eye

With the **critical eye** you converse with yourself as you write: These are tired ideas, look for more original ones. If you don't concentrate, you'll never make the deadline. That's a good pathway—follow it—push it some more. Say this first, then it will be easier to say the other thing later. You're not as clearheaded as you were before, so why not take a break and come back to this tomorrow morning. This would be an effective last line.

The Intuitive Eye

With the **intuitive eye** you steadily see the possibility of your essay. You see an essay with the emotional tone of a teenager like yourself, with quick changes from high moods to low. You see an essay which brings a slow smile to your dad's lips; you see an essay worthy of a warm hug.

Traditional Essay

Below is a sample essay labeled to illustrate opening, developmental, and closing paragraphs, as well as transitional and linking devices of a traditional essay. (Note that the details in this essay are arranged in chronological order. This arrangement combines with "repetition" to form a series of strong transitions between paragraphs.)

America — The Land of Plenty?

Opening Paragraph

America had long been a nation of plenty. Even during its bleakest hours, America had always found the resources to keep surging ahead. During the 1960's and early '70s, America was at perhaps an all-time peak—it prospered as never before. More and more Americans enjoyed "all the comforts of home," including their own home. Nearly anything could be purchased on credit, and nearly everyone had plenty of that. No one would have believed it could all change so quickly or so drastically as it did in the summer of 1973. *It was in the summer of that year that America saw its* **dream** *of forever being the "land of plenty"* **slowly dim.**

Thesis Statement

Transition

It was early in the summer of '73 that the **first sign of this fading dream appeared.** It appeared in the front windows of gasoline stations across the land: the sign read simply "Closed." Closed for good reason. The product these stations needed to operate was not available—at least not to them. This substance, which had long been cheap and plentiful, was suddenly anything but cheap and even less plentiful. This suddenly rare commodity was gasoline. The gasoline Americans had taken for granted for so long was nothing to take for granted in the summer and fall of 1973. It was often difficult to find and just as difficult to get once you found it. People often waited in block-long lines for an hour or more to get their **"ration"** of six, eight, or perhaps ten gallons.

Transition

Later in the year, it appeared as if even a **six-gallon ration** might be too much to expect. It was in November that the Arab oil-producing nations cut off all oil shipments to the United States because it continued to support Israel in the Middle East war. The supply of gas was immediately at a critical low. The

Parallel Structure Links {

American home owners responded by voluntarily turning down their thermostats by an average of two degrees. American business and labor leaders responded by voluntarily shortening working hours and by cutting back on unnecessary energy use. Unneeded lighting was turned off. Slower driving was encouraged; Sunday driving, discouraged. Still, most Americans felt the gasoline shortage was contrived to drive up prices and that the cries of **"energy crisis" were greatly exaggerated.**

Transition

But **then, before the year had ended,** the **reality of the crisis** hit home. A mandatory fuel allocation program was announced to take effect within thirty days. It called for a ten percent cutback in heating fuel for industries, a fifteen percent cutback for stores and other commercial establishments. It also called for a fifty-mile-per-hour speed limit nationwide. Airline flights were reduced in number, and perhaps most shocking of all, outdoor Christmas lights were banned. In all, Americans were told to reduce their energy consumption by ten percent immediately or the crisis would become a catastrophe. Nearly everyone reduced—a catastrophe was avoided.

Transition

Even though **most Americans still felt** the crisis was only temporary, they came to realize—many of them for the first time—that America was not a land of "unlimited" plenty. There was indeed a limit to the supply of energy products which even America would be allowed to consume. It was this limit which America had both reached and exceeded in the summer and fall of 1973. In that short, significant time, America had awakened from its dreamlike sleep long enough to catch a glimpse of its own future—a future filled with many of the same hopes and dreams it had always had, but one also tempered with the reality of its limitations.

Closing Paragraph

Creative Essay

Below is a sample essay labeled to illustrate the development of a creative essay. (Note how the opening paragraph sets the emotional tone and focuses on the topic, and how the developmental paragraphs logically expand the topic through a series of questions and answers. The concluding lines force a reader to reflect further on the topic of the essay.)

Why Did Kamal Die?

Opening paragraph sets the emotional tone.

In two days Kamal would have been four years old, but his wasted body now lies under a pile of rocks behind his family's hut.

First question (also the title) focuses on the topic.

Why did Kamal die? The too-easy answer is malnutrition. A lack of vitamins and protein opened him to an intestinal infection and two fatal weeks of diarrhea. He could have been saved with a simple solution of boiled water, salts, and sugar which the UNICEF distributes in a free kit called "oral rehydration therapy" (ORT). But Kamal's mother, forced to work 18-hour days at home and in the fields, had missed the rural health-care worker's demonstration in the village.

Second question

Why was Kamal malnourished in the first place? He and his six brothers and sisters had known starvation all their lives. His father and mother scraped at five dry acres of government land, earning no more than $500.00 (U.S.) even in a good year. For the past seven years, however, an unrelenting drought had dried up the wells and withered the cassava and rice crops. Kamal's family had become desperate for food.

Third question

Then was the weather to blame? Not really. In fact, during those seven famine years, the government had raised surpluses of cotton, sugarcane, and tea on large, well-irrigated government farms. These surpluses they sold to industrial countries in Europe and North America. With the proceeds, they paid off interest on huge debts, bought new pesticides and irrigation pumps for the cash-crop plantations, and invested in new military equipment—rifles, land rovers, and rocket launchers. The government stored no food surpluses and did little to help small sharecroppers survive. The weather could be blamed for the drought, but cruel government policies created the famine.

Lack of respect for human rights is partly to blame for the policies that killed Kamal, yet those policies came about in response to heavy pressures. The government, propped up by U.S. support, has tried to suppress Soviet-aided rebels on the southern border and, in the process, has shoved tens of thousands of refugees and poor sharecroppers like Kamal's parents onto tracts of hilly land. Desperate to make a living, the refugees have cleared land and ripped out trees for firewood. But instead of creating usable farmland, they have wiped out vegetation and caused terrible erosion.

Fourth question

If U.S. aid has primarily been used for military matters, couldn't Kamal have been saved by one of the giant international relief agencies that make those moving appeals on TV? As a matter of fact, more than $70 million was raised for immediate relief work by Bob Geldof's 16-hour international rock concert, Live Aid, starring Michael Jackson, Lionel Ritchie, Tina Turner, Bruce Springsteen, and many others. More millions of dollars were raised by private religious organizations. Sacks of grain and medical supplies were already on their way in loaded trucks and many lives had already been saved when torrents of rain suddenly broke the seven-year drought, flashing down the parched gullies, turning roads and railways to quagmires. For weeks the aid trucks were sidelined until the roads could be rebuilt. During that short period, Kamal died.

Alarming statistic connects Kamal's death to worldwide crisis.

Around the world, according to expert Roy Prosterman (The Hunger Project Papers, May 1984), 18 children die of hunger every sixty seconds. Thirty-five thousand people every day. Between 13 and 18 million people every year. In the two minutes it may have taken you to read these words, another 36 children died. Because this situation is considered "normal," their deaths will not make the evening news.

Repeated title forces reader to reflect further on the topic.

You call it. Why did Kamal die?

Writing Terms

Argumentation: Writing or speaking in which reasons or arguments are presented in a logical way.

Arrangement: The order in which details are placed or arranged in a piece of writing.

Audience: Those people who read or hear what you have written.

Balance: The arranging of words or phrases so that two ideas are given equal emphasis in a sentence or paragraph; a pleasing rhythm created when a pattern is repeated in a sentence.

Body: The paragraphs between the introduction and conclusion which develop the main idea(s) of the writing.

Brainstorming: Collecting ideas by thinking freely and openly about all the possibilities; used most often with groups.

Central idea: The main point or purpose of a piece of writing, often stated in a thesis statement or topic sentence.

Clincher sentence: The sentence which summarizes the point being made in a paragraph, usually located last.

Coherence: The arrangement of ideas in such a way that the reader can easily follow from one point to the next.

Composition: A process in which several different ideas are combined into one, unified piece of writing.

Data: Information which is accepted as being true—facts, figures, examples—and from which conclusions can be drawn.

Deductive reasoning: The act of reasoning from a general idea to a specific point or conclusion.

Description: Writing which paints a colorful picture of a person, place, thing, or idea using concrete, vivid details.

Details: The words used to describe a person, convince an audience, explain a process, or in some way support the central idea; to be effective, details should be vivid, colorful, and appeal to the senses.

Emphasis: Placing greater stress on the most important idea in a piece of writing by giving it special treatment; emphasis can be achieved by placing the important idea in a special position, by repeating a key word or phrase, or by simply writing more about this idea than the others.

Essay: A piece of prose writing in which ideas on a single topic are presented, explained, argued, or described in an interesting way.

Exposition: Writing which explains.

Extended definition: Writing which goes beyond a simple definition of a term in order to stress a point; it can cover several paragraphs and include personal definitions and experiences, similes and metaphors, quotations, and even verse.

Figurative language: Language which goes beyond the normal meaning of the words used; writing in which a figure of speech is used to heighten or color the meaning.

Focus: Concentrating on a specific subject to give it emphasis or clarity.

Form: The arrangement of the details into a pattern or style; the way in which the content of writing is organized.

Free writing: Writing openly and freely on any topic; *focused* free writing is writing openly on a specific topic or angle.

Generalization: An idea or statement which emphasizes the general characteristics rather than the specific details of a subject.

Grammar: Grammar is the study of the structure and features of a language; it usually consists of rules and standards which are to be followed to produce acceptable writing and speaking.

Idiom: A phrase or expression which means something different from what the words actually say. An idiom is usually understandable to a particular group of people. (Example: *over his head* for *didn't understand.*)

Inductive reasoning: Reasoning which leads one to a conclusion or generalization after examining specific examples or facts; drawing generalizations from specific evidence.

Inverted sentence: A sentence in which the normal word order is inverted or switched; usually the verb comes before the subject.

Issue: A point or question to be decided.

Journal: A daily record of thoughts, impressions, and autobiographical information; a journal is often a source of ideas for writing.

Juxtaposition: Placing two ideas (words or pictures) side by side so that their closeness creates a new, often ironic, meaning.

Limiting the subject: Narrowing the subject to a specific topic which is suitable for the writing or speaking task.

Literal: The actual or dictionary meaning of a word; language which means exactly what it appears to mean.

Loaded words: Words which are slanted for or against the subject.

Logic: The science of correct reasoning; correctly using facts, examples, and reasons to support your point.

Modifier: A word, phrase, or clause which limits or describes another word or group of words. (See *adjective* and *adverb*.)

Narration: Writing which tells a story or recounts an event.

Objective: Relating information in an impersonal manner; without feelings or opinions.

Observation: Paying close attention to people, places, things, and events to collect details for later use.

Overview: A general idea of what is to be covered in a piece of writing.

Personal narrative: Personal writing which covers an event in the writer's life; it often contains personal comments and observations as well as a description of the event.

Persuasion: Writing which is meant to change the way the reader thinks or acts.

Poetic license: The freedom a writer has to bend the rules of writing to achieve a certain effect.

Point of view: The position or angle from which a story is told.

Premise: A statement or point which serves as the basis of a discussion or debate.

Process: A method of doing something which involves several steps or stages; the writing process involves prewriting, composing, revising, and proofreading.

Prose: Prose is writing or speaking in the usual or ordinary form; prose becomes poetry when it takes on rhyme and rhythm.

Purpose: The specific reason a person has for writing; the goal of writing.

Revision: Changing a piece of writing to improve it in style or content.

Spontaneous: Doing, thinking, or writing without planning. (See Free writing, 045.)

Subjective: Thinking or writing which includes personal feelings, attitudes, and opinions.

Syntax: The order and relationship of words in a sentence.

Theme: The central idea in a piece of writing (lengthy writings may have several themes); a term used to describe a short essay.

Thesis statement: A statement of the purpose, intent, or main idea of an essay.

Tone: The writer's attitude toward the subject; a writer's tone can be serious, sarcastic, tongue-in-cheek, solemn, objective, etc.

Topic: The specific subject of a piece of writing.

Transitions: Words or phrases which help tie ideas together.

Unity: A sense of oneness; writing in which each sentence helps to develop the main idea.

Universal: A topic or idea which applies to everyone.

Usage: The way in which people use language; language considered to be standard (formal and informal) or nonstandard. Only standard usage is acceptable in writing.

Vivid details: Details which appeal to the senses and help the reader see, feel, smell, taste, and hear the subject.

Writing About a Person _____

119   Whenever possible, write about someone you know—or would like to know. Follow the steps in the writing process; use the suggested prewriting techniques (031) and gather as much information and as many specific details as you can. The suggestions which follow can help you think about your topic on a variety of levels.

1. Observe Begin gathering details by observing the person you are describing; notice in particular those details of personality and character which set your subject apart from other people.

2. Investigate Talk to your subject (in person, by phone, or by letter). Have some specific questions ready ahead of time, but be prepared to add or follow up as you go along. What are your subject's goals, dreams, attitudes, concerns, pet peeves, hobbies . . . ? Quote your subject directly whenever possible (use a tape recorder). Read about your subject if he or she is well known and not available for an interview.

3. Define Determine what type of person it is you are describing (child . . . adult; student . . . doctor; shy . . . mischievous; friend . . . stranger) and how he or she is like/not like other people of the same type.

4. Describe List the important physical characteristics, mannerisms, and personality traits, especially those which make your subject unique or worth reading about. (Remember: Show, don't tell. Include people and action in your writing and let them "show" the reader what your subject is like. See 051.)

5. Recall Add details (anecdotes and stories) recounting things your subject has said and done in the past. Try to recall at least one specific incident which reveals the kind of person your subject really is.

6. Compare Compare (and contrast) your subject to other people. Who is he or she most like? a little bit like? not at all like? What object, thing, place, word, sport, plant, . . . could he or she be compared to?

7. Analyze Ask others about your subject and notice how they react to the questions. Their reaction can tell you (and your reader) a great deal about the kind of person your subject truly is. What are your subject's strengths, weaknesses, influences?

8. Evaluate Determine why this person is important to you, to others, to the community.

After you have collected enough details, decide what overall impression your subject has made on you. Use this impression as a starting point and begin your first draft. Write freely and naturally as if you were talking directly to your reader. Include anecdotes, stories, quotations, comparisons, and anything else you feel is worth sharing with your readers.

Avoid Using Cliches or Overused Expressions

autumn of his years	graceful as a swan	runs like a deer
bull in a china shop	heart of gold	sings like a bird
busy as a bee (beaver)	memory of an elephant	sly as a fox
chip off the old block	mind like a sponge	strong as an ox
doesn't pull any punches	quiet as a mouse	stubborn as a mule
fish out of water	red as a beet	stuck-up

Possible Topics _____

I know a special person, a person who . . .

is clever/funny	is a living legend	is a little weird	is the ultimate fan
is stubborn	is always happy	is always in trouble	is always upset
is helpful/kind	is everyone's friend	is afraid of nothing	is always talking
is very talented	is very patriotic	is a perfectionist	is always in a panic
is phony	is a complainer	is always around	is always collecting

Writing About a Place _____

120   Whenever possible, write about a place you know well or one which left a distinct impression on you or is an important part of your life. Follow the steps in the writing process and gather enough details to make your writing interesting to you and your reader. The suggestions below should help get you started.

1. Observe Continue gathering details by observing (firsthand, in books, pictures) your subject and the people, events, and feelings that contribute to making this place unique. Notice the way people react to it and what their general attitude seems to be.

2. Investigate Talk to others about this place, its past, its future. Talk to the place. Talk to a place? Why not. Try something like "If this place could talk, what would it say?" Or, wonder out loud or on paper: "I wonder what this place thinks, feels, hears . . .?"

3. Define Determine what type of place it is you are writing about (land, landmark, building, . . .) and to what degree it is or is not like other places of the same type. What is its function or purpose? (See 122.)

4. Describe Describe the age, size, shape, color, and other important physical features. Where is it located or where does it spend most of its time? What is its most outstanding feature? Show, don't tell. Include people and action in your writing (including yourself) to show the reader what this place is really like—what it feels, smells, tastes, and sounds like—as well as how it looks.

5. Recall Add information you remember from the past. Stories or anecdotes are especially important.

6. Compare Compare (and contrast) your subject to other places. What other place is it most like? a little bit like? sometimes like? not at all like?

7. Analyze Talk to other people about your subject. What do they remember or how do they feel about this place? Does it remind them of other places? In what way? What is its future? its strengths? its weaknesses?

8. Evaluate Why is this place important to you, to others, to the community? What would things be like if this place were no longer there?

Remember to breathe life into your writing. Captivate your readers with a series of thought-provoking questions they can't ignore. As always, write naturally and freely and consider using observations, stories, imaginary dialogue, and maybe even a little poetry in what you share with your readers.

Avoid Using Cliches or Overused Expressions

blanket of snow	mantle of snow	raining cats and dogs
blue as the sky	ocean's roar	sea of faces
covered like a blanket	ominous silence	silhouetted against the sky
cold as ice	flat as a pancake	smooth as glass
crack of dawn	fresh as a daisy	smooth as silk
dawn breaks	God's country	trees like sentinels
dry as dust	green as grass	white as snow

Possible Topics _____

a nursing home	a fishing or sailing boat
the school library	the park after a picnic
the principal's office	the stadium before a concert
the dentist's office	your favorite classroom
a music store	a deserted house
a church or chapel	an unusual hole on a golf course
your favorite hangout	a shoreline or beach
an auto salvage yard	a polluted river

Writing About an Object

121   As with any type of writing, select a subject which interests you. Do some free writing or clustering about your subject to find a focus, angle, or slant that you think might make it more interesting for your reader. Continue other prewriting activities if need be until you have gathered enough information to get you started. The suggestions below may also help.

   1. Observe Observe the object closely to determine how it works. Also notice how other people use this object and how they feel about it.

   2. Investigate Ask other people about their experiences, attitudes, and feelings about this object. Read about it.

   3. Define What class or category does this object fall into? (See 122.) How is this object similar to or different from other objects in this same category?

   4. Describe Describe the color, size, shape, and texture of your subject (but don't overdo it). Describe the important parts and how they fit together. Not surprisingly, you are reminded once again that showing is better than telling. (See 051.) Surround your object with people, action, and places so that the reader can get a true picture of your subject and its importance.

   5. Recall Try to remember an interesting incident or story involving this object which will help the reader better understand your subject.

   6. Compare What other objects is your subject most like? least like? not at all like? What person (or type of person) does it remind you of? what season? what foreign country?

   7. Analyze Try to find out when this object was discovered, built, first used, etc. What are its strengths and weaknesses? What changes would you make in it if you were able?

   8. Evaluate Why is this object important? Does it have any practical value? any aesthetic (artistic) value? any historical value?

   Once you have gathered enough details, begin writing. Think of an unusual way to approach your subject. (How about a news report or fairy tale or parody or TV drama or rap poem or . . . ?) You can always go back to a more traditional form if it doesn't work out.

Writing a Definition

122   One of the most common "operations" students are asked to perform in their academic writing is that of *defining*. "Define capitalism." "Define realism." "Define sanity." When next you are asked to "define," use the guidelines which follow.

   First, place the term you are attempting to define into the next larger class or category of similar objects. Then, add the special characteristics which make this object different from the rest of the objects in that class. Note the following example:

   Term — *A computer . . .*

   Class — *is an electronic machine . . .*

   Characteristic — *which stores, retrieves, and manipulates*
   information.

   Note: Avoid the temptation of using the term or a variation of it in your definition. ("A computer is an electronic machine that computes data.")

   If all you are required to write is a simple or limited definition, you need go no further. If, however, you are expected to expand or extend your definition to make it come alive for the reader, you have only begun. You must now gather details and make this subject come to life for your readers. (See "Writing about a Person . . . Place . . . Object.")

Writing About an Event

123   Writing about an event is actually writing about a feeling or attitude ... and people ... and places ... and objects. The central question you must answer is which one (or more) of these is most important or makes the event memorable and worth writing about. It is important that you write about an event you have actually been a part of or witnessed firsthand. (An exception might be watching the event on television or interviewing someone who was part of the event.) Follow the steps in the writing process and the suggestions below.

1. Observe Look closely for any special details which will help your reader "see" or "feel" the event in the same way you did. Notice things which happened before the event began, especially those which help set the mood. (Include all the senses: see, smell, feel, taste, and hear.)

2. Investigate Talk to other people about the event. Get their impressions, feelings, disappointments, surprises, etc. Listen for the comments of others throughout the event. Talk to an "expert" on the subject or someone who can explain the special appeal of this kind of event. Read about its history.

3. Describe List the *who, what, when, where, why,* and *how* of the event—or at least those which are important to a complete understanding of the event. Write freely about these six questions as if you were describing it to someone else. More than ever, showing is better than telling. Include the background, people, actions, feelings, conversations, and all the other specific details which make this event special.

4. Define What kind or type of event is it you are writing about? How is it similar to or different from other events in the same category?

5. Compare Compare (contrast) this event to similar ones you have witnessed or heard about.

6. Speculate How might this event have been more noteworthy or memorable?

7. Evaluate Why is this event important or worthwhile to you? to others? to the community? Argue for or against the value of this event happening again.

8. Analyze, explain, criticize, recommend. . . .

Avoid Cliches or Worn-out Expressions

assembled multitude	eyes of the world	cold sweat
slowly but surely	broad daylight	lock, stock, and barrel
few and far between	out of the blue	more easily said than done
clockwork precision	Mother Nature	raining cats and dogs
sadder but wiser	festive occasion	bury the hatchet
over a barrel	par for the course	drop like flies
gala event	sell like hotcakes	

Possible Topics

an early snowstorm	an air or water show
a protest march	a wedding
a prom or dance	a parade
my proudest moment	the first day of school
winning a prize	a near accident
a concert or show	a time to remember
a cherished moment	a surprise visit
a vacation stop	a fire/accident
something lost/found	a real mess
the big showdown	an act of charity

Writing an Explanation ————————

124 Explanations are common in school settings. Before a particular class can even begin, your teacher will have to explain the classroom procedures, the grading system, the daily requirements, and on and on. When the class finally begins, the explanations will most likely continue. Teaching often involves explaining (*defining, reviewing, demonstrating, clarifying*). When you explain something in writing, you are, in effect, teaching or making something easier to understand. Keep this in mind when you begin writing. The suggestions below should help.

  1. Observe Whenever possible, observe the person, place, thing, idea, event, or process you are going to explain in your writing. Notice the parts, steps, or details which will help you explain your subject to your reader.

  2. Investigate Talk to "experts" and others who have an understanding of your subject. Listen to their explanations and ask questions about anything you don't understand. Ask the *what, when, where, why, how,* and *to what extent* questions.

  3. Define Write a simple, concise definition of your subject. (See 122.) Check reliable books on the topic and expand your definition to include the specific characteristics which make this person, place, thing, or idea different from others like it.

  4. Describe List each step, part, cause, etc. needed to understand your subject. List examples or instances which clarify each point in your explanation. Describe the size, shape, color, sound, and smell to help your reader picture what it is you are trying to explain.

  5. Compare Compare your subject to others which are simpler or more familiar to your reader. Tell what your subject is "not" like.

  6. Analyze Break down your subject into its parts or steps. How do the parts work together to form the whole? What is the history or future or present condition of your subject?

  7. Evaluate Why is your subject important or worth knowing about? How might it help your reader?

  Explanations must be clear. Test what you have written by reading it out loud—and by reading it to someone else if at all possible. Revise accordingly. Maybe you need more examples, illustrations, or comparisons. Maybe you have to explain each point (step) more carefully or more fully.

  Remember: Your purpose is to make what may at first seem very technical or complicated seem clear and understandable.

Writing to Persuade _____

125   When you write to persuade, you write to prove a point, to change someone's opinion, to clarify an issue. Persuading someone to change his or her mind or take a stand is not always easy. It requires careful thinking and planning, strong evidence or support, and a thorough understanding of the topic.

More than any other type of writing, persuasive writing requires that you select a subject which truly interests you, one which you have strong feelings about. Your subject (*issue*) should be current and controversial.

1. Reflect Begin collecting material by free writing, clustering, or listing your personal feelings about the issue and the reasons you feel the way you do. This may be the most important stage in the persuasive writing process; you simply cannot be convincing unless you have "you" on your side.

2. Investigate Talk to other people about the issue. What are their feelings about the issue and why do they feel this way? What personal experiences have they had that make them feel this way? What would they suggest be done to solve or lessen the problem? Listen carefully, especially to those with whom you disagree. They will give you a preview of the response you can expect from your audience. Test your opinions and reasons on them. You must understand well what you are up against if you hope to write persuasively.

3. Read Read as much as you can about the issue. Understand fully the history of the issue and what events or circumstances led up to the way things are today. Gather facts, figures, evidence, examples, and quotations—on both sides of the issue. Read current periodicals so that you are both informed and up-to-date.

4. Think For writing to be persuasive, it must be founded in logic. (See "Thinking Logically.") Use a calm, reasoning tone throughout your writing. Rely on logic, not emotion. Be diplomatic. Give credit to the reasonable arguments on the other side of the issue; then point out clearly the weaknesses of each. Admit that this issue, as with most, is not a black and white issue. Then, convince your reader that your perspective is the most sensible, logical one.

5. Organize Persuasive writing should be well organized.

Here are some suggestions:

    a. Write out a clear statement of the purpose behind your persuasive writing. This statement (often called a *proposition*) should spell out what you propose to prove in your writing. State your proposition in positive terms. ("School officials should be prohibited from secretly searching student lockers," rather than "... officials should not be allowed to . . . .")

    b. Place your topic (*proposition*) at the top of your paper. List your reasons underneath; under each reason, list the facts, figures, examples, or quotations which help support it.

    c. Use specific examples to illustrate your main points. Build strong images: "Each day this country throws out enough garbage to completely cover the state of Rhode Island." Use statistics sparingly and, when you do, round them off: "Each day we throw out nearly 50 million tons of garbage."

    d. Appeal to the needs of your reader. Let each of them know what's in it for him or her. Prove to them that they have something to gain by taking the same stand as you. Use stylistic devices (if needed) to draw attention to the important points you are trying to make.

    e. Choose your words carefully. Remember that words convey feeling (*connotation*) as well as meaning (*denotation*). Select words which your reader will react to positively. (Define any words which your reader may not be familiar with.)

    f. Consider ending your writing with one of your strongest examples or reasons. Your readers may well hold judgment until the very end, waiting for "the bottom line."

Searching & Researching

"Research is the recreation of the truly curious and committed."

What is a Research Paper?

A research paper is a documented essay which requires careful planning, searching, studying, and writing. The length of a research paper depends on the nature of the project. Some personal research projects that you might develop into papers will be rather brief (two to five pages), but most academic research papers will be at least five pages in length. Quite often a research paper is called a term paper because a term (a quarter or semester) is the length of time given for its completion. Instructors often establish a minimum number of pages for term papers, usually eight to ten pages.

What does it mean to be a researcher?

135   To Henry David Thoreau it meant living alone for seven years at Walden Pond. It meant "driving life into a corner, and reducing it to its lowest terms." It meant trying to make some sense out of Life with a capital *L*. To John Howard Griffin, author of *Black Like Me*, it meant having his skin temporarily darkened by medical treatments to pass as a black man. It meant traveling throughout the South for more than a month and discovering what it was like to be treated as a second-class citizen. To Joanne Hauser, a student researcher, it meant four weeks worth of reading, interviewing, observing, and volunteering her time. It meant assessing her community's day-care services.

What will researching mean to you? It should mean the same to you as it did to these three researchers. It should be a process that helps you better understand your present, your past, your place in the scheme of things. This should be the goal of all research no matter how broad or limited the initial itch that starts the process.

"Research paper — report — what's the difference?"

Join one of Ms. Marmalade's more "notorious" students during a writing conference and learn what it means to write a research paper.

You Ain't Nothin' But a Hound Dog

Ms. Marmalade: Your first draft is interesting, Elvis, but it really isn't a *research paper*. I would call this a *report*.

Elvis: Research paper—report—what's the difference? I went to two different encyclopedias and a book about the history of rock, and I wrote down everything there was about the origins of rock and roll. I wrote the same paper—I mean the same kind of paper—in junior high.

Ms. Marmalade: That was fine for a report. But a research paper requires a more active brand of thinking.

Elvis: I was sure active. My head was splittin' by the time I was through.

Ms. Marmalade: By "active" I mean *intellectually* active. In a report, you collect, organize, and compile information. You depend on experts to ask the right questions and give the right answers. You're an observer. Thus your role is essentially passive.

Elvis: Well, I worked up a mighty big sweat for being passive.

Ms. Marmalade: I'm sure you did, Elvis. But in a research paper, you're no longer simply an observer. You choose a topic that is open for debate. Then you gather information from many different sources and develop your own position.

Elvis: But half the time, they don't even agree!

Ms. Marmalade: Exactly. That's why you must formulate your own position or thesis and develop it as no one has ever done before. You become an authority on your topic by borrowing, comparing, rejecting, or agreeing with your sources; and explaining your own thinking as you go. That can be quite satisfying, Elvis.

Elvis: I get your point. *Now* will you take a peek at my new song?

Ms. Marmalade: I would be delighted. Hm. Very good. However, "ain't" is not proper diction, and "ain't nothin' " is a double negative. "Hound dog" is redundant and a bit general as well. This is a charming little tune, Elvis, but as you see, it needs some editing. A correct title would be, "You Are Nothing But a Bassett Hound." Be more careful when you edit the final draft of your research paper.

Elvis: Ms. Marmalade? No offense, ma'am, but you're stepping on my blue suede shoes, if you know what I mean. "Blue suede . . . you can do anything, but . . ."— hot dawg! I just got me an idea for another song!

Research Update

For years, student researchers have been burdened with the form of their finished product. If you have ever written a research paper with endnotes or footnotes, a working or complete bibliography, title page, etc., you know how much time and effort it takes just to understand the form of a research paper. Form so consumed student writers that content often became a secondary issue. What was said, in essence, was less important than how it was presented.

Current research style has changed this. The most widely used styles developed by the Modern Language Association of America (MLA) and the American Psychological Association (APA) are simple and efficient. They allow student researchers to devote most of their time to the important issue—developing meaningful research. A writer no longer has to struggle, for example, with footnotes at the bottom of a page or variations in line spacing. Preparing the finished product has become the important final step in the research process rather than an all-consuming one.

138 Personalized Research

As students become more involved in developing their own sources of information (interviews, surveys, direct observation, etc.), it is becoming more acceptable to use the first person (I) in the written text. Who better than the researcher himself can explain the reason for conducting the research in the first place, the context of an interview, or the circumstances surrounding a firsthand experience? This does not mean that a researcher should dominate a text with constant references to himself. It does mean, however, that personal comments are important if they serve to clarify or improve the reader's understanding of a researcher's finding.

One Approach: Writer and instructor Ken Macrorie felt so strongly about the lack of real feelings in research that he developed (over a number of years) the **I-Search**, a process which naturally lends itself to personalized research. An I-Search begins with an individual's own natural curiosity about something. One person might, for example, wonder if she has what it takes to become an emergency-room nurse. Another person might wonder what home computer is best for his family. Once a personal need is established, an I-Searcher then sets out in search of information and answers.

An I-Searcher relies on interviews, correspondence, visits, and firsthand experiences as much as possible during the search. Books and periodicals play a secondary role and are usually referred to upon the recommendation of an interviewee. The end product of an I-Search is the story of an individual's own searching adventure, a story which naturally lends itself to genuine thoughts and feelings.

139 Getting Involved

What do these developments in research mean to you? Get involved in projects that interest you, and take an active role in each one of them. Don't, for example, rely exclusively on published studies or reports if you have the time and the means to conduct your own firsthand research. And don't rely solely on the critics' interpretations of a piece of literature. If your own personal reading of the piece tells you something different, then that should be reported in your findings as well.

Question, discuss, and evaluate your research as it develops. You might find it worthwhile to keep track of your thoughts and activities during the research process in a log or journal. A record of your thoughts and actions will often mean as much or more to you than the actual information you uncover.

Present your findings in a format that makes sense to you and benefits your readers. If that means presenting a personal anecdote (story) to open your paper or providing personal insights into parts of your research, then do so. A research paper without personality can be like ice cream without flavor—little worth the bother. *(Note:* Be sure to follow the guidelines established by your instructor for any academic research project.)

140 Keep Time on Your Side

It is late Friday afternoon, a time when most students have WEEKEND on their minds. Yet here is John searching for books in the school library. He has already stacked a number of them on the checkout counter, and he is out among the aisles looking for a few more titles that might help him with his research. A casual observer might think that John is dedicated to learning, a real student.

John's a real student all right; unfortunately he is all too real. You see, John isn't collecting books because he wants to. He would rather join his friends for a movie, a game, or a pizza. But he has no time for socializing this weekend. In two and one-half days he has to turn in an eight-page research paper, a paper that was assigned weeks ago, a paper that he has essentially put off until now. Sound familiar?

If you have ever put yourself into this situation, you know what kind of weekend John has ahead of him. Writing a research paper under the gun is pure frustration. And just the thought of another last-ditch, kamikaze effort should be enough to sour any stomach. Meaningful research requires a great deal of time to develop because there is so much planning, searching, studying, and writing involved. That is why your instructors assign research projects early in the semester or term, and that is why they encourage you to budget your time throughout the project.

Follow whatever timetable your instructors give you for a research project, and keep time on your side as much as possible. Instructors know what it takes to develop a worthwhile finished product. If they leave this up to you, use the general timetable which follows to help you plan your way. This is based on a research paper assigned at midterm and due at the end of the semester: eight to nine weeks. Adjust accordingly.

141 Research Timetable

Prewriting: (four weeks)

Selecting a subject and making a list of potential sources (one week)

Searching for information, reading, and note taking (two weeks)

Studying your information, finalizing a thesis statement, developing an outline (one to two weeks)

Writing the First Draft: (one week)

Revising: (two weeks)

Allow for at least two revisions.

Set aside work between revising sessions (take in a movie, enjoy a pizza) and let your ideas incubate.

Editing: (one week)

Preparing the final draft

Proofreading the finished product (one day)

Steps in the Process ▅▅▅▅▅▅▅

"My idea of research is to look at the thing from all sides; the person who has seen the animal, how the animal behaves, and so on."
—**Marianne Moore**

142 Prewriting ▅▅▅▅▅▅▅▅▅▅▅▅▅

1. Select an interesting subject. Your most meaningful research will satisfy a personal need: a question you want to answer, a condition you want to investigate, an issue you want to explore. Keep four important points in mind when selecting a subject:

- Select a subject that is well suited to your interests and background.

- Make sure there is some information available on your subject.

- Make sure you have enough time to develop it.

- Make sure it meets the requirements of your instructor.
 (See "Prewriting Techniques," 031, for help.)

2. Do some preliminary investigating. Check area and school libraries for material on the subject and select a number of books or articles to read. Begin your initial reading with a general reference book, an encyclopedia perhaps. Check the list of *related articles* and *see references* located at the end of most reference articles. This information can be helpful in finding a specific focus for research.

You might also talk with someone in your community or school who may have personal information about your research subject. Consider using one of the computer programs designed to help researchers in a subject search. Ask your local or school librarian about the availability of such programs in your area.

3. Limit your subject. After you have done some investigating, develop a preliminary focus or thesis statement which makes clear what you plan to cover in your research paper. Make sure that you have enough current sources of information to adequately develop your focus. Check your timetable, too. Do you have enough time to develop this idea? (*Note:* Don't be surprised if your thesis changes as your research develops. You will probably consider a number of focuses before you settle upon the one you will finally use for your paper.)

Helpful Hint: Complete one of the ideas given below if you have trouble forming a preliminary focus statement.

- I want to learn more about . . .
- I want to find out . . .
- I want to better understand . . .
- I want to see if . . .

143 **Searching for Information**

4. Prepare a preliminary bibliography. Using the card catalog, *Readers' Guide to Periodical Literature,* the vertical file, and other reference publications (including computer data bases, if available), compile a list of materials available on your subject. Place this information on 3- by 5-inch bibliography cards and arrange them in alphabetical order by the author's last name. If the name of the author is not known, alphabetize by the first word in the title (except *a, an,* or *the*). Number each card in the upper right-hand corner; place the call number of each book in the upper left-hand corner.

Whenever possible, check the reliability of potential sources before you include them in your list.

- Take note of the author's credentials on the title page or in a special section called "Contributors" in journals.
- Check your source's reputation. Do other writers refer to the source?
- Check your source's bias. Does he or she represent a certain school of thought?
- Check your source's performance. Is the writing well researched? Clear? Logical? Thorough?
- Ask an instructor or other professional in the field about the author's credibility.

Sample Bibliography Card

Chambers, Rick. "No Place to Lay Their Heads." The Church Herald 16 Sept 1988: 9–11

Sample Note Card

Homeless -- personal closeup

A man sleeping on a New York sidewalk during the afternoon has a sign at his feet which reads: "Won't you help me? I'm cold and homeless and lonely. God Bless You."

(p. 11)

5. Begin taking notes. As you read the material listed in your preliminary bibliography, take notes on ideas and jot down quotations which you feel might be useful in your research. Place this information on note cards; follow the guidelines below:

- Use cards of the same size and style (4- by 6-inch cards are recommended).
- Place one main idea or quotation on each card. Be sure to list the page numbers on

which you found the material as well as the bibliography card number of your source. (Place the card number in the upper right-hand corner.)

- Use abbreviations and phrases.
- Place all verbatim (word for word) notes in quotation marks.
- Use the ellipsis when necessary. (See 601.) Place any information which you add to these direct quotes in brackets [like this].
- Use a diagonal (/) to indicate where a quote has gone from one page to another in the original source. This will be very useful when you are citing the exact page of a quote in a parenthetical reference.
- Look up any unfamiliar words you come across in your reading. If you find that a particular word is important, copy the definition onto a note card.
- Leave space at the bottom of each card for notes on how and where you might use the information.
- Place a descriptive slug (heading) at the top of each card. The slug should be a word or phrase which highlights the main idea of each note.

Note Taking: A Closer Look _____

There are three ways in which you can take notes.

1. You can **summarize.** Summarize (in your own words) as you take notes unless there is good reason to retrace the thinking of a source or to quote a source directly. When you summarize, you narrow or reduce what you have read to a few important points.

2. You can **paraphrase.** Paraphrasing is restating in your own words what you have read. It is a helpful note-taking technique when you are trying to retrace the thinking of one of your sources. Put quotation marks around key words or phrases you borrow directly from the source. (See 181 for guidelines and examples.)

3. You can **quote directly.** Use a source's exact words when they include essential information, when the source's language is unique or distinctive, and when the source is considered an expert on the subject. Put this information in quotation marks.

Special Note: Work each source of information into your own thinking before you take notes on it. This is the best way to avoid plagiarism. (See 151.)

6. Collect information from other sources. Consider creating your own sources of information by conducting interviews, reading diaries or personal papers, implementing questionnaires or surveys, or carrying out firsthand observations or experiences.

144 Designing a Plan

7. Write your working outline. Organize your note cards into their most logical order and use them to construct a preliminary or working outline. Your descriptive slugs may be used as main and subpoints in your outline. (See 110.)

8. Continue your research. Search for any additional information which is needed to support your thesis. Review your preliminary thesis statement and rework it if necessary. Your thoughts about it might have changed as you gathered information.

9. Revise your outline. Revise your working outline as needed when you find new information.

> *". . . having something to say means having a good stock of facts."*
> **—Rudolph Flesch**

10. Write your first draft. Begin with an introduction which establishes the purpose of your research (your thesis). You might also work one or more of the following elements into your **introduction:**

- information your reader needs to understand your research findings
- definitions of complex terms or concepts
- your reason for choosing this subject
- an opening anecdote or quotation
- additional background information

The next step is to develop or prove your thesis in the **body** of the paper. You can develop this section in one of two ways: spontaneously or systematically.

146 Writing Spontaneously

You can put your outline and note cards aside and write as much as you can on your own. Refer to your note cards only when you need a quotation or specific facts and figures. After you have completed the initial writing, you can then review your outline and note cards to see if you have missed or misplaced any important points.

147 Writing Systematically

Or, you can approach the body in a more systematic fashion. Begin by laying out one section of note cards at a time (cards with the same heading) so that you can see all or most of them at one time.

- Write a general statement which covers the main idea of that section of cards; then determine which cards contain the best information to support this statement. Repeat this process for each section of note cards.
  Note: If you find that your general statement is valid, but you do not have enough information to support it, gather more information or drop it from consideration.

- Make sure that you write your paper using your own words; use direct quotes only when the point being made is stated precisely as you want it to be in the original source. As you sort through your cards, examine each for possible use as a transition.

- Work to achieve a style which is semiformal. (See 021.) Do not use fragments, abbreviations, or substandard language (slang and colloquialisms). And do not try to impress your reader by using language which is too lofty or flowery. This will only be a distraction to the reader and cause him or her to question your understanding of the subject.

- Present your ideas honestly and clearly. If you feel strongly about your research and have something meaningful to offer your readers, you are bound to write an interesting paper.

- Aim for objectivity in your writing. This means you should focus on the discoveries you have made during your research rather than on your feelings or attitudes toward them. Don't, however, ignore your personal insights or observations if they add meaning to your paper.

The final section or **conclusion** of your paper should leave the reader with a clear understanding of the significance of your research. This is usually done by reviewing the important points you have made and drawing a final conclusion(s). You might, however, take a more personal approach in the closing of your paper. For instance, you might discuss how your research has changed or confirmed your thinking about your subject; or you might simply discuss what you have learned from your searching and researching.

> *"An effective piece of writing has focus. There is a controlling vision which orders what is being said."*
>
> **—Donald Murray**

11. Revise your first draft at least two times. Revise at least once to clarify your thinking on the content of your paper, and one more time to refine the style of your writing. (See 016 and 050 for an explanation of revising and style.)

12. Include all necessary parenthetical references. Give credit for quoted materials and the general ideas of your sources. (See "Documenting Sources," 151, for an explanation if using MLA style and 970 if using APA style.) Also assemble the "Works Cited" list if using MLA style or "References" list if using APA style.

149 Preparing the Final Paper ━━━━━━━━━━━━

> *"A sentence should read as if its author, had he held a plough instead of a pen, could have drawn a furrow deep and straight to the end."*
>
> **—Henry David Thoreau**

13. Edit your final revision. Check for punctuation, capitalization, usage, and grammar. (See "Re-marks" for help.)

Note: The guidelines which follow refer to MLA style. See 970 for guidelines and examples for APA style.

14. Prepare your final copy. Type your paper (or write in ink) on good quality typing paper. Do not use erasable paper unless you plan on using a good photocopier to make your final copy. If you use a word processor, try to print with a letter-quality printer. Leave a margin of one inch on all sides, except for page numbers. Double-space your entire paper, including long quotations and the "Works Cited" section. (See 171 for an example.)

15. Arrange and number your pages. Begin numbering with the first page of the essay and continue through the "Works Cited" section. Type your last name before each page number. Place the page numbers in the upper right-hand corner, one-half inch from the top and even with the right-hand margin.

16. Add your title. A title page is usually not required for a research paper. Simply type the author's name, instructor's name, course title, and date in the upper-left corner of the first page of the paper. (Begin one inch from the top and double-space throughout.) Center the title (double-space before and after); then type the first line of the paper.

Note: If a title page is required, center the title one-third of the way down from the top of the page; likewise, center the author's name, instructor's name, and any additional information two-thirds of the way down. (See 169.)

17. Type your final outline. Add, delete, or rearrange material as is necessary to make your outline consistent with the final version of your paper. Use either a topic or sentence outline (as your instructor requires); do not mix the two in the same outline. (See 170.) If your outline is more than one page in length, number it with small Roman numerals (i, ii, iii, iv). Double-space throughout.

18. Proofread your paper for typing errors. Check the final draft from beginning to end. Submit your research paper as "error free" as you can possibly make it.

Your Responsibility as a Researcher

"Advice to young writers? Always the same advice: learn to trust your own judgment, learn inner independence . . . ."

—Doris Lessing

150   If you are submitting a paper as your own research, then you have a responsibility to present your own findings. Too often, student researchers essentially piece together the ideas of others, documented or not, and call it a research paper. A research paper like any other type of meaningful writing should be a personal process of discovery. What sense of discovery or accomplishment can there be if you don't thoughtfully study the information you gather during research and make it your own?

How do you make research your own? First, gain control over the information you plan on using in your research. If you don't understand a particular resource, get help clarifying it or don't use it. Consider points in which your sources agree and disagree on related issues, and decide which ones offer the best arguments and why. Then, determine how these findings stand up to your own thinking. This is when research becomes meaningful and becomes your own.

Remember: Responsible and meaningful research develops when you do the following:

- Commit yourself to the subject of your research.
- Give yourself enough time to develop it thoroughly.
- Get actively involved and conduct some firsthand research.
- Understand the information you've collected.
- Study, question, discuss, and write about your research as it develops.

151 Documenting Sources

When you make your research your own, two things will naturally follow. First, your writing will sound like it comes from you, a student researcher committed to presenting his or her findings as clearly and sincerely as possible. Second, your writing will be honest because you won't lean on the ideas of others for the main support of your research. Your writing instead will reflect the results of your planning, searching, and studying.

You owe it to your sources, your readers, and yourself to give credit for the ideas you do borrow in your research, unless the ideas are common knowledge or widely accepted. Failure to do so results in **plagiarism,** the act of presenting someone else's ideas as your own. In essense, plagiarism is a form of intellectual thievery carried out, intentionally or unintentionally, by researchers who fail to do their own mind work.

Plagiarism generally appears in one of the following ways: There is *word-for-word* plagiarism which occurs when a researcher repeats the exact words of a source without giving the necessary credit. There is the *paraphrase* or restated form in which a researcher says basically the same thing as an original source with only a few words changed. And there is the paraphrase in which a researcher uses a source's key words or phrases as his own rather than placing them in quotation marks.

152 What is "common knowledge"?

In research you should cite everything you borrow unless that information is common knowledge. Sometimes, however, it is difficult to tell. Consider information common knowledge

- if reliable authors refer to it without citing its source,

- if most people knowledgeable in the field accept it as a fact,

- if few experts would dispute it,

- and, if it is reported in most introductory textbooks or basic reference books on the subject.

Note: But remember your audience. What is common knowledge among brain surgeons may not be common knowledge among patrons of the local coffee shop. You must decide what is "news" to your audience. If in doubt, cite the source.

153 Using Quoted Material

A quotation can be anything from a single word to an entire paragraph(s). As a writer you must keep quotations in perspective. Choose quotations carefully, keep them as brief as possible, and use them only when they are interesting, revealing, or necessary in the development of your text. A paper that is quote heavy usually means a writer has done little independent thinking. Spelling, capitalization, and punctuation should reflect the original work as much as possible. Any changes you make should be clear to your readers. Note the quidelines for quoted material which follow.

Short Quotations

1. If a quotation runs four or less typed lines, work it into the text of your paper. Put the quoted material within quotation marks.

2. Use a colon to formally introduce a quotation.

Long Quotations

3. Quotations of more than four typed lines should be set off from the rest of the text. Indent each line ten spaces and double-space the material without quotation marks. In quoting two or more paragraphs, indent the first line of each paragraph three spaces. (Skip two spaces after a longer quote before you cite a parenthetical reference.)

Quoting Poetry

4. Lines of verse should be worked into your text and punctuated with quotation marks. Use a slash (/) between lines of verse in the text. For verse quotations of four or more lines, follow the steps in the previous guideline.

5. The omission of a line(s) of verse is signified by a line of periods the approximate length of the lines quoted.

Partial Quotations

6. If you want to omit part of the original material, use an ellipsis to signify the omission. An ellipsis (. . .) is three periods with a space before and after each one. If an ellipsis is at the end of a sentence, add a fourth period with no space before the first one. *Special Note:* Anything you take out of a quotation should not alter the author's original meaning.

Adding to Quotations

7. Use brackets [like this] to signify any explanatory material you add within a quotation.

MLA Parenthetical References

154   The 1988 edition of the *MLA Handbook for Writers of Research Papers* suggests giving credit in the text rather than in footnotes or endnotes. This can be done by inserting the appropriate information (usually author and page number) in parentheses after the words or ideas borrowed from another source. Use as few parenthetical references as accuracy allows. Place them where a pause would naturally occur to avoid disrupting the flow of your writing (usually at the end of a sentence).

Keep two points in mind when documenting sources: First, your references must clearly refer to sources listed in the "Works Cited" section of your paper. Second, indicate as precisely as you can the location of cited references with page numbers, volume numbers, acts, chapters, etc. (Use the sample references which follow as your guide for documentation; or see 970-978 for a guide to the APA style.)

One Author: Citing a Complete Work

No parenthetical reference is needed if you identify the author and work in your text. Give the author's last name in a reference if it is not mentioned in the text.

With Author in Text

In No Need for Hunger, Robert Spitzer recommends that the U.S. government develop a new foreign policy to help Third World countries overcome poverty and hunger.

Without Author in Text

No Need for Hunger recommends that the U.S. government develop a new foreign policy to help Third World countries overcome poverty and hunger (Spitzer).

Note: A parenthetical reference could begin with an editor, translator, speaker, or artist instead of the author if that is how a work is listed in the Works Cited section.

One Author: Citing Part of a Work

Cite the necessary page numbers in your reference if you borrow from a particular passage in a work. Leave a space between the author's last name and the page reference. No punctuation is needed.

With Author in Text

Mathews reports that President Reagan cut the housing budget from $30 billion in 1981 to $7.3 billion in 1987 (58).

Without Author in Text

President Reagan cut the housing budget from $30 billion in 1981 to $7.3 billion in 1987 (Mathews 58).

Two or Three Authors

Give the last names of every author in the reference in the order that they appear in the Works Cited section.

Students learned more than a full year's Spanish in ten days using the complete supermemory method (Ostrander and Schroeder 51).

More Than Three Authors

Give the first author's last name as it appears in the Works Cited section followed by et al. (and others) with no punctuation in between.

According to Guerin et al., Huck Finn reflects "those same nightmarish shadows that even in our own time threaten to obscure the American Dream" (149).

Corporate Author

If the corporate name is long, include it in the text to avoid disrupting the flow of your writing. Use a shortened form of the name in the text and in references—i.e., *Task Force* for *Task Force on Education for Economic Growth*—after stating the full title at least once.

> The thesis of the Task Force's report is that economic success depends on our ability to improve large scale education and training as quickly as possible (14).

No Author

Give the title or a shortened version of the title as it is listed in the Works Cited section. No page numbers are needed for single-page articles or nonprint sources.

> The World Almanac states that 513,000 refugees from Ethiopia, Uganda, Chad, and Zaire are living in Sudan (608).

Two or More Works by the Same Author

Give the author's last name (unless it appears in the text), the title or a shortened version, and the page reference.

> The average person will have taken more than 2,600 quizzes, tests, and exams if he or she finishes college (Von Oech, Whack 21).

Literary Works

To cite classic prose works, list more than the page reference if the work is available in several editions. Give the page reference first, and then add a chapter, section, or book number in abbreviated form after a semicolon.

> In Cry, the Beloved Country, Alan Paton presents Steven Kumalo as "a man who lives in a world not made for him, whose own world is slipping away, dying, being destroyed, beyond recall" (14; ch. 3).

Cite classic verse plays and poems by divisions (act, scene, canto, book, part) and lines. Use periods to separate the various parts. If you are citing lines only, use the words line or lines in your first reference and numbers only in additional references.

> It is hard to develop an affection for someone [Lady Macbeth] who makes such a demonic request: "Come, you spirits/that tend on mortal thoughts, unsex me here,/And fill me, from the crown to the toe, top full/of direst cruelty" (I.v.41-4).

Note: Bible is not underlined in biblical references. The books of the Bible are abbreviated in parenthetical references.

Indirect Source

If you cite an indirect source—someone's remarks published secondhand—give the abbreviation *qtd. in* (quoted in) before the indirect source in your reference.

> Paton improved the conditions in Diepkloof by "removing all the more obvious aids to detention. The dormatories are open at night: the great barred gate is gone" (qtd. in Callan xviii).

Note: Avoid citing indirect sources whenever possible and go to original sources.

One or More Works in a Reference

Cite each work as you normally would; separate the references with a semicolon.

> Both poet-teachers strongly believe in the benefits of dream writing for beginning writers (Koch 137; Ziegler 34).

Works Cited ▬▬▬▬▬

The Works Cited section (bibliography) lists all of the sources you have cited in your text. It is found at the end of your research paper. Begin your list on a new page (the next page after the text) and number each page, continuing the numbering from the text. The guidelines which follow describe the form of the Works Cited section in detail.

155 Guidelines for the Works Cited Section

1. Type the page number in the upper right-hand corner, one-half inch from the top of the page.
2. Center the title *Works Cited* one inch from the top. Double-space before the first entry.
3. Begin each entry flush with the left margin. If the entry runs more than one line, indent additional lines five spaces.
4. Double-space each entry; also double-space between entries.
5. List each entry alphabetically by the author's last name. If there is no author, use the first word of the title (disregard *A, An, The*).

156 The Form for an Entry

An entry generally has three main divisions: author, title, and publication information. A basic entry for a **book** would be as follows:

> Spitzer, Robert R. No Need for Hunger. Danville: Interstate, 1981.

(**Double-space** after the author and title. **Single-space** the publication information.)

A basic entry for a **periodical** (a magazine) would be as follows:

> Whitman, David. "Hope for the Homeless." U.S. News and World Report 29 Feb. 1988:
> 26-35.

(**Double-space** after the author and the title of the article. **Single-space** the rest of the entry.)

157 Works Cited Entries: Books ▬▬▬▬▬

The entries which follow illustrate the information needed to cite books, sections of a book, pamphlets, and government publications.

One Author

> Spitzer, Robert R. No Need for Hunger. Danville: Interstate, 1981.

Two or Three Authors

> Ostrander, Sheila, and Lynn Schroeder. Superlearning. New York: Delacorte, 1979.

More Than Three Authors

> Guerin, Wilfred L., et al. A Handbook of Critical Approaches to Literature. New York:
> Harper, 1966.

A Single Work from an Anthology

> Morris, William. "The Haystack in the Floods." Nineteenth Century British Minor
> Poets. Ed. Richard Wilbur and W.H. Auden. New York: Dell, 1965. 265-79.

Note: If you cite a complete anthology, begin the entry with the editors.

Two or More Books by the Same Author

Von Oech, Roger.   A Kick in the Seat of the Pants.   New York: Perennial-Harper, 1986.

---.   A Whack on the Side of the Head.   New York: Warner, 1983.

Note: List the books alphabetically according to title. After the first entry, substitute three hyphens for the author's name.

A Corporate (group) Author

Task Force on Education for Economic Growth.   Action for Excellence.   Washington:

Education Commission of the States, 1983.

No Author

The World Almanac and Book of Facts.   New York: Newspaper Enterprise Assoc., 1985.

One Volume of a Multivolume Work

Ziegler, Alan.   The Writing Workshop.   Vol. 2.   New York: Teachers and Writers, 1984.

Note: If you cite two or more volumes in a multivolume work, give the total number of volumes after the title.

An Introduction, Preface, Foreword, or Afterword

Callan, Edward.   Introduction.   Cry, the Beloved Country.   By Alan Paton.   New York:

Macmillan, 1987.   xv-xxvii.

Note: Give only the author's last name after *By* if he is the author of the piece cited and the complete work.

Cross-References

Abbey, Edward.   "The Most Beautiful Place on Earth."   Hall 225-41.

Baldwin, James.   "Notes of a Native Son."   Hall 164-83.

Hall, Donald, ed.   The Contemporary Essay.   New York: Bedford-St. Martin's, 1984.

Note: To avoid unnecessary repetition when citing two or more entries from a larger collection, you may cite the collection once with complete publication information (see *Hall*). The individual entries (see *Abbey* and *Baldwin*) can then be cross-referenced (listed) by author, title, last name of the editor of the collection, and page numbers.

An "Edition"

Shakespeare, William.   Macbeth.   Ed. Sylvan Barnet.   New York: Signet-NAL, 1963.

Note: An "edition" refers to the work of one person prepared by another person(s), an editor (Ed.).

A Translation

Vergil.   The Aeneid.   Trans. Patric Dickinson.   New York: Mentor-NAL, 1961.

An Article in a Reference Book

"Ethnocentrism."   Webster's New Universal Unabridged Dictionary.   2nd ed.   1983.

Note: It is not necessary to give full publication information for familiar reference works (encyclopedias and dictionaries). If an article is initialed, check in the index of authors (in the opening section of each volume) for the author's full name.

Signed Pamphlet

Laird, Jean E.   The Metrics Are Coming.   Burlington: National Research Bureau, 1976.

Pamphlet with No Author or Publication Information

>   Pedestrian Safety. [United States]: n.p., n.d.

Note: List the country of publication [in brackets] if known. Insert *N.p.* before the colon if the country of publication is unknown.

Government Publications

>   United States. Congressional Quarterly Service. Congress and the Nation: A Review of
>   Government in the Postwar Years. Washington: GPO, 1965.

Note: State the name of the government (country, state, etc.) followed by the name of the agency.

A Book in a Series

>   Bishop, Jack. Ralph Ellison. Black Americans of Achievement. New York: Chelsea
>   House, 1988.

Note: Give the series name and number (if any) before the publication information.

A Publisher's Imprint

>   Solzhenitsyn, Alexander. One Day in the Life of Ivan Denisovich. Trans. Ralph Parker.
>   New York: Signet-NAL, 1963.

Note: The name of a publisher's imprint appears above the publisher's name on the title page. Give the imprint followed by a hyphen and the name of the publisher. (Signet-NAL)

Special Note: If more than one city is listed for a publisher, list the first one.

A Book with a Title within a Title

>   Harte, Bret. "The Outcasts of Poker Flat" and Other Stories. New York: Signet-NAL,
>   1961.

Note: If the title contains a title normally underlined, do not underline it in your entry.

158 Works Cited Entries: Periodicals _____

The entries which follow illustrate the information and arrangement needed to cite periodicals.

Signed Article in a Magazine

>   Mathews, Tom. "What Can Be Done?" Newsweek 21 Mar. 1988: 57-58.

Unsigned Article in a Magazine

>   "Then There's Rent Control." The New Republic 11 Apr. 1988: 22.

An Article in a Scholarly Journal

>   Cameron, John. "A Proposed Model for Imagination and Creativity."
>   Wisconsin Academy Review 34.3 (1987): 33-36.

Note: Journals are usually issued no more than four times a year: 34.3 refers to the volume and issue number. The issue number is not needed if the pagination in a volume continues from one issue to the next.

Signed Newspaper Article

>   Lee, Jessica. "Bush Plans 'to Build on' Budget." USA Today 10 Jan. 1989: 4A.

Note: 4A refers to page four in section A of the newspaper. Cite the edition of a major daily newspaper (if given) after the date. (10 Jan. 1989, late ed.: 4A)

Unsigned Newspaper Article

"Some Better Ways to Curb Teen Drinking." Editorial. Milwaukee Journal 17 June
  1979, sec. 2: 15.

Note: For an unsigned story, omit editorial.

A Letter to the Editor

Stassen, Harold E. Letter. Chicago Tribune 10 Jan. 1989, sec. 1: 16.

A Review

Foote, Timothy. "The Eye of the Beholder." Rev. of Testimony and Demeanor,
  by John Casey. Time 7 July 1979: 66.

Note: If you cite the review of a work by an editor or translator, use *ed.* or *trans.* instead of
by.

A Title or Quotation within an Article's Title

Merrill, Susan F. "'Sunday Morning' Thoughts." English Journal 76.6 (1987): 63.

Note: Use single quotation marks around the shorter title if it is a title normally
punctuated with quotation marks.

Works Cited Entries:
159 # Other Print and Nonprint Sources _____

Computer Software

Wordstar Professional. Vers. 4. Computer software. MicroPro, 1987. IBM PC-DOS
  2.0, 256KB, disk.

Note: At the end of an entry, add any information needed for operation—the system for
which the program is designed (IBM PC-DOS 2.0), the units of memory (256KB), and the
program form (disk, cassette, cartridge).

Television and Radio Programs

"An Interview with Sadat." 60 Minutes. CBS. WITI, Milwaukee. 11 Nov. 1979.

Note: If your reference is primarily to the work of an individual, cite that person before
the title. Otherwise, other pertinent information (writer, director, producer, narrator, etc.)
may be given after the main title of the program (underlined).

Recordings

Guthrie, Woody. Woody Guthrie Sings Folk Songs. With Leadbelly, Cisco Houston,
  Sonny Terry, and Bess Hawes. Intro. by Pete Seeger. Folkways Records, FA 2483,
  1962.

Note: FA 2483 refers to the catalog number. A person cited first in a recording (the
composer, conductor, performer, etc.) depends on the reason for the entry. If citing jacket
notes, give the author's name, the title of the material (if given), and the words *Jacket
notes* before the regular bibliographic information.

Films

Rebel without a Cause. Dir. Nicholas Ray. With James Dean, Natalie Wood, Sal Mineo,
  and Dennis Hopper. Warner, 1955.

Note: Cite the size and length of the film (if important) after the date.

Filmstrips, Slide Programs, and Videotapes

> Going Back, A Return to Vietnam.　Videocassette.　Virginia Productions, 1982.　55 min.

Note: Cite the medium (filmstrip, slide program, videocassette, etc.) after the title.

Performances

> Les Miserables.　By Alain Boublil and Claude-Michel Schonberg.　Dir. Trevor Nunn and
> John Caird.　Broadway Theatre, New York.　5 Apr. 1988.　Based on Victor Hugo's
> Les Miserables.

Note: If you are citing the efforts of an individual, give the person's name first.

Musical Compositions

> Beethoven, Ludwig van.　Symphony no. 8 in F major, op. 93.

Note: Do not underline a composition known only by form, number, and key.

Works of Art

> Renior, Pierre-Auguste.　Portrait of Claude Monet.　Louvre, Paris.　Plate 13 in Renior.
> By Elda Fezzi.　London: Thames and Hudson, 1968.

Note: If you cite the original work, give the artist, title, and location of the work of art.

Published Letters

> Bottomley, Edwin.　"To Father."　6 Dec. 1843.　An English Settler in Pioneer Wisconsin:
> The Letters of Edwin Bottomley.　Ed. Milo M. Quaife.　Madison: State Historical
> Society, 1918.　60-62.

Note: "To Father" and *6 Dec. 1843* refer to the cited letter.

Letter Received by the Author (Yourself)

> Thomas, Bob.　Letter to the author.　10 Jan. 1989.

Published or Recorded Interview

> Orbison, Roy.　"Roy Orbison: 1936-1988."　By Steve Pond.　Rolling Stone.
> 26 Jan. 1989: 22+.

Note: Type the word *Interview* after the interviewee's name if the interview is untitled.

Personal Interview

> Brooks, Sarah.　Personal interview.　15 Oct. 1988.

Note: If you spoke to your interviewee by phone, cite the entry as a *Telephone interview.*

Maps and Charts

> Wisconsin Territory.　Map.　Madison: Wisconsin Trails, 1988.

Lectures, Speeches, and Addresses

> Angelou, Maya.　Address.　Opening General Sess.　NCTE Convention.　St. Louis, 18
> Nov. 1988.

Note: If known, give the speech's title in quotation marks instead of *Address, Lecture,* or *Speech.*

Cartoons

> Trudeau, Garry.　"Doonesbury."　Cartoon.　Chicago Tribune 23 Dec. 1988, sec. 5: 6.

Additional Styles and Systems for Documentation

160   Most academic disciplines have their own manuals of style for documentation. The MLA author/page style, which is highlighted in red in this handbook, is most widely accepted in the humanities (literature, history, fine arts, philosophy, etc.). It is also the style you will likely be asked to follow for much of your academic research. Another common style of documentation is the author/date system explained in the American Psychological Association (APA) style manual and in *The Chicago Manual of Style* (CMS) and the related *A Manual for Writers*. (The APA author/date style is highlighted in blue in the "Appendix.") The author/date system is often used in the social sciences, business, education, and psychology. Note in the chart below how each of these style manuals presents a parenthetical reference and a corresponding bibliographic entry.

MLA (Borroff 37)

> Borroff, Marie.   Language and the Past: Verbal Artistry in Frost, Stevens, and Moore.
> Chicago: U of Chicago P, 1979.

APA (Borroff, 1979, p. 37)

> Borroff, Marie.   (1979).   Language and the past: Verbal artistry in Frost, Stevens, and
> Moore.   Chicago: University of Chicago Press.

CMS (Borroff 1979, 37)

> Borroff, Marie.   1979.   Language and the past: Verbal artistry in Frost, Stevens, and
> Moore.   Chicago: University of Chicago Press.

Special Note: Make sure you know which documentation style your instructor wants you to follow before you prepare a research paper.

161 Endnotes and Footnotes

You might be instructed to give credit for sources in endnotes or footnotes. Endnotes appear at the end of a text on a separate page(s), footnotes at the bottom of pertinent pages in the text. The first endnote or footnote to a work contains the publication information found in the Works Cited section or bibliography. Second and later references to a particular work contain less information.

Note: Since the first note to a work contains complete publication information, you might not need to compile a Works Cited list or bibliography. Check with your instructor.

162 MLA Guidelines for Footnotes and Endnotes _____

1.   Number notes consecutively throughout a paper.

2.   Place numbers at points in the text that preserve a paper's coherence (preferably, at the end of a sentence or a clause).

3.   Raise note numbers slightly above the typed line; leave one space after the number.

4.   Indent the first line of each endnote or footnote five spaces.

5.   For endnotes, center the title *Notes* one inch from the top of the endnote page. Double-space, indent five spaces, and type the note number slightly above the line. Leave one space and enter the reference. Succeeding lines to a note should be flush with the left-hand margin. (Double-space throughout.)

6.   For footnotes, double-space twice between the last line of the text on a page and the first footnote. Single-space each entry and double-space between them. If a note continues to the next page, type a line one double space below the text. Double-space again and continue the footnote.

Model Notes

163   The model notes which follow illustrate the information needed in first and succeeding entries.

164   Books: First References⎯⎯⎯⎯⎯⎯⎯⎯

One Author

[1] Robert R. Spitzer, No Need for Hunger (Danville: Interstate, 1981) 75.

Two or Three Authors

[2] Sheila Ostrander and Lynn Schroeder, Superlearning (New York: Delacorte, 1979) 57.

More Than Three Authors

[3] Wilfred L. Guerin, et al., A Handbook of Critical Approaches to Literature (New York: Harper, 1966) 149.

A Single Work From an Anthology

[4] William Morris, "The Haystack in the Floods," Nineteenth Century British Minor Poets, ed. Richard Wilbur and W.H. Auden (New York: Dell, 1965) 265-270.

Note: If you cite a complete anthology, begin the entry with the editors.

A Corporate Author

[5] Task Force on Education for Economic Growth, Action for Excellence (Washington: Education Commission of the States, 1983) 14.

No Author

[6] The World Almanac and Book of Facts (New York: Doubleday, 1961) 75.

One Volume in a Multivolume Work

[7] Alan Ziegler, The Writing Workshop, vol. 2 (New York: Teachers and Writers, 1984) 12.

An Introduction, Preface, Foreword, or Afterword

[8] Edward Callan, introduction, Cry, the Beloved Country, by Alan Paton (New York: Macmillan, 1987) xvi.

An "Edition"

[9] William Shakespeare, Macbeth, ed. Sylvan Barnet (New York: Signet-NAL, 1963) 14.

A Translation

[10] Vergil, The Aeneid, trans. Patric Dickinson (New York: Mentor-NAL, 1961) 131.

An Article in a Reference Book

[11] "Ethnocentrism," Webster's New Universal Unabridged Dictionary, 2nd ed., 1983.

A Pamphlet

[12] John E. Laird, <u>The Metrics Are Coming</u> (Burlington: National Research Bureau, 1976) 2-3.

Government Publications

[13] United States, Congressional Quarterly Service, <u>Congress and the Nation: A Review of Government in the Postwar Years</u> (Washington: GPO, 1965) 98.

A Book in a Series

[14] Jack Bishop, <u>Ralph Ellison</u>, Black Americans of Achievement (New York: Chelsea House, 1988) 48-51.

A Publisher's Imprint

[15] Alexander Solzhenitsyn, <u>One Day in the Life of Ivan Denisovich</u>, trans. Ralph Parker (New York: Signet-NAL, 1963) 113.

A Book with a Title within Its Title

[16] Bret Harte, <u>"The Outcasts of Poker Flat" and Other Stories</u> (New York: Signet-NAL, 1961) 12-15.

165   Periodicals: First References ━━━━━━

Article in a Magazine

[17] Tom Mathews, "What Can Be Done?" <u>Newsweek</u> 21 Mar. 1988: 58.

An Article in a Scholarly Journal

[18] John Cameron, "A Proposed Model for Imagination and Creativity," <u>Wisconsin Academy Review</u> 34.3 (1987): 35.

Newspaper Article

[19] Jessica Lee, "Bush Plans 'to Build on' Budget," <u>USA Today</u> 10 Jan. 1989: 4A.

A Letter to the Editor

[20] Harold E. Stassen, letter, <u>Chicago Tribune</u> 10 Jan. 1989, sec. 1: 16.

A Review

[21] Timothy Foote, "The Eye of the Beholder," rev. of <u>Testimony and Demeanor</u>, by John Casey, <u>Time</u> 7 July 1979: 66.

A Title or Quotation within an Article's Title

[22] Susan F. Merrill, "'Sunday Morning' Thoughts," <u>English Journal</u> 76.6 (1987): 63.

Other Print and Nonprint Sources:
166   First References ━━━━━━

Computer Software

[23] <u>Wordstar Professional</u>, computer software, MicroPro, 1987.

Television and Radio Programs

24 "An Interview with Sadat," 60 Minutes, CBS, WITI, Milwaukee, 11 Nov. 1979.

Recordings

25 Woody Guthrie, Woody Guthrie Sings Folk Songs, with Leadbelly, Cisco Houston, Sonny Terry, and Bess Hawes, intro. by Pete Seeger, Folkways Records, FA 2483, 1962.

Films

26 Rebel without a Cause, dir. Nicholas Ray, with James Dean, Natalie Wood, Sal Mineo, and Dennis Hopper, Warner, 1955.

Filmstrips, Slide Programs, and Videotapes

27 Going Back, A Return to Vietnam, videocassette, Virginia Productions, 1982 (55 min.).

Performances

28 Les Miserables, by Alain Boublil and Claude-Michel Schonberg, dir. Trevor Nunn and John Caird, Broadway Theatre, New York, 5 Apr. 1988.

Published Letters

29 Edwin Bottomley, "To Father," 6 Dec. 1843, An English Settler in Pioneer Wisconsin: The Letters of Edwin Bottomley, ed. Milo M. Quaife (Madison: State Historical Society, 1918) 60-62.

Letter Received by the Author (Yourself)

30 Bob Thomas, letter to the author, 10 Jan. 1989.

Published or Recorded Interview

31 Roy Orbison, "Roy Orbison: 1936-1988," by Steve Pond, Rolling Stone 26 Jan. 1989: 22.

Personal Interview

32 Sarah Brooks, personal interview, 15 Oct. 1988.

Maps and Charts

33 Wisconsin Territory, map (Madison: Wisconsin Trails, 1988).

Lectures, Speeches, and Addresses

34 Maya Angelou, address, Opening General Sess., NCTE Convention, St. Louis, 18 Nov. 1988.

Cartoons

35 Garry Trudeau, "Doonesbury," cartoon, Chicago Tribune 23 Dec. 1988, sec. 5: 6.

Second and Later References: Books and Periodicals _____

If a work has been fully documented in an endnote or footnote, succeeding references need only include the author's last name (or the title if no author) and the pages cited.

One Author

[36] Spitzer 48.

[37] Spitzer 90-93.

Note: Simply repeat the necessary information—the author or title and page numbers—even when you are referring to the same work two or more times in sequence. (The use of *ibid.* and *op. cit.* is no longer recommended.)

Two Authors

[38] Ostrander and Schroeder 57.

Multivolume Work

[39] Ziegler 12.

Note: If a volume other than the one listed in the first note is referred to, add the new volume number after the author's name.

Two Works by the Same Author

[40] Von Oech, A Kick 30.

[41] Von Oech, A Whack 21.

Play or Long Poem

[42] Macbeth V.v.23-26.   or   Macbeth 5.5.23-26.

Note: Use periods (no spacing) between act, scene, and lines.

Periodical Article (Unsigned)

[43] "Then There's Rent Control" 22.

Reference Book

[44] "Ethnocentrism."

Note: Add author, if given, to a second and later reference book note.

Abbreviations for the Research Paper _____

anon.	anonymous	ibid.	in the same place as			opere citato	
bk., bks.	book(s)		quoted above; *ibidem*	p., pp.		page(s)	
©	copyright	i.e.	that is; *id est*	pub. (or		published by, publica-	
chap., ch., chs.	chapter(s)	ill., illus.	illustration, illustrated	publ.), pubs.		tion(s)	
col., cols.	column(s)		by	rev.		revised	
comp.	compiler, compiled, compiled by	introd.	(author of) introduc-tion, introduced by,	rpt.		reprinted (by), reprint	
ed., eds.	editor(s), edition(s), or		introduction	sc.		scene	
	edited by	l., ll.	lines(s)	sec., secs.		section(s)	
e.g.	for example; *exempli gratia*	loc. cit.	in the place cited; *loco citato*	sic		thus (used with brackets to indicate an error is that way in the original)	
et al.	and others; *et alii*	MS, MSS	manuscript(s)				
et seq.	and the following; *et sequens*	narr., narrs.	narrated by, narrator(s)	tr., trans.		translator, translation	
		n.d.	no date given	v., vv. (or		verse(s)	
ex.	example	no., nos.	number(s)	vs., vss.)			
f., ff.	and the following page(s)	n. pag.	no pagination	viz.		namely; *videlicet*	
		N.p.	no place of publication and/or no publisher	vol., vols.		volume(s): capitalize when used with	
fig., figs.	figure(s)		given			Roman numerals	
GPO	Government Printing Office, Washington, D.C.	op. cit.	in the work cited;				

Helping the Homeless

**Center title
one-third
from top.**

Amy Douma
Mr. VanderMey
English 202
11 Dec. 1988

**Center identifying
information
two-thirds from
top. Double-space.**

Title centered one inch from top. Double-space throughout.

Helping the Homeless

Introduction - Who are the homeless and why are they so?

   I.   Classifying the homeless

       A.   Traditionally unemployed males

       B.   More and more entire families

  II.   Ineffective government programs the primary cause

       A.   Temporary Emergency Food Assistance Program

           1.   Homeless can't store food

           2.   Have no place to prepare food

       B.   Voucher System

           1.   "Rewards" homeless

           2.   Requires a far more adequate housing supply

       C.   Rent-Control System

           1.   Creates "housing gridlock"

           2.   Primary cause of homelessness in rent-controlled cities

 III.   Steps to alleviate homelessness

       A.   Federal government acceptance of responsibility

           1.   During Reagan administration, decrease in housing funds

           2.   Drop in housing production

       B.   Increase proper housing

           1.   Soup kitchens important

           2.   Transitional housing more important

           3.   Permanent housing most important

       C.   Monitor facilities

           1.   Satisfactory for the homeless using them?

           2.   Offer support groups

Conclusion - The homeless need help immediately from the federal government.

Douma 1

Amy Douma

Mr. VanderMey

English 202

11 Dec. 1988

Helping the Homeless

On a chilly February afternoon, an old man sits
sleeping on the sidewalk outside a New York hotel while
the lunchtime crowd shuffles by. At the man's feet is
a sign which reads: "Won't you help me? I'm cold and
homeless and lonely. God Bless You" (Chambers 11).
Imagine, for a moment, the life this man leads. He
probably spends his days alone on the street begging
for handouts, and his nights searching for shelter from
the cold. He has no job, no friends, and nowhere to
turn. Although most Americans would like to believe
that cases like this are rare, the National Coalition
for the Homeless estimates that as many as 3 million
citizens of our country share this man's lifestyle
(Tucker 34). Who are these people we call "the
homeless," and what factors have contributed to their
plight?

According to Pastor Walker, the director of
the Gospel Missions Shelter in Sioux City, Iowa, most
of the homeless are unemployed males, and from 40 to
50 percent have alcohol or drug-related problems.
Walker is quick to note, however, that the image of
the "typical" homeless person is changing. He says,
for instance, that the average age of the homeless has
dropped from fifty-five to thirty in the last ten
years (Walker interview). National studies have confirmed that the composition of America's homeless
population is changing. A recent study by the U.S.
Conference of Mayors, for example, found that one-

Name and page number are one-half inch from the top.

Title is centered.

Writer uses a personal close-up to create emotional involvement in the topic.

Concludes with a question which focuses on the subject of the paper.

Writer cites personal interview from her "field research"; uses paraphrase.

third of the homeless population consists of families with small children, and 22 percent of the homeless have full- or part-time jobs (Mathews 57).

Statistics seem to show that more and more of the homeless are entire families who have simply become the victims of economic hardship.

Why are these people still on the streets, despite the billions of dollars that are spent on the homeless each year? Some blame the national housing shortage, arguing that the 2 percent vacancy rate is not great enough to fill the country's need for shelter (Marcuse 426). Further study of the problem, however, suggests that government programs and policies are more likely to blame. These current programs fall into several categories. Some are handout programs designed to provide food or clothing to all of the needy, not just the homeless. An example of this type of program is the Temporary Emergency Food Assistance Program, which was created by the federal government in 1981 in order to make surplus agricultural commodities available to those in need. Other programs, such as the experimental voucher program and the rent-control system, are intended specifically to provide housing for low-income families that need shelter. Despite the good intentions behind these programs, however, none of them have provided sufficient help for the homeless.

Why have these programs been ineffective in alleviating homelessness? In some cases, the answer is that the programs are not designed to fit the special needs of the homeless. It was estimated in October of 1986, for instance, that 99 percent of the food supplied by the Temporary Emergency Assistance Program had gone to those who were not homeless. The reason? As Anna

Use of question signals a shift in the development of the paper from a profile of the homeless to the causes of their homelessness.

Writer blends examples and comments.

Question signals a closer look at the problem.

Kondratas of the Department of Agriculture says, "When you're homeless, you don't carry around a five-pound block of cheese" (qtd. in Whitman 34). Food programs such as this are of value only to those who already have facilities to store and prepare the food they are given. The homeless, therefore, are unable to take full advantage of programs of this nature.

Not all programs designed specifically to make housing available to those with low incomes have been effective, either. An example is the voucher system, a federal program created in 1983 which allows low-income families to live wherever they can find housing, regardless of cost. The only stipulation is that families must pay at least 30 percent of their incomes in rent. Although this system has been successful in finding shelter for some needy families, the program has several flaws which render it unacceptable as a long-term solution to homelessness. One problem is that most families who rely on the voucher system pay a lower percent of their income for rent than those who currently rent apartments on their own. Therefore a family could raise its income simply by becoming "homeless" (Coulson 16). The voucher program could begin a trend that contributes to the problem of homelessness instead of alleviating it. The second problem with the program is that it needs an ample housing supply to be effective. Says Democratic Congressman Thomas Downey of Long Island, "The voucher system would make sense if there were housing, but there is just not enough. It doesn't in any way address the problem" (qtd. in Hull 23).

The program that has had the worst results, however, is the rent-control system, which now covers

Quotation found in secondary source.

Writer uses lengthy paraphrase.

Discussion of "rent control" placed last in series of failed government programs; will be developed most extensively.

approximately 12 percent of America's housing. Rent
control is a program set up by local governments to
limit the amount of rent that a landlord can charge
his tenants. Its existence dates back to the latter
part of World War II, when New York tenants became
worried about impending rent increases following the war.
In 1947, these tenants persuaded politicians to extend
the rent limits into permanent housing regulations.
Since that time, nine states and many major cities, such
as Los Angeles and Washington, D.C., have adopted rent-
control policies (Fleetwood 19).

At first glance, it would appear that rent control
should benefit the homeless by insuring that low-rent
housing is made available. The problem is that most of
the rent-controlled housing is currently occupied by
those of the middle to upper class, who have either
received their apartments as family heirlooms or
acquired them by bribery. Leaving their current
apartments in order to find housing more appropriate
for their income bracket would mean exchanging a below-
market rent for a rent well above the average market
price. Most of these tenants would rather cling to a
cheap apartment that really doesn't suit them than
confront the cost of moving elsewhere. This results in
a condition known as "housing gridlock," in which no
one moves out of the low-rent housing. Seymour Durst,
a developer-philosopher from Manhattan, describes the
situation this way: "We've got plenty of low-income
housing in New York. We've just got upper-income
people living in it" (qtd. in Tucker 43).

This situation has had a drastic effect on the
poor of New York City. Unless they have access to a
rent-controlled apartment, they are forced to find

Writer refers to
"common
knowledge"
available in
numerous
sources, known
by anyone
familiar with
the field.

Writer
identifies
source with an
explanatory
phrase.

housing at middle- to upper-income prices. Some
estimate that those who find an apartment in these
areas are consequently paying 20 to 100 percent more
for housing than they would have without the rent-
control program ("Then There's Rent"). Those who can't
afford these higher rent payments are often left without a place to live. Therefore, the abuses of the
rent-control program are contributing to the problem
of homelessness rather than alleviating it.

Throughout the nation, rent control has had
effects similar to those in New York. According to
William Tucker, a writer who has done extensive
research on rent control and the homeless, the
existence of rent control is the primary factor that
determines the number of homeless a city will have,
regardless of location. For example, the extent of
homelessness in Santa Monica, California, is so great
that the city has been dubbed "The Homeless Capital of
the West Coast." The only characteristic of this city
that distinquishes it from others in the same area is
its extremely strict rent-control policy. Other cities
in Tucker's study that have rent-control programs also
have a much higher rate of homelessness than the
national average. In fact, Tucker asserts that where
rent control is practiced, homelessness is 250 percent
greater than in cities without rent control (41).

Since these government programs have not solved
the problems of homelessness, what should be done
instead? There is no guaranteed answer to this
question, but the most promising solution consists of
three steps. First of all, the federal government must
accept responsibility for providing shelter for the
homeless. During the Reagan administration, the

Citation of one-page article with no author.

Writer identified with an explanatory phrase to establish authority.

Source named in text; only page number cited in parentheses.

Question signals a shift in the development of the paper from the causes of the problem to possible solutions.

federal government attempted to shift this burden to
state and local governments by slashing federal funds
for housing. Between the years of 1981 and 1987,
Reagan cut the housing budget from $30 billion to $7.3
billion, expecting local governments and private
contributions to make up for the decrease in funds
(Mathews 58). Unfortunately, Reagan's plan has not
worked as well as he expected. In New York City, for
instance, only $500 million has been spent on the
homeless since the cutbacks, while the need has been
estimated at $12.5 billion (Chambers 11).

Statistics have been used to support claims.

The decrease in funds has been coupled with a
recent drop in housing production. Only 60,000 new
housing units have been created in New York during the
past three years, compared to 265,000 between the years
1960 and 1963. Many other cities have experienced
similar cutbacks. This decrease in new housing units
has undoubtedly contributed to the nation's housing
shortage. In addition, some existing subsidized
federal housing units from the 1960's will soon be free
from the rent restrictions placed on them at that time.
The result will probably be a substantial rise in the
amount of rent charged, which will put much of the
current low-income housing out of the reach of the poor
(Mathews 57-58). In order to avoid the drastic effects
that these decreases in low-rent housing could cause,
more housing must be created immediately. According to
community groups, renewed federal support will be
essential to accomplish this task (Hull 22).

A second step necessary for helping the homeless
is insuring that the proper type of housing is made
available. According to Peter Marcuse, a professor of
urban planning at the Columbia University Graduate

School of Architecture, Planning, and Preservation, shelter for the homeless falls into three categories. The first and simplest type is the soup kitchen, a temporary emergency shelter that provides food and, sometimes, a place to sleep. Shelters of this type are especially important in places where little food is available or weather conditions are unfavorable. The second type of housing is the transitional shelter, which also provides housing for a limited amount of time. Transitional housing is unique, however, in that it provides job counseling and other social services, which are intended to help the homeless permanently rejoin society. The third type of shelter is permanent housing, the type of shelter most likely to bring about an end to homelessness (428). Permanent shelter could be provided by constructing low-cost prefabricated housing modules, or by renovating buildings that are currently uninhabited (Coulson 16). Unfortunately, most current housing programs focus on temporary soup kitchens, as they are the least expensive to build and maintain. Although soup kitchens have an important role to play, more transitional and permanent housing will be necessary for the homeless to fully readjust to society.

The final step to ending homelessness is forming an organization that will periodically make certain that those who are provided with shelters are satisfied with their facilities and surroundings. This function should be coupled with psychiatric care for those who are not yet ready to rejoin society. Studies have shown that neglecting the more personalized care of the homeless often makes previous efforts to aid them futile. These people tend to return to living on the

Writer uses summary. ("The first and simplest type . . . .")

Source cited at the beginning of the paragraph; only page number cited in parentheses.

Final step anticipates possible objections by readers. ("Studies have shown . . . .")

streets unless they are offered some type of support group (Whitman 27). An organization of this type could either take the form of a government agency or work through one of the existing social groups. This third step must be included in any plan intended to alleviate homelessness.

When we discuss "ending" homelessness, however, we must remember that it is a problem that will probably never be truly eliminated. There will always be those who refuse any help offered to them, the ones who prize their freedom of lifestyle above personal comfort. While we must respect the rights of such people, we cannot use them as an excuse to do nothing about the homeless. Most of those living on the streets are there, not by choice, but because they have no alternative. It is these people that we must try to help immediately, with the support of the federal government. If we begin now, we may be able to make homelessness simply a matter of choice.

Writer offers concession to make argument realistic, but reaffirms claim that increased federal support is needed.

Works Cited

Chambers, Rick. "No Place to Lay Their Heads." The
Church Herald 16 Sept. 1988: 9-11.

Coulson, C. "The $37,000 Slum." The New Republic
19 Jan. 1988: 15-16.

Fleetwood, Blake. "There's Nothing Liberal about Rent
Control." The Washington Monthly June 1986:
19-23.

Hull, Jennifer. "Building from the Bottom Up." Time
9 Feb. 1987: 22-23.

Marcuse, Peter. "Why Are They Homeless?" The Nation
4 Apr. 1987: 426-29.

Mathews, Tom. "What Can Be Done?" Newsweek
21 Mar. 1988: 57-58.

"Then There's Rent Control." The New Republic
11 Apr. 1988: 22.

Tucker, William. "Where Do the Homeless Come From?"
National Review 25 Sept. 1987: 32-43.

Walker, Harry. Personal interview. 20 Dec. 1988.

Whitman, David. "Hope for the Homeless." U.S. News
and World Report 29 Feb. 1988: 26-35.

"Works Cited"
centered one
inch from the
top.

Writing with a Computer

173   Let's suppose as part of a research project, you survey groups of young writers in computer writing labs. Your survey opens with the following general question: Has the computer helped you with your writing? Almost everyone will answer with an enthusiastic yes. If you ask them to explain their answer, they will tell you that they stay at a piece of writing longer with a computer, that they experiment more, that they like the way they can manipulate information on the monitor, that they have a better attitude about writing in general. (These explanations reflect the findings of current research.)

     Ask the teachers of these writers, and they will tell you the same thing: Computers have helped students with their writing. Many of them, however, will want to qualify their answer. They will tell you that computers are better suited for certain tasks during the writing process than they are for others. This is the consensus among writing teachers and writing researchers. The section which follows discusses the up side and the down side of computer-assisted writing as seen by the experts. Use it as a guide when you develop your own writing with a computer.

Prewriting

> *"For better or worse, less of me will remain unsaid because of the speed and ease and even intimacy of computer-assisted writing."*
>
> *– Peter Stillman*

Up Side:

     +Some researchers generally claim that young writers do more prewriting and planning on a computer than on paper because they can turn their attention from handwriting and legibility to developing their ideas.

     + Prewriting and planning programs are available to help writers select and develop a writing subject.

Down Side:

     –Research also claims that writers may do less prewriting and planning on a computer.

     – Computer-assisted writers have been observed to concentrate on the order rather than the development of ideas.

     – Some types of prewriting are difficult to manipulate on the screen. For example, it would be difficult to cluster on a computer.

     – The monitor is too tempting for some young writers; they constantly stop and read what they have written. Solution: Turn the resolution of the monitor down until first thoughts are developed.

Best Advice: Do most of your prewriting and planning on paper. However, keep in mind that a computer might also be of use to you during the initial stages of writing. For some writers, simply changing from pen and paper to computer to printout encourages new ideas.

Special Note: Save your work on a data disk at frequent intervals throughout a writing project. If at all possible, make a backup copy of your work as well.

Writing the First Draft
Up Side:

     + Some writers and instructors feel a computer helps a writer stay with a piece of writing longer and develop it more thoroughly.

+ Computers allow a writer to concentrate on ideas rather than the finished copy.

+ Drafting on a computer in a writing lab enhances a sharing of ideas since a writer's work is more public. Writers become more aware of a real audience.

Down Side:

– Some writers can't resist making changes, and this may disrupt the free flow of their ideas.

– Deleting sections of copy might be too tempting for some writers. Most writers feel it is important to save all of their ideas in early drafts.

Best Advice: Do your drafting on your computer. If you can't resist the temptation to make a lot of changes during first drafts, turn down the resolution on your monitor. If this doesn't work, start drafting with pen and paper.

Revising

> *"For me it [the word processor] was obviously the perfect new toy. I began playing on page 1— editing, cutting, and revising— and have been on a rewriting high ever since."*
>
> *– William Zinsser*

Up Side:

+ A computer relieves a writer from the toil of writing or typing revision after revision. (A computer is a godsend when it comes to revising longer essays and research papers.)

+ A computer makes revising easier since a writer can move, delete, and add information very simply with function keys.

Down Side:

– Some research suggests that the quickness of computer-assisted revision discourages reflection, experimenting, and testing—qualities of meaningful writing.

– The computer will encourage some writers to concentrate on only one revision draft rather than many because the ease of revision is too tempting.

Best Advice: Use your computer for revising. No one should rewrite or retype drafts during revising when they can do it so much easier on a computer. Make sure, however, that you allow yourself some "mulling over" periods during revising for reflection and rethinking. Always have a printed copy of your writing on hand when you revise to make quick notes, to experiment, and to have an original version of your text after you've made changes on your computer.

Editing and Proofreading

Up Side:

+ A computer encourages a writer to produce clean final copy because it makes changing elements so easy.

+ Programs are available that help students prepare their writing for publication. The spell checkers and *search* and *replace* capabilities in some word processing programs are especially helpful.

+ Programs are also available to help students format endnotes, tables of contents, and indexes for research papers.

Down Side:

–Again, the ease of making changes on a computer promotes quickness, but not always thoughtful writing.

Best Advice: Definitely do your editing and proofreading on a computer. Almost all writers agree that the computer is of most benefit in preparing a paper for publication.

Writing
SUMMARIES

The best test of how well you understand something you've read is whether you can write in your own words an accurate summary of the important ideas. Adding summary writing to your study routine can increase your ability to understand and remember what you have read. There are three popular forms of summary writing— the abstract, the paraphrase, and the précis.

The Abstract

180   The abstract is a shortened form of a written selection using the important words of the selection itself. An abstract should have the same style and essential content as the original. Words and phrases are taken from the original and used as part of the abstract. There should be no attempt at originality. You simply select the important words and connect them into a shortened, readable version of the original selection.

Original

The human brain, once surrounded by myth and misconception, is no longer such a mystery. It is now understood to be the supervisory center of the nervous system, and, as such, it controls all voluntary (eating and thinking) and most involuntary behavior (blinking and breathing). The brain functions by receiving information from nerve cells which are located throughout the body. Recent research has provided a clear picture of exactly what happens when information first reaches the brain. It has been discovered that the cells in the cortex of the brain which receive the information are arranged in a regular pattern in columns. The columns are, in turn, arranged into a series of "hypercolumns." Each cell within each column has a specific responsibility to perceive and analyze certain kinds of incoming information. Within the columns, the analysis of this information follows a formal sequence. Eventually, the information is relayed to the higher centers of the brain where a complete picture is assembled. The brain then evaluates the information and either sends a return message to the muscles and glands or stores the information for later use. The return message travels through the body in the form of electrical and chemical signals via the billions of nerve cells (neurons). When the message reaches its destination, the muscles or glands respond with the appropriate reaction. With each additional experience, the brain is better able to analyze, evaluate, and respond to the information it receives each day.

Abstract

The human brain controls all voluntary and most involuntary behavior. The brain functions by receiving information from nerve cells which are located throughout the body. The cells in the cortex of the brain which receive the information are arranged in columns; each cell within each column has a specific responsibility to perceive and analyze certain kinds of incoming information. After the information has been analyzed following a formal sequence, it is relayed to the higher centers of the brain where a complete picture is assembled. The brain then evaluates the information and either sends a return message to the muscles and glands or stores the information for later use.

181 The Paraphrase

A paraphrase is a restatement of someone else's ideas written in your own words. A paraphrase states fully and clearly the meaning of a complex piece of writing. Because a paraphrase often includes your interpretation of complicated phrases and ideas, it can actually be longer than the original. A paraphrase is used to clarify the meanings of poems, proverbs, legal documents, and any other writing which is obscure or symbolic.

Original

Nothing Gold Can Stay

Nature's first green is gold,	(1)
Her hardest hue to hold.	(2)
Her early leaf's a flower;	(3)
But only so an hour.	(4)
Then leaf subsides to leaf.	(5)
So Eden sank to grief,	(6)
So dawn goes down to day.	(7)
Nothing gold can stay.	(8)

—Robert Frost

Paraphrase

The first growth of spring is more gold in color than green.	(1)
But this golden shade of green doesn't last very long.	(2)
The first leaf is actually a blossom or flower,	(3)
but it remains for only a very short time.	(4)
Then the buds and blossoms give way to full, green leaves.	(5)
In the same way, the Garden of Eden was taken away;	(6)
and dawn's glow gives way to the harsher light of day.	(7)
Nothing in nature—especially those things most beautiful—	
lasts forever.	(8)

182 The Précis

A précis is perhaps the most useful kind of summary writing for general studying. A précis is a summary in your own words of something you have just read. You select only the most important ideas and combine them into clear, concise sentences. A précis of a paragraph, for example, may be only one sentence long. In most cases your précis should be no more than one-third as long as the original. Follow the guidelines below the next time you need to write a summary of something you have read.

──Guidelines for Writing a Précis──

1. Skim the selection to get the overall meaning.

2. Reread the selection carefully, paying particular attention to key words and phrases. (Check the meaning of any words with which you are unfamiliar.)

3. List the major ideas on your own paper.

4. Quickly skim the selection a final time so that you have the overall meaning clearly in mind as you begin to write.

5. Write a summary of the major ideas, using your own words except for those "few" words in the original which cannot be changed. Keep the following points in mind as you write your précis:

   a. Your opening (topic) sentence should be a clear statement of the main idea of the original selection.

   b. Stick to the essential information — names, dates, times, places, and similar facts are usually essential; examples, detailed data, and adjectives are usually not.

c.   Try to state each important idea in one clear sentence.

   d.   Arrange your ideas into the most logical order, and link your sentences with effective connecting words so that your précis becomes a complete paragraph in itself.

   e.   Use vivid, efficient words which help keep the précis to no more than one-third the length of the original.

   f.   Use a concluding sentence which ties all of your points together and brings your summary to an effective end.

6.   Check your précis for accuracy and conciseness by rereading the original passage and comparing it thought for thought with your précis. Ask yourself the following questions:

   a.   Have I kept the original writer's point of view in my précis?

   b.   Have I cut or compressed the supporting details contained in the original?

   c.   Could another person get the main idea of the original selection by simply reading my précis?

7.   Proofread your précis for mechanical errors and overall effectiveness. (Follow the same checklist or proofreading guidelines you use for your paragraph or essay writing.)

Original

   "Acid rain" is precipitation with a high concentration of acids. The acids are produced by sulfur dioxide, nitrogen oxide, and other chemicals which are created by the burning of fossil fuels. Acid rain is known to have a gradual, destructive effect on plant and aquatic life. The greatest harm from acid rain is caused by sulfur dioxide, a gas produced by the burning of coal. As coal is burned in large industrial and power plant boilers, the sulfur it contains is turned into sulfur-dioxide gas. This invisible gas is funneled up tall smokestacks and released into the atmosphere some 350-600 feet above the ground. As a result, the effects of the gas are seldom felt immediately. Instead, the gas is carried by the wind for hundreds and sometimes thousands of miles before it floats back down to earth. For example, sulfur dioxide produced in Pennsylvania at noon on Monday may not show up again until early Tuesday when it settles into the lakes and soil of rural Wisconsin. Adding to the problem is the good possibility that the sulfur dioxide has undergone a chemical change while in flight. By simply taking on another molecule of oxygen, the sulfur dioxide could be changed to sulfur trioxide. Sulfur trioxide, when mixed with water, creates sulfuric acid—a highly toxic acid. If the sulfur trioxide enters a lake or stream, the resulting acid can kill fish, algae, and plankton. This, in turn, can interrupt the reproductive cycle of other life forms, causing a serious imbalance in nature. If the sulfur enters the soil, it can work on metals such as aluminum and mercury and set them free to poison both the soil and water. Damage from acid rain has been recorded throughout the world, from the Black Forest in Germany to the lakes in Sweden to the sugar maple groves in Ontario, Canada. The result is a growing concern among scientists and the general public about the increasing damage being done to the environment by acid rain.

Précis

   "Acid rain," the term for precipitation which contains a high concentration of harmful chemicals, is gradually damaging our environment. The greatest harm from acid rain is caused by sulfur dioxide, a gas produced from the burning of coal. This gas, which is released into the atmosphere by industries using coal-fired boilers, is carried by the wind for hundreds of miles. By the time this gas has floated back to earth, it has often changed from sulfur dioxide to sulfur trioxide. Sulfur trioxide, when mixed with water, forms sulfuric acid—a highly toxic acid. This acid can kill both plant and aquatic life and upset the natural balance so important to the cycle of life.

Using the
LIBRARY

"Knowledge is of two kinds. We know a subject ourselves, or we know where we can find information upon it."

— Samuel Johnson

A student writer has two sources of material—his own experiences, ideas, and knowledge plus that of other people. This second kind of material can be collected firsthand by observing, listening, and talking to other people. Unfortunately, you are restricted in both the amount and kind of information you can gather firsthand. There is one place, however, where you are not restricted. It is a place where you can freely gather information from all times, places, and people. You can share in the experiences, ideas, and knowledge of thousands of other people. The place, of course, is your library.

Before you can take full advantage of any library, however, you must become acquainted with the kinds of information contained there and how to use each kind. Most libraries contain the following sections:

1. Card Catalog
2. Fiction books
3. Nonfiction books
4. Reference books
5. Reserved books
6. Vertical file
7. New/special books
8. *Readers' Guide*
9. Magazines/newspapers
10. Audiovisual materials

The Card Catalog

190   Of all these sections, the **card catalog** is among the most important. The card catalog is an index (listing) of nearly all the materials in the library. All books, for example, are listed in the card catalog by *subject, author,* and *title.* This means you can find a book you are interested in even if you don't know the author or the exact title. The **catalog cards** list the following information: call number, author, title, subject, publisher, illustrator, copyright date, number of pages, and information about the content of the book. (See the sample cards on the following page.)

Sample Catalog Cards

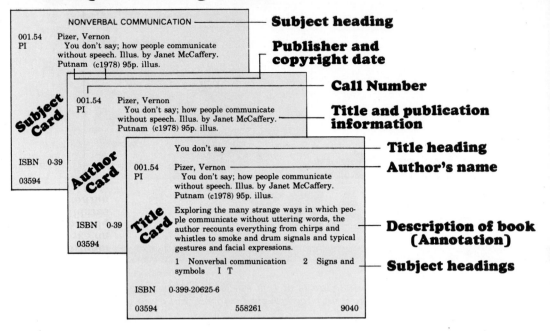

NONVERBAL COMMUNICATION —— **Subject heading**

001.54
PI   Pizer, Vernon
        You don't say; how people communicate
     without speech. Illus. by Janet McCaffery.   **Publisher and**
     Putnam (c1978) 95p. illus.   **copyright date**

Subject Card

ISBN 0-39

03594

—— **Call Number**

Title and publication information

001.54
PI   Pizer, Vernon
        You don't say; how people communicate
     without speech. Illus. by Janet McCaffery. —
     Putnam (c1978) 95p. illus.

Author Card

ISBN 0-39

03594

You don't say —————————— **Title heading**

001.54   Pizer, Vernon ——————— **Author's name**
PI   You don't say; how people communicate
             without speech. Illus. by Janet McCaffery.
             Putnam (c1978) 95p. illus.

Title Card

Exploring the many strange ways in which peo-
ple communicate without uttering words, the   **Description of book**
author recounts everything from chirps and   **(Annotation)**
whistles to smoke and drum signals and typical
gestures and facial expressions.

1 Nonverbal communication   2 Signs and   —— **Subject headings**
symbols   I T

ISBN   0-399-20625-6

03594   558261   9040

191   The cards in the card catalog are arranged alphabetically and filed in drawers similar to those shown below. Each drawer is labeled clearly so that you can see at a glance which cards are contained in that drawer.

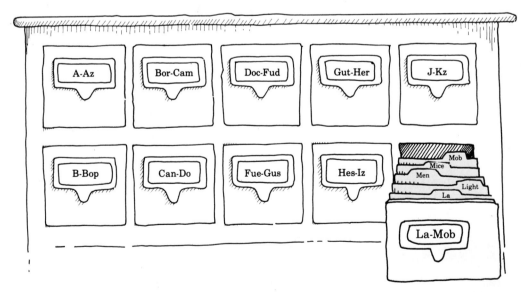

192   By checking in the appropriate drawer for the title, you can determine quickly whether the library has the book you are interested in finding. If you aren't able to locate that particular book, you can check elsewhere in the card catalog for other books on the same subject. By reading the annotations on the subject cards, you can determine which books best suit your needs.

To use the card catalog efficiently, it is important to know that certain words, numbers, and abbreviations are handled in a special way when they are first in a title. Look carefully at the samples and guidelines below:

McCarthy, Mary
Magnificent Seven (The)
MEDICINE—HISTORY
Medicine Before Physicians
1,000,000's of Everything
Mr. Chips Takes a Vacation

Titles

- If a title begins with an article (*a, an, the*) the article is ignored and the title is filed alphabetically by the second word. **Example:** The title card for *The Magnificent Seven* is placed in the *M* drawer under *Magnificent*.

- If a title begins with a number, the card is placed in alphabetical order as if the number were spelled out. **Example:** The title card for *1,000,000's of Everything* is placed in the *M* drawer under *millions*.

- If the title begins with an abbreviation, the title is filed as if the abbreviation were spelled out. **Example:** The title card for *Mr. Chips Takes a Vacation* is placed in the *M* drawer under *Mister*.

Authors

- Authors are listed by last name first. **Example:** McCarthy, Mary

- Last names beginning with *Mc* are filed as if they were written *Mac*.

Subjects

- Subject cards are listed alphabetically and are placed before titles which begin with the same word. **Example:** The subject card for MEDICINE — HISTORY comes before the title card for *Medicine Before Physicians*.

Finding a Book: The Call Number

Once you have located your card in the card catalog, you must next locate the book in the library. To do this, you will need to copy down the **call number** of the book and locate that number on the library shelves. Nonfiction books, the type used most often for school reports and research papers, are arranged by subject according to one of two systems of classifications, the *Dewey Decimal* or *Library of Congress* system. This means that books with similar contents are placed together on the shelves, making your job of locating a variety of material on a particular topic much easier.

193 The Dewey Decimal System

In the **Dewey Decimal System,** all knowledge is divided into ten main *classes,* each of which is assigned a set of numbers. Each of these classes is further divided into *divisions.* (See the chart on the following page.)

Each division is then divided into ten *sections,* each with its own number. These sections are divided into as many *subsections* as are needed for that particular topic. Together these numbers make up the **class number** of a book.

Divisions of the Dewey Decimal Class Number		
900	History	Class
970	History of North America	Division
973	History of the United States	Section
973.7	History of the U.S. Civil War	Subsection
973.74	History of Civil War Songs	Subsection

The Dewey Decimal System

000	**Generalities**	340	Law	670	Manufactures processible
010	Bibliographies and catalogs	350	Public administration	680	Assembled and final products
020	Library science	360	Welfare and association	690	Buildings
030	General encyclopedic works	370	Education		
040	General collected essays	380	Commerce	700	**The Arts**
050	General periodicals	390	Customs and folklore	710	Civic and landscape art
060	General organizations			720	Architecture
070	Newspapers and journalism	400	**Language**	730	Sculpture and the plastic arts
080	General collections	410	Linguistics and nonverbal lang.	740	Drawing and decorative arts
090	Manuscripts and book rarities	420	English and Anglo-Saxon	750	Painting and paintings
		430	Germanic languages	760	Graphic arts
100	**Philosophy and related**	440	French, Provencal, Catalan	770	Photography and photographs
110	Ontology and methodology	450	Italian, Romanian, etc.	780	Music
120	Knowledge, cause, purpose, man	460	Spanish and Portuguese	790	Recreation (Recreational arts)
130	Pseudo- and parapsychology	470	Italic languages		
140	Specific philosophic viewpoints	480	Classical and Greek	800	**Literature and Rhetoric**
150	Psychology	490	Other languages	810	American Literature in English
160	Logic			820	Engl. and Anglo-Saxon literature
170	Ethics (Moral philosophy)	500	**Pure sciences**	830	Germanic languages literature
180	Ancient, med., Oriental philos.	510	Mathematics	840	French, Provencal, Catalan lit.
190	Modern Western philosophy	520	Astronomy and allied sciences	850	Italian, Romanian, etc. literature
		530	Physics	860	Spanish and Portuguese literature
200	**Religion**	540	Chemistry and allied sciences	870	Italic languages literature
210	Natural religion	550	Earth sciences	880	Classical and Greek literature
220	Bible	560	Paleontology	890	Lits. of other languages
230	Christian doctrinal theology	570	Anthropolog. and biol. sciences		
240	Christ. moral and devotional theol.	580	Botanical sciences	900	**General geog./history**
250	Christ. pastoral, parochial, etc.	590	Zoological sciences	910	General geography
260	Christ. social and eccles. theol.			920	General biog., geneal., etc.
270	Hist. and geo. of Christ. church	600	**Technology** (Applied science)	930	Gen. history of ancient world
280	Christ. denominations and sects	610	Medical sciences	940	Gen. history of modern Europe
290	Other religions and compar. rel.	620	Engineering and allied operations	950	Gen. history of modern Asia
		630	Agriculture and agric. industries	960	Gen. history of modern Africa
300	**The social sciences**	640	Domestic arts and sciences	970	Gen. history of North America
310	Statistical method and statistics	650	Business and related enterprises	980	Gen. history of South America
320	Political science	660	Chemical technology, etc.	990	Gen. history of rest of world
330	Economics				

In addition to its class number, a **call number** contains the first letter of the author's last name. It may also contain a cutter number assigned by the librarian to help in shelving the book and the first letter of the title's first significant word. The call number determines where a book is located in the library.

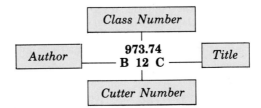

Note: The exceptions to this classification system are fiction books and the individual biography. Fiction is usually kept in a separate section of the library where the books are arranged by the author's last name. (Classic literature is, however, listed and shelved in the literature class.) Biographies are arranged on separate shelves by the last name of the person written about.

194 The Library of Congress System

In the **Library of Congress** system of classifying books, the call number begins with a letter rather than a number. The letter(s) used in this system represent the twenty subject classes; each is listed on the next page alongside the corresponding Dewey Decimal number.

The Library of Congress and Dewey Decimal Systems

L C Category		Dewey Decimal	L C Category		Dewey Decimal
A	General Works	000-099	K	Law	340-349
B	Philosophy	100-199	L	Education	370-379
	Psychology	150-159	M	Music	780-789
	Religion	200-299	N	Fine Arts	700-799
C	History:	910-929	P	Language and	400-499
	auxiliary sciences			Literature	800-899
D	History:	930-999	Q	Science	500-599
	general and Old World		R	Medicine	610-619
E-F	History:	970-979	S	Agriculture	630-639
	American		T	Technology	600-699
G	Geography	910-919	U	Military Science	355-359,
	Anthropology	571-573			623
	Recreation	390-399	V	Naval Science	359, 623
		790-799	Z	Bibliography and	010-019
H	Social Sciences	300-399		Library Science	020-029
J	Political Science	320-329			

Note: Under the Library of Congress system, the books are placed on the shelves first by letter(s), then by the numbers which follow.

Locating Books by Call Number

195   When you go to the shelves to get your book, you must remember to look carefully at the call numbers. Because some numbers contain several decimal points and are longer than others, they can easily distract you into looking in the wrong place for your book. For instance, the call number 973.2 is located on the shelf after a book with the call number 973.198. (See the illustration below.) Also, you will most likely find several books with the same Dewey Decimal number. Whenever this happens, the books are arranged alphabetically by author abbreviation.

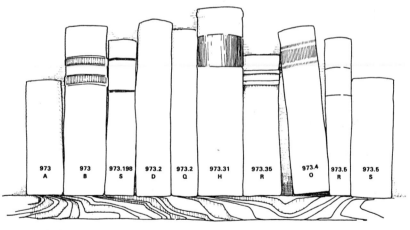

Readers' Guide to Periodical Literature

196   *The Readers' Guide to Periodical Literature* is another useful index to library information. It indexes magazine articles by subject and author. If you are looking for information on a current topic, the *Readers' Guide* will direct you to specific magazine articles which contain more recent information than most books. It will also help you find magazine articles from years ago. To use the *Readers' Guide,* simply select a volume which covers the appropriate year(s) and search alphabetically for the author or subject in which you are interested. When you find a listing for an article you would like to read, fill out a request form (*call slip*) or put the title, date, and volume of the magazine

ENGLER, PAUL   AUTHOR ENTRY

Oil Shortage today. Beef tomorrow? por Farm J 99:B16 Mr '75

ENGLISH

ENVIRONMENTAL engineering (buildings)

Architecture, energy, economy, and efficiency. G. Soucie. Audubon 77:122 S '75

Autonomous living in the Ouroboros house. S.J. Marcovich. il Pop Sci 207:80-2+ D '75   NAME OF AUTHOR

Conditioned air gets used three times in an energy-conscious design. il Archit Rec 158:133-4 N '75

Energy house from England aims at self-sufficiency. D. Scott. il Pop Sci 207:78-80 Ag '75

Houses designed with nature: their future is at hand; Ouroboros and integral projects. S. Love. bibl il Smithsonian 6:46-53 D '75   DATE

OCF presents awards for energy conservation. il Archit Rec 158:34 D '75

PM visits a house full of energy-saving ideas. J.F. Pearson. il Pop Mech 144:59+ Ag '75

Profession and industry focus on solar energy. il Archit Rec 158:35 Ag '75   NAME OF MAGAZINE

Round table: toward a rational policy for energy use in buildings; with introd by W. F. Wagner, Jr. il Archit Rec 158:8, 92-9 mid-Ag '75

Solar energy systems: the practical side. il Archit Rec 158:128-34 mid-Ag '75   VOLUME

ENVIRONMENTAL health

Environmental hazards and corporate profits. Chr Cent 92: 404 Ap 23 '75

See also

Environmental diseases   "SEE ALSO" CROSS REFERENCE

ENVIRONMENTAL impact statements. See Environmental policy

ENVIRONMENTAL indexes. See Environment—Statistics

ENVIRONMENTAL law

Capitol watch. G. Alderson Liv Wildn 38:60 Wint '74; 39:33 Spr; 42 Jl; 41 O '75   PAGE NUMBER

How to save a river; Bellport, N.Y. high students, sponsoring Carmans River bill.

A. Rubin, Sr Schol 105:4-7 Ja 16 '75

Overview: law. A.W. Reitze Jr and G.L. Reitze. See issues of Environment

See also   SUBJECT ENTRY

Air pollution — Laws and legislation

Land utilization — Laws and regulations

ENVIRONMENTAL movement

After setbacks — new tactics in environmental crusade. J. McWethy. il U.S. News 78:62-3 Je 9 '75   TITLE OF ARTICLE

Be a part of Food day every day. Org Gard & Farm 22:32+ Ap '75

Dialogue: C. Amory versus environmental groups on hunting issue. R.E. Hall. Conservationist 29:1 Ap '75

Ecological view. J. Marshall. Liv Wildn 39: 5-10 Spr '75

Environment, a mature cause in need of a lift. L.J. Carter. Science 187:45-6+ Ja 10 '75

Junior leagues focus on community education; environmental projects. M.D. Poole, por Parks & Rec 10:21+ D '75

Obligation and opportunity. R.F. Hall. Conservationist 29:1 Je '75   "SEE" CROSS REFERENCE

Organic living almanac. See issues of Organic gardening and farming

Prophets of shortage; address, July 11, 1975. D. Hodel. Vital Speeches 41:621-5 Ag 1 '75

What conservationists think about conservation; results of questionnaire. H. Clepper. il Am For 81:28-9+ Ag '75

See also

Canada-United States environmental council

Industry and the environmental movement   SUBTOPIC

Exhibitions

See also

International exposition on the environment. 1974

Material from the Readers' Guide to Periodical Literature is reproduced by permission of the H.W. Wilson Company.

on a piece of paper and take it to the librarian. The librarian will get the magazine for you.

Look closely at the sample page from the *Readers' Guide*. Notice the following:

- The *Readers' Guide* is cross referenced, giving you other subject headings where you may find additional articles on related topics.

- Articles are arranged alphabetically by subject and author; the title is listed under one of these two entries.

- Each subject entry is divided into subtopics whenever there are a large number of articles on the same subject listed together.

The Reference Section

198   Another special section of the library is the **reference section.** Students are usually familiar with the reference section because this is the section where the encyclopedias are kept. But there are a number of other helpful reference books with which all students should be familiar. The most popular titles are listed below:

Information Please Almanac is an atlas and yearbook which is published annually. The book contains facts, statistics, and short articles. Information is not arranged according to a specific pattern, but a detailed index makes information easy to find.

Statesman's Yearbook is a statistical and historical annual of the nations of the world. The information about each country includes facts concerning its government, geographical area, population, religions, education, judicial system, social welfare, and so on. A bibliography follows each entry.

The World Almanac and Book of Facts is an annual publication which contains facts and statistics concerning the following subjects: industry, politics, history, finances, religion, education, and social institutions or programs. In addition to this information, the book also includes a chronological review of major events in the past year. The book has a very detailed index.

The McGraw-Hill Encyclopedia of World Biography is a twelve-volume set which contains 5,000 biographies of world figures. The last volume contains a detailed index.

Webster's Dictionary of Proper Names has more than 10,000 entries. Entries include real people, fictional characters, literary works, events, sports figures, political personalities, specific terms, and acronyms.

Current Biography is published monthly and annually. Each article includes a photo of the individual, a biographical sketch, and information concerning the person's birthdate, address, occupation, etc. Each yearbook contains an index of names, an index of professions, and a cumulative index.

Dictionary of American Biography is prepared under the direction of the American Council of Learned Societies. It includes biographies of noteworthy persons who lived in the United States. It does not include biographies of people living today.

American Writers: A Collection of Literary Biographies is a four-volume set which includes a series of reports on American authors. Each report contains a brief biographical sketch, a selected bibliography, and a rather lengthy evaluation of the writer's work.

Contemporary Authors is a biographical dictionary of authors who have written fiction, juvenile books, general nonfiction, and books on social sciences. Most entries are American writers. Each entry gives basic biographical information including titles written, honors given, etc. This publication is printed semiannually.

Something About the Author: Facts and Pictures About Contemporary Authors and Illustrators of Books for Young People contains about 200 biographical sketches. Each edition is a two-volume set and each volume contains an index. Entries are similar in content to those found in *Contemporary Authors*.

Bartlett's Familiar Quotations contains 20,000 quotations arranged in chronological order from ancient times to the present.

Peter's Quotations; Ideas for Our Time by Laurence J. Peter is a collection of useful and often witty quotations arranged by subject.

Brewer's Dictionary of Phrase and Fable contains real, fictitious, and mythical names from history, romance, the arts, science, fables, phrases, superstitions, and customs. Entries are grouped under key words and names.

Granger's Index to Poetry indexes 514 volumes of poetry anthologies containing works of 12,000 poets and translators. Poems are arranged according to subject, author, title, and first line.

199 Other Special Sections

Books, magazines, and reference materials are important sources of information, but they are not the only resources available in the library. Many libraries have *newspapers* with today's news and *vertical files* of older newspaper clippings and current pamphlets. Vertical files are arranged in alphabetical order by subject. Valuable current information can be found there. Records, tapes, slides, picture and photograph files, and numerous other *audiovisual materials* may be features of your library. If they are, they are probably color coded in the card catalog.

Note: Ask your librarian to explain the various resources of your library. *Remember:* The librarian is the best resource you have in the library.

Parts of a Book

200   If the book you have searched for and located in the library is a nonfiction book which you need for a research paper or assignment, it is necessary to understand how to use that book efficiently. Below you will find a brief description of each part of a book. It is especially important, for instance, to make full use of the index when using nonfiction books. (Additional information on using books is included in the *Reading, Study Skills,* and *Research Paper* sections of the Handbook.)

The **title page** is usually the first printed page in a book. It gives you (1) the full title of the book, (2) the author's name, (3) the publisher's name, and (4) the place of publication.

The **copyright page** is the page right after the title page. It is here you will find the year in which the copyright was issued which is usually the same year the book was published.

The **preface** (also called **foreword, introduction,** or **acknowledgment**) comes before the table of contents and is there to give you an idea of what the book is about and why it was written.

The **table of contents** is one section most of you are familiar with since it shows you the major divisions of the book (*units, chapters,* and *topics*). It comes right before the body of the book and is used to help locate major topics or areas to be studied.

The **body** of the book, which comes right after the table of contents, is the main section or *text* of the book.

Following the body is the **appendix.** This supplementary section gives extra information, usually in the form of maps, charts, tables, diagrams, letters, or copies of official documents.

The **glossary** follows the appendix and is the *dictionary* portion of the book. It is an alphabetical listing of technical terms, foreign words, or special words, with an explanation or definition for each.

The **bibliography** is a list of books or articles used by the author when preparing to write the book.

The **index** is probably the most useful of all the parts of a book. It is an alphabetical listing of all important topics appearing in the book. It is similar to the table of contents, except that the index is a much more detailed list. It will tell you on what page you can find practically anything you would need to locate in that book.

The **thesaurus** has been a welcome companion to generations of students and writers. A thesaurus is, in a sense, the opposite of a dictionary. You go to a dictionary when you know the word but need the definition. You go to a thesaurus when you know the definition but need the word. For example, you might want a word that means *fear*, but specifically the kind of fear that causes more worry than pain. You need the word to fill in the blank of the following sentence:

> Joan experienced a certain amount of
> _____ over the upcoming exam.

If you have a thesaurus which is in dictionary form, simply look up the word *fear* as you would in a dictionary. If, however, you have a more traditional thesaurus, you must first look up your word in the INDEX at the back of the thesaurus. The index is arranged alphabetically. You will find this entry for *fear* in the index:

> **FEAR 860**
> **fearful** *painful* 830
> *timid* 862

The numbers after *fear* are GUIDE NUMBERS, not page numbers. (Guide numbers are similar to the topic numbers in your Handbook index.) The boldface guide numbers indicate that the word in the index is the heading or key word for that particular group of synonyms. For instance, if you look up number 860 in the body of the thesaurus, you will find (on page 259) a long list of synonyms for the word *fear*. These include *timidity, diffidence, apprehensiveness, fearfulness, solicitude, anxiety, care, misgiving, mistrust, suspicion,* and *qualm.* You select the word *anxiety* and your sentence becomes

> Joan experienced a certain amount of
> *anxiety* over the upcoming exam.

Another feature of the traditional thesaurus is the useful placement of synonyms and antonyms directly before or after the other. Suppose you wanted a word that meant the opposite of *fear*. You could look up *fear* as you did above (guide number 860) and find that guide word 861 is *courage*. The guide word is then followed by a list of antonyms of fear such as *boldness, daring, gallantry, heroism,* and *confidence.*

259	*PERSONAL AFFECTIONS*	859-861

860. FEAR. — *N.* **fear,** timidity, diffidence, apprehensiveness, fearfulness, solicitude, anxiety, care, apprehension, misgiving, mistrust, suspicion, qualm; hesitation.

trepidation, flutter, fear and trembling, perturbation, tremor, quivering, shaking, trembling, palpitation, nervousness, restlessness, disquietude, funk *[colloq.].*

fright, alarm, dread, awe, terror, horror, dismay, consternation, panic, scare; stampede *[of horses].*

intimidation, bullying; terrorism, reign of terror; terrorist.

V. **fear,** be afraid, apprehend, dread, distrust; hesitate, falter, funk *[colloq.],* cower, crouch, skulk, take fright, take alarm; start, wince, flinch, shy, shrink, fly.

tremble, shake, shiver, shudder, flutter, quake, quaver, quiver, quail.

frighten, fright, terrify, inspire (*or* excite) fear, bulldoze *[colloq.],* alarm, startle, scare, dismay, astound; awe, strike terror, appall, unman, petrify, horrify.

Adj. **afraid,** frightened, alarmed, fearful, timid, timorous, nervous, diffident, fainthearted, tremulous, shaky, afraid of one's shadow, apprehensive; aghast, awe-struck, awe-stricken, horror-stricken, panic-stricken.

861. [Absence of fear] COURAGE — *N.* courage, bravery, valor, resoluteness, boldness, spirit, daring, gallantry, intrepidity, prowess, heroism, chivalry, audacity, rashness, dash, defiance, confidence, self-reliance; manhood, manliness, nerve, pluck, mettle, grit, virtue, hardihood, fortitude, firmness, backbone.

Using the Dictionary

Too often a dictionary is used only when someone needs to know the meaning of a word. Even though this is the main reason for the existence of the dictionary, it is only one of several reasons. A dictionary can serve many of your needs, including several you have probably never associated with the dictionary before. Below are some of the most important ways a dictionary can help you. *(All are illustrated following this section.)*

Spelling Not knowing how to spell a word can make it difficult to find in the dictionary but not impossible. You will be surprised at how quickly you can find a word by following its *sounded-out* spelling.

Capital Letters If you need to know whether a certain word is capitalized, it is probably going to be faster (certainly more accurate) to look it up in the dictionary than to ask a friend who thinks he knows.

Syllabication Other than for meaning and pronunciation, the dictionary is most often used to determine where you can divide a word. This is especially important when you are typing a paper or when you are working with strict margin requirements.

Pronunciation Many times people become lost or confused when they look at a word because they don't *hear* the word properly. They may even know the meaning of the word, but without the correct pronunciation they cannot recognize it. To remember a word and its meaning, you must know the correct pronunciation of it. (The dictionary gives you a **Pronunciation Key** at the bottom of all right-side pages.)

The **Parts of Speech** The dictionary uses nine abbreviations for the parts of speech:

n.	noun	v.t.	transitive verb	adj.	adjective
pron.	pronoun	interj.	interjection	adv.	adverb
v.i.	intransitive verb	conj.	conjunction	prep.	preposition

Etymology (History) Just after the pronunciation and part of speech, you will find [in brackets] the history of that particular word. The value of this section will be clear later when you must recall the meaning of a word; if you know a little about the history of each word you look up, it is going to be much easier to remember a meaning when the need arises. This is especially true of many Greek and Latin words where entire stories or myths are told to dramatize the origin of a particular word. (See 444.)

Restrictive Labels There are three main types of labels used in a dictionary: **subject labels,** which tell you that a word has a special meaning when used in a particular field *(mus.* for *music, med.* for *medicine, zool.* for *zoology,* etc.); **usage labels,** which tell you how a word is used *(slang, colloq.* for *colloquial, dial.* for *dialect,* etc.); and **geographic labels,** which tell you the region of the country where that word is mainly used *(N.E.* for *New England, West, South,* etc.).

Synonyms and Antonyms Even though the best place to look for synonyms and antonyms is a thesaurus (201)—a dictionary of synonyms and antonyms—a dictionary will quite often list and label synonyms and antonyms after the meaning.

Illustrations Whenever a definition is difficult to make clear with words alone, a picture or drawing is used. These sketches can be extremely helpful since the mind can grasp more easily (also remember longer) definitions which are well illustrated.

Meaning Even though you probably know how to look up the meaning of a word, it is not quite as easy to figure out what to do with *all those meanings* once you have found them. The first thing to do is to read (or at least skim) all the meanings given. It is important to realize that most dictionaries list their meanings chronologically. This means the oldest meaning of the word is given first, then the newer or technical versions. You can see why it is extremely dangerous to simply take the first meaning listed—it is quite possible that this first one is not the meaning you are after at all. Remember to read all the meanings, and then select the one which is most appropriate for your use.

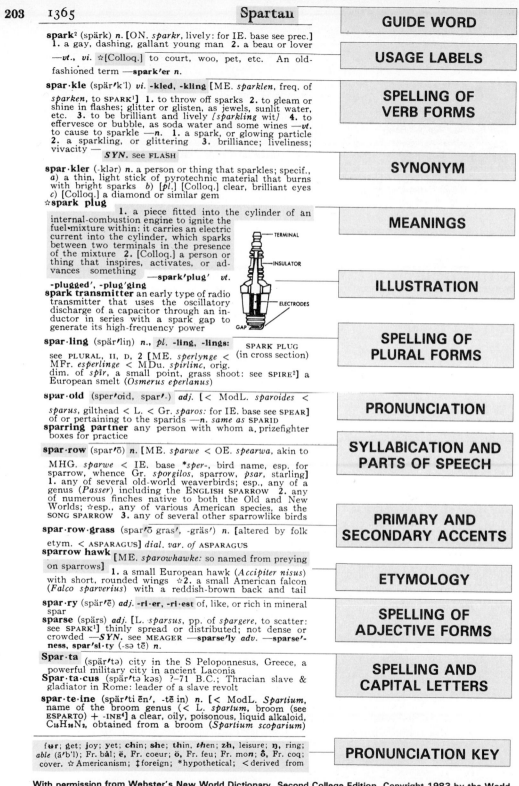

spark² (spärk) *n.* [ON. *sparkr*, lively: for IE. base see prec.] **1.** a gay, dashing, gallant young man **2.** a beau or lover —*vt.*, *vi.* ☆[Colloq.] to court, woo, pet, etc. An old-fashioned term —**spark′er** *n.*

GUIDE WORD

USAGE LABELS

spar·kle (spär′k'l) *vi.* **-kled, -kling** [ME. *sparklen*, freq. of *sparken*, to SPARK¹] **1.** to throw off sparks **2.** to gleam or shine in flashes; glitter or glisten, as jewels, sunlit water, etc. **3.** to be brilliant and lively [*sparkling* wit] **4.** to effervesce or bubble, as soda water and some wines —*vt.* to cause to sparkle —*n.* **1.** a spark, or glowing particle **2.** a sparkling, or glittering **3.** brilliance; liveliness; vivacity — *SYN.* see FLASH

SPELLING OF VERB FORMS

spar·kler (-klər) *n.* a person or thing that sparkles; specif., *a*) a thin, light stick of pyrotechnic material that burns with bright sparks *b*) [*pl.*] [Colloq.] clear, brilliant eyes *c*) [Colloq.] a diamond or similar gem

SYNONYM

☆**spark plug 1.** a piece fitted into the cylinder of an internal-combustion engine to ignite the fuel·mixture within: it carries an electric current into the cylinder, which sparks between two terminals in the presence of the mixture **2.** [Colloq.] a person or thing that inspires, activates, or advances something —**spark′plug′** *vt.* **-plugged′, -plug′ging**

MEANINGS

TERMINAL

INSULATOR

ELECTRODES

GAP

SPARK PLUG (in cross section)

ILLUSTRATION

spark transmitter an early type of radio transmitter that uses the oscillatory discharge of a capacitor through an inductor in series with a spark gap to generate its high-frequency power

spar·ling (spär′liŋ) *n., pl.* **-ling, -lings:** see PLURAL, II, D, 2 [ME. *sperlynge* < MFr. *esperlinge* < MDu. *spirlinc*, orig. dim. of *spîr*, a small point, grass shoot: see SPIRE²] a European smelt (*Osmerus eperlanus*)

SPELLING OF PLURAL FORMS

spar·oid (sper′oid, spar′-) *adj.* [< ModL. *sparoides* < *sparus*, gilthead < L. < Gr. *sparos:* for IE. base see SPEAR] of or pertaining to the sparids —*n. same as* SPARID

sparring partner any person with whom a. prizefighter boxes for practice

PRONUNCIATION

spar·row (spar′ō) *n.* [ME. *sparwe* < OE. *spearwa*, akin to MHG. *sparwe* < IE. base *sper-*, bird name, esp. for sparrow, whence Gr. *sporgilos*, sparrow, *psar*, starling] **1.** any of several old-world weaverbirds; esp., any of a genus (*Passer*) including the ENGLISH SPARROW **2.** any of numerous finches native to both the Old and New Worlds; ☆esp., any of various American species, as the SONG SPARROW **3.** any of several other sparrowlike birds

SYLLABICATION AND PARTS OF SPEECH

spar·row·grass (spar′ō gras′, -gräs′) *n.* [altered by folk etym. < ASPARAGUS] *dial. var.* of ASPARAGUS

PRIMARY AND SECONDARY ACCENTS

sparrow hawk [ME. *sparowhawke:* so named from preying on sparrows] **1.** a small European hawk (*Accipiter nisus*) with short, rounded wings ☆**2.** a small American falcon (*Falco sparverius*) with a reddish-brown back and tail

ETYMOLOGY

spar·ry (spär′ē) *adj.* **-ri·er, -ri·est** of, like, or rich in mineral spar

sparse (spärs) *adj.* [L. *sparsus*, pp. of *spargere*, to scatter: see SPARK¹] thinly spread or distributed; not dense or crowded —*SYN.* see MEAGER —**sparse′ly** *adv.* —**sparse′ness, spar′si·ty** (-sə tē) *n.*

SPELLING OF ADJECTIVE FORMS

Spar·ta (spär′tə) city in the S Peloponnesus, Greece, a powerful military city in ancient Laconia

Spar·ta·cus (spär′tə kəs) ?–71 B.C.; Thracian slave & gladiator in Rome: leader of a slave revolt

spar·te·ine (spär′ti ēn′, -tē in) *n.* [< ModL. *Spartium*, name of the broom genus (< L. *spartum*, broom (see ESPARTO) + -INE⁴] a clear, oily, poisonous, liquid alkaloid, $C_{15}H_{26}N_2$, obtained from a broom (*Spartium scoparium*)

SPELLING AND CAPITAL LETTERS

fur; get; joy; yet; chin; she; thin, *th*en; zh, leisure; ŋ, ring; *able* (ā′b'l); Fr. bâl; ë, Fr. coeur; ö, Fr. feu; ô, Fr. mon; ö, Fr. coq; cover. ☆ Americanism; ‡foreign; *hypothetical; <derived from

PRONUNCIATION KEY

Special Forms of Writing

" . . . somehow there's a trick of letting go to let the best writing take place."

Good fiction writers often "let themselves go" when they start a new writing project. That is, they push themselves beyond predictability in search of new and fresh ideas. News writers, on the other hand, are not necessarily looking for new ideas, unless they happen to be feature writers or columnists. They are primarily interested in collecting facts and presenting them clearly and accurately. Writers in the workplace are even more conservative. Their business letters, memos, and résumés follow prescribed formats, so structure and form are more important to them than their ability to explore and experiment in their writing. This section will help you understand and develop many forms of writing, including **short fiction, newswriting,** and **business writing.** Some of these forms lend themselves well to "letting go."

The Poet in You

If, like millions of others, you would claim to hate poetry, let us notice where poetry already intersects with your life. When you were a baby, you probably smiled at the cradle rhythms of "Rockabye baby, in the treetop, / When the wind blows," etc., etc. A few years later and you were twirling a rope, chanting, "Hank and Freda, sittin' in a tree / K-I-S-S-I-N-G; / First comes love, then comes marriage, / Then comes Hubert in a baby carriage!" Lots of fun. Poetry.

Today, you are more sophisticated, of course, but you may still have a favorite jingle on TV or a favorite rock lyric. Even when you say, "This day started like a brass band and ended like a kazoo," you are expressing yourself poetically.

205 **What is a Poem?**

First, let us distinguish **poetry** from **verse.** Verse is a composition of metrical or rhythmic lines; it earns the name poetry when it becomes distinctly a work of thoughtful, imaginative art in which sounds, figures of speech, expressive structures, and some degree of make-believe play an important role. A poem may be any length and may use the whole range of sound effects possible in a language, but it certainly need not be filled with jingly rhythms, mushy sentiment, and rhymes that chime. (See 343 for more definitions and terms.)

While here, let us try a poetic definition of poetry. Since a poem looks both *out* on a world of imagination (the *what* of the poem) and *in* on itself (the *how* of the poem), we might say that a poem is

**Words
dreaming in a bed
of language.**

206 Where Short Story and Poem Overlap

Like a story, a poem always has a speaker. Sometimes that speaker is a clearly identifiable narrator with a specific point of view and an intriguing tale to tell. Like a story, a poem may focus on character. Like a story, a poem always *enacts* its ideas, sometimes dramatizing scenes. A poem always uses vivid language, appealing to the senses while conveying emotions and thoughts. Like a story, a poem typically has a sort of plot: entrance into an idea; deepening of its significance; development toward a question, crisis, or key insight; and final resolution (or deepening, or explosion) of meaning. Almost any poem is a seed from which a story could be grown.

Here the major similarities end. Poems differ from stories in many ways: 1) poems usually detach themselves from any specific, physical setting; 2) poems make more exclusive use of compact figures of speech like symbols, metaphors, similes, metonymy, synecdoche, and so on; thus they create the impression of achieving meaning through more indirect means; 3) through indirection, poems zero in on the emotional-logical heart of a matter without dwelling on outward circumstances; 4) poems are self-consciously artificial; thus the real plot of a poem is the unveiling of its own form.

207 The Form of Poetry

Our century has seen the rise of *free verse*, poetry whose lines are free of the requirements of regular length, meter, or rhyme. Before any poet claims the somewhat dangerous freedom of free verse, however, he or she must realize that poetry is practically as old as civilization and that as it has developed, many major achievements in poetic form have become conventions and taken on a life of their own.

By convention, lines in most English poetry are labeled according to basic meter (*iambic, anapestic*, etc.) and length (*trimeter, pentameter*, etc.). Groups of lines, comparable to paragraphs in prose, are called stanzas and designated according to number of lines (*couplet, tercet, quatrain, sestet, octave*, etc.). Furthermore, certain overall forms — like the haiku, ballad, limerick, sonnet, and so on — have, by convention, more or less exact specifications for line length, meter, rhyme scheme, and stanza length. Some forms are specified to the exact number of syllables in each line.

Whole books have been devoted to the formal conventions in poetry. Here we need add only two comments:

First, the form of a poem involves much more than simply rhyme, meter, line length, and shape of stanza; *any* recognizable elements in the poem — letters, grammatical structures, figures of speech, types of images, connotations, even empty spaces — can be repeated, contrasted, sequenced, juxtaposed, or in some other way set in meaningful relation. Relation is the basis of pattern, pattern is the basis of form, and poetic form *speaks*.

Second, formal conventions restrict the poet, that is true. But restricting is not the same as stifling. When you put a nozzle on a garden hose, you restrict the water. But why? So you can shoot farther and shape the spray! Formal restrictions in poetry, similarly, should be seen as enhancers of the spirit of sport in the poem. That, perhaps, is what the poet Robert Frost was implying when he commented that writing poetry without rhyme is like playing tennis without the net.

208 The Sound of Poetry

" 'Tis not enough no harshness gives offense.
The sound must seem an echo to the sense."

—**Alexander Pope**

Thus, the sense of a poem may be silly, and likewise the sound:

I fished up in Saskatchewan—
Alas, I did not catch a one!

The sound may seem to imitate other sounds in nature:

Through hiss of spruce, a single drop

Or perhaps the very variety in a poet's use of vowels and consonants creates a sense of richness and life appropriate to the poem's theme:

Nine bean-rows will I have there, a hive for the honey-bee
And live alone in a bee-loud glade.

—**W.B. Yeats**

In each case the sound is self-consciously crafted to help evoke the thought. The poet has at his disposal all the devices of rhyme (end rhyme, internal rhyme, perfect rhyme, slant rhyme, etc.), alliteration, assonance, consonance, repetition, contrast, pause, and rhetorical emphasis with which to build formal patterns of sound. (See 343.)

Such patterns are valueless, of course, as soon as they draw undue attention to themselves. Many a beginning poet, writing an alliterated line like "The grapes, grey-green and golden, tasted great," thinks he has discovered something, when what he has discovered is simply a new brand of monotony.

209 The Meaning of Poetry

Here are three common false notions about the meanings of poems:

1. Poems have no meaning. (Only a person who, through careless reading, lack of exposure to poetry, or deep skepticism, has never found personal meaning in a poem would dare to say this.)

2. Poems can mean anything you want them to. (This is really the same falsehood as the first, with the added belief that in the absence of obvious external meaning, one's private feelings are of ultimate importance. You can use your mother's fried chicken for a doorstop, too, if you feel like it, but you won't get much nutrition that way.)

3. Every poem should have one basic meaning which can be stated in a sentence. (If the meaning of a poem could be stated in a sentence, all good poets would quit. Each good poem is the shortest way of saying *all* that it says.)

210 The Uses of Poetry

We may use poems for placemats and greeting cards if we wish, but poetry can be suited for more dignified uses, too. Poems can celebrate an occasion or time of joy; praise God or a famous person; preserve an insight; mourn someone's death; probe a mystery; dramatize a problem; call the universe for help; crack a joke; intensify a ritual; tell the history of a nation; and on and on. Taken together, the poems from a given civilization are the keenest record available of the vision of its people.

How to Read a Poem

211   Here is a list of methods for reading poems for more understanding and enjoyment:

1. **Read slowly**, syllable by syllable. You wouldn't comb your hair with a garden rake; don't speed-read a poem.

2. **Read aloud** (except in the library). Ignore the smirks of strangers.

3. **Read a poem over and over again,** once to let the strangeness wear off, again to recognize the form, a third time to assimilate the themes and images, a fourth time to hear the music of the language, and as many more times as you wish to probe the questions raised by the earlier readings. The best poems will give back far more than you ask of them.

4. **Try to catch the "arc" of the whole poem** rather than stopping at individual lines as if they could stand by themselves. The "drift" of the whole poem may provide a clue to some of the difficult phrases. Conventional forms like the sonnet or ballad often have conventional "arcs," but when you have recognized the familiar pattern, pay special attention to any notable variations from that pattern. Remember, too, that blank spaces may also be informative parts of the structure.

5. **Listen for voices.** A poet will sometimes purposely mimic the speech of other types of people. If you miss the false voice, you'll miss the irony of the poet's technique, and you may get the meaning of the poem just backwards.

6. **Call up your own past sensations** when you encounter imagery appealing to the senses ("bee-loud glade"); do not treat images as slot-filling pieces of data. Feel the smallness of the bees, hear the electric energy of their buzzing; sense the sheltered coolness of a glade, and finally sense the poet's seeming pleasure (or other emotion) in the whole scene.

7. **Take pleasure in the artfulness of poetic language,** even if the poem is about suicide, lost love, or some hopeless state of affairs. Poetry always has two faces; one face may look on life's ugliness and despair, but the other always looks hopefully on the power of language to express the theme in fitting form.

8. **Use your memory.** First, use memory to hold the early lines of a poem in mind as you pass on to the succeeding ones; doing so is necessary if you want to catch patterns as they develop. Second, use your memory to recall any feelings you have had similar to those presented in the poem; doing so will place you in a dialogue with the poem, a technique guaranteed to improve comprehension of whatever you read.

9. **Trust the poet,** even if you do not immediately grasp the poem's meaning. If there is any doubt that the poet is in control of his words and ideas, give the poet the benefit. If after the 352nd reading, however, the poem still makes no sense, you may begin to suspect that the poet doesn't understand it either.

10. **Anticipate, in two ways.** First, as you read the poem, try to play the role of poet and guess where the poem will go next. You will then be reading creatively, even if the poem completely reverses your expectations. Second, approach the poem with the expectation that as a result of reading it, you may learn to view some aspect of life in a whole new way. Not to read with that sort of openness is not to appreciate fully the power of poetry.

Writing a Poem

"A poem is never a put-up job so to speak. It begins as a lump in the throat, a sense of wrong, a homesickness, a lovesickness. It is never a thought to begin with." **—Robert Frost**

212   How do you write a poem—a good poem? Here we step a few feet into a land of mystery. No one knows exactly how good poems are written, not even poets. Without a doubt, however, the best preparation for writing poetry is reading good poetry. A few hours of deep communion with a short poem by Shakespeare, Emily Dickinson, or W.B. Yeats, for example, will teach you more than twenty-seven sweaty afternoons with a poetry manual. Nevertheless, a few hints may help.

213 Choosing a Subject

Anything looked at closely is worth seeing, as one poet has said. The point is this: That anything looked at closely — from a drop under a microscope to a galaxy in deep space — is worth writing a poem about.

1. Try making "found poetry" by searching pamphlets, newspapers, magazine ads, etc. for snatches of prose which, when yanked out of context and cut into poetic lines, make a new kind of sense.

2. Think of an animal that impresses you and try to write about it in such a way that your language mirrors the animal's manners.

3. Think of an important event in your life but try writing a poem about the moments just prior to it or just after.

4. Think of a subject that "eats away at you" but write a poem about it in the form of a newspaper account that gets more and more out of hand.

5. Write a poem celebrating a time, place, or thing that no one else seems ever to have noticed (the oil spot under your car, or the moment after the dishwater has drained from the sink but the suds remain, talking to you).

6. Write a poem about something you love but in the voice of someone who hates it.

7. Write a poem in the form of a dialogue between two inanimate objects.

8. Write a poem in which each line has exactly nine syllables.

9. Look up, in your mind, at something much bigger than you and write a poem addressing it.

10. Write a poem about a time when you felt slightly crazy, using language that is slightly crazy.

If in the course of writing these or any other poems you discover that something larger is at stake, let the poem expand to take it in. Many poems are truly discovered in the process of writing another one. It may be worth starting a horrendously bad poem just so you can shake the good one out of your grey matter.

214 Tips on Technique

The following suggestions may save you from some of the errors most common among beginning writers of poetry:

1. If your poem is about overly sentimental subjects like puppies, kittens, little birdies, or pretty flowers, avoid writing it if you can.

2. If you spot a cliche anywhere in your poem — a tired phrase like "raining cats and dogs," "green with (of course) envy," or "happy as a (yawn) lark" — cross it out and approach the idea from a new angle.

3. Avoid overused, cute forms such as last lines that step
down
     like
        this.

4. Use *enjambment* occasionally to break up a pattern of too many end-stopped lines in a row. *Enjambment* is the spilling over of one line into the next:

> The end-stopped line is strong and bold.
> But in the spilling of a line one
> Now and then may strike poetic gold.

5. Certain metric schemes may give the verse a comical flavor when you least intend it. Anapests, for example, when used without interruption, tend to sound as if the poet is riding a toy horse:

> I would like to be serious but, lo I cannot.
> Anapestic tetrameter makes the verse trot.

Similarly, any rhythmic scheme, used without variation, tends to sound like a caricature of poetry.

6. Use rhyme if you wish to pair two words meaningfully; *use* rhyme, that is, but don't let it use you. Certain chiming old rhyming pairs will seem almost to have written themselves. If "Moon" appears, for example, can "June" be far behind?

7. Like certain meters, certain rhymes are likely to sound comical despite your most serious intentions, especially when three-syllable words are made to rhyme perfectly.

> Despite my somber intention,
> This rhyme follows comic convention.

8. The universal response to a pun is a groan. Be sure a groan is the response you want before you use a pun prominently in your poem. Used well, of course, a pun can be subtle, suggestive, and meaningfully ambiguous.

9. Alliteration is one of the easiest sound devices to use in English verse, but its very availability makes it prone to overuse. It works best when woven with other sound devices like assonance and contrast. Try to keep the technical machinery of your language hidden, or clearly subordinate to your themes, unless you are trying specifically to write a sound poem.

10. Many a fine image or figure of speech in poetry has been ruined when the poet went on to state the same basic idea in different words. Repetition is a useful element of design in a poem, but redundancy (unintentional looping back over ground already covered) is a logical flaw which often seems to stem from the poet's anxiety that the first expression of the idea was not effective. More broadly speaking, whenever a poet uses more words than necessary, the poetry in the poem dies at that point. Poetry is motion.

> *"There are three things, after all, that a poem must reach: the eye, the ear, and what we may call the heart or the mind. It is most important of all to reach the heart of the reader."*
> **—Robert Frost**

Writing about Poetry

215   Before you can possibly begin writing about a poem, you must first understand what the poem is saying. You must consider the poem as a whole and as the sum of its parts. This requires careful attention to the details, rhymes, rhythms, and symbolism which together create poetry. Follow the suggestions given earlier in this unit on how to read a poem and get as close to the meaning and significance of the poem as you possibly can. Then follow the suggestions below:

1. **Paraphrase** (put in your own words) **the poem.** Your paraphrase will be the *prose meaning,* or denotative meaning, of the poem. It may be a simple story, a brief description, or a statement of an emotion or feeling. Putting the poem in your own words will give you only the surface-level meaning of the poem, not the *total meaning.* However, this is an essential first step whenever you write about poetry.

2. **Interpret the poem.** In other words, put into writing what the poem means to you. (It is important to remember that each word in a poem has three parts: sound, denotation, and connotation.) Because the total meaning of a poem is based on

sound and feeling as well as print, you must read the poem out loud before you attempt to interpret it. Your interpretation will then be based on the sounds, feelings, and images, as well as the "words," of the poem. Be prepared to support your interpretation with references to the poem.

3. **Examine the poem.** Look carefully at the individual elements which make up the poem and how each element contributes to the overall effectiveness of the poem. In other words, try to figure out what makes this poem work (or not work). Among the elements to examine are the theme, the tone, the structure, the central purpose, the speaker and the occasion, the use of figurative language, and the use of rhyme, rhythm, and repetition.

4. **Evaluate the poem.** Based on your examination of the poem, decide where and how the poem succeeds or fails. (Remember, the value of a poem is determined by the impact it has on the reader; if the poem had an effect on you, it has value.) Support your feelings by referring to specific passages in the poem.

   a.   Does the poem appeal to *the ear*? Does it sound good? Does the poem use rhyme, rhythm, and repetition effectively? Or does the poem follow a pattern which becomes predictable or monotonous?

   b.   Did the poem touch you in some way? Is it likely the poem will have a similar effect on other readers?

   c.   Does the poem bring the reader a new outlook or a better understanding of the subject? Does it recreate a worthwhile experience and allow the reader to participate in it?

   d.   Is the poem powerful enough to involve not only the reader's senses, but also his intelligence, emotions, and imagination?

   e.   Does the poem contain language which appeals to the reader's senses? Does the language help create an effective image of what is being described?

   f.   Does the poet use figurative language effectively (simile, metaphor, allusion, personification, symbol, etc.)?

   g.   Does the poet use language which is unusual or language which is difficult to understand (archaic, colloquial, ornate, rhetorical)?

   h.   Is the poet's tone (attitude) exactly what it appears to be, or does he use language which is intentionally ambiguous, mocking, or contradictory (irony, paradox, pun, understatement, overstatement)?

   i.   What is your overall feeling about the poem?

5. **Compare your poem.** You can compare the poem you are writing about to another poem, a short story, a novel, a film, or some other literary work. You will most likely compare only one element of the poem to the other work although it is possible several points may be comparable.

6. **Read other poems.** This might include other poems written by the same author, poems written in the same form or style, or poems written on the same theme. Reading of this kind should give you additional insight into the poem you are writing about.

7. **Read related material.** Among the materials which would prove beneficial would be biographical sketches or articles about the poet, books on how poetry is written or analyzed, and books written about the particular time period referred to in the poem.

Writing Windfalls

216 For Poetry

* Poetry is a language of indirection — "by indirection, find directions out."
* Write the spaces as well as the words.
* Sometimes a "mistake" makes your poem; don't let the good ones pass you by.
* Speak with a new voice, and you will think new thoughts.
* Six excellent lines of poetry are worth more than 600 pretty ones.
* The power of what you say is in what you don't say.
* Form speaks louder than words.
* Listen for poetry at the bus stop and on the beach.

Always Write a Poem Like This

> *When you don't really feel*
> *Like writing. Why wait*
> *Until your head is clear*
> *And you're sputtering along*
> *Like a piece of bacon, all set*
> *To start the morning right?*
> *Some atrocity is sure to pop up,*
> *Buttered with enthusiasm*
> *On both sides.*
> *No, write it now*
> *While your head is empty*
> *Like a belly; you'll be glad*
> *You started off at nothing*
> *So that*
> *Something could arise.*

> **—Randall VanderMey**

217 For Short Stories

* Write about what you know — or would like to know.
* There are no new stories in the world, only fresh ones.
* Observe closely; then write with all your senses.
* The "I" in your story is not you.
* If you care for a character in your story, give it a kick in the pants.
* Show, don't tell. (Getting people into your writing will help you show.)
* Practice new and different kinds of writing — satire, parody, dialogue, editorials, definitions, etc.
* Read! And especially read as many different kinds of writing as you can.
* Share your writing. Talk about your writing with others (before, during, after).
* A good critic and a good friend are two different things.
* Keep writing . . . even when you sleep.

Writing the
SHORT STORY

"I have never written a story in my life that didn't have a very firm foundation in actual human experience."

—**Katherine Anne Porter**

By the time you finish high school, you will have seen and felt enough of life to fill a Nobel prize-winning novel, not to mention a good short story or two. Putting that experience on paper in artistic form is, of course, the problem.

But you know the difference between interesting and boring, between deep and shallow, between fresh and worn out, between detailed and general, between *zip* and *thud*. The artist is one who can make that knowledge work. The artist, in other words, can be you.

Broadly speaking, a short story is a piece of prose fiction short enough to be read comfortably in one sitting. Because it is fiction, it shows us a world which is plausible in the imagination but not literally true; in that sense, it is different from prose forms such as the essay, the research paper, the report, the biography, the autobiography, or the sermon. And because it is short, it details best with only a handful of characters, a short stretch of time, and a concentrated action; a novel, by contrast, may introduce us to a rainbow of characters spanning several generations and caught up in a complicated web of events.

The Writer's Aim

"Whatever our theme in writing, it is old and tired. Whatever our place, it has been visited by the stranger, it will never be new again. It is only the vision that can be new; but that is enough."

—**Eudora Welty**

218   When you write your short story, aim high. Aim at capturing truth about human experience, even if you have to *discover* that truth in the very writing of the story, even if that "truth" turns out to be a whole new set of questions. You'll first have to get rid of your favorite truisms, cliches, and stereotypes. Leave all your "safe" ideas behind: maybe might *doesn't* make right, maybe not *all* Dutchmen are penny-pinchers, maybe you *should* cry over spilt milk!

The whole truth of a short story, however, is never in a statement some character coughs up, never in a moral you as author tack on at the end. Instead, it is in the shape of the events you describe, in the depth of character, in the texture or "feel" of life you describe and the texture of language you use. The truth of a story can only come out of your secret store of knowledge about life. So let this be your aim: *to write the story that only you can write.*

Anatomy of a Short Story Writer

219   Writing a short story will involve your whole self, though some parts of you will play more important roles than others. Your success will depend, however, on how well you can blend the work of your brain, your five senses, your heart, and your hands. Let's study the anatomy of a writer more closely.

Brain: Brain physiologists claim that the left half of a human brain works best at grasping facts, thinking logically, processing speech, and the like; the right half, by contrast, deals best with feelings, intuitions, recognition of images, and so on. Let your whole brain, left and right halves both cooperating, go to work. In other words, "think feelingly."

Eye: Your eyes must be used to see these two things: 1) the world as it is, and 2) your writing as it is. To see the world with insight, merely opening your eyes is not enough. You must *look, see, notice,* and *comprehend.* Look at the sky, see the cloud, notice its anvil shape, and comprehend that hail may be pounding some farmer's wheat field. Look at your bloodhound, see his swollen nose, notice the three scarlet pricks at the tip, and comprehend that Old Blue turned up a porcupine again. This is the way an artist sees, and *anyone can do it!*

If this kind of seeing becomes a habit, you will soon begin to crave words that express the concrete nuances of your thought—words like "sallow," "inferno," and "dragoon"—where once you might have settled for general terms like "sick-looking," "fire," and "soldier." Your trained eye should then be able to tell you whether your story places a living world before the eye of imagination; if not, back you must go to the drawing board.

Ear: Your ears — if used, like your eyes, to notice and comprehend — can discover for you not only the sounds of nature (the plops, razzes, and hiccups) but also the sounds of human nature, especially that of human speech. How does a grandmother complain about her arthritis so that you *know* she is really thinking about her husband who died three years ago on that date? How many different things could a kid mean by the words, "Stop it, you guys"? Your ears can tell you, if they are kept clean and ready. Written dialogue, which appears somewhere in almost every short story, can be a dead giveaway that a writer's imagination is in a coma, or it can be the spark and proof of life. Some writers like to record dialogues, real and imaginary, in a journal, just to keep their skill alive. You might give it a try.

Other Senses

Ear and eye easily dominate the other senses, but people are blessed with five senses, not two. Everyone knows what a rock concert sounds like, but what does it *smell* like? What sensations does your skin *feel* on a two-hour bus ride in 90-degree heat? What does a camp out *taste* like? Throw open all five windows on the world: look, listen, smell, taste, and feel. The words in a vivid description should play all five senses like chords on a piano.

Voice: Your voice is more than your vocabulary; it is the unique combination of pace, pattern of repetition and contrast, use of detail, level of energy, pitch of excitement, and so on, that, like your fingerprint, distinguishes you from every other person alive. Those who waste all their effort trying to sound unique ultimately will sound uniquely boring. Better to be yourself, speaking an honest tongue. If your self needs *improving,* then work at that, but always be yourself. After all, a frog with the voice of a prince is still a frog.

Heart: To have "heart" can mean both to have courage and to have a capacity for love. The short story writer needs both. Why courage? Because if a short story is not the taking of a chance, it is not worth writing. Why love? Because only love of life and of language can make the hard work of writing, rewriting, and re-rewriting seem worthwhile.

Hands: Pen in hand, the writer manipulates the various elements of the short story, such things as characterization, plot, setting, point of view, tone, atmosphere, and language. The way you handle these elements is called your craft. Many techniques of craft in short story writing have become established by common practice and common sense over many years. The following is a list of basic instructions in the craft of short story writing. But a warning is in order: Abiding by rules may be a way to produce acceptable writing, but the best short stories are produced as often by the breaking as by the obeying of rules, if the breaking of rules makes a more powerful sense.

Elements of the Short Story

220 Character / Characterization

Note the difference between these two terms: character is something a person in a story *has*, while characterization is something the author *does*. The character in a story supposedly has a personality too complicated to describe in full, just as you do. But the writer must *select, order,* and *highlight* certain features of that personality (in other words, "characterize" the character) in order to focus and emphasize that character's role in the action.

It is not enough, however, to say that a character has this trait or that. The main character, especially, must be tested against circumstances outside or inside of himself. He must be forced to rethink his basic vision of life. Unfortunately, many a beginning writer fails at this point by falling so much in love with his main character that he tries to protect that character against suffering. That's silly. What would you say about a drummer who loved his drum so much that he refused to beat it? The lesson is this: don't coddle your characters. Make them sweat. Action is essential to character and vice versa.

> *"Sometimes you know the story. Sometimes you make it up as you go along and have no idea how it will come out. Everything changes as it moves. That is what makes the movement which makes the story."*
>
> **—Ernest Hemingway**

221 Plot

If you start with a character and set him in *motion* (shaving, brushing his teeth, putting on a sport coat, etc.) you still do not have a story. Now if you add *conflict* (man against man, man against woman, man against nature, man against God, man against toothbrush, etc.) you have a story, but still no plot. Plot arises when you select, arrange, and present the parts of the story in such a way that they seize and hold a reader's interests. Plot, in other words, is the artificial but effective arrangement of action in a story.

The novelist Kurt Vonnegut has been heard to say that plot is simple: all you need is a character who wants something, plus something that stands in his way, plus his effort to get it anyway. The classic plot structure shows this same pattern; it calls for an introduction to a situation, a series of developments arranged in a pattern of rising tension, a climax in which the central character's fate is determined, a falling action in which the implications of the climactic moment are gradually discovered, and a wrap-up, or *denouement,* in which loose ends are tied up.

However, not all stories follow this classic pattern. Some use subplots to parallel or contrast with the main action. Some save a major surprise for the end, but such neatly ironic "O'Henry" stories, as they are called, are likely to seem gimmicky today and should ordinarily be avoided. Many modern stories hinge on a subtle, psychological change or realization in the protagonist. Others, in which the protagonist is a hapless, dumpy "anti-hero," may show a series of frustrations and dead ends rather than a smoothly rising action. Experiment with plot, if you will, to serve your own purposes, but remember that conflict is useless unless something valuable or significant is at stake — not only a person's wealth, but perhaps his sense of self-worth, happiness, or ability to hope. A reader is more likely to enjoy your story if he feels that he might want the same thing if he were the protagonist.

Where should a plot begin? Preferably, in the middle of things, near to the heart of the matter, and in motion. You would then be wise to dramatize, close up, only those scenes that are crucial in the development and climax of the conflict, while using brief narrative bridges ("Three days later . . .") to pass over those scenes that are of lesser interest. Somehow the story writer has to find a proper blend between *telling* (to set up or interpret the conflict) and *showing* (to focus on the heart of the drama). The exact blend will be determined by the nature of the action and by your purpose in presenting it to your audience. If this sounds like show biz, you aren't far from the truth.

222 Setting

Since space is very limited in a short story, and since character and action are normally supreme, descriptions of setting should ordinarily play a supporting, not leading, role in the story. Yet description need not be crossed out; if it is blended into the description of action, it can make the action sparkle. Note, for example, how physical description dominates the following paragraph:

> The secondhand store looked more like an attic than a shop on street level; molding sea lockers, chipped white bassinets, and shadeless lamps elbowed one another like patients in a waiting room. But here, in a dark corner, a surprised Duane found the moose antlers he was searching for.

Not bad, you might say. But here is that same setting *blended* with the action:

> Tired of bumping his knees on old sea lockers and chipped white bassinets, and slightly irritated by the gaze of so many headless lamps, Duane resolved to leave; only then, knocking his ankle on something horizontal, did he reach down into a half century of dust and touch a raspy plate that turned out to belong, oh joy, to the moose antlers of his dream.

One plus one adds up to more than two.

223 Point of view

As a short story writer, you must create the illusion of a narrator who tells the story for you. You may use the first-person narrator ("*I* was hopping mad"), the objective or dramatic third-person narrator ("*Her* face suddenly flushed with anger"), or a compromise between the two extremes, the third-person *limited omniscient* narrator (*She felt* herself grow suddenly angry"), who freely takes the reader into the mind of the main character (though not into the minds of others). Skillful writers may vary and combine these basic points of view when they can achieve a more appropriate effect by doing so.

Furthermore, the narrator must have a position in time. Does he report an action after it has happened ("I *was* mad," "She *appeared* angry," "She *felt* herself growing angry")? Or does the narrator report an action as it is happening now ("I *am* mad," "She *flushes* with anger," "She *feels* herself growing angry")?

Whatever limitation you place on your narrator to clarify his point of view, stick with it. Don't commit the narrative "sin," as so many beginning writers do, of jumping without warning from one point of view to another. The reader can't appreciate your story if he has to keep asking, "Who's talking now?"

224 Mood

By choosing certain words rather than others and by weaving their connotations together, you can give whole settings and scenes a kind of personality, or mood. Note the difference if you describe a tall, thin tree as "erect like a steeple," "spiked like a witch's hat," "a leafy spear," or "rather inclining toward the slim." However, no single image can work alone; mood can only arise from a steady pressure in your language toward one major atmospheric effect. That effect should support your main purpose for writing the story.

You might have fun by choosing a mood *first* — say, the throat-tightening anxiety of a piano recital — then let a story grow out of it.

225 Tone

Tone is your (not necessarily your narrator's) overall outlook or attitude toward your material. Ironic, matter-of-fact, bemused, outraged, curiously respectful, disdainful — how do you feel about the fragment of life you display in your story? The curious thing about tone is that it may *change*, but it must never *waver*.

226 Style

Your personal writing style is the outward boundary of your energy, the sum and pattern of all your choices. Styles do sort into general types; no one would confuse Ernest Hemingway's tight style with the ballooning, throbbing style of William Faulkner. But style is often identified as well by what in it is odd, daring, and never before heard.

Should you labor to improve your style? Maybe. But that's a fine way, alas, to develop a labored-sounding style. Much better that you labor to live more fully, more deeply, more honestly. Travel, read, learn a language, fight for a cause, discover what you value. Learn what makes your reader tick. But above all, labor to learn the capacity of the English language to do your bidding. After all that, style will happen. Count on it.

"A writer really writes for an audience of about ten persons. Of course, if others like it, that is clear gain.   But if those ten are satisfied, he is content."

—Alfred North Whitehead

The Story Writer's Audience

227   "He who writes to please himself, caters to a fool." All right, you win — nobody ever really said this, until now. And yet it bears a grain of truth, namely this: We are all, generally speaking, too easily pleased with ourselves. We need to strike the iron of our minds against the flint of someone else's to produce fire in writing. That means that the short story writer must know as much as he or she can about human nature and write to engage that nature. About a good writer we might say, "He seems to speak from his heart." But about a *great* writer we are most likely to say, "He seems to speak from within *us.*"

Unfortunately, the readers of your story are not likely to help you as much as you might like. Mom and Dad will, of course, think your story is wonderful. Your worst critics will use it to wrap fish, while your best critics, most of them, will keep agonizingly quiet. And your teacher, as always, may have some good things to say and some bad.

Where does that leave you? Ultimately, alone. For that reason you must become an uncompromising critic of your own work, if you can. Try to be more fair but also more demanding than any other reader will be. The poet and critic John Ciardi has written, "A writer can, in fact, develop only as rapidly as he learns to recognize what is bad in his writing." If you write to please that critic in you, and forgive yourself when you fall short, you will have a wise man or woman for a reader.

Writing the NEWS STORY

The Structure of a News Story

When a wave breaks, it sends a wall of water thundering toward shore. This initial surge might pick up some momentum as it rushes forward, but usually the real strength in a wave lasts a relatively brief period of time. As a wave progresses, it normally loses power and size until it washes gently onto shore. Only a few great waves crash onto a beach with force.

A news story progresses in much the same way. It breaks forcefully with an attention-getting **headline** and a strong **lead** which attract the reader and send a story on its way. The news story picks up momentum in the **body** with supporting and background details which answer questions readers will have after reading the lead. These details, however, much like the advancing surge of a wave, lose their power and importance as the story continues. By the time a news story ends, the details have little impact on the story. Only when a story is of great news value or of great complexity will details in the latter part of the story be important to a reader. (See 247 for a model news story.)

The Newswriting Process

230 Prewriting:

Keep your eyes and ears open. Look and listen for important news. Sound advice for news writers who must be prepared for important news when it breaks. A writer spots a potential story mainly by judging its **news value.** News has value when it exhibits at least one of the following traits:

Impact: News has impact when it makes a difference in the lives of the readers. For example, new requirements for graduation, a change in the maximum speed limit, or a change in the minimum wage would have impact because each would make a difference to high school readers.

Timeliness: News is timely when it is current and new. And an experienced news writer knows that a story lives a short life: what is currently interesting often is not interesting when the next issue of the newspaper comes out.

Proximity: News which is local has news value. Readers are interested in people and events connected to their own schools, neighborhoods, cities, and states. *Note:* Important news which is not local should be "localized" either by showing how the story affects the readers or by finding a local person to comment on it.

Prominence: News of people with status, prominence, and notoriety has news value. People who make decisions and people who are involved in important events are obviously newsworthy. For example, a story about outstanding athletes forming a SADD (Students Against Drunk Driving) chapter in a school would have news value because it involves prominent members of a school.

Human Interest: News which is touching, stirring, or otherwise interesting has news value. For example, a janitor retiring after 30 years of service to a school or the school chorus singing Christmas carols at a local senior citizens center would have news value because both stories would touch the readers' emotions.

Special Note: News value determines not only what makes a story newsworthy but also where details go in a story. Those details with the greatest news value come first in a story.

231 Designing a Plan:

Most news writers, once they have a story of news value, concentrate on the lead to set the story in motion. The lead usually summarizes the substance or main points of a news story in one or two sentences. News writers often develop the lead by asking themselves the five W's and H—*who, what, when, where, why,* and *how*—of a story. They then put the answers to these questions—at least the questions which are important—in the opening sentence(s) of the story.

Note: The lead of a news story functions in much the same way as the topic sentence in a paragraph and the thesis statement in an essay or research paper.

Once a lead has been formed, a news writer must evaluate what he or she knows about the story and what additional facts and details must be uncovered. Enough information must be gathered to answer any important questions a reader might have after reading the headline and the lead paragraph. You probably won't know everything you need to know when you start writing your story so be prepared to do some background research and interviewing. (See 238 for interviewing guidelines.)

As you compile and organize your information, you should begin to visualize what your story will look like in its finished form. That is, you should begin to see what facts and details you will include in your story and in what order you will include them.

Remember: A typical reader will not stay with a story until the end. The important information, therefore, must be included early.

If the story is a very routine one, try to put the facts in a perspective that will offer something new to your readers. For example, most situations can be compared with similar ones in other places or in previous years. Without such comparisons, your readers cannot grasp the full significance of the facts you give them.

Few news writers bother with an outline for a story. They don't have the time or necessarily the need since news stories usually aren't that complex. You should, however, have all of your notes in front of you. Highlight and organize those facts and details you plan to use in your story.

232 Writing the First Draft:

If you have thoroughly researched and prepared a story, writing the first draft should be easy. Begin with the lead and follow with the facts and details you feel are necessary to the story. Write freely at this point, and don't be afraid to move, add, or take out detail.

233 **Revising:**

Begin your revision with a general reading. Make sure that the story flows smoothly and that the sentences are clear and direct. Then check for any missing information and information that might be misleading or misplaced. Also, double-check names, facts, dates, and spellings. A news writer is credible only if he presents clear and accurate information.

Carefully reread the lead as well. Earlier versions of the lead put the story into focus, but the final version must also grab the readers' attention. You should also write a headline for your story at this point, mainly as a test of your story's substance. If you have difficulty forming a headline, your story might lack a clear main idea.

Note: Unless you have a very small news staff, an editor will write the final headline for your story.

234 **Editing:**

Finally, check for errors in word choice, mechanics, and spelling, even though a copy editor will do so as well. A news story that is clean or free of careless errors reflects favorably on you and on your newspaper. (See the "Traits of Newswriting Style" which follow for help with revising and editing.)

Traits of Newswriting Style

235   1. **Sentences and Paragraphs**   News sentences and paragraphs are typically short and direct; paragraphs seldom contain more than three sentences. Each new paragraph should not depend on the following paragraph for explanation. A story can then end after any paragraph. (This is of great help during production since the layout staff can quickly and efficiently cut a story.)

2. **Clarity**   The facts in a news story must be clearly stated. Make sure it is clear who did what to whom, when things happened, and in what sequence they happened.

3. **Accuracy**   The facts in a news story must be accurately stated as well. Readers will not tolerate mistakes in times and dates, and sources will not tolerate being misquoted. Always verify facts before you turn in a story.

4. **Details**   Since news is information, a news story must contain a lot of detail. Include descriptions of people and places and exact quantities (final scores, total amounts, estimates, etc.). Remember to get complete names, addresses, and class or age of people involved in a news story.

5. **Objectivity**   A news story must be presented without any favoritism. Let the facts speak for themselves. No sports story should include a statement like "all fans should get out there tonight and support the team"—unless it is a quote from a source. Personal feelings and opinions should appear in editorials and columns. Reporters who state their own opinions in a news story are guilty of editorializing.

6. **Brevity**   A news story must get to the point quickly and concisely. Unnecessary words, phrases, and information clog a news story.

7. **Quotes**   Most news stories rely on good quotes. Alternate direct quotes (a source's exact words) with indirect quotes. Use direct quotes for authoritative, colorful, or memorable words. The example passage which follows begins with an indirect quote and ends with a direct quote.

> After Northwestern got a 20-point lead, the players began to get tired, Coach Douma said. "It was our third game in four days. They were emotional games, which made them even more tiring."

8. **Attribution**   Any time you report a quotation, opinion, estimate, prediction, or a fact that is not common knowledge in a news story, you must identify the source. For example, if you wrote, "An explosion in the science lab destroyed the entire supply of chemicals," you must add "the fire chief said" or some other statement of attribution.

Use *said* for your verb of attribution most of the time. Verbs like *insisted, replied,* and *protested* should be used only when they are clearly more appropriate.

9. **Names**   The first time a person is mentioned, use the full name along with an appropriate title. Use just the last name for additional references unless two or more people have the same last name. (In such cases use a first name to help readers separate them.) The example passage which follows includes a first and second reference to a name.

> Dr. Roy Anker, a respected film reviewer, lists "Tender Mercies" among his favorite films. Anker said he especially admires the film's cinematography.

10. **Titles**   Quotation marks rather than italics (underlining) indicate titles of books, movies, poems, musical works, plays, and TV programs. Quotation marks are not needed for titles of newspapers and magazines.

11. **Abbreviations**   Abbreviate months except May, June, and July, but spell out the names of days:

> School starts on Sept. 4 and ends on June 6, a Friday.

Abbreviate Street, Avenue, and Boulevard when they appear with a street number:

> She moved from 220 Wolf Road to 220 Woolf Blvd.

Abbreviate most formal titles preceding a name:

> Sen. Tom Harkin opposed the aid bill, but Rep. Fred Grandy favored it.

Traits of Headlines and Leads

236 Headlines

In every issue of a newspaper, there may be several stories for which the headline could follow the "X defeats Y" formula—*Broncos defeat Whippets, Council considers budget, Director discusses play.*   But good news writers avoid such headlines because they look routine and draw little attention. A news story is not complete until you have identified and written into the headline the important difference in a game, meeting, or event—*Reserves spark Whippet comeback, Council snubs teen center, Flu virus delays play opening.*

A headline is basically a statement with a subject and a verb (as you can see in the headlines above). Sometimes the subject or verb is implied rather than stated. In the following headline the verb "says" is implied. *Director: The talent in this band won't quit.* In the next headline the subject (probably "weather service") is implied: *Predicts severe weather.* Such omissions keep headlines brief and informative.

Note: Always search for specific words for your headline. Also, make sure that your headline is clear so that it can't be misread by a reader.

237 Leads

A reader will automatically scan the lead of your news story if the headline attracts his attention. The lead should state the main news point of your story in such a way that those readers who have most reason to be interested in your story will want to read it. Stress what is most important, most unusual, or most recent about the main point of your news story.

Avoid using questions in your lead, and do not start with routine words or phrases. For example, a lead beginning with the time and date of a meeting—On Monday, Sept. 24, at 7 p.m. the Council met...—will not attract very many readers.

Occasionally a news story will have two or three main points. For example, two important pieces of news might develop in a particular meeting. The usual practice in such a case is to write a multiple-element lead in which all of the main points are identified, the most important one first. Note the two-element lead which follows:

> Two juniors will spend their senior year as exchange students in another country. Three other juniors plan to spend their summer months in a foreign exchange program.

You can use a delayed lead to prepare the reader for the main news point, especially in those stories with human interest appeal. For example, if the team you are covering has just lost its 14th game in a row, rather than beginning "The Knights dropped another contest Friday night," you might begin "Knight forward Mike Kell shook his head in disbelief after the final buzzer sounded." You could then get to the main point of the story—the team suffering another defeat—and then work in something more—the effect of another defeat on one of the participants.

238 Interviewing

As a news writer, you are a current events broker. You gather news from investigating and researching important events, you decide which events to develop into stories, and you then share what you have learned about these stories with your readers. Your most important single source of information as you select and develop news stories is the interview. Firsthand accounts of current events and the insights of experts are indispensible elements of newswriting. The following guidelines will help you conduct an effective interview:

1. Unless you have only one or two brief questions, make an appointment for your interview and reveal what general questions you plan to ask.

2. Prepare for the interview. Good background research leads to good questions. Arrive at your interview with your main questions written out.

3. During the actual interview use your prepared questions to get the conversation going, but never limit yourself to just these questions. Your best material will often come from follow-up questions.

4. If the interview focuses on personality, include some details about *setting, action, gesture,* and *tone* of the particular person. These help make a person more real to the reader.

5. Take abbreviated notes during the interview. Then fill in the gaps and make your notes readable right after the interview. At the same time, begin to shape your story by selecting the strongest quotes and most telling details from the interview.

6. Offer to call your source(s) before a story is printed to verify the accuracy of quotes and facts you have used.

The Structure of a Feature Story

A feature story runs a much different course than a news story. The lead of a feature essentially invites a reader into a story whereas the lead in a news story reveals all of the story's main points. A steady stream of interesting and important facts and details which follows in the body of a feature eventually breaks into a strong conclusion. A news story, as you know, offers facts and details according to their importance, and it has no real conclusion. It simply ends after the least important details are reported. Since every part of a feature is important, it is never cut at production time.

A feature story is meant to entertain and inform. It often highlights an interesting or engaging angle of a straight news story. For example, a feature might describe a particular scene, present a memorable character, clarify a complex issue, or communicate a particular mood. Let's say a straight news story during the state basketball tournament summarizes a particular game. A feature story might highlight the reactions of a certain spectator or describe the "action" around the concession stand during the game.

239 Types of Features

There are five general types of features, all of which present an entertaining and informative look at the readers' world.

1. **News Feature**   A news feature is based on a current news story. It often provides related background information. For example, suppose a news story announces the schedule of events for homecoming week. A news feature might highlight the difficulties the homecoming committee had in scheduling the homecoming parade.

2. **Informative Feature**   An informative feature presents an interesting and appealing story not necessarily related to a timely news story. It is based on a news writer's interviews, observations, and reading. For example, suppose you were interested in architecture. You might research school architecture and develop an informative feature which proposes the ideal layout for a high school.

3. **Historical Feature**   A historical feature often evolves from a timely news story. For example, suppose a news story reports on the track team's first conference championship in 25 years. A historical feature might review the last championship track team.

4. **Personality Story**   A personality story presents a story about an individual who will be of interest or appeal to readers. For example, a day-in-the-life story of a college freshman will be of interest to high school readers, especially if those readers know the student and/or plan on attending college.

5. **Firsthand Account**   A firsthand account develops from a feature writer's personal experiences. For example, a writer might recreate his or her driver's test or first day on the job.

240 Writing the Feature Story

Prewriting: A feature writer has much more freedom than a straight news writer. While the news writer operates entirely with the facts of a story, a feature writer has many options. He can dart in and out of the main body of facts in a related, more inventive story. He can head for deeper water and do a reflective piece of writing. Or, he can explore uncharted waters for a truly original story.

You will discover plenty of inviting ideas for features. The large body of current news alone supplies any number of potential feature stories. (See "Sample Writing Topics," 034, for story ideas.) Your challenge will be to make your particular story inviting to your readers. The success of your feature ultimately will depend on your willingness to develop your story thoroughly and imaginatively. Feature writing demands careful observation of sights and sounds, insightful interviewing, and colorful writing.

Designing a Plan: Naturally you must start with a good story idea, but the angle in which you develop this idea is equally important. Think of the angle as your special approach to a story. For example, let's say you decide to feature the "action" at a state tournament concession stand in a story. You might offer your readers a close look at the art of garnishing a hot dog, that is, if you witnessed a number of interesting subjects. This angle would appeal to a large number of readers, and it would help you focus your attention on one specific aspect of the concession stand activity.

A feature, like any story, is competing for the readers' attention. Without an attractive and imaginative headline and lead, it will be passed over. The headline you can save for later, but the lead, that important opening to your feature, demands your immediate attention once you have a story angle. You must somehow set your story in motion and do so in such a way that your reader gets excited, curious, or somehow involved in your story. For example, in a story about the art of garnishing a hot dog, few readers could resist a story starting in this way:

Ketchup.
Mustard.
Sweet relish.
Onions.
Sauerkraut.
Chili peppers.
They all make their way onto stadium hot dogs at tournament time.

Remember: A feature story generally does not begin with a summary lead as in a news story. (See "Types of Original Leads" below for explanations and examples of different leads.)

Writing the First Draft: Once you have established your lead, you are ready to write the first draft of your feature. Include plenty of lively details, entertaining or informative quotes, and your own imaginative ideas to help the reader share in your story. Do not, however, become too cute. A feature, like any good news story, should have something to say that is informative or enlightening.

Note: Whenever possible include one or two anecdotes—brief summaries of humorous or amusing events—in your feature stories. Readers enjoy these entertaining digressions.

The conclusion should effectively bring your story to a close. You might refer to something important in your lead. You might generally confirm your feature's significance if you have written a serious feature. Or, you might leave your reader with an amusing parting shot if you have written a light or humorous feature. An example of an amusing concluding statement follows:

If it is true that we are what we eat, then there are a lot of sweet and sour basketball fans in our state.

Revising and Editing: When you are ready to revise your feature, refer to the section on revising and editing the straight news story (233) for help. Also, since a feature story closely resembles the personal or informative essay, refer to the section in your handbook on the essay (105) for additional guidance.

Note: Pay special attention to the lead and conclusion when you revise. Make sure they effectively reflect the focus of your story.

241 Types of Original Leads

Save summary leads for straight news stories, and start your feature stories imaginatively. The ideas for original leads which follow will help you develop your own inventive openings.

1. **Quick Bursts Lead**—a series of short, direct statements: Begin with beads of mustard and ketchup. Continue with sprinkles of onion and relish. And finish with a shower of sauerkraut. A stadium hot dog is ready.

2. **Surprise Lead**—an eye-opening beginning: A dog with the works is worth the indigestion.

3. **Contrast Lead**—an opening with opposites or differences: Some fans attend to quality when garnishing a hot dog, while others attend to quantity.

4. **Figurative Lead**—an opening figure of speech: The garnishes for stadium hot dogs are either crown jewels or a crown of thorns depending on the strength of your stomach.

5. **Allusion Lead**—an opening reference to literature: Double, bubble, toil and trouble. Your stomach may bubble and toil after a stadium dog with the works.

6. **Expert Lead**—an opening quote from an expert: "A dog is man's best friend, at least if you're talking about stadium hot dogs," said Mary Jordan, concession manager. "Our customers are almost all males."

7. **Suspense Lead**—an open-ended beginning: Should he hold the pickle relish? Bob Youmans couldn't decide. He had already spread mustard, ketchup, and onions on his hot dog.

8. **Question Lead**—an opening question: Have you ever watched a true hot-dog connoisseur in action?

242 Rights and Responsibilities of Student Journalists

Student journalists have somewhat less freedom than professional journalists. The Supreme Court has recently ruled that principals have the right to censor student publications. You should not respond by "playing dead" to controversial issues. You should instead practice responsible reporting so that your administrators allow you considerable press freedom.

Ensure administrators that you understand the sensitivity inherent in controversial stories. Demonstrate your professionalism by asking three questions before you print any delicate story: (If you answer no to any of these questions, hold the story.)

a. Are you sure that the story is accurate and fair to all parties involved?

b. Are you sure the story offers real benefit to readers?

c. Will this benefit clearly outweigh the potential damage?

The Structure of an Editorial

243   An editorial is generally a short persuasive essay which develops from a writer's reaction to a timely news story. Its primary function is to influence readers to a particular way of thinking. (An editorial writer might argue that the school student council does not represent the entire student body after a controversial council action.)

A good editorial is much like a challenging stretch of river in that it is direct, forceful, and absorbing. Readers do not quickly forget an effective editorial. They will be moved to agree or disagree with the writer's argument or at least to reexamine the initial issue once they slip into calmer waters.

Not all editorials take issue with current news developments, however. There are four less argumentative duties which editorials carry out.

1. Some editorials inform like straight news stories. Usually informative editorials deal with complex issues which require careful explanation and interpretation. (The effects of cost control measures on certain programs in a school might be addressed in an informative editorial.)

2. Some editorials promote worthy activities. (The formation of a SADD [Students Against Drunk Driving] group might be promoted in an editorial.)

3. Some editorials commend worthy individuals or events. (The individuals who remodeled a computer lab or a Wellness Day event might be commended in an editorial.)

4. And some simply encourage or entertain their readers. (A serious or satiric What-To-Do-In-Our-Town piece might be developed in an editorial.)

244 Writing the Editorial

Prewriting: Choose a timely subject for your editorial, and make sure it is a subject that is of genuine interest to you and to a large portion of your audience. Don't, for example, address the cancellation of a particular elective simply because you signed up for it. Take issue with an event like this only if you feel it will have a significant impact on a number of students.

Designing a Plan: Start your editorial with a clearly stated proposition. A proposition is a statement of what you propose to prove in your writing.

Note: Don't be afraid to take a controversial or unpopular stand in your editorial as long as it is a stand you support.

State your proposition in positive terms. *(Student council should represent the entire student body* rather than *Student council does not represent the entire student body.)* Then plan your editorial carefully so that you're not surprised by any unforeseen snags in your argument. The questions which follow will help you develop a convincing editorial.

Developing a Convincing Editorial

1. What facts or evidence will support the case you're making? If you don't have this evidence now, where can you find it?

2. Can you get testimony from written sources or from authorities that will support your main point?

3. Can you use comparisons or analogies to advance your argument?

4. Can you project confidence and insight into your argument?

5. Is there a particular image or picture that you can use to strengthen your argument?

6. Can you effectively check counterarguments (opposing viewpoints)?

7. Can you effectively argue that the action you recommend is sound and will be seen as desirable? *Special Note:* Since an editorial is a special type of persuasive essay, refer to "Writing to Persuade," 125, for help when you plan your stories.

An editorial should be a brief run. A 200-word editorial is appropriate for high school newspapers. You must quickly come to your point, speak from authority, and present a clear, forceful case. As in other types of news stories, the lead of an editorial must get the readers' attention as well as state the subject of the story. Open with a surprising statement, a quotation, a brief anecdote, or any other appealing opening. (See 237 and 241 for example leads.)

Writing the First Draft: The body of an editorial should develop logically with clear and accurate details and examples. Present your strongest arguments first and last. Give credit to any counterarguments early, and point out the weaknesses in each. Offer a solution or a call to action in your conclusion. And maintain a positive and reasonable tone throughout: excessive emotion, sermonizing, or moralizing will weaken your argument.

Revising and Editing: Ideally you will write an editorial sooner than the straight news stories so that you have more time for revision. Consider the general effectiveness and validity of your argument before you worry about the mechanics of a piece. An editorial should be as appealing, succinct, and forceful as you can make it before it goes to print. Use the checklist which follows to help you revise your editorials.

245 Checklist for Revising Editorials _____

_____ 1. Consider the clarity and appeal of your proposition, the persuasiveness and accuracy of your general argument, and the effectiveness of your recommendations or solutions. (See "Using Evidence and Logic," 552, for help when evaluating the strength of your argument.)

_____ 2. Deal in principles. Your editorial should not be a character attack. Also, whenever possible, commend rather than criticize.

_____ 3. Let the facts speak for themselves. Don't preach, moralize, or dictate.

_____ 4. Keep paragraphs brief and direct. A few effective examples or illustrations in an editorial are far more effective than a barrage of details and statistics. *Note:* Short editorials on different aspects of an issue are more effective than one lengthy editorial.

_____ 5. Consider the timing and importance of the story. Don't write about old news or news that is not important to a large number of readers. Also, avoid cheerleading. (Promoting school spirit or studying hard would be considered cheerleading.)

_____ 6. Evaluate the clarity and directness of your ideas. Honesty and accuracy are absolutes. If you can't uncover important facts, don't run the story.

_____ 7. Keep the language in your editorial simple and direct. Don't "impress" your reader with your extensive vocabulary.

_____ 8. Don't become too dramatic. Deadly seriousness is usually not necessary in an editorial. Readers appreciate tasteful humor or whimsy on the editorial page.

_____ 9. Make sure that you have acted responsibly in developing your argument. (See "Rights and Responsibilities of Student Journalists," 242, for an explanation of responsible journalism.)

246 Journalism Terms

Angle: A particular point of view or way of looking at a subject.

Banner: One-line head extending all the way across the top of the page.

Beat: A specified territory regularly covered by a reporter.

Bleed: Illustration that extends beyond usual margins, generally to the edge of the page.

Boldface: Heavier version of a type style (abbreviated *bf*): boldface.

Byline: Credit line at the beginning of a story telling who wrote it.

Caption: Description or comment that goes with an illustration. Also called a *cutline*.

Copyreader (Copy Editor): Person who corrects or improves stories to get them ready for typesetting.

Cropping: Marking or cutting a photo to eliminate parts of it that do not suit the purpose for which it is being used.

Cutline: See *Caption*.

Display Type: Any type larger than body type—used mostly for headlines and ads.

Downstyle: In headlines, using normal sentence capitalization rather than capitalizing the first letter of all important words as is done in book titles.

Dummy: Diagram of a particular page layout or of general appearance for a publication.

Editor: Person who prepares copy for publication. Also, a person with a defined area of staff leadership which may not include working with copy.

Editorial: An article which reflects the opinion of the writer or the management of the news organization.

Editorializing: The fault of injecting personal opinion into a news story.

Evergreen Stories: Items which can be held back when space is unavailable and used when they are needed.

Feature: A story which appeals to an audience because of the human interest of its contents rather than the importance of its content.

Flag: The *nameplate* or printed inscription containing the name of the newspaper.

Flush-Left or Flush-Right: Copy or headlines aligned with the margin, left or right.

Folio: Page number.

Folio Line: Information run with the page number, usually including the publication's name, the date of publication, and sometimes information about the contents of the page.

Font: An assortment of one style or size of type.

Grabber: An attention-getting lead.

Gutter: Space between columns; more often, the wider space where adjoining pages meet.

Halftone: A negative of a photo or art which converts the image into dots suitable for printing. On the final page, large black dots will appear black, medium sized ones appear as shades of gray, and small ones look white.

Inverted-Pyramid Structure: A method of organizing a news story such that the most important information is in the lead; the remaining information is presented in order of decreasing importance.

Italic: Type which slants to the right: *italic*.

Jump: To continue a story on another page.

Jumphead: Headline over a jumped part of a story.

Jump Line: Brief information telling where to find the rest of a continued story.

Justified: Type with lines adjusted to be flush with both left and right margins. Unjustified type, with only the left margin flush, is called ragged right.

Kicker: A smaller emphasis headline appearing above a larger head.

Lead (Pronounced *leed*): Opening of a story, usually a summary of its most significant information.

Libel: Written or printed material that defames a person's character or

exposes him to ridicule.

Masthead: The identification statement usually placed on the editorial page. It includes the *nameplate*, policy statement, key personnel, and so on.

Mug Shot: A photo showing someone's face or sometimes head and shoulders.

Pasteup: A layout sheet with copy and heads pasted down and positions for illustrations indicated.

Pica: Unit of measure used by printer and page designers. Six picas roughly equal an inch.

Point: A printer's unit used to designate the height of a line of copy or headline or the thickness of a ruling line; 12 points equals one pica and 72 points equals one inch.

Proofreading: Carefully checking printed copy for errors before the publication goes to press.

Serif: Small finishing stroke at the ends of many letters in some type styles. Styles that do not have such strokes or lines are called sans-serif (serif ... sans-serif).

Tombstoning: Placing similar headlines side-by-side (which may cause readers to confuse them).

Typo: Common abbreviation for typographical error.

X-Height: The height of a lowercase x and thus all letters without vertical strokes extending above or below such letter.

247 Sample News Story

<table>
<tr><td>Statement
Headline</td><td>

Apple IIGS computer stolen

</td></tr>
<tr><td>Byline</td><td>*by Jamie Siegrist*</td></tr>
<tr><td>Lead
Paragraph</td><td>An Apple IIGS computer and its color monitor, two disk drives, and a printer were stolen from the Learning Resource Center early Monday morning, according to Rob Robinson, director of the center.

Robinson said the equipment was worth $2,000. He added that the center received it only a month ago.</td></tr>
<tr><td>Explanation
and
Amplification</td><td>Software and manuals for the equipment were also taken from the LRC circulation desk, leading investigators to believe that the person who stole it knew the computer center fairly well. Robinson said police are investigating, but to his knowledge there are no suspects yet.

"Students would be the last people I would suspect because they are more trustable than the average person, and they have the most to lose if caught," said Robinson.</td></tr>
<tr><td>Background
Information</td><td>There were no signs of entry, but it is suspected that someone may have hidden in the center until after it was locked up. It is also possible that someone made a key, according to Robinson. He said a better security system is being discussed.

Last year, six VCRs were stolen from the A-V room adjacent to the computer center, but the VCRs in the center were untouched, so it was thought that the center was safe. After that theft, locks in the A-V room were changed.</td></tr>
</table>

"If I read a book that impresses me, I have to take myself firmly in hand before I mix with other people; otherwise they would think my mind rather queer."

—**Anne Frank**

Writing about
LITERATURE

What do you usually do after you've seen a good movie or heard an outstanding concert? Tell others about it or avoid mixing with them? I would guess that if you're like most people you would tell them about it—enthusiastically! Sharing good news about a movie or concert is something most of us do with little coaxing. But what about a good book? Are we just as quick—or ready—to share the good news? If not, maybe it's because it isn't always easy describing in words *why* a story was good— why it moved you, touched you, changed you. The "whys" are often very personal, developing slowly over the days and weeks you spent sharing a slice of life with the characters in your book.

This may be why books are written about as much as they are talked about. When you write, you have time to think, and plan, and remember. There is so much you can say about a "good" book, part of the challenge in writing a book review is deciding what is important or interesting enough to include. The information in this chapter should help you first, to understand your choices, and, second, to make the right ones.

What is a Book Review?

250   A book review is not simply a plot summary or an unsupported opinion of how well the reader did or did not like the book. A book review includes information about the key elements of the book (plot, characters, setting, theme, etc.) and the reviewer's opinion of how well the author has succeeded in using those elements to write an effective story. A good book review presents evidence to support this opinion, and, in the process, helps the reader gain an insight into the story. In general, the writer of a book review gives enough information to help the reader decide whether he or she wants to read the book, but not so much as to spoil the joy of discovery which comes from reading a good book.

To do a good job of reviewing a book, the writer must know the book thoroughly. This requires a careful, attentive reading (and rereading of certain parts). The writer must also know what kind of book it is he or she is reading (romance novel, biography, historical novel, science fiction, etc.) and what characterizes good literature of this type. For example, it would be wrong to criticize a biography because it lacked a strong plot or to find fault with a science fiction novel because it had an unrealistic setting. As you read, consider the following points.

As You Read

1. **Determine the author's purpose.** Read the preface and introduction—they often contain clues and occasionally a specific statement of the author's purpose or intention.

2. **Consider the title and subtitle.** Sometimes (but not always) the title or subtitle can provide an important clue as to the "meaning" of the book.

3. **Take notes.** Write down anything which you feel could be useful to you later when you attempt to piece everything together. (*Example:* "The author's description of the character's first day of school is very believable. The overly friendly attitude of the teacher is especially effective.")

4. **Collect samples.** Make a list of especially good or especially weak passages, as well as any passages which you might use as quotations in your review.

5. **Summarize each chapter** (or every 15-20 pages). React to your summaries: Are you enjoying the story to this point? Why or why not? Are you confused about anything in the story? What questions would you like to ask someone else about the book? Keep a reading log. (See 257.)

Before You Write

1. **Read about the author** in other sources, especially if you find yourself needing to know more about his or her background, qualifications, or philosophy. (Include this information in your actual review only if it will help the reader understand the book or your review more clearly.)

2. **Read related material.** Find books or articles which discuss the kind of literature you are reviewing or which cover the historical time period in which the story was written or is set.

3. **Consider your theme.** Decide what the theme or central focus of your review is going to be. Be sure you have a significant and well-defined theme. Avoid themes which are too obvious, too general, or vague. Word your theme (*thesis statement*) carefully, making certain you understand all the key literary terms used.

4. **Revise your notes.** Locate and list the evidence (examples, quotations, summaries, etc.) which supports your theme. You might use a support sheet similar to the one below:

   Thesis: Gatsby is a true crusader for the American Dream, but a crusader with a flaw.

   1. We could all admire Gatsby if it weren't for the obscure hint of tarnish on his armor or those tiny, black rumors that float among his party guests like the "foul dust" Nick speaks of (147).

   2. We know of Gatsby's shady dealings and his "connections," yet we cannot really accuse him of being wrong because we can see into his fanciful dreams and unrealized ambitions (98).

   3. The trouble with Gatsby is that he gets some of the important things in his life a little mixed up--one of them is love. He thinks he is in love with a wealthy girl by the name of Daisy Fay; in fact, it is her wealth he has fallen in love with (47).

   4. Perhaps Gatsby's greatest flaw is his inability to comprehend the difference between the rich and the wealthy--between his world and Daisy's. The rich have the money, but not the culture, tradition, or standing of the wealthy (49).

   5. Gatsby continued to believe that one day he would achieve his goals and that one day Daisy would come back to him. "Gatsby believed in the green light,

the orgiastic future that year by year recedes before us. It eluded us then, but that's no matter--tomorrow we will run faster, stretch our arms farther. . . . And one fine morning . . . " (187).

6.   But Gatsby has little chance of realizing his goals: "So we beat on, boats against the current, borne back ceaselessly into the past" (201).

5.   **Design a plan.** Arrange into an outline, map, or list all the "evidence" and other points you plan to cover in your review. Make sure that all of the information in your outline relates to your theme and is important enough to include. Arrange your points in a logical way so that the reader will be able to follow your thinking and will understand how you came to the conclusion you did.

253 Getting Started

After you have read your book, determined a focus or theme, collected evidence and details, and designed a plan—it is time to see just how everything fits together.

Using your plan (or outline) as a guide, write freely about the book. You might also try a focused writing or two using other general questions or prompts about the book: What is your general impression of the book? Was it exciting or dull and predictable? Did you learn anything from it? What is most real or believable about it? Which parts are especially good or memorable? Which characters are most believable or lifelike? What truth about life is revealed? What seems to be the point, lesson, or theme of the story?

After your free and focused writings, you may be ready to work on an opening or introduction for your review. This can help you to focus specifically on your theme and help you organize your details to fit your design or plan. There are a number of possibilities you might try. You might, for example, use one (or combine several) of the suggestions below into an opening paragraph:

1.   Summarize the novel very briefly. Include in this summary the title, author, and type of book. This can be done with a statement of "what and how" about the book. (*Example:* In his allegorical novel, Lord of the Flies, William Golding writes about [*what?*] the evil side of man [*how?*] by describing what happens to a group of young boys who are marooned on a deserted island with no adults to control their actions.)

2.   Use a passage from the book and follow it with a comment on how this quotation is typical (or not typical) of what is contained in the book.

3.   You might begin with what you believe to be the author's purpose in writing the book and how well you think he or she achieves this purpose.

4.   You can discuss briefly the theme or major problem dealt with in the book.

5.   You can present information about the author and his or her background, qualifications, or philosophy.

6.   Finally, state your specific theme.

In the body of your review, you must decide how to arrange the details that support your theme. No matter what method you choose, the body must be developed with a clear focus and a specific sense of direction and purpose. It can be helpful to present your theme early in your review and follow with these three steps: 1. *State* each of your ideas about your theme clearly (*generalization*). 2. *Support* each of your generalizations with specific details from the story (*evidence*). 3. *Explain* how each of these specific details proves your point (*interpretation*). Continue to focus on your theme as you add and analyze your details; remember that it is very easy to get off the track.

Make each new paragraph in your review a continuation of your central theme. Be careful not to leave any thought gaps as you switch from one paragraph to another. Tie your paragraphs together with ideas related to your theme; very often in a book review, a key word or phrase can be used as a linking device. Resist the temptation to rely heavily on plot for transitional material. Build your theme to a high point, finally bringing all your ideas together.

End your review with a paragraph (or two) which brings your theme into final focus for the reader. You might, for instance, arrive at a specific conclusion about your theme, about the author's purpose, or about the overall effectiveness of the story.

Writing about Content

254   With a general idea of how you might start, end, and develop your review, you should write your first draft. If you are reviewing a book, you will most likely write something about each of the four main elements of fiction: *plot, character, setting,* and *theme.* You will give most of your attention to the element(s) which is most important to the overall effectiveness of the novel.

1. **Plot** — Discuss only as much of the plot as is necessary to give your reader a general idea of the story. Never give away the ending or any unusual twist in the plot.

2. **Character** — You should pay particular attention to the characters and the author's method of developing these characters throughout the story. If there is one character who is central to the entire novel, you should point this out to your reader. You might trace the changes this character goes through and comment on the reasons for these changes. You can consider what forces—internal and external—motivate a particular character or shape his personality. You can discuss how a particular character does or does not adjust to new situations which arise in the story. Or you can write about the characters in general and to what extent they are believable, consistent, and interesting.

3. **Setting** — The setting is very important in some novels, not nearly so important in others. Typically, setting is most important in historical novels, science fiction novels, and those in which atmosphere or mood are especially important. If it is essential for your reader to know the specific time and place in which a story takes place, include a description of the setting in your review.

4. **Theme** — You should always pay some attention to the theme of the story and how well the author has developed this theme. Sometimes a theme can be stated as a moral or lesson: "If you give someone too much power, he is bound to abuse it." Other times a story is based on one or more general themes: ambition, charity, duty, fame, freedom, greed, guilt, happiness, hypocrisy, jealousy, love, loyalty, patriotism, poverty, prejudice, pride, responsibility, sacrifice, survival, tradition, etc. Decide how important the theme is to the overall effectiveness of the story and give it appropriate attention.

5. **Other Elements** — If the author uses other elements (*symbolism, satire, irony,* etc.) to add impact to his story, you should mention this in your review. If these elements are present in the story, but do not contribute significantly to the overall effectiveness, you need not write about them.

If the book you have read includes a good deal of symbolism or satire, you should consider the different levels of meaning which may be present. The plot will provide the first and most obvious level, but there may be a deeper meaning which is closer to the author's purpose. Look carefully at the author's use of symbolism, irony, satire, personification, and other figures of speech (313); then develop your interpretation of the piece. You might discuss your ideas with someone else who has read the book and compare thoughts. Then decide whether your interpretation is valid enough to share with your readers.

If the author is attempting to convey a strong message of political or social importance, you should comment on how well this message comes across and whether it enhances or detracts from the story.

Finally, include your opinion or reaction to the book. Point out where the book succeeds or fails and support your opinion with specific references or examples from the book.

255 Revising and Proofreading Your Review

One of the most important stages in the process of writing a book review is revising. No reader is going to take seriously a review which is filled with incomplete thoughts or careless errors. Follow the suggestions below when preparing the final copy of your review.

1. Let your review sit for a day or two before you go back to revise it. This will allow you to be more objective about what you have written and judge the review much as your readers will. You will also bring to your review the renewed energy needed to make the necessary changes.

2. Read your review out loud as you revise. The ear will often pick out errors and awkward expressions your eye does not.

3. Read especially for clarity and unity. Poorly written book reviews tend to hop from one point to the next with little sense of continuity. Work carefully to tie all parts of your review into one coherent piece of writing.

4. Check your quotations for accuracy and appropriateness. Also, do not overload your review with quotations which simply sound good. Double-check your use of quotation marks and punctuation (ellipses, period and comma placement at the end of quoted material, etc.).

5. Follow the same guidelines you would for any formal writing assignment and write or type your final copy neatly on unlined paper.

——— Things Not to Do in Your Review ———

256 1. Do not attempt to write a review unless you have read the book carefully and completely.

2. Do not simply write a plot or character summary, or include so much summary that it buries your interpretation.

3. Do not make general statements about the book without supporting them with specific examples or quotations.

4. Do not turn your review into a mere string of quotations; the explanations which tie these quotations together should be the heart of your review.

5. Do not, however, make your review a "running commentary" on one quotation after another; comment on those quotations which need explanation and leave the others to speak for themselves.

6. Do not include so much factual information in your review that it becomes more of a "report" than a review. Use personal, colorful language and include your opinions, interpretations, and observations.

257 **Keeping a Reading Log**

A reading log is a place to react to what you read. You can discover exactly how you feel about what you're reading, gather new insights, and expand your enjoyment. Reading logs can be excellent sourcebooks for book reviews. When you have a source of compelling ideas, memorable lines, details, questions, and personal reactions, you have the ingredients for an outstanding book review—one which reflects honest and original thinking.

If you have trouble saying anything interesting about the books you read, you need to start a reading log. Also, if you seldom enjoy reading, you should experiment with a reading log.

All of us actively respond to what happens around us each day. This is normal. We laugh, get angry, feel sad, become confused, encourage others, wonder, ask questions. It is just as normal to respond to what is happening in the inner world of a book. Reading logs provide a place for you to participate with the author and the world he has created. This participation makes you an active reader.

The following questions will help you to react openly and honestly to what you read. These are only suggestions to get you started. You will soon discover your own questions, build relationships with characters and authors in your own way, and discover new techniques to help you become an active reader. Your own ideas will become the primary source for your reading-log entries.

258 **Sample Reading Log Questions**

1. What were your feelings after reading the opening chapter(s)? After reading half the book? After finishing the book?

2. Did this book make you laugh? cry? cringe? smile? cheer? explode? Record some of your reactions.

3. Are there connections between the book and your own life?

4. What character would you like to be in this book? Why?

5. Would you like to acquire a personality trait of any particular character? Describe the trait and explain why you like it.

6. Would you have used a different name for any character or place? What name? Why?

7. What makes you wonder in this book?

8. What confuses you in this book?

9. Is there an idea that makes you stop and think or prompts questions? Identify the idea and explain your responses.

10. What are your favorite lines/quotes? Copy them into your reading log.

11. What questions would you like to ask the author of this book?

12. How have you changed after reading this book?

13. What do you know now that you didn't know before?

14. What questions about this book would you like answered?

15. Who else should read this book? Why?

16. Who shouldn't read this book? Why?

17. Would you like to read more books by this author? Why?

18. If X-rays were taken, what would a certain character's heart look like? his soul? his brain?

More Than Mere Words

Sketches: Sometimes we grow a bit weary of words. Some of us are artists and draftsmen. Some of us are interested in settings and costumes. All of these are good reasons to include sketches in your reading logs. You can draw portraits of the characters, design settings, and draw costumes appropriate to the time and place.

Poems: You might try writing a bio-poem about one or more of the characters in a book. The form for a bio-poem is:

Bio-Poem

Line 1:   Your character's first name

Line 2:   Four words that describe this character

Line 3:   Brother or sister of . . .

Line 4:   Lover of . . . (three ideas or people)

Line 5:   Who feels . . . (three ideas)

Line 6:   Who needs . . . (three ideas)

Line 7:   Who gives . . . (three ideas)

Line 8:   Who fears . . . (three ideas)

Line 9:   Who would like to see . . .

Line 10: Resident of . . .

Line 11: His or her last name

The following bio-poem was written by a student who had finished reading *Grapes of Wrath.* You can feel how well he had come to understand Noah Joad.

Sample Bio-Poem

Noah

Tall, strange, calm, puzzled

Brother of Tommy

Lover of peace, isolation, silence

Who feels laid-back, calm, nothing

Who needs a sense of direction, a place in society, pride

Who gives peace, amazement, a wondering look

Who fears life, other people, himself

Who would like to see feelings, caring, temptation

Resident of Oklahoma

Joad.

Sometimes you may find it necessary to alter the suggested bio-poem format because of the nature or lack of information about a book character.

Conversations: Would you like to have a conversation with a character you meet in a book? Write a dialogue between you and that character. Would you like to interview the author? What questions would you ask and what responses would he or she give?

Note: Check the "Writing to Learn" section in this handbook for other ways to respond in your reading logs. *Also note:* As you continue to write more and more about books you will probably want to use many literary terms. For a list of useful terms, see 275-371.

Below is a sample list of things which you might include in a book review. (This list was used by the student who wrote the review of *Black Like Me*.)

a. an excerpt from the book and a follow-up comment
b. the point of view and setting
c. the plot and how it contributes to the development of the theme
d. the topic or theme and its importance in our society today
e. the accuracy or truth of the theme
f. the believability of the characters
g. the author's background
h. the author's tone and style
i. the diction or language used
j. the overall ease/difficulty of reading
k. a personal reaction/opinion

Black Like Me: A Student Review

Rest at pale evening . . .
A tall slim . . .
Night coming tenderly
Black like me.

John Howard Griffin, the author of **Black Like Me**, used the verse above to describe himself in a strange world where friends were lacking and hate stares were everywhere.

Griffin tells his readers how he had undergone a series of treatments and medications to temporarily darken the color of his skin. He literally abandoned his white world and crossed the line into an atmosphere of hate, fear and hopelessness — the world of the American black man. To make his exit complete, he was compelled, for a time, to give up his family, friends, and the life that was familiar to him in Mansfield, Texas.

During his six weeks in the Southern states, Griffin learned about the struggles and hardships a

---

2

black man must go through day after day. Even though he was rejected and pushed around, Griffin never stopped trying to understand the white man's point of view. He describes the contrast between the two races: "The atmosphere of a place is entirely different for Negro and White. The Negro sees and reacts differently not because he is Negro, but because he is suppressed. Fear dims even the sunlight."

Every time he stepped onto a bus, sat down in a diner, or checked into a hotel, Griffin was reminded of the burden of being **black**. It was as if having black skin meant you were afflicted with a contagious disease. But Griffin was an exception; his time for pain and suffering was only temporary. As soon as the dark color wore out of his skin, he would once again join the white race. But the thought of this did not appeal to Griffin. If it weren't for his wife and children, he might have rather continued living as a Black and helping them in their struggle for Civil Rights, as opposed to existing in an atmosphere of bigotry. Griffin was often reminded of the cruelty of white men in his dreams.

It was the same nightmare I had been having recently. White men and women, their faces stern

---

3

and heartless, closed in on me. The hate stares burned through me. I pressed back against a wall. I could expect no pity, no mercy. They approached slowly and I could not escape them. Twice before, I had awakened myself screaming.

On December 14, Griffin was ready to return to his home in Mansfield. The dark pigment had worn out of his skin, allowing him to resume his white identity once again. Through newspaper and magazine articles, photographers, and television broadcasters, Griffin's project became known to people throughout the country. Although he was anxious to be reunited with his family and friends, he was not nearly so anxious to return to the bigoted part of society: "I felt the greatest love for this land and the deepest dread of the task that now lay before me — the task of telling truths that would make me and my family the target of all the hate groups."

Griffin's wife and children welcomed him with hugs and kisses, while many of his "friends" greeted him with abusive phone calls and hateful remarks.

In one instance, some racists went so far as to hang his effigy on Main Street. The dummy, half black — half white, with Griffin's name on it and a

---

4

yellow streak painted down its back, was hanging from the center red-light wire in downtown Mansfield. This aroused the town even more and caused riots between the Blacks and the Whites. Griffin was very aware of what was happening. He was also conscious of the bad consequences it could have on his family's life. So, in order to restore a normal existence for themselves, the Griffins moved from their home in Mansfield, Texas, to start a new life in Mexico.

It was at his new home that Griffin laid the foundations for his book, **Black Like Me.** The project was undertaken to discover how deeply America was involved in the practice of racism against Blacks. Most Whites denied any stain of bigotry and claimed to believe that in this land we judge every man by his qualities as an individual human being.

Reading this book really opened my eyes and helped me understand the Negro and his plight in this country. I think John Howard Griffin did an excellent job of conveying the feelings as well as the facts. By traveling through the Southern states and living as a Negro for six weeks, Griffin was able to experience, rather than just see, how a black man is mistreated and how different his world is from that of the white man. I, too, was able to experience that.

The following review of *The Great Gatsby* concentrates on the central character of the novel, Jay Gatsby. However, in the process of discussing this character, the reviewer ties in important information about plot, setting, and theme as well.

The Great Gatsby

The Roaring Twenties: A curious concoction of prosperity and immorality, the rise of the self-made man, and the birth of the American Dream--the Great Gatsby era.

Before reading the book by F. Scott Fitzgerald, I never understood just what the Great Gatsby was. I honestly thought it was a dance like the Charleston. Now, however, I am much wiser. I know that Gatsby is a person who stands for that time in America when young and boisterous crowds combed the cities at night, slept through the morning, and made their fortunes in the afternoon. Gatsby is a true crusader for the American Dream, but a crusader with a flaw.

Gatsby is, as the title implies, a great person. Knowing him, we feel he would be able to accomplish anything he set out to do. In the beginning of the novel, our narrator, Nick Carroway, gives us this description of Gatsby:

> If personality is an unbroken series of successful gestures, then there was something gorgeous about him, some heightened sensitivity to the promises of life. . . . It was an extraordinary gift for hope, a romantic readiness such as I have never found in any other person. . . . No, Gatsby turned out all right at the end; it is what preyed on Gatsby, what foul dust floated in the wake of his dreams that

2

temporarily closed out my interest in the abortive sorrows and shortwinded elations of men. (147)

We know Gatsby has what it takes, from his winning smile to his boyhood "list of improvements." Yet, there is something wrong with Gatsby. We would all be justified in admiring him if it weren't for the obscure hint of tarnish on his armor or those tiny, black rumors that float among his party guests like the "foul dust" that Nick speaks of. We know of his shady dealings and his "connections," yet we cannot really accuse him of being wrong because we can see into his fanciful dreams and unrealized ambitions. We feel instead that some injustice has been done here. We feel a sorrow for Gatsby--an unreal man in a real world.

The trouble with Gatsby is that he gets some of the very important things in life a little mixed up. One of them is love. He finds himself, by some extraordinary circumstance, trespassing in a garden of wealth, and he dares to pick a flower; her name is Daisy Fay. Daisy Fay on the white, wicker porch of her grand, grand home, in her beautiful dresses, with a voice that jingles like a pocket full of gold--she feeds him all the sweetness of her wealth, and that is what Gatsby loves: not the girl, but the gold.

This infatuation is Gatsby's driving force for five years, and his conviction that what he feels really is love makes this force all the stronger. In reality, Daisy and Gatsby can never be together simply

3

because Daisy is too weak to ever stand by his side. Out of necessity, she marries while he is away because it is time for her life to be "shaped." Gatsby, on the other hand, is the shaper of his own life and never simply gives up on his dreams.

But Gatsby's fondest dream never comes true, the reason being the difference between someone who is rich and someone who is wealthy. Perhaps the greatest tragedy of all is that Gatsby is unable to comprehend this difference, a difference best illustrated by the setting of the story. It is set on two small islands off the tip of Manhattan, New York: East Egg and West Egg. Daisy lives on East Egg among the stately mansions and the wealthy people. Gatsby lives on West Egg which is looked upon, by the East Eggers, as being somewhat tacky because it has about it an air of "eccentric impulsiveness." This is to be expected, however, as it is the home of the rich--those who have the money, but not the "culture" of the wealthy.

In several places throughout the novel, reference is made to the light on the end of Daisy's dock on East Egg, a light which Gatsby can see from his yard on West Egg. It is green like a crisp, new dollar bill, and it stands for everything Gatsby is striving for. The first time Nick sees Gatsby, he is standing with his arms outstretched toward the light as if he is trying to somehow touch it, somehow reach his goal; and he believes he can do it just as he believed that Daisy would actually show up at one of his extravagant parties.

4

Gatsby believed in the green light, the orgiastic future that year by year recedes before us. It eluded us then, but that's no matter--tomorrow we will run faster, stretch our arms farther. . . . And one fine morning. . . . (187)

Yes, one fine morning, in Gatsby's mind, Daisy will come back to him, and they will live happily ever after. But, in reality, Daisy and Gatsby are two different people in two different worlds, separated by one large body of water. Gatsby has as much a chance of getting Daisy back as he has of making it across that water on foot.

The last line of the book states it well: "So we beat on, boats against the current, borne back ceaselessly into the past." Similarly, I can see Gatsby as a man trying to go up a down escalator. He climbs and climbs and climbs, yet he gets nowhere. It is unfortunate that he has access only to down escalators, but on West Egg, that is the only kind. All of the up escalators are on East Egg where the people have only to stand still, and they rise to the top. That is the injustice of this story, the reason for the foul dust and the tarnish on the armor. That is why we put ourselves behind owl-eye glasses at the grave of the Great Gatsby; and that is why, when I read this story, I want no more escalators, those ugly machines that thoughtlessly deposit people here and there and trip them getting on and off. Instead, I want to take the hand of Gatsby and show him to the stairway.

Understanding
LITERATURE

Literary Terms

275 An **abstract** word or phrase refers to an idea rather than a concrete object or thing. *Liberty, prejudice, love,* and *freedom* are examples of abstract words.

276 **Action** is what happens in a story: the events or conflicts. If the action is well organized, it will develop into a pattern or plot.

277 **Allegory** is a story in which people, things, and actions represent an idea or generalization about life; allegories often have a strong moral or lesson.

278 An **allusion** is a reference in literature to a familiar person, place, thing, or event.

279 An **analogy** is a comparison of two or more similar objects so as to suggest that if they are alike in certain respects, they will probably be alike in other ways as well.

280 **Anecdote** is a short summary of a funny or humorous event. Abe Lincoln was famous for his anecdotes, especially this one:

> Two fellows, after a hot dispute over how long a man's legs should be in proportion to his body, stormed into Lincoln's office one day and confronted him with their problem. Lincoln listened intently to the arguments given by each of the men and after some reflection rendered his verdict: "This question has been a source of controversy for untold ages," he said, slowly and deliberately, "and it is about time it should be definitely decided. It has led to bloodshed in the past, and there is no reason to suppose it will not lead to the same in the future.
> "After much thought and consideration, not to mention mental worry and anxiety, it is my opinion, all side issues being swept aside, that a man's lower limbs, in order to preserve harmony of proportion, should be at least long enough to reach from his body to the ground."

281 **Antagonist** is the person or thing working against the protagonist or hero of the work. When this is a person, he is usually called the *villain*.

152   *Understanding Literature*

282 **Autobiography** is an author's account or story of her own life.

283 **Biography** is the story of a person's life written by another person.

284 **Caricature** is a picture or imitation of a person's features or mannerisms exaggerated as to be comic or absurd. (See illustration on previous page.)

285 **Character** is a person in a story or poem.

286 **Characterization** is the method an author uses to reveal or describe his characters and their various personalities.

287 **Cliche** is a word or phrase which is so overused that it is no longer effective in most writing situations, as in "as busy as a bee" and "I slept like a log."

288 **Climax** is the high point or turning point in a work, usually the most intense point.

289 **Comedy** is literature dealing with the comic or the serious in life in a light, humorous, or satiric manner. In comedy, human errors or problems appear funny.

290 A **concrete** word refers to an object which can be heard, seen, felt, tasted, or smelled. *Wall, desk, car,* and *cow* are examples of concrete words. (See 275.)

291 **Conflict** is the "problem" in a story which triggers the action. There are five basic types of conflict:

> *Man vs. Man:* One character in a story has a problem with one or more of the other characters.
> *Man vs. Society:* A character has a conflict or problem with some element of society — the school, the law, the accepted way of doing things, and so on.
> *Man vs. Himself:* A character has trouble deciding what to do in a particular situation.
> *Man vs. Nature:* A character has a problem with some natural happening: a snowstorm, an avalanche, the bitter cold, or any of the other elements common to nature.
> *Man vs. Fate* (God): A character has to battle what seems to be an uncontrollable problem. Whenever the problem seems to be a strange or unbelievable coincidence, fate can be considered as the cause of the conflict.

292 **Connotation** is all the emotions or feelings a word can arouse, such as the negative or bad feeling associated with the word *pig* or the positive or good feeling associated with the word *love.*

293 **Context** is the environment of a word; that is, the words, sentences, and paragraphs which surround a particular word and help to determine or deepen its meaning.

294 **Denotation** is the literal or dictionary meaning of a word. (See *Connotation.*)

295 **Denouement** is the final solution or outcome of a play or story.

296 **Description** is a type of writing which emphasizes the characteristics or qualities of a person, place, or thing in an attempt to create a clear word picture.

297 **Dialogue** is the conversation carried on by the characters in a literary work.

298 **Diction** is an author's choice of words based on their correctness, clearness, or effectiveness.

> **Archaic** words are those which are old-fashioned and no longer sound natural when used, as *"I believe thee not"* for *"I don't believe you."*
>
> **Colloquialism** is an expression which is usually accepted in informal writing or speaking but not in a formal situation, as in *"Hey, man, what's happenin'?"*
>
> **Jargon** (technical diction) is the specialized language used by a specific group as with those who use computers: *override, interface, download.*
>
> **Profanity** is language which shows disrespect for someone or something which is regarded as holy or sacred.
>
> **Slang** is the language used by a particular group of people among themselves;

it is also language which is used in fiction and special writing situations to lend color and feeling: *awesome, rad,* and *narly.*

Trite expressions are those which lack depth or originality, or are overworked or not worth mentioning in the first place.

Vulgarity is language which is generally considered common, crude, gross, and, at times, offensive. It is sometimes used in fiction to enhance the realism of a work.

299 A **didactic** literary work has as its main purpose to present a moral or religious statement. It can also be, as in the case of Dante's *Divine Comedy* and Milton's *Paradise Lost,* a work which stands on its own as valuable literature.

300 **Drama** is the form of literature known as *plays;* but drama also refers to the type of serious play that is often concerned with the leading character's relationship to society rather than with some tragic flaw within his personality.

301 **Dramatic monologue** is a poem in which a simple character speaks either to himself or to another character who is not present in a way which reveals much about that character.

302 **Empathy** is putting yourself in someone else's place and imagining how that person must feel. The phrase "What would you do if you were in my shoes?" is a request for one person to empathize with another.

303 **Epic** is a long narrative poem which tells of the deeds and adventures of a hero.

304 **Epigram** is a brief, witty poem or saying often dealing with its subject in a satirical manner: "There never was a good war or a bad peace" (Ben Franklin).

305 **Epitaph** is a short poem or verse written in memory of someone.

306 **Epithet** is a word or phrase used in place of a person's name; it is characteristic of that person: *Alexander the Great, Hammerin' Hank,* and *Mr. Nice Guy.*

307 **Essay** is a piece of prose which expresses an individual's point of view; usually, it is a series of closely related paragraphs which combine to make a complete piece of writing.

308 **Exaggeration** *(hyperbole)* is overstating or stretching the truth for literary effect: "My shoes are killing me."

309 **Exposition** is writing which is intended to make clear or explain something which might otherwise be difficult to understand; in a play or novel, it would be that portion which helps the reader to understand the background or situation in which the work is set.

310 **Falling action** is the action of a play or story which works out the decision arrived at during the climax. It ends with the resolution.

311 **Farce** is literature which has one purpose: to make the audience laugh.

312 **Figurative language** is language which cannot be taken literally since it was written to create a special effect or feeling.

313 # Figure of speech is a literary device used to create a special meaning through emotional and connotative use of words. The most common types are *antithesis, apostrophe, hyperbole, litotes, metaphor, metonymy, personification, simile, symbol, synecdoche,* and *understatement* (371).

Antithesis is an opposing or contrast of ideas: "Ask not what your country can do for you. Ask what you can do for your country" (President John F. Kennedy).

Apostrophe is a poetic device in which the poet talks to an absent person, place, or thing as if it were present: "O Captain! My Captain! Our fearful trip is done" (Walt Whitman addressing the deceased Abraham Lincoln).

Hyperbole (hi-pur´ba-li) is an exaggeration or overstatement: "My dad had a bird when he saw my grades."

Litotes (li´ta-tez) is a form of understatement in which something is expressed by the negation of the contrary: "He was a man *of no small means*" (meaning *of considerable means*).

Metaphor is a comparing of two unlike things in which no words of comparison *(like* or *as)* are used: "That new kid in our class is really a squirrel."

Metonymy (ma-tonʹa-mi) is the substituting of one word for another which is closely related to it: "The *White House* has decided to provide a million more public service jobs." (*White House* is substituting for *president.*)

Personification is a literary device in which the author elevates an animal, object, or idea to the level of a human such that it takes on the characteristics of a human personality: "The rock stubbornly refused to move."

Simile is a comparison of two unlike things in which a word of comparison *(like* or *as)* is used: "Mr. Kosinski's eyes are like charging bulls when he's mad."

Symbol is a concrete object used to represent an idea. A black object usually symbolizes death or sorrow.

Synecdoche (si-nekʹ da-ki) is using part of something to represent the whole: *"All hands* on deck." (*Hands* is being used to represent the whole person.)

314 **Flashback** is returning to an earlier time in a story for the purpose of making something in the present more clear.

315 **Foreshadowing** is a suggestion of what is to come later in the work by giving hints and clues.

316 **Form** is the way a work is organized or designed; it is the structure or frame into which the story is written.

317 **Genre** is a French word often used as a synonym for *form* or *type* when referring to literature. The novel, essay, and poem are three of the many genres or forms of literature.

318 **Gothic novel** is a type of fiction which is usually characterized by gloomy castles, ghosts, and supernatural or sensational happenings—all of which is supposed to create a mysterious, chilling, and sometimes frightening story. Mary Shelley's *Frankenstein* as well as several works by Edgar Allen Poe are probably the best known gothic works still popular today.

319 **Imagery** is used to describe the words or phrases which bring forth a certain picture or image in the mind of the reader.

320 **Impressionism** is the recording of events or situations as they have been impressed upon the mind. Impressionism deals with vague thoughts and remembrances; realism, with objective facts. In "A Child's Christmas in Wales," Dylan Thomas remembers his winters in Wales as they impressed him as a boy:

> ". . . we waited to snowball the cats. Sleek and long as jaguars and horrible-whiskered, spitting and snarling, they would slink and sidle over the white back-garden walls, and the lynx-eyed hunters, Jim and I, fur-capped and moccasined trappers from Hudson Bay, off Mumbles Road, would hurl our deadly snowballs at the green of their eyes. The wise cats never appeared."

321 **Irony** is using a word or phrase to mean the exact opposite of its literal or normal meaning. There are three kinds of irony:

> **dramatic irony,** wherein the reader or the audience sees a character's mistakes or misunderstandings which the character is unable to see himself.
> **verbal irony,** in which the writer says one thing and means another.
> **irony of situation,** in which there is a great difference between the purpose of a particular action and the result.

322 **Limerick** is a light, humorous verse of five lines with an *aabba* rhyme scheme:

> There was a young lady from Maine,
> Who was as thin as a cane;
> When her bathing was done
> And the water did run,
> She slid through the hole in the drain.

323 **Local color** is the use of details which are common in a certain region or section of the country.

324 **Malapropism** is the type of pun or play on words which results when two words become jumbled in the speaker's mind. The term comes from a character in Sheridan's comedy, *The Rivals.* The character, Mrs. Malaprop, is constantly mixing up her words, as when she says "as headstrong as an *allegory* [she means *alligator*] on the banks of the Nile." Both words fit in the sentence, which is precisely what makes a malapropism a pun rather than a simple mistake.

325 **Melodrama** is an exaggerated, sensational form of drama which is intended to appeal to the emotions of the audience, as with many of the television soap operas.

326 **Mood** is the feeling a piece of literature arouses in the reader: happy, sad, peaceful, etc.

327 **Moral** is the particular value or lesson the author is trying to get across to the reader. The "moral of the story" is an especially popular phrase in Aesop's fables and other children's literature.

328 **Motif** is a term for an often-repeated character, incident, or idea in literature. The hero's saving a damsel in distress is a common *motif* of American melodrama.

329 **Myth** is a traditional story which attempts to explain or justify a certain practice, belief, or natural phenomenon of a people.

330 **Narration** is the type of writing which relates an event or series of events: a story. **Narrator** is the person who is telling the story.

331 **Naturalism** is an extreme form of realism in which the author tries to show the relation of man to his environment. Often, the author finds it necessary to show the base or ugly side of that relationship.

332 **Novel** is a term which covers a wide range of prose materials which have two common characteristics: they are fictional and lengthy.

333 **Oxymoron** is a combination of contradictory terms as in *cruel kindness.*

334 **Parable** is a short, descriptive story which illustrates a particular belief or moral.

335 Paradox is a statement that is seemingly contrary to common sense yet is, in fact, true; a self-contradictory statement: "The coach considered this a good loss."

336 Parallelism is the repeating of phrases or sentences that are similar (parallel) in meaning and structure, as with "of the people, by the people, and for the people."

337 Parody is a literary form which is intended to mock a particular literary work or its style; a *burlesque* or comic effect is created.

338 Pathos is a Greek root meaning *suffering* or *passion*. It is usually applied to the part in a play or story which is intended to bring out pity or sorrow from the audience or reader.

339 Plagiarism is using someone else's writing or ideas and trying to pass them off as your own.

340 Plot is the action in a story. It is usually a series of related incidents which builds and grows as the story develops. There are five basic parts or elements in a plot which make up a *plot line.*

341 Plot line is the graphic representation of the action or events in a story: *exposition, rising action, climax, falling action, resolution.*

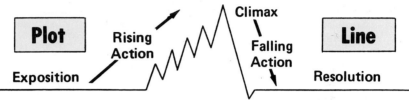

342 Poetic justice is a term which describes a character "getting what he deserves" in the end, especially if what he deserves is punishment. The purest form of poetic justice is when one character plots against another but ends up being caught in his own evil trap.

343 Poetry is language which reflects imagination, emotion, and thinking in verse form. There are many elements used in writing effective poetry:

> **Alliteration** is the repetition of initial consonant sounds in neighboring words as in "rough and ready." Many poetic examples of alliteration can be found in today's songs: " . . . though the *tangled trails* of *time* have led us far astray, the memory seems to stay" (from "Lonely People," Harry Chapin).
>
> **Assonance** is the repetition of vowel sounds without the repetition of consonants as in "...my words like silent raindrops fell..." (from "Sounds of Silence," Paul Simon).
>
> **Ballad** is a poem which tells a story and usually rhymes every other line.
>
> **Blank verse** is an unrhymed form of poetry which normally consists of ten syllables in which every other syllable, beginning with the second, is stressed. Since blank verse is often used in very long poems, such as Frost's *Death of the Hired Man,* it may depart from the strict pattern from time to time to avoid monotony.
>
> **Canto** is a division of a long poem.
>
> **Caesura** is a pause or sudden break in a line of poetry.
>
> **Cinquain** is a form of poetry, invented by Adelaide Crapsey, with lines of 2, 4, 6, 8, and 2 syllables. Another form of cinquain is word cinquain with lines of 1, 2, 3, 4, and 1 word.

Syllable Cinquain

Line 1:	Title	2 syllables
Line 2:	Description of title	4 syllables
Line 3:	Action about the title	6 syllables
Line 4:	Feeling about the title	8 syllables
Line 5:	Synonym for title	2 syllables

Word Cinquain

Line 1:	Title	**1 word**
Line 2:	Description of title	**2 words**
Line 3:	Action about the title	**3 words**
Line 4:	Feeling about the title	**4 words**
Line 5:	Synonym for title	**1 word**

Closed couplet (See "Stanza.")

Consonance is the repetition of consonant sounds, especially in poetry. Consonance is similar to alliteration except that it is not limited to the first letter of each word as is alliteration: "...and high school girls with clear skin smiles..." (from "At Seventeen," Janis Ian).

Elegy is a formal poem mourning the death of a certain individual.

End rhyme is the rhyming of words which appear at the ends of two or more lines of poetry.

Enjambment is the running over of a sentence or thought from one verse or line to another.

Foot is a unit of meter which denotes the combination of stressed and unstressed syllables. (See "Verse.")

Iambic: an unstressed followed by a stressed syllable (repeat)
Anapestic: two unstressed followed by a stressed syllable (interrupt)
Trochaic: a stressed followed by an unstressed syllable (older)
Dactylic: a stressed followed by two unstressed syllables (openly)
Spondaic: two stressed syllables (heartbreak)
Pyrrhic: two unstressed syllables (Pyrrhic is very rare and seldom appears by itself.)

Free verse is poetry that does not have a regular meter or rhyme scheme: Edgar Lee Master's *Silence* is written in free verse.

Haiku is a form of Japanese poetry which has three lines; the first line has five syllables, the second has seven syllables, and the third has five syllables. The subject of the haiku has traditionally been nature as in:

> **Behind me the moon**
> **Brushes shadows of pine trees**
> **Lightly on the floor.**

Heroic couplet *(closed couplet)* consists of two successive rhyming lines which contain a complete thought. It is usually written in iambic pentameter.

Internal rhyme occurs when the rhyming words appear in the same line of poetry: "We'll drink a *toast* to those who *most* believe in what they've won" (from "Tea and Sympathy," Janis Ian).

Lyric is a short verse which is intended to express the emotions of the author; quite often these lyrics are set to music.

Meter is the repetition of stressed and unstressed syllables in a line of poetry. (See "Foot.")

Ode is a lyric poem written to someone or something. It is serious and elevated in tone. Allen Tate's "Ode to the Confederate Dead" is a eulogy (words of high praise) written for the Southern soldiers after the Civil War.

Onomatopoeia is the use of a word whose sound suggests its meaning, as in *clang, buzz,* and *twang.*

Paradox is a statement which at first seems contradictory but which turns out to have a profound meaning as in Bob Dylan's lyric: "I was so much older then; I'm younger than that now."

Pastoral is a poem or dramatic work which was originally characterized by an ideal look at shepherd and rustic life. The term has since been extended to include any work which deals with the subject of rural life.

Psalm is a sacred or religious song or lyric.

Refrain is the repetition of a line or phrase of a poem at regular intervals, especially at the end of each stanza. The refrain in a song is called the *chorus*.

Repetition is the repeating of a word or phrase within a poem or prose piece to create a sense of rhythm: "But I sometimes think the difference is just in how I think and feel, and that the only changes *going on* are *going on* in me" (from "Changes," Harry Chapin).

Rhyme is the similarity or likeness of sound existing between two words. *Sat* and *cat* are perfect rhymes because the vowel and final consonant sounds are exactly the same.

Rhymed verse is verse with end rhyme; it usually has regular meter.

Rhythm is the ordered or free occurrences of sound in poetry. Regular rhythm which recurs is called meter. Free occurrence of sound is called free verse.

Scansion is the analysis of verse to show its meter.

Stanza is a division of poetry named for the number of lines it contains:

Couplet:	two-line stanza	**Sestet:**	six-line stanza
Triplet:	three-line stanza	**Septet:**	seven-line stanza
Quatrain:	four-line stanza	**Octave:**	eight-line stanza
Quintet:	five-line stanza		

(Note: All others are called nine-, ten-, eleven-, and so on, line stanzas.)

Verse is a metric line of poetry. It is named according to the kind and number of feet composing it: *iambic pentameter, anapestic tetrameter . . . . (See "Foot.")*

Monometer:	one foot	**Pentameter:**	five feet
Dimeter:	two feet	**Hexameter:**	six feet
Trimeter:	three feet	**Heptameter:**	seven feet
Tetrameter:	four feet	**Octometer:**	eight feet

Verse is usually found in one of three forms: *rhymed, blank,* or *free verse.*

344 **Point of view** is the vantage point from which the story is told. In the **first-person** point of view, the story is told by one of the characters: *"I'm not reading that stupid book."* In the **third-person** point of view, the story is told by someone outside the story: *"He felt justified in refusing to read. After all, he couldn't read that book—it was too hard."* There are three basic **third-person points of view.** (See next page.)

345 **Protagonist** is the main character or hero of the story.

346 **Pseudonym** means *false name* and is usually applied to the name writers use in place of their natural name. Mark Twain, which is probably the most famous pseudonym in literature, was assumed by the Hannibal, Missouri, writer Samuel Langhorne Clemens.

347 **Pun** is a word or phrase which is used in such a way as to suggest more than one possible meaning. Words used in the pun are words that sound the same (or nearly the same) but have different meanings: "I really don't mind going to school; it's the *principal (principle)* of the thing."

348 **Realism** is literature which attempts to represent life as it really is by paying close attention to what otherwise might be considered insignificant details.

349 **Renaissance,** which means *rebirth,* is the period of history following the Middle Ages. This period began late in the fourteenth century and continued through the fifteenth and sixteenth centuries. Milton (1608-1674) is often regarded as the last of the great Renaissance poets. The term now applies to any period of time in which intellectual and artistic interest is revived or reborn.

Omniscient is a viewpoint which allows the narrator to relate the thoughts and feelings of all the characters; a *godlike* intuition.

Limited omniscient allows the narrator to relate the thoughts and feelings of only one character.

Camera view (Objective view) is seeing and recording the action from a neutral or unemotional point of view.

350 **Resolution** is the portion of the play or story where the problem is solved. It comes after the climax and falling action and is intended to bring the story to a satisfactory end; *denouement*.

351 **Rising action** is the series of conflicts which build a play toward a climax.

352 **Romance** is a form of literature which presents life as we would like it to be rather than as it actually is. Usually, it has a great deal of adventure, love, and excitement.

353 **Romanticism** is a literary movement with an emphasis on the imagination and emotions.

354 **Sarcasm** is the use of praise to mock someone or something, as in "He's a real *he-man*," or "She's a real *winner*."

355 **Satire** is a literary tone used to ridicule or make fun of human vice or weakness.

356 **Setting** is the time and place in which the action of a literary work occurs.

357 **Slapstick** is a form of low comedy which makes its appeal through the use of violent and exaggerated action. The "pie in the face" routine is a classic piece of *slapstick* as are the Charlie Chaplin and Mack Sennett films.

358 **Slice of life** is a term which describes the type of realistic or naturalistic writing which accurately reflects what life is really like. This is done by giving the reader a sample or *slice* of life.

359 **Soliloquy** is a speech delivered by a character when he is alone on stage.

360 **Sonnet** is a poem which usually consists of fourteen lines of iambic pentameter. There are two popular forms of the sonnet, the Italian (or Petrarchan) and the Shakespearean (or English).

> **Italian (Petrarchan)** sonnet has two parts: an octave of eight lines and a sestet of six lines, and usually rhyming *abbaabba, cdecde*. Often a question is raised in the octave and answered in the sestet.

> **Shakespearean (English** or **Elizabethan)** sonnet consists of three quatrains and a final rhyming couplet. The rhyme scheme is *abab, cdcd, efef, gg*. Usually, the question or theme is set forth in the quatrains while the answer or resolution appears in the final couplet.

361 **Stereotype** is a pattern or form which does not change. A character is "stereotyped" if he has no individuality and fits the mold of that particular kind of person. For many years, Blacks were stereotyped in literature as maids, butlers, shoe-shine boys, and other servant-type characters.

362 **Stream of consciousness** is a style of writing in which the thoughts and feelings of the writer are recorded as they occur.

363 **Structure** is the form or organization a writer uses for his literary work. There are a great number of possible forms or structures used regularly in literature: *parable, fable, romance, satire, farce, slapstick,* and so on.

364 **Style** is *how* the author writes (form) rather than *what* he writes (content).

365 **Theme** is the statement about life a particular work is trying to get across to the reader. In stories written for children, the theme is often spelled out clearly at the end when the author says, "...and so, the moral of the story is: Never tell your mother or father something that isn't true or they may not believe you when you tell the truth." In more complex literature, the theme may not be so moralistic in tone, or at least not so clearly spelled out.

366 **Tone** is the attitude of the author toward his audience and characters. This attitude may be *serious, mock-serious, humorous, satiric,* and so on.

367 **Total effect** is the final, overall impression left with the reader by a literary work.

368 **Tragedy** is a literary work in which the hero is destroyed by some flaw within his character and by forces which he cannot control.

369 **Tragic hero** is a character who experiences an inner struggle because of some flaw within his character. That struggle ends in the defeat of the hero.

370 **Transcendentalism** is a philosophy which requires that man go beyond (transcend) reason in his search for truth. Man can arrive at the basic truths of life through spiritual intuition or instinct if he takes the time to meditate or think seriously about it.

371 **Understatement** is the stating of an idea with considerable restraint or holding back so as to emphasize what is being talked about. Mark Twain once described Tom Sawyer's Aunt Polly as being "prejudiced against snakes." Since she could not stand snakes, this way of saying so is called *understatement*.

Writing LETTERS, MEMOS, and RESUMES

Today's workers find that most good jobs require a number of specific job-related skills. (If you are going to be a plumber, you have to know how to plumb.) No surprises here. But what may surprise you is that most good jobs also require a number of writing-related skills. In fact, sixty million people regularly have to write as part of their jobs. Therefore, if you plan to get and keep a good job, you will need to know how to write. If you plan to succeed in that job, you will need to know how to write well.

There is no doubt that writing will continue to be a very important skill in the business world, regardless of what new technology is used to type, copy, or transmit the product of that writing. Writing is thinking, and so far, people, not machines, must do the thinking.

410 The Advantages of a Written Message

1. Written language usually has more impact than spoken language, especially in the business world. It can be corrected and edited before it is sent.

2. A letter provides the writer with plenty of time to think about what he or she wants to say.

3. A letter communicates a very specific message. Too often a phone conversation wanders from one topic to another and people can be left with several impressions of what was said.

4. A letter not only communicates a specific message, but it also provides the receiver with a copy of the message and the specific details of what action must be taken.

5. A letter is a written reminder to both parties of when and why the message was sent. This makes it more likely that the appropriate action will be taken and taken on time.

6. A letter can also serve as an official record of what was agreed upon by the two parties; for this reason, people in business often follow up a phone conversation with a letter so that they have a written record of what was discussed. Some businesses operate on the philosophy that if it isn't written down, it doesn't exist.

As you might imagine, business letters are written for "business" reasons: to make a request, to order materials, to file a complaint, to apply for a job, and so on. A business letter is usually concise and to the point. Preferably, it should fit on one page. Business documents also have a very businesslike appearance and follow a specific pattern of form, style, and spacing.

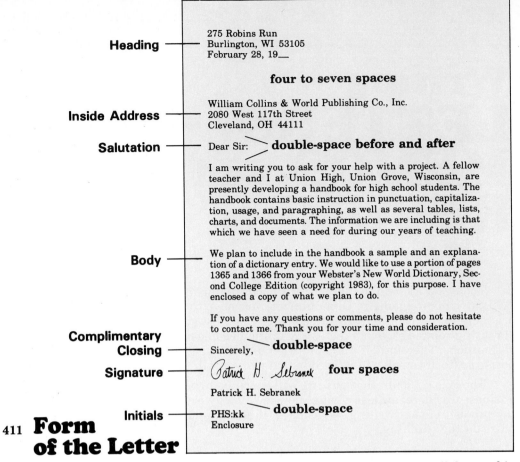

Heading

275 Robins Run
Burlington, WI 53105
February 28, 19___

four to seven spaces

Inside Address

William Collins & World Publishing Co., Inc.
2080 West 117th Street
Cleveland, OH 44111

Salutation

Dear Sir: **double-space before and after**

I am writing you to ask for your help with a project. A fellow
teacher and I at Union High, Union Grove, Wisconsin, are
presently developing a handbook for high school students. The
handbook contains basic instruction in punctuation, capitalization, usage, and paragraphing, as well as several tables, lists,
charts, and documents. The information we are including is that
which we have seen a need for during our years of teaching.

Body

We plan to include in the handbook a sample and an explanation of a dictionary entry. We would like to use a portion of pages
1365 and 1366 from your Webster's New World Dictionary, Second College Edition (copyright 1983), for this purpose. I have
enclosed a copy of what we plan to do.

If you have any questions or comments, please do not hesitate
to contact me. Thank you for your time and consideration.

Complimentary Closing

Sincerely, **double-space**

Signature

Patrick H. Sebranek **four spaces**

Patrick H. Sebranek

Initials

PHS:kk **double-space**
Enclosure

411 Form of the Letter

The **heading** for the business letter includes the complete address and full date and is
placed about an inch from the top of the page. (*Note:* If letterhead stationery is used,
only the date need be placed in the heading position. The date should be placed several
spaces below the letterhead.)

The **inside address** is placed on the left margin several (approximately four to seven)
line spaces below the heading. It should include the name and address of the person and/or
company the letter is being sent to. (*Note:* If the person you are writing to also has a
title with the company he represents, place that title after his name. Separate the two
with a comma. Place the title on the next line if it is two or more words long.)

The **salutation** is placed two spaces below and directly under the inside address. The
most common salutations when addressing a company or firm are *Gentlemen:, Dear Sirs:,*
or *Dear (Company Name).* If you are writing to an individual within that company, you
should address him or her *Dear Mr. . . . , Dear Miss . . . , Dear Ms. . . . , Dear President . . . .*

The **body** of the business letter is the same in form as the body of any letter. It should
be single-spaced (unless it is very short: seven lines or less) with a double-space between
paragraphs. If the body carries over to a second page, the name of the addressee should
be typed at the top left margin. Two line spaces should be placed after the name.

The **closing** comes between the body and the signature. The most commonly used clos-
ings for the business letter include *Very truly, Very truly yours, Yours truly, Sincerely
yours,* etc. *Respectfully yours* is often used when writing to an employer or government
official. In each case, the closing is followed by a comma.

The **signature** of a business letter should always include a handwritten signature of
the writer, followed by the typed name and title of the writer. If someone other than

the writer types the letter, it is customary to place the typist's initials after those of the writer against the left margin, two or three spaces below the typed signature. If an enclosure is sent with the letter, this fact should be made clear by placing the word *Enclosure(s)* or *Enc.* below the signature.

Styles of the Business Letter

Semi-Block   Block   Full Block

—Guidelines for Writing a Business Letter

412

1. A good business letter is written for a definite purpose; know what your purpose is and make it clear early in the letter. (It can be helpful to actually write this purpose out on a piece of paper and keep it in front of you as you write.)

2. Collect all the information you will need for your letter and jot down the basic order in which you plan to cover this information. Organize your material in the most natural or most persuasive order.

3. Keep your reader in mind as you write, and select a tone for your letter which is appropriate for the reader and the "business" you are writing about. Your tone might be friendly, but firm; tactful, but insistent; etc. Whatever the tone, however, you must always be courteous. Use positive rather than negative words.

4. Use a writing style which is natural and easy to read; business letters need not be boring or complicated. Avoid the use of words and phrases which are stiff, technical, or overused. (See the "Expressions to Avoid in Business Writing," 417.)

5. Read your first draft out loud to test it for overall "sound" and effectiveness. Be sure your letter states clearly what it is you want your reader to do after he or she reads your letter. List only as many of the specific details as your reader needs to know. End your letter with a pleasant statement and a reminder of what action you hope your reader will take.

6. Follow the correct form for the kind of letter you are writing and use that form throughout your letter. For example, if you indent one paragraph, indent them all. If you place the heading along the left margin, place the closing there as well.

7. Make sure your final copy is typed or written (in ink) neatly and is attractive in appearance. Change typewriter ribbons if yours is light or inconsistent. Use a good quality paper whenever possible, and erase or cover your errors completely.

8. Revise and proofread your letter the same way you would any other piece of writing. Look for errors in sentence structure, usage, punctuation, spelling, capitalization, etc. (Use a proofreading checklist.)

9. Fold your letter following the method used with a standard-sized (4¼" x 9½") business envelope.

10. Address the envelope carefully, using either the traditional system of upper and lowercase letters or the new postal system of all capital letters and no punctuation.

413 **Folding the Letter**

The *preferred* method for folding a letter is used with a standard-sized (4¼" x 9½") business envelope.

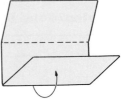

1. Begin by folding the bottom edge of the letter so that the paper is divided into thirds.

2. Next, fold the top third of the letter down and crease the edges firmly.

3. Finally, insert the letter into the envelope with the open end at the top.

A second method of folding is used when your envelope is smaller than the traditional business envelope.

1. Begin by folding the letter in half.

2. Next, fold the letter into thirds.

3. Insert the letter into the envelope.

414 **Addressing the Business Envelope**

Addressing your letter correctly can be critical to the promptness of its delivery. The destination address on the envelope must be exactly the same as the inside address on the letter, and the return address must match the heading. The destination address begins in the center of the envelope, and the return address is placed in the upper left-hand corner.

There are two acceptable formats for business addresses. In the older, traditional system, both upper and lowercase letters are used, as are punctuation and abbreviations. The newer system is preferred by the postal system. Their bulletins state: "You will get the best possible service if you remember these four important steps in addressing your letters:

1. Capitalize everything in the address.

2. Use the list of common abbreviations found in the National ZIP Code Directory. (See 706.)

3. Eliminate all punctuation.

4. Use the special state (two-letter) abbreviations found in the ZIP Directory." (See 706.)

Old System	Ms. Sarah Johnson 719 State Street Boston, MA 02101	**New System**	MS SARAH JOHNSON 719 STATE STREET BOSTON MA 02101

415 **Alternate Forms of Addresses**

There are various combinations for addresses. Here are some examples:

MISS TRISH DATON BOX 77 HOUSTON TX 77008	NORTHERN CORP ATTN D J HENKHAUR XYZ CORP RM 4A MAJOR INDUSTRIAL PARK CLEVELAND OH 44135	MR TEDDY BARE PRESIDENT ACME TOY COMPANY 4421 RANDOLPH ST CHEYENNE WY 82001
	ACCOUNTING DEPT STEVENSON LTD BLDG 18 2632 FOURTH ST DULUTH MN 55803	MS JOAN JACKSON 261 MASON ST APT 44 TORONTO ONTARIO CANADA

Note: There are some instances when both the post office box number and a street address may be used. The important thing to remember is that the mail will be delivered to the line immediately above the bottom line, once it reaches the correct city and ZIP area. For example:

	LAKE GINEVRA INN		LAKE GINEVRA INN
Mail will be	444 LAWN DRIVE	Mail will be	PO BOX 20
delivered here:	PO BOX 20	delivered here:	444 LAWN DRIVE
	PORTLAND OR 92713		PORTLAND OR 92713

416   The Letter of Complaint

A letter of complaint should be written following the same guidelines as any other business letter. In addition, it is very important to include all the essential information surrounding the complaint so that the appropriate action can be taken by the reader.

1. Begin your letter with a brief description of the **product** (or service), including the brand name, model number, and where and when you bought the product.

2. Also include a description of just what the **problem** is, when you first noticed it, and what you think may be the **cause** of the problem.

3. If you have already tried to resolve the problem, explain what you did and what the result of that **action** was. Include the names of those people you talked to about the problem.

4. Finally, suggest what action you would like the reader to take to **solve** the problem.

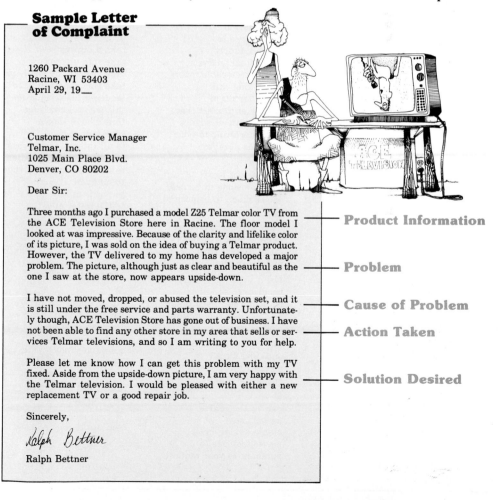

Sample Letter of Complaint

1260 Packard Avenue
Racine, WI 53403
April 29, 19__

Customer Service Manager
Telmar, Inc.
1025 Main Place Blvd.
Denver, CO 80202

Dear Sir:

Three months ago I purchased a model Z25 Telmar color TV from the ACE Television Store here in Racine. The floor model I looked at was impressive. Because of the clarity and lifelike color of its picture, I was sold on the idea of buying a Telmar product. However, the TV delivered to my home has developed a major problem. The picture, although just as clear and beautiful as the one I saw at the store, now appears upside-down.   — **Product Information** / — **Problem**

I have not moved, dropped, or abused the television set, and it is still under the free service and parts warranty. Unfortunately though, ACE Television Store has gone out of business. I have not been able to find any other store in my area that sells or services Telmar televisions, and so I am writing to you for help.   — **Cause of Problem** / — **Action Taken**

Please let me know how I can get this problem with my TV fixed. Aside from the upside-down picture, I am very happy with the Telmar television. I would be pleased with either a new replacement TV or a good repair job.   — **Solution Desired**

Sincerely,

Ralph Bettner

Ralph Bettner

A
above-mentioned
accidents will happen
acid test
a factor in the problem
after all is said and done
all boils down to
all in all
all things being equal
all things considered
along this line
a matter of concern
and/or
are in receipt of
as a last resort
as a matter of fact
as per
at an early date
attached hereto
at the present writing
at this point in time
at your earliest convenience

B
bear in mind
belabor the point
benefit of the doubt
best foot forward
be that as it may
better late than never
beyond the shadow of a doubt
bit off more than I can chew
break the ice
bring the matter up
burning my candle at both ends
by and large
by leaps and bounds
by no means
by the same token

C
calm before the storm
cart before the horse
come through with flying colors
conspicuous by its absence
constructive criticism

D
days on end
don't rock the boat

E
earliest possible moment
easier said than done
enclosed herewith
enclosed please find
explore every avenue

F
face the fact

fall down on the job
far be it from me
far-reaching effects
few and far between
fill the bill
food for thought
for your information

G
get down to brass tacks
get down to business

H
have on good authority
heart of the matter
honesty is the best policy

I
I beg to remain
I beg to stay
I'd like to share
if and when
in conclusion
in reference to
in short supply
in the final analysis
in the foreseeable future
in the long run
in the matter of
in view of the fact that
it goes without saying
it is interesting to note
it stands to reason

L
last but not least
leave no stone unturned
leaves much to be desired

M
make a concerted effort
make a long story short
make contact with
map out a plan

N
needless to say
no action has been taken
no time like the present
now or never

O
once and for all
on the right track
out of the blue

P
par for the course
permit me
please advise me
please feel free to
pursuant to your request

Q
quick as a flash

R
rank and file
red-letter day
regarding the matter of
rest assured

S
sadder but wiser
see eye-to-eye
sell like hotcakes
sharp as a tack
shift into high gear
shot in the arm
slowly but surely
so richly deserved
status quo
stitch in time saves nine
straight and narrow path
strike while the iron is hot

T
take a dim view
take into account
take the bull by the horns
take this opportunity to
tendered his resignation
this will acknowledge
thus I have shown
time is money
to all intents and purposes
token of our appreciation
to make a long story short
to no avail
to put it mildly
to the bitter end
tried and true

U
unaccustomed as I am

V
venture to predict

W
water under the bridge
we are pleased to advise
we wish to state
with reference to
words are inadequate
words cannot describe
words cannot express
words fail to express
word to the wise

Y
you are hereby advised

Form and Appearance

☐ 1. The letter is neatly written in ink or typed with no smudges or obvious corrections.

☐ 2. The letter contains all necessary parts of a business letter.

☐ 3. The letter is centered on the page, with spacing equal above and below and on left and right. Correct spacing is also necessary between parts of the letter. (See sample letter, 411.)

☐ 4. All left-hand margins are exactly even.

☐ 5. The right-hand margin of the body of the letter is fairly even.

☐ 6. The signature is legible and written in blue or black ink.

Punctuation

☐ 1. A comma always separates the city and state. There is no comma between the state and ZIP code.

☐ 2. A comma separates the day of the month from the year in the heading.

☐ 3. A colon is used after the salutation.

☐ 4. A comma is used after the closing.

Capitalization

☐ 1. The names of streets, cities, and people in the heading, inside address, or body are capitalized.

☐ 2. The month in the heading is capitalized.

☐ 3. The title of the person you are writing to and the name of the department and company listed in the inside address are capitalized.

☐ 4. The word *Dear* and all nouns in the salutation are capitalized.

☐ 5. Only the first word of the closing is capitalized.

Spelling

☐ 1. The numbered street names up to ten are spelled out. Figures are used for numbers above ten.

☐ 2. The names of cities, streets, and months in the heading and inside address are spelled out. The state may be abbreviated, but make sure it is abbreviated correctly.

Wording

☐ 1. Avoid using words and expressions which are phony, vague, or sexist.

Avoid these expressions .... **Use these instead**

ceased functioning	quit working
excessive amount	too many
furthermore	then, also
likewise	and, also
numerous	many
subsequent	next
chairwoman	chair, moderator
foreman	supervisor
mailman	letter carrier
salesman	sales representative
manpower	work force

Writing In-House Messages

Memos, bulletins, and short reports which are well written make good impressions on co-workers and bosses. This fact alone is reason enough to learn how to write them well. Below are several basic guidelines to follow when writing in-house papers.

*State the purpose in the first sentence.
*Include the date and time.
*Be specific.
*Write neatly and clearly.
*Use only those abbreviations that are clearly understood.
*Arrange information in the order that will be most useful to the reader.

Writing Memorandums

A standard form is used within many organizations for writing longer messages, including memorandums, bulletins, and short reports. It is usually written to a number of people, not just one. It can be used to help organize a meeting, to report on the meeting, or to circulate useful information about the meeting. This form might be circulated to specific people (*memorandum*), or it could be posted for all interested parties to see (*bulletin*).

INTER-TECH, INC.

Memorandum   **Date:** October 21, 19___

To: Secretarial Staff

From: Jane Brand, Personnel Director

Subject: Career Advancement Program

This month's meeting will be held next Thursday at 8:00 p.m. It will feature Dr. G.F. Gillis, a professor at City Technical College. He will speak on moving up the career ladder, a topic which I'm sure interests all of us. He is planning a winter term training program which will feature all facets of office administration and communication. Sign up with me if you plan to attend.

BULLETIN

To: All Sales People   **Subject:** Inventory

To keep our inventory information up to date, please indicate the type of record or tape sold on each sales slip. Choose one of the following categories:

Popular	--P	Folk	--F
Classical	--C	Rock	--R
Jazz	--J		

Use the first letter of each category and put it next to the price on the sales slip.

Signed: _Hill U. Tally_

Writing Messages

420

On-the-job skills often include writing short but important messages to fellow employees. In many cases, standardized forms are used throughout an office or business. However, if no standardized form is available, you can use the 5 W's as a guideline of what to include.

Who - Who is the message for?
Who is the message from?
Who is writing the message?

What - What is the message? (Be brief but complete)

When - When was the message written? (Date and time)
When is the meeting, appointment, etc. mentioned in the message?

Where - Where is the receiver of the message to go?

Why - Why is there a need for a meeting, appointment, etc.?

Note: When writing down any message (telephone or personal), be sure to get all the facts correctly. Accuracy and clarity are essential. Telephone numbers must include area codes; names must be spelled correctly. Ask the caller to clarify any information which you are unsure of. Each good message you write will help establish your reputation as an efficient, dependable worker.

421 **Using A Standard Message Form**

Message When No Form Is Used

MESSAGE

To: *Mr. Smith* Date: *Sept. 5, 1984* Time: *10:00 a.m.*

From: *Elinor Stacey of the Daily Press*

Telephone:

☐ Telephoned: ☐ Please call
☐ Called to see you   ☐ Will call again
☑ Returned your call   ☐ URGENT

Message: *There will be no problem in rescheduling your interview. She will meet you at the dump site on Thursday, Sept. 14, at 9:00 a.m.*

By: *Stan Killberg*

Mr. Smith, you received a call from Elinor Stacey of the Daily Press at 10:00 a.m. today (Sept. 5, 1984). She said there would be no problem in rescheduling your interview. She will meet you at the dump site on Thursday, Sept. 14, at 9:00 a.m.

Stan Killberg

The Letter of Application and Résumé

422   In the very near future and several times throughout your lifetime, you will be applying for a job. Some authorities estimate that a worker entering the work force in the next several years will change jobs an average of six times in his or her lifetime. The competition for good jobs is bound to increase as the job market changes. Those workers who know how to go about applying for a job will be at a distinct advantage. One very important part of applying for and landing a job is the letter of application and personal résumé.

Your **letter of application** is your introduction, your calling card. It creates that all-important first impression and usually determines whether or not you will be considered and interviewed for the job. The effectiveness of your letter will depend in large part on how well you tell your own story — how well you communicate your qualifications for the job and what it is you can contribute to the employer. There are two types of job application letters: the cover letter, which is sent with a résumé, and the independent letter of application, which contains much of the information normally contained in a résumé.

A **résumé** is an organized summary of the job applicant's background and qualifications. It lists the applicant's education, work experience, talents, skills, etc. It should be a vivid word picture of the person applying for the job. It must be organized in such a way that the prospective employer can see at a glance whether the applicant has the necessary background for the job.

The content and format of résumés may vary slightly, but generally all résumés contain the following information:

Personal data	Employment objective
Educational background	Work experience
Special skills or knowledge	Other experience (military, clubs
Accomplishments	and organizations, volunteer
References (on a separate sheet)	work, etc.)

When you use a résumé to apply for a job, you also need a short **cover letter**. The cover letter should not simply repeat information given in the résumé; instead, it should begin by identifying the job for which you are applying and telling how you heard about it. You can then add any other information not included in the résumé which might be important for this particular job. Finally, request an interview; include your phone number and when you can be reached.

On the pages which follow you will find samples of a **cover letter**, a **résumé**, an **independent letter of application**, and a **follow-up letter**.

——Guidelines for Writing a Cover Letter——

423   **Do. . .**

1. Address the letter to a specific individual whenever possible.
2. Develop a bridge between yourself and employer at the very beginning — tell how you learned of the vacancy.
3. Give a brief statement emphasizing your qualifications for this position.
4. Use words directly from the job ad to describe what you can do.
5. Emphasize what you can do for an employer rather than what he can do for you.
6. Highlight parts of the enclosed résumé which specifically pertain to the job offered.
7. Indicate the dates you are available for interviewing.
8. Show enthusiasm throughout your letter.
9. Sign each letter.
10. Follow up the mailing with a telephone call.

Don't . . .

1. Don't use awkward salutations as, "To Whom It May Concern" or "Dear Sir or Madam."

2. Don't begin each sentence or paragraph with "I."

3. Don't fill the page; stick to three or four short paragraphs.

4. Don't use cliches or overused expressions.

5. Don't change from one style to another in the same letter. Stick to either block or semi-block.

6. Don't send out duplicated letters.

Guidelines for Writing a Résumé

424   **Do . . .**

1. Put your name (in caps), address, and phone number (and when you are available at that number) at the top of your résumé.

2. List your career aims and objectives. This allows you an opportunity to express enthusiasm for the job as well as to list your general qualifications for the job.

3. Include information about your educational background.

4. Be specific when describing your achievements — use numbers and figures (. . . graduated in top five percent, . . . maintained a *B* average, . . . missed only one day of school, . . . supervised seven other workers).

5. List your work experience. Include positions held, names of employers, specific duties, and dates you held each position.

6. Include information about related experiences. List volunteer work, club duties, family responsibilities, and any other experience or activities which reflect positively on your ability to work in a responsible, dependable manner.

7. Keep the résumé as brief as possible. Cover all the essential information clearly and concisely; try to limit your résumé to one typed page (never more than two pages).

8. Arrange the information within the résumé in order of the most impressive or most important to the job for which you are applying.

9. Proofread carefully for spelling, punctuation, and typographical errors.

10. Experiment with the layout of the résumé for overall appearance and readability.

11. Get someone else's reaction before typing the final copy.

12. Use only typed originals (or high-quality photocopies or offset printed copies).

13. Be timely in responding to ads.

Don't . . .

1. Don't emphasize what you want in a job; stress how you fit into the employer's needs.

2. Don't use the same résumé for every job application — custom design each résumé to fit that particular job.

3. Don't list personal statistics such as your weight, height, and age.

4. Don't use "big" words or long, complicated sentences.

5. Don't use unfamiliar abbreviations or unnecessary jargon.

6. Don't include information about salaries or wages.

7. Don't include references on the same sheet as the résumé. (Have them available on a separate sheet in case the employer requests them.)

8. Don't include strictly personal references such as a neighbor or friend.

5340 Tower Avenue
Bolton, MA 01437
September 29, 1989

Mr. David Schroeder
Schroeder Chevrolet and Pontiac
1320 Highland Avenue
Bolton, MA 01437

Dear Mr. Schroeder:

Mrs. Burton, your office manager, mentioned that you are
in need of an auto mechanic in your shop. The enclosed
résumé will show you that automotive repair has been my
occupation and my recreation.

A successful dealership like yours depends on reputation. I
have had good customer relations all the time I worked at
Frank's Texaco. My stock car experience has made me
familiar with a variety of parts and engines.

May I call you after 2:30 p.m. on Thursday, October 3, to set
up a time and date for an interview? If this is not a convenient time, please call me any day after 2:30 at 848-7653.
I look forward to meeting you.

Thank you for your consideration.

Sincerely,

Bob Keefe

Bob Keefe

BK:skj
Enclosures

Sample Résumé

ROBERT E. KEEFE

5340 Tower Avenue	(413) 848-7653
Bolton, MA 01437	(after 2:30 p.m.)

JOB OBJECTIVE: Automobile mechanic in car dealership

EDUCATION: Northwest Technical College
Large engine repair (night courses)
Bolton High School - Graduated June,
1983
Major course emphasis:
Auto Mechanics I, II, III
Small Engine Repair
Power Mechanics

EXPERIENCE:
1981 - present Frank's Texaco Service
Auto mechanic, gas station attendant
(part-time)
*Numerous customers
request me to do their work.
*88% customer satisfaction
*Own automotive tools
1980 - present Restored several stock cars
*Was asked to display one car
at Bolton Mall.
*Sold two cars at 50% profit.

AWARDS AND
MEMBERSHIPS:
1981-1983 Member, Bolton High School
Automotive Club
1983 Stock car entry took 3rd place, Dade
County Fair.

REFERENCES: Available upon request.

MOLLY C. KEYES

Present	Permanent
310 North Ninth, Apt. B	409 West Spring Street
La Crosse, Wisconsin 54601	Burlington, Wisconsin 53105
(608) 784-4722	(414) 763-9705

EDUCATION

University of Wisconsin-La Crosse
La Crosse, Wisconsin 54601

* Certified to teach grades 1-8, certification number
  118 of the Wisconsin code.
* Bachelor of Science Degree received May 1984
* Major: Elementary Education
  Minor: Special Education
* Experienced a comprehensive view of the field of
  education
* Aware of current trends and issues in education
* Obtained direction in the methods and ideology of an
  effective teacher
* Financed total education

PROFESSIONAL EXPERIENCE

Student Teacher, Ludwig Middle School
La Crosse, Wisconsin 54601

* Taught in a variety of curriculum areas including
  math, science, reading, spelling, health, and the
  language arts
* Developed and implemented daily lesson plans
* Participated in unit and faculty meetings
* Acquainted with the daily
  duties of the teacher

**Sample Résumé
of College
Graduate Applying
for First Job**

Activity Assistant, Coulee Region Infant Development
Center, La Crosse, Wisconsin 54601

* Assisted with activities for the developmentally
  disabled on a weekly basis
* Aided in the daily living instruction in both the EMR
  and TMR rooms

WORK EXPERIENCE

Tour Guide/Tourist Coordinator,
La Crosse Area Convention and Visitors Bureau (Riverside
USA), La Crosse, Wisconsin 54601

* Greeted and welcomed tourists to La Crosse
* Helped tourists find hotel and restaurant
  accommodations
* Maintained the operation of Riverside USA
* Supervised the employees of Riverside USA

Waitress, Natale's
Burlington, Wisconsin 53105

* Maintained public relations with customers
* Established a working relationship with the staff

CREDENTIALS

Available upon request.

Career Services, Wilder Hall
University of Wisconsin-La Crosse
La Crosse, Wisconsin 54601
(608) 785-8514

Guidelines for the Letter of Application

427
1. Follow the "Guidelines for Writing a Business Letter," 412.

2. Include essentially the same information as that which is included in a résumé.

3. Keep the letter as short as possible while still including the essential information. (Three-quarters to one full sheet is an acceptable length.)

4. Use a separate letter for each job opening; include information about the specific job for which you are applying.

5. Tell why you are writing, identify the job you are applying for, and tell how you heard of the opening. Do this in the opening sentence(s).

6. Show an understanding of the requirements of the job and point out how you are able to fill those requirements.

7. List your qualifications, personal data, and your references. (Include the "optional" information if it is appropriate for the job for which you are applying.)

Qualifications	Personal Data	References (optional)
Job experience	Educational background	Teachers, coaches
Related experience	Grades, accomplishments	Clergymen
Special training	Age, health (optional)	Former employers
Career plans	Work habits, attitude	Professional acquaintances

8. Be positive and enthusiastic — sell yourself. Don't, however, claim to be qualified for something you are not.

9. Keep the tone of the letter honest and natural. Avoid cliches and overused phrases.

10. Request an interview; list your phone number and when you can be reached.

---

415 Empire Avenue
Glen Ellyn, IL 60137
January 17, 19__

Sample Letter of Application

Ethel Richards, Manager
Sea 'n' Sky Travel Agency
4444 Burright Building
Glen Ellyn, IL 60137

Dear Ms. Richards:

Mr. Lee Underhill, our work-study program advisor here at Central High, pointed out your advertisement for a part-time office assistant. I would like you to consider me for the position.

I know I might at first seem young for this job, but I assure you I have the necessary office skills. My grades are the highest in the business classes I take, and I have completed both basic and advanced computer courses. The second qualification I have for this job is my experience in traveling. I have visited all but four of our states and have toured in Europe, Africa, and Mexico in the last five years. I speak Spanish fluently and can communicate passably in French. I intend to continue my studies in languages next year at City College and work toward my goal of being an interpreter for the United Nations.

I am finished with classes every day at noon, so I am free to work afternoons, evenings, and weekends. Please contact me at home to arrange for an interview at your convenience. My number is 763-2532. Since I enjoy meeting people and am enthusiastic about the joys of traveling, I feel I could be a good addition to your staff.

Sincerely,

Richard Greggs

Richard Greggs

---

428 The Letter of Request

One of the most important parts of the job-hunting process is lining up good references. In many cases, it is the recommendation of a respected member of the community which can make the difference between getting or not getting a job. Before you can list a person as a reference on your résumé or letter of application, however, you must first get his or her permission. The letter below is one example of how a letter of request can be worded. Make your letter personal whenever possible; always make it clear why you are writing.

429 The Follow-Up Letter

Another important step in the job-hunting process, one that is often ignored, is the follow-up letter sent after the interview. A follow-up letter will get your name before the interviewer one more time; it is your chance to further influence the decision. A good follow-up letter should contain the following:

1. A thank-you-for-the-interview comment.
2. A statement that reaffirms your interest in the position and your value as an employee in that position.
3. A statement that you will be available for further interviews at their convenience.

Letter of Request

4149 Osage Drive
Burlingame, IA 54321
December 2, 19—

Fr. Jerry Sawill
195 Smith Street
Farwell, ND 53467

Dear Fr. Sawill:

I am writing to request your permission to use your name as a reference. I am going to begin to apply for part-time jobs to save money for next year's college tuition.

You have known me as long and as well as anyone, except for my parents, of course. I would greatly appreciate it if you would serve as a personal reference. I will send this semester's grades when they arrive and any other recent information that you might be able to use.

We really miss seeing you and our other friends since we moved here to Iowa. I will stop in to see you when we come to visit over the Christmas holidays.

Sincerely,

Sue Fugate

Sue Fugate

Follow-Up Letter

6455 North Lincoln Street
Chicago, IL 60606
February 16, 19__

Mr. George Carter
Bart Wholesale Furniture Company
7194 Shermac Drive
Chicago, IL 60606

Dear Mr. Carter:

Thank you for your time and courtesy yesterday. I enjoyed meeting you and all your employees at the store. The tour you gave me answered all the questions I had. I was especially impressed with the efficiency exhibited throughout your store.

My enthusiasm for gaining the position of sales manager is even greater now that I have seen the possibilities. I believe that my managerial ability, coupled with the positive attitudes and talents of the present staff, could lead to an increase in overall sales.

I have already begun considering a number of ideas for improvements which I would try if hired. If you have any further questions, I will continue to be available for additional interviewing at your convenience.

Sincerely,

Jackie Penkotti

Jackie Penkotti

Reading & Learning

"Reading [and learning] is to the mind what exercise is to the body."

Do important points during lectures go in one ear...and right out the other? Are your notes impossible to decipher? Do you find it difficult to make important ideas part of your own thinking? Don't worry. If you answer yes to these questions, you're not a mental wreck. You've just become a little lazy about your learning, or perhaps you've picked up some bad habits that make learning and retaining information difficult. Or then again, you may never have "learned how to learn." In any case, what you need are some techniques (or should we say exercises) to get you in shape for learning.

This section will offer insights into the learning process and many learning techniques which will help you with everything from **reading** and **listening** to **note taking** and **test taking**.

Reading to Learn

By the time most students get to high school, the word "reading" has an entirely different meaning to them than it did just a few years ago. The emphasis has switched from "learning to read" to "reading to learn." Reading now means studying, note taking, summarizing, reviewing, and so on, not just reading. It is a means to an end, a way of getting and learning information you cannot get firsthand.

430   Here are some of the reading techniques which can help you improve your ability to "read to learn":

1.   First, you must learn to "analyze" each reading assignment carefully and completely: WHAT? WHEN? WHERE? WHY? HOW?

2.   Since each reading assignment is different, you must learn how to vary your reading rate depending upon the difficulty of the material (and your reason for reading it).

3.   Learn how to use a reading-study method such as SQ3R.

4.   Learn how to improve your comprehension (and vocabulary) skills by using context clues as you read.

5. Learn how to handle unfamiliar words you come across by using both the context and structure of each word.

6. Learn how to take good notes, as well as how to write summaries, outlines, maps.

7. Learn how to personalize what you have read. Using a journal or learning log is highly recommended. (See 471.)

8. Learn how to use good reading habits—and how to get rid of some bad ones.

431 Determining a Purpose and Plan

Before you can expect to improve any of your reading-to-learn skills, you must first understand—clearly—the purpose or point of each reading assignment you are given: WHAT am I supposed to read? WHERE will I find it? WHY is it important? WHEN is it due? HOW am I supposed to react to it (take notes, do a journal entry, answer some questions)? Write down the information your teacher gives you and anything else that comes to mind which might help when you sit down to read.

Secondly, you must think about the assignment and what it will take for you to get it done properly. HOW long will it take me? (Plan accordingly.) WHEN am I going to do this assignment? (Try doing your reading at the same time each day and at a time when you're not overly hungry, tired, or distracted.) WHERE? (Read in a place that is quiet and comfortable.) WHAT materials will I need to complete the assignment? (Bring your textbook, notebook, handouts, reference book, whatever you need.) WHY am I doing this reading? (Focus on your purpose: fulfilling a course requirement, researching a writing idea, preparing for a class or group discussion, etc.)

Note: If you expect to make an assignment part of your own thinking, you must personalize the reading. Probably the best way to do this is to keep a "learning or reading log" for each class. (A learning log is a notebook or journal in which you react to material presented in reading assignments, discussions, or lectures. Your entries can be sentences, paragraphs, poems, summaries—whatever it takes to make the material your own. See 471.)

432 Reading to Learn

With all the preliminaries out of the way, you are ready to read. If it is going to take more than an hour to finish your assignment, plan to take a break or two (but only after completing a major section, chapter). Read your directions and notes over carefully and decide what the appropriate "reading rate" would be for this assignment. In other words, how carefully do you have to read (and reread) this material to get the job done?

433 Adjusting Your Purpose and Rate

There are three general purposes for reading: to **enjoy,** to **learn,** and to **skim.** For most assignments, you will be reading to learn. And, depending upon how difficult the material is and what you have to get out of it, you will be reading at a rate suitable for studying (taking notes, rereading, summarizing). Because each assignment is different, though, you must be ready to adjust your rate as you go from one paragraph and one page to another.

The very fastest form of "study-reading" is skimming. It is actually a form of previewing (recommended for all study-reading) and can be used to get a quick overview of the material or to find the answers to specific questions. The most "serious" form of study-reading requires that you use a specific method or systematic approach to reading. There are several methods you can use, but each covers the same basic steps: previewing, questioning, reading, stating, and testing (the PQRST method). Perhaps the most popular of these methods is the SQ3R, a method developed by the army to help its recruits read and remember the technical information in its training manuals. The **SQ3R** stands for **Survey, Question, Read, Recite, Review.**

SQ3R
A Method for Your Reading Madness:

Survey: To **survey** is to look over the entire reading assignment in a brief but planned way before you actually begin "reading." The goal is to get a general idea (an overview) of what the entire assignment is about:

1. Read the title, author, date, and any other background information important to your purpose or the assignment.

2. Read the headnote (the paragraph between the title and the body of the reading material) and the first two or three paragraphs.

3. Read all the subheadings, chapter titles, and boldfaced or italicized words. (Do not, however, stop to read about them.)

4. Examine illustrations, graphs, charts, pictures, and other graphic information.

5. Read the last paragraph and any questions which follow the selection.

6. Study the author's style, especially his method of arranging sentences and paragraphs. (Main ideas followed by details, or details first?)

7. Finally, try to put into a sentence or two what the overall idea of the reading is.

Question: To **question** is to "wonder" about the material and what it covers. After you finish your survey, you will most likely have many unanswered questions floating around in your head. Write down those questions which seem important and keep the others in mind. This will help you establish a positive, "inquiring-mind" attitude for the actual reading. The more (and better) questions you ask yourself during the survey, the more likely you are to find what you are looking for.

Read: To **read** is to read—carefully—the entire selection from start to finish. Keep your purpose (and your teacher's instructions) in mind as you look for main ideas, important details, and answers to the questions you have raised. Take notes, and when you come across an answer or a major idea, stop reading and write a summary—in your own words. (This will personalize the material and make it much easier to remember, especially several weeks or months later.) For long, complex readings, it is a good idea to break up your reading by chapters, sections, or major ideas. Stop to summarize, organize, and preview (again) before continuing on to the next portion.

Recite: To **recite** is to think about what you have just read by answering out loud (or verbalizing to yourself) all of the major questions covered in the reading. This should be done at the end of each major section and again at the end of the entire reading. Apply the WHO, WHAT, WHEN, WHERE, WHY, and HOW questions. If you have never tried reciting as you read, you are in for a pleasant surprise. It will help you not only get through the reading, but will also help you remember the material for a much longer time than simply reading and walking away.

Review: To **review** is to look over all of what you have written, scribbled, or drawn as you were reading. Depending upon what you are preparing for (test, discussion, demonstration), you may want to review with another person. Try explaining the main ideas of what you have read to this other person as if you were teaching it to her or him. Ask questions of one another to make sure your explanation will hold up under careful examination. When you review alone, consider using note cards or study sheets (with covered answers) so that you can ask yourself the necessary questions.

That's the SQ3R—a better way to handle your *reading-to-learn* assignments. Give it a try the next time you are faced with a complicated reading assignment. (For a closer look at note taking, outlining, and summarizing, check your handbook index for topic numbers.)

Remembering What You Have Read

In addition to using a study-reading method (such as SQ3R) and personalizing what you have read, there are several specific memory techniques which you can use to help you remember your reading material.

435 Association

The **association method** is a memory technique in which each idea being studied is tied (*associated*) with a more memorable word, picture, or idea. For example, if you were supposed to remember the first ten amendments to the Constitution (Bill of Rights), you would begin by setting up an association for the first amendment. What do most people "see" when they visualize the early colonists who helped set up the Bill of Rights? Pilgrims (*religion*), Benjamin Franklin (*printing press*), Patrick Henry (*speech*), Boston Tea Party (*protest or petition*)? You may see an entirely different set of images when you ask yourself this question, maybe from a classroom project in grade school or a film you watched or book you read.

Or maybe you are unable to visualize much of anything to help you remember the Bill of Rights. If that is the case, try a verbal (word) association. Since *Bill* has four letters and also begins with *B*, how about "four basic rights" as an association for the first amendment? (Some associations won't make much sense at first, but because you make them up, they are often surprisingly easy to remember.)

436 Acronym

Now remember—*Bill* of Rights, *four* basic rights. And what are the four basic rights? Freedom of religion, speech, press, and petition. And how will you remember that? By setting up a second association, of course. Perhaps, an **acronym,** a "word" created by using the first letter(s) of several related words. (VISTA, for example, is an acronym for Volunteers In Service To America.) The acronym would have to be made up of the first letter(s) of the words *press, religion, petition,* and *speech.* One possibility is the word (acronym) *preps* which is made up of the "re" from religion and the first letter from the other three. The first amendment can easily be associated with firsts, or beginnings, *prep*arations; the acronym *preps* can then be used to help you remember the first four basic rights, which are? Without looking!

437 Strange Sentences

A slightly different version of the acronym technique is to compose a sentence which is silly or strange enough that you will have no trouble remembering it. Say for example, you needed to remember the countries of Central America and match them to their place on a map. These countries are (from top to bottom) Mexico, Belize, Guatemala, Honduras, El Salvador, Nicaragua, Costa Rica, and Panama. Your sentence would have to contain words beginning (in order) with M . . . b . . . g . . . h . . . e . . . n . . . c . . . p. Want to give it a try? How about, "My brother George has extremely noisy cassette players" ? Anything equally strange will work.

438 Rhymes, Songs, Jingles, and Raps

Many students who have a hard time remembering the capitals of even nearby states have no trouble remembering the words to dozens of popular songs. Why? First, because the songs mean something to them, they like singing along. Second, repetition. It is not unusual to hear the same song five, six, maybe ten times a day on the radio. Just try to forget them! Also, anything that has rhyme and rhythm is always much easier to remember. Remember either of these: *i before e, except . . ., In 1492, Columbus . . .*? Put your imagination (and talent) to work: Compose rhymes, songs, jingles, and raps to help you remember ideas and facts. Try to make up a rap, with the towns on a map (or) use a song that you know, to remember the . . . . You get the idea.

Guidelines for Reading to Learn

439

1. Know exactly what the reading assignment is, when it is due, and what you must do to complete it successfully.

2. Gather any additional materials you may need to complete your assignment (notebook, handouts, reference books, etc.).

3. Decide how much time you will need to complete the assignment and plan accordingly.

4. Decide when and where (library, study hall, home) you will do your assignment; read in a quiet, comfortable place whenever possible.

5. If you have trouble doing your reading assignments as you should, try doing them at the same time each day. This will help you control the urge to wait until you are "in the mood" before starting.

6. Do not plan your study-reading when you are either especially hungry or tired.

7. Plan to take breaks only after completing major sections of each assignment and stick to that schedule.

8. Read and follow all directions carefully.

9. Know your textbooks and what they contain; use the index, glossary, and footnotes.

10. Use a specific approach to your study-reading—the SQ3R approach, for example—and avoid the most common poor reading habits: head movement, pointing, regressions, and subvocalizing. (See "The Mechanics of Reading.")

11. Preview each chapter or assignment before you begin reading to get an overall picture of what the reading selection is about; if there are questions, read them over before you begin reading.

12. Use the titles, headings, and subheadings before and while you are reading to ask yourself questions about the material.

13. Try to identify the main idea of each paragraph as well as the important supporting details; notice words or phrases which are in italics or boldface.

14. Attempt to figure out the author's pattern of organization or development as you read.

15. Look closely at maps, charts, graphs and other illustrations to help you understand and remember important information.

16. Take good notes of everything you read—summarize, outline, star, underline, highlight, or whatever else works best for you.

17. Use all of your senses when you read. Try to imagine what something looks, feels, and tastes like and draw illustrations in your notes.

18. Realize that some reading material is much more difficult than other material; vary your reading speed and concentration accordingly.

19. Use sound, structure, and context clues to figure out the meaning of unfamiliar words; look up any words which you cannot figure out and write them in your notebook.

20. Practice summarizing out loud what you have read whenever possible.

21. Try hard to reason out difficult material by rereading first; then ask someone for an explanation or find a simpler explanation in another book.

22. Make out note cards or flash cards of difficult material to study later.

23. Keep a list of things you want to check on or ask your teacher about.

24. Keep a separate list of things you feel may appear on tests.

25. Remember that reading is thinking and often requires a good deal of effort and concentration. Have a specific purpose and positive attitude each time you read.

440 Using Context to Improve Reading

One of the biggest challenges for readers in high school and beyond is handling new or difficult words or concepts. They seem to show up regularly in study-reading and can make reading a real chore. They slow you down—distracting, confusing, and sometimes frustrating you in the process. So get out the dictionary, right? Well, yes, but. . . . But don't use it unless you have to. Instead, try getting the meaning of each new word from the context. The *context* of a word is its environment (the words which surround it). By looking closely at these surrounding words and the message they are sending out, you can pick up valuable hints or clues as to the meaning of the new word.

Most good readers use context regularly and are generally aware of the different types of context clues. Knowing something about the types of context clues can help sharpen your word-attack skills and improve your overall reading ability. The chart which follows shows you seven types of context clues. Look them over. Then use them the next time you run across an unfamiliar word or idea.

▬ Types of Context Clues ▬▬▬▬▬▬▬▬▬▬▬▬▬▬▬▬▬▬▬

1) Clues supplied through **synonyms:**
   Carol is fond of using *trite,* worn-out expressions in her writing. Her favorite is "You can lead a horse to water, but you can't make him drink."
2) Clues contained in **comparisons and contrasts:**
   As the trial continued, the defendant's guilt became more and more obvious. With even the slightest bit of new evidence against him, there would be no chance of *acquittal.*
3) Clues contained in a **definition or description:**
   Peggy is a *transcriptionist,* a person who makes a written copy of a recorded message.
4) Clues through **association** with other words in the sentence:
   Jim is considered the most troublesome student ever to have walked the halls of Central High. He has not passed a single class in his four years there and seldom makes it through an entire hour of class without falling asleep or getting sent to the office. His teachers consider him completely *incorrigible.*
5) Clues which appear in a **series:**
   The *dulcimer,* fiddle, and banjo are all popular among the Appalachian Mountain people.
6) Clues provided by the **tone and setting:**
   The streets filled instantly with *bellicose* protesters, who pushed and shoved their way through the frantic bystanders. The scene was no longer peaceful and calm as the marchers had promised it would be.
7) Clues derived from **cause and effect:**
   Since nobody came to the first voluntary work session, attendance for the second one is *mandatory* for all the members.

441 Direct and Indirect Clues

Context clues are made up of synonyms, definitions, descriptions, and several other kinds of specific information helpful to understanding the meaning of a passage or a particular word. In addition, clues can help strengthen and deepen the meaning of words you already know. Context clues can help explain how something works, where or when an event takes place, what the purpose or significance of an action is, and on and on.

Some context clues are not so direct as those listed above. They might be examples, results, or general statements rather than direct definitions or descriptions. Still, indirect clues can be very helpful. Finally, you should realize that context clues do not always appear immediately before or after the word you are studying. In a lengthy piece of writing, the clues might not appear until several paragraphs later (or earlier). As an alert reader, you will want to be aware of this so that you can find these clues wherever they appear. The more clues you find, the closer you can get to the specific meaning of a word and—more importantly—to the overall meaning of the passage itself.

442 Now You Try It

See how well you can apply context clues. Look carefully at the boldfaced words in the sample passage taken from Jack London's *Call of the Wild*. Then look for direct and indirect context clues which help you understand the meaning of those words. In addition to the clues available in this single paragraph, any reader of this novel would enjoy the added advantage of having read the first 46 pages. Taken together, there is a good chance the reader could figure out the meaning of at least some of the boldfaced words. Using context clues intelligently can make a big difference in a reader's overall efficiency. See how your efficiency improves (a little at a time) now that you understand a bit more about context clues.

> They made Sixty Miles, which is a fifty-mile run, on the first day; and the second day saw them booming up the Yukon well on their way to Pelly. But such splendid running was achieved not without great trouble and **vexation** on the part of Francois. The **insidious** revolt led by Buck had destroyed the **solidarity** of the team. It no longer was as one dog leaping in the traces. The encouragement Buck gave the rebels led them into all kinds of petty **misdemeanors.** No more was Spitz a leader greatly to be feared. The old awe departed, and they grew equal to challenging his authority. Pike robbed him of half a fish one night and gulped it down under the protection of Buck. Another night Dub and Joe fought Spitz and made him forego the punishment they deserved. And even Billee, the good-natured, was less good-natured, and whined not half so **placatingly** as in former days. Buck never came near Spitz without snarling and bristling **menacingly.** In fact, his conduct approached that of a bully, and he was given to swaggering up and down before Spitz's very nose.

Improving Vocabulary Skills

443 Using Word Parts

Having a "good" vocabulary is extremely important to overall reading efficiency. The truth is, without a good vocabulary, it is very difficult to significantly improve your reading rate or comprehension. But, once again, there is hope. You can improve your vocabulary, and not simply by studying longer lists of vocabulary words. The answer—or at least one of them—is to learn more about the structure of words, the basic parts of words.

By studying the structure of a single word (the *prefix, root,* and *suffix* which make up the word), it is possible to understand the meaning of that word. Before you can "study" the structure of a word, however, you will have to know the meanings of the most widely used prefixes, roots, and suffixes. This could be as few as 50 (most of which you already know) or as many as 500 (the number included in this handbook). This will depend upon the amount of time and energy you are willing to put into the project.

By learning three to five new word parts a day (and a word each is used in), you will soon become an expert on word parts and word structure. What makes this form of vocabulary study especially good is that the number of words added to your vocabulary will be much greater than the number of word parts you learn. For instance, the root *hydro* is found in the word *hydrogen,* where it means *water,* and in the words *hydroelectric, hydrofoil, hydroid, hydrolysis, hydrometer, hydronaut, hydrophobia, hydroplane,* and *hydrosphere* where, in each case, it also means *water*. Not all roots are found in as many as 10 different words. Many are, however, and some are found in as many as 30 or 40 different words. (Sounds like a deal from late-night television: "All this for only . . . and there's more.") The bottom line is that if you are willing to invest some time learning the most common word parts, you will be paid back many times over.

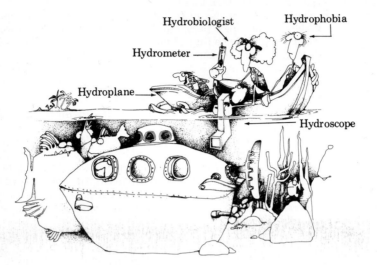

444 "Picking Up" a Vocabulary

Oftentimes, you can "pick up" new words when you least expect to—from television, radio, music, commercials, magazines, conversation. Be smart. Remember those words worth remembering and make them part of your permanent vocabulary. The same thing is true in school. We know that you are going to hear lots of new words in science, math, social studies, and other classes. You are no stranger to the word lists, glossaries, and special terms needed to survive in these classes; however, you may not be quite so familiar with other "opportunities" to improve your vocabulary during the school day.

One opportunity can be found in Greek and Roman mythology, a popular unit in many English and literature courses. These units contain many stories (myths) covering a variety of topics from the adventures of Hercules to the origin of the weeping willow tree. Scattered throughout these myths are characters, themes, and words which have become part of our language. "Herculean," for example, means "having great strength or size." It comes from the tale of Hercules, the godlike hero who performed twelve seemingly impossible tasks.

The reason for all the fuss about these special words is that they are words with strong associations and, therefore, easy words to remember. Beyond that, they are words which carry with them strong images. Such words are especially valuable when you become the writer of someone else's reading material.

445 Using the Dictionary and Thesaurus

When all else fails—look it up in the dictionary. And, while you are in there looking up the meaning of a word, read over (and think about) all of the definitions listed, not just the one you need at the moment. By knowing all its meanings, you will deepen your understanding of the word. (You might also sneak a peak at the synonyms and antonyms listed after the definitions.)

A Dictionary of Prefixes

a, an [not, without] amoral (without a sense of moral responsibility), atheism, anemia, atypical, atom (not cutable), apathy (without feeling)

ab, abs, a [from, away] abnormal, avert (turn away)

acro [high] acropolis (high city), acrobat, acrogen (of the highest class), acronym, acrophobia (fear of height)

ad (ac, af, ag, al, an, ap, ar, as, at) [to, towards] admire (look at with wonder), attract, admit, advance, allege, announce, assert, aggressive, accept

ambi, amb [both, around] ambidextrous (skilled with both hands), ambiguous, amble

amphi [both] amphibious (living on both land and water), amphitheater

ana [on, up, backward] analysis (loosening up or taking apart for study), anatomy, anachronism

ante [before] antedate, anteroom, antebellum, antecedent

anti, ant [against] anticommunist, antidote, anticlimax, antacid, antarctic

apo [from, off] apostasy (standing from, abandoning a professed belief), apology, apothecary, apostle

be [on, away] bedeck, belabor, bequest, bestow, beloved

bene, bon [well] benefit, benefactor, benevolent, benediction, bonus, bona fide, bonanza

bi, bis, bin [both, double, twice] bicycle, biweekly, binoculars, bilateral, biscuit

by [side, close, near] bypass, bystander, by-product, bylaw, byline

cata [down, against] catalogue, catapult, catastrophe, cataclysm

circum, circ [around] circumference, circumnavigate, circumspect

co (con, col, cor, com) [together, with] compose, copilot, conspire, collect, concord

coni [dust] coniosis (disease which comes from inhaling dust)

contra, counter [against] controversy, contradict, counterpart

de [from, down] demote, depress, degrade, deject, deprive

di [two, twice] dilemma, diatom, dissect, diploma

dia [through, between] diameter, diagonal, diagram, diagnosis, dialogue

dis, dif [apart, away, reverse] dismiss, distort, distinguish, diffuse

dys [badly, ill] dyspepsia (digesting badly, indigestion), dystrophy

em, en [in, into] embrace, enslave

epi [upon] epidermis (upon the skin, outer layer of skin), epitaph, epithet, epigram, epitome

eu, ev [well] eulogize (speak well of, praise), eupepsia, euphony, eugenics

ex, e, ec, ef [out] expel (drive out), exmayor, exit, exorcism, eccentric (out of the center position), eject, emit

extra, extro [beyond, outside] extraordinary (beyond the ordinary), extracurricular, extrovert, extraneous

for [away or off] forswear (to renounce an oath)

fore [before in time] foretell (to tell beforehand), forecast, foreshadow, foregone, forefather

hemi, demi, semi [half] hemisphere, hemicycle, semicircle, demitasse

homo [man] Homo sapiens, homicide, homunculus, hominid

hyper [over, above] hypercritical, hyperemia, hypersensitive, hypertensive, hyperactive

hypo [under] hypodermic, hypothesis, hypotension

idio [private, personal] idiom, idiosyncrasy, idiomatic

il (ir, in, im) [not] incorrect, illegal, immoral, irregular

in (il, im) [into] inject, inside, illuminate, impose, illustrate, implant, imprison

infra [beneath] infrared

inter [between] intercollegiate, interfere, intervene, interrupt (break between)

intra [within] intramural, intravenous (within the veins)

intro [into, inward] introduce, introvert (turn inward)

macro [large, excessive] macrodent (having large teeth), macrocosm

mal [badly, poor] maladjusted, malnutrition, malfunction, malady

meta [beyond, after, with] metabolism 'thrown beyond, literally; hence, chemical and physical change), metaphor, metamorphosis, metaphysical

mis [incorrect, bad] misuse, misprint

miso [hating, wrong] misanthropist, misogamist, miser

mono [one] monoplane, monotone, monogamy, monochrome, monocle

multi [many] multiply, multiform, multilateral

neo [new] neopaganism, neoclassic, neologism, neophyte

non [not] nontaxable (not taxed), nontoxic, nonexistent, nonsense

ob (of, op, oc) [towards, against] obstruct, offend, oppose, occur

para [beside, almost] parasite (one who eats beside or at the table of another), paraphrase, parody, parachute, paramedic, parallel

penta [five] pentagon (figure or building having five angles or sides), Pentateuch, pentameter, pentathlon

per [throughout, completely] pervert (completely turn wrong, corrupt), perfect, perceive, permanent, persuade, pervade

peri [around] perimeter (measurement around an area), periphery, periscope, pericardium, period

poly [many] polygon (figure having many angles or sides), polygamy, polyglot, polychrome

post [after] postpone, postwar, postscript, postseason

pre [before] prewar, preview, precede, prevent, premonition

pro [forward, in favor of] project (throw forward), progress, pro-abortion, promote, prohibition

pseudo [false] pseudonym (false or assumed name), pseudo, pseudopodia

re [back, again] reclaim, revive, revoke, rejuvenate, retard, reject, return

retro [backwards] retrospective (looking backwards), retroactive, retrorocket, retrogression

se [aside] seduce (lead aside), secede, secrete, segregate

self [by oneself] self-determination, self-employed, self-service, selfish

sesqui [one and a half] sesquicentennial (one and one-half centuries)

sub [under] submerge (put under), submarine, subhuman, subject, substitute, subsoil, suburb

suf (sug, sup, sus) [from under] suffer, suggest, support, suspect, sufficient, suspend

super, supr, sur [above, over, more] supervise, superman, survivor, supreme, supernatural, superior

syn (sym, sys, syl) [with, together] sympathy, system, synthesis, symphony, syllable, synchronize (time together), synonym

trans, tra [across, beyond] transoceanic, transmit, traverse (lying across as a bridge over a stream), transfusion

tri [three] tricycle, triangle, tripod, tristate

ultra [beyond, exceedingly] ultramodern, ultraviolet, ultraconservative

un [not, release] unfair, unnatural, unbutton, unfasten

under [beneath] underground, underling

uni [one, below] unicycle, uniform, unify, universe, unique

vice [in place of] vice-president, vice-admiral, viceroy

Suffixes

able, ible [able, can do] capable, agreeable, edible, visible (can be seen)

ad, ade [result of action] monad (a unit, an individual), blockade (the result of a blocking action), lemonade

age [act of, state of, collection of] salvage (act of saving), storage, forage

al [relating to] sensual, gradual, manual, natural (relating to nature)

algia [pain] neuralgia (nerve pain)

an, ian [native of, relating to] Czechoslovakian (native of Czechoslovakia), African

ance, ancy [action, process, state] assistance, allowance, defiance, resistance

ant [performing, agent] assistant, servant, defiant

ar, er, or [one who, that which] doctor, baker, miller, teacher, racer, amplifier

ard, art [one who] drunkard, dullard, braggart

ary, ery, ory [relating to, quality, place where] dictionary, dietary, bravery, dormitory (a place where people sleep)

asis, esis, osis [action, process, condition] genesis, hypnosis, neurosis

ate [cause, make] enumerate, liquidate, segregate (causing a group to be set aside)

cian [having a certain skill or art] logician, musician, beautician, magician, physician

cide [kill] homicide, pesticide, genocide (killing a race of people)

cule, ling [very small] molecule, ridicule, duckling (very small duck), sapling

cy [action, function] hesitancy, prophecy, normalcy

dom [quality, realm, office] boredom, freedom, kingdom, stardom, wisdom (quality of being wise)

ee [one who receives the action] employee, devotee, nominee (one who is nominated), refugee, trustee

en [made of, make] silken, frozen, oaken (made of oak), wooden, lighten

ence, ency [action, state of, quality] difference, conference, proficiency (quality of being proficient), urgency

er (see ar)

ery (see ary)

esce [to become] acquiesce (become restful, peaceful), coalesce

escent [in the process of] convalescent, obsolescent

ese [a native of, the language] Japanese, Vietnamese

esis (see *asis*)

esque [*in the style of*] burlesque, arabesque

ess [*female*] actress, goddess, lioness

et, ette [*a small one, group*] midget, octet, baronet, bassinet

fic [*making, causing*] scientific, specific

ful [*full of*] frightful, careful, helpful (full of help)

fy [*make*] fortify (make strong), simplify, terrify, amplify

hood [*order, condition, quality*] manhood, womanhood, brotherhood

ible (see *able*)

ic [*nature of, like*] acidic, metalic (of the nature of metal), heroic, poetic

ice [*condition, state, quality*] justice, malice

id, ide [*a thing connected with or belonging to*] fluid, fluoride

ile [*relating to, suited for, capable of*] domicile, agile, juvenile, senile (related to being old), missile

ine [*nature of*] feminine, masculine, genuine, medicine

ion, sion, tion [*act of, state of, result of*] action, injection, infection, suspension (state of suspending)

ish [*origin, nature, resembling*] foolish, Irish, clownish (resembling a clown)

ism [*doctrine, system, manner, condition, characteristic*] alcoholism, exorcism, heroism (characteristic of a hero), Communism, realism

ist [*one who, that which*] artist, dentist, violinist, racist

ite [*nature of, quality of, mineral product*] expedite, Israelite, graphite, sulfite, dynamite (quality of being powerful)

ity, ty [*state of, quality*] captivity, chastity, fraternity, clarity

ive [*causing, making*] assertive, abusive (causing abuse), affirmative, exhaustive

ize [*make*] emphasize, liberalize (make liberal), idolize, penalize, publicize

less [*without*] baseless, careless (without care), artless, fearless, helpless

ling (see *cule*)

ly [*like, manner of*] carelessly, fearlessly, hopelessly, shamelessly

ment [*act of, state of, result*] contentment, alignment, amendment (state of amending), achievement

mony [*a resulting thing*] patrimony, alimony, acrimony

ness [*state of*] carelessness, restlessness, lifelessness

oid [*like, resembling*] asteroid, spheroid, tabloid, anthropoid

ology [*study, science, theory*] biology, anthropology, geology, neurology

or (see *ar*)

ory (see *ary*)

osis (see *asis*)

ous [*full of, having*] gracious, nervous, vivacious (full of life), spacious

rhea [*flowing, discharge*] pyorrhea, diarrhea, gonorrhea (discharge from the reproductive organs)

ship [*office, state, quality, skill, profession*] friendship, authorship, scholarship, dictatorship

some [*like, apt, tending to*] lonesome, threesome, gruesome

tude [*state of, condition of*] gratitude, multitude (condition of being many), aptitude, solitude

ure [*state of, act, process, rank*] culture, literature, pressure, rupture (state of being broken)

ward [*in the direction of*] eastward, forward, backward

y [*inclined to, tend to*] cheery, crafty, faulty, dirty, itchy

448
Roots

acer, acid, acri [*bitter, sour, sharp*] acerbic (bitter, harsh), acerbate (embitter), acidity (sourness), acrid, acrimony

acu [*sharp*] acute, acuity, acupuncture

ag, agi, ig, act [*do, move, go*] agent (doer), agenda (things to do), agile, navigate (move by sea), pedagogue (childmover, teacher), ambiguous (going both ways, not clear), retroactive, agitate

ali, allo, alter [*other*] alias (a person's other name), alternative, alibi, alien (from another country), alter (change to another form), allotment, allocate

altus [*high, deep*] altimeter, exalt, altitude, alto

am, amor [*love, liking*] amiable, amorous, enamored

anim [*mind, will*] unanimous, animosity, equanimity, magnanimous, animal

anni, annu, enni [*year*] anniversary, annually (yearly), centennial (occurring once in 100 years), per annum, annuity

anthrop [*man*] anthropoid (man-like, e.g., an ape), anthropology (study of mankind), misanthrope (hater of mankind), philanthropic (love of mankind)

antico [*old*] antique, antiquated, antiquity

arch [*chief, first, rule*] archangel (chief angel), architect (chief worker), archaic (first; very early), archives, monarchy (rule by one person), matriarchy (rule by the mother), patriarchy (rule by the father), archeology

aster, astr [*star*] aster (star flower), asterisk, asteroid, disaster (originally a bad happening from a contrary influence by a star), astrology (lit., star-speaking; pseudoscience of influence by stars and planets), astronomy (star law), astronaut (lit., star traveler; space traveler)

aud, aus [*hear, listen*] audible (can be heard), auditorium, audio, audition, audience, auditory, auscultate

aug, auc [*increase*] augment, auction, augur

auto, aut [*self*] automobile (self-moving vehicle), autograph (self-writing; signature), automatic (self-acting), autonomy (lit., self-laws; self-government), autobiography (lit., self-life writing)

belli [*war*] rebellion, belligerent (warlike or hostile), bellicose

bibl [*book*] Bible, bibliography (writing, list of books), bibliomania (craze for books), bibliophile (book lover)

bio [*life*] biology (study of live things), amphibious, biography, biophysics, biopsy (cutting living tissue for examination), microbe (small, microscopic living thing), biogenesis

breve [*short*] breve, brevity, abbreviate, brief

bursa [*purse, payment*] reimburse, disbursements (money paid out)

cad, cas [*to fall*] cadaver, cadence, caducous (falling off), cascade

calor [*heat*] calorie (a unit of heat), calorify (to make hot), caloric, nonchalant

cande [*shine*] candor, candelabra, candid

cap, cip, cept [*take*] capable, capacity, capture, anticipate, participate, principal, accept, except, conception, deceptive, perception, conceive, receive, forceps

capit, capt [*head*] decapitate (to remove the head from), capital, captain, caption, recapitulate

carn [*flesh*] carnal, carnage, carnivorous (flesh eating), incarnate, reincarnation

caus, caut [*burn, heat*] cauterize, cauldron, caustic

cause, cuse, cus [*cause, motive*] because, excuse (to attempt to remove the blame or cause; exonerate), accusation

ced, ceed, cede, cess [*move, yield, go, surrender*] cede (yield), antecedent (moving, occurring before), accede, concede, intercede, precede, recede, secede (move aside from), proceed (move forward), success

chrom [*color*] chrome (color purity), chromatic, chromosome (color body in genetics), Kodachrome, monochrome (one color), polychrome (many colored)

chron [*time*] chronological (in order of time), chronometer (time-measured), chronicle (record of events in time), synchronize (make time with, set time together), anachronism (lit., back in time; anything backwards in historical time)

cide [*kill*] suicide (self-killer or self-killing), homicide (man, human killer or killing), genocide (race killing), tyrannicide (tyrant killer or tyrant killing), pesticide (pest killer), germicide (germ killer), insecticide (insect killer)

cise [*cut*] decide (cut off uncertainty), precise (cut exactly right), concise, incision, scissors, criticize

cit [*to call, start*] incite, citation, cite

civ [*citizen*] civic (relating to a citizen), civil, civilian, civvies (citizen clothing), civilization

clam, claim [*cry out*] exclamation, clamor, proclamation, reclamation, acclamation, declamation, claim

clemen [*merciful*] inclement (not merciful), clemency, clement

clud, clus, claus [*shut*] include (to take in), recluse (one who shuts himself away from others), claustrophobia (abnormal fear of being shut up, confined), conclude, include, preclude, seclude, close, closet

cognosc, gnosi [*know*] prognosis (forward knowing), diagnosis (thorough knowledge), recognize (to know again), incognito (not known), agnostic (not knowing about God)

cord, cor, card [*heart*] cordial (hearty, heartfelt), accord, concord, discord, record, courage, encourage (put heart into), discourage (take heart out of), core, coronary, cardiac

corp [*body*] corporation (a legal body), corpse, corps, corporal, corpulent

cosm [*universe, world*] cosmos (the universe), cosmic, cosmology, cosmopolitan (world citizen), cosmonaut, microcosm, macrocosm

crat [*rule, strength*] autocracy, democratic

crea [*create*] creature (anything created), recreation, creation, creator

cred [*believe*] creed (statement of beliefs), credo (a creed), credence (belief), credit (belief, trust), credulous (believing too readily, easily deceived)

cresc, cret, crease, cru [*rise, grow*] crescendo (growing in loudness or intensity), crescent (growing, like the moon in first quarter), accretion, concrete (grown together, solidified), increment (amount of growth), increase, decrease, accrue (to grow, as interest in money)

crit [*separate, choose*] critical, criterion (that which is used in choosing), diacritical, hypocrisy

cub, cumb [*lie down, lean back*] incubate (to hatch by keeping), encumber (to place a burden upon), cumbersome, succumb, incumbent

cur, curs [*run*] current (running or flowing), concurrent, concur (run together, agree), curriculum (lit., a running, a course), cursory (done hastily, "on the run"), incur (run into), precursor (fore-runner), recur, occur, courier

cura [care] manicure (caring for the hands), curator, curative

cus, cuse (see cause)

cycl, cyclo [wheel, circular] Cyclops (a mythical giant with one eye in the middle of his forehead), cyclone (a wind blowing circularly; a tornado), unicycle, bicycle

deca [ten] decade, decalogue, decapod (ten feet), Decapolis, decathlon

dem [people] democracy (people-rule), demagogue (people-leader, one who stirs up people for selfish ends), demography (vital statistics of the people: deaths, births, etc.), epidemic (on or among the people; general), pandemonium

dent, dont [tooth] dental (relating to teeth), orthodontist (a dentist who practices orthodontia), denture, dentifrice

derm [skin] hypodermic (under skin; injected under the skin), dermatology (skin study), epidermis (on skin; outer layer), taxidermy (arranging skin; mounting animals)

dic, dict [say, speak] diction (how one speaks, what one says), dictionary, dictate, dictator, dictum (a saying), dictaphone, dictagraph, dictatorial, edict, predict, verdict, contradict, adjudicate (to speak the law, to judge), benediction

domin [master] dominate, dominion, domain, predominant, Anno Domini (in the year of our Lord, abbreviated A.D.)

don [give] donate (make a gift), condone

dorm [sleep] dormant, dormitory

dox [opinion, praise] doxy (belief, creed, or ism), orthodox (having the correct, commonly accepted opinion), heterodox (differing opinion; contrary, self-contradictory), doxology (statement or song of praise), paradox

drome [to run, step] syndrome (run together; symptoms) hippodrome (a place where horses run)

duc, duct [lead] duke (leader), induce (lead into, persuade), seduce (lead aside), traduce (lead across in public disgrace, vilify), aquaduct (water leader, artificial channel), subdue, ductile (easily drawn out or hammered thin), viaduct, conduct, conduit, produce, reduce, educate

dura [hard, lasting] durable, duration, duramen, endurance

dynam [power] dynamo (power producer), dynamic, dynamite, hydrodynamics (lit., water power), dyne (unit of power, force), dynamometer, dynasty (power, rule by successive members of a family)

end, endo [within] endoral (within the mouth), endocardial (within the heart), endoskeletal, endoplasm

equi [equal] equinox, equilibrium

erg [work] energy, erg (unit of work), allergy, ergophobia (morbid fear of work), ergometer, ergograph

fac, fact, fic, fect [do, make] factory (the place where workmen are employed in making goods of various kinds), fact (a thing done, a deed), facsimile, facility, manufacture, faculty, amplification, affect

fall, fals [deceive] fallacious, falsify, fallacy

fer [bear, carry] ferry (carry by water), odoriferous (bearing an odor), coniferous (bearing cones, as a pine tree), pestiferous (bearing disease), fertile (bearing richly), defer, infer, refer, suffer (bear under, as under yoke), referee, referendum, circumference

fic, fect (see fac)

fid, fide, feder [faith, trust] fidelity, confident, confidante, infidelity, infidel, fiduciary (held in trust, confidential), perfidy (breaking faith), bona fide (in good faith), federal, confederacy, Fido

fila, fili [thread] filament (a threadlike conductor heated by electrical current), filiform (having the shape of a thread), filter, filet

fin [end, ended, finished] final, finite, infinite, finish, confine, fine, refine, define, finale

fix [fix] fix (a difficult position), transfix (to hold motionless), fixation (the state of being attached), fixture, affix, prefix, suffix

flex, flect [bend] flex (bend), reflex (bending back), flexible, flexor (muscle for bending), inflexibility, reflect, deflect, genuflect (bend the knee)

flu, fluc, fluv [flowing] influence (to flow in), fluctuate (to wave in an unsteady motion), fluviograph (instrument for measuring the flow of rivers), fluid, flue, flush, fluently, affluent

form [form, shape] form, uniform, conform, deform, reform, perform, formative, formation, formal, formula

fort, forc [strong] fort, fortress (a strong point, fortified), fortify (make strong), forte (one's strong point), forte (strong, loud in music), fortitude (strength for endurance), force, effort, comfort, pianoforte, force (power)

fract, frag [break] fracture (a break), infraction, fragile (easy to break), fraction (result of breaking a whole into equal parts), refract (to break or bend, as a light ray), refractive, fragment

fum [smoke] fume (smoke; odor), fumigate (destroy germs by smoking them out), perfume

gam [marriage] bigamy (two marriages), monogamy, polygamy (lit., many marriages), exogamy, endogamy, gamete, gambit

gastro [stomach] gastric, gastronomic, gastritis (inflammation of the stomach)

gen [birth, race, produce] genesis (birth, beginning), Genesis, genus, genetics (study of heredity), eugenics (lit., well-born), genealogy (lineage by race, stock), generate, progeny (offspring), genitals (the reproductive organs), congenital (existing as such at birth), indigenous (born, growing or produced naturally in a region or country), genetic, hydrogen (lit., water-borne element)

geo [earth] geometry (earth measurement), geography (lit., earth-writing), geocentric (earth centered), geology, geochemistry, geophysics

germ [vital part] germination (to grow), germ (seed; living substance, as the germ of an idea), germane

gest [carry, bear] congest (bear together, clog), suggestion (mental process by which one thought leads to another), congestive (causing congestion), gestation, suggestion, gesture

gloss, glot [tongue] polyglot (many tongues), epiglottis, glossary, glottic

glu, glo [lump, bond, glue] conglomerate (bond together), agglutinate (make to hold in a bond)

grad, gress [step, go] grade (step, degree), gradual (step by step), graduate (make all the steps, finish a course), graduated (in steps or degrees), aggressive (stepping toward, pushing), transgress (step across limits, break a law)

graph, gram [write, written] graph, graphic (written; vivid), autograph (self-writing, signature), photography (light-writing) graphite (carbon used for

writing), phonograph (sound-writing), bibliography, monograph (writing on one subject), telegram (far writing)

grat [pleasing] congratulate (express pleasure over success), gratis (as a favor, free), gratuitous (gratis), gratuity (mark of favor, a tip), grateful, gracious, ingrate (not thankful; hence, unpleasant), ingratiate

grav [heavy, weighty] grave, gravity, aggravate, gravitate

greg [herd, group, crowd] gregarian (belonging to a herd), congregation (a group functioning together), segregative (tending to group aside or apart), aggregation

hab, habit [have, live] habitat (the place in which one lives), inhabit (to live in; to establish as residence), rehabilitate, habitual

helio [sun] heliograph (as instrument for using the sun's rays), heliotrope (a plant which turns to the sun)

hema, hemo [blood] hematid (red blood corpuscle), hemotoxic (causing blood poisoning), hemorrhage, hemoglobin, hemophilia, hematose

here, hes [stick] adhere, cohere, inherent

hetero [different] heterogeneous (different in birth; miscellaneous), heterodox, heterochromatic (of different colors), heteromorphic (of different forms), superheterodyne, heterosexual (with interest in opposite sex)

homo [same] homogeneous (of same birth or kind), homonym (word with same name or pronunciation as another), homosexual (with sex desire for those of the same sex), homologous (same-minded, agreeing), homogenize

hum, human [earth, ground, man] humility (quality of lowliness), humane (marked by sympathy, compassion for other human beings and animals), humus, exhume, humanity

hydr, hydro, hydra [water] dehydrate (take water out of; dry), hydrant (water faucet), hydraulic (pertaining to water or to liquids), hydraulics, hydrogen, hydrophobia (fear of water), hydrodynamics, hydroelectric

hypn [sleep] hypnoidal (relating to hypnosis or sleep), hypnosis, Hypnos (god of sleep), hypnotherapy (treatment of disease by hypnosis)

ignis [fire] ignite, igneous, ignition

ject [throw] deject, inject, project (throw forward), eject, object, ejaculate

join, junct [join] junction (act of joining), enjoin (to lay an order upon; to command), juncture, conjunction, joint, adjoining, injunction

jud, judi, judic [judge, lawyer] judge (a public officer who has the authority to give a judgment), abjure (reject the case), judicial (relating to administration of justice), judicious, prejudice

jur, jus [law] justice (a just judgment; as justice must be served), conjure (to swear together; to imagine; to entreat; as, conjure the king to be merciful), juror, jurisdiction

juven [young] juvenile, juvenescent (becoming young), rejuvenate (to make young again)

later [side, broad] lateral, latitude

laut, lav, lot, lut [wash] lavish (flowing like water), dilute (to make a liquid thinner and weaker), ablution (a washing away), launder (to wash and iron clothes), lavatory, laundry, lotion, deluge

leg [law] legal (lawful; according to law), legislate (to enact a law), legislature (a body of persons who can make laws), legitimize (make legal), legacy

letter, lit, liter, litera [*letters*] litany (prayer consisting of invocations and responses), literary (concerned with books and writing), literature (the best works written during the century), literal, alliteration, obliterate

levis [*light*] alleviate (lighten a load), levitate, levity

lic, licit [*permit*] license (freedom to act), licit (permitted; lawful; conceded), illicit (not permitted), licentious (taking liberties; disregarding rules, especially in morals)

lith [*stone*] monolith (one stone, a single mass), lithography (stone writing, printing from a flat stone or metal plate), neolithic (new stone, of the layer stone age), paleolithic (ancient stone)

liver, liber [*free*] liberal (relating to liberty), delivery (freedom; liberation), liberalize (to make more free: as, to liberalize the mind from prejudice), deliverance

loc, loco [*place*] locomotion (act of moving from place to place), locality (locale; neighborhood), allocate (to assign; to place; apportion), relocate (to put back into their homes)

log, logo, ology [*word, study, speech*] Logo (the word, Jesus), logic (orig., speech; then reasoning), prologue, epilogue, dialogue, catalogue, logorrhea (a flux of words; excessively wordy), zoology (animal study), psychology (mind study), theology (god study)

loqu, locut [*talk, speak*] eloquent (speaking out well and forcefully), loquacious (talkative), colloquial (talking together; conversational or informal), obloquy (a speaking against, a reproach), circumlocution (talking around a subject), soliloquy

luc, lum, lus, lun [*light*] Luna (the moon goddess), lumen (a unit of light), luminary (a heavenly body; someone who shines in his profession), translucent (letting light come through), luster (sparkle; gloss; glaze), illuminate

lude [*play*] ludicrous, prelude (before play), interlude

magn [*great*] magnify (make great, enlarge), magnificent, magnanimous (great of mind or spirit), magnate, magnitude, magnum

man [*hand*] manual, manage, manufacture, manacle, manicure, manifest, maneuver, emancipate

mand [*command*] mandatory (commanded), remand (order back), writ of mandamus (written order from a court), countermand (order against, cancelling a previous order), mandate

mania [*madness*] mania (insanity; craze; excessive craving), monomania (mania on one idea), kleptomania (thief mania; abnormal tendency to steal), pyromania (insane tendency to set fires), dipsomania (uncontrollable craving for alcoholic drink), manic, maniac

mar, mari, mer [*sea, pool*] mermaid (fabled marine creature, half fish), marine (a sailor serving on shipboard), marsh (wetland, swamp), maritime

matri, matro, matric [*mother*] matrimony (state of wedlock), maternal (relating to the mother), matriarchate (rulership of a woman), matris (mother goddess of the Hindu deities), matron

medi [*half, middle, between, halfway*] mediate (come between, intervene), medieval (pertaining to the middle ages), mediterranean (lying between lands), medium (a person having the faculty to make contact with the supernatural), mediocre

mega [*great*] megaphone (great sound), megacephalic (great-headed), megalith,

megalopolis (great city; an extensive urban area including a number of cities), megacycle (a million cycles), megaton (force of a million tons of TNT), omega (great)

mem [*remember*] memorandum (a note; a reminder), commemoration (the act of observing by a memorial or ceremony), memento, memoir, memo, memorable

meter [*measure*] meter (a measure), gravimeter (instrument for measuring weight and density), voltameter (instrument to measure volts in an electric circuit), barometer, thermometer

micro [*small*] microscope, microfilm, microcard, microwave, micrometer (device for measuring very small distance), micron (a millionth of a meter), microbe (small living thing), microorganism, omicron (small)

migra [*wander*] migrate (to wander), emigrant (one who leaves a country), immigrate (to come into the land to settle), migrator (one who roves; a wanderer)

mit, miss [*send*] emit (send out, give off), remit (send back, as money due), submit, admit, commit, permit, transmit (send across), omit, intermittent (sending between, at intervals), mission, missile

mob, mot, mov [*move*] mobile (capable of moving), motionless (without motion), motor (that which imparts motion; source of mechanical power), emotional (moved strongly by feelings), motivate, promotion, demote

mon [*warn, remind*] admonish (warn), admonition, monitor, premonition (forewarning), monument (a reminder or memorial of a person or event), reminisce

monstr, mist [*show*] demonstrate (to display; show) muster (to gather together; collect; put on display) demonstration, monstrosity

mori, mort, mors [*mortal, death*] mortal (causing death or destined for death), immortal (not subject to death), mortality (rate of death), immortality, mortician (one who buries the dead), mortification

morph [*form*] amorphous (with no form, shapeless), anthropomorphic (man form), Morpheus (the shaper, god of dreams), morphine (drug making sleep and dreams), metamorphosis (a change of form, as a caterpillar into a butterfly), morphidite

multi, multus [*many, much*] multifold (folded many times), multilinguist (one who speaks many languages), multiped (an organism with many feet), multiply (to increase a number quickly by multiplication)

nasc, nat [*to be born, to spring forth*] nature (the essence of a person or a thing), innate (inborn, inherent in), international (between or among nations), renascence (a rebirth; a revival), natal, native, nativity

neur [*nerve*] neuritis (inflammation of a nerve), neuropathic (having a nerve disease), neurologist (one who practices neurology), neural, neurosis, neurotic

nom [*law, order*] autonomy (self-law, self-government), astronomy, Deuteronomy (lit., second law, as given by Moses), gastronomy (lit., stomach law; art of good eating), agronomy (lit., field law; crop production), economy (household law, management)

nomen, nomin [*name*] nomenclature, nominate, nominal

nounce, nunci [*warn, declare*] announcer (one who makes announcements publicly), enunciate (to pronounce carefully),

pronounce (declare; articulate), renounce (retract; revoke), denounce

nov [*new*] novel (new; strange; not formerly known), renovate (to make like new again), novice, nova, innovate

nox, noc [*night*] nocturnal, equinox (equal nights), noctiluca (something which shines by night)

null [*none*] null, nullification, nullify, nullifidian (one who has no faith), nulliparous

number, numer [*number*] numeral (a figure expressing a number), numeration (act of counting), numberable (can be numbered), enumerate (count out, one by one), innumerable

omni [*all, every*] omnipotent (all powerful), omniscient (all knowing), omnipresent (present everywhere), omnivorous (all eating), omnibus (covering all things)

onus [*burden*] onerous (burdensome), onus, exonerate (to take out or take away a burden)

onym [*name*] anonymous (without a name), pseudonym (false name), antonym (against name; word of opposite meaning), synonym

oper [*work*] opera (a work which has been set to music and is sung instead of spoken), operate (to labor; function), opus (a musical composition or work), cooperate (work together)

ortho [*straight, correct*] orthodox (of the correct or accepted opinion), orthodontist (tooth straightener), orthopedic (originally pertaining to straightening a child), orthography (correct writing, spelling), unorthodox

oss, osteo [*bone*] ossicle (a small bone), ossification (the process of making into bone), osteopath (one who practices osteopathy), osteoporosis (a condition in old age when bones become porous and fragile)

pac [*peace*] pacifist (one for peace only; opposed to war), pacify (make peace, quiet), Pacific Ocean (peaceful ocean)

pan [*all*] Pan American, panacea (cureall), pandemonium (place of all the demons; wild disorder), pandemic, panchromatic (sensitive to all colors), pantheism (all-god belief; belief that God is all and all is God)

pater, patr [*father*] patriarch (the head of the tribe, family), patron (a wealthy person who supports as would a father), paternity (fatherhood, responsibility, etc.), patriot

path, pathy [*feeling, suffering*] pathos (feeling of pity, sorrow), pathetic, sympathy, antipathy (against feeling), apathy (without feeling), empathy (feeling or identifying with another), telepathy (far feeling; through transference), pathogenic (disease being born; causing suffering or disease)

ped, pod [*foot*] pedal (lever for a foot), impede (get the feet in a trap, hinder), impediment, pedestal (foot or base of a statue), pedestrian (foot traveler), centipede, tripod (three-footed support), podiatry (care of the feet), antipodes (opposite feet; parts of the earth diametrically opposed)

pedo [*child*] orthopedic, pedagogue (child leader, teacher), pedant (narrowminded teacher), pediatrics (medical care of children)

pel, puls [*drive, urge*] compel, dispel, expel, repel, impel, propel, pulse, impulse, pulsate, compulsory, expulsion, repulsive

pend, pens, pond [*hang, weigh*] pendant (a hanging object), appendix, pendulum, depend, impend, suspend, perpendicular, pending, dispense, pensive (weighing thought), appendage, ponderous (weighty)

phan, phen [*show, appear*] phantom, phenomenal, fantasy

phemi [*speak*] euphemism (speak well of), prophet

phil [*love*] philosophy (love of wisdom), philanthropy, philharmonic, bibliophile, Philip, Philadelphia (city of brotherly love)

phobia [*fear*] phobia (abnormal fear), claustrophobia (fear of closed places), acrophobia (fear of high places), photophobia (fear of light), aquaphobia (fear of water), pyrophobia (fear of fire)

phon [*sound*] phonograph, phonetic (pertaining to sound), phonology, symphony (sounds with or together), polyphonic (having many sounds or tunes), dictaphone, euphony (pleasing sound)

photo [*light*] photograph (light-writing), photoelectric, photoflash, photogenic (artistically suitable for being photographed), photometer (light meter), photon (a quantum of light energy), photosynthesis (action of light on chlorophyll to make carbohydrates)

pict [*paint*] pictograph (writing with pictures or symbols), picture (make a mental image), depiction (the act of depicting or representing), picturesque, pictorial

plac, plais [*please*] placid (calm, unruffled), placatory (appeasing, soothing), placebo, placate, complacent (self-satisfied)

plenus [*full*] plenary, replenish, plentiful, plenteous

plic, pli, ply [*fold*] inexplicable, pliable, implicate

plu, plur, plus [*more*] plus (indicating that something is to be added), plural (more than one), pluralist (one who holds two or more jobs), plurisyllabic (having more than one syllable)

pneuma, pneumon [*breath*] pneumatic (pertaining to air, wind or other gases), pneumonia (disease of the lungs), pneumatogram (tracing of respiratory movements)

pod (see *ped*)

poli [*city*] metropolis (mother city; main city), police, politics, Indianapolis, megalopolis, Acropolis (high city, fortified upper part of Athens), cosmopolite (world citizen)

pon, pos, pound [*place, put*] postpone (put afterward), component, opponent (one put against), proponent, depose, expose, impose, purpose, propose deposit, deposition, expound, compound, posture (how one places himself), position, post

pop [*people*] population (the number of people in an area), Populist (a member of the Populist party), populous (full of inhabitants), popular

port [*carry*] porter (one who carries), portable, transport (carry across), report, export, import, support, comport, deportment (how one carries himself, behaves), portage, transportation, port, disport

portion [*part, share*] portion (a part; a share, as a portion of pie), proportion (the relation of one share to others), portionless (without portion; without dowry)

posse, potent [*power*] posse (an armed band; a force with legal authority), possible, potent, potentate, omnipotent, impotent

prehend [*seize*] apprehend (seize a criminal, seize an ideal), comprehend (seize with the mind), comprehensible,

comprehensive (seizing much, extensive), reprehensible (needing to be seized back, rebuked)

prim, prime [*first*] primacy (state of being first in rank), prima donna (the first lady of opera), primitive (from the earliest or first time), primary, primal

proto [*first*] prototype, protocol, protagonist, protozoan

psych [*mind, soul*] psyche (soul, mind), psychic (sensitive to forces beyond the physical), psychiatry (healing of the mind), psychology, psychopath (mind feeling; one with mental disease), psychosis (serious mental disorder), psychotherapy (mind treatment), psychogenic (of psychic birth, origin)

punct [*point, dot*] punctual (being exactly on time), punctum (a dot; a point), compunction (remorse; points of guilt), punctuation, puncture, acupuncture

put [*think*] computer (a computing or thinking machine), deputy, reputable (honorable; estimable; a thinker), dispute, repute

quies [*be at rest*] acquiesce, quiescent, quiet

reg, recti [*straighten*] regular, rectify (make straight), regiment, rectangle, correct, direct, erect, incorrigible

ri, ridi, risi [*laughter*] ridicule (laughter at the expense of another; mockery), deride (make mock of; jeer at), risible (likely to laugh), ridiculous

rog, roga [*ask*] prerogative (privilege; asking before), interrogation (questioning; the act of questioning), surrogate, derogatory

rupt [*break*] rupture (break), interrupt (break into), abrupt (broken off), disrupt (break apart), erupt (break out), incorruptible (unable to be broken down)

salv, salu [*safe, healthy*] salvation (act of being saved), salvage (that which is saved after appearing to be lost), salvable, salubrious (healthy), salutary (promoting health), salute (wish health to)

sat, satis [*enough*] sate (to satisfy, sate with food), satisfy (to give pleasure to; to give as much as is needed), satient (giving pleasure, satisfying), satiate, saturate

sci [*know*] science (knowledge), conscious (knowing, aware), omniscient (knowing everything), prescient (knowing beforehand)

scope [*see, watch*] scope (extent one can see), telescope, microscope, kaleidoscope (instrument for seeing beautiful forms), periscope, horoscope (hourwatcher), episcopal (overseeing; pertaining to a bishop), stethoscope

scrib, script [*write*] scribe (a writer), scribble, inscribe, describe, subscribe, prescribe, ascribe, scrivener, manuscript (written by hand), scripture (the Bible)

sed, sess, sid [*sit*] sedentary (characterized by sitting), sedate (sitting, settled, dignified), preside (sit before), president, reside, subside, sediment (that which sits or settles out of a liquid), session (a sitting), obsession (an idea that sits stubbornly in the mind), possess

sen [*old*] senior, senator, senescent (growing old), senile (old; showing the weakness of old age)

sent, sens [*feel*] sentiment (feeling), presentiment (feeling beforehand), assent, consent, resent, dissent, sentimental (having strong feeling or emotion), sense, sensation, sensitive, sensory, dissension

sequ, secu, sue [*follow*] sequence (following of one thing after another), sequel, consequence, subsequent, obsequious (blindly following), prosecute, execute, consecutive (following in order), ensue, pursue, second (following first)

serv [*save, serve*] servant, service, subservient, servitude, servile, reservation, preserve, conserve, deserve, observe, conservation

sign, signi [*sign, mark, seal*] signal (a gesture or sign to call attention), signature (the mark of a person written in his own handwriting), design, insignia (distinguishing marks), signify

silic [*flint*] silicon (a nonmetallic element found in the earth's crust), silicosis (a disease prevalent among miners and stone cutters who breathe much dust)

simil, simul [*like, resembling*] similar (resembling in many respects), simulate (pretend; put on an act to make a certain impression), simulation (pretense; counterfeit display), assimilate (to make similar to), simile

sist, sta, stit, stet [*stand*] assist (to stand by with help), circumstance, stamina (power to withstand, to endure), persist (stand firmly; unyielding; continue), stanchion (a standing brace or support), substitute (to stand in for another), status (standing), state, static, stable, stationary

solus [*alone*] solo, soliloquy, solitaire, solitude

solv, solu [*loosen*] solvent (a loosener, a dissolver), solve, solvency, insolvency, absolve (loosen from, free from), resolve, soluble, solution, resolution, resolute, dissolute (loosened morally)

somnus [*sleep*] somnific, insomnia (not being able to sleep), somnambulant (a sleepwalker)

soph [*wise*] sophomore (wise fool), philosophy (love of wisdom), sophisticated (worldly wise), sophistry, sophist, theosophy (wise about God)

spec, spect, spic [*look*] specimen (an example to look at, study), specific, spectator (one who looks), spectacle, speculate, aspect, expect, inspect, respect, prospect, retrospective (looking backwards), suspect (look under), perspective, circumspect, introspective, conspicuous, despicable

sphere [*ball, sphere*] sphere (a planet; a ball), stratosphere (the upper portion of the atmosphere), hemisphere (half of the earth), biosphere, spheroid

spir [*breathe*] spirit (lit., breath), conspire (breathe together; plot), inspire (breathe into), aspire (breathe toward), expire (breathe out, die), spirant, perspire, respiration

spond, spons [*pledge, answer*] sponsor (one who pledges responsibility to a project), correspond (to communicate by letter; sending and receiving answers), irresponsible, respond

stereo [*solid*] stereotype (to fix in lasting form), stereome (strengthening tissue in plants), stereograph

string, strict [*draw, tight*] stringent (draw tight, rigid), astringent (drawing tightly, as skin tissue), strict, restrict, constrict (draw tightly together), boa constrictor (snake that constricts its prey)

stru, struct [*build*] structure, construct, instruct, obstruct, construe (build in the mind, interpret), destroy, destruction, instrument (originally, a tool for building)

sume, sump [*take, use, waste*] assume (to take; to use), consume (to use up), presume (to take upon oneself before knowing for sure), presumption, sump pump (a pump which takes up water)

tact, tang, tag, tig, ting [*touch*] contagious (transmission of disease by touching), contact (touch), tact (sense of touch for the appropriate), intact (untouched, uninjured), intangible (not able to be touched), tangible, contingent (touching together, depending on something), tactile

techni [*skill, art*] technician (one who is skilled in the mechanical arts), pyrotechnics (display of fireworks), technique, technology

tele [*far*] telephone (far sound), telegraph (far writing), telegram, telescope (far look), television (far seeing), telephoto (far photograph), telecast, telepathy (far feeling), teletype, teleprompter

tempo [*time*] tempo (rate of speed), pro tem (for the time being), extemporaneously, contemporary (those who live at the same time), temporary, temporal

ten, tin, tain [*hold*] tenacious (holding fast), tenant, tenure, untenable, detention, retentive, content, pertinent, continent, obstinent, abstain, contain, pertain, detain, obtain, maintain

tend, tent, tens [*stretch, strain*] tendency (a stretching; leaning), extend, intend, contend, pretend, superintend, tender, tent, tension (a stretching, strain), tense, tensile, attention

terra [*earth*] territory, terrestrial, terrain, terrarium

test [*to bear witness*] testament (a will; bearing witness to someone's wishes), detest, attest (certify; affirm; bear witness to), testimony, contest, intestate

the, theo [*God, a god*] monotheism (belief in one god), polytheism (belief in many gods), atheism (belief there is no god), pantheism (belief that God is all things), theogony (birth, origin of the gods), theology

therm [*heat*] therm (heat unit), thermic, thermal, thermometer, thermos bottle, thermostat (heat plus stationary; a device for keeping heat constant), hypothermia (subnormal body temperature), thermonuclear

thesis, thet [*place, put*] antithesis (place against), hypothesis (place under), synthesis (put together), epithet

tom [*cut*] atom (not cutable; smallest particle of matter), appendectomy (cutting out an appendix), tonsillec-

tomy, epitome (cut on; a summary), dichotomy (cutting in two; a division), anatomy (cutting, dissecting to study structure)

tort, tors [*twist*] torsion (act of twisting, as a torsion bar), torture (twisting to inflict pain), retort (twist back, reply sharply), extort (twist out), distort (twist out of shape), contort, tortuous (full of twists, as a mountain road)

tox [*poison*] toxic, intoxicate, antitoxin

tract, tra [*draw, pull*] tractable (can be handled), abstract (to draw away), tractor, attract, subtract, subtrahend (the number to be drawn away from another)

trib [*pay, bestow*] tribute (a fine paid to a conquering power), distribute (to divide among many), redistribute, contribute (to give money to a cause), attribute, retribution, tributary

trophy [*nourishment, development*] dystrophy (badly nourished), atrophy

tui, tuit, tut [*guard, teach*] tutor (one who teaches a pupil), tuition (payment for instruction or teaching fees), intuent (knowing by intuition)

turbo [*disturb*] turbulent, turmoil, disturb, turbid

typ [*print*] type, prototype (first print, model), typical, typography, typewriter, typology (study of types, symbols), typify

ultima [*last*] ultima (last; final; most remote), ultimate (man's last destiny), ultimatum (the final or last offer that can be made)

unda [*wave, flow*] abundant, inundate, undulation, redundant

uni [*one*] unicorn (a legendary creature with one horn), uniface (a design that appears only on one side), unify (make into one), university, unanimous, universal

vac [*empty*] vacate (to make empty), vacuum (a space entirely devoid of matter), evacuate (to remove troops or people), vacation, evacuee, vacant

vale, vali, valu [*strength, worth, valor*] valor (value; worth), validity (truth; legal strength), equivalent (of equal worth), evaluate (find out the value; appraise actual worth), valedictorian, valiant, value

ven, vent [*come*] convene (come together, assemble), intervene (come between), circumvent (coming around), adventure, invent, subvention, venturesome, convent, inventory, venture, venue, event, eventually, souvenir, contravene (come against), avenue, advent, convenient, prevent

ver, veri [*true*] verity (truth), very, verify (show to be true), verisimilitude, aver (say to be true, affirm), verdict

vert, vers [*turn*] avert (turn away), divert (turn aside, amuse), invert (turn over), introvert (turn inward, one interested in his own reactions), extrovert (turn outward, one interested in what is happening outside himself), controversy (a turning against; a dispute), reverse, versatile (turning easily from one skill to another), convertible, adversary, adverse

vest [*clothe, to dress*] vest (an article of clothing; vestment), investor (one who has laid out money for profit), travesty, vestry, vestment

vic, vicis [*change, substitute*] vicarious, vicar, vicissitude

vict, vinc [*conquer*] victor (conqueror, winner), evict (conquer out, expel), convict (prove guilty), convince (conquer mentally, persuade), invincible (not able to be conquered), evince, eviction

vid, vis [*see*] video (television), vision, evident, provide, providence, visible, revise, supervise (oversee), vista, visit, visage

viv, vita, vivi [*alive, life*] revive (make live again), survive (live beyond, outlive), vivid (full of life), vivify (enliven), convivial (fond of "living it up" with friends), vivisection (surgery on a living animal), vitality, vivacious (full of life)

voc [*call*] vocation (a calling), avocation (occupation not one's calling), convocation (a calling together), invocation (calling in), evoke, provoke, revoke, advocate, provocative, vocal, vocation, vocabulary

vol [*will*] malevolent, benevolent (one of good will), volunteer, volition

vola [*to fly*] volatile (able to fly off or vaporize), volley, volery, volitant

volcan, vulcan [*fire*] Vulcan (Roman god of fire), volcano (a mountain erupting fiery lava), volcanize (to undergo volcanic heat), vulcanist

volvo [*turn about, roll*] voluble (easily turned about or around), voluminous, volution, revolt

vor [*eat greedily*] voracious, carnivorous (flesh-eating), herbivorous (plant-eating), omnivorous (eating everything), devour (eat greedily)

zo [*animal*] zoo (short for zoological garden), zoology (study of animal life), zoomorphism (attributing animal form to God), zodiac (circle of animal constellations), protozoa (first animals; one-celled animals)

---

449   Numerical Prefixes

Prefix	Symbol	Multiples and Submultiples	Equivalent	Prefix	Symbol	Multiples and Submultiples	Equivalent
tera	T	10^{12}	trillionfold	centi	c	10^{-2}	hundredth part
giga	G	10^9	billionfold	milli	m	10^{-3}	thousandth part
mega	M	10^6	millionfold	micro	u	10^{-6}	millionth part
kilo	k	10^3	thousandfold	nano	n	10^{-9}	billionth part
hecto	h	10^2	hundredfold	pico	p	10^{-12}	trillionth part
deka	da	10	tenfold	femto	f	10^{-15}	quadrillionth part
deci	d	10^{-1}	tenth part	atto	a	10^{-18}	quintillionth part

The Mechanics of Reading

Reading is such an automatic activity for most of us that we seldom take time to think about what actually takes place "physically" when we read, what the *mechanics* of the reading process are. Since you are probably now quite curious, let's take a closer look.

450 Translating Words into Thoughts

When you read, your eyes move. Actually, they move, then stop. They move and they stop . . . and move again . . . and stop again . . . and move again . . . as many as ten or fifteen times per line. Not my eyes, you say? I'll prove it to you.

Get a friend to help you perform the following experiment: Both of you sit down (about two feet apart) facing each other. Give your friend something to read and ask her to hold it about nose high, so that you can see her eyes as she reads. Now, tell her to begin reading. Watch her eyes as they move across the page. Do you see the starts and stops? See if you can count the number of stops (called *fixations*) she makes per line. You will have to count very quickly. Each fixation takes only a split second. Count for several lines until the number becomes fairly predictable. Now switch around and let her see what you saw.

The most important thing to remember about this exercise is that your eyes "read" only when they are stopped—and they do not stop for very long. As your eyes move from one fixation to the next, you are not able to read because the words are blurred. Another way of thinking about this is to recall what happens when you take a picture at the same time your camera is bumped or moved: the picture is blurred and out of focus. It is the same way with your eyes. Unless they are stopped, even for a fraction of a second, the picture (words) will appear blurred. As a reader, you do not see this blur, fortunately, because the brain is programmed to blot it out. If the brain did not have this built-in blotter, reading would be an impossible task.

451 A Highway to the Brain

Once the eyes pick up a word, it is transferred to the brain in one of three ways:

1. The **direct route** (*see-thought*) is the most efficient and desirable of the three routes. The eyes "see" the words on the page and send them directly to the brain for interpretation. There is no delay or "detour" and, therefore, less chance for an important idea to become lost or confused along the way.

2. The **indirect route** (*see-hear-thought*) includes one unnecessary and time-consuming step: subvocalization. When you subvocalize, you say each word to

yourself and think about its meaning as you "hear" it, somewhat like a recorded tape delay. This extra step slows your reading rate considerably. This slower rate in turn affects your comprehension because words are "read" one at a time, rather than two or three at a time as they should be. (*Exception:* If the material you are reading is especially difficult or complex, subvocalizing can actually help you concentrate on one idea at a time.)

3. The **interrupted route** (*see-say-hear-thought*) includes two unnecessary steps, "say-hear." These extra steps can cause a complete interruption of the reading process. In this situation, you actually say (vocalize, mumble) each word and then listen to yourself read. Rather than being a simple "see-thought" process as it should be, reading becomes a "see-say-hear-thought" process. This is the least efficient of the three kinds of reading.

452 Getting Rid of Bad Habits ————————

Now that you know a little more about the mechanics of reading, it might be a good idea to see how well you are using them. First, do you have any bad reading habits? Do you move your head, point to each word, accidentally skip sentences, or have some other habit that gets in the way of reading efficiently? If so, concentrate on breaking these habits. In many cases, it is simply a matter of practicing. Just as you picked up these habits through faulty practice, you can now correct them through positive practice. (*Note:* Ask your teacher or a reading specialist for help if you have some especially stubborn habits or suspect poor eyesight or some other physical problem.)

Regressions: Needless Detours

A **regression** takes place every time you skip or misread a phrase, sentence, or passage and have to go back over what you have already read. (This is not the same as going back to reread something because it was especially difficult or complex.) Regressions happen to everyone, even "good" readers. But they can be a serious problem for readers who are trying to improve their efficiency and can't break the habit. Regressions can be caused by any of several factors: distractions, weak vocabulary, poor vision, or lack of concentration.

Whatever the cause, you can cut down on the number of regressions with a rather simple technique. Use a card or bookmark as a "pacer." Move the pacer down the page at a steady pace (slightly faster than you are used to) just above the line you are reading. Since the card quickly covers what you have just read, there is little or no chance for you to go back for a second reading. Continue practicing until you have trained your eyes and mind to concentrate on what you are reading and get it right the first time.

Now the Good News ————————————

You have no "bad" habits, you say, but still don't read as efficiently as you would like? Then, read on. There are several techniques which you can use to help you stop less, read more, and get more out of what you read.

453 Thought Groups

To make yourself a more efficient reader, you must work to reduce the number of fixations (stops) in each line you read. To do this, you can use any of a number of *eye-stretching* exercises including those which follow. These exercises will help you learn to read words in groups rather than one at a time, just as you once learned to read letters in groups (words) instead of one letter at a time. In this way you become a "thought" reader instead of a "word" reader. The phrase "eight cylinder engine," for example, should be read as a thought, not as three separate words.

Increasing Recognition Span

In order to read in thoughts, most of you will have to increase your **recognition span**, the peripheral vision of reading. Your recognition span is determined by the number of words you can physically see or read at one time (in one fixation). People who read one word at a time have a recognition span of one word. People who read thought groups have a span of from three to five words, cutting down significantly on the number of stops they have to make.

In the next exercise, you are to follow the line down the middle of the columns. Do not move your head or your eyes either left or right. The objective is to "stretch" your eye or recognition span by forcing your eyes to use more of their peripheral vision. (*Note:* You will not be able to see or focus on every word in this exercise. If you practice, however, you will "see" or recognize the meaning behind the words.) Go ahead and try the exercise. Then find some old newspapers or magazines, draw a line down the middle of the columns, and get to work. Remember to focus on the lines and eliminate all left and right movement.

Increasing Recognition Span Exercise

Along with the fitness and exercise craze that has swept America have come sore muscles, pulled tendons, and torn ligaments. Many of these injuries could be avoided if proper warm-up and conditioning routines were followed. Most beginners start out exercising too hard and too fast. A thorough warm-up before any exercising is a must. The warm-up serves two important functions—stretching the muscles in preparation for a workout, and getting the heart pumping.

The stretch should begin at the top of the body and work slowly down to the ankles. The routine should consist of basic stretches such as head rotations to relax the neck, arm circles to loosen the shoulders, and trunk rotations to stretch the back and stomach muscles. Stretching out the leg muscles is also very important as most exercising involves much use of the legs. Toe touches, calf stretches, and ankle rotations are just some of the exercises that can be used to loosen the leg muscles. It is important to remember that these are warm-up stretches. Stretching does not mean bouncing or jerking the muscles. Such action could easily lead to pulls, sprains, or tears.

Space Reading

The first exercise was aimed at increasing your recognition span—the number of words you can recognize in one fixation. The next exercise will encourage you to read thought groups rather than individual words. The "space reading" technique which follows is designed to draw your attention to the horizontal line just above the line of print. By focusing your eyes on this line and moving quickly from left to right, you should be able to sense your eyes stretching outward and downward. You should be able to recognize the thought groups without first focusing on each of the words. (Again, use newspapers and magazines to practice. If classmates are also practicing, exchange articles and discuss your progress.)

Space Reading Exercise

What do refrigerators, plastic hamburger trays, foam insulation, and aerosol

spray cans have in common? They all can release chemicals called chloro-

fluorocarbons (CFC's) into the air. Since CFC gases are inert, that is, unable

to bond with other chemicals, they were once thought to be completely safe.

But scientists now know that they can be very dangerous. CFC's blow away in

the wind. However, they do not disappear. Instead they drift up in the atmosphere, unchanged, until they reach the ozone layer, a thin blanket of gas which protects the whole world from being French-fried by the sun's powerful ultraviolet rays. When CFC's reach the ozone, ultraviolet rays bombard them, breaking them into their three chemical parts: chlorine, fluorine, and carbon. Chlorine seems to be the culprit; it starts a chain reaction which finally breaks down ozone. The result? CFC's seem to be eating big holes in the ozone layer, like moths on a sweater. The biggest hole appears over Antarctica every spring. Scientists are now studying what that hole may tell us about the future of our world's delicate atmosphere. Will a trip to the beach someday be a life-threatening deed? It may, unless the human race can learn to live without belching clouds of CFC's into the air.

456 Anticipating Thought Groups

Another technique for improving thought grouping is one which trains your eyes to *anticipate* groups by recognizing clues in the sentence. Phrases and clauses, for example, are by definition a group of related words—a thought group. A prepositional phrase is easy to anticipate. It is a preposition followed by two or more related words. These words combine with the preposition to form a thought group: *on the floor, near the door, above his head, beneath the bed*—you get the idea. Nouns are also found quite often as key words in thought groups. Usually they are combined with an article (*a, an, the*) and one or more modifiers to form a noun phrase or thought group: *the wrong turn, the right way, a cute puppy, a full-grown mutt, my mom's taxi, the crosstown bus.*

A very simple exercise for increasing awareness of thought groups is to go through an article in a newspaper or magazine and divide the entire article into thought groups (see next exercise). Then read each of the marked articles several times. You should start to feel yourself reading with a rhythmic or bouncy pace. This indicates you are beginning to read in thoughts rather than words.

Anticipating Thought Groups Exercise

The laws of physics / state that all matter / constantly runs / toward a state / of disorganization. / The person / who discovered / this scientific phenomenon / must have observed / my bedroom. / It's truly / a scientific wonder / how quickly and drastically / a room can change. / For example, / those clothes / I didn't hang up / the other day / really don't make / that much of a mess / until they are added / to that pile / that has been accumulating / for the past week. / In addition / to the clothes, / there are / the empty bags and boxes / from numerous bedtime snacks / which have been shoved aside / to make room / for the latest one. / This supports the hypothesis / that the amount of matter / entering my room / is far greater / than the amount leaving. / The laws of physics / also state that / a certain amount of energy / is required / to return anything disorganized / to a state of orderliness. / I guess that explains / why my bedroom / is still a mess.

457 The Bottom Line

As with any suggestion or advice, the information on improving reading efficiency is good only when it is put into practice. It's now up to you. If you have found a suggestion or two that sound pretty good, give them a try. And give them time—improvement only comes with practice.

CLASSROOM
Skills

Listening Skills

460   Listening is the most common of all ways to learn. Yet, for some, it is the most difficult of all the learning skills to master.

Why? First, listening is not something we do automatically. Most of us were born with the ability to hear, but not with the tendency to listen. We have to be taught or at least reminded (sometimes repeatedly) to listen. Listening requires concentration and mental discipline. It is easy for our minds to wander, daydream, or stray rather than concentrate on what is being said.

Second, listening requires us to think about what another person is saying. When you read or write or think, you are forming the thoughts within your mind—you are in control. But when you listen, you are like a passenger in a car. The speaker is the driver and controls the speed, brakes, and direction; you are along only for the ride.

But most speakers drive too slowly. You, like most other students, can think four times as fast as the average person can talk. As a result, your mind will often have time to spare, time to wander. Only by focusing your attention on the task at hand (listening to the speaker and what he or she has to say) can you hope to become a good listener.

Instead of allowing your mind to wander, you must listen carefully not only to what the speaker is saying, but also to what he is "saying" between the lines. You can further help your mind stay on track by thinking about possible test questions, putting the speaker's statements into your own words, reviewing the main points made so far, anticipating the next major idea, separating fact from opinion, and continually challenging yourself to get the most out of what you are hearing.

Guidelines for Improving Listening Skills _____

The guidelines listed below will help you understand better all that is involved in the listening process. Read and think about each guideline. Then begin working to improve your listening skills by following these suggestions.

Adjust your attitude . . .

1. Have a positive attitude toward the listening situation; if you are motivated to listen well, you probably will.

2. Prepare to listen by reading or thinking beforehand about what you may hear; write down any questions you may have and be ready to ask them. Bring the rest of your notes with you as well.

3. Keep an open mind about the speaker and the topic; do not conclude beforehand that you are not going to like or benefit from what is about to be said.

4. Avoid poor listening habits such as daydreaming, pretending to listen, giving up when the material becomes difficult, being distracted, prejudging the speaker or the topic, and getting too emotionally involved.

5. Have a purpose or goal. Take time to figure out why you are listening (to gather information for tests, to learn how to . . ., etc.).

Listen carefully . . .

6. Determine the speaker's purpose. Try to figure out why the speaker is telling you what he is (to motivate, to explain, to clarify, to inform, etc.).

7. Concentrate on the speaker and his use of voice intonation, facial expression, and other gestures. This may help you determine which points are most important as well as what the speaker is implying (saying between the lines).

8. Listen for directions and follow them carefully. Listen for the speaker's plan of organization or sequence in presenting main points, important supporting details, and examples. This can help you anticipate what is going to be covered next.

9. Listen for the speaker's transitions or signal words and phrases like *as a result, next, secondly, more importantly,* etc. These signals can help you follow the speaker from one point to the next.

10. Listen for bias or prejudice on the part of the speaker. Is the speaker using emotional appeals or propaganda techniques to sway his listeners? (See "Fallacies of Thinking.") Is the speaker making clear what is fact and what is opinion?

Think and write . . .

11. Think about what is being said. How does this material relate to me? What can I associate it with in my personal life to help me remember? How might I use this information in the future?

12. Listen with pen in hand. Take notes on any information you have to remember for tests or discussions; do not, however, take so many notes that you miss some of the more important points or the overall idea of what is being said.

13. Summarize each main point as it is discussed and draw conclusions about the importance of each; it can also be helpful to distinguish between new and old ideas in your notes.

14. Write down questions you would like to ask; ask them as soon as it is appropriate to do so.

15. End on a positive note. Clarify any questions you may still have and ask for additional information if necessary. Summarize the entire talk in one or two sentences as a final test of whether or not you understood what was said.

Note-Taking Skills

462   Memory experts tell us that the average person forgets at least half of what he or she learns within 24 hours of learning it. This is especially true of information which we gather passively, information which we merely hear about in a classroom lecture, for example. It is not true, however, if we gather information actively or experience something firsthand as in a science experiment or small group discussion. The more actively and personally involved we are in the learning process, the more likely we are to remember what we have learned.

Note taking is a skill worth knowing. It is an active approach to learning—or at least it should be. Taking notes gets you personally involved in the learning process and helps you focus on the most important information. It changes information you would otherwise have only heard about into ideas you have actively worked with and thought about. This active involvement will make learning and remembering easier and more meaningful.

Students who have not studied the techniques of note taking very often end up with one of the following kinds of notes:

1. notes which are so disorganized and so poorly written they are almost impossible to read later on;

2. notes which are so short and incomplete they are of little use when they are needed for a test or paper; or

3. notes which are so full of details, lines, arrows, and examples they are impossible to use efficiently.

Fortunately, note-taking skills can be improved. With a little time and effort, you can turn note taking into an active, efficient way to record and remember information you may need to refer to a week, a month, or a semester after it was presented in class. The most important thing to understand about note taking is that it's not simply hearing and writing; it's *listening, thinking, reacting, questioning, summarizing, organizing, listing, labeling, illustrating* — and *writing*.

Guidelines for
463 ## Improving Note-Taking Skills _____

The guidelines below will help you understand better what you must do to improve your note-taking skills. Read and follow each suggestion carefully.

Be attentive . . .

1. Listen for and follow any special instructions, rules, or guidelines your classroom teacher may have regarding notebooks and note taking.

2. Place the date and the topic of each lecture or discussion at the top of each page of notes.

3. Write your notes in ink, on one side of the paper, and as neatly as time will allow; leave space in the margin for revising or adding to your notes later.

4. Begin taking notes immediately. Don't wait for something new or earthshaking before you write your first note.

5. Relate the material you are noting to something in your life by writing a brief personal observation or reminder.

Be concise . . .

6. Remember, taking good notes does not mean writing down everything; it means summarizing the main ideas and listing only the important supporting details.

7. Write as concisely as you can. Leave out words that are not essential to the

meaning; write your notes in phrases and thoughts rather than complete sentences.

8. Use as many standard abbreviations, acronyms, and symbols (U.S., avg., in., ea., lb., vs., @, #, $, %, &, +, =, w/o, etc.) as you can.

9. Develop your own system of abbreviations or a personal shorthand method. Consider using abbreviations for words or phrases used in a particular class. (Example: CW for Civil War in history class)

10. Draw simple illustrations, charts, or diagrams in your notes whenever it would help make the point clearer.

Be organized . . .

11. Write a title or heading for each new topic covered in your notes.

12. Listen for transitions or signal words to help you organize your notes. Number all related ideas and information presented in time sequence.

13. Ask questions when you don't understand.

14. Use a special system of marking your notes to emphasize important information (underline, star, check, indent).

15. Label or indicate in some way information which is related by cause and effect, comparison or contrast, or any other special way.

Be smart . . .

16. Always copy down (or summarize) what the teacher puts on the board or an overhead projector.

17. Circle those words or ideas which you will need to ask about or look up later.

18. Don't let your notes sit until it is time to review for a test. Read over the notes you have taken within 24 hours and recopy, highlight, or summarize as necessary. (Consider using a colored marker or pen to highlight those notes which you feel are especially important.)

19. Share your note-taking techniques, abbreviations, or special markings with others; you can then learn from what they share with you.

20. Consider switching to a new system of note taking (outlining, mapping, 2-column) if you are unhappy with your present method.

464   Using Your Outline as a Note-taking Guide

Use your outline of reading notes as a classroom note-taking guide. Follow it during the classroom review of the reading material. As you do, you will be prepared to answer any questions your teacher may ask you about the assignment and take notes as well. For your outline to work efficiently, you must leave room on your page for taking notes. (Use the left two-thirds of your paper for the outline summary; use the right one-third for class notes.) Follow your outline and jot down anything which helps to clarify or adds to your understanding of what you have read. By combining your reading and classroom summaries in this way, you should end up with a well-organized set of study notes.

Chapter 10: "The Disinherited"	
Outlined Reading Assignment	Class Notes
I. The Clash of Cultures	Early settlers had
A. Pioneer attitude toward the Indian	few problems; as more trappers and
1. Inferior being	hunters moved in,
a. lacked "civilization"	conflicts started
b. lacked "religion"	Indians labeled
2. Easily exploited	"pagans"; until
a. Swindled in trades	Indians retaliated
b. Set against other tribes	followed.
3. No property rights	
a. A "squatter on gov. land	Some argued that
b. False promises	because Indians did
c. Forced off land	not have the right
B. Indian reaction to treatment	to vote, they could
1. Bitterness surfaced	not own property.
a. Resulting action	
1) Move	Serious clashing
2) Defend	of the cultures
3) Attack	followed.

Cooperative Group Skills

Being able to work together in a group is an invaluable skill, a skill which some people seem to come by naturally. Most people, however, have to "work" at being a good group member. You already practice some of these skills. Taking turns, which you have been practicing since before kindergarten, is an example of a basic group skill. Making eye contact when talking or listening is another. These skills, along with the others needed for effective group work, fall into three general categories: *active involvement, meaningful interaction,* and *honest encouragement.*

465 Active Involvement

Active involvement is the essential element in successful group work. When you listen well, propose ideas and opinions sincerely, challenge tactfully, and make good decisions, you are actively involved.

1. Listening: To work well in any group, you must have a positive attitude. You must listen carefully and actively to others and have an open mind each time someone in the group speaks. Focus on the words and ideas rather than the person. Think about what is being said. Ask yourself how this person's ideas relate to the group and its work. Take notes that will help you follow the discussion and pull everything together later on.

2. Proposing: A group is only as good as the individual members make it. When you have a useful idea or opinion, offer it to the group. If the idea or feeling you express builds on or alters the ideas of someone else in the group, make that known: "After Janae said ... I was reminded of .... " Always speak in a way that shows consideration for other's feelings.
Note: Use "I statements" when you propose ideas. This tells the listener that you are accepting responsibility for what you say.

3. Challenging: Challenge the thinking of others. Make sure, however, that you challenge the ideas, not the person. Instead of saying, "I disagree with you," say, "I don't agree with your first point because .... " Make sure that you have a valid reason for challenging an idea, and make sure you base your challenge on accurate information. You can also make your concerns known by questioning an individual. This can lead to a less threatening give and take of ideas. *Note:* Don't feel personally insulted when your ideas are challenged. Remember it is your idea that is being questioned, not you.

4. Making Decisions: Decisions made by a group can be as democratic or autocratic as you like.

> **Leader's Choice** - The group leader can make a decision based on choices offered by group members.
>
> **Voting** - Group members can vote on a list of choices.
>
> **Forming a Consensus** - Group members can continue discussing choices until everyone in the group agrees.
>
> **Research** - Group members can agree to get more information before a decision is made.
>
> **Gallup Poll** - A vote or survey can be taken of individuals outside of the group.
>
> **Expert's Choice** - An expert can be asked to make the decision.

Meaningful Interaction _____

For you to be an effective member of a group, you must interact cooperatively. Meaningful "interaction" keeps a group moving forward toward an intended goal. To accomplish this, you must work your ideas into the discussion, ask relevant questions, and evaluate the group's performance (including your personal performance).

1. Integrating Ideas: Before you can ask relevant questions, you must first make the ideas already presented part of your own thinking. Obviously, listening carefully and taking notes can do this. So can summarizing or paraphrasing.

2. Asking Relevant Questions: Asking good questions is perhaps the most important of all group skills. It not only keeps group members actively involved in meaningful thinking and discussing, but it also keeps a group focused on its task.

Connect your questions to ideas which were previously made. You might, for example, say: "Josie, it seems to me that your point about ... is very important, but I'm not sure I understand ...." When a group gets bogged down or loses direction, a good question can help members refocus on the task at hand. You might, for example, say, "Tom, what do you think about Martha's last observation?" or "This discussion is going nowhere. Let's go back to the original idea and ...."

3. Evaluating Performance: At the end of a group session, it is helpful to evaluate individual and group performance. To do this, you must identify the most useful contributions, the direction and value of the overall discussion or group work, and the amount of progress made. By stopping to reflect on how the discussion went and how it might have gone better, you are learning from firsthand experience what it takes to make a group work.

Honest Encouragement _____

Encouragement is important to success in all areas. This is especially true of groups (teams, committees, families, classrooms). Building trust, promoting participation, and establishing (re-establishing) group rapport are all important in creating a positive, encouraging atmosphere.

1. Building Trust: Trust usually develops among individuals when they know that they won't be put down, ridiculed, interrupted, or ignored during group work. Complimenting one another, showing genuine concern for another's opinion, and being sincere and honest all contribute to building trust and cohesiveness in a group.

2. Promoting Participation: "A group that works together learns together." Get everyone involved. Don't let any one person dominate the discussion or use the group as an audience. To promote participation, consider the following activity: Give each member of the group the same number of tokens at the beginning of a session. Each time a group member makes a meaningful contribution to the group, he or she passes in one of her tokens. When a member's tokens are spent, he or she cannot contribute another idea until every member of the group has spent at least one (or two or three) tokens.

3. Maintaining Rapport: It is very important for groups to maintain a positive attitude toward their work. As a group member, you cannot, however, ignore disruptions or problems which crop up. Confront problems head-on with statements like, "Jason, we were finally making some progress. Can't you think of a better way ..." or "Jim, I think you misunderstood. Tom was suggesting we reconsider ..." or "We're getting off track. Let's go back to Ellen's point ...."

Cooperative Group Skills
—The Bottom Line———————————

Get Actively Involved

1. Listen carefully (and actively) during group sessions.
2. Contribute ideas to the discussion. (Use "I statements.")
3. Challenge the thinking of others. (Challenge the idea, not the person.)
4. Establish a system for decision making.

Interact

5. Integrate the ideas of others into your own thinking.
6. Ask relevant questions.
7. Evaluate your individual and group performance.

Offer Encouragement

8. Build trust among group members.
9. Promote participation among all members.
10. Build group rapport.

Writing to LEARN

"To write is to write is to write is to write is to write ..."
—Gertrude Stein

What might Ms. Stein have had in mind when she made this statement? Why the unending repetition of "to write is to write" ? Was she unsure of herself—unsure of what it means to write or to be a writer? Of course not. She was a writer of great stature, and writing was of supreme importance to her. The lofty place writing held in her life echoes in the line. As far as she was concerned, nothing more needed to be said on the subject.

What would cause a writer to become so committed to the process of writing? Was it seeing her work in print? Was it the recognition? Not really (although any writer likes to feel her work is appreciated). The real fascination that writers have with writing is the frame of mind that it puts them in. The act of filling up a page with words stimulates their thought processes; it allows them to dig deeply into their minds to unlock new and interesting ideas. That is the main attraction writers find in writing. They know that it leads to exciting and meaningful learning.

Writing to Learn
How can writing help you learn?

469   First, you must approach writing as a means to stimulate learning rather than a means to simply showcase what you already know. Second, you must recognize that writing doesn't have to lead to an end product. A series of questions, a list, or a cluster can constitute meaningful writing if it enhances your thinking and understanding. Third, you should work at writing if you expect writing to work for you. Make it an important part of your learning routine. And fourth, you should read the opening section on the writing process in your handbook (if you have not already done so) to better understand writing as a process of learning and discovery.

Once you commit yourself to writing to learn, you will benefit in a number of ways:

Interest You will develop a greater interest in learning.

Understanding You will improve your ability to retain and understand concepts.

Thinking You will make use of higher levels of thinking.

Attitude You will approach your course work with a more positive attitude.

Learning You will gain a new learning technique, one which you can use for a lifetime.

Journal Writing

"The more you experience writing, the more writing shapes your experiences."

—Dave Kemper

470   One of the most rewarding writing-to-learn activities is the personal journal since it helps you make meaning out of your own experiences. All it takes on your part is a pen or pencil, a notebook, and a personal commitment to write honestly—and often. If you make personal writing part of your daily routine, you will benefit in three ways: 1) you will learn new things about your world, 2) you will become more comfortable with writing, and 3) you will become more confident in its benefits for you. The guidelines which follow will get you started. (Also, see 001 for a detailed discussion of personal writing.)

— Guidelines for Journal Writing —

1. Reserve a notebook for your personal journal. When you fill one up, start another.

2. Find a comfortable place to write. Enjoy yourself. Vary the setting if your writing starts to grow stale.

3. Write whatever you like, whatever is on your mind. This is your personal writing-to-learn journal. (See 032 and 034 for a list of writing topics if you have trouble getting started.)

4. Try writing nonstop. This is how you will get the most mileage out of your writing. Your goal should be to write for ten minutes at a time.

5. Date your journal entries to help you keep track of your writing.

6. Underline ideas in your journal that you like. Maybe a particular idea helped clarify your thinking or brought a whole new way of thinking to mind. Continue exploring interesting or stimulating ideas in future entries.

7. When you've discovered an especially interesting idea in your writing, "push" it as far as you can to see what additional ideas you can uncover. On the other hand, if an unrelated idea bumps into your writing, go with it if you feel it will lead to a more exciting line of thinking.

8. Vary the type of writing you do. There are any number of ways to write in a journal. Consider clustering, imaginary dialogues, unsent letters, parodies, ads, etc. Don't be afraid to experiment. (See 031 and 033 for an explanation of various prewriting techniques.)

9. Share entries with friends or classmates. Discussing your writing usually leads to additional writing and learning.

10. If you continue to write, ask yourself why you've become a "regular" writer in one of your entries.

"The man who has ceased to learn ought not to be allowed to wander around loose...."

—M.M. Coady

Learning Logs

471   Another meaningful writing-to-learn activity is keeping a log of what goes on in a particular course. A learning log (or subject journal) gets you actively involved in your course work, and, more specifically, it gives you the opportunity to explore important ideas and concepts presented in the course. A learning log is most meaningful if you write as freely as possible since a free flow of ideas promotes meaningful learning. (Use the guidelines for journal writing on the previous page to get you started in your learning log, and refer to the list which follows for writing ideas.)

Guidelines to Keeping a Learning Log

1. Write about class activities—anything from a class discussion to an important exam. Consider what was valuable, confusing, interesting, humorous, etc.

2. Discuss new ideas and concepts. Consider how this new information relates to what you already know.

3. Evaluate your progress in a particular class. Consider your strengths, your weaknesses, your relationship with members of the class.

4. Discuss your course work with a particular audience: a young child, a foreign exchange student, an object, an alien from another planet.

5. Question what you are learning. Dig deeply into the importance of the concepts presented. Consider writing this in the form of a dialogue.

6. Confront ideas and concepts which confuse you. Back them into a corner until you better understand the problem.
(Consider giving a copy of your thoughts to your teacher so that he or she has a better idea of how you and the class are doing.)

7. Describe your assignments in your own words.

8. Plan the activities for tomorrow's class. Or, develop a mock essay test for your class. Make sure to answer one or more of the questions. (This is a very effective study method.)

9. Keep a record of your thoughts and feelings during an extended lab or research assignment. This will help you evaluate your progress. And the ideas which develop in your log entries will often add new meaning to your work.

10. Set aside a section in your log for a proofreader's "Most Wanted" list. Keep track of errors in grammar or mechanics that repeatedly appear in your writing. Review this list from time to time, and refer to it when you proofread your compositions. Adjust it accordingly throughout the course. (See "Re-marks," 600, for help with grammar and mechanics.)

11. Set aside a section in your log for a glossary of important and interesting vocabulary words. Use these words in your log entries.

12. Argue for or against anything that came up in a discussion, in your reading, or in a lecture.

472 Active Note Taking

An effective variation of the basic learning log is to record your thoughts and feelings alongside your course notes. This makes note taking an active, stimulating activity, and it helps you make new ideas and concepts part of your own thinking. To engage in this writing-to-learn activity, divide each page in your notebook in half. Use one side for traditional notes from lectures, discussions, and reading. Use the other side to react to these notes. Your responses could include the following:

a **comment** on what memory or feeling a particular idea brings to mind,

a **reaction** to a particular point you strongly agree or disagree with,

a **question** about a concept that confuses you,

a **paraphrase** of a difficult or complex idea,

a **discussion** of the importance or significance of the material,

or a **response** to an idea that confirms or questions a particular belief.

Writing-to-Learn Activities

473   Writing to learn is essentially exploratory writing. What form your writing takes is strictly up to you as long as it encourages thinking and learning. You might be perfectly satisfied with free, nonstop writing; others might find clustering or listing meaningful. Still others might enjoy a variety of writing activities. (See 031 or 033 in your handbook for an explanation of activities which promote writing to learn.)

Refer to the list of activities which follow for additional writing-to-learn ideas:

1. **Unsent Letters** Draft letters to anyone (or anything). The topic of your letter should be something you are concerned about, studying, or reading.

2. **First Thoughts** Write or list your immediate impressions about something you are studying, reading, or concerned about. These thoughts will help you focus on the task at hand, and they will serve as a point of reference to measure your learning.

3. **Dramatic Scenarios** Project yourself into a unit of study and develop a scenario (plot) in your writing. Let's say you are studying World War II. You might put yourself in President Truman's shoes the day before he decided to drop an atomic bomb on Hiroshima. The thoughts going through his mind might be the focus of your writing.

4. **Free Association** Begin with one word and see where it takes you in your writing.

5. **Synergize** Generate ideas in pairs. (Synergize simply means "to work together.") Alternate statements or questions and answers related to your course work. The point is to work from each other's ideas. This works well as a reviewing exercise.

6. **Acrostics** Write acrostic poems for vocabulary words. The letters of each vocabulary word are used as the first letter of each line in the poems.(Another good reviewing idea.)

7. **Word Works** Use as many vocabulary words as you can in a writing-to-learn entry. The writing that you develop can be as crazy as you want it to be. Try to use each vocabulary word correctly, however.

8. **Nutshelling** Try writing down in one sentence the importance or relevance of something you've heard, seen, or read.

9. **Pointed Questions** Keep asking yourself WHY in your writing. Keep pressing the question until you can't push it any further. Sum up what you've learned.

10. **Debate** Try splitting your mind into two "persons." Have one side debate (disagree with) your thinking on a subject, and have the other side defend it. Keep the debate going as long as you can.

Note: See 257 for guidelines and activities for reading logs.

Guidelines for Writing Assignments

474 Planning Your Work Session

1. First of all, know exactly what the writing assignment is, when it is due, and what you must do to complete it successfully.

2. Gather any materials you may need to complete your assignment (journal, notebook, handouts, dictionary, handbook, etc.)

3. Decide how much time you will need to complete the assignment and plan accordingly.

4. Decide when and where (library, study hall, home) you will do your assignment; write in a quiet, comfortable place whenever possible.

5. If you have trouble doing your writing assignments as you should, try doing them at the same time and place each day. This will help you control the urge to wait until you are "in the mood" before starting.

6. Do not plan to do your writing when you are either hungry or tired.

7. Plan to take breaks only after completing a certain amount of each assignment and stick to that schedule. If necessary, ask your family not to disturb you and hold any phone calls you may get.

Preparing to Write

8. Remember that writing is thinking and often requires a good deal of effort and concentration. Have a specific purpose and positive attitude each time you sit down to write.

9. Remember, too, that some writing assignments are more difficult than others; vary your pace and concentration accordingly.

10. Begin the actual writing by reviewing carefully all the directions and guidelines your teacher may have given you for this assignment. Look up any words you are unsure of and write down the meaning of each.

11. Keep a list of things you need to check on or ask your teacher about. (Remember, all writing is basically an attempt to solve a problem. You must clearly understand a problem before you can solve it.)

Selecting and Supporting Your Topic

12. If you have not been given a specific topic to write about, begin listing possibilities. Try first to think of topics you are interested in or know something about. Consider the suggestions given by your teacher; look in newspapers or magazines for ideas; if necessary, consult any lists of topics you may have available.

13. When you have a topic you feel will work for this assignment, place a clear, concise statement of that topic and how you plan to handle it at the top of your paper. This statement can serve as the controlling idea (thesis statement) for your assignment.

14. Next list all your initial thoughts and ideas about the topic, including details you may want to include later in your writing.

15. Continue to gather information (from as many sources as necessary) until you have enough to support your topic sentence or thesis statement. (It is always a good idea to collect more information than you think you actually need.)

Arranging Your Information

16. Look carefully at your information and begin arranging it into the best possible order: order of importance, chronological (time) order, order of location, etc. Even though you may later add details or change their order, it is always a good idea to start with a specific plan or design.

17. Put your main points into a working outline. This will help you spot any gaps which may exist and make clear where you must add more details.

Writing Your Assignment

18. Continue writing. Listen to your ideas as you are putting them on paper. Good writing sounds natural and honest. Here are some pointers which may help you keep your writing sincere and clear:

    a. Don't go hunting for a big word when a small one will do — a big word is one you probably wouldn't use in a classroom conversation.

    Do, however, use your thesaurus when you need a word which is more specific or more exact than the word you first used.

    b. Don't use slang — not all your readers will understand it — or qualifiers like *kind of, sort of, quite,* or *a bit* which add nothing to what you have already said.

    Do, however, use contractions if they sound more natural.

    c. Don't use cliches or euphemisms — they tend to make your writing sound phony.

    Do, however, use words and phrases which "sound" good and make your writing more appealing. To be appealing, your writing should have a certain bounce or rhythm to it.

    d. Don't use filler or padding — when you have said all that needs to be said, stop writing.

    Do, however, include enough details (examples, reasons, comparisons, etc.) to prove your point or paint a complete picture.

    e. Don't use adverbs or adjectives when they are unnecessary: return *back, complete* monopoly, *more* perfect, screamed *loudly, muffled* silence, *individual* person, *final* result.

    Do use verbs which are vivid and nouns which are concrete; by doing so, you eliminate the need for additional modifiers:

    sprinted, dashed, scampered, bolted — not *ran fast*

    engineer, conductor, porter, fireman — not *railroad worker*

19. Work for an ending which leaves the reader with a good feeling about what he has just read. A good ending will give the reader something to take with him and share with others.

Revising and Proofreading

20. Check your writing for fragments and run-ons. (Reading each paragraph backwards one sentence at a time can help you locate these errors.)

21. Revise and proofread your writing carefully. (Use a checklist if necessary.) Always check for spelling, usage, and punctuation errors. Most of these errors are avoidable and should never find their way into a final copy.

Writing Your Final Copy

22. Follow the directions of your teacher when it comes to writing or typing your final copy. Keep your final copy in a safe, clean, dry place. Don't let your paper get wrinkled or dirty; also, don't fold your paper.

23. Turn your writing assignment in on time and be open to any suggestions your teacher may give you for future improvement. The only way to improve your writing is to write, rewrite, and write again. There are no substitutes or shortcuts, so welcome the advice you are given as an opportunity to improve your writing and to better yourself.

Taking
TESTS

The key to doing well on any test is being well prepared. This is never more true than when you are preparing for an essay test. You must begin by organizing and reviewing what you have studied. You review the important names, dates, and places and prepare to work them into an essay which makes clear what these details add up to. Even though this is often easier said than done, there are a number of steps which can be taken to improve your ability to handle an essay test. Studying the guidelines below is a good first step.

Guidelines for Taking an Essay Test

475   1. Make sure you are ready for the test both mentally and physically. (See the "Guidelines for Taking Tests," 481.)

2. Listen carefully to the final instructions of the teacher. How much time do you have to complete the test? Do all the questions count equally? Can you use any aids such as a dictionary or handbook? Are there any corrections, changes, or additions to the test?

3. Begin the test immediately and watch the time carefully. Don't spend so much time answering one question that you run out of time before answering the others.

4. Read all the essay questions carefully, paying special attention to the key words.

5. Ask the teacher to clarify any question you may not understand.

6. Rephrase the question into a controlling idea for your essay answer.

7. Think before you write. Jot down all the important information and work it into a brief outline. Do this on the back of the test sheet or on a piece of scrap paper.

8. Use a logical pattern of organization and a strong topic sentence for each paragraph.

9. Write concisely without using abbreviations or nonstandard language.

10. Emphasize those areas of the subject you are most sure of.

11. Keep your test paper neat with reasonable margins. Neatness is always important; readability is a must, especially on an exam.

12. Revise and proofread as carefully and completely as time will permit.

476 Understanding the Essay Test Question

Understanding what the teacher is asking for in an essay test question is very important. Too many students make the error of thinking the best way to answer an essay question is to write down everything and anything about the topic as fast as they can. This frenzied method of handling an essay test has the pen flying across the paper in a desperate attempt to fill as many pages as is physically possible. No time is taken to think about the essay test question or to organize an appropriate answer. The resulting grade is usually disappointing.

The poor result is not necessarily from the student's lack of knowledge about the subject, but from his lack of the basic skills needed to write a good essay test answer.

The first step in correctly handling an essay test question is to read the question several times until you are sure you know what the teacher is asking. As you read, you must pay special attention to the key words found in every essay question. Your ability to understand and respond to these key words is a basic skill necessary to handling the essay question. For example, if you are asked to *contrast* two things on a test and you *classify* them instead, you have not given the teacher the information requested. Your score will obviously suffer.

477 Key Words

A list of key terms, along with a definition and an example of how each is used, can be found on the next three pages. Study these terms carefully. It is the first step to improving your essay test scores.

Classify   To **classify** is to place persons or things (especially plants and animals) together in a group because they are alike or similar. In science there is an order which all groups follow when it comes to **classifying** or **categorizing**: *phylum* (or *division*), *class, order, family, genus, species,* and *variety*.

Compare   To **compare** is to bring both points of *similarity* and *difference,* but generally with the greater emphasis on similarities.

"Compare the British and American forms of government."

Contrast   To **contrast** is to particularly stress *differences.* In a sense, *compare* covers this, but with less emphasis on *differences.*

"Contrast the views of the North and the South on the issue of States' Rights."

Criticize   To **criticize** is to point out the *good* points and the *bad* points of a situation or idea. To be a "critic" is *not* simply to be *negative;* a good critical analysis must deal with both sides of the issue.

"Criticize Roosevelt's foreign policy during the middle 1930s."

Define   To **define** is to give a clear, concise meaning for a term. Generally, to define consists of identifying the class to which a term belongs and how it differs from other things in that class. (See the section on "Writing a Definition," 122.)

"Define what is meant by the term *filibuster.*"

Describe   To **describe** is to recount, sketch, or relate something in sequence or story form. What is called for here is to give a good *word picture* of the concept.

"Describe Scout's appearance on the night of the Halloween party."

Diagram   To **diagram** is to organize in some pictorial way — a flow chart, a map, or some other graphic device. Generally, a good diagram will include appropriate labeling of both the whole figure and each of its parts.

> "Diagram the levels of authority and responsibility of our town's government officials."

Discuss   To **discuss** is to examine and talk about an issue *from all sides*. A **discussion** answer is usually fairly long and must be carefully organized.

> "Discuss the long-range effects of the atomic bomb on the people of Hiroshima."

Enumerate   To **enumerate** (root: *numer* or *number*) is to write in list or outline form a set of related facts, ideas, objects, or issues. Though actual numbering isn't truly demanded by this term, it often helps.

> "Enumerate the causes of the Great Depression of 1929."

Evaluate   To **evaluate** is to make a *value* judgment, a statement of negative and/or positive worth. Generally speaking, it is better to back up this type of answer with *evidence* (facts, figures, instances, etc.) rather than simply with appeals to authority (the opinions of particular *experts*).

> "Evaluate the contributions of the automobile to the average American's overall standard of living."

Explain   To **explain** (*ex* = out; *plain* = open space) is to bring out into the open, to make clear, to analyze, and to clarify. This term is similar to *discuss* but implies more of an emphasis on cause-effect relationships or step-by-step sequences.

> "Explain the immediate effects of the atomic bomb on Hiroshima."

Illustrate   To **illustrate** is, according to its definition, to show by means of a picture, a diagram, or some other graphic aid. At times, however, the term may be used to call forth specific examples or instances which *illustrate* a law, rule, or principle.

> "Illustrate the relationships between the Senate and the House of Representatives."

Interpret   To **interpret** is to explain, translate, or show a specific application (how it works) of a given fact or principle. Generally, an *interpretation* should go beyond previously cited examples or instances.

> "Interpret the following statement: Power corrupts, and absolute power corrupts absolutely."

Justify   To **justify** is to tell why a position or point of view is good, right, or proper. A *justification* should be mostly *positive*; stress the *advantages* of a position over its *disadvantages*.

> "Justify the U.S.A.'s intervention into Cuban-Russian relations during Kennedy's administration."

List   To **list** is like enumerating but calls even more clearly for a formal *numbering* or *sequencing*.

> "List three examples of naturalism in Jack London's *Call of the Wild*."

Outline   To **outline** is to organize a set of facts or ideas in terms of main points and sub points. Though a formal system of identifying these points one from another is not necessarily *demanded* by this term, it is usually a good idea. (See 110.)

> "Outline the events in the Tom Robinson affair."

Prove   To **prove** means to give evidence, to present facts, to use logic as a base for clear, forthright argumentation.

> "Attempt to prove that capital punishment is **not** an effective deterrent to crime."

Relate   To **relate** is to show how two or more things are connected because of similar reasons for being, similar results, or similar characteristics. Don't confuse this use of the word with the verb *to relate* meaning simply *to tell,* as in "He related the story of his life."

> "Relate the invention of the cotton gin to the spread of slavery into the territories of the West during the early 1800s."

Review   To **review** (to view again) is to reexamine or to summarize the key characteristics or major points of an overall body of facts, principles, or ideas. Generally speaking, a **review** should present material in *chronological* (in the order in which it happened) or in *decreasing order* of importance or concern.

> "Review the steps leading to the founding of the United States."

State   To **state** means *to say.* However, to state also means to present a *brief,* concise statement of a position, fact, or point of view. Usually a **statement** requires a shorter response than discussion.

> "State your reasons for having taken the position you now hold on the issues of States' Rights versus Federal Power."

Summarize   To **summarize** (root: *sum*) is to present the main points of an issue in *condensed, shortened* form. Details, illustrations, and examples are not given.

> "Summarize Lincoln's reasons for issuing the Emancipation Proclamation."

Trace   To **trace** is to present — in step-by-step sequence — a series of facts which are somehow related either in terms of time, order of importance, or cause and effect. The approach used most frequently is *time-order.*

> "Trace the events leading up to the attempted secession of several Southern states from the Union."

Reprinted by permission. Adapted from Dr. Kenneth L. Dulin's "The Vocabulary of Essay Questions."

---

478   Planning and Writing the Essay Test Question

In addition to a basic understanding of the key words mentioned above, you must also understand how to go about writing the essay answer. The steps below should help:

1. **Read** the question several times or until you clearly understand what is being asked for. (Pay specific attention to the "key word" being used in the question.)

2. **Rephrase** the question into a statement which can serve as the thesis statement for your essay answer or the topic sentence for a one-paragraph answer. *Note:* It often works well to drop the key word and not attempt to include it in your thesis statement.

   > **Question:** <u>Explain</u> the immediate effects of the atomic bomb on Hiroshima. *Thesis statement:* The immediate effects of the atomic bomb on Hiroshima were devastating.

3. **Outline** the main points you plan to cover in your answer. Time will probably not allow you to include all supporting details in your outline. (Using a topic outline rather than a sentence outline will also save time.)

4. **Write** your essay. Your opening sentence will be your thesis statement (the reworded question). Follow this with any background information which is necessary for a complete understanding of your answer.

Sample Essay Answer

One-paragraph Answer   If you feel that only one paragraph is needed to answer the question, use the main points of your outline as supporting details for your thesis statement. (Your thesis statement now serves as the topic sentence of your single-paragraph answer.)

Multi-paragraph Answer   If the question is too complex to be handled in one paragraph, your opening paragraph will include only your thesis statement and background information. (See step 4.) Begin your second paragraph by rephrasing one of the main points from your outline into a suitable topic sentence. Support this topic sentence with examples, reasons, or other appropriate details. (Additional paragraphs should be handled in the same manner as paragraph two.) If time permits, add a summary or concluding paragraph to bring all of your thoughts to a logical close. By adding or changing an appropriate word or two, your original thesis statement can be used as a closing sentence (*clincher sentence*) for your essay answer.

I. The Explosion
   A. A "noiseless flash"
   B. A wave of pressure
II. The Fire
   A. Ignited by bomb
   B. Ignited by debris
III. The Fallout
   A. Black rain
   B. Contamination

The immediate effects of the atomic bomb on Hiroshima were devastating.

The initial explosion of the atomic bomb on Hiroshima has often been described by those who survived it as a "noiseless flash." The bomb which was dropped on this island city was equal in power to 13,000 tons of TNT; incredibly, no explosion was heard by the residents of Hiroshima. Instead, they recall an enormous flash of blinding light followed by a tremendous wave of pressure. The wave and the violent wind which followed did an unbelievable amount of damage. Train cars, stone walls, and bridges as far as two miles away from the impact area were toppled. Of the 90,000 buildings in Hiroshima, an estimated 62,000 were destroyed in an instant. In that same instant, the smoke and dust carried by the wind turned day into night.

The darkness quickly gave way to light as fires sprang up throughout the city. Buildings near the center of the explosion were ignited at once by the tremendous heat (estimated at 6,000 degrees C) which was generated by the splitting atoms. Away from the impact area, it was simply a matter of time before the splintered wreckage was ignited by exposed wiring and over-turned cooking stoves. By late afternoon of the first day, very nearly every building in Hiroshima was ablaze.

As the fires raged, additional effects of the bomb became evident. Huge drops of "black rain" began to fall. The explosion had lifted tremendous amounts of smoke, dust, and fission fragments high into the atmosphere over Hiroshima. Soon a condensed moisture, blackened by the smoke and dust and contaminated with radiation, began to fall like rain on the city. The radioactive "fallout" polluted the air and water adding to the problems of those who had survived the blast and fires.

Before the day had ended, the devastation from the bomb was nearly complete. Very little of Hiroshima remained.

Guidelines for Taking Tests

Organizing and Preparing Test Material

1. Ask the teacher to be as specific as possible about what will be on the test.

2. Ask how the material will be tested (true/false, multiple choice, essay).

3. Review your class notes and recopy those sections which are especially important. When you recopy your notes, use a different method of organizing. If, for instance, your history notes are arranged chronologically, copy them over by definition, by *good* and *bad*, by nation, etc.

4. Get any notes or materials you may have missed from the teacher or another student.

5. Set up a specific time(s) to study for an exam and schedule other activities around it.

6. Make a list of special terms important in each subject and study that list thoroughly.

7. Look over quizzes and exams you took earlier in that class.

8. Prepare an outline of everything to be tested to get an overview of the unit.

9. Prepare a detailed study sheet for each part of your outline.

10. Attempt to predict test questions and write practice answers for them.

11. Set aside a list of questions to ask the teacher or another student.

Reviewing and Remembering Test Material

1. Begin reviewing early. Don't wait until the night before the test.

2. Whenever possible, relate the test material to your personal life or to other subjects you are taking.

3. Look for patterns of organization in the material you study (cause/effect, comparison, chronological, etc.).

4. Use association techniques by relating the unfamiliar to the familiar.

5. Use maps, lists, diagrams, acronyms, rhymes, or any other special memory aids.

6. Use flash cards or note cards and review with them whenever time becomes available.

7. Recite material out loud whenever possible as you review.

8. Skim the material in your textbooks, noting key words and ideas; practice for the test by summarizing the importance of these ideas.

9. Study with others only after you have studied well by yourself.

10. Test your knowledge of a subject by teaching or explaining it to someone else.

11. Review especially difficult material just before going to bed the night before the exam.

12. Go over your material as often as possible on exam day.

Taking the Test

1. Make sure you are ready for the test both mentally and physically.

2. Check to see that you have all the materials you need for a particular test.

3. Report to the room as quickly as possible on the day of the exam.

4. Review especially difficult material right up to the time the test starts.

5. Listen carefully to the final instructions of the teacher. How much time do you have to complete the test? Do all the questions count equally? Can you use any aids such as a dictionary or handbook? Are there any corrections, changes, or additions to the test?

6. Begin the test immediately and watch the time carefully.

7. Read the directions carefully, underlining or marking special instructions.

8. Follow all special instructions, like showing your work on math tests.

9. Read all questions carefully, paying attention to words like *always, only, all,* and *never.*

10. Answer the questions you are sure of first.

11. Use context clues to help you with unfamiliar words.

12. Use material on the test itself to help you answer more difficult questions.

13. When being tested on long passages, read the questions before you read the passage.

14. Move on to the next question when you get stuck on a particular question. You might *code* each question you skip. You can do this by writing a *3* next to very difficult questions, a *2* next to difficult ones, and a *1* next to those you think you know the answers to. After you've gone through all the questions, go back to the *1's* first.

482 Taking the Objective Test

True/False Test

1. Read the entire question before answering. Often the first half of a statement will be true or false, while the second half is just the opposite. For an answer to be true, the entire statement must be true.

2. Read each word and number carefully. Pay special attention to names and dates which are similar and could easily be confused. Also, watch for numbers which contain the same numerals but in a different order (*Example:* 1619 . . . 1691).

3. Be especially careful of true/false statements which contain words like *all, every, always, never,* etc. Very often these statements will be false simply because there is an exception to nearly every rule.

4. Watch for statements which contain more than one negative word. *Remember:* Two negatives make a positive. (*Example:* It is *unlikely* ice will *not* melt when the temperature rises above 32 degrees F.)

5. Remember that if one part of the statement is false, the whole statement is false.

Matching Test

1. Read through both lists quickly before you begin answering. Note any descriptions which are similar and pay particular attention to the details that make them different.

2. When matching word to phrase, read the phrase first and look for the word it describes.

3. Cross out each answer as you find it — *unless* you are told that the answers can be used more than once.

4. If you get stuck when matching word to word, determine the part of speech of each word. If the word is a verb, for example, match it with another verb.

5. Fill in the blanks with capital letters rather than lower-case letters since they are less likely to be misread by the person correcting the test.

Multiple Choice Test

1. Read the directions very carefully to determine whether you are looking for the *correct* answer or the *best* answer. Also check to see if some questions can have two (or more) correct answers.

2. Read the first part of the question very carefully, looking for negative words like *not, never, except, unless,* etc.

3. Try to answer the question in your mind before looking at the choices.

4. Read all the choices before selecting your answer. This is especially important in tests where you are to select the best answer or on tests where one of your choices is a combination of two or more answers (*Example:* c. Both a and b, d. All of the above, e. None of the above).

5. As you read through the choices, eliminate those which are obviously incorrect; then go back and reconsider the remaining choices carefully.

6. Use words and context clues in the question to help you figure out difficult answers. Guess at an answer only as a last resort.

Fill in the Blanks

1. If the word before the blank is *a*, the word you need probably begins with a consonant; if the word before the blank is *an*, your answer should begin with a vowel.

2. If the missing word is the subject of the sentence, the verb will tell you whether your answer should be singular or plural.

3. The length of the blank will often tell you how long your answer should be.

4. If there are several blanks in a row, it could well indicate the number of words which are needed in your answer.

5. If you don't know the answer immediately, read the statement again and look closely for clues which might help you determine the probable answer.

"Make the most of yourself for that is all there is of you."
— **Ralph Waldo Emerson**

COLLEGE-PREP
Skills

Preparing for College

Well, you've finally made THAT decision—you're going to college. Your parents are happy, you're happy, but now the real work begins. You have to start looking at different schools and asking yourself a number of questions: Are my grades good enough? Are my PSAT, SAT, or ACT scores high enough to get into the colleges that I'm considering? What activities and awards have I received that will help me get accepted into a college? What are the requirements of the colleges that I'm interested in? Should I get other opinions about which college I should attend? Where can I get information about these colleges?

If all this (and more) is going through your mind, don't worry. The questions and uncertainty are very normal. That doesn't mean you don't have your work cut out for you. We know that this is a busy and confusing time for you, so we have tried to ease the burden. In the next few pages, you will find a number of checklists and ideas to help you make the right choice. The rest is up to you.

Deciding on a College

485   To help decide if the college you're interested in is right for you, consider these following questions.

1. Where is the school located? Will I be comfortable that close to or far from home?

2. Is the school in a city or a small town? Do I want the excitement of an urban setting or the peacefulness of a more secluded campus?

3. Is the school a 4-year, 2-year, technical, extension, state, private, or religious college? Which do I prefer? Which is "right" for me?

4. What is the enrollment of this school? Is the campus size best for me?

5. Is the school run on semesters or trimesters? Which schedule will work best for me?

6. Does this school have the major that I'm interested in? How competitive is the course of study at this school? Do I have the skills and background to succeed in my major at this school?

7. What is the availability of housing on this campus? How early do I need to apply to get into a dorm?

8. Are there tutorial and support services located on or near campus if I need them?

9. Considering tuition, room and board, books, personals, and the rest, can I afford this school? Are my parents willing/able to help me financially?

10. Do I qualify for grants, loans, scholarships, and/or work-study positions to help me pay for this school?

11. Are different ethnic and cultural groups well represented on this campus?

12. What activities and social events are offered on or near campus? Are enough of my interests served?

Getting Ready for College

486 It may surprise you that college preparations begin as early as the ninth grade. But by starting to plan now, you can be assured you will not suddenly discover you have forgotten to take care of something important later on.

Ninth Grade

_____ Get to know your guidance counselor, teachers, and principal.

_____ Plan a tentative college-prep schedule for the next four years. (It's definitely not too early to begin planning for college.)

_____ Talk to your parents about college. If possible, talk to someone in the career area you are considering.

_____ Begin looking and listening for information about colleges and admission requirements.

_____ If you haven't already done so, find a quiet place where you can really concentrate when you have important studying to do. (Keep a dictionary, thesaurus, and your English handbook nearby whenever you study.)

_____ Learn how to listen and take good notes in class; then learn how to prepare for and take exams, especially essay exams. (See these sections in your handbook and see your teacher if you need additional help.)

_____ Work on your writing. No other single skill is more critical to success in college than your ability to write well in a variety of situations. (Keep a journal of free writings or a learning log—or both.)

_____ Begin a plan or program to build your vocabulary. (Consider including regular study of prefixes, suffixes, and roots. See 446.)

_____ Begin saving your English, math, science, and social studies notebooks so that you will have them to study for your college entrance exams.

_____ Get involved in cocurricular activities. (Remember that speech, drama, yearbook, exchange student programs, and similar activities can be especially good experiences for college prep.)

_____ Finally, relax and enjoy high school.

_____ Make sure you are still following a college-prep schedule. (See your counselor if you have any doubts.)

_____ Become familiar with the career information available in your school and community in those fields you are considering. Send away for more information if necessary.

_____ Look over the *PSAT, SAT,* or *ACT* study booklets to get an idea of what college entrance exams are like. (Begin learning/reviewing those prefixes, suffixes, and roots which often show up on these exams.)

_____ Begin organizing your time (use an actual chart if necessary) so that you do not have to rush or cram to complete important projects on time.

_____ Become familiar with research and resource materials. (See 190.) These materials will help you handle high school and college research projects.

_____ Make a list of all those colleges you have an interest in attending and collect information on each. (If you haven't already done so, visit a college campus. It will give you a good idea of what lies ahead.)

_____ Sign up for the *ACT* or *SAT* for next year. (Consider taking the PSAT—or other preliminary test—this year, or early next fall.)

_____ Continue working on your writing, thinking, and study skills. (Essays of comparison and contrast, for example, are popular college assignments.)

_____ Read! In addition to the Recommended Reading List, get into the habit of reading newspapers and magazines. A clear understanding of what is going on in the world around you will become more and more important.

_____ Continue to save your academic notebooks.

_____ Look for a summer job, summer school program at a nearby college, or a summer trip that will be both educational and enriching.

_____ Sign up to take the *PSAT* if you haven't already taken it.

_____ Continue to review college guides and catalogs. Write to the colleges you are still considering for their latest catalogs, requirements, applications, and other materials.

_____ Read available reference books which list important information about colleges—admission requirements, tuition, degrees offered, financial assistance, etc.

_____ Go to any college or career days offered in your area; also, meet with college representatives visiting your school.

_____ Plan a visit to one or more of the colleges you are still considering. Arrange a meeting with a college official during your visit. Also, visit any students you may know attending that school.

_____ Prepare to take the *SAT* or *ACT.* (Review analogies and prefix, suffix, root definitions.)

_____ Meet with your guidance counselor to evaluate your progress and continue your college planning. (Ask your counselor about college credit courses available at your high school.)

_____ Begin discussing specific financial considerations with your parents. Send for financial-aid forms, scholarship applications, work-study information, etc.

_____ Continue working on your writing and study skills. Talk to college students you know about what skills they wish they had worked harder on in high school.

_____ Continue reading books from the suggested reading list. (The upcoming summer would be a good time to catch up if you are not able to read much more than what is required during the school year.)

_____ Look forward to next year: it should be an exciting and memorable year.

_____ You should be ready to narrow your choice of colleges to two or three by mid-September. Get application forms immediately and send them back in early fall. Many colleges have enrollment limits and cutoff dates for application.

_____ Submit your financial-aid and scholarship applications as soon as possible. Again, see your counselor for help. Often there are numerous local scholarships which are not well known.

_____ Request letters of recommendation from teachers as they are needed for various applications.

_____ Keep up with current national and international events—refer to newspapers and magazines as well as television. (Can you locate on a map those areas being discussed in the news?)

_____ Become familiar with the "levels of thinking" frequently called for in college essays and exams. (See the thinking tips in your handbook.)

_____ Continue reading from the recommended reading lists.

_____ Discuss effective methods of reading, writing, and studying in college with your parents, teachers, and college students.

_____ Tie up loose ends before graduation and get ready to move up and out in the world.

_____ Good luck! By working hard, especially in the first semester, you'll do just fine!

Recommended Reading Lists

"There are books and there is literature."
—**Elizabeth Hardwick**

487   Several hundred college and university professors who were surveyed recently suggested that students considering college should read as many of the following classics as possible. If you can, find out which of these titles are required reading in grades 9 through 12. Then select several other titles to read on your own. (You might get together with several classmates to read and discuss the same titles.) A strong background in reading and writing are still considered the keys to succeeding in college.

Grade 9

All Quiet on the Western Front . . Remarque
Black Like Me . . . . Griffin
Bury My Heart at Wounded Knee . . . Brown
The Good Earth . . . . Buck
Great Expectations . . . . Dickens
Great Tales and Poems of
    Edgar Allen Poe . . . . Poe
Hound of the Baskervilles . . . . Doyle
Iliad . . . . Homer
The Little Prince . . . . Saint Exupery
Lord of the Flies . . . . Golding
Odyssey . . . . Homer
The Old Man and the Sea . . . . . Hemingway
A Separate Peace . . . . Knowles
To Kill a Mockingbird . . . . Lee
The Yearling . . . . Rawlings

Grade 10 or 11
(Classic American Literature)

The Adventures of Huckleberry
    Finn . . . . Twain
Autobiography and
    Other Writings . . . . Franklin
The Crucible . . . . Miller
Death of a Salesman . . . . Miller
For Whom the Bell Tolls . . . . . . Hemingway
Grapes of Wrath . . . . Steinbeck
The Great Gatsby . . . . Fitzgerald
Moby Dick . . . . Melville
My Antonia . . . . Cather
Narrative of the Life
    of Frederick Douglass . . . . Douglass
Of Mice and Men . . . . Steinbeck
Our Town . . . . Wilder
The Red Badge of Courage . . . . Crane
The Scarlet Letter . . . . Hawthorne
Walden . . . . Thoreau

Grade 10 or 11
(English Literature)

Animal Farm . . . . Orwell ✓
Brave New World . . . . Huxley
Canterbury Tales . . . . Chaucer
Gulliver's Travels . . . . Swift
Heart of Darkness . . . . Conrad
Jane Eyre . . . . C. Bronte
Lord Jim . . . . Conrad
1984 . . . . Orwell
Pride and Prejudice . . . . Austen ✓
Return of the Native . . . . Hardy
Saint Joan . . . . Shaw
Silas Marner . . . . Eliot
Tale of Two Cities . . . . Dickens
Turn of the Screw . . . . James
Wuthering Heights . . . . E. Bronte

Grade 12
(World Literature)

The Aeneid . . . . Vergil
Anna Karenina . . . . Tolstoy
Chekhov: The Major Plays . . . . . . Chekhov
Candide . . . . Voltaire
Crime and Punishment . . . . Dostoyevsky
Cry, the Beloved Country . . . . Paton
Cyrano de Bergerac . . . . Rostand
A Doll's House . . . . Ibsen
Don Quixote . . . . Cervantes
Ghandi: His Life and Message
   for the World . . . . Fischer
Madame Bovary . . . . Flaubert
Oedipus . . . . Sophocles
One Day in the Life of
   Ivan Denisovich . . . . Solzhenitsyn
Plato's Dialogues . . . . Plato
The Stranger . . . . Camus

Notes to the College Freshman . . .
from Someone Who's Just Been There

488

You're probably thinking that college is going to be the ultimate experience of freedom, but that it's also a little scary. Both are true. College is definitely a time to test your wings, but it's also a time when you suddenly have a lot to think about and be responsible for. I know exactly how you feel because I've just finished four years of the most exciting and confusing time of my life. Here are some tips that might help you prepare for your first year:

1. **Roommates:** Sometimes, roommates hit it off beautifully! Other times, well. . . . The best approach is to think of meeting your roommate as a learning experience, part of your education. No one's perfect—not you, and not your roommate. You will enjoy many things together but will not see eye-to-eye on everything. Remember that you two are now partners. It's up to both of you to make it work: communicate honestly and make decisions together about your room, your phone bill, etc.

2. **Responsibility:** Take control of your life; you have to be responsible for yourself now. This involves eating well, getting enough rest and exercise, and not getting too caught up in the party scene. Keep your health and academics ahead of everything else. If you need help, get a tutor or see a counselor—that's what they're there for.

3. **Budgeting:** Open a checking account. Set a budget and stick to it. Get a part-time or work-study job if you absolutely need to. (Avoid doing this the first semester/year if at all possible.)

4. **Parents:** Keep in touch with them and let them know how you're doing in your classes. If you need advice or financial help, ask for it; but don't depend on it. If you feel they're still "taking care" of you, tell them— they may not realize they're overdoing it. Find out what they expect of you when you're home on weekends or on breaks. And by all means, be grateful for any help they give you.

5. **Studying:** Make studying your first priority from day one. Never put it off! Make a schedule so that studying becomes routine. If you use your

time wisely, it's amazing what you can get done ... and with all of the long-term assignments, it's important to get something done every day so you aren't stuck doing it all at the last minute.

6. **Instructors:** Give college and your classes a chance if you're unhappy at first. Get to know your professors and teaching assistants. They'll be happy to help you with your assignments as well as give you advice on how to study for their courses.

7. **Courses:** See a university advisor just before the end of each semester so you can plan for the next one. You will save yourself a lot of hassles later if you know which courses will and will not fulfill your degree requirements.

8. **Growing:** Be open-minded and explore new areas of interest. Make new friends. Listen to other ideas and opinions and be comfortable in expressing your own. Respect the rights and values of other people, and appreciate your own.

9. **Goals:** Think about career goals often. A successful student will become aware of her strengths and weaknesses, her interests and background. Ask yourself what you really want to do. Write down classes that you want to take in the future and keep your eyes open for jobs (summer or part-time) that may give you experience in your field. Overall, be realistic but ambitious!

10. **Rewards:** Finally, enjoy the time you spend in college. Take time to think about where you're going and don't forget to reward yourself for the things you accomplish.

The Well-Prepared College Student

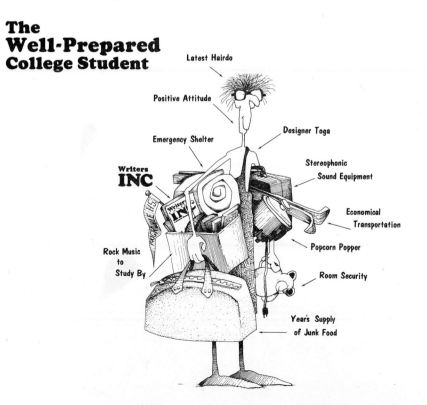

Latest Hairdo

Positive Attitude

Emergency Shelter

Designer Toga

Stereophonic Sound Equipment

Writers INC

Economical Transportation

Rock Music to Study By

Popcorn Popper

Room Security

Year's Supply of Junk Food

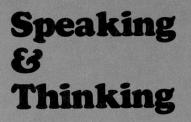

Speaking & Thinking

"Half the world is composed of people who have something to say and can't and the other half who have nothing to say and keep on saying it."

Having something to say and saying it well have been important preoccupations of people for centuries. In ancient Greece and Rome, for example, the notable public speakers were revered individuals; their speeches were masterpieces in style and substance. A public speaker learned his craft in school where instructors trained their students to be clear and logical thinkers so they could develop purposeful and effective speeches. Included in the study were rhetoric (speaking), logic, and grammar.

This section looks at the classical link between style and substance in speaking. The opening chapter provides insights into preparing, practicing, and evaluating a speech. The following chapters offer insights into the thinking process in general, as well as insights into the thinking which produces clear, creative, and logical speeches and compositions.

Starting Your Speech

490   The best place to begin when you are faced with the prospect of giving a speech is with the purpose behind the presentation. The questions which follow will help get you going.

1. Why am I giving this speech? to inform my audience? to persuade them? to amuse or entertain? to stimulate or move them?

2. Who will be in my audience? my teacher and classmates? my boss and coworkers? my family and friends?

3. Does my speech have to be about a particular topic, or am I free to select a topic I like and one which I think my audience might like as well?

4. Is there any time limit or other important restriction or guideline?

5. Will the occasion be formal or informal?

6. Will the place, occasion, and topic be suited to the use of visual aids?

Selecting and Narrowing the Topic

Once you have thought about your purpose, audience, and occasion, you are ready to begin your search for an appropriate topic. There are several worthwhile things to keep in mind as you begin to look for a specific topic:

Rule nothing out. Nearly any subject can be made to work as a topic for a speech. Only those which are clearly wrong for the occasion or the audience should be ruled out. Keep an open mind as you search and try to fashion each new subject you come across into a speech topic. (See "Guidelines for Selecting a Subject, 031.")

Consider "first-person" topics. If there is a subject which interests you—one which you may have some personal experience with—consider that subject first. Using a familiar topic allows you to talk of things you care about or have firsthand knowledge of. You can then communicate your ideas and feelings on a more personal level. This acquaintance with the subject will help you to feel more self-confident and enthusiastic.

Consider other sources. If you are not able to use a firsthand topic and have no other workable ideas, you will need to find help from some other source. Possibly one of your teachers or a close friend will have some suggestions for you. If not, the next logical place for you to look is in the library. There you will find numerous sources for ideas which can stimulate your thinking:

1. The vertical file, which is a file of newspaper clippings, brochures, pamphlets, and other miscellaneous material can provide you with hundreds of ideas on current topics. It can also serve as a source of current information for the later writing of the speech.

2. The *Readers' Guide to Periodical Literature,* which is an ongoing publication listing magazine articles by author and subject, will keep you thinking for hours about possible topics. It will also give you an indication of how much information is available on each subject you are considering.

3. A newspaper or magazine will update you on the major issues of the day. With this information, you can decide whether it would be worthwhile to look more closely at a particular topic or issue.

4. A special display set up in the library to feature new or popular books might provide you with an idea. These displays usually feature high-interest or current material which is what makes displays good sources for a speech topic.

5. Even though they are often frowned upon by teachers as the primary source of any writing assignment, encyclopedias can be very helpful tools when it comes to finding a speech topic. You would do well, however, to check out other books, magazines, newspapers, etc., and not rely too heavily on the encyclopedia for information.

Test your topic. Once you have found a possible topic, start searching for specific information. Test your specific topic by free writing, clustering, or skimming several articles. Try to determine just how much information there is on the subject, especially how much new or interesting information is available.

Find a focus. If you are satisfied that this topic will work, focus on the particular area which seems best suited for the time limit, the audience, and the occasion. This narrowed-down version becomes your specific topic.

State your topic. You should now be able to state your topic and purpose in one declarative sentence, often referred to as your *thesis statement.* You can begin the wording of your thesis statement with "My purpose is . . ." and follow that with one of the four main goals of public speaking: *to inform, to convince, to stimulate, to interest.* Lastly, add your specific, narrowed-down topic to complete your thesis statement.

Example: "My purpose is to convince my audience that high school study halls are inefficient and, therefore, should be done away with."

> *"What this country needs is more free speech worth listening to."*
> **—Hansell B. Duckett**

492 Searching and Planning

Once you have determined your topic and purpose, you are then ready to gather material for support. Set aside a portion of your notebook and begin writing down personal remembrances, experiences, and thoughts related to the topic. Continue to jot down ideas which come to you from radio, television, classroom discussion, magazines, and so on. This continued attention will provide you with many good details which you can use when you are writing your speech. (These notes can also be arranged into your working outline.)

Next, go to your library and take full advantage of the material which is available there. (Refer to the "Using the Library" section of this handbook for a detailed description of the card catalog, *Readers' Guide,* and other helpful materials. Also, if your speech assignment calls for extensive research with note cards or some form of documentation, turn to "The Research Paper" for additional steps to follow.)

Writing the Speech

493 Writing a speech is much the same as writing a paragraph or an essay. You must write in a clear, concise manner and use a logical pattern of organization which has a beginning, a middle, and an end. Your writing should move smoothly and naturally from one point to the next.

But it cannot be said that a speech is entirely the same as other forms of writing. It is not. A speech is written to be heard rather than read. It must, therefore, "sound" good as well as look good on paper. It must be written in such a way that your audience can transcribe what they hear into a clear, colorful picture—a picture which they can take with them and talk about later.

494 Using Your Senses

When an audience listens to your speech, they will need strong images to help them visualize your ideas. They need to see, hear, feel, smell, and taste what you are describing. They must experience with you the emptiness of walking into a new school alone, the sounds of laughter made louder by your fear, and the unfamiliar stares of your soon-to-be classmates. Through the use of vivid sensory details, you can paint a picture your audience will remember long after they have forgotten the statistical data too often heavily relied upon in public speaking.

495 Creating an Effective Style and Tone

As with any piece of writing, the **style** of a speech has to be colorful and appealing, otherwise it has little chance of either getting your ideas across or of getting a favorable response from your audience. To make your speech colorful, write as naturally and honestly as possible. If you then feel a need to "add" color, rhythm, and sound, consider using a *stylistic device.*

Closely related to the style of your speech is the **tone.** Tone is the attitude or feeling which you bring to each of the words, phrases, or sentences in your speech. Tone is especially important in writing which is intended to be spoken because your attitude or feeling is sure to be reflected in your voice. This "tone of voice" is nearly as important as the words themselves in determining the success or failure of a speech. As you work with your speech, be aware of the tone it is taking on. Select words, phrases, and stylistic devices which help to create the appropriate tone.

A Closer Look at Style

More than any other president of recent times, John F. Kennedy is remembered for the appealing style and tone of his speeches. By looking at sample portions of his speeches, you should get a better feel for how style and tone can help strengthen the spoken word. (The tone of each sample is listed above the excerpt and labeled as an **appeal**—a word which reflects both the writer's personal feelings and attitudes and the feelings he hopes his audience will also experience.)

497 **Parallel structuring** is the repeating of phrases or sentences which are similar (parallel) in meaning and structure; **repetition** is the repeating of the same word or phrase to create a sense of rhythm and emphasis.

Appeal for Commitment

Let every nation know, whether it wishes us well or ill, that we shall *pay any price, bear any burden, meet any hardship, support any friend, oppose any foe,* in order to assure the survival and the success of liberty (Inaugural Address, 1961).

(Note: In this sample, the three-word phrases in italics are parallel because each begins with the same kind of word—a verb—and each ends with the same kind of word—a noun. These parallel phrases also contain repetition in the form of the word *any.)*

498 **Analogy** is a comparison of an unfamiliar idea to a simple, familiar one. The comparison is usually quite lengthy, suggesting several points of similarity. An analogy is especially useful when attempting to explain a difficult or complex idea.

Appeal to Common Sense

In our opinion the German people wish to have one united country. If the Soviet Union had lost the war, the Soviet people themselves would object to a line being drawn through Moscow and the entire country. If we had been defeated in war, we wouldn't like to have a line drawn down the Mississippi River. . . (Interview, November 25, 1961).

499 **Alliteration** is the repetition of initial consonant sounds in neighboring words as in *wet, wild,* and *wooly.*

Appeal to the Democratic Principle

I ask you to look into your hearts—not in search of charity, for the Negro neither wants nor needs condescension—but for the one *plain, proud,* and *priceless* quality that unites us all as Americans: a sense of justice (Message to Congress, 1963).

500 **Allusion** is a reference in a speech to a familiar person, place, or thing.

Appeal to the Democratic Principle

One hundred years of delay have passed since *President Lincoln* freed the slaves, yet their heirs, their grandsons, are not fully free (Radio and television address, 1963).

501 **Metaphor** is comparing two things without using words of comparison *(like or as).*

Appeal for Involvement, Commitment

Let the word go forth from this time and place, to friend and foe alike, that the *torch* has been passed to a new generation of Americans. . . (Inaugural Address, 1961).

(Note: In this instance, the word *torch* is used metaphorically. The changing of the presidents is being compared to the passing of the torch, a traditional symbol of ongoing causes.)

502 **Simile** is comparing two unlike things using *like* or *as.*

Appeal to the Democratic Principle

Only an educated and informed people will be a free people; . . . the ignorance of one voter in a democracy impairs the security of all, and . . . if we can, as Jefferson put it, "enlighten the people generally . . . tyranny and the oppressions of mind and body will vanish, *like the evil spirits at the dawn of the day."*

503 **Irony** is using a word or phrase to mean the exact opposite of its literal meaning or to show a result which is the opposite of what would be expected or appropriate.

Appeal to Common Sense

They see no harm in paying those to whom they entrust the minds of their children a smaller wage than is paid to those to whom they entrust the care of their plumbing (Vanderbilt University, 1961).

504 **Antithesis** is balancing or contrasting one word or idea against another, usually in the same sentence.

Appeal to Common Sense, Commitment

Let us never negotiate out of fear. But let us never fear to negotiate (Inaugural Address, 1961).

Mankind must put an end to war or war will put an end to mankind (Address to the U.N., 1961).

505 **Anecdote** is a short story told to illustrate a point.

Appeal to Pride, Commitment

Frank O'Connor, the Irish writer, tells in one of his books how as a boy, he and his friends would make their way across the countryside and when they came to an orchard wall that seemed too high and too doubtful to try and too difficult to permit their voyage to continue, they took off their hats and tossed them over the wall—and then they had no choice but to follow them.

This Nation has tossed its cap over the wall of space, and we have no choice but to follow it. Whatever the difficulties, they will be overcome (San Antonio Address, November 21, 1963).

506 **Negative definition** is describing something by telling what it is *not* rather than, or in addition to, what it is.

Appeal for Commitment

. . . members of this organization are committed by the Charter to promote and respect human rights. Those rights are not respected when a Buddhist priest is driven from his pagoda, when a synagogue is shut down, when a Protestant church cannot open a mission, when a cardinal is forced into hiding, or when a crowded church service is bombed (United Nations, September 20, 1963).

507 **Extended definition** is defining a concept through the use of several different devices or approaches.

Appeal to Common Sense

World peace, like community peace, does not require that each man love his neighbor—it requires only that they live together in mutual tolerance, submitting their disputes to a just and peaceful settlement.

Genuine peace must be the product of many nations, the sum of many acts. It must be dynamic, not static, changing to meet the challenge of each new generation. For peace is a process—a way of solving problems.

Peace is a daily, a weekly, a monthly process, gradually changing opinions, slowly eroding old barriers, quietly building new structures. And however undramatic the pursuit of peace, the pursuit must go on (From two addresses, 1963).

508 **Quotations,** especially of well-known individuals, can be effective in nearly any speech.

Appeal for Emulation or Affiliation

At the inauguration, Robert Frost read a poem which began "the land was ours before we were the land's"—meaning, in part, that this new land of ours sustained us before we were a nation. And although we are now the land's—a nation of people matched to a continent—we still draw our strength and sustenance . . . from the earth (Dedication speech, 1961).

509 **Rhetorical question** is a question posed for emphasis of a point, not for the purpose of getting an answer.

Appeal to Common Sense, Democratic Principle

"When a man's ways please the Lord," the Scriptures tell us, "he maketh even his enemies to be at peace with him." And is not peace, in the last analysis, basically a matter of human rights—the right to live out our lives without fear of devastation—the right to breathe air as nature provided it—the right of future generations to a healthy existence? (Commencement Address, 1963)

510 **Pun** is a play on words which is either humorous or witty. In either case, it involves using words in a way or in a situation different from their normal use.

Appeal to a Sense of Humor

What more can be said today, regarding all the dark and tangled problems we face, than: Let there be light (University of Washington, 1961).

Appeal to Hope

For every apparent blessing contains the seeds of danger—every area of trouble gives out a ray of hope—and the one unchangeable certainty is that nothing is certain or unchangeable (State of the Union, 1962).

511 Below you will find a sample speech labeled for stylistic devices.

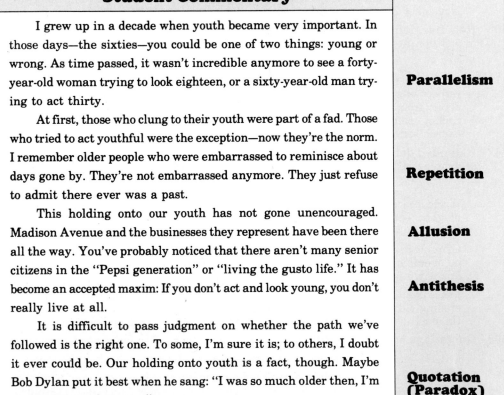

Student Commentary

I grew up in a decade when youth became very important. In those days—the sixties—you could be one of two things: young or wrong. As time passed, it wasn't incredible anymore to see a forty-year-old woman trying to look eighteen, or a sixty-year-old man trying to act thirty. — **Parallelism**

At first, those who clung to their youth were part of a fad. Those who tried to act youthful were the exception—now they're the norm. I remember older people who were embarrassed to reminisce about days gone by. They're not embarrassed anymore. They just refuse to admit there ever was a past. — **Repetition**

This holding onto our youth has not gone unencouraged. Madison Avenue and the businesses they represent have been there all the way. You've probably noticed that there aren't many senior citizens in the "Pepsi generation" or "living the gusto life." It has become an accepted maxim: If you don't act and look young, you don't really live at all. — **Allusion** / **Antithesis**

It is difficult to pass judgment on whether the path we've followed is the right one. To some, I'm sure it is; to others, I doubt it ever could be. Our holding onto youth is a fact, though. Maybe Bob Dylan put it best when he sang: "I was so much older then, I'm younger than that now." — **Quotation (Paradox)**

The Elements of a Speech

512 **The Introduction:** After you have finished wording your speech, you must arrange your details into an introduction, body, and conclusion. You should, for example, use an especially interesting detail in your opening or **introduction.** It should be combined with other thoughts so as to accomplish the following:

- Gain the attention of your audience.
- Motivate your audience to want to listen to you.
- State clearly the purpose and central idea of your talk (thesis statement).
- Serve as a transition or bridge into the main part of your speech.

513 You can structure your opening remarks using any of the stylistic devices discussed earlier in this section or by selecting one of the following techniques:

- an appropriate quotation
- a startling statement
- a challenging question or series of questions
- a humorous story
- a short demonstration
- an attention-capturing incident or illustration
- an immediate issue or challenge

514 **The Body:** The **body** of the speech should be arranged so that it builds to a climax. This can be a growing, dramatic build *(crescendo)* which reaches an intense, emotional peak at the conclusion. In this instance, the voice works with the written copy to heighten and amplify the climax. The climax can also be a slow, diminishing fade which captivates your audience much like a whisper in a dramatic scene. It pinpoints a specific idea or emotion and draws your speech to a thoughtful, quiet close much the same as a eulogy or memorial reading.

515 **The Conclusion:** The **conclusion** you choose will depend a great deal on which of the two styles of climax you choose. It must, in either case, draw your important thoughts into a final, meaningful focus. It should leave your audience with a picture which is clear and vivid—one which they will remember whenever this subject is mentioned in the future.

Preparing the Speech for Delivery

516 Once you are satisfied that the written portion of your speech is in its final form, you can write or type your final copy. Follow the suggestions listed below when you type:

1. Always double-space your copy and leave an extra-wide margin at the bottom.

2. Never run a sentence from one page to another.

3. Keep your copy neat and clean.

4. Never abbreviate unless you intend the material to be delivered as an abbreviation. *Example:* FCC, YMCA, and FBI may be abbreviated because they will be delivered as abbreviations.

5. Number the pages (beginning with page one) in the upper right-hand corner.

517 ## Practicing the Delivery

You must next turn your attention to the delivery of the speech. The best way to assure a smooth, effective presentation is to practice out loud as often as you can. Try to get an audience of family or friends to listen to you. They can offer a more realistic setting than an empty room and can also offer suggestions for improvement. If you cannot find an audience, a reasonable substitute would be a recorder. By listening to your playback (or listening and watching if you have access to video tape equipment), you will be in a better position to make improvements in your written copy as well as in your delivery technique.

518 **Marking for Interpretation**

As you decide what changes you want to make, note them on your speech copy. This applies to changes in delivery technique as well. Noting delivery techniques on your paper is called "marking your copy" and involves using a set of symbols to represent voice patterns. These special symbols will remind you to pause in certain key places during your presentation, to emphasize a certain word or phrase, or to add color to a word which might otherwise be misunderstood, and so on. Below is a sample list of copy-marking symbols:

Copy-Marking Symbols
Inflection *(arrows)* . . . . for a rise in pitch, for a drop in pitch.
Emphasis *(underlining)* . . . . for additional <u>drive</u> or <u>force</u>.
Color *(curved line)* . . . . for additional feeling or intonation.
Pause *(dash, diagonal, ellipsis)* . . . . for a pause—or / break . . . in the flow.
Rate *(hyphen)* . . . . for a rapid-or-connected-rate.

519 **Marking for Pronunciation**

Whenever you are unsure of the correct pronunciation of a word, look it up in the dictionary. There is no quicker or surer way to lose credibility as a speaker than to mispronounce a key word. Each word in a dictionary is labeled with special marks (called diacritical markings) which show you the correct way to say a word. Copy this diacritically marked word immediately following the difficult word on your speech copy. You can refer to these markings when you get to that word during your presentation. You should practice saying the word enough so that it sounds natural when you pronounce it.

520	**Student Editorial: Pet Peeve**

As far as I'm concerned, it's already too late to talk about Union High School students and their study halls. I believe changes should have been made <u>long</u> ago. Unluckily, we're <u>still</u> talking.

A relatively large portion of this school's student population / have gone through the process of <u>receiving</u> a pass, <u>going</u> to the principal's office, and being <u>confronted</u> with evidence <u>proving</u> they have skipped study hall. It's obvious to me that a great deal of effort is being exerted by students and the administration / to avoid being caught and attempting to catch, respectively. (REE SPEK TIV LEE)

With all the time and trouble both sides are going to, you'd expect <u>someone</u> to suggest a solution to the problem. But no one seems to care that much about <u>why</u> students skip study hall. The big concern is in <u>rounding</u> them up and getting them back in. I suspect that if you were to take the time to ask students why they skip, you would hear a great many tell you it's because the study halls are useless and boring. I feel they'd be right.

It's time we stop "<u>dealing</u> with skippers"; it's time we stop <u>complaining</u> about the people who skip; and, above all else, it's time we <u>stop</u> <u>avoiding</u> the <u>real</u> problem and start looking at why skipping occurs in the first place.

The administration, school board, and students have spent too much time worrying about the insignificant aspects of the skipping issue / and too <u>little</u> time on the problem itself. Continued neglect won't make skipping go away; reasonable solutions will.

521 **Evaluating Your Speech**

As you continue to prepare the delivery portion of your speech, remember to review the voice characteristics necessary for effective speaking. The "Speech Evaluation Form" which follows can serve as a reminder of the things you should or should not do when delivering a speech. You may also want to refer to the list of "Speech Terms," 524, when reviewing the aspects of voice which are important in a speech.

Speech Evaluation Form

Speaker _____ Date_____

Title/Subject of Presentation_____

	Rating	Comments
Subject Significant topic? Clear purpose? Appropriate to the audience?		
Research/Analysis Full investigation? Clear and logical analysis? Sources documented?		
Organization Introduction as an attention-getter? Introduction states purpose/links? Body logically arranged? Appropriate conclusion?		
Language Suited to the audience? Clear and direct? Original and appealing? Vivid word picture? Appropriate tone?		
Stylistic Technique Use of effective repetition/parallelism? Appeal to emotion/logic? Call for involvement? Anecdotes/Analogies? Figurative language?		
Delivery Appropriate action and gestures? Eye contact? Loudness and quality of voice? Pronunciation/Enunciation? Drive/Pause/Rate/Color?		
Overall Effectiveness Attention maintained? Enthusiasm and concern shown throughout? Purpose met?		
FINAL RATING		

Evaluated by_____

Giving Your Speech

522   If you have practiced often and well, giving the actual speech should be easy. You may feel a little nervous at first, but if you relax and keep the following suggestions in mind, you have nothing to fear.

1. Speak loudly and clearly.

2. Don't rush. Take your time and let your voice naturally add color and interest to your topic.

3. Use your hands. Sometimes you will need your hands to hold a chart or a poster. Other times, your hands will be busy operating part of your demonstration. At the very least, let your hands hold your note cards or paper (if they are allowed). Never leave your hand movements to chance. They'll end up picking lint off your shirt or dangling nervously at your side.

4. Look at your audience as you speak.

5. Keep both feet firmly on the floor. Don't slouch, sway, or teeter.

6. Show enthusiasm for your topic from start to finish.

— Speech Checklist ————————

523   1. Choose a topic both you and your audience will like.

2. Make sure your topic fits the assignment and time limit.

3. Do a good job of thinking about and researching your topic. Explore all sides of the topic.

4. Think about the topic information you have gathered and use only the details which will work well for you.

5. Write an introduction which will gain the interest of your audience as well as introduce your topic.

6. Think about how you can move from one point to another smoothly.

7. Use your own language. Write as if you were actually talking to someone.

8. Don't use a "big" word when a small one will do.

9. Make sure everything you say is clear and understandable.

10. Speak loudly enough so everyone can hear you.

11. Don't rush.

12. Use your hands to help you in some way.

13. Keep both feet on the floor.

14. Show enthusiasm for your topic.

15. Look at your audience.

16. End with a strong, interesting idea.

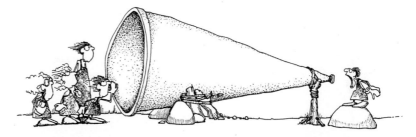

Acoustics: The science of sound or the way the walls, floor, ceiling, and other parts of a room react to sound. The quality of speech sounds depends in part on the acoustics of the room in which they are produced.

Ad Lib: Making up or composing the words to a speech as you deliver it.

Articulation: The uttering of speech sounds in a clear, distinct manner. The tongue, lips, teeth, cheeks, palate, and uvula all partake in the articulation process.

Cadence: The rhythm or flow of a speech. A smooth, even flow is described as being *legato;* a bouncy, jerky flow is called *staccato.*

Climax: The high point or peak in a speech.

Color: The emotional treatment given certain key words in a speech to convey the special meanings or connotations of those words. The voice is greatly inflected and the force usually increased to accomplish this distinct vocal appeal.

Commentary: An organized group of remarks or observations on a particular subject; an interpretation, usually of a complex social issue.

Continuity: The state or quality of being continuous or unbroken. A speech with continuity will move smoothly from the introduction through the conclusion by way of effective linking or transitional devices.

Editorial: A carefully organized piece of writing in which an opinion is expressed.

Emphasis: Giving more attention to a particular word or phrase than to the others. This can be done by varying the force, pace, pitch, or color of the voice.

Enunciation: The clearness or crispness of a person's voice. If a speaker's enunciation is good, it will be easy to understand each sound or word he creates.

Eye Contact: The communicating a speaker does with his eyes during a speech. It is very important that a speaker establish sincere eye contact with his audience so that full communication can take place.

Force (Drive): The amount of pressure or punch behind the speaker's voice; *loudness.*

Gesture: The motion a speaker uses to emphasize a point. Hand and facial gestures are usually effective additions to a speech, although they can also be visual distractions and take away from the speaker's effectiveness. The important thing to remember is to keep gestures as natural as possible and not to overuse them.

Inflection: The rising and falling in the pitch of the voice.

Monotone: A voice which is unchanging in inflection or color; *dullness.*

Oratory: The art of public speaking.

Pace: The rate of movement of a speech. It is often a combination of rates, selected for their appropriateness to the message and the audience.

Pause: The momentary stopping in a speech to give additional emphasis to a particular word, phrase, or idea.

Pitch: The highness or lowness of a voice. By properly varying the pitch of the voice, the speaker can emphasize or color the words in his script.

Presence: The sense of closeness of the speaker to his audience. If a speaker is sincere and open with his audience, his degree of presence or believability will be high.

Projection: Directing or throwing the voice so it can be heard at a distance.

Rate: The speed (fastness or slowness) of the speech pattern.

Repetition: The repeating of words or phrases to add a sense of balance and rhythm to a piece of writing as in Lincoln's Gettysburg Address: ". . . of the people, by the people, and for the people."

Resonance: The prolonging of a sound through vibration. In the speech process, the resonance is intensified by the chest, throat, and nose. The quality of the resulting sound will be determined by whichever of these three cavities acts as the primary resonator.

Script (Manuscript): The written copy of the speech used during a presentation.

Speech: The process of communicating with the voice through a combination of breathing, resonating, and articulating.

Stage Fright: The tension or nervousness a speaker feels when he is preparing to deliver or is actually delivering a speech.

The Thinking
PROCESS

Opening Thoughts

You don't have to *be* a brain to *use* your brain. In fact, as you read this page, you are already using the thinking skills a nuclear physicist, a fine artist, or a philosopher would use. You observe, name, add, distinguish, compare, analyze parts, shape parts into new wholes, form general ideas, evaluate things, and solve problems. Moreover, you were using those skills already in first grade, without even "thinking."

Apart from age and life experience, what is the difference between a first grader and a thinker like you? You have become more skilled over the years. You did it by

- using your brain more often,
- using more of your brain's potential,
- enlarging your aims,
- more consciously controlling the thinking process, and
- learning helpful techniques.

525   Before you go on, remember one thing. Only a small portion of a person's thinking takes place on the conscious level. Most of it goes on in the dark caverns of the subconscious mind. No logical rules or creative techniques can ever capture the whole process. Thoughts have to fight their way upstream like salmon. They swarm toward their destination like bees. They churn like a potful of boiling soup. Formal guidelines may help you start, stop, or steer your thoughts, but when they begin to stifle subconscious thoughts, they have lost their usefulness. Don't put your genius behind bars. Stay flexible. Keep it fun.

The section which follows will help you better understand and appreciate the thinking process. First, you'll take stock of your reasons for thinking; then you'll meet someone with a "thinking attitude"; and, finally, you'll learn about your thinking organ—the brain.

526 **Why Do We Think?**

1. **We can't help it.** Our bodies keep sending nerve impulses to the brain—rumbling stomach, stubbed toe, musky perfume, saccharine taste, olive green, sound of a garage band. The brain interprets these and tells the body how to respond.

2. **We want to.** By studying our experiences, thoughts, and feelings, we shape our lives into a continuing story. Memories preserve our past; perceptions and reflections guide us in the present; plans and wishes lead us into the future.

3. **We have to.** Parents, teachers, employers, and others send out the messages: Think, or you will fail. Be imaginative, accurate, and quick. Don't be dull, confused, or slow.

4. **We enjoy it.** Thinking can be suspenseful, dramatic, satisfying. It puts the thrill in basketball, chess, debate, the movies, falling in love, and other sports.

5. **We need to.** Clear thinking and lively imagination help us solve some problems, reach some decisions, or grasp larger concepts.

527 **A Thinking Attitude**

Frank is always coming up with new ideas. You can always count on him for good advice. Hank, well, he's more of a follower. He gets most of his ideas from Frank.

Both guys have about the same level of intelligence. What makes Frank the better thinker?

Unlike Hank, Frank has a **thinking attitude**. He's…

Patient

Frank assumes that problems are complex and that his head will be crowded with other business. If ideas don't pop up like slices of toast, he waits and keeps working.

Curious

Whereas Hank feels safe with what he knows, Frank enjoys surprises. He lifts the lids from boxes to see what's inside. He often asks "Why" and "What if," just as children do.

Able to Concentrate

Under pressure, Frank blocks out all distractions. He "glues" himself to the main point, even in a noisy room. Hank seems almost grateful to be interrupted.

Respectful of Evidence

Frank insists on evidence to back up general statements. If he uncovers a disturbing new fact, he will change his opinions. Hank gathers only the sort of evidence that proves what he already believes.

Skeptical

Frank questions the evidence out of habit. He'll say: "Hold on. We're forgetting something" or "Who said that?" or "Is that up-to-date?" Hank is more gullible. He figures if he read it in a book, it must be true.

Open to Other Perspectives

Frank sometimes plays "devil's advocate" to test for weaknesses in his own viewpoint. Opposing views don't threaten him. He reminds himself that both he and the other person are still searching; the truth probably lies somewhere in between.

Ready to Change

Frank expects to change his opinions in the course of research or a good discussion. Hank hopes that nothing important will come up to disturb his way of thinking.

Tolerant of Ambiguity

Frank can live with unresolved questions. He is fascinated by problems that seem to have two contradictory solutions. When Hank sees a paradox like that, he throws up his hands and sighs, "That's ridiculous."

If Hank can't solve a problem in one swoop, his brain is ready for a siesta. Frank won't put the problem down. He'll look at it from the back, from below, from inside, from above. He sees an image of himself solving the problem and struggles until the image becomes a reality.

An attitude like Frank's can improve your thinking power. It takes the fear out of thinking and keeps you involved in the thinking process. With a thinking attitude you will gather in more to think about and think more thoroughly about it. Above all, a thinking attitude will put you in charge of your own thoughts. As the poet William Blake once said, "You must build your own system or you will be enslaved by someone else's."

528 **Getting to Know Your Brain**

Knowing your own brain is a bit like knowing what is under the hood of your car. You are more likely to keep your "engine" in tune if you know how it works. Below is a profile of the brain with a key to its parts and their functions:

Structure and Function

Key:

A. CORTEX
—thin blanket of nerve cells, covers the cerebrum
—has many wrinkles, which increase the total surface area

B. CEREBRUM
—about 85% of brain mass
—seat of conscious thought processes
—subparts (or "lobes"):
    a) frontal lobe: thought, speech, body movements
    b) parietal lobe (top middle): bodily sensations, shape, texture, position
    c) occipital lobe (rear): sight, reading, visual imagery
    d) temporal lobe: smell, memory for music, memory images, speech

C. CEREBELLUM
—automatically coordinates movement, posture, and balance with sense perceptions

D. CORPUS CALLOSUM
—bridge of nerve fibers, connects left and right halves

E. PONS
—relays nerve impulses between cerebrum and cerebellum

F. MEDULLA OBLONGATA
—lower portion of brain stem
—controls automatic movements: swallowing, breathing, heartbeat, circulation, posture, intestinal movements

G. SPINAL CORD
—conducts brain impulses to body and vice versa
—controls reflexes

529 **A Closer Look at the Brain**

Millions of nerve cells, or neurons, are grouped in bundles called ganglia. These intertwine with millions of capillaries, which feed blood, and therefore oxygen, to the brain tissues. Despite the unimaginable number of nerve pathways and chemical transactions in the brain, the brain's response to stimuli is almost instantaneous.

You won't need to think of the brain's structure every time you brace yourself for some serious thinking, but here are several important observations you should make. The brain is...

● **Specialized**. Some parts respond to the body and some respond to other parts of the brain. Some parts produce thoughts, some parts help process thoughts, and some parts store thoughts. Some parts produce the thinking mankind is best known for: conscious reflection. Other parts produce and coordinate animal reflexes as well as automatic functions of the body. The parts most essential for survival, the brain stem and medulla, are huddled deep inside masses of brain tissue. Injury to one part of the brain can remove a single function, e.g., speaking ability, while leaving other functions unharmed.

● **Delicate**. The brain's hard shell, the skull, protects its soft nerve ganglia from all but the hardest knocks. If the brain is going to be hurt, it will probably be hurt from within, through the bloodstream and nerve paths, by alcohol, poor diet, cigarettes, coffee, drugs, lack of sleep, or disease.

● **Layered**. At any given time, the brain may be working on several levels: conscious reasoning, memory, physical motion, imagination, automatic movement, reflex, and so on.

● **Coordinated**. The brain is like a miniature world in which the parts, like countries, trade with one another. Sometimes they act in concert, sometimes in conflict, as when the pleasure-seeking parts of the brain want a bag of jelly donuts that the rational mind says would blow your diet.

530 **Left Brain/Right Brain**

From the top, the brain looks something like a shelled walnut, with two wrinkled halves connected by a narrow bridge across a deep fissure running from front to rear:

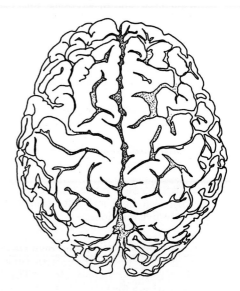

The two halves look like mirror opposites and function that way, too. The right half handles nerve impulses to the left side of the body. The left half serves the right side of the body. The two nerve pathways crisscross at the corpus callosum.

Researchers have shown that the two halves think in quite different ways. You need both ways to be a well-rounded thinker. In general, the left brain is a "splitter." In other words, it is best at breaking down thoughts into parts and logical sequences. The right brain, by contrast, is a "lumper"—it composes wholes and grasps them imaginatively.

On the next page you'll find a more detailed contrast, adapted from a table by Gabriele Lusser Rico, who surveyed split-brain research and applied the results to the teaching of writing.

Left Brain	**Right Brain**
1. Recognizes parts: e.g., trees	Recognizes wholes: e.g., forest
2. Processes items one by one: e.g., fries, root beer, hamburger	Processes items all at once: e.g., supper
3. Thinks logically: e.g., "If this flops, then we're in trouble, unless we adopt plan B."	Thinks in analogies and resemblances: e.g., "This is a time bomb."
4. Sees detail: e.g., brushstrokes	Sees overall designs: e.g., a landscape
5. Grasps information: e.g., "I have just stepped on a snail."	Grasps emotional subtlety: e.g., "Yuck!"
6. Bounded by rules: e.g., "Subject must agree with verb in number."	Unbounded, open: "This essay is powerful, like a bull, a train, a thunderstorm."
7. Remembers complicated sequences of actions: e.g., the motions required for a spike in volleyball	Remembers complex sequences of imagery: e.g., the appearance of a spike
8. Uses language: e.g., apple	Uses pictures: e.g.,
9. Perceives words as verbal signs: e.g., "I" + "love" + "you"	Perceives words as rhythmic, artful patterns: e.g., "a loaf of bread, a jug of wine, and thou"

531 Thinking Phase

Notice that the right brain specializes in the kind of thinking that makes children so fresh and creative: thinking in images, in terms of wholes, in resemblances, in emotions, in pictures, and in rhythms. But also notice that the left brain specializes in the kinds of thinking that are more and more emphasized in school as you grow older: information, analysis, detail, rules, logic, grammar, syntax, language.

According to Rico, children go through three major phases as their minds develop:

1. **Innocent Phase** (ages 2-7): the right brain dominates. A child feels much wonder, emotion, curiosity, and delight in pattern.

2. **Conventional Phase** (ages 8-16): the left brain begins to dominate. Thinking is more bound by rules, habits, rational realism, conventional patterns, cliche.

3. **Cultured Phase** (ages 17 and up): increased collaboration and "orchestration" between right and left hemispheres. Recovery of some right-brain, imaginative, intuitive functions.

Take stock of your own ways of thinking. If you discover weaknesses in either "half," try to bring the two types of thinking into better balance. (The sections on "Thinking Creatively," "Thinking Clearly," and "Thinking Logically" offer suggestions for better utilizing your left-brain and right-brain thinking abilities.)

> *"To know is nothing at all; to imagine is everything."*
> **—Anatole France**

Thinking
CREATIVELY

Successful short stories and poems offer readers something new, something unexpected, something—at times—even outrageous. They originate from initial perceptions which are then bent, twisted, played with, and eventually reworked by writers into new and exciting shapes. The section which follows describes the creative "mind set" which triggers these new shapes. Use it as your guide to creative thinking and writing.

What Is Creativity?

532   It's the power of a four-year-old to invent new words—her classmates are curled up on their rugs like "boa and arrow constrictors." Ginger ale, says another, "tastes like your foot's asleep."

It's the flash of inspiration that makes a photographer see Stonehenge in a pile of old tires.

It's your power to see a similarity between a toaster and the family's old car; your power to imagine what the school of tomorrow might be like; your power to turn a near-fight into new friendship.

The Creative Process

533   You've heard the old saying, "Success is 10% inspiration, 90% perspiration." The same is true of the creative process, as any successful artist or writer could tell you.

The creative process is not a step-by-step procedure. Rather, it is the use of an array of methods for preparing the mind, stimulating the mind, opening the mind, and guiding the mind as it spins out bright ideas.

Where dull thinking (DT) plucks a sandbur off his socks and throws it away, creative thinking (CT) invents Velcro. DT stays angry because somebody ripped off his CD player. CT wins one hundred dollars in a literary contest with a story told from the point of view of the thief.

534 An Overview of the Creative Process

Creativity starts with sensory **perceptions**: seeing, hearing, smelling, tasting, and touching. Sensory perceptions in turn trigger memories. The process is set in motion.

The first **stirring** of a creative idea may come from a memory, a fresh perception, or a prompt from another person. Often the stirring will occur while your mind is occupied with something else. While the left brain is away, the right brain will play.

Then a period of **exploring** and **gathering** may begin. Information starts to fall in line and gravitate toward a center.

Next many creative thinkers go through a period of **resting** and waiting, sometimes called "incubation." The idea may seem to be forgotten, but the brain keeps working on it subconsciously, trying out different angles.

After all that preparation, **inspiration** may strike. Inspiration literally means "breathed into." So it seems. The mind, like a lung, fills itself with possibilities, plans, inklings, and waking dreams. "Aha!" you might shout. Or "Eureka!"

For inspiration to last, the creative thinker must soon begin **shaping** thought through drawing, dancing, sculpting, or in this case, writing.

The last phase of the creative process is **revising** or reworking whatever one has thought and written about in order to make it a more perfect expression of the idea.

535 The Creative Process: A Closer Look

1. **Look closely!** Don't just look at something. Study it. Empty yourself of all ideas about it. Keep on studying until it gives you news about itself. That's the creative way of sensing the world.

2. **Catch the stirrings.** Creative stirrings are of no use to you unless you are ready to catch them. A personal journal makes a good net.

3. **Explore freely and energetically.** Gather uncritically. Save the shaping for later. This is the time to try out, have fun, make mistakes, act foolish, be surprised.

4. **Don't become impatient.** If you have time to think, use it. Incubation is not a failure to think; it's a different mode of thinking. People who are familiar with the thinking process often include "down time" in their plans.

5. **The creativity begins!** It is tempting to see inspiration as the destination and reward of thinking. But inspiration is more like a launching pad. The fun, the work, the real creativity begins there. Belt yourself in and take off.

6. **Catch new ideas.** As you work out the details of your creative idea, keep the spirit of creativity alive. Expect to catch new ideas as they stir up from your field of thought.

7. **Swerving along.** Don't force yourself to work straight through from start to finish. Your inspiration may lead you from the center to the shores or from puddle to puddle. Work out connections later.

8. **Fine-tune your ideas.** Make the spirit of your imagination sparkle even in the tiniest details.

The Creative Mind in Action

Without creativity you might look at an ordinary object like a pencil and think, "There's a pencil. Something to write with. It looks brand new. It's probably worth less than a dime."

But if you look at the same pencil with a creative mind—not just look at it but notice it and feel it as it is—it can set all sorts of mental imagery in motion. Here's proof:

The No. 2 Pencil Meets a Creative Mind

- First, notice the parts: lead point, hexagonal wooden barrel painted yellow, words "Dixon Ticonderoga 1388—2 Soft" stamped along one side in green ink on gold, triple-striped green and yellow metal collar holding a powdery pink eraser, not yet rubbed raw.

- Imagine the manufacturing process—the wood gluers, the planes, the slicers, the paint vats, the dryers, the stamps, and so on.

- Think of the tree the wood was once a part of. Where did it grow? Where on the tree was this pencil's wood located? Where are the other parts of the tree now?

- Imagine being the paint. Now imagine being covered all over with yellow paint and stamped with green and gold letters.

- See the pencil as a bridge stretching between two places. What are they?

- Imagine the pencil as a pillar. What is it holding up?

- Who will hold this pencil before it is worn to a nub? What will be the most important thing ever written with it? What will be the funniest thing?

- How strong is it? How much weight would be needed to break it? The weight of a safe? Of a hamster? A frying pan? A six-year-old boy? A rainbow trout?

- Now it is being used as a pointer. Who is pointing it and what are they pointing at? Why?

- Imagine an occasion when this pencil might be given as a gift. What is the occasion?

- If the pencil could think, what would it be thinking as it is locked away in a drawer? How about as it is being used to write a letter?

- How would you feel if you were turned upside down and your head, ground to a point, were scraped in loops and squiggles across a piece of paper?

- Imagine a world in which the pencil is a sacred object. What would that world be like?

- Look at the pencil—what does it resemble?

- Listen to the sounds it makes—what do they remind you of?

- Smell it—what does the smell remind you of?

- Bite it—what does it taste like?

- Roll the pencil around in your fingers—what does its texture bring to mind?

Get the idea? What other new ways of experiencing the pencil can you think of? Always be on the alert, thinking of new ways to look at old objects and ideas. *Remember:* When your brain has nothing to do, it has a way of freezing up. Use your brain, your creativity. See Velcro, not sandburs.

Thinking
CLEARLY

"There is nothing we imagine that we do not already know."
— **Stephen Spender**

Thinking Clearly

The purpose of thinking clearly is not to fly through the air but to cover the ground. In other words, the purpose is not to create imaginative new connections but to choose logical steps that you can follow as you think through a problem or task. Maybe this procedure sounds completely separate from "right brain" creativity, but it is not. Creative thinking is always at work and serves as a constant guide for your rational thinking. It is simply forced into the background when the more disciplined and formal reasoning process is at work.

Get Ready, Get Set, Think

Before you engage in the active process of clear, rational thinking, establish the right frame of mind by "getting ready" and "getting set" to think.

537 Get Ready

Getting ready to think is something you have always done. Your readiness comes from your lifestyle, your mental background, and your immediate circumstances.

Lifestyle: Regular sleep, vigorous exercise, and a healthy diet help to clear and energize your mind. Nicotine, alcohol, and other drugs cloud and dull it.

Mental background: Your brain is able to store almost all you've ever thought and experienced in your lifetime, as well as all the ideas you've gathered from books or conversation. Enrich your storehouse by developing good habits: talk with interesting people, read challenging books, travel, spend time alone in deep thought, record ideas in a journal, go on in school, pay attention to small details. It is never too late to start.

Immediate circumstances: Respect deadlines. By framing your task in time, you can prod yourself to get on with the job. Solitude and silence are ideal for most thinkers, but some claim to need distraction—music, a room full of friends, a droning television set. Having paper and pencil or books or even a tape recorder on hand may enhance your thinking.

538 Get Set

Getting set to think means you mentally square off to meet a thinking challenge. It depends on your ability to identify the challenge, clarify your purpose, and overcome any mental hang-ups you might have. Deliberately getting set to think can help you concentrate as you go along.

Indentify your challenge: What is your thinking supposed to do? Solve a problem? Lead you to a decision? Explore a broad concept? Test your conscience? Whatever you want the challenge to be, accept it. At the moment you take personal responsibility for the outcome, your energies will begin to focus and your thoughts will begin to form meaningful patterns.

Clarify your purpose: Why do you want to accept this challenge? What is the purpose? Having a worthy purpose in mind, to borrow from Garrison Keillor, gives a shy person the courage to get up and do what has to be done.

Get rid of mental hang-ups: A mental hang-up is anything that freezes your mind or throws it "off the scent." Here are a few to watch out for:

> **Emotional hangover:** If you are upset about something, don't let it spoil the thinking task at hand.

> **Personality conflicts:** Ignore the dweeboid who sits next to you in study hall. The challenge lies between you and your thinking task, not between you and the dweeboid.

> **Stock opinions:** Every mind is littered with stock opinions—popular ideas we accept without proof. Clear thinking cuts through them like a razor.

> **Peer pressure:** Maybe it's totally uncool to approach a thinking challenge attentively and purposefully. Tell peer pressure where to get off; go ahead and apply yourself to your challenge.

539 Think

Rational thinking falls into two categories: *metacognition*—the act of "thinking about thinking"—and *cognition*—the act or process of thinking. Metacognition allows you to supervise your thinking. You can, in a sense, watch yourself work through a thinking task. The result is that your rational thinking is very flexible. You can speed up, slow down, zoom in, combine operations, back up, skip steps, or switch tactics whenever you want. Your mind does not run on a rigid track. It can steer wherever it must to solve problems. (See 115 for an example of metacognition at work.)

Metacognition

Metacognition consists of three basic elements: 1) developing a plan of action, 2) maintaining the plan, and 3) evaluating the plan. When you develop a plan of action, ask yourself questions like the following: *What in my past experience will help me with this particular task? In which direction do I want my thinking to take me? What should I do first?* Maintain your train of thought as it develops with questions like these: *How am I doing? Am I on the right track? How should I proceed? Should I move in a different direction?* And evaluate the outcome of your thinking with questions like these: *How well did I do? Did my particular course of thinking produce more or less than I had expected? What could I have done differently? How might I apply this line of thinking to other problems?*

Cognition

Cognition is a difficult process to describe, but it essentially begins when you make a basic thinking move—maybe you *identify* a certain relationship between two or more things. You then use an initial distinction or idea—that *A* is like *B*—to make additional distinctions if necessary. You might, for example, make the distinction that *A* and *B* add solid evidence to support an argument. You continue to apply basic thinking moves which follow from previous decisions until you reach a point that satisfies your "thinking." You never really know where your cogitating will take you until you actually get at it. This should sound familiar to you since the same holds true for the process of writing. Thinking and writing are interdependent skills. **You think to write and you write to think.**

Note: Clear thinkers often evaluate the results of their thinking by seeing how they stand up to the reasoning of others. If they discover that their ideas are too rigid, too general, or too narrow, they will qualify or abandon them.

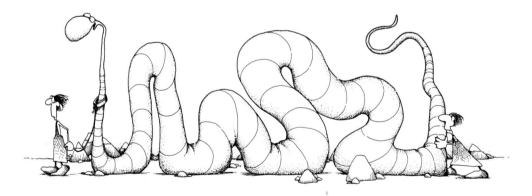

Basic Thinking Moves

The basic moves any thinking person makes are classified below according to their level of complexity. You will note that *recalling* information is a simple thinking operation whereas an operation like *analyzing* is rather complex. You can't perform a complex thinking operation without some understanding of the operations that precede it in the thinking hierarchy. If you are assigned, for example, to *evaluate* something you've read, you should know that your ability to do so depends on your ability to *recall* the material, *understand* it, *apply* it, and so on.

Thinking Operations

Level (simple to complex)	Key words	

Knowledge
(Recalling learned material)
    Remembering **A** and **B**
Memorizing a poem;
    clustering; recognizing
("That's a toad.")
	Recall
	Underline
	List
	Name
	Record
		Label
		Cluster
		Match
		Memorize
		Define

Comprehension (Understanding the material) **A = B** *Explaining* ("My dad's a baker.") *Changing* ("That's not a Toyota.")	Understand Show Summarize Explain Describe	Demonstrate Review Cite Restate Locate
Application (Using the learned material) First **A,** then **B** *Modeling* ("This is how you delete copy on your disk.")	Apply Select Model Organize Illustrate	Utilize Choose Imitate Demonstrate Use

Analysis
(Break material down to
increase understanding)
    A resembles **B, A** differs
        from **B**
Choosing ("This shampoo
has the same ingredients as
that one.")
Classifying ("I mean country
rock, not country western.")
	Analyze
	Compare
	Contrast
	Classify
	Map
		Characterize
		Divide
		Break Down
		Choose
		Examine

Synthesis (Reshaping material into a new form or composition) **A x B = C** *Constructing* ("Your brawn and my brains make a great combination.") *Speculating* ("My history class and my science class make me wonder about the history of science.")	Construct Speculate Design Compose Create	Develop Invent Blend Propose Formulate
Evaluation (Judging the worth of the material) **A>B or C; A<B** *Convincing* ("Spivak for Student Body President") *Arguing* ("*Apartheid* is institutional racism.")	Evaluate Convince Argue Judge Criticize	Rate Measure Persuade Assess Recommend

> *"The best argument is that which seems merely an explanation."*
>
> —Dale Carnegie

Thinking
LOGICALLY

Building Arguments

When you want to build an argument, in either speaking or writing, first consider the direction of your travel between reasons and conclusions. **Inductive argument** leads from observed facts to a general conclusion: "He has a temperature of 103°F...he has white spots on his tonsils...so he may have mononucleosis." **Deductive argument** starts with a general statement called a "premise," and applies it to a specific case in order to reach a conclusion about the specific case: "People with mononucleosis generally have white spots on their tonsils; he has mononucleosis; therefore, he probably has white spots on his tonsils."

The more premises assumed in an argument, the greater the logical "leap" needed to get through it. A good mental habit is to notice logical gaps and think of steps that would be needed to fill them. Logical weaknesses will often be found there.

543 Syllogisms: The Deductive Argument

A brief deductive argument reduced to a single "major premise," followed by a single "minor premise," leading to a "conclusion," is called a **syllogism**:

    p1 Every band member performed in the Rose Bowl Parade.
    p2 Brunhilde is a band member.
    C Brunhilde performed in the Rose Bowl Parade.

Notice that if the two premises are true, the conclusion is undeniable, and the syllogism is said to be "valid."

Usually we don't spell out all the steps in the syllogisms underlying our everyday speech; a syllogism with one of its premises taken for granted, such as the following, is called an **enthymeme**:

> Those brass knuckles must have been confiscated; we saw them on a shelf in the principal's office. (For this conclusion to be true, the unstated premise must also be true: Only confiscated items are put on the shelf in the principal's office.)

248   *Thinking Skills*

Developing a
Formal Argument

544   For term papers, speeches, debates, committee meetings, intense discussions and the like, you may need to organize your thoughts to a high degree and defend them against people who would disagree with you. To do your best in these situations, remember the chief stages of formal argument which follow:

Stages of the Formal Argument

Decide on your **purpose** for argument.

Gather **information** related to your topic.

Make a central **claim** which you can defend.

Add **qualifiers** to "round off" the claim.

Offer **definitions** for any unclear terms.

Use minor claims to **support** the central claim.

Use further evidence to **reinforce** the support.

Explain why the supports **warrant** acceptance as evidence.

Consider possible **objections** to your claim.

Make necessary **concessions** to the strongest objections.

Make clear **rebuttals** against the weaker objections.

Then **refine** your central claim

and **reaffirm** it.

Finally, **urge** its acceptance.

Note: You will not necessarily address every one of these stages in every argument. Each argument demands different treatment. Several of these key terms in an argument are explained below.

Key Stages in the Formal Argument

545   **Claim:**   Claims fall into three main groups: claims of **fact**, claims of **value**, and claims of **policy**.

Claims of fact assert that something is true or not true. If facts can be easily verified by observation or experiment, don't waste your time arguing about them. Brenda has 32 teeth—count 'em. But some "facts" are disputable:

1. Television violence causes violent behavior in children.
2. Sugar is bad for your health.
3. This bridge will not last another 10 years.

Claims of value assert that something has or does not have worth. Claims of value are impossible to defend when they are based on private taste or unfounded opinion.

To be strong, they must say what something has value for: Is a shoe best for hiking, tennis, sailing? And they ought to be based on a set of relevant criteria; for shoes, the criteria might be cost, durability, and style.

Claims of policy assert that something ought to be done or not done:
1. The Three Mile Island nuclear reactors ought to be dismantled.
2. We need a law to prevent any more farmland from being turned into suburban housing tracts.
3. Ms. Anderson should receive the "Teacher-of-the-Year Award."

546 Qualifiers: These are terms that make a claim more flexible. Note the difference between this claim:

Teachers ignore students' excuses.

and this one:

Some teachers **tend to** ignore students' excuses.

The second is easier to defend because it makes a qualified or moderated claim, rather than an absolute one. It leaves room for exceptions. Other useful qualifiers are:

almost	likely	most	to some extent
frequently	may	often	typically
hardly	maybe	probably	usually
if . . . , then . . .	might	sometimes	very
in most cases			

547 Support: Your central claim will not stand up just because you make it. It needs evidence for support; the more kinds of evidence you offer and the stronger the evidence, the sturdier your argument will be.

- For claims of **fact**, the following kinds of support may be helpful:

Observation: "I saw the northern lights twice last week."
Expert Testimony: "Carl Sagan says . . ."
Calculations: "It takes the solar wind X hours to reach earth."
Analogy: "The aurora borealis works much like the excited gases in a flourescent light bulb."
Records: "According to the latest reports from NASA . . ."
Inference: "For the aurora borealis to appear, there must have been solar flares within the previous 24 hours."

- For claims of **value**, these kinds of support may be helpful:

Comparison: "The movie was almost as exciting as *Star Wars*."
Expert Critique: "Siskel and Ebert gave it two thumbs up."
Experience: "I've seen it three times."
Demonstration: "This scene looks bad in slow motion."
Analysis: "The plot hinges on the secret that . . ."
Reputation: "Moviegoers all over the country have been saying that . . ."

- For claims of **policy**, try offering these types of support:

Precedent: "This curfew policy failed once before."
Prediction: "An early curfew is likely to do more harm than good."
Expert Testimony: "Sergeant O'Malley reported 17 cases of vandalism since . . ."

Demonstration: "An early curfew is in effect in the nearby town of Fairview and it has . . ."

548   Reinforcement: Sometimes support itself needs to be supported. If you quote an authority, for example, you may need to tell what her position is and her area of expertise. If your analysis needs to be clarified, give concrete examples and define key terms.

549   Warrant: A warrant is an idea that connects the support to your claim. It may be a simple reason or a complex line of reasoning. Here are some sample warrants with claims of fact, value, and policy:

> **Claim:**   *No life exists on Mars.*
> **Support:**   *Space photographs show a planet too dry to support life.*
> **Warrants:** *The photographs are of excellent resolution; they show all of Mars; we know of no life forms that can live without water.*
>
> **Claim:**   *Smoking is bad for your health.*
> **Support:**   *The surgeon general says so.*
> **Warrant:**   *The surgeon general has access to the best available research.*
>
> **Claim:**   *Cigarette advertising should be banned from magazines.*
> **Support:**   *It has already been banned from TV.*
> **Warrants:** *TV advertising is comparable to magazine advertising; TV audiences are comparable to magazine readers; cigarette advertising was banned from magazines for good reasons.*

Often a warrant is so obviously true that it need not be stated. But sometimes a warrant needs to be explained, illustrated, and defended. The warrant is a miniature argument within the larger argument. If the warrant fails, the entire argument sags and may collapse, unless there are other supports with better warrants.

550   Concession: Concessions are "points" that you let the other side score. When your argument has some true weaknesses—vagueness, incompleteness, lack of support—it is best to admit the fact. Giving away "points" will not weaken your argument if it was not strong there to begin with. In fact, a crucial concession takes away the major weapon of the opposition.

Some Useful Expressions for Making Concessions	
Admittedly	I concede that
Certainly . . ., but	It goes without saying that
Even though	Perhaps . . ., yet
Granted	Undoubtedly
I cannot argue with	While it is true that

551   Rebuttal: A rebuttal can mean either an objection against your argument or a reply that points out a weakness in an objection—an objection to an objection.

To find the weakness in an objection, try to uncover its logical "skeleton" and pick it apart bone by bone, or syllogism by syllogism. Sometimes a rebuttal will flatly deny the assumption made in an objection. Sometimes a rebuttal will point out previously ignored information. Sometimes it will redefine basic terms. Sometimes it will interpret old evidence in a new way. Sometimes it will quote one authority who contradicts the other. Sometimes a rebuttal will expose the personal bias, or emotional slant, in an opponent's argument.

Rebuttals help to "sweep the deck" of all the "debris" leftover in an argument so you can make a clean reaffirmation of your well-tested central claim.

Using Evidence and Logic

552   An argument is a chain of reasons which a person uses to support a conclusion. To use argument well, you need to know both how to draw logical conclusions from sound evidence and how to recognize and avoid false arguments. **Logical fallacies** are sometimes described in the complicated terms of formal logic, but more often they are cataloged according to informal types.

The informal fallacies described in this section are the bits of fuzzy or dishonest thinking that crop up often in our own speaking and writing, as well as in the advertisements, political appeals, editorials, and so on that we daily consume.

Logical fallacies are fairly harmless (though not excusable) when they are used to support an argument which is true anyway on other grounds. But they are dishonest and dangerous when a person uses them deliberately to satisfy some greedy, prejudiced, or spiteful desire. After all, an argument may be completely false and yet *effective* in swaying an audience which is not equipped to resist its emotional appeal. In fact, it is mainly *because* fallacies are effective that they are so often used as improper shortcuts to persuasion.

Fallacies of Thinking

A logical way of grouping the many types of logical fallacies is according to the part of the argument that they chiefly falsify. Some distort the original question; some are used to sabotage the whole argument; others make use of improper evidence or language; and still others draw faulty conclusions from the evidence available. In the list below, traditional Latin names are provided in italics if they are still in common use.

553 ## Distorting the Question

1. **The Bare Assertion**   ("That's just how it is.") The most basic way to distort a question is to deny that there is one. Refusing to back up a disputed claim with proper reasons is an irresponsible argument stopper.

2. **Begging the Question**   This fallacy consists of *assuming* in a definition or in the premises of your argument the very point you are trying to prove. Note how circular this sort of reasoning is:

> Phil: I hate Mr. Baldwin's class because I'm never happy in there.
> (But what's wrong with the *class*?)

3. **Oversimplification**   Beware of phrases like, "It all boils down to. . . . " or "It's a simple question of. . . . " Almost no dispute among reasonably intelligent people is "a simple question of. . . . " Anyone who feels, for example, that capital punishment "all boils down" to a matter of protecting society ought to question, in succession, a doctor, an inmate on death row, his wife, a sociologist, a minister, and a political philosopher.

4. **Black and White Thinking**   ("Either . . . or . . . . ") This familiar fallacy consists of reducing all possible options to two extremes: "America: Love It or Leave It." "Put up or shut up." "If you can't stand the heat, get out of the kitchen." Usually when a person eliminates all "greys" from consideration like this, that person leaves little doubt about which option he or she considers white and which black. Thus, the black/white fallacy usually appears in the argument of someone who is not listening for a reply.

5. **Complex Question**   Sometimes by phrasing a question a certain way, you may ignore or cover up an even larger, more urgent question. For example, Roger asks the high school principal, "Why can't I get academic credit for monitoring the bathroom?"; he ignores the larger question whether *anyone* should get credit for monitoring a bathroom.

Sabotaging the Argument

6. Red Herring   *Red herring* refers to a stinky smoked fish dragged across a trail to throw a tracking dog off the scent. Certain issues are like that: so volatile and controversial that, once introduced into a discussion, they tend to sidetrack everyone involved. Let's say you are discussing the need for tobacco subsidies in the federal budget and somebody asserts, beside the point, that all restaurants should have no-smoking sections — off you go, chasing that tasty fish.

7. Misuse of Humor   Jokes have a healthy way of lightening the mood, but when humor is used the way an octopus squirts ink — to blind and befuddle, and possibly to injure — it qualifies as a subversive activity (a kind of logical guerrilla warfare) and is a confession of weakness in the saboteur's position.

8. Appeal to Force   ("Might makes right.") One simple way of sabotaging an argument is to break the opponent's leg. On a more subtle level, someone may imply that your argument cannot be true because his own is in the majority. Needless to say, one needs a degree of courage to resist such "logic."

Misusing Evidence

9. Impressing with Large Numbers   ("Hop on the bandwagon.") This fallacy can take at least two forms. One person can try to "snow" another by slinging impressive figures. ("I paid $6,958.36 for this bomb — isn't she a beaut?") Just as commonly, one person will try to make his claim sound reasonable by saying that "everybody" agrees. ("The pain reliever used by one out of three Americans . . . .") This uncritical use of numbers can easily lead to absurdity: "Eat garbage — 7 billion flies can't be wrong!"

10. Irrelevant Appeals to Authority   You can take Dr. Carl Sagan's word on the composition of Saturn's rings, but the moment he, like the famous quarterback Joe Namath a few years ago, tries to peddle pantyhose on TV, watch out!

11. Appeal to Popular Sentiment   (*Argumentum ad populum*)   Associating your cause with all the popular virtues — flag-waving patriotism, baseball, apple pie, fluoride in drinking water — may seduce your listeners into smiling agreement, but it bases your argument on unfulfillable promises. If the other guy is unscrupulous, he may use the same tactic.

12. Appeal to Personal Factors   (*Argumentum ad hominem,* or argument directed "at the man")   By focusing on a person's lifestyle or other personal qualities, one may evade the true issue at hand. *Ad hominem* arguments can have either a positive or a negative thrust. For example, while campaigning <u>for</u> Senator Buzof, you might say, "Senator Buzof is a family man and a former Eagle Scout." You might turn that same fact <u>against</u> him: "Would you trust this Buzof fellow in your Congress? He has a mind like a Boy Scout!"

When personal factors are cited in an argument to undercut an opponent's credibility or to assassinate his character, the fallacy is called "Poisoning the Well." Supposedly, if the "well" is polluted, no good argument could ever come of it.

Another type of *ad hominem* argument goes by the name *tu quoque* (or, "you're another"). If someone charges you with some shortcoming or wrongdoing, you "defend" yourself, fallaciously, by asserting that the other person is equally guilty. Children are experts in this fallacy: "Suzy did it, too!" But the most famous user of this fallacy was Adam in the Garden of Eden who, with his cheeks still fat with apple, pointed the accusing finger at Eve.

13. Appeal to Pity   (*Argumentum ad misericordiam*)   This fallacy may be heard in courts of law when an attorney begs for leniency because his client's mother is ill, his brother is out of work, his cat has a hairball, and blah, blah, blah. The strong tug on the heartstrings has a classic variant in the classroom when the student says to the teacher, "May I have an extension on this paper? I worked till my eyeballs fell out, but it's still not done."

14. **Appeal to Ignorance** *(Argumentum ad ignorantiam)* One commits this fallacy by claiming that since no one has ever proved a claim it must therefore be false. ("Show me one study that proves marijuana leads to harder drugs.") Or, vice versa, one may claim that some belief must be true since no one can disprove it. ("Sure I believe in flying saucers — half of all sightings have never been explained.") This fallacy unfairly shifts the burden of proof onto someone else.

15. **Hypothesis Contrary to Fact** ("If only . . . . ") This false argument bases its claim on what one supposes would have happened if one thing or another had not happened instead. Such claims, being pure speculation, cannot be tested by logic.

16. **False Analogy** Sometimes you may argue that *X* is good (or bad, or promising, etc.) because it is like *Y* (which, in its own turn, is good, bad, or promising, etc.). Such an analogy may be helpful if it illuminates the subject. But the analogy weakens an argument if it is *improper,* if the grounds for comparison are too *vague,* or if the analogy is *stretched too far.*

556 **Misusing Language**

All of the fallacies listed in this section could be termed "misuses of language," but the following three fallacies are all based specifically on a misleading selection of words.

17. **Obfuscation** ("Fuzzy Language") Technical buzzwords (*interface, inverse efficiency ratio, streamlined target refractory system, community sanitary output,* etc.), sometimes combined with twisted language, may obscure behind their brilliant facade the fact that the passage of speech or prose in which they occur means practically nothing.

18. **Ambiguity** Sometimes a word or sentence structure will allow for two or more opposite interpretations, as in the following: "We were introduced to the head hunter; the next day he had us for lunch." When ambiguity appears in argument, it is sometimes an unintended result of careless thinking, a kind of joke that recoils on the teller. At other times, however, a speaker or writer may deliberately be ambiguous to avoid being pinned down.

19. **Slanted Language** By choosing words with strongly positive or negative connotations, a person can add a persuasive emotional charge to an argument. Such words may be used to express genuine and appropriate feeling, or they may be the vehicle for mindless prejudice. The philosopher Bertrand Russell once illustrated the bias involved in slanted language when he compared three synonyms for the word "stubborn": "I am *firm.* You are *obstinate.* He is *pigheaded.*"

557 **Drawing Faulty Conclusions**

20. **Hasty Generalization** A reasonable conclusion must be backed by sufficient evidence. Basing conclusions on inadequate evidence, on the other hand, is always a fallacy, even if the conclusion could be justified by a different set of proofs. ("I saw the principal drive away at noon. He must have another job somewhere on the side.")

21. **Composition and Division** The twin fallacies of composition and division are based, respectively, on the belief that the whole of something will have the same quality as each of its parts and the converse belief that each part will have the quality of the whole. The fallacy of composition is clear when a choir director says after an audition, "All of the singers were excellent. What an excellent choir we shall have." The result? Forty-six excellent altos, one excellent baritone, and one less-than-excellent choir!

22. **False Cause** (*Post hoc, ergo propter hoc,* or "after this, therefore because of this") If *A* precedes *B*, it need not therefore be the cause of *B*, even though we may lazily assume that it is. *A* may have been the only sufficient cause of *B*; it may also have been one of several necessary causes; or, finally, *A* and *B* may be entirely coincidental. Notice the fallacy of "false cause" at work in the following: "Since that new school was built, drug use among our young people has skyrocketed. Better that it would never have been built."

Your Final RE-marks

A Proofreader's Guide

A Proof-reader's Guide

Marking
PUNCTUATION

Period

600   A **period** is used to end a sentence which makes a statement, or which gives a command that is not used as an exclamation.

> **"That guy is coming over here."**
> **"Don't forget to smile when you talk."**
> **"Hello, Big Boy."**
> **"Hi."**

It is not necessary to place a period after a statement which has parentheses around it and is part of another sentence.

> **Euny gave Jim an earwich (an earwich is one piece of buttered bread slapped on each ear) and ran for her life.**

601   An **ellipsis** (three periods) is used to show that one or more words have been omitted in a quotation. (Leave one space before and after each period when typing.)

> **"Give me your tired . . . yearning to breathe free."**

If an omission occurs at the end of a sentence, the ellipsis is placed after the period which marks the conclusion of the sentence.

> **"Ernest Hemingway was fond of fishing. . . . His understanding of that sport is demonstrated in many of his writings."**

Note: If the quoted material is a complete sentence (even if it was not in the original) use a period, then an ellipsis.

An ellipsis also may be used to indicate a pause.

> **"Well, Dad, I . . . ah . . . ran out of gas . . . had two flat tires . . . and ah . . . there was a terrible snowstorm on the other side of town."**

602   A period should be placed after an initial.

> **Dena W. Kloosterman, Thelma J. Slenk, D. H. Lawrence**

603 A period is placed after each part of an **abbreviation** — unless the abbreviation is an acronym. An **acronym** is a word formed from the first (or first few) letters of words in a set phrase. (See 706-708.)

> **Abbreviations: Mr., Mrs., Ms., A.M., P.M., Dr., A.D., B.C.**

> **Acronyms: WAC (Women's Army Corps); Radar (Radio Detecting and Ranging); NATO (North Atlantic Treaty Organization)**

When an abbreviation is the last word in a sentence, only one period should be used at the end of the sentence.

> **When she's nervous, she bites her nails, wrings her hands, picks at her clothes, etc.**

604 Use a period as a decimal and to separate dollars and cents.

> **6.1 percent**   **28.9 percent**   **$3,120.31**

▄ Comma ▬▬▬▬▬▬▬▬▬▬

605 A comma may be used between two independent clauses which are joined by coordinating conjunctions such as these: *but, or, nor, for, yet, and, so.*

> **My friend smokes constantly,** *but* **he still condemns industry for its pollution.**

Note: Do not confuse a sentence with a compound verb for a compound sentence.

> **My friend** *smokes* **but still** *condemns* **industry for its pollution.** (This is a simple sentence with a compound verb; use no comma.)

606 Commas are used to separate individual words, phrases, or clauses in a series. (A series contains at least three items.)

> **I used a rapalla, a silver spoon, a nightcrawler harness, and a Swedish pimple.**
> **The bait I used included kernels of corn, minnows, bacon rind, larva, and spawn sacks.**

Note: Do not use commas when the words in a series are connected with *or, nor,* or *and.*

> **I plan to catch bass** *or* **trout** *or* **sunfish.**

607 Commas are used to enclose an explanatory word or phrase inserted in a sentence.

> **Spawn,** *or fish eggs,* **are tremendous bait.**

An **appositive**, a specific kind of explanatory word or phrase, identifies or renames a preceding noun or pronoun. (Do not use commas with *restrictive appositives.* See the third example below and 611.)

> **My father,** *an expert angler,* **uses spawn to catch brook trout.**
> **The objective,** *to hook fish,* **is easier to accomplish with spawn.**
> **The word** *angleworm* **applies to an earthworm used for fishing.**

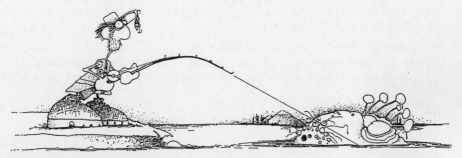

608 Commas are used to separate coordinate adjectives, adjectives which *equally* modify the same noun.

> **Trout gobble up the** *small, soft, round* **eggs.**

Notice in the example above that no comma separates the last adjective from the noun.

> *Most small* **panfish also eat spawn.**

In the example above, *most* and *small* are not separated by a comma because the two adjectives do *not* equally modify *panfish.* To determine whether adjectives modify equally, use these two tests: 1) Shift the order of the adjectives; if the sentence is clear, the adjectives modify equally. (If *most* and *small* were shifted in the example above, the sentence would be unclear.) 2) Insert *and* between the adjectives; if the sentence reads well, use a comma when *and* is omitted.

Note: If the first adjective modifies the second adjective *and* the noun, use a comma.

> **He sat down on the** *soft, velvet* **cushion.**

609 Commas are used to separate contrasted elements from the rest of the sentence and are often used to show word omission in certain grammatical constructions.

> **We need strong minds, not strong emotions, to solve our problems.**
> **Wise people learn from the mistakes of others; fools, from their own.**
> (The comma is used to show that the word *learn* has been omitted from the second half of the sentence.)

610 A comma should separate an adverb clause or a long modifying phrase from the independent clause which follows it.

> **"If you cannot get rid of the family skeleton, you may as well make it dance."** —*George Bernard Shaw*

Note: A comma is usually omitted if the phrase or adverb clause follows the independent clause.

> **"This will never be a civilized country until we expend more money for books than we do for chewing gum."** —*Elbert Hubbard*

611 Commas are used to enclose **nonrestrictive** phrases and clauses. Nonrestrictive phrases or clauses are those which are not essential or necessary to the basic meaning of the sentence. **Restrictive** phrases or clauses — those which are needed in the sentence because they restrict or limit the meaning of the sentence — are not set off with commas. Compare the following examples with their nonrestrictive and restrictive phrases.

> **Rozi,** *who is making funny faces,* **is my sister.**
> (*Note:* The clause, *who is making funny faces,* is merely additional information; it is nonrestrictive [not required]. If the clause were left out of the sentence, the meaning of the sentence would remain clear since the name of the girl is given.)

> **The girl** *who is making funny faces* **is my sister.**
> (*Note:* This clause is restrictive. The clause, *who is making funny faces,* is needed to identify the girl.)

Compare the following examples:

> **The novelist** *Sinclair Lewis* **was the first American writer to win a Nobel Prize for literature. (restrictive)**

> **Sinclair Lewis,** *a novelist,* **was the first American writer to win a Nobel Prize for literature. (nonrestrictive)**

612 Commas are used to set off items in an address and items in a date.

> **They live at 2341 Pine Street, Willmar, Minnesota 56342, during the summer.** (*Note:* Do not use a comma to separate the state from the ZIP code.)

> **Democracy would be dead by Wednesday, July 4, 1984, according to**

George Orwell. Orwell wrote that in July 1949 with pen in cheek. (*Note:* If only the month and year are given, it is not necessary to separate them with a comma.)

613 Commas are used to set off the exact words of the speaker from the rest of the sentence.

> **"Didn't you know," she exclaimed, "that dirty socks can stunt your growth?"**

614 A comma is used to separate an interjection or weak exclamation from the rest of the sentence.

> *Hey,* **will you do me a favor?**
> *Yes,* **I'd be happy to.**
> *Wow,* **that was quite a tip!**

615 Commas are used to set off a word, phrase, or clause that interrupts the movement of a sentence. Such expressions usually can be identified through the following tests: 1) They may be omitted without changing the substance or meaning of a sentence. 2) They may be placed nearly anywhere in the sentence without changing the meaning of the sentence.

> *As a general rule,* **the safest way to double your money is to fold it and put it in your pocket. That is,** *however,* **only true for those with deep pockets.**

616 Commas are used to separate a series of numbers in order to distinguish hundreds, thousands, millions, etc.

> **The Democrats wasted $720,806 on a foolish domestic program. The Republicans invested $1,320,252 to prove that the Democrats wasted money.**

617 Commas are used to enclose a title or initials and names which follow a surname.

> **J. L. Vanderlaan, Ph.D., and G. S. Bruins, M.D., sat in their pajamas playing Old Maid.**
> **Asche, H., Hickok, J. B., and Cody, William F., are three popular Western heroes.**
> **Casey Jones, Jr., was a good friend of John Henry, Sr.**

618 Commas are used to separate a **vocative** from the rest of the sentence. (A *vocative* is the noun which names the person/s spoken to.)

> **Don't you realize,** *George,* **that you're the very first president who thinks we need independence?**
> *Benedict, honey,* **stop giggling. Don't you know it's dangerous to let the little Franklin boy play with your kite in such awful weather?**

619 A comma may be used for clarity or for emphasis. There will be times when none of the traditional comma rules call for a comma, but one will be needed to prevent confusion or to emphasize an important idea. Use a comma in either case.

> **Several days before, he had complained of headaches.** (*clarity*)
> **What she does, does matter to us.** (*clarity*)
> **Those who can, tell us what happened.** (*clarity*)
> **"They can't yank a novelist like they can a pitcher. A novelist has to go the full nine, even if it kills him."** —*Ernest Hemingway (emphasis)*

Note: **Do not use a comma** which could cause confusion. There should be no comma between the subject and its verb or the verb and its object. Also, use no comma before an indirect quotation. (The circled commas should not be used.)

> **The man who helped us unload the truck⊙is my uncle.**
> **Uncle Hank said⊙he would never again move my player piano.**

▬ Semicolon ▬

620 A semicolon is used to join two or more independent clauses which are not connected with a coordinating conjunction. (This means that each of the clauses could stand alone as separate sentences.)

>**I once had a '55 Chevy with a 283; that was the first V-8 I ever owned.**

Note: The exception to this rule can occur when the two clauses are similar, short, or conversational in tone.

>**To rule is easy, to govern difficult.**

621 A semicolon is used to join two independent clauses within a compound sentence — when the clauses are connected only by a conjunctive adverb. (Common conjunctive adverbs are these: *also, as a result, besides, for example, furthermore, however, in addition, instead, meanwhile, moreover, nevertheless, similarly, then, therefore, thus.*)

>**My neighbor proudly brags that he is free from racism;** *however,* **he also feels compelled to say that one of his childhood friends was black.**

622 A semicolon is used to separate independent clauses which are long or contain commas.

>**Someone righteously cleansed the library of all "dirty literature"; so the library now contains only "clean" classics such as** *Romeo and Juliet, Gulliver's Travels,* **and** *The Canterbury Tales.*

623 A semicolon is used to separate groups of words or phrases which already contain commas.

>**I packed a razor, toothbrush, and deodorant; blue jeans, bathing suit, and jacket; tennis balls, fish hooks, and golf clubs.**

▬ Colon ▬

624 A colon may be used after the salutation of a business letter.

>**Dear Ms. Asche:**   **Dear President Bush:**

625 A colon is used between the parts of a number which indicate time.

>**8:32 a.m.**   **11:03 p.m.**

626 A colon may be used to emphasize a word, phrase, clause, or sentence which explains or adds impact to the main clause.

>**Television entertains America's children with the most popular theme of the day: violence. In a single evening children can witness rapes, robberies, fistfights, riots, and murders: all in the quiet confines of their living rooms.**

627 A colon is used to introduce a list.

>**Debbie dropped the purse and out spilled the contents: fingernail clipper, calculator, car keys, wallet, and a ragged old nylon.**

628 A colon should not separate a verb from its object or complement, and it should not separate a preposition from its object.

>**Incorrect:** **Hubert hated: spelling, geography, history, and reading (separates verb from objects).**
>
>**Correct:**   **Hubert hated his subjects: spelling, geography, history, and reading.**
>
>**Correct:**   **Hubert hated these: spelling, geography, history, and reading.**
>
>**Incorrect:** **He just looked at: his fingernails, the ceiling, the teacher, and girls (separates preposition from objects).**

Correct:	He just looked at other subjects: his fingernails, the ceiling, the teacher, and girls.

629 The colon is used to distinguish between title and subtitle, volume and page, and chapter and verse in literature.

> *The Write Source: A Student Handbook*
> *Encyclopedia Americana* IV: 211
> Psalm 23:1-6

630 A colon may be used to formally introduce a sentence, a question, or a quotation.

> **It was John F. Kennedy who said these words: "Ask not what your country can do for you. Ask what you can do for your country."**

▬ Dash ▬▬▬▬▬▬▬▬▬▬▬▬▬▬▬▬▬▬▬▬▬▬

631 The dash is used to indicate a sudden break or change in the sentence.

> **"The sun—the bright sun, that brings back, not light alone, but new life, and hope, and freshness to man—burst upon the crowded city in clear and radiant glory."**
> **—*Charles Dickens***

632 A dash may be used to emphasize a word, series, phrase, or clause.

> **He ran downstage, glared at the audience, screamed his terrible epithet—and his pants fell down.**

> **"The writer is by nature a dreamer—a conscious dreamer."**
> **— *Carson McCullers***

A dash is used to set off an introductory series from the clause that explains the series.

> **Health, friends, and family—we are not sufficiently thankful for these.**

633 A dash is used to show interrupted or faltering speech in dialogue. (*Note:* A dash is indicated by two hyphens- -without spacing before or after- -in all handwritten and typed material.)

> **Why, hello, Dear- -yes, I understand- -no, I remember- -oh, I want to- - of course I won't- -why, no, I- -why, yes, I- -it was so nice to talk with you again, Dear.**

Note: A dash may also be used to show that words or letters are missing.

> **Listen, you d— Yankee!**

▬ Hyphen ▬▬▬▬▬▬▬▬▬▬▬▬▬▬▬▬▬▬▬▬

634 The **hyphen** is used to make a compound word.

> **great-great-grandfather, run-of-the-mill, mother-in-law, three-year-old, twenty-six-year-old songwriter, teacher-poet (coequal nouns) The Ford-Carter debates helped make peanut butter as patriotic as apple pie.**

Note: Don't use a single hyphen when a dash (two hyphens) is required.

635 A hyphen is used between the elements of a fraction, but not between the numerator and denominator when one or both are already hyphenated.

> **four-tenths   five-sixteenths   (7/32) seven thirty-seconds**

Note: Use hyphens when two or more words have a common element which is omitted in all but the last term.

> **We have cedar posts in four-, six-, and eight-inch widths.**

636 A hyphen is used to join a capital letter to a noun or participle.

> **U-turn   A-center   T-shirt   V-shaped**

637 A hyphen is usually used to form new words beginning with the prefixes *self, ex, all, great,* and *half.* It is also used to join any prefix to a proper noun, a proper adjective, or the official name of an office. A hyphen is used with the suffix *elect.*

> **ex-mayor, self-esteem, all-knowing, pro-American, post-Depression, mid-May, president-elect, governor-elect, great-grandson, half-baked**

Note: Use a hyphen with other prefixes or suffixes to avoid confusion or awkward spelling.

> **re-cover (not *recover*) the sofa** 　　　　　**shell-like (not *shelllike*)**

638 The hyphen is used to join the words in compound numbers from *twenty-one* to *ninety-nine* when it is necessary to write them out. (See 710-712.)

639 The hyphen is used to separate a word at the end of a line of print. A word may be divided only between syllables, and the hyphen is always placed after the syllable at the end of the line—never before a syllable at the beginning of the following line.

Additional Guidelines for Using the Hyphen

1. Always leave enough of the word at the end of the sentence so that the word can be identified.
2. Never divide a one-syllable word: *rained, skills, through.*
3. Avoid dividing a word of five letters or less: *paper, study, July.*
4. Never divide a one-letter syllable from the rest of the word: *omit-ted,* not *o-mitted.*
5. Always divide a compound word between its basic units: *sister-in-law,* not *sis-ter-in-law.*
6. Never divide abbreviations or contractions: *shouldn't,* not *should-n't.*
7. Avoid dividing the last word in a paragraph.
8. Never divide the last word in more than two lines in a row.
9. When a vowel is a syllable by itself, divide the word after the vowel: *epi-sode,* not *ep-isode.*
10. Avoid dividing a number written as a figure: *1,000,000;* not *1,000,-000.* (If a figure must be broken, divide it after one of the commas.)
11. Always check a dictionary if you are uncertain where a word should be divided.

---

640 Use the hyphen to join two or more words which serve as a single adjective (a *single-thought* adjective) before a noun.

> **slow-moving tank**　　　**mud-caked shoes**　　　**five-year-old child**
>
> **"A pessimist is a person who looks both ways before crossing a one-way street."**
> 　　　　　　　　　　　　　　　　　　　　　　　　　　　　　**—*L.J. Peters***

Note: When words forming the adjective come after the noun, do not hyphenate them.

> **The tank ahead of us was slow moving.**　　**Max's shoes are mud caked.**

When the first of the words is an adverb ending in *ly,* do not use a hyphen; also, do not use a hyphen when a number or letter is the final element in a one-thought adjective.

> **fresh*ly* painted barn**　　**Grade *A* milk**　　**number *360* sandpaper**

641 The hyphen is used to join numbers which indicate the life span of an individual, the scores of a game, the term of an event, etc.

> **The child lived a short life: 1971-1973.**
> **The score, 78-27, suggests the nature of the Elk Rapids-Traverse City basketball game.**

Question Mark

642 A **question mark** is used at the end of a direct question.

> **Are your relatives mushy when you visit them?**
> **Are your grandparents heavy on the kissy-huggy stuff?**

No question mark is used after an indirect quotation.

> **My aunt always asks how I am doing in school.**
> **I always wonder what "doing in school" means.**

643 When two clauses within a sentence both ask questions, one question mark is used.

> **Does your uncle greet you as mine greets me — with a "cootchy-coo" under the chin and a "How old are you now, little lady?" Do you think he would feel insulted if I gave him a "cootchy-coo" in the beard and said, "I'm seventeen, Uncle, and how old are you getting to be?"**

644 The question mark is placed within parentheses to show uncertainty.

> **Although my cousin is only 18 (?), he looks down his nose when he says "Hello" to his younger cousins.**

645 A short question within parentheses is punctuated with a question mark.

> **You may visit me next week (is that possible?) as long as your handshake is firm and you don't pat my head.**

646 Only one question mark should punctuate a question. The following punctuation is both silly and incorrect.

> **Do you mean that kid with the purple socks???**
> **Really! Why did you ever date him???**

Exclamation Point

647 The **exclamation point** is used to express strong feeling. It may be placed after a word, a phrase, or a sentence. (The exclamation point should be used sparingly.)

> **Help! Mom! Help!**
> **Wow, man, what a way to go!**
> **Please! Tell me that's not a cop!**

648 Never write more than one exclamation point; such punctuation is incorrect and looks foolish.

> **Isn't kissing fun!!!**
> **Who even thinks about the germs!!!**

Quotation Marks

649 **Quotation marks** are placed before and after direct quotations. Only the exact words quoted are placed within quotation marks.

> **"I really don't know," he said, "whether this year's drought will result in higher food prices, food shortages, or both."** (*Note:* The words *he said* are not in quotation marks because the person did not say them. Also, the word *whether* is not capitalized because it does not begin a new sentence.)

650 Quotation marks are placed before and after each passage being quoted.

> **"My brother built a horse which could walk, buck, trot, and gallop. The torso of this 'creation' was a telephone pole. One end of the pole was bolted to the hitch of a tractor. The other end of the pole was bolted to a fifty-gallon barrel (a saddle was tied on the barrel). The**

center of the pole was straddled by a metal *U-frame*. **One end of a large spring was connected to the top of the** *U*. **The other end of the spring was connected to the pole and suspended in the center of the** *U*. **The legs of this** *U* **were carried by spoked metal wheels—the centers of which were welded off center. The mechanical horse could perform an interesting variety of tricks—depending on the direction and the speed of the tractor."**

651 If more than one paragraph is quoted, quotation marks are placed before each paragraph and at the end of the last paragraph **(Example A).** Quotations which are more than four lines on a page are usually set off from the text by indenting ten spaces from the left margin ("block form"). Quotation marks are placed neither before nor after the quoted material unless they appear in the original **(Example B).**

Example A	Example B
" _____	_____
_____	_____
_____ .	_____
" _____	_____
_____	_____
_____ .	_____ .
" _____ ."	_____ .

Note: Although it is no longer the preferred method, lengthy quotations are sometimes indented five spaces from both the left and right side and typed using single spacing.

652 Quotation marks also may be used (1) to distinguish a word which is being discussed, (2) to indicate that a word is slang, or (3) to point out that a word is being used in a special way. *(Note:* Italics may be used in place of quotation marks for each of these three functions. Also remember, in handwritten material or in typed material, each word which should be in italics is underlined. See 659.)

> **I am "firm," you are "stubborn," he is "pigheaded."**
> **Ray is one of those "no problem" types who somehow manage to screw up everything.**
> **In order to be popular, she works very hard at being "cute."**

653 Single quotation marks are used to punctuate a quotation within a quotation. Double and single quotation marks are alternated in order to distinguish a quotation within a quotation within a quotation.

> **"I never read 'The Raven'!"**
> **"Did you hear him say, 'I never read "The Raven" '?"**

654 Quotation marks are used to punctuate titles of songs, poems, short stories, lectures, courses, episodes of radio or television programs, chapters of books, unpublished works, and articles found in magazines, newspapers, or encyclopedias. (For punctuation of other titles, see 660-661.)

> **"Born in the U.S.A."** (song)
> **"Uncle Wiggly Loses His Pants"** (short story)
> **"The Raven"** (poem)
> **"Fundamentals of Oil Painting"** (course title)

(*Note:* When you punctuate a title, capitalize the first word, the last word, and every word in between *except* articles, short prepositions, and short conjunctions. See 694.)

655 Periods and commas are always placed inside quotation marks.

> **"I don't know," said Albert. Albert said, "I don't know."**

656 An exclamation point or a question mark is placed inside quotation marks when it punctuates the quotation; it is placed outside when it punctuates the main sentence.

> **I almost croaked when he asked, "That won't be a problem for you, will it?"**
> **Did the teacher really say, "Finish this by tomorrow"?**

657 Semicolons or colons are placed outside quotation marks.

> **I wrote about Wallace Stevens' "Thirteen Ways of Looking at a Blackbird"; "Sunday Morning" was too deep for me.**

▬ Underlining (Italics) ▬▬▬▬▬▬▬▬

658 Italics is a printer's term for a style of type which is slightly slanted. In this sentence the word *happiness* is typed in italics. In handwritten or typed material, each word or letter which should be in italics is underlined.

> **The novel <u>To Kill a Mockingbird</u> tells an important story. (typed)**
> **The novel *To Kill a Mockingbird* tells an important story. (printed)**

659 Underlining (*italics* in print) is used to indicate a foreign word which has not been adopted in the English language; it also designates scientific names.

> **<u>Angst</u> is a painful state of mind. (foreign word)**
> **The chills and fever of malaria result from a bite by the <u>anopheles</u> mosquito.**

Underlining (*italics* in print) is used to designate a word, number, or letter which is being emphasized or discussed (referred to as a thing in itself). (See 652.)

> **I got an <u>A</u> on my test because I understood the word <u>classify</u>.**

660 Underlining (*italics*) is used to indicate the titles of magazines, newspapers, pamphlets, books, plays, films, radio and television programs, book-length poems, ballets, operas, lengthy musical compositions, record albums, legal cases, and the names of ships and aircraft. (See 654.)

> **<u>A Tale of Two Cities</u> (novel)**
> **<u>Attack of the Killer Tomatoes</u> (film)**
> **<u>MASH</u> (television program)**
> **<u>Motorists Handbook</u> (pamphlet)**
> **<u>U.S.S. Arizona</u> (ship)**
> **<u>New York Times</u> or New York <u>Times</u>**

(*Note:* When the name of a city is used as part of the name of a newspaper, the name of the city need not be underlined.)

Exceptions: Do not underline or put in quotation marks sacred writings (including the Bible and its many books) or the names of any series, edition, or society which might appear alongside (or in place of) the actual title. Also, do not underline or put in quotation marks your own title at the top of your page.

> **Bible, Genesis, Talmud (sacred writings)**
> **NCTE Research Report No. 9 (series)**
> **The Baltimore Edition of the Complete Works of Poe (edition)**

661 When one title appears within another title, punctuate as follows:

> **"Upstairs, Downstairs Is Back" (television program in an article)**
> **"An Interpretation of 'The Raven' " (poem in an article)**
> **A Tale of Two Cities as History (book in the title of another book)**

▬ Parentheses ▬

662 **Parentheses** are used to enclose explanatory or supplementary material which interrupts the normal sentence structure.

> **Abraham Lincoln began his political career in Springfield (Ill.) where he served four terms as a state legislator. Following his fourth term, Lincoln tried unsuccessfully to capture the Whig Party's nomination. (Lincoln later joined the Republican Party.) After failing a second time to secure the nomination, Lincoln decided to make one last effort; if he failed, he would retire from politics. His third attempt was a major triumph, for Lincoln won not only the nomination but the election as well (1846). He was soon off to Washington, D.C., where he was to become one of the most controversial of all U.S. Presidents (Sandburg 42).**

Note: Punctuation is placed within parentheses when it is intended to mark the material within the parentheses. Punctuation is placed outside parentheses when it is intended to mark the entire sentence, of which the parenthetical material is only a part. Also note that words enclosed by parentheses do not have to begin with a capital letter or end with a period—even though the words may compose a complete sentence.

663 For unavoidable parentheses within parentheses, use brackets (. . . [. . .] . . .).

Note: Avoid excessive use of parentheses by using phrases or clauses set off by commas.

▬ Brackets ▬

664 Brackets are used before and after material which a writer adds when quoting another writer.

> **"Sometimes I think it [my writing] sounds like I walked out of the room and left the typewriter running."**   *—Gene Fowler*

(Note: The brackets indicate that the words, *my writing,* were not part of the quotation but were added for clarification.)

665 Place brackets around material which has been added by someone other than the author or speaker.

> **"Congratulations to the astronomy club's softball team which put in, shall we say, a 'stellar' performance." [groans]**

666 Place brackets around an editorial correction.

> **The French [Germans] relish sauerkraut.**

667 Brackets should be placed around the letters *sic* (Latin for "as such"); the letters indicate that an error, appearing in quoted material, was created by the original speaker or writer.

> **"No parent can dessert [sic] his child without damaging a human life."**

▬ Apostrophe ▬▬▬▬▬▬▬▬▬▬▬▬▬▬▬▬▬▬▬▬▬▬▬▬▬▬

668   An **apostrophe** is used to show that one or more letters have been left out of a word to form a contraction.

> **don't**—*o* is left out; **she'd**—*woul* is left out; **it's**—*i* is left out

An apostrophe is also used to show that one or more letters or numbers have been left out of numerals or words which are spelled as they were actually spoken.

> **class of '85**—*19* is left out; **good mornin'**—*g* is left out

Note: When two apostrophes are called for in the same word, simply omit the second one.

> **Follow closely the** *do's* **and** *don'ts* **(not** *don't's*) **on the checklist.**

669   An apostrophe and *s* are used to form the plural of a letter, a number, a sign, or a word discussed as a word.

> **A—A's; C—C's; 8—8's.**
> You use too many **and's** in your writing.

670   The possessive form of singular nouns is usually made by adding an apostrophe and *s*.

> **Spock's ears; John Lennon's assassination**

Note: When a singular noun ends with an *s* or *z* sound, the possessive may be formed by adding just an apostrophe. When the singular noun is a one-syllable word, however, the possessive is usually formed by adding both an apostrophe and *s*.

> **Dallas' sports teams (or) Dallas's sports teams**
> **Kiss's last concert; my boss's generosity (one-syllable)**

671   The possessive form of plural nouns ending in *s* is usually made by adding just an apostrophe. For plural nouns not ending in *s*, an apostrophe and *s* must be added.

> **Joneses' great-grandfather; bosses' office; children's book**

Remember! The word immediately before the apostrophe is the owner.

> kid's guitar . . . . *kid* is the owner
> kids' guitar . . . . *kids* are the owners
> boss's office . . . . *boss* is the owner
> bosses' office . . . . *bosses* are the owners
> (Please don't write, "My sisters' hip is out of joint.")

672   When possession is shared by more than one noun, use the possessive form for the last noun in the series.

> **VanClumpin, VanDiken, and VanTulip's fish (All three own the same fish.)**
> **VanClumpin's, VanDiken's, and VanTulip's fish (Each guy owns his own fish.)**

673   The possessive of a compound noun is formed by placing the possessive ending after the last word. (See 846.)

> **his mother-in-law's (singular) mouth; the secretary of state's (singular) wife**
> **their mothers-in-law's (plural) husbands; the secretaries of state's (plural) wives**

674   The possessive of an indefinite pronoun is formed by placing an apostrophe and *s* on the last word. (See 865.)

> **everyone's; anyone's; somebody else's**

675   An apostrophe is used with an adjective which is part of an expression indicating time or amount.

> **yesterday's news; a day's wage; a month's pay**

Brace

676 The **brace** is used to join related matter. The brace is not a standard punctuation mark, but it is used often in notes, forms, or letters.

$$\text{pizzas} \left. \begin{array}{l} \text{10 in.} \\ \text{12 in.} \\ \text{14 in.} \end{array} \right\} \quad \$2.98 \text{ - } 4.76$$

Asterisk

677 The omission of one or more paragraphs from a quotation is indicated by centering three **asterisks** on one line. No other material should be printed on that line.

*   *   *

678 An asterisk may be used in a short paper to indicate to the reader that additional information is included in a footnote at the bottom of the page.

> **His first year* was very difficult.**
> ***1968**

Diagonal

679 A diagonal is used to form a fraction. Also, place a diagonal (also *slash*) between *and* and *or* to indicate that either is acceptable. (Avoid this use of the diagonal in formal writing.)

> **His hat size used to be 8-1/2; with his hair cut, it's 6-7/8.**
> **Use calamine lotion and/or aloe to soothe those spider bites.**

680 When quoting more than one line of poetry, use a diagonal at the end of each line.

> The following three lines from Frost's "The Road Not Taken" hint at both the costs and rewards of nonconformism: **"Two roads diverged in a wood, and I—/I took the one less traveled by/ and that has made all the difference."**

681

	PUNCTUATION MARKS			
´	Accent, acute	¨ (ö)	Dieresis	
`	Accent, grave	. . .	Ellipsis	
'	Apostrophe	!	Exclamation point	
*	Asterisk	-	Hyphen	
(or)	Brace	. . .	Leaders	
[ ]	Brackets	¶	Paragraph	
∧	Caret	( )	Parentheses	
؜ (ç)	Cedilla	.	Period	
^	Circumflex	?	Question mark	
:	Colon	" "	Quotation marks	
,	Comma	§	Section	
†	Dagger	;	Semicolon	
—	Dash	˜	Tilde	
/	Diagonal/Slash	___	Underscore	

Checking
■MECHANICS■

■ Capitalization ■

685 Capitalize all proper nouns and all proper adjectives (adjectives derived from proper nouns). The chart below provides a quick overview of capitalization rules. The information following the chart explains specific or special uses of capitalization.

Capitalization at a Glance

Days of the week .... Sunday, Monday, Tuesday
Months .... June, July, August
Holidays, holy days .... Thanksgiving, Easter, Hanukkah
Periods, events in history .... Middle Ages, the Renaissance
Special events .... the Battle of Bunker Hill
Political parties .... Republican Party, Socialist Party
Official documents .... Declaration of Independence
Trade names .... Oscar Mayer hot dogs, Pontiac Sunbird
Formal epithets .... Alexander the Great
Official titles .... Mayor John Spitzer, Senator Kennedy
Official state nicknames .... the Badger State, the Aloha State
Geographical names
    Planets, heavenly bodies .... Earth, Jupiter, the Milky Way
    Continents .... Australia, South America
    Countries .... Ireland, Grenada, Sri Lanka
    States, provinces .... Ohio, Utah, Nova Scotia
    Counties .... Juneau, Racine
    Cities, towns, villages .... El Paso, Burlington, Wonewoc
    Streets, roads, highways .... Park Avenue, Route 66, Interstate 90
    Sections of a country or continent .... the Southwest, the Far East
    Landforms .... the Rocky Mountains, the Sahara Desert
    Bodies of water .... Nile River, Lake Superior, Pumpkin Creek
    Public areas .... Yellowstone National Park

686 Capitalize words like *father, mother, uncle,* and *senator* when they are parts of titles which include a personal name or when they are substituted for proper nouns (especially in direct address).

> Hi, **Uncle** Duane! *(Uncle* is part of the name.)
> My **uncle,** Duane, likes me. *(Uncle* is not part of the name.)
> Did you know that **Senator** Proxmire kissed my mother?
> The **senator,** Bill Proxmire, is a cool guy.
> **Mom** has been appointed **postmaster general** of the United States.
> We are relieved to see you, **Ambassador.**

Note: To test whether a word is being substituted for a proper noun, simply read the sentence with a proper noun in place of the word. If the proper noun fits in the sentence, the word being tested should be capitalized; if the proper noun does not work in this sentence, the word should not be capitalized. *(Further note:* Usually the word is not capitalized if it follows a possessive—*my, his, our,* etc.)

> Did **Mom (Sue)** say we could go? *(Sue* works in this sentence.)
> Did your **mom (Sue)** say you could go? *(Sue* does not work here; the word *mom* also follows the possessive *your.)*

687 Words such as *home economics, history,* and *science* are proper nouns when they are the titles of specific courses, but are common nouns when they name a field of study.

> That guy failed his **home economics** assignment because he tried to cook eggs in the microwave oven. (a field of study)
> "Who teaches **History 202**?" (title of a specific course)
> "The same guy who teaches that **sociology** course." (a field of study)

Note: The words *freshman, sophomore, junior,* and *senior* are not capitalized unless they refer to an entire class or they are part of an official title: the *Sophomore Class* of Elkhorn High School, *Junior Prom, Senior Banquet.*

688 Words which indicate particular sections of the country are proper nouns and should be capitalized; words which simply indicate direction are not proper nouns.

> Skiing is popular in the **North.**
> Sparrows don't fly **south** because they are lazy.
> We visited some friends in **western** Wisconsin.

689 Nouns or pronouns which refer to the Supreme Being are capitalized.

> **God, Him, Jehovah,** the **Lord,** the **Savior, Allah**

690 The word *Bible* and the books of the Bible are capitalized; likewise, the names for other holy books and sacred writings are capitalized.

> **Bible, Book of Psalms, Ecclesiastes,** the **Koran**

691 Capitalize the first word in every sentence and the first word in a full-sentence direct quotation.

> **He** never saw a snake he didn't like.
> **The** old lady shouted up the stairs, "**You** kids stop fightin' this minute or I'll spank the both of ya!"

Capitalize the first word in each sentence which is enclosed in parentheses if that sentence comes before or after another complete sentence.

> Converted Republican Ronald Reagan won the '84 election by a comfortable margin. (**He** won 49 of the 50 states.)

Do not capitalize a sentence which is enclosed in parentheses and is located in the middle of another sentence.

> Converted Republican Ronald Reagan (**he** was an active member of the Democratic Party early in his career) won the '84 election by a comfortable margin.

Capitalize a complete sentence which follows a colon *only* if that sentence is a formal statement or a quotation. Also, capitalize the sentence following a colon if you want to emphasize that sentence.

> It was Ralph Waldo Emerson who made the following comment: **"What** you do speaks so loud that I cannot hear what you say."

> "All that mankind has done, thought, gained or been: **It** is lying as in magic preservation in the pages of books." *—Thomas Carlyle*

692 Capitalize the first word in a line of poetry *only* when the author does the same.

> **"The** colors of their tails   **"wholly** to be a fool
> **Were** like the leaves themselves"   **while** Spring is in the world"
> — *Wallace Stevens*   — *e.e. cummings*

693 Capitalize races, nationalities, languages, and religions. *Note:* Today some authors capitalize *Black* and *White* when the words are used as proper nouns in place of *Negro* and *Caucasian.*

> Negro   Navajo   Canadian   Caucasian
> Black   Hebrew   Catholic   White

694 Capitalize the first word of a title, the last word, and every word in between except articles (*a, an, the*), short prepositions, and short conjunctions. Follow this rule for titles of books, newspapers, magazines, poems, plays, songs, articles, films, works of art, pictures, and stories.

> **Bible; Milwaukee Journal; A Midsummer Night's Dream; Sports Illustrated; The Red Badge of Courage; Building Self-Respect**

695 Capitalize the name of an organization, association, or team and its members.

> **New England Historical Society; Elk Rapids High School Drama Club; Burlington Memorial Hospital Auxiliary; Fond du Lac Jaycees; the Boy Scouts; the Red Cross; Green Bay Packers; Republican, Democratic Party**

696 Capitalize abbreviations of titles and organizations. (Some other abbreviations are also capitalized. See 706-709.)

> **U.S.A.; NAACP; M.D.; Ph.D.; A.D.; B.C.; R.R.; No.**

Also capitalize the letters used to indicate form or shape.

> **U-turn, I-beam, S-curve, A-bomb, T-shirt**

697 **Do not capitalize** any of the following: 1) a prefix attached to a proper noun, 2) seasons of the year, 3) a common noun shared by (and coming after) two or more proper nouns, 4) words used to indicate direction or position, 5) the word *gods* or *goddesses* when they are referring to mythology, or 6) common nouns which appear to be part of a proper noun.

Capitalize	Do Not Capitalize
American	*un*-American
January, February	*winter, spring*
Lakes Erie and Michigan	Missouri and Ohio *rivers*
The South is quite conservative.	Turn *south* at the stop sign.
Are you going to the Junior Prom?	Only *juniors* are welcome.
Duluth Central High School	a Duluth *high school*
Governor Michael Dukakis	Michael Dukakis, our *governor*
President George Bush	George Bush, our *president*
The planet Earth is egg shaped.	The *earth* we live on is good.
I'm taking History 101.	I'm taking *history.*

▬ Plurals ▬▬▬▬▬▬▬▬▬▬▬▬▬▬▬▬▬▬▬▬▬

698 The plurals of most nouns are formed by adding *s* to the singular.

> **cheerleader — cheerleaders; wheel — wheels**

The plural form of nouns ending in *sh, ch, x, s,* and *z* are made by adding *es* to the singular.

> **lunch — lunches; dish — dishes; mess — messes; fox — foxes; buzz — buzzes**

Note: Some nouns remain unchanged when used as plurals: *deer, sheep, salmon,* etc.

699 The plurals of common nouns which end in *y* (preceded by a consonant) are formed by changing the *y* to *i* and adding *es.*

> **fly — flies; jalopy — jalopies**

The plurals of nouns which end in *y* (preceded by a vowel) are formed by adding only *s.*

> **donkey — donkeys; monkey — monkeys**

Note: The plurals of proper nouns ending in *y* are formed by adding *s.*

700 The plurals of words ending in *o* (preceded by a vowel) are formed by adding *s.*

> **radio — radios; rodeo — rodeos; studio — studios**

Most nouns ending in *o* (preceded by a consonant) form plurals by adding *es.*

> **echo — echoes; hero — heroes; tomato — tomatoes**

Exception: Musical terms always form plurals by adding *s;* consult a dictionary for other words of this type.

> **alto — altos; banjo — banjos; solo — solos; piano — pianos**

701 The plurals of nouns that end in *f* or *fe* are formed in one of two ways: if the final *f* sound is still heard in the plural form of the word, simply add *s;* if the final sound is a *ve* sound, change the *f* to *ve* and add *s.* (*Note:* Several words are correct with either ending.)

> Plural ends with *f* sound: **roof — roofs; chief — chiefs**
> Plural ends with *ve* sound: **wife — wives; loaf — loaves**
> Plural ends with either sound: **hoof — hoofs, hooves**

702 Foreign words (as well as some of English origin) form a plural by taking on an *irregular* spelling; others are now acceptable with the commonly used *s* or *es* ending.

Foreign Words		English Words	
crisis	crises	child	children
criterion	criteria	goose	geese
appendix	appendices/appendixes	ox	oxen
radius	radii	die	dice

703 The plurals of symbols, letters, figures, and words considered as words are formed by adding an *apostrophe* and an *s.*

> He wrote three **x's** in place of his name.
> **"Hello's"** and **"Hi there's"** were screamed at my dad.

Note: Some writers omit the apostrophe when the omission does not make the sentence confusing. The examples above must have apostrophes; the example below need not.

> Give me four **5's (5s)** for a twenty.

704 The plurals of nouns which end with *ful* are formed by adding an *s* at the end of the word.

three pailfuls; two tankfuls

Note: Do not confuse these examples with three *pails full* (when you are referring to three separate pails full of something) or two *tanks full.*

The plurals of compound nouns are usually formed by adding *s* or *es* to the important word in the compound.

brothers-in-law; maids of honor; secretaries of state

705 Pronouns referring to a collective noun may be singular or plural. A pronoun is singular when the group (noun) is considered a unit. A pronoun is plural when the group (noun) is considered in terms of its individual components.

The faculty forgot **its** promise. (group as a unit)
The faculty forgot **their** detention pads. (group as individuals)

▬ Abbreviations ▬

706 **An abbreviation** is the shortened form of a word or phrase. The following abbreviations are always acceptable in both formal and informal writing:

Mr., Mrs., Miss, Ms., Messrs., Dr., a.m., p.m. (A.M., P.M.), A.D., B.C.

Do not abbreviate the names of states, countries, months, days, units of measure, or courses of study in formal writing. Do not abbreviate the words *Street, Road, Avenue, Company,* and similar words when they are part of a proper name. Also, do not use signs or symbols (%, &, #, @) in place of words. The dollar sign is, however, appropriate when numerals are used to express an amount of money ($325).

State Abbreviations

	Standard	Postal
Alabama	Ala.	AL
Alaska	Alaska	AK
Arizona	Ariz.	AZ
Arkansas	Ark.	AR
California	Calif.	CA
Colorado	Colo.	CO
Connecticut	Conn.	CT
Delaware	Del.	DE
District of Columbia	D.C.	DC
Florida	Fla.	FL
Georgia	Ga.	GA
Guam	Guam	GU
Hawaii	Hawaii	HI
Idaho	Idaho	ID
Illinois	Ill.	IL
Indiana	Ind.	IN
Iowa	Iowa	IA
Kansas	Kan.	KS
Kentucky	Ky.	KY
Louisiana	La.	LA
Maine	Maine	ME
Maryland	Md.	MD
Massachusetts	Mass.	MA
Michigan	Mich.	MI
Minnesota	Minn.	MN
Mississippi	Miss.	MS
Missouri	Mo.	MO
Montana	Mont.	MT
Nebraska	Neb.	NE
Nevada	Nev.	NV
New Hampshire	N.H.	NH
New Jersey	N.J.	NJ
New Mexico	N.M.	NM
New York	N.Y.	NY
North Carolina	N.C.	NC
North Dakota	N.D.	ND
Ohio	Ohio	OH
Oklahoma	Okla.	OK
Oregon	Ore.	OR
Pennsylvania	Pa.	PA
Puerto Rico	P.R.	PR
Rhode Island	R.I.	RI
South Carolina	S.C.	SC
South Dakota	S.D.	SD
Tennessee	Tenn.	TN
Texas	Texas	TX
Utah	Utah	UT
Vermont	Vt.	VT
Virginia	Va.	VA
Virgin Islands	V.I.	VI
Washington	Wash.	WA
West Virginia	W.Va.	WV
Wisconsin	Wis.	WI
Wyoming	Wyo.	WY

Address Abbreviations

	Standard	Postal
Avenue	Ave.	AVE
Boulevard	Blvd.	BLVD
Court	Ct.	CT
Drive	Dr.	DR
East	E.	E
Expressway	Expy.	EXPY
Heights	Hts.	HTS
Highway	Hwy.	HWY
Hospital	Hosp.	HOSP
Junction	Junc.	JCT
Lake	L.	LK
Lakes	Ls.	LKS
Lane	Ln.	LN
Meadows	Mdws.	MDWS
North	N.	N
Palms	Palms	PLMS
Park	Pk.	PK
Parkway	Pky.	PKY
Place	Pl.	PL
Plaza	Plaza	PLZ
Ridge	Rdg.	RDG
River	R.	RV
Road	Rd.	RD
Rural	R.	R
Shore	Sh.	SH
South	S.	S
Square	Sq.	SQ
Station	Sta.	STA
Terrace	Ter.	TER
Turnpike	Tpke.	TPKE
Union	Un.	UN
View	View	VW
Village	Vil.	VLG
West	W.	W

Common Abbreviations

abr. abridge; abridgment

ac, AC alternating current

ack. acknowledge; acknowledgment

acv actual cash value

A.D. anno Domini (usually small capitals A.D.)

a.m. Also **A.M.** ante meridiem (usually small capitals A.M.)

ASAP as soon as possible

avg., av. average

BBB Better Business Bureau

B.C. 1. before Christ (usually small capitals B.C.) 2. British Columbia

bibliog. bibliographer; bibliography

biog. biographer; biographical; biography

C 1. Celsius 2. centigrade 3. coulomb

c. circa (about)

cc cubic centimeter

cc. chapters

CDT, C.D.T. Central Daylight Time

cm. centimeter

c.o. Also **c/o** care of

COD, C.O.D. 1. cash on delivery 2. collect on delivery

co-op. cooperative

CST, C.S.T. Central Standard Time

cu. Also **c** cubic

D.A. district attorney

d.b.a. doing business as

dc, DC direct current

dec. deceased

dept. department

disc. discount

DST, D.S.T. Daylight-Saving Time

dup. duplicate

ea. each

ed. edition; editor

EDT, E.D.T. Eastern Daylight Time

e.g. for example (Latin *exempli gratia*)

EST, E.S.T. Eastern Standard Time

etc. and so forth (Latin *et cetera*)

ex. example

F Fahrenheit

FM, fm frequency modulation

F.O.B., f.o.b. free on board

ft foot

g 1. gravity 2. gram

gal. gallon

gds. goods

gloss. glossary

GNP gross national product

hdqrs. headquarters

hgt. height

Hon. Honorable (title)

hp horsepower

Hz hertz

id. the same (Latin *idem*)

i.e. that is (Latin *id est*)

illus. illustration

inc. incorporated

IQ, I.Q. intelligence quotient

IRS Internal Revenue Service

ISBN International Standard Book Number

JP, J.P. justice of the peace

jr., Jr. junior

K 1. kelvin (temperature unit) 2. Kelvin (temperature scale)

kc kilocycle

kg kilogram

km kilometer

kn. knot

kt. karat

kw kilowatt

l liter

lat. latitude

lb pound (Latin *libra*)

l.c. lower-case

lit. literary; literature

log logarithm

long. longitude

ltd., Ltd. limited

m meter

M.A. Master of Arts (Latin *Magister Artium*)

man. manual

Mc megacycle

M.C., m.c. master of ceremonies

M.D. Doctor of Medicine (Latin *Medicinae Doctor*)

mdse. merchandise

mfg. manufacture; manufactured

mg milligram

mi. 1. mile 2. mill (monetary unit)

misc. miscellaneous

ml milliliter

mm millimeter

mpg, m.p.g. miles per gallon

mph, m.p.h. miles per hour

MS 1. manuscript 2. Mississippi (with ZIP code) 3. multiple sclerosis

Ms., Ms Title of courtesy for a woman

MST, M.S.T. Mountain Standard Time

neg. negative

n.s.f., N.S.F. not sufficient funds

O.D. Doctor of Optometry

oz, oz. ounce

PA 1. Pennsylvania (with ZIP code) 2. public-address system

pct. percent

pd. paid

Pfc, Pfc. private first class

pg. page (also **p.**)

p.m. Also **P.M.** post meridiem (usually small capitals P.M.)

P.O. 1. Personnel Officer 2. Also **p.o.** petty officer; post office 3. postal order

pop. population

POW, P.O.W. prisoner of war

pp. pages

ppd. 1. postpaid 2. prepaid

PR 1. Also **P.R.** public relations 2. Puerto Rico (with ZIP code)

psi, p.s.i. pounds per square inch

PST, P.S.T. Pacific Standard Time

PTA, P.T.A. Parent-Teachers Association

qt. quart

RD rural delivery

RF radio frequency

rpm, R.P.M. revolutions per minute

r.s.v.p., R.S.V.P. please reply

SOS 1. international distress signal 2. Any call or signal for help

Sr. 1. senior (after surname) 2. sister (religious)

SRO, S.R.O. standing room only

ST standard time

St. 1. saint 2. strait 3. street

std. standard

syn. synonymous; synonym

tbs., tbsp. tablespoon

TM trademark

uhf, UHF ultra high frequency

USSR Union of Soviet Socialist Republics

V 1. *Physics:* velocity 2. *Electricity:* volt 3. volume

VA 1. Also **V.A.** Veterans Administration 2. Virginia (with ZIP code)

vhf, VHF very high frequency

VIP *Informal* very important person

vol. 1. volume 2. volunteer

vs. versus

W 1. *Electricity:* watt 2. *Physics:* (Also **w**) work 3. West

whse., whs. warehouse

whsle. wholesale

wkly. weekly

w/o without

wt. weight

yd yard (measurement)

zool. zoological; zoology

708 Most abbreviations are followed by a period. **Acronyms** are exceptions. An acronym is a word formed from the first (or first few) letters of words in a set phrase.

> **radar (radio detecting and ranging), CARE (Cooperative for American Relief Everywhere), VISTA (Volunteers in Service to America), UNICEF (United Nations International Children's Emergency Fund)**

709 An **initialism** is similar to an acronym except that the initials used to form this abbreviation cannot be pronounced as a word.

> **CIA — Central Intelligence Agency** (*initialism*)
> **NASA — National Aeronautics and Space Administration** (*acronym*)

Common Acronyms and Initialisms

CIA	Central Intelligence Agency	NATO	North Atlantic Treaty Organization
FAA	Federal Aviation Administration	NYC	Neighborhood Youth Corps
FBI	Federal Bureau of Investigation	OEO	Office of Economic Opportunity
FCC	Federal Communications Commission	OEP	Office of Emergency Preparedness
FDA	Food and Drug Administration	REA	Rural Electrification Administration
FDIC	Federal Deposit Insurance Corporation	SSA	Social Security Administration
FHA	Federal Housing Administration	TVA	Tennessee Valley Authority
FmHA	Farmers Home Administration	VA	Veterans Administration
FTC	Federal Trade Commission	VISTA	Volunteers in Service to America
IRS	Internal Revenue Service	WAC	Women's Army Corps
NASA	National Aeronautics and Space Administration	WAVES	Women Accepted for Volunteer Emergency Service

Numbers

710 **Numbers** from one to nine are usually written as words; all numbers 10 and over are usually written as numerals.

> **two; seven; nine; 10; 25; 106; 1,079**

Exception: If numbers are used infrequently in a piece of writing, you may spell out those that can be written in no more than two words.

> **ten; twenty-five; fifty thousand;** *but* **3½; 101; 2,020**

Note: Numbers being compared or contrasted should be kept in the same style.

> **8 to 11 years old** *or* **eight to eleven years old**

711 Use numerals to express numbers in the following forms: money, decimal, percentage, chapter, page, address, telephone, ZIP code, dates, time, identification numbers, and statistics.

> **$2.39; $3; 26.2; 8 percent; chapter 7; pages 287-89; 2125 Cairn Road; July 6, 1945; 44 B.C.; A.D. 79; 4:30 P.M.; Highway 36; a vote of 23 to 4; 34 mph**

Exception: If numbers are used infrequently in a piece of writing, you may spell out amounts of money and percentages when you can do so in two or three words.

> **nine cents; one hundred dollars; eight percent; thirty-five percent**

Note: Always use numerals with abbreviations and symbols.

> **5'4"; 8%; 10 in.; 3 tbsp.; 6 lbs. 8 oz.; 90° F**

712 Use words to express numbers in the following constructions:

a. Numbers which begin a sentence.

> **Fourteen** students "forgot" their assignments.

> (Adapt the sentence structure if this rule creates a clumsy construction.)
> Clumsy: *Six hundred and thirty-nine* teachers were victims of
> the layoff this year.
> Better: This year, 639 teachers were victims of the layoff.

b. Numbers which precede a compound modifier that includes a figure.

> The chef prepared **two 10-foot** sub sandwiches.
> The basket was woven from **sixty-two 11-inch** ropes.

Note: You may use a combination of words and numerals for very large numbers.

> **1.5 million; 3 billion to 3.2 billion; 6 billion**

▬ Spelling Rules ▬

713 Rule 1: Write *i* before *e* except after *c*, or when sounded like *a* as in *neighbor* and *weigh*.

> Eight of the **exceptions** are included in this sentence:
> Neither sheik dared leisurely seize either weird species of financiers.

When the *ie/ei* combination is not pronounced *ee*, it is usually spelled *ei*.

> **Examples: reign, foreign, weigh, neighbor**
> **Exceptions: fiery, friend, mischief, view**

Rule 2: When a one-syllable word *(bat)* ends in a consonant *(t)* preceded by one vowel *(a)*, double the final consonant before adding a suffix which begins with a vowel *(batting)*.

When a multi-syllable word *(control)* ends in a consonant *(l)* preceded by one vowel *(o)*, the accent is on the last syllable *(con trol')*, and the suffix begins with a vowel *(ing)*—the same rule holds true: double the final consonant *(controlling)*.

> **sum—summary; god—goddess; prefer—preferred; begin—beginning;**
> **forget—forgettable; admit—admittance**

Rule 3: If a word ends with a silent *e,* drop the *e* before adding a suffix which begins with a vowel.

> **state—stating—statement; like—liking—likeness; use—using—useful;**
> **nine—ninety—nineteen**

(Notice that you do *not* drop the *e* when the suffix begins with a consonant. Exceptions include *judgment, truly, argument,* and *ninth.)*

Rule 4: When *y* is the last letter in a word and the *y* is preceded by a consonant, change the *y* to *i* before adding any suffix except those beginning with *i*.

> **fry—fries; hurry—hurried; lady—ladies; ply—pliable; happy—happiness;**
> **beauty—beautiful**

When forming the plural of a word which ends with a *y* that is preceded by a vowel, add *s*.

> **toy—toys; play—plays; monkey—monkeys**

Steps to Becoming a Better Speller

1. Be patient. Learning to become a good speller takes time.

2. Check the correct pronunciation of each word you are attempting to spell. Knowing the correct pronunciation of each word is important to remembering its spelling.

3. As you are checking the dictionary for pronunciation, also check on the meaning and history of each word. Knowing the meaning and history of a word can provide you with a better notion of how and when the word will probably be used. This fuller understanding will help you remember the spelling of that particular word.

4. Before you close the dictionary, practice spelling the word. You can do this by looking away from the page and trying to "see" the word in your "mind's eye." Write the word on a piece of paper. Check the spelling in the dictionary and repeat the process until you are able to spell the word correctly.

5. Learn some spelling rules. The four rules in this handbook are four of the most useful, although there are others.

6. Make a list of the words which you misspell. Select the first ten and practice spelling them.

   Step A: Read each word carefully, then write it on a piece of paper. Look at the written word to see that it's spelled correctly. Repeat the process for those words which you misspelled.

   Step B: When you have finished your first ten words, ask someone to read the words to you so you can write them again. Again check for misspellings. If you find none, congratulations! Repeat both steps with your next ten words.

7. Write often. As noted educator Frank Smith said, "There is little point in learning to spell if you have little intention of writing."

714 A

ab-bre-vi-ate	ad-vis-able	anx-ious	at-tend-ance	bliz-zard
a-brupt	ad-vise (v.)	any-thing	at-ten-tion	book-keep-er
ab-scess	ae-ri-al	a-part-ment	at-ti-tude	bough
ab-sence	af-fect	a-pol-o-gize	at-tor-ney	bought
ab-so-lute (-ly)	af-fi-da-vit	ap-pa-ra-tus	at-trac-tive	bouil-lon
ab-sorb-ent	a-gain	ap-par-ent (-ly)	au-di-ble	bound-a-ry
ab-surd	a-gainst	ap-peal	au-di-ence	break-fast
a-bun-dance	ag-gra-vate	ap-pear-ance	au-thor-i-ty	breath (n.)
ac-cede	ag-gres-sion	ap-pe-tite	au-to-mo-bile	breathe (v.)
ac-cel-er-ate	a-gree-able	ap-pli-ance	au-tumn	brief
ac-cept (-ance)	a-gree-ment	ap-pli-ca-ble	aux-il-ia-ry	bril-liant
ac-ces-si-ble	aisle	ap-pli-ca-tion	a-vail-a-ble	Brit-ain
ac-ces-so-ry	al-co-hol	ap-point-ment	av-er-age	brought
ac-ci-den-tal-ly	a-lign-ment	ap-prais-al	aw-ful	bro-chure
ac-com-mo-date	al-ley	ap-pre-ci-ate	aw-ful-ly	bruise
ac-com-pa-ny	al-lot-ted	ap-proach	awk-ward	budg-et
ac-com-plice	al-low-ance	ap-pro-pri-ate **B**	bach-e-lor	bul-le-tin
ac-com-plish	all right	ap-prov-al	bag-gage	buoy-ant
ac-cor-dance	al-most	ap-prox-i-mate-ly	bal-ance	bu-reau
ac-cord-ing	al-ready	ar-chi-tect	bal-loon	bur-glar
ac-count	al-though	arc-tic	bal-lot	bury
ac-crued	al-to-geth-er	ar-gu-ment	ba-nan-a	busi-ness
ac-cu-mu-late	a-lu-mi-num	a-rith-me-tic	band-age **C**	busy
ac-cu-rate	al-ways	a-rouse	bank-rupt	caf-e-te-ria
ac-cus-tom (ed)	am-a-teur	ar-range-ment	bar-gain	caf-feine
ache	a-mend-ment	ar-riv-al	bar-rel	cal-en-dar
a-chieve (-ment)	a-mong	ar-ti-cle	base-ment	cam-paign
ac-knowl-edge	a-mount	ar-ti-fi-cial	ba-sis	can-celed
ac-quaint-ance	a-nal-y-sis	as-cend	bat-tery	can-di-date
ac-qui-esce	an-a-lyze	as-cer-tain	beau-ti-ful	can-is-ter
ac-quired	an-cient	as-i-nine	beau-ty	ca-noe
ac-tu-al	an-ec-dote	as-sas-sin	be-come	can't
a-dapt	an-es-thet-ic	as-sess (-ment)	be-com-ing	ca-pac-i-ty
ad-di-tion (-al)	an-gle	as-sign-ment	be-fore	cap-i-tal
ad-dress	an-ni-hi-late	as-sist-ance	beg-gar	cap-i-tol
ad-e-quate	an-ni-ver-sa-ry	as-so-ci-ate	be-gin-ning	cap-tain
ad-journed	an-nounce	as-so-ci-a-tion	be-hav-ior	car-bu-ret-or
ad-just-ment	an-noy-ance	as-sume	be-ing	ca-reer
ad-mi-ra-ble	an-nu-al	as-sur-ance	be-lief	car-i-ca-ture
ad-mis-si-ble	a-noint	as-ter-isk	be-lieve	car-riage
ad-mit-tance	a-non-y-mous	ath-lete	ben-e-fi-cial	cash-ier
ad-van-ta-geous	an-swer	ath-let-ic	ben-e-fit (-ed)	cas-se-role
ad-ver-tise (-ment)	ant-arc-tic	at-tach	be-tween	cas-u-al-ty
ad-ver-tis-ing	an-tic-i-pate	at-tack (ed)	bi-cy-cle	cat-a-log
ad-vice (n.)	anx-i-ety	at-tempt	bis-cuit	ca-tas-tro-phe

caught
cav-al-ry
cel-e-bra-tion
cem-e-ter-y
cen-sus
cen-tu-ry
cer-tain
cer-tif-i-cate
ces-sa-tion
chal-lenge
change-a-ble
char-ac-ter (-is-tic)
chauf-feur
chief
chim-ney
choc-o-late
choice
choose
Chris-tian
cir-cuit
cir-cu-lar
cir-cum-stance
civ-i-li-za-tion
cli-en-tele
cli-mate
climb
clothes
coach
co-coa
co-er-cion
col-lar
col-lat-er-al
col-lege
col-lo-qui-al
colo-nel
col-or
co-los-sal
col-umn
com-e-dy
com-ing
com-mence
com-mer-cial
com-mis-sion
com-mit
com-mit-ment
com-mit-ted
com-mit-tee
com-mu-ni-cate
com-mu-ni-ty
com-par-a-tive
com-par-i-son
com-pel
com-pe-tent
com-pe-ti-tion
com-pet-i-tive-ly
com-plain
com-ple-ment
com-plete-ly
com-plex-ion
com-pli-ment
com-pro-mise
con-cede
con-ceive
con-cern-ing
con-cert

con-ces-sion
con-clude
con-crete
con-curred
con-cur-rence
con-demn
con-de-scend
con-di-tion
con-fer-ence
con-ferred
con-fi-dence
con-fi-den-tial
con-grat-u-late
con-science
con-sci-en-tious
con-scious
con-sen-sus
con-se-quence
con-ser-va-tive
con-sid-er-ably
con-sign-ment
con-sis-tent
con-sti-tu-tion
con-tempt-ible
con-tin-u-al-ly
con-tin-ue
con-tin-u-ous
con-trol
con-tro-ver-sy
con-ven-ience
con-vince
cool-ly
co-op-er-ate
cor-dial
cor-po-ra-tion
cor-re-late
cor-re-spond
cor-re-spond-ence
cor-rob-o-rate
cough
couldn't
coun-cil
coun-sel
coun-ter-feit
coun-try
cour-age
cou-ra-geous
cour-te-ous
cour-te-sy
cous-in
cov-er-age
cred-i-tor
cri-sis
crit-i-cism
crit-i-cize
cru-el
cu-ri-os-i-ty
cu-ri-ous
cur-rent
cur-ric-u-lum
cus-tom
cus-tom-ary
cus-tom-er
D cyl-in-der
dai-ly

dair-y
dealt
debt-or
de-ceased
de-ceit-ful
de-ceive
de-cid-ed
de-ci-sion
dec-la-ra-tion
dec-o-rate
de-duct-i-ble
de-fend-ant
de-fense
de-ferred
def-i-cit
def-i-nite (-ly)
def-i-ni-tion
del-e-gate
de-li-cious
de-pend-ent
de-pos-i-tors
de-pot
de-scend
de-scribe
de-scrip-tion
de-sert
de-serve
de-sign
de-sir-able
de-sir-ous
de-spair
des-per-ate
de-spise
des-sert
de-te-ri-o-rate
de-ter-mine
de-vel-op
de-vel-op-ment
de-vice
de-vise
di-a-mond
di-a-phragm
di-ar-rhe-a
di-a-ry
dic-tio-nary
dif-fer-ence
dif-fer-ent
dif-fi-cul-ty
di-lap-i-dat-ed
di-lem-ma
din-ing
di-plo-ma
di-rec-tor
dis-agree-able
dis-ap-pear
dis-ap-point
dis-ap-prove
dis-as-trous
dis-ci-pline
dis-cov-er
dis-crep-an-cy
dis-cuss
dis-cus-sion
dis-ease
dis-sat-is-fied

dis-si-pate
dis-tin-guish
dis-trib-ute
di-vide
di-vine
di-vis-i-ble
di-vi-sion
doc-tor
does-n't
dom-i-nant
dor-mi-to-ry
doubt
drudg-ery
du-al
du-pli-cate
dye-ing
E dy-ing
ea-ger-ly
ear-nest
eco-nom-i-cal
econ-o-my
ec-sta-sy
e-di-tion
ef-fer-ves-cent
ef-fi-ca-cy
ef-fi-cien-cy
eighth
ei-ther
e-lab-o-rate
e-lec-tric-i-ty
el-e-phant
el-i-gi-ble
e-lim-i-nate
el-lipse
em-bar-rass
e-mer-gen-cy
em-i-nent
em-pha-size
em-ploy-ee
em-ploy-ment
e-mul-sion
en-close
en-cour-age
en-deav-or
en-dorse-ment
en-gi-neer
En-glish
e-nor-mous
e-nough
en-ter-prise
en-ter-tain
en-thu-si-as-tic
en-tire-ly
en-trance
en-vel-op (v.)
en-ve-lope (n.)
en-vi-ron-ment
equip-ment
equipped
e-quiv-a-lent
es-pe-cial-ly
es-sen-tial
es-tab-lish
es-teemed
et-i-quette

ev-i-dence
ex-ag-ger-ate
ex-ceed
ex-cel-lent
ex-cept
ex-cep-tion-al-ly
ex-ces-sive
ex-cite
ex-ec-u-tive
ex-er-cise
ex-haust (-ed)
ex-hi-bi-tion
ex-hil-a-ra-tion
ex-is-tence
ex-or-bi-tant
ex-pect
ex-pe-di-tion
ex-pend-i-ture
ex-pen-sive
ex-pe-ri-ence
ex-plain
ex-pla-na-tion
ex-pres-sion
ex-qui-site
ex-ten-sion
ex-tinct
ex-traor-di-nar-y
ex-treme-ly
F fa-cil-i-ties
fal-la-cy
fa-mil-iar
fa-mous
fas-ci-nate
fash-ion
fa-tigue (d)
fau-cet
fa-vor-ite
fea-si-ble
fea-ture
Feb-ru-ar-y
fed-er-al
fem-i-nine
fer-tile
fic-ti-tious
field
fierce
fi-ery
fi-nal-ly
fi-nan-cial-ly
fo-li-age
for-ci-ble
fore-go
for-eign
for-feit
for-mal-ly
for-mer-ly
for-tu-nate
for-ty
for-ward
foun-tain
fourth
frag-ile
fran-ti-cal-ly
freight
friend

G
ful-fill
fun-da-men-tal
fur-ther-more
fu-tile
gad-get
gan-grene
ga-rage
gas-o-line
gauge
ge-ne-al-o-gy
gen-er-al-ly
gen-er-ous
ge-nius
gen-u-ine
ge-og-ra-phy
ghet-to
ghost
glo-ri-ous
gnaw
gov-ern-ment
gov-er-nor
gra-cious
grad-u-a-tion
gram-mar
grate-ful
grat-i-tude
grease
grief
griev-ous
gro-cery
grudge
grue-some
guar-an-tee
guard
guard-i-an
guer-ril-la
guess
guide
guid-ance
guilty
gym-na-si-um
gyp-sy
gy-ro-scope

H
hab-i-tat
ham-mer
han-dle (d)
hand-ker-chief
hand-some
hap-haz-ard
hap-pen
hap-pi-ness
ha-rass
har-bor
hast-i-ly
hav-ing
haz-ard-ous
height
hem-or-rhage
hes-i-tate
hin-drance
his-to-ry
hoarse
hol-i-day
hon-or
hop-ing

hop-ping
horde
hor-ri-ble
hos-pi-tal
hu-mor-ous
hur-ried-ly
hy-drau-lic
hy-giene
hymn
hy-poc-ri-sy

I
i-am-bic
i-ci-cle
i-den-ti-cal
id-io-syn-cra-sy
il-leg-i-ble
il-lit-er-ate
il-lus-trate
im-ag-i-nary
im-ag-i-na-tive
im-ag-ine
im-i-ta-tion
im-me-di-ate-ly
im-mense
im-mi-grant
im-mor-tal
im-pa-tient
im-per-a-tive
im-por-tance
im-pos-si-ble
im-promp-tu
im-prove-ment
in-al-ien-able
in-ci-den-tal-ly
in-con-ve-nience
in-cred-i-ble
in-curred
in-def-i-nite-ly
in-del-ible
in-de-pend-ence
in-de-pend-ent
in-dict-ment
in-dis-pens-able
in-di-vid-u-al
in-duce-ment
in-dus-tri-al
in-dus-tri-ous
in-ev-i-ta-ble
in-fe-ri-or
in-ferred
in-fi-nite
in-flam-ma-ble
in-flu-en-tial
in-ge-nious
in-gen-u-ous
in-im-i-ta-ble
in-i-tial
ini-ti-a-tion
in-no-cence
in-no-cent
in-oc-u-la-tion
in-quir-y
in-stal-la-tion
in-stance
in-stead
in-sti-tute

in-sur-ance
in-tel-lec-tu-al
in-tel-li-gence
in-ten-tion
in-ter-cede
in-ter-est-ing
in-ter-fere
in-ter-mit-tent
in-ter-pret (-ed)
in-ter-rupt
in-ter-view
in-ti-mate
in-va-lid
in-ves-ti-gate
in-ves-tor
in-vi-ta-tion
ir-i-des-cent
ir-rel-e-vant
ir-re-sis-ti-ble
ir-rev-er-ent
ir-ri-gate
is-land
is-sue
i-tem-ized
i-tin-er-ar-y
it's

J
jan-i-tor
jeal-ous (-y)
jeop-ard-ize
jew-el-ry
jour-nal
jour-ney
judg-ment
jus-tice
jus-ti-fi-able

K
kitch-en
knowl-edge
knuck-les

L
la-bel
lab-o-ra-to-ry
lac-quer
lan-guage
laugh
laun-dry
law-yer
league
lec-ture
le-gal
leg-i-ble
leg-is-la-ture
le-git-i-mate
lei-sure
length
let-ter-head
li-a-bil-i-ty
li-a-ble
li-ai-son
li-brar-y
li-cense
lieu-ten-ant
light-ning
lik-able
like-ly
lin-eage
liq-ue-fy

liq-uid
lis-ten
lit-er-ary
lit-er-a-ture
live-li-hood
liv-ing
log-a-rithm
lone-li-ness
loose
lose
los-ing
lov-able
love-ly
lun-cheon
lux-u-ry

M
ma-chine
mag-a-zine
mag-nif-i-cent
main-tain
main-te-nance
ma-jor-i-ty
mak-ing
man-age-ment
ma-neu-ver
man-u-al
man-u-fac-ture
man-u-script
mar-riage
mar-shal
ma-te-ri-al
math-e-mat-ics
max-i-mum
may-or
mean-ness
meant
mea-sure
med-i-cine
me-di-eval
me-di-o-cre
me-di-um
mem-o-ran-dum
men-us
mer-chan-dise
mer-it
mes-sage
mile-age
mil-lion-aire
min-i-a-ture
min-i-mum
min-ute
mir-ror
mis-cel-la-neous
mis-chief
mis-chie-vous
mis-er-a-ble
mis-ery
mis-sile
mis-sion-ary
mis-spell
mois-ture
mol-e-cule
mo-men-tous
mo-not-o-nous
mon-u-ment
mort-gage

mu-nic-i-pal
mus-cle
mu-si-cian
mus-tache

N
mys-te-ri-ous
na-ive
nat-u-ral-ly
nec-es-sary
ne-ces-si-ty
neg-li-gi-ble
ne-go-ti-ate
neigh-bor (-hood)
nev-er-the-less
nick-el
niece
nine-teenth
nine-ty
no-tice-able
no-to-ri-ety
nu-cle-ar
nui-sance

O
o-be-di-ence
o-bey
o-blige
ob-sta-cle
oc-ca-sion
oc-ca-sion-al-ly
oc-cu-pant
oc-cur
oc-curred
oc-cur-rence
of-fense
of-fi-cial
of-ten
o-mis-sion
o-mit-ted
o-pin-ion
op-er-ate
op-por-tu-ni-ty
op-po-nent
op-po-site
op-ti-mism
or-di-nance
or-di-nar-i-ly
orig-i-nal
out-ra-geous

P
pag-eant
paid
pam-phlet
par-a-dise
para-graph
par-al-lel
par-a-lyze
pa-ren-the-ses
pa-ren-the-sis
par-lia-ment
par-tial
par-tic-i-pant
par-tic-i-pate
par-tic-u-lar-ly
pas-time
pa-tience
pa-tron-age
pe-cu-liar
per-ceive

per-haps
per-il
per-ma-nent
per-mis-si-ble
per-pen-dic-u-lar
per-se-ver-ance
per-sis-tent
per-son-al (-ly)
per-son-nel
per-spi-ra-tion
per-suade
phase
phe-nom-e-non
phi-los-o-phy
phy-si-cian
piece
planned
pla-teau
plau-si-ble
play-wright
pleas-ant
pleas-ure
pneu-mo-nia
pol-i-ti-cian
pos-sess
pos-ses-sion
pos-si-ble
prac-ti-cal-ly
prai-rie
pre-cede
pre-ce-dence
pre-ced-ing
pre-cise-ly
pre-ci-sion
pre-cious
pred-e-ces-sor
pref-er-a-ble
pref-er-ence
pre-ferred
prej-u-dice
pre-lim-i-nar-y
pre-mi-um
prep-a-ra-tion
pres-ence
prev-a-lent
pre-vi-ous
prim-i-tive
prin-ci-pal
prin-ci-ple
pri-or-i-ty
pris-on-er
priv-i-lege
prob-a-bly
pro-ce-dure
pro-ceed
pro-fes-sor
prom-i-nent
pro-nounce
pro-nun-ci-a-tion
pro-pa-gan-da
pros-e-cute
pro-tein
psy-chol-o-gy
pub-lic-ly
pump-kin

pur-chase
pur-sue
pur-su-ing
pur-suit

Q
qual-i-fied
quan-ti-ty
quar-ter
ques-tion-naire
qui-et
quite
quo-tient

R
raise
rap-port
re-al-ize
re-al-ly
re-cede
re-ceipt
re-ceive
re-ceived
rec-i-pe
re-cip-i-ent
rec-og-ni-tion
rec-og-nize
rec-om-mend
re-cur-rence
ref-er-ence
re-ferred
re-hearse
reign
re-im-burse
rel-e-vant
re-lieve
re-li-gious
re-mem-ber
re-mem-brance
rem-i-nisce
ren-dez-vous
re-new-al
rep-e-ti-tion
rep-re-sen-ta-tive
req-ui-si-tion
res-er-voir
re-sis-tance
re-spect-a-bly
re-spect-ful-ly
re-spec-tive-ly
re-spon-si-bil-i-ty
res-tau-rant
rheu-ma-tism
rhyme
rhythm
ri-dic-u-lous
route

S
sac-ri-le-gious
safe-ty
sal-a-ry
sand-wich
sat-is-fac-to-ry
Sat-ur-day
scarce-ly
scene
scen-er-y
sched-ule
sci-ence
scis-sors

sec-re-tary
seize
sen-si-ble
sen-tence
sen-ti-nel
sep-a-rate
ser-geant
sev-er-al
se-vere-ly
shep-herd
sher-iff
shin-ing
seige
sig-nif-i-cance
sim-i-lar
si-mul-ta-ne-ous
since
sin-cere-ly
ski-ing
sol-dier
sol-emn
so-phis-ti-cat-ed
soph-o-more
so-ror-i-ty
source
sou-ve-nir
spa-ghet-ti
spe-cif-ic
spec-i-men
speech
sphere
spon-sor
spon-ta-ne-ous
sta-tion-ary
sta-tion-ery
sta-tis-tic
stat-ue
stat-ure
stat-ute
stom-ach
stopped
straight
strat-e-gy
strength
stretched
study-ing
sub-si-dize
sub-stan-tial
sub-sti-tute
sub-tle
suc-ceed
suc-cess
suf-fi-cient
sum-ma-rize
su-per-fi-cial
su-per-in-tend-ent
su-pe-ri-or-i-ty
su-per-sede
sup-ple-ment
sup-pose
sure-ly
sur-prise
sur-veil-lance
sur-vey
sus-cep-ti-ble

sus-pi-cious
sus-te-nance
syl-la-ble
sym-met-ri-cal
sym-pa-thy
sym-pho-ny
symp-tom
syn-chro-nous

T
tar-iff
tech-nique
tele-gram
tem-per-a-ment
tem-per-a-ture
tem-po-rary
ten-den-cy
ten-ta-tive
ter-res-tri-al
ter-ri-ble
ter-ri-to-ry
the-ater
their
there
there-fore
thief
thor-ough (-ly)
though
through-out
tired
to-bac-co
to-geth-er
to-mor-row
tongue
to-night
touch
tour-na-ment
tour-ni-quet
to-ward
trag-e-dy
trai-tor
tran-quil-iz-er
trans-ferred
trea-sur-er
tried
tries
tru-ly
Tues-day
tu-ition
typ-i-cal
typ-ing

U
unan-i-mous
un-con-scious
un-doubt-ed-ly
un-for-tu-nate-ly
unique
u-ni-son
uni-ver-si-ty
un-nec-es-sary
un-prec-e-dent-ed
un-til
up-per
ur-gent
us-able
use-ful
using
usu-al-ly

V
u-ten-sil
u-til-ize
va-can-cies
va-ca-tion
vac-u-um
vague
valu-able
va-ri-ety
var-i-ous
veg-e-ta-ble
ve-hi-cle
veil
ve-loc-i-ty
ven-geance
very
vi-cin-i-ty
view
vig-i-lance
vil-lain
vi-o-lence
vis-i-bil-i-ty
vis-i-ble
vis-i-tor
voice
vol-ume
vol-un-tary
vol-un-teer

W
wan-der
war-rant
weath-er
Wednes-day
weird
wel-come
wel-fare
where
wheth-er
which
whole
whol-ly
whose
width
wom-en
worth-while
wor-thy
wreck-age
wres-tler
writ-ing
writ-ten
wrought

Y
yel-low
yes-ter-day
yield

> *"English is a stretch language; one size fits all. That does not mean anything goes; in most instances, anything does not go. But the language, as it changes, conforms itself to special groups and occasions: There is a time for dialect, a place for slang, an occasion for literary form. What is correct on the sports page is out of place on the op-ed [editorial] page; what is with-it on the street may well be without it in the classroom. The spoken language does not have the same standards as the written language . . . ."*
>
> **—William Safire**

Using the
RIGHT WORD

Do you put much thought into the spoken words you use each day? Of course you don't. Using the language is basically a spontaneous act. If you stopped to think about each and every word, your language would become stilted, unnatural, and hard to follow. Listen to a government official during a press conference. A skilled bureaucrat analyzes everything he says and presents his ideas so deliberately and carefully that it's easy to lose track of what he is actually trying to say. Listen to politicians in a debate. Most of their arguments are "canned," prepared ahead of time. They spend little, if any, time in the spontaneous give-and-take of ideas. Read a legal brief or land abstract and see if you can make sense of this *legalese,* the specialized form of English often used in legal documents. In each of these cases, a great deal of time and effort has gone into saying things carefully, correctly, properly. But in each case the message is unclear and unnatural. So why all the concern about usage? Does it really matter if you use *who* or *whom, different than* instead of *different from?*

It depends on *who* you talk to. (*Whom* is actually the correct form, but "on *whom* you talk to" just doesn't sound right to most people.) Your friends probably think correct usage is about as important as a balanced diet. Your parents . . . well, that depends. Some parents adhere strictly to correct usage; other parents are not so strict. Some of your teachers "guard" the language against corruption with red pens flaring; others are quite comfortable with language that sounds sincere and natural.

What should you do? First, you should know when correct usage is important. You'll quickly learn which teachers demand "*as* Thoreau writes" rather than "*like* Thoreau writes." And it won't take you long to realize many other situations when proper word choice is important: a letter to a university director of admissions, a formal essay or research paper, a presentation to a local church or civic group. Second, you should become familiar with the words which are commonly misused by reviewing this section in your handbook. Third, you should refer to this section whenever you have a usage question. (*Note:* If your handbook doesn't answer your question, refer to a high school or collegiate dictionary.) Finally, you should make every effort to keep your writing both "correct" and natural.

715 a, an: *A* is used before words which begin with a consonant sound; *an* is used before words which begin with a vowel sound.

> **Examples:** *a* heap; *a* uniform; *an* idol; *an* urban area; *an* honor; *a* historian.

716 ability, capacity: *Ability* is the power of applying knowledge; *capacity* is the power of receiving and retaining it.

> **Example:** My mother has the *ability* to make liver and onions; I, unfortunately, don't have the *capacity* to eat it.

717 accept, except: The verb *accept* means to receive; the verb *except* means to leave out or take out. The preposition *except* means other than.

> **Examples:** Melissa graciously *accepted* defeat. Mike *excepted* the wasp from his collection (verb). Everyone *except* Zach agreed on the theme for the winter carnival.

718 acrost, acrossed: Neither is correct. Use *across*.

719 adapt, adopt: *Adapt* means to make fit or suitable by changing or adjusting; *adopt* means to choose and treat as your own (a child, an idea).

> **Example:** The puppy we *adopted* from the shelter had to *adapt* to its new surroundings.

720 adverse, averse: *Adverse* means to be against or to oppose; *averse* means to have a dislike for something.

> **Example:** The father's *aversion* to rock music prompted an *adverse* reaction—jumping up and down on his son's radio.

721 affect, effect: *Affect* means to influence; the verb *effect* means to produce.

> **Examples:** Mark's giggle *affected* the preacher. Mark's giggle *effected* a pinch from his mother.

The noun *effect* means the result.

> **Example:** The *effect* of the pinch was a sore leg.

722 allusion, illusion: *Allusion* is an indirect reference to something; *illusion* is a false picture or idea.

> **Example:** The person who makes many *allusions* to his strength tries to reinforce the *illusion* that he's strong.

723 alot: *Alot* is not one word; *a lot* (two words) is a vague descriptive phrase which should not be used in formal writing.

> **Example:** "You can observe *a lot* just by watching." (Yogi Berra)

724 already, all ready: *Already* is always an adverb.

> **Examples:** My little girl reads *already*. The class was *all ready* "to try out" the substitute.

725 alright: *Alright* is the incorrect form of *all right*. (Please note, the following are spelled correctly: *always, altogether, already, almost.)*

726 altogether, all together: *Altogether* is always an adverb.

> **Examples:** This is *altogether* too much noise. "*All together* now: 'Tie me kangaroo down sport . . . .' "

727 among, between: *Among* is used when speaking of more than two persons or things. *Between* is used when speaking of only two.

> **Examples:** Putrid socks were scattered *among* sweaty uniforms. "Ya want a fist *between* your eyes?"

728 amount, number: *Amount* is used for bulk measurement. *Number* is used to count separate units. (See also 765.)

> **Examples:** The soft drink produced a large *number* of burps. The burps were the result of a large *amount* of gas.

729 annual, biannual, semiannual, biennial, perennial: An *annual* event happens once every year. A *biannual* event happens twice a year *(semiannual* means the same as *biannual).* A *biennial* event happens every two years. A *perennial* event is active throughout the year and continues to happen every year.

730   **ant, aunt:** *Aunt* is a relative. *Ant* is an insect.
       Example: Do not say, "I carefully inspected my tiny *aunt's* crazy legs."

731   **anyways:** This is the incorrect form of *anyway*. (Also, watch out for *nowhere*.)

732   **ascared:** *Ascared* is not standard English. Use either *scared* or *afraid*.

733   **ascent, assent:** *Ascent* is rising; *assent* is agreement.
       Example: The pilot *assented* that the plane's *ascent* was unusually bumpy.

734   **base, bass:** *Base* is the foundation or the lower part of something. *Bass* is a deep sound or tone. *Bass* (*a* pronounced as in *fast)* is a fish.

735   **be, bee:** *Be* is the verb. *Bee* is the insect.

736   **be sure and:** Use *be sure to* instead. (Also avoid similar phrases which use *and* instead of *to*.)

737   **berth, birth:** *Berth* is a space or compartment. *Birth* is the process of being born.
       Example: We give up our most comfortable *berths* through *birth*.

738   **beside, besides:** *Beside* means by the side of. *Besides* means in addition to.
       Examples: Jeff set his books *beside* his plate. *Besides* some burned toast, Bernice served some sunny-side up sliders (interesting looking eggs).

739   **blew, blue:** *Blew* is the verb. *Blue* is the color.

740   **board, bored:** *Board* is a piece of wood. *Board* also means an administrative group or council.
       Example: The School *Board* approved the purchase of fifty 1" x 6" pine *boards*.

       Bored may mean to make a hole by drilling or to become weary out of dullness.
       Example: Dissecting fish *bored* Joe, so he took his tweezers and *bored* a hole in the tail of the perch.

741   **brake, break:** *Brake* is a device used to stop a vehicle. *Break* means to separate or to destroy.
       Example: I hope the *brakes* on my car never *break*.

742   **bring, take:** *Bring* means the action is directed toward the speaker; *take* means the action is directed away from the speaker.
       Example: "Guards, *take* this advisor away, and *bring* me another one. I don't like his advice."

743   **by, buy:** *By* is the preposition. *Buy* is the verb meaning to purchase.
       Example: You're the sixth person to stop *by* the house to ask if I would *buy* some dried fruit for the band fund-raiser.

744   **can, may:** *Can* suggests ability while *may* suggests permission.
       Example: "*Can* I go to the library?" literally means, "Do I have the skill to handle the business?"

745   **cannon, canon:** A *cannon* is a big gun; a *canon* is a rule or law made by an authority in a church or organization.

746   **canvas, canvass:** *Canvas* is a heavy cloth; *canvass* means to go among the people asking them for votes or opinions.

747   **capital, capitol:** The noun *capital* refers to a city or to money. The adjective *capital* means major or important. *Capitol* refers to a building.
       Examples: The *capitol* building is in the *capital* city for a *capital* reason. The city government contributed *capital* for the building expense.

748   **cent, sent, scent:** *Cent* is a coin; *sent* is the past tense of the verb *send; scent* is an odor or smell.
       Examples: For twenty-two *cents,* I *sent* my girlfriend a mushy love poem in a perfumed envelope. She adored the *scent* but hated the poem.

749   **chord, cord:** *Chord* may mean an emotion or feeling, but it also may mean the combination of two or more tones sounded at the same time, as with a guitar *chord*. A *cord* is a string or rope.

750   **chose, choose:** *Chose* (choz) is the past tense of the verb *choose* (chooz).
> **Example:** This afternoon Mom *chose* tacos and hot sauce; this evening she will *choose* Alka-Seltzer.

751   **coarse, course:** *Coarse* means rough or crude; *course* means a path or direction taken. *Course* also means a class or series of studies.
> **Example:** As Heidi pursued her *course* to success, she encountered a few *coarse* individuals.

752   **collaborate, corroborate:** *Collaborate* (root: *labor*) means to labor or work together; *corroborate* means to confirm or support.

753   **compare to, compare with:** Things of the same class are *compared with* each other; things of a different class are *compared to* each other.
> **Examples:** An acorn, when *compared with* a black walnut, isn't all it's cracked up to be. A penny *compared to* a skunk makes no "sense" at all.

754   **complement, compliment:** *Complement* refers to that which completes or fulfills. *Compliment* is an expression of admiration or praise.
> **Example:** I *complimented* Aunt Betty by saying that her new shoes *complemented* her outfit.

755   **continual, continuous:** *Continual* refers to something which happens again and again; *continuous* refers to something which doesn't stop happening.
> **Example:** Sunlight hits Peoria, Iowa, on a *continual* basis; but sunlight hits the world *continuously*.

756   **counsel, council:** When used as a noun, *counsel* means advice; when used as a verb, *counsel* means to advise. *Council* refers to a group which advises.
> **Examples:** The jackrabbit *council counseled* all bunnies to keep their tails out of the old man's garden. That's good *counsel*.

757   **dear, deer:** *Dear* means loved or valued; *deer* are animals. *(Note:* People will think you're strange if you write that you kissed your *deer* in the moonlight.)

758   **desert, dessert:** *Desert* is barren wilderness. *Dessert* is food served at the end of a meal.
> **Example:** The scorpion tiptoed through the moonlit *desert*, searching for *dessert*.

The verb *desert* means to abandon; the noun *desert* also may mean deserving reward or punishment.
> **Example:** The burglar's cover *deserted* him when the spotlight swung his way; his subsequent arrest was his just *desert*.

759   **die, dye:** *Die (dying)* means to stop living. *Dye (dyeing)* is used to change the color of something.

760   **different from, different than:** Use *different from* in formal writing; use either form in informal or colloquial settings.
> **Example:** He is as *different from* his sister as *Mad Magazine* is from *War and Peace*.

761   **disinterested, uninterested:** *Disinterested* means indifferent, unbiased by personal opinion; *uninterested* means having no interest or concern.
> **Examples:** A *disinterested* referee will judge a basketball game fairly. An *uninterested* referee will sit down on the centerline and smoke his pipe.

762   **eminent, imminent:** *Eminent* means strong, distinguished, prominent. *Imminent* means close or near.
> **Example:** Embarrassment was *imminent* when the *eminent* politician quickly puckered his lips under the bonnet which lay nestled in the lady's left arm; he had not noticed the thick hairy tail which protruded from under her right arm.

763 **faint, feign, feint:** *Faint* means to be feeble, without strength; *feign* is a verb which means to present something in a pretended or false manner; *feint* is a noun which means a move or activity which is pretended or false.

> **Example:** The little boy *feigned* a bruised, blood-spattered face and fell to the floor in a *feint;* his teacher, who didn't notice that the blood smelled like catsup, *fainted* beside him.

764 **farther, further:** *Farther* refers to a physical distance; *further* refers to additional time, quantity, or degree.

> **Examples:** Alaska is *farther* north than Iceland. If you have any *further* questions, ask your mother.

765 **fewer, less:** *Fewer* refers to the number of separate units; *less* refers to bulk quantity.

> **Example:** Modern families spend *less* time preparing meals, so they eat *fewer* fresh foods.

766 **flair, flare:** *Flair* means a distinctive and natural talent; *flare* means to light up quickly or burst out.

> **Example:** Hotheads have a *flair* for tempers which *flare.*

767 **for free:** Use *free* or *for nothing* instead.

768 **good, well:** *Good* is an adjective; *well* is nearly always an adverb.

> **Examples:** The strange flying machines flew *well.* (The adverb *well* modifies *flew.*) They looked *good* as they flew overhead. (The adjective *good* modifies *they.*)
> **Exception:** When used to indicate state of health, *well* is an adjective.
> **Examples:** The pilots looked *good* at the start of the race. Not all of them looked so *well* at the finish.

The race made a *good* story for the young reporter. He wrote *well* and made the event come alive for his readers.

769 **hanged, hung:** Men are *hanged;* things are *hung.*

> **Example:** "I'll be *hanged!* That young carpenter *hung* my back door crooked."

770 **heal, heel:** *Heal* means to mend or restore to health. A *heel* is the back part of a human foot.

> **Examples:** "Oh, that injury will *heal.* Just don't get another *heel* in the solar plexus."

771 **healthful, healthy:** *Healthful* means causing or improving health; *healthy* means possessing health.

> **Example:** *Healthful* foods build *healthy* bodies.

772 **hear, here:** You *hear* with your ears. *Here* means the area close by.

773 **heard, herd:** *Heard* is the past tense of the verb *hear; herd* is a large group of animals.

> **Example:** The *herd* of grazing mares raised their heads when they *heard* the neigh of the stallion.

774 **heir, air:** *Heir* is a person who inherits something; *air* is a gas.

> **Example:** I'm *heir* to some dirty *air* thanks to those antiquated factories.

775 **hole, whole:** A *hole* is a cavity or hollow place. *Whole* means entire or complete.

776 immigrate, emigrate: *Immigrate* means to come into a new country or environment. *Emigrate* means to go out of one country to live in another.

> **Examples:** Martin Ulferts *immigrated* to this country in 1882. He was only three years old when he *emigrated* from Germany.

777 imply, infer: *Imply* means to suggest or express indirectly; *infer* means to draw a conclusion from facts. (A writer or speaker *implies*; a reader or listener *infers*.)

> **Example:** The editor *implied* carelessness; the reader *inferred* corruption.

778 inter-, intra-: *Inter-* means between; *intra-* means among.

> **Example:** *Inter*scholastic basketball is played *between* schools; *intra*mural basketball is played by teams from *within* a school.

779 it's, its: *Its* is the possessive form of *it*. *It's* is the contraction of *it is*.

> **Example:** *It's* obviously a watchdog; it prefers to watch thieves rather than bark for *its* master.

780 kind of, sort of: These expressions are clumsy in formal writing. However, when either one is used, no article *(a, an,* or *the)* should follow.

> **Example:** This *kind of* movie is raunchy. (Not: This *kind of a* movie is raunchy.)

781 knew, new: *Knew* is the past tense of the verb *know*. *New* means recent or novel.

> **Example:** I already *knew* that the zoo had acquired a number of *new* gnus.

know, no: *Know* means to understand or to realize. *No* means the opposite of *yes*.

782 last, latest: Use *last* in the sense of final; *latest* in the sense of most recent.

> **Examples:** "We meet at *last,* Dr. Moriarty, on terms of my own choosing. Watson and I have uncovered your *latest* diabolical scheme."

783 later, latter: *Later* means after a period of time. *Latter* refers to the second of two things mentioned.

> **Example:** *Later* in the year 1965, Galen married Sam; the *latter,* Sam, is a lady.

784 lay, lie: *Lay* means to place. *Lay* is a transitive verb. (See 877.)

> **Examples:** Today I *lay* an empty bag of M & M's on my reading table. Yesterday I *laid* a half-empty bag of M & M's on my reading table. I *have laid* many bags of M & M's on my reading table.

Lie means to recline. *Lie* is an intransitive verb. (See 880.)

> **Examples:** The mutt *lies* down. It *lay* down yesterday. It *has lain* down before.

785 lead, led: *Lead* is the present tense of the verb meaning to guide. The past tense of the verb is *led*. When the words are pronounced the same, then *lead* is the metal.

> **Examples:** "Hey, Nat, get the *lead* out!" "Hey, cool it, man! Who gave you a ticket to *lead* me around?"

786 learn, teach: *Learn* means to get information; *teach* means to give information.

> **Examples:** "Don't try to *teach* me about credit cards, money cards, and checking accounts. I *learned* a long time ago that a budget boils down to this: pay with cash or go without."

787 leave, let: *Leave* means to allow something to remain behind. *Let* means to permit.

> **Examples:** Jesse's free spirit said, *"Let* those assignments slide tonight." Her sense of duty said, "If you *leave* all of that work in your locker, school will be a real merry-go-round tomorrow."

788 lend, borrow: *Lend* means to give for temporary use; *borrow* means to receive for temporary use.

> **Example:** If Hulk Hogan were to *lend* you $10, I hope you'd have enough sense to *borrow* it with the intent of paying it back.

789 liable, likely: *Liable* means responsible according to the law or exposed to an adverse action; *likely* means in all probability.

> **Example:** The "flat tire on the freeway in rush-hour traffic" seems a *likely* story; but I still think you're *liable* to be in deep trouble for missing your final exam.

790 **like, as:** *Like* is a preposition meaning similar to; *as* is a conjunction. The conjunction "as" has several meanings. *Like* usually introduces a phrase; *as* usually introduces a clause.

> **Example:** *Like* the other people in my lab group, I work on an experiment *as* a real scientist would—carefully and thoroughly.

791 **loose, lose, loss:** *Loose* (loos) means free, untied, unrestricted; *lose* (looz) means to misplace or fail to find or control; *loss* (los) means a losing or an amount that is lost.

792 **mail, male:** *Mail* refers to letters or packages handled by the postal service. *Male* refers to the masculine sex.

793 **meat, meet:** *Meat* is food or flesh; *meet* means to come upon or to encounter.

794 **metal, meddle, medal, mettle:** *Metal* is an element like iron or gold. *Meddle* means to interfere. *Medal* is an award. *Mettle,* a noun, refers to quality of character.

> **Examples:** The golden snoop cup is a *metal medal* which is awarded to the greatest *meddler.* Snooping is a habit of people of low *mettle.*

795 **miner, minor:** A *miner* digs in the ground for valuable ore. A *minor* is a person who is not legally an adult. A *minor* problem is one of no great importance.

The use of *minors* as *miners* is no *minor* problem.

796 **moral, morale:** *Moral* relates to what is right or wrong. *Morale* refers to a person's mental condition.

> **Examples:** *Hoosiers* (the movie) was an entertaining, *morale*-building movie. It contained little preaching or *moralizing.*

797 **of, have:** *Of* should not be used in place of *have.* "I *should have* (not *should of*) known that."

798 **off of:** Drop the *of.* "How many times do I have to tell you to stay *off* (not *off of*) my blue suede shoes?"

799 **orientate:** The correct word is *orient.*

> **Example:** Once I *orient* (not *orientate*) myself to my new job, I'll be able to work much faster.

800 **pain, pane:** *Pain* is the feeling of being hurt. *Pane* is a flat side or a single section of a window.

801 **past, passed:** *Passed* is a verb. *Past* can be used as a noun, as an adjective, or as a preposition.

> **Examples:** That Escort *passed* my 'Vette (verb). Many senior citizens hold dearly to the *past* (noun). I'm sorry, Sweetheart, but my *past* life is not your business (adjective). Old Rosebud walked *past* us and never smelled the apples (preposition).

802 **peace, piece:** *Peace* means tranquility or freedom from war. *Piece* is a part or fragment.

> **Example:** Someone once observed that *peace* is not a condition, but a process—a process of building goodwill one *piece* or one person at a time.

803 **people, persons:** Use *people* to refer to populations, races, large groups; use *persons* to refer to individuals or human beings.

> **Examples:** What the American *people* need is a good insect repellent. The forest ranger recommends that we check our *persons* for wood ticks when we leave the woods.

804 **personal, personnel:** *Personal* means private. *Personnel* are people working at a particular job.

805 **plain, plane:** *Plain* means an area of land which is flat or level; it also means clearly seen or clearly understood.
  Example: My teacher told me to "check the map" after I said it was *plain* to me why the early settlers had trouble crossing the Rockies on their way to the Great *Plains*.
  Plane means flat, level, and even; it is also a tool used to smooth the surface of wood.
  Example: I used a *plane* to make the board *plane* and smooth.

806 **pore, pour, poor:** A *pore* is an opening in the skin. *Pour* means a constant flow or stream. *Poor* means needy or pitiable.
  Example: Tough exams on late spring days make my *poor pores pour*.

807 **principal, principle:** As an adjective, *principal* means primary. As a noun, it can mean a school administrator or a sum of money. *Principle* means idea or doctrine.
  Examples: His *principal* gripe is lack of freedom. "Hey, Charlie, I hear the *principal* chewed you out!" After twenty years, the amount of interest was higher than the *principal*. The *principle* of *caveat emptor* is "Let the buyer beware."

808 **quiet, quit, quite:** *Quiet* is the opposite of noisy. *Quit* means to stop. *Quite* means completely or entirely.

809 **quote, quotation:** *Quote* is a verb; *quotation* is a noun.
  Example: "The *quotation* I used was from Woody Allen. You may *quote* me on that."

810 **real, very, really:** Do not use *real* in place of the adverbs *very* or *really*.
  Examples: Pimples are *very* (not *real*) embarrassing. This cake is *really* stale—I mean, it's just about fossilized.

811 **right, write, wright, rite:** *Right* means correct or proper; it also refers to that which a person has a legal claim to, as in copyright. *Write* means to inscribe or record. *Wright* is a person who makes or builds something. *Rite* is a ritual or ceremonial act.
  Example: Did you *write* that it is the *right* of the ship*wright* to perform the *rite* of christening—breaking a bottle of champagne on the stern of the ship?

812 **scene, seen:** *Scene* refers to the setting or location where something happens; it also may mean sight or spectacle. *Seen* is part of the verb *see*.
  Example: An exhibitionist likes to be *seen* making a *scene*.

813 **seam, seem:** *Seam* is a line formed by connecting two pieces. *Seem* means to appear to exist.
  Example: The ragged *seams* in his old coat *seem* to match the creases in his face.

814 **set, sit:** *Sit* means to put the body in a seated position. *Set* means to place. *Set* is transitive; *sit* is intransitive. (See 877-880.)

"How can you just *sit* there and watch as I *set* all these chairs in place?"

815　**sight, cite, site:** *Sight* means the act of seeing. *Cite* means to quote or to refer to. *Site* means location or position.
　　Examples: What an incredible *sight!* The judge *cited* a young boy and his dog for defacing a downtown job *site*.

816　**sole, soul:** *Sole* means single, only one; *sole* also refers to the bottom surface of the foot. *Soul* refers to the spiritual part of a person.
　　Example: A blistered *sole* heals quickly, but a *soul* that is blistered may need time to heal.

817　**some, sum:** *Some* refers to a certain unknown number or part. *Sum* means an amount.
　　Example: The total *sum* was stolen by *some* thieves.

818　**stationary, stationery:** *Stationary* means not movable; *stationery* refers to the paper and envelopes used to write letters.

819　**steal, steel:** *Steal* means to take something without permission; *steel* is a metal.

820　**than, then:** *Than* is used in a comparison; *then* tells when.
　　Examples: *Then* he cried and said that his big brother was bigger *than* my big brother. *Then* I cried.

821　**their, there, they're:** *Their* is the possessive personal pronoun. *There* is an adverb used to point out location. *They're* is the contraction for *they are*.
　　Examples: You see those trees over *there* with *their* trunks tagged? *They're* next on the city's hit list.

822　**threw, through:** *Threw* is the past tense of throw. *Through* means passing from one side of something to the other.
　　Example: She wildly *threw* the discus *through* the shop window.

823　**to, at:** *To* should not be used in place of *at* in a sentence like this: He is *at* (not *to)* school.

824　**to, too, two:** *To* is the preposition which can mean in the direction of. *To* also is used to form an infinitive. *Too* is an adverb indicating degree. *Two* is the number.
　　Example: The *two* divers were careful not *to* swim *to* the sunken ship *too* quickly.

825　**vain, vane, vein:** *Vain* means valueless or fruitless; it may also mean holding a high regard for one's self. *Vane* is a flat piece of material set up to show which way the wind blows. *Vein* refers to a blood vessel or a mineral deposit.
　　Example: The weather *vane* indicates the direction of the wind; the blood *vein* determines the direction of flowing blood; the *vain* mind moves in no particular direction or on any specific course and is content to think only about itself.

826　**verbal, oral:** *Verbal* is anything in words; anything spoken is *oral*.
　　Examples: My neighbor made a *verbal* commitment with a fly-by-night landscaper. He'll be the first to tell you that an *oral* agreement means nothing.

827　**waist, waste:** *Waist* is the part of the body just above the hips. The verb *waste* means to wear away, decay; the noun *waste* refers to material which is unused or useless.
　　Example: Large *waists* and much *waste* are sad symbols of our wealth.

828　**wait, weight:** *Wait* means to stay somewhere expecting something. *Weight* refers to a degree or unit of heaviness.

829　**ware, wear, where:** *Ware* refers to a product which is sold; *wear* means to have on or to carry on one's body; *where* asks the question, in what place? or in what situation?
　　Example: The little boy who sold pet fleas boasted, "Anybody can *wear* my *ware* any*where* and he'll always know right *where* it is."

830　**way, weigh:** *Way* means path or route. *Weigh* means to measure weight.
　　Example: After being *weighed* at Weight Watchers club, the two sad friends walked the long *way* home . . . past the malt shop.

831   **weather, whether:** *Weather* refers to the condition of the atmosphere. *Whether* refers to a possibility.
 Examples: I'm a fair-*weather* fan. The temperature and not our football team's success will determine *whether* I go to the next game.

832   **which, witch:** *Which* is the relative pronoun used to refer to something. *Witch* is an evil female who is believed to cast spells and keep company with black cats.
 Example: The cool *witch* drives a broomstick *which* has a tachometer.

833   **who, which, that:** *Which* refers to nonliving objects or to animals; *which* should never refer to people. *Who* is used in reference to people. *That* may refer to animals, people, or nonliving objects.

834   **who, whom:** *Who* is used as the subject of a verb; *whom* is used as the object of a preposition or as a direct object.
 Examples: *Who* ordered the weird pizza with anchovies and pineapple? This weird pizza was ordered by *whom?*
 Note: To test for who/whom, arrange the parts of the clause in a subject, verb, object order *(who* works as the subject, *whom* as the object).

835   **who's, whose:** *Who's* is the contraction for *who is. Whose* is the possessive pronoun.
 Examples: *"Who's* that kid with the red ears?" *"Whose* ears are you talking about, big mouth?"

836   **wood, would:** *Wood* is the stuff which trees are made of; *would* is part of the verb *will.*
 Examples: The captain who had a *wooden* leg *would* always be shortening his trousers whenever termites were on board.

837   **your, you're:** *Your* is a possessive pronoun. *You're* is the contraction for *you are.*
 Examples: "Tell me, Dear, are *your* kisses always this short?" "No, Sweetheart, only when *you're* standing on my feet."

"Grammar is Glamour"

Understanding
■GRAMMAR■

Parts of Speech

840 **Parts of speech** refers to the ways in which words are used in sentences. Words can be used in eight different ways; therefore, there are eight parts of speech: *noun, pronoun, verb, adjective, adverb, preposition, conjunction, interjection.*

■ Noun ■

841 A **noun** is a word which is the name of something: a person, place, thing, or idea.

> **Grandma Ulferts, uncle; Dordt College, school;**
> **John Deere tractor, carburetor; Christmas, holiday**

842 Nouns fall into certain groups. Nouns are grouped according to their *form* (number, gender, and case), their *function* (subject, object, complement, appositive, and modifier), and their *class* (proper, common, concrete, abstract, and collective). The two main classes of nouns are **proper** and **common.**

A **proper noun** is the name of a particular person, place, thing, or idea. Proper nouns are always capitalized.

> **Corizon Aquino, Central America, Grand Ole Opry,**
> **Corvette, Friday, December, Saskatchewan, Tanzania**

A **common noun** is any noun which does not name any particular person, place, thing, or idea. Common nouns are not capitalized.

> **child, country, rainbow, tortilla, nincompoop,**
> **winter, rhinoceros, happiness, love**

843 Nouns are also grouped according to the kind of thing (concrete or abstract) they name. A **concrete noun** names a thing that is tangible (can be touched, heard, smelled, or tasted). Concrete nouns are either proper or common.

> **Afghanistan, White House, Tolstoy,**
> **nations, guitar, grits, whisper, author**

An **abstract noun** names an idea, a doctrine or thought, a theory, a concept, a condition, or a feeling; in other words, an object that cannot be touched or seen. Abstract nouns are either common or proper.

**New Deal, Judaism, satisfaction, poverty, illness,
euphoria, excellence, relativity, creation, evolution**

844 Another type of noun is the **collective noun.** A collective noun names a group or unit. Collective nouns are either common or proper. (See 926.)

**United States, New York Jets, Peace Corps,
class, faculty, audience, herd, flock**

845 Nouns are also grouped according to their **number.** Number indicates whether the noun is singular or plural.

A **singular noun** refers to one person, place, thing, or idea.

singer, stage, rock festival, benefit

A **plural noun** refers to more than one person, place, thing, or idea.

singers, stages, rock festivals, benefits

846 A **compound noun** is a noun made up of two or more words. Some compound nouns are written as one word *(football),* some as two words *(high school),* and some as hyphenated words *(brother-in-law).*

847 Nouns can be classified according to **gender** or sex.

masculine . . . . . . **uncle, brother, men, bull, rooster** *(male)*
feminine . . . . **mother, hostess, women, cow, hen** *(female)*
neuter . . . . **tree, cobweb, fishing rod, spices, closet**
         (without sex)
indefinite . . . . . . **president, pastor, doctor, parent, lawyer,**
         baby, duckling, clerk, assistant *(male or
         female)*

848 Nouns are also grouped into one of three **cases.** Their case tells how nouns are related to the other words used with them. There are three cases: **nominative, possessive,** and **objective.**

A noun is in the **nominative case** when it is used as the **subject** of the verb.

The old **senator** pleaded with his colleagues to approve a freeze on nuclear weapons. "Even **survivors** are victims of a nuclear holocaust."

A noun is also in the **nominative case** when it is used as a **predicate noun** (or predicate nominative). A predicate noun follows a form of the *be* verb *(is, are, was, were, been)* and repeats or renames the subject. (In the examples below, *loser* renames *winner* and *death* renames *life.)*

"Therefore," he asserted, "even the *winner is* a **loser** in a nuclear confrontation. *Life* for the survivors *would be* little more than a slow and painful **death."**

A noun is in the **possessive case** when it shows possession or ownership.

The younger **senator's** face curled into a smile as he spoke. "Nuclear weapons are **humanity's** salvation from war; fear of their use is our assurance that no one will dare to use them."

A noun is in the **objective case** when it is used as the direct object, the indirect object, or the object of the preposition.

A third senator spoke quietly, "In a nuclear age, winners and losers are obsolete. The human race needs **peacemakers."** *(Peacemakers* is the direct object of *needs.)*

"And even they can't promise **mankind** peace." *(Mankind is the indirect object of the verb can promise.)*

"Our best hope for peace lies within the **hearts** of the common **people.**" *(Hearts is the object of the preposition within; people is the object of the preposition of.)*

▬Pronoun▬

849 A **pronoun** is a word used in place of a noun.

> **I, you, she, it, which, that, themselves, whoever,
> me, he, they, whatever, my, mine, ours**

850 All pronouns have antecedents. An **antecedent** is the noun which the pronoun refers to or replaces.

> The **judge** coughed and reached for the glass of water. The water touched *his* lips before *he* noticed the **fly** *which* lay bathing in the cool liquid. *(Judge is the antecedent of his and he; fly is the antecedent of which.)*

Note: Each pronoun must agree with its antecedent in *number, person,* and *gender.* (See 930-931.)

851 Pronouns are distinguished according to their *type, class, number, gender, person,* and *case.* There are three **types.**

> **Simple . . . I, you, he, she, it, we, you, they, who, what**
> **Compound . . . myself, yourself, himself, herself, ourself, itself,
>   whatsoever**
> **Phrasal . . . one another, each other**

852 The following are five **classes** of pronouns: **personal, relative, indefinite, interrogative,** and **demonstrative.**

853 The form of a personal pronoun indicates its **number** (singular or plural), **gender** (masculine, feminine, or neuter), **person** (1st, 2nd, 3rd), and **case** (nominative, possessive, or objective).

854 The **number** of a pronoun can be either singular or plural. **Singular** personal pronouns are these: I, you, he, she, it. **Plural** personal pronouns are these: we, you, they. Notice that the pronoun *you* can be singular or plural.

> You (plural) can't all fit in our Yugo.
> You (singular) are the only one I trust at the wheel.

855 The **person** of a pronoun indicates whether that pronoun is speaking, is spoken to, or is spoken about.

> A **first person** pronoun is used in place of the name of the speaker.

>> **I** feel foolish.
>> **We** won't fall for that trick a second time.

> **Second person** is used to name the person or thing spoken to.

>> Eliza, will **you** please stop bickering!
>> **You** dogs stop growling right now!

> **Third person** is used to name the person or thing spoken about.

>> **She** said that garbage is good fertilizer.
>> **He** always uses **it.**

856 The **case** of each pronoun tells how it is related to the other words used with it. There are three cases: **nominative, possessive,** and **objective.**

857 A pronoun is in the **nominative case** when it is used as the **subject** of the verb. The following are nominative forms: I, you, he, she, it, we, they.

I like myself when things go well.
You must live life in order to love life.

858 A pronoun is also in the **nominative case** when it is used as a **predicate nominative**. A predicate nominative follows a form of the *be* verb (am, is, are, was, were, been) and it repeats the subject.

"It is **I**," growled the big wolf from under Grandmother's bonnet.
"It is **he!**" shrieked Little Red as she twisted his snout into a corkscrew.

859 A pronoun is in the **possessive case** when it shows possession or ownership. An apostrophe, however, is not used with a personal pronoun to show possession.

my, mine, our, ours, his, her, hers, their, its, yours

860 A pronoun is in the **objective case** when it is used as the direct object, indirect object, or object of a preposition.

Nathaniel hugged **me**. (*Me* is the direct object of the verb *hugged*.)
Benji told **me** a story. (*Me* is the indirect object of the verb *told*.)
Teddy Snappers, our dog, listened because the story was about **him**. (*Him* is the object of the preposition *about*.)

861 ## Number, Person, and Case of Personal Pronouns

Singular			
	Nominative Case	Possessive Case	Objective Case
1st Person	I	my, mine	me
2nd Person	you	your, yours	you
3rd Person	he	his	him
	she	her, hers	her
	it	its	it
Plural			
	Nominative Case	Possessive Case	Objective Case
1st Person	we	our, ours	us
2nd Person	you	your, yours	you
3rd Person	they	their, theirs	them

862 A personal pronoun is called a **reflexive pronoun** when it reflects on the subject or refers to it. A reflexive pronoun can act as a direct object or indirect object of the verb, the object of a preposition, or a predicate nominative.

He loves **himself**.   (direct object of *loves*)
He gives **himself** birthday presents. (indirect object of *gives*)
He smiles at **himself** in the mirror. (object of preposition *at*)
He is truly **himself** only when he sleeps. (predicate nominative)

863 A reflexive pronoun is called an **intensive pronoun** when it intensifies or emphasizes the noun or pronoun it refers to.

Leo **himself** taught his children to invest their lives in others.
The lesson was sometimes painful—but they learned it **themselves**.

864 A **relative pronoun** relates one part of a sentence to a word in another part of the sentence. Specifically, a relative pronoun shows that a dependent clause describes a noun in the independent clause. (The noun is underlined in each example; the relative pronoun and dependent clause are in boldface.)

The girl **who had been hit by a drunken driver** regained consciousness and cried because she did not feel pain.

The accident **which had happened ten days earlier** had left her entire body paralyzed and numb.

It was a drunk's decision to drive **that destroyed the girl's opportunity to choose how to live.**

865 An **indefinite pronoun** is indefinite because its antecedent (the word being referred to by the pronoun) is vague or unknown.

The teacher stopped chewing, glanced at his sandwich, then glared at his snickering students and screamed, **"Whoever** put this caterpillar in here will be kicked out of school!" (The antecedent of *whoever* is unknown.)

866 An **interrogative pronoun** asks a question.

"Who is knocking on the door, and **what** do you want?" grunted Little Pig No. 1.

867 A **demonstrative pronoun** points out or identifies a noun without naming the noun.

"That sounds too much like a growling stomach," whimpered Little Pig No. 2. "And **those** don't look like Mommy's toenails under the door," squealed Little Pig No. 3.

868

Classes of Pronouns

Relative
who, whose, whom, which, what, that

Demonstrative
this, that, these, those

Interrogative
who, whose, whom, which, what

Intensive and Reflexive
myself, himself, herself, yourself, themselves, ourselves

Indefinite Pronouns

all	both	everything	nobody	several
another	each	few	none	some
any	each one	many	no one	somebody
anybody	either	most	nothing	someone
anyone	everybody	much	one	something
anything	everyone	neither	other	such

Verb

869 A **verb** is a word which expresses action or state of being. A verb has different forms depending on its **number** (singular or plural); **person** (first, second, third); **voice** (active, passive); **tense** (present, past, future, present perfect, past perfect, future perfect); and **mood** (indicative, imperative, subjunctive).

870 **Number** indicates whether a verb is singular or plural. The verb and its subject both must be singular, or they both must be plural.

One large **island floats** off Italy's "toe." (singular)
Five small **islands float** inside Michigan's "thumb." (plural)

871 **Person** indicates whether the subject of the verb is **1st, 2nd,** or **3rd person** and whether the subject is **singular** or **plural.** Verbs usually have a different form only in *third person singular* of the *present tense*.

	Singular	Plural
1st Person	I sniff	we sniff
2nd Person	you sniff	you sniff
3rd Person	he/she/it *sniffs*	they sniff

872 **Voice** indicates whether the subject is acting or being acted upon. **Active voice** indicates that the subject of the verb is acting—doing something.

> As Verne sat helplessly by, Clyde **rolled** the winning total.

Note: Active verbs "show" rather than "tell"; they can add life and movement to your writing.

Passive voice indicates that the subject of the verb is being acted upon. A passive verb is a combination of a *be* verb and a past participle.

> The winning total **was rolled** by Clyde as Verne sat helplessly by.

Active voice: As Verne sat helplessly by, Clyde **rolled** the winning total.
Passive voice: The winning total **was rolled** by Clyde as Verne sat helplessly by.

873 **Tense** indicates time. Each verb has three principal parts: the **present, past,** and **past participle.** All six of the tenses are formed from these principal parts. The past and past participle of regular verbs are formed by adding *ed* to the present form. The past and past participle of irregular verbs are usually different words; however, some irregular verbs remain the same in all three principal parts.

Present tense expresses action which is happening at the present time, or which happens continually, regularly.

> In September sophomores **smirk** and **joke** about the "little freshies" entering high school.

Past tense expresses action which is completed at a particular time in the past.

> They **forgot** that just ninety days separated them from freshman status.

Future tense expresses action which will take place in the future.

> They **will remember** in a few years when they will be freshmen again.

Present perfect tense expresses action which began in the past but continues in the present or is completed at the present.

> Our boat **has weathered** worse storms than this one.

Past perfect tense expresses action which began in the past and was completed in the past.

> They **had supposed,** wrongly, that the hurricane would miss the island.

Future perfect tense expresses action which will begin in the future and be completed by a specific time in the future.

> By this time tomorrow, the hurricane **will have smashed** into the coast.

874

Tense	Active Voice		Passive Voice	
	Singular	Plural	Singular	Plural
Present Tense	I find you find he/she/it finds	we find you find they find	I am found you are found he/she/it is found	we are found you are found they are found
Past Tense	I found you found he found	we found you found they found	I was found you were found he was found	we were found you were found they were found
Future Tense	I shall find you will find he will find	we shall find you will find they will find	I shall be found you will be found he will be found	we shall be found you will be found they will be found
Present Perfect	I have found you have found he has found	we have found you have found they have found	I have been found you have been found he has been found	we have been found you have been found they have been found
Past Perfect	I had found you had found he had found	we had found you had found they had found	I had been found you had been found he had been found	we had been found you had been found they had been found
Future Perfect	I shall have found you will have found he will have found	we shall have found you will have found they will have found	I shall have been found you will have been found he will have been found	we shall have been found you will have been found they will have been found

Common Irregular Verbs and Their Principal Parts

Present Tense	Past Tense	Past Participle	Present Tense	Past Tense	Past Participle	Present Tense	Past Tense	Past Participle
am, be	was, were	been	fly	flew	flown	shine (light)	shone	shone
begin	began	begun	forsake	forsook	forsaken	shine (polish)	shined	shined
bid (offer)	bid	bid	freeze	froze	frozen	show	showed	shown
bid (order)	bade	bidden	give	gave	given	shrink	shrank	shrunk
bite	bit	bitten	go	went	gone	sing	sang, sung	sung
blow	blew	blown	grow	grew	grown	sink	sank, sunk	sunk
break	broke	broken	hang (execute)	hanged	hanged	sit	sat	sat
bring	brought	brought	hang			slay	slew	slain
burst	burst	burst	(suspend)	hung	hung	speak	spoke	spoken
catch	caught	caught	hide	hid	hidden, hid	spring	sprang, sprung	sprung
choose	chose	chosen						
come	came	come	know	knew	known	steal	stole	stolen
dive	dived	dived	lay	laid	laid	strive	strove	striven
do	did	done	lead	led	led	swear	swore	sworn
drag	dragged	dragged	lie (recline)	lay	lain	swim	swam	swum
draw	drew	drawn	lie (deceive)	lied	lied	swing	swung	swung
drink	drank	drunk	raise	raised	raised	take	took	taken
drown	drowned	drowned	ride	rode	ridden	tear	tore	torn
drive	drove	driven	ring	rang	rung	throw	threw	thrown
eat	ate	eaten	rise	rose	risen	wake	woke, waked	waked
fall	fell	fallen	run	ran	run	wear	wore	worn
fight	fought	fought	see	saw	seen	weave	wove	woven
flee	fled	fled	set	set	set	wring	wrung	wrung
flow	flowed	flowed	shake	shook	shaken	write	wrote	written

875 The **mood** of the verb indicates the tone or attitude with which the statement is made.

Indicative mood is used to state a fact or to ask a question.

> Can any theme capture the essence of the complex 1960's U.S. culture? President John F. Kennedy's directives (stated below) represent one ideal popular during the decade.

Imperative mood is used to give a command.

> "Ask not what your country can do for you. Ask what you can do for your country."

The **subjunctive mood** is no longer commonly used; however, it continues to be used by careful writers to express the exact manner in which their statements are made.

1) Use the subjunctive *were* to express a condition which is contrary to fact.

> If I **were** you, I wouldn't giggle in front of Dad.

2) Use the subjunctive *were* after *as though* or *as if* to express doubt or uncertainty.

> Dad looks as if he **were** about to ground you. Well . . . maybe not. Actually, he looks as though he **were** about to ring your neck!

3) Use the subjunctive *be* in "that clauses" which express necessity, parliamentary motions, or legal decisions.

> "It is moved and supported that 6,000,000 quad **be used** to explore the planet."
> "Ridiculous! Knowing earthlings is bound to help us understand ourselves! Therefore, I move that the sum **be amended** to 12,000,000 quad."
> "Stupidity! I move that all missions **be postponed** until we have living proof of life on earth."

876 **Auxiliary verbs** or helping verbs *help* to form some of the **tenses** (873), the **mood** (875), and the **voice** (872) of the main verb. In the following examples, the auxiliary verbs are in boldface, and the main verbs are italicized.

> Two of Grandma Ulfert's fourteen children **had** *died* at birth.
> One child, Uncle Harry, **has** *been* severely retarded since birth.
> Grandma **will** *nurture* him until he dies because she loves all life.

Common auxiliary verbs are these: *shall, will, would, should, must, can, may, have, had, has, do, did;* and the various forms of the *be* verb: *is, are, was, were, am, been.*

877 Verbs are **transitive** or **intransitive**. A **transitive verb** communicates action and is always followed by an object which receives the action. An object must receive the action of a transitive verb in order to complete the meaning of the verb.

> The city council **passed** a strict noise ordinance.

A transitive verb in the **active voice** directs the action from the subject to the object.

> The *students* **protested** the noise *ordinance* with a noisy demonstration.
> The *police* quietly **enforced** the *ordinance* with several arrests.

(In the first example, the object *ordinance* receives the action of the verb *protested* from the subject *students.* In the second example, *ordinance* receives the action of *enforced* from the *police.*)

Note: If a transitive verb is in the **passive voice,** the subject of the sentence receives the action. (In the following example, the *ordinance* receives the action of the verb.)

> The *ordinance* **was debated** by students and parents at a public meeting.

The name of the actor that creates the action in a passive verb is not always stated. (In the following example, the subject receives the action of the verb. However, the sentence does not say who did the overturning.)

> The *ordinance* **was overturned.**

878 The object of a transitive verb is called the **direct object** if it receives the action directly from the subject.

> The boy kicked his **skateboard** forward. (*Skateboard* is the direct object.)

879 An **indirect object** receives the action of a transitive verb, indirectly. An indirect object names the person (or *thing*) to whom (or *to what*) or for whom (or *for what*) something is done.

> Then he gave **me** a real show. (*Me* is the indirect object.)

Note: When the word naming the indirect receiver of the action is contained in a prepositional phrase, it is no longer considered an indirect object.

> Then he put on a real show for **me**. (*Me* is the object of the preposition *for*.)

880 An **intransitive verb** refers to an action which is complete in itself. It does not need an object to receive the action.

> He and his skateboard **flew** as one. Both **jumped** and **flipped** and **twisted**.

Note: Some verbs can be either **transitive** or **intransitive**.

> He had **pushed** himself to the limit. (transitive)
> He also **pushed** for recognition. (intransitive)

881 A **linking verb** is a special type of intransitive verb which links the subject to a noun or adjective in the predicate. Common linking verbs are the various forms of the *be* verb (*is, are, was, were, been, am*) and verbs such as *smell, look, taste, remain, feel, appear, sound, seem, become, grow, stand, turn*.

> On his skateboard, the *boy* **felt** *cool. He* **was** *somebody*.

In the first example above, the adjective *cool* is linked to the subject *boy; cool* is called a **predicate adjective.** In the second example, the noun *somebody* is linked to the subject *he; somebody* is called a **predicate noun** or **predicate nominative.**

882 A **verbal** is a word which is derived from a verb, has the power of a verb, but acts as another part of speech. Like a verb, a verbal may take an object, a modifier (adjective, adverb), and sometimes a subject; but unlike a verb, a verbal functions as a noun, an adjective, or an adverb. Three types of verbals are **gerunds, infinitives,** and **participles.**

A **gerund** is a verb form which ends in *ing* and is used as a noun.

> **Smoking** cigarettes rotted my lungs. (subject)
> I started **smoking** at fourteen. (direct object)
> The result of all that **smoking** is my cancer. (object of the preposition)

An **infinitive** is a verb form which is usually introduced by *to;* the infinitive may be used as a *noun,* as an *adjective,* or as an *adverb.*

> **To smoke** so much for so long has cost me greatly. (subject)
> If it had been illegal **to smoke** in public places twenty years ago, things might now be different. (adverb)
> The right **to smoke** in public is now in serious question. (adjective)

A **participle** is a verb form ending in *ing* or *ed.* A participle functions as a verb because it can take an object; a participle functions as an adjective because it can modify a noun or pronoun.

> That man **smoking** the cigar is dangerous. The pile of **smoked** cigars grows deeper each day. (*Smoking* functions as an adjective because it modifies *man. Smoking* functions as a verb because it has an object, *cigar. Smoked* modifies the noun *cigars;* this participle does not have an object.)

▬ Adjective ▬▬▬▬▬▬▬▬▬▬▬▬▬▬▬▬▬▬▬▬

883 An **adjective** describes or modifies a noun or pronoun. Articles *a, an,* and *the* are adjectives.

> **Little** people peek through **big** steering wheels.
> (*Little* modifies *people; big* modifies *steering wheels.*)

Adjectives can be common or proper. Proper adjectives are created from proper nouns and are capitalized.

> **Canada (proper noun)** is a land of many cultures and climates.
> **Canadian (proper adjective)** winters can be long and harsh.

884 A **predicate adjective** follows a form of the *be* verb (a linking verb) and describes the subject.

> Late autumn seems **grim** to those who love summer.
> (*Grim* modifies *autumn.)*

885 Adjectives have three forms: **positive, comparative,** and **superlative.**

The **positive form** describes a noun or pronoun without comparing it to anyone or anything else.

> Superman is **tough.** Superman is **wonderful.**

The **comparative form** *(-er)* compares two persons, places, things, or ideas.

> Tarzan is **tougher** than Superman.
> Tarzan is **more wonderful** than Superman.

The **superlative form** *(-est)* compares three or more persons, places, things, or ideas.

> But I, Big Bird, am the **toughest** of all!
> But I, Big Bird, am the **most wonderful** of all!

▬ Adverb ▬▬▬▬▬▬▬▬▬▬▬▬▬▬▬▬▬▬▬▬▬

886 An **adverb** modifies a verb, an adjective, or another adverb. An adverb tells *how, when, where, why, how often,* and *how much.*

> She kissed him **loudly.** (*Loudly* modifies the verb *kissed.)*
> Her kisses are **really** noisy. (*Really* modifies the adjective *noisy.)*
> The kiss exploded **very** dramatically. (*Very* modifies the adverb *dramatically.)*

887 Adverbs can be cataloged in four basic ways: **time, place, manner,** and **degree.**

    a.   Adverbs of **time.** (They tell *when, how often,* and *how long.)*
        today, yesterday   daily, weekly   briefly, eternally

    b.   Adverbs of **place.** (They tell *where, to where,* and *from where.)*
        here, there   nearby, yonder   backward, forward

    c.   Adverbs of **manner.** (They often end in *-ly* and tell *how* something is done.)
        precisely   regularly   regally   smoothly   well

    d.   Adverbs of **degree.** (They tell *how much* or *how little.)*
        substantially   greatly   entirely   partly   too

Note: Some adverbs can be written with or without the *-ly* ending. When in doubt, use the *-ly* form. (**Examples:** slow, slowly; loud, loudly; fair, fairly; tight, tightly; deep, deeply; quick, quickly)

Also note: Adverbs, like adjectives, have three forms: **positive, comparative,** and **superlative.** (See Handbook 885.)

Positive	Comparative	Superlative
well	better	best
badly	worse	worst
fast	faster	fastest
remorsefully	more remorsefully	most remorsefully
passively	less passively	least passively

▬Preposition▬

888 A **preposition** is a word (or group of words) that shows the relationship between its object (a noun or a pronoun that follows the preposition) and another word in the sentence.

> To make a mustache, Natasha placed the hairy caterpillar **under** her nose. (*Under* shows the relationship between the verb *placed* and the object of the preposition *nose. Note:* The first noun or pronoun following a preposition should be its object.)

> The drowsy insect clung obediently **to** the girl's upper lip. (*To* shows the relationship between the verb *clung* and the object of the preposition *lip*. Note that *girl's* is an adjective. Therefore, the first noun following *to* is *lip*.)

889 There are three kinds of prepositions: **simple** (*at, in, of, on, with*), **compound** (*within, outside, underneath*), and **phrasal** (*on account of, on top of*).

890 A **prepositional phrase** includes the preposition, the object of the preposition, and the modifiers of the object. A prepositional phrase may function as an adverb or as an adjective.

> Some people run **away from caterpillars.** (The phrase, functioning as an adverb, modifies the verb *run*.)

> However, little kids **with inquisitive minds** enjoy their company. (The phrase functions as an adjective modifying the noun *kids*.)

891 A **preposition** which lacks an object may be used as an adverb.

> Natasha never played with caterpillars **before.** (The object of the preposition is understood: before *this time* or before *today*. *Before* modifies *played*, a verb.)

892

List of Prepositions

aboard	at	despite	in regard to	opposite	together with
about	away from	down	inside	out	through
above	back of	down from	inside of	out of	throughout
according to	because of	during	in spite of	outside	till
across	before	except	instead of	outside of	to
across from	behind	except for	into	over	toward
after	below	excepting	like	over to	under
against	beneath	for	near	owing to	underneath
along	beside	from	near to	past	until
alongside	besides	from among	notwithstanding	prior to	unto
alongside of	between	from between	of	regarding	up
along with	beyond	from under	off	round	up to
amid	but	in	on	round about	upon
among	by	in addition to	on account of	save	with
apart from	by means of	in behalf of	on behalf of	since	within
around	concerning	in front of	onto	subsequent to	without
aside from	considering	in place of	on top of		

▬ Conjunction ▬▬▬▬▬▬▬▬▬▬▬▬▬▬▬▬▬▬▬

893 A **conjunction** connects individual words or groups of words.

> A puffer fish is short **and** fat. (The conjunction *and* connects the word *short* to the word *fat*.)
> The puffer puts his lips on a snail **and** sucks out the flesh. (The conjunction *and* connects the phrase *puts his lips on a snail* to the phrase *sucks out the flesh*.)

894 A **coordinating conjunction** connects a word to a word, a phrase to a phrase, or a clause to a clause. The words, phrases, or clauses joined by a coordinating conjunction must be *equal* or of the *same type*. (Examples by Ernest Hemingway)

> When we came back to Paris, it was clear **and** cold **and** lovely. (The conjunction *and* connects equal adjectives.)

> I would sit in front of the fire **and** squeeze the peel of the little oranges into the edge of the flame **and** watch the sputter of blue that they made. (*And* connects equal phrases, each one part of the compound predicate.)

> I always worked until I had something done, **and** I always stopped when I knew what was going to happen next. (*And* connects equal clauses.)

895 **Correlative conjunctions** are coordinate conjunctions used in pairs. (*either, or; neither, nor; not only, but also; both, and; whether, or; just, as; just, so; as, so*)

> **Neither** rain **nor** sleet **nor** dark of night shall keep them from their appointed rounds.

896 A **subordinating conjunction** is a word or group of words that connect, and show the relationship between, two clauses which are *not* equally important. A subordinating conjunction connects a dependent clause to an independent clause in order to complete the meaning of the dependent clause.

> A brown trout will study the bait **before** he eats it. (The clause *before he eats it* is dependent. It depends on the rest of the sentence to complete its meaning.)

897

Kinds of Conjunctions	
Coordinating:	and, but, or, nor, for, yet
Correlative:	either, or; neither, nor; not only, but also; both, and; whether, or; just, as; just, so; as, so
Subordinating:	after, although, as, as if, as long as, as though, because, before, if, in order that, provided that, since, so, so that, that, though, till, unless, until, when, where, whereas, while

Note: Relative pronouns (864) and conjunctive adverbs (621) can also connect clauses.

▬ Interjection ▬▬▬▬▬▬▬▬▬▬▬▬▬▬▬▬▬▬

898 An **interjection** is included in a sentence in order to communicate strong emotion or surprise. Punctuation (often a comma or exclamation point) is used to set an interjection off from the rest of the sentence.

> **Oh, no!** The TV broke. **Good grief!** I have nothing to do! **Yipes,** I'll go mad!

Note: Interjections can be very effective in adding realism to dialogue.

304 *Understanding Grammar*

Sentences
— Understanding the Elements ———————

899 A **sentence** is made up of one or more words which express a complete thought. *(Note: A sentence begins with a capital letter; it ends with a period, question mark, or exclamation point.)*

> **It was mid-July on a Thursday night. School was out, right? "We've got nothing to do but relax," said one of the three boys. "Tonight belongs to us. We're in charge!"**

900 A sentence must have a **subject** and **predicate** which express a complete thought. The subject is the element of the sentence about which something is said. The predicate is the element of the sentence which says something about the subject. (The primary part of a predicate is the word or words which function as a verb.)

> **The boys passively flopped onto the couch. Almost instinctively they flipped on the tube.**

Note: In the first sentence *boys* is the subject—the sentence talks about the boys. *Flopped,* a verb, is the primary part of the predicate—it says something about the subject.

Either the subject or the predicate or both may be "missing," but both must be clearly understood.

> **"What's on?"** *(What* is the subject; the predicate is expressed by the contraction: *'s* for *is.)*

> **"Nothing."** *(Nothing* is the subject; the predicate *is* is understood.)

> **"Shut up and turn the channel."** (The subject *you* is understood; *shut up and turn* is the predicate.)

901 A **simple subject** is the subject without the words which modify it.

> The younger **boy** grabbed the controller and shifted to channel four.

902 A **complete subject** is the simple subject and all the words which modify it.

> **A muscular, heavily armed, sweating male** leaped out on the screen.

903 A **compound subject** is composed of two or more simple subjects.

> A rocket **launcher** and a twenty-millimeter **cannon** blazed at him from the two Apache choppers that hovered above.

904 The **subject** is always a noun or a word or phrase which functions as a noun such as a pronoun, infinitive, gerund, or noun clause.

> The **jungle** around the muscled man exploded in flame and smoke. **(noun)**

> Perched on the lip of a rocky ravine, **he** looked out from his dusky inferno. **(pronoun)**

> **To run back toward the choppers** would bring death from above. **(infinitive phrase)**

> **Leaping into the ravine** would bring death from below. **(gerund phrase)**

> **That the dauntless hero was doomed** seemed inevitable. **(noun clause)**

905 A **predicate** is the part of the sentence which says something about the subject.

> Then it **happened!**

A **simple predicate** is the predicate without the words which describe or modify it.

Little people **can talk** faster than big people. *(Can talk* is the simple predicate; *faster than big people* describes how little people *can talk.)*

A **complete predicate** is the simple predicate and all the words which modify or explain it.

Little people **can talk faster than big people.**

A **compound predicate** is composed of two or more simple predicates.

Big people **talk** slowly but **eat** fast.

906 A sentence may have a **compound subject** and a **compound predicate.**

Sturdy **tongues,** long **lips,** and thick **teeth say** sentences slowly but **chew** food quickly.

907 A sentence may also have a **direct object**—something which receives the action of the predicate. (See 878.)

Chickens eat **oyster shells.** *(Oyster shells* receives the action of *eat.* It answers the question *Chickens eat what?)*

The **direct object** may be **compound.**

Chickens eat **oyster shells** and **grit.**

___ Phrases and Clauses ___

908 A **phrase** is a group of related words which lacks either a subject or a predicate or both.

ran very fast (The predicate lacks a subject.)
the young colt (The subject lacks a predicate.)
down the steep slope (The phrase lacks both a subject and a predicate.)
The young colt ran very fast down the steep slope. (Together, the three phrases present a complete thought.)

909 Phrases appear in several types: **noun, verb, verbal, prepositional, appositive,** and **absolute.**

910 A **noun phrase** consists of a noun and its modifiers; the whole phrase functions as a simple noun would.

The next kid in line has to sit on the dunking stool. (subject)

I could twist those skinny balloons into a **flying purple people eater.** (object of preposition)

911 A **verb phrase** consists of a verb and its modifiers.

Gina **quickly sat down on the tiny chair** when the music stopped. *(Quickly, down* and *on the tiny chair* all modify *sat;* the six words combined make up the whole verb phrase.)

912 A **verbal phrase** is a phrase based on one of the three types of verbals: **gerund, infinitive,** or **participle.** (See 882.)

A **gerund phrase** is based on a gerund and functions as a noun.

Heading a soccer ball is hard for a unicorn. (subject)

I was tired of his **popping our soccer balls.** (object of preposition)

An **infinitive phrase** is based on an infinitive and functions as a noun, an adjective, or an adverb.

To err is human; **to forgive,** divine. *(To err* and *to forgive* are subjects.)

The old man tried **to stop intruders** by installing iron bars on his windows. (direct object of the verb *tried)*

306 *Understanding Grammar*

The old man installed iron bars on his windows **to stop intruders.** (adverb modifying *installed*)

Did he give his permission **to paint a mural on this wall?** (adjective modifying *permission*)

A **participial phrase** consists of a past or present participle and its modifiers; the whole phrase functions as an adjective.

Scooping up the chihuahua, he took off for the end zone. (adjective modifying the pronoun *he*)

His voice, **cracked by fatigue,** sounded eighty years old. (adjective modifying the noun *voice*)

913 A **prepositional phrase** consists of a preposition, its object, and any modifiers.

Zach won the wheelchair race **in spite of having a broken wrist.** (adverb modifying the verb *won*)

Reach for that catnip ball **behind the couch.** (adjective modifying *catnip ball*)

914 An **appositive phrase** consists of a noun and its modifiers which stands beside another noun and renames it. An appositive adds new information but does not modify any other word as an adjective would.

My mother, **the woman with the strange face,** must have blinked as the shutter snapped. (The appositive phrase; *the woman with the strange face,* renames *my mother,* though it does not modify the phrase.)

915 An **absolute phrase** consists of a noun and a participle (plus the object of the participle and any modifiers). Because it has a subject and a verbal, an absolute phrase resembles a clause; however, the verbal does not have the tense and number found in the main verb of a clause. (*Note:* The absolute phrase can be placed anywhere within the sentence but has no direct grammatical relation with any part of it.)

Her whistle blasting repeatedly, the lifeguard cleared the pool. (*Whistle* is the noun; *blasting* is a present participle modifying *whistle.*)

916 A **clause** is a group of related words which has both a subject and a predicate.

An **independent clause** presents a complete thought and can stand as a sentence; a **dependent clause** does not present a complete thought and cannot stand as a sentence.

In the following sentences, the dependent clauses are in boldface, and the independent clauses are in *italics.*

A small pony can attack a large horse **if it kicks its heels in the horse's belly.**

Sparrows make nests in cattle barns **so they can stay warm during the winter.**

▬Utilizing the Types▬▬▬▬▬▬

917 A **sentence** may be classified according to the type of statement it makes, the way it is constructed, and the arrangement of material within the sentence.

918 Sentences make different kinds of statements according to the **mood** of their main verbs: **declarative, interrogative, imperative, exclamatory,** or **conditional.**

Declarative sentences make statements. They tell us something about a person, place, thing, or idea.

The Statue of Liberty stands in New York Harbor.
For nearly a century, it has greeted immigrants and visitors to America.

Interrogative sentences ask questions.

> **Did you know that the Statue of Liberty is made of copper and stands over 150 feet tall?**

Imperative sentences make commands. They often contain an understood subject *(you)*.

> **Go see the Statue of Liberty.**
>
> **After a few weeks of physical conditioning, climb its 168 stairs.**

Exclamatory sentences communicate strong emotion or surprise.

> **What do you mean climbing 168 stairs sounds like a dumb idea! Whatever happened to that old pioneering spirit, that desire to take a chance, to try something new, that never-say-die attitude that made America great!**

Conditional sentences express wishes ("if . . . then" statements) or conditions contrary to fact.

> **If you were to climb to the top of the statue, then you could share in the breathtaking feeling experienced by our forefathers.**

919 The structure of a sentence may be **simple, compound, complex,** or **compound-complex,** depending on the relationship between independent and dependent clauses in it.

A **simple sentence** may have a simple subject or a compound subject. It may have a simple predicate or a compound predicate. But a simple sentence has only one independent clause, and it has no dependent clauses. A simple sentence may contain one or more phrases.

> My **back aches.** (simple subject; simple predicate)
> My **teeth** and my **eyes hurt.** (compound subject; simple predicate)
> My **hair** and my **muscles are deteriorating** and **disappearing.** (compound subject; compound predicate)
> **I must be getting over the hill.** (simple subject: *I;* simple predicate: *must be getting;* phrase: *over the hill)*

A **compound sentence** consists of two independent clauses. The clauses must be joined by a coordinating conjunction, by punctuation, or by both.

> Energy is part of youth, **but** both are quickly spent.
> My middle-aged body is sore; my middle-aged face is wrinkled.

A **complex sentence** contains one independent clause (in italics) and one or more dependent clauses (in boldface).

> *People often say wise things* **like age is a state of mind.** (independent clause; dependent clause)
>
> *Youth seems past,* however, **when my back aches before the day is even half over.** (independent clause; two dependent clauses)

A **compound-complex sentence** contains two or more independent clauses (in italics) and one or more dependent clauses (in boldface).

> *My body is rather old, and age is not a state of mind* **unless my bald head is an illusion.** (independent clause; independent clause; dependent clause)

920 Depending on the arrangement of material and the placement of emphasis, a sentence may also be classified as **loose, balanced, periodic,** or **cumulative.**

A **loose sentence** expresses the main thought near the beginning and adds explanatory material as needed.

We bashed the pinata for 15 minutes without denting it, although we at least avoided denting one another's craniums and, with masks raised, finally pried the candy out with a screwdriver.

A **balanced sentence** is constructed so that it emphasizes a similarity or contrast between two or more of its parts, including words, phrases, or clauses.

Joe's unusual security system **invited burglars** and **scared off friends.** (*Invited* contrasts with *scared off* and *burglars* contrasts with *friends.*)

A **periodic sentence** is one which postpones the crucial or most surprising idea until the end.

Following my mother's repeated threats of being grounded for life, I decided it was time to propose a compromise.

A **cumulative sentence** places the general idea in the main clause and gives it greater precision with modifying words, phrases, or clauses placed before it, after it, or in the middle of it.

Eyes squinting, puffy, always on alert, *he showed the effects of a week in the forest,* **a brutal week, a week of staggering in circles driven by the baying of wolves.** (The phrases *eyes squinting, puffy,* and *always on alert* look forward to the pronoun *he* in the main clause; the phrases after the word *forest* look back toward the word *week.*)

Keeping the Parts in Agreement
▬ Agreement of Subject and Verb ▬▬▬▬▬

The subject and verb of any clause must agree in both person and number. There are **three persons:** the **first person** *(I)* is the speaker, the **second person** *(you)* is the person spoken to, and the **third person** *(he, she, it)* is the person or thing spoken about. There are **two numbers: singular** refers to one person or thing; **plural** refers to more than one person or thing.

921 A verb must agree in number (singular or plural) with its subject.

The *student was* **proud of her quarter grades.** (Both the subject *student* and the verb *was* are singular; they are said to agree in number.) The student's *parents were* **also proud of her.**

Note: Do not be confused by other words coming between the subject and verb.

The *manager* **as well as the players** *is* **required to display good sportsmanship.** *(Manager,* **not** *players,* **is the subject.)**

Note: Do not neglect agreement in sentences in which the verb comes before the subject. In these inverted sentences, the true *(delayed)* subject must be made to agree with the verb.

There *are* **many hardworking** *students* **in our schools. There** *is* **present among many students today a** *will* **to succeed.** *(Students* **and** *will* **are the true subjects of these sentences, not** *there.)*

922 Compound subjects connected with *and* usually require a plural verb.

Strength **and** *balance are* **necessary for gymnastics.**

Note: When the nouns joined by *and* are considered as one unit, the verb is singular.

Macaroni **and** *cheese is* **an inexpensive meal.**

923 Singular subjects joined by *or* or *nor* take a singular verb.

Neither *Bev* **nor** *Connie is* **going to the street dance.**

Note: When one of the subjects joined by *or* or *nor* is singular and one is plural, the verb is made to agree with the subject nearer the verb.

Neither *Mr. Kemper* **nor his** *students are* **able to find the photographs. (The plural subject** *students* **is nearer the verb; therefore, the plural verb** *are* **is used to agree with** *students.***)**

924 The indefinite pronouns *each, either, neither, one, everybody, another, anybody, everyone, nobody, everything, somebody,* and *someone* are singular; they require a singular verb.

Everybody is **invited to the cafeteria for refreshments.**

Note: Do not be confused by words or phrases which come between the indefinite pronoun and the verb.

Each **of the boys** *is* **(not** *are)* **required to bring a bar of soap on the first day of class.**

925 The indefinite pronouns *all, any, half, most, none,* and *some* may be either singular or plural when they are used as subjects. These pronouns are singular if the number of the noun in the prepositional phrase is singular; they are plural if the noun is plural.

Half **of the bottles** *were* **missing.** *(Bottles,* **the noun in the prepositional phrase, is plural; therefore, the pronoun** *half* **is considered plural, and the plural verb** *were* **is used to agree with it.)**

Half **of the movie** *was* **over by the time we arrived. (Because** *movie* **is singular,** *half* **is also singular.)**

926 Collective nouns *faculty, committee, team, congress, species, crowd, army, pair, assembly, squad)* take a singular verb when they refer to a group as a unit; collective nouns take a plural verb when they refer to the individuals within the group.

The *faculty is* **united in its effort to make this school a better place to be.** *(Faculty* **refers to a group as a unit; therefore, it requires a singular verb:** *is.***)**

The *faculty are* **required to turn in their keys before leaving for the summer. (In this example,** *faculty* **refers to the individuals within the group. If the word** *individuals* **were substituted for** *faculty,* **it would become clear that the plural verb** *are* **is needed in this sentence.)**

927 Some nouns which are plural in form but singular in meaning take a singular verb: *mumps, measles, news, mathematics, economics, gallows, shambles.*

Measles is **still considered a serious disease in many parts of the world.**

Note: Other nouns plural in form take plural verbs: *scissors, trousers, tidings.*

The *scissors are* **missing again.**

Note: Some nouns ending in *ics (athletics, acoustics, gymnastics, politics, statistics)* are singular when referring to an organized body of knowledge; they are plural when they refer to activities, qualities, or opinions.

Politics is **an interesting field of study.** *(Politics* **here means an organized body of knowledge.) The** *politics* **of a presidential campaign** *are* **intense.** *(Politics* **refers to the activities of an election campaign.)**

Note: Phrases containing mathematical calculations usually take a singular verb.

Three and three *is* **six. Five times six** *is* **thirty.**

928 When a relative pronoun *(who, which, that)* is used as the subject of a clause, the number of the verb is determined by the *antecedent* of the pronoun. (The *antecedent* is the word to which the pronoun refers.)

This is one of the *books which are* **required for geography class. (The relative pronoun** *which* **requires the plural verb** *are* **because its antecedent** *books* **is plural. To test this type of sentence for agreement, read the** *of* **phrase first:** *Of the books which are . . . .)*

929 When a sentence contains a form of the *to be* verb—and a noun comes before and after that verb—the verb must agree with the subject even if the *complement* (the noun coming after the verb) is different in number.

The *cause* **of his problem** *was* **his bad** *brakes.* **His bad** *brakes were* **the** *cause* **of his problem.**

Agreement of Pronoun and Its Antecedent

930 A pronoun must agree in number, person, and gender (sex) with its *antecedent.* (The *antecedent* is the word to which the pronoun refers. See 850.)

Bill **brought** *his* **gerbil to school. (The antecedent in this sentence is** *Bill;* **it is to** *Bill* **that the pronoun** *his* **refers. Both the pronoun and its antecedent are singular, third person, and masculine; therefore, the pronoun is said to agree with its antecedent.)**

The *teachers* **brought** *their* **gerbils to school.**

931 Use a singular pronoun to refer to such antecedents as *each, either, neither, one, anyone, anybody, everyone, everybody, somebody, another, nobody,* and *a person.*

One **of the rowboats is missing** *its* **(not** *their)* **oars.**

Note: When *a person* or *everyone* is used to refer to both sexes or either sex, you will have to choose whether to use masculine pronouns in a universal sense (meaning mankind) or offer optional pronouns. (See 940.)

A person **must learn to wait** *his* **turn.**
A person **must learn to wait** *his or her* **turn.**
(Those writers who find neither of the above choices acceptable may choose to avoid the problem by rewriting the sentence.)
People **must learn to wait** *their* **turn.** (rewritten)

932 Two or more antecedents joined by *and* are considered plural; two or more antecedents joined by *or* or *nor* are referred to by a singular pronoun.

Tom **and** *Bob* **are finishing** *their* **assignments. Either** *Connie* **or** *Sue* **left** *her* **headset in the library.**

Note: If one of the antecedents is masculine and one feminine, the pronouns should likewise be masculine and feminine.

Is either *Dave* **or** *Phyllis* **bringing** *his* **or** *her* **frisbee?**

Note: If one of the antecedents joined by *or* or *nor* is singular and one is plural, the pronoun is made to agree with the nearer antecedent.

Neither the *manager* **nor the** *players* **were willing to wear** *their* **new polka-dot uniforms.**

Treating the Sexes Fairly

When you box people in or put them down just because of their sex, that is called "sexism." When you identify all human virtues with only one sex, or when you identify one sex with the whole human race, that, too, is sexism. And when you bring in sexual distinctions where they don't belong, that, too, is sexism. Sexism is unfair. And it hurts. Ask anyone who has been a victim of it.

To change our centuries-old habits of sexist thinking, we must try to change our language, for our traditional ways of speaking and writing have sexist patterns deeply imprinted in them. The assumptions built into our language teach even little children who they are and how they relate to others. For their sakes and our own, we must seek a language which implies equal value, equal potential, and equal opportunity for people of either sex.

What NOT to Do   ## What to DO

Portraying the Sexes in News Stories, Fiction, Speeches . . .

933 Don't typecast all men as leaders, professionals, breadwinners, etc.; don't typecast all women as subordinates, homebodies, helpers, and dependents.

Do show both women and men as doctors and nurses, principals and teachers, breadwinners and housekeepers, bosses and secretaries, grocery store owners and cashiers, pilots, plumbers, TV repairers, social workers, etc.

934 Don't associate courage, strength, brilliance, creativity, independence, persistence, and seriousness only with men and boys; don't associate only emotionalism, passivity, and fearfulness with women and girls.

Do portray people of both sexes along the whole range of potential human strengths and weaknesses.

935 Don't refer to women according to their physical appearance and to men according to their mental abilities or professional status:

The admirable Dr. Hicks and his wife Mary, a smashing redhead, both showed up at the party.

Do refer to both on the same plane, either physical or professional:

The dashing Dr. Hicks and his wife Mary, a smashing redhead,

or

The admirable Dr. Hicks and the much-admired Mrs. Hicks. . . .

936 Don't take special notice when a woman does a "man's job" or vice versa:

lady doctor
male nurse
coed

Do treat men's or women's involvement in a profession as normal, not exceptional:

doctor
nurse
student

937 Don't portray women as the posses-
sions of men:

> Fred took his wife and kids on a
> vacation.

**Do portray women and men,
husbands and wives, as equal
partners:**

> **Fred and Wilma took their kids
> on a vacation.**

938 Don't use demeaning, patronizing, or
sexually-loaded labels when
referring to women.

> girl (for secretary)
> career girl
> the weaker sex
> better half, little woman
> chick, fox, bombshell,
>   knockout

**Do use respectful terms rather
than labels; consider what the
woman herself might wish to be
called:**

> **secretary, Helen, Ms. Jones
> career person, professional
>   women
> wife, spouse
> woman, girl, attractive woman,
>   young woman**

Referring to People in General . . .

939 Don't use "man-words" to refer to
all people or a person in general:

> mankind
> man's history
> man-made
> the best man for the job
> man-hours

**Do use "gender-inclusive" alter-
natives to "man-words":**

> **humanity, people, human
>   beings, the human race
> human history, our history
> synthetic, artificial,
>   manufactured
> the best person (or, best one)
>   for the job
> hours, employee hours**

940 Don't use masculine pronouns—*he,
his, him*—when you want to refer
generically to a human being:

> A politician can kiss privacy good-
> bye when he runs for office.

**There are several ways to avoid
sexism like this:**

> *Reword the sentence:* **Campaign-
> ing for office robs a politician
> of privacy.**
> *Express in the plural:* **Politicians
> can kiss privacy goodbye when
> they run for office.**
> *Offer optional pronouns:* **A politi-
> cian can kiss privacy goodbye
> when he or she runs for office.**

Addressing Your Reader . . .

941 Don't assume that your reader is
male:

> You and your wife will be shocked
> at these prices.
> After the morning shave, one
> feels a bit clearer in the head.

**Do assume that your reader is
either male or female:**

> **You and your spouse (or, loved
> one) will be shocked at these
> prices.
> After gargling, one feels a bit
> clearer in the head.**

942 In the salutation of a business letter to someone you do not know, don't use a male word:

> Dear Sir:
> Dear Gentlemen:

If the reader could be male or female, *either* address both:

> Dear Madam or Sir:
> Dear Ladies and Gentlemen:

or address a position:

> Dear Personnel Officer:
> Dear Members of the Pee Wee Herman Fan Club:

Referring to Men and Women Together . . .

943 Don't give special treatment to one of the sexes:

> The men and the ladies came through in the clutch.
> I now pronounce you man and wife.
> Hank and Miss Jenkins
> Mr. Bubba Gumm, Mrs. Bubba Gumm

Do use equal language for both sexes:

> The men and the women came through in the clutch.
> I now pronounce you husband and wife.
> Hank and Mimi
> Mr. Bubba Gumm, Mrs. Lotta Gumm

Using Occupational Titles . . .

944 Don't use "man-words" for titles, whether or not the person in question is a male:

> foreman
> chairman
> salesman
> mailman
> insurance man
> fireman
> cameraman
> businessman
> congressman

Do use neutral titles whenever possible:

> supervisor
> chair; presiding officer; moderator
> sales representative; sales clerk; salesperson
> mail carrier; postal worker; letter carrier
> insurance agent
> firefighter
> camera operator
> executive; manager; businessperson
> member of Congress; representative; senator; Congressman Flintstone and Congresswoman Rubble

945 Don't use special diminutive titles to distinguish female workers from males:

> steward, stewardess
> usher, usherette
> policeman, policewoman
> poet, poetess
> author, authoress
> maid, houseboy

Do use neutral terms for both men and women:

> flight attendant
> usher
> police officer
> poet
> author
> housekeeper, servant

The
APPENDIX

≡ fog
∞ haze; dust haze
⊤ thunder
< sheet lightning
⊾ thunderstorm
\ direction
☉ or ☼ sun
● or ⬤ new moon
☽ first quarter
○ or ☻ full moon
☾ last quarter

● rain
* snow
⊠ snow on ground
▲ hail
△ sleet
∨ frostwork

SHAPES

▭ rectangle
▱ parallelogram
○ circle
⌒ arc of circle
⟂ equilateral
≜ equiangular

∥ parallel
⊥ perpendicular
∠ angle
∟ right angle
△ triangle
□ square

MATH

+ plus
− minus
± plus or minus
∓ minus or plus
× multiplied by
÷ divided by
= equal to
≠ or ≢ not equal to
≈ or ≑ nearly equal to
≡ identical with
≢ not identical with
⌁ equivalent
∼ difference
≅ congruent to
> greater than
≯ not greater than
< less than

≮ not less than
≧ or ≥ greater than or equal to
≦ or ≤ less than or equal to
√ radical; square root
∛ cube root
∜ fourth root
Σ sum
∞ infinity
∫ integral
ƒ function
: is to; ratio
:: as; proportion
π pi
∴ therefore
∵ because

MISC

© copyright
% per cent
℅ care of
a/c account of
@ at
# number
& or & and
Ω ohm
℞ take (from Latin *Recipe*)
ĀĀ or Ā or āā of each (doctor's prescription)
♂ or ♂ male
♀ female
lb pound
℥ ounce
ℨ dram
ƒℨ fluid ounce
ƒℨ fluid dram
° degree
′ minute
″ second

GREEK

Forms	Name	Sound
A α	alpha	a
B β	beta	b
Γ γ	gamma	g (n)
Δ δ	delta	d
E ε	epsilon	e
Z ζ	zēta	z
H η	ēta	ē
Θ θ	thēta	th
I ι	iota	i
K κ	kappa	k
Λ λ	lambda	l
M μ	mu	m

Forms	Name	Sound
N ν	nu	n
Ξ ξ	xi	x
O o	omicron	o
Π π	pi	p
P ρ	rhō	r (rh)
Σ σ ς	sigma	s
T τ	tau	t
Υ υ	upsilon	u
Φ φ	phi	ph
X χ	khi	kh
Ψ ψ	psi	ps
Ω ω	ōmega	ō

HAND SIGNS

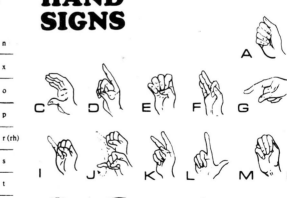

Multiplication and Division Table

A number in the top line (11) multiplied by a number in the extreme left-hand column (12) produces the number where the top line and side line meet (132).

A number in the table (208) divided by the number at the top of the same column (13) results in the number (16) in the extreme left-hand column. A number in the table (208) divided by the number at the extreme left (16) results in the number (13) at the top of the column.

1	2	3	4	5	6	7	8	9	10	11	12	13	14	15	16	17	18	19	20	21	22	23	24	25
2	4	6	8	10	12	14	16	18	20	22	24	26	28	30	32	34	36	38	40	42	44	46	48	50
3	6	9	12	15	18	21	24	27	30	33	36	39	42	45	48	51	54	57	60	63	66	69	72	75
4	8	12	16	20	24	28	32	36	40	44	48	52	56	60	64	68	72	76	80	84	88	92	96	100
5	10	15	20	25	30	35	40	45	50	55	60	65	70	75	80	85	90	95	100	105	115	115	120	125
6	12	18	24	30	36	42	48	54	60	66	72	78	84	90	96	102	108	114	120	126	132	138	144	150
7	14	21	28	35	42	49	56	63	70	77	84	91	98	105	112	119	126	133	130	147	154	161	168	175
8	16	24	32	40	48	56	64	72	80	88	96	104	112	120	128	136	144	152	160	168	176	184	192	200
9	18	27	36	45	54	63	72	81	90	99	108	117	126	135	144	153	162	171	180	189	198	207	216	225
10	20	30	40	50	60	70	80	90	100	110	120	130	140	150	160	170	180	190	200	210	220	230	240	250
11	22	33	44	55	66	77	88	99	110	121	132	143	154	165	176	187	198	209	220	231	242	253	264	275
12	24	36	48	60	72	84	96	108	120	132	144	156	168	180	192	204	216	228	240	252	264	276	288	300
13	26	39	52	65	78	91	104	117	130	143	156	169	182	195	208	221	234	247	260	273	286	299	312	325
14	28	42	56	70	84	98	112	126	140	154	168	182	196	210	224	238	252	266	280	294	308	322	336	350
15	30	45	60	75	90	105	120	135	150	165	180	195	210	225	240	255	270	185	300	315	330	345	360	375
16	32	48	64	80	96	112	128	144	160	176	192	208	224	240	256	272	288	304	320	336	352	368	384	400
17	34	51	68	85	102	119	136	153	170	187	204	221	238	255	272	289	306	323	340	357	374	391	408	425
18	36	54	72	90	108	126	144	162	180	198	216	234	252	270	288	306	324	342	360	378	396	414	432	450
19	38	57	76	95	114	133	152	171	190	209	228	247	266	285	304	323	342	361	380	399	418	437	456	475
20	40	60	80	100	120	140	160	180	200	220	240	260	280	300	320	340	360	380	400	420	440	460	480	500
21	42	63	84	105	126	147	168	189	210	231	252	273	294	315	336	357	378	399	420	441	462	483	504	525
22	44	66	88	110	132	154	176	198	220	242	264	286	308	330	352	374	396	418	440	462	484	506	528	550
23	46	69	92	115	138	161	184	207	230	253	276	299	322	345	368	391	414	437	460	483	506	529	552	575
24	48	72	96	120	144	168	192	216	240	264	288	312	336	360	384	408	432	456	480	504	528	552	576	600
25	50	75	100	125	150	175	200	225	250	275	300	325	350	375	400	425	450	475	500	525	550	575	600	625

Animal Crackers

Animal	Male	Female	Young	Collective	Gestation	Longevity	(Record)
Ass	Jack	Jenny	Foal	Herd	340-385	18-20	(63)
Bear	He-bear	She-bear	Cub	Sleuth	180-240	18-20	(34)
Cat	Tom	Queen	Kitten	Clutter/Clowder	52-65	10-12	(27)
Cattle	Bull	Cow	Calf	Drove/Herd	280	9-12	(25)
Chicken	Rooster	Hen	Chick	Brood/Clutch	21	7-8	(14)
Deer	Buck	Doe	Fawn	Herd	140-250	10-15	(26)
Dog	Dog	Bitch	Pup	Pack	55-70	10-12	(24)
Duck	Drake	Duck	Duckling	Brace/Herd	21-35	10	(15)
Elephant	Bull	Cow	Calf	Herd	515-760	30-40	(98)
Fox	Dog	Vixen	Cub/Kit	Skulk	51-60	8-10	(14)
Goat	Billy	Nanny	Kid	Tribe, Trip	135-163	12	(17)
Goose	Gander	Goose	Gosling	Flock/Gaggle	30		
Horse	Stallion	Mare	Filly/Colt	Herd	304-419	20-25	(50+)
Lion	Lion	Lioness	Cub	Pride	105-111	10	(29)
Monkey	Male	Female	Boy/Girl	Band/Troop	149-179	12-15	(29)
Rabbit	Buck	Doe	Bunny		27-36	6-8	(15)
Sheep	Ram	Ewe	Lamb	Flock/Drove	121-180	12	(16)
Swan	Cob	Pen	Cygnet	Bevy	30		
Swine	Boar	Sow	Piglet	Litter	101-130	10	(15)
Tiger	Tiger	Tigress	Cub		105	19	
Whale	Bull	Cow	Calf	Gam/Pod	276-365	37	
Wolf	Dog	Bitch	Pup	Pack	63	10-12	(16)

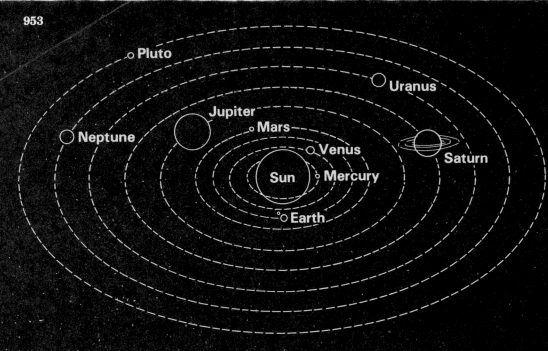

Our solar system is located in the Milky Way Galaxy. Even though this galaxy contains approximately 100 billion stars, our solar system contains only one star—the sun. The sun, which is the center of our solar system, has 9 planets and a myriad of asteroids, meteors, and comets orbiting it. The planets are large, nonluminous bodies which follow fixed elliptical orbits about the sun. (See the illustration above.) The planets are divided into two categories: the terrestrial planets—Mercury, Venus, Earth, Mars, and Pluto—which resemble the Earth in size, chemical composition, and density; and the Jovian planets—Jupiter, Saturn, Uranus, and Neptune—which are much larger in size and have thick, gaseous atmospheres and low densities. (See the table below.)

Planet Profusion

	Sun	Moon	Mercury	Venus	Earth	Mars	Jupiter	Saturn	Uranus	Neptune	Pluto
Orbital Speed (in miles per second)		.6	29.8	21.8	18.5	15.0	8.1	6.0	4.1	3.4	2.9
Rotation on Axis	24 days 16 hr. 48 min.	27 days 7 hr. 38 min.	59 days	243 days	23 hr. 56 min.	1 day 37 min.	9 hr. 50 min.	10 hr. 8 min.	10 hr. 46 min.	18 hr. 12 min.	6 days 9 hr.
Mean Surface Gravity (Earth = 1.00)		0.16	0.33	0.87	1.00	0.37	2.64	1.15	.99	1.27	0.5 (less than)
Density (times that of water)	100	3.3	5.4	5.3	5.5	3.9	1.3	0.7	1.2	1.6	1.0
Mass (times that of earth)	333,000	0.012	0.055	0.8	6×10^{21} metric tons	0.1	318	95	15	17	0.002
Approx. weight of a Human (in pounds)		25	49	130	150	55	396	172	148	190	75
Number of Satellites	9 planets	0	0	0	1	2	16	17	5	2	1
Mean Distance to Sun (in millions of miles)		93.0	36.0	67.22	93.0	141.6	483.5	886.5	1,785	2,793	3,664
Revolution around Sun		365.25 days	88.0 days	224.7 days	365.25 days	686.99 days	11.86 years	29.46 years	84.0 years	164.8 years	247.6 years
Approximate Surface Temperature (degrees Fahrenheit)	27,000,-000°	lighted side 200° dark side -230°	lighted side 800° dark side -275°	900°	60°	-60°	-200°	-300°	-355°	-330°	-382°
Diameter (in miles)	867,000	2,155	3,031	7,680	7,921	4,218	88,700	74,940	32,190	30,760	3,600

A Table of
Common Parliamentary Motions

Motion	Purpose	Needs Second	Debatable	Amend-able	Vote	May Interrupt Speaker	Subsidiary Motion Applied
I. Original or Principal Motion							
1. Main Motion (general) Main Motions (specific)	To introduce business	Yes	Yes	Yes	Majority	No	Yes
a. To reconsider	To reconsider previous motion	Yes	When original motion is	No	Majority	Yes	No
b. To rescind	To nullify or wipe out previous action	Yes	Yes	Yes	Majority or two-thirds	No	No
c. To take from the table	To consider tabled motion	Yes	No	No	Majority	No	No
II. Subsidiary Motions							
2. To lay on the table	To defer action	Yes	No	No	Majority	No	No
3. To call for previous question	To close debate and force vote	Yes	No	No	Two-thirds	No	Yes
4. To limit or extend limits of debate	To control time of debate	Yes	No	Yes	Two-thirds	No	Yes
5. To postpone to a certain time	To defer action	Yes	Yes	Yes	Majority	No	Yes
6. To refer to a committee	To provide for special study	Yes	Yes	Yes	Majority	No	Yes
7. To amend	To modify a motion	Yes	When original motion is	Yes (once only)	Majority	No	Yes
8. To postpone indefinitely	To suppress action	Yes	Yes	No	Majority	No	Yes
III. Incidental Motions							
9. To rise to point of order	To correct error in procedure	No	No	No	Decision of chair	Yes	No
10. To appeal from decision of chair	To change decision on procedure	Yes	If motion does not relate to indecorum	No	Majority or tie	Yes	No
11. To suspend rules	To alter existing rules and order of business	Yes	No	No	Two-thirds	No	No
12. To object to consideration	To suppress action	No	No	No	Two-thirds	Yes	No
13. To call for division of house	To secure a countable vote	No	No	No	Majority if chair desires	Yes	Yes
14. To close nominations	To stop nomination of officers	Yes	No	Yes	Two-thirds	No	Yes
15. To reopen nominations	To permit additional nominations	Yes	No	Yes	Majority	No	Yes
16. To withdraw a motion	To remove a motion	No	No	No	Majority	No	No
17. To divide motion	To modify motion	No	No	Yes	Majority	No	Yes
IV. Privileged Motions							
18. To fix time of next meeting	To set time of next meeting	Yes	No, if made when another question is before the assembly	Yes	Majority	No	Yes
19. To adjourn	To dismiss meeting	Yes	No	Yes	Majority	No	No
20. To take a recess	To dismiss meeting for specific time	Yes	No, if made when another question is before the assembly	Yes	Majority	No	Yes
21. To raise question of privilege	To make a request concerning rights of the assembly	No	No	No	Decision of chair	Yes	No
22. To call for orders of the day	To keep assembly to order of business	No	No	No	None unless objection	Yes	No
23. To make a special order	To ensure consideration at specified time	Yes	Yes	Yes	Two-thirds	No	Yes

Movable Holidays

Christian and Secular

Ash Wednesday	Easter	Pentecost	Labor Day	Election Day	Thanksgiving	1st Sunday Advent	
March 4	April 19	June 7	Sept. 7	Nov. 3	Nov. 26	Nov. 29	1987
Feb. 17	April 3	May 22	Sept. 5	Nov. 8	Nov. 24	Nov. 27	1988
Feb. 8	March 26	May 14	Sept. 4	Nov. 7	Nov. 23	Dec. 3	1989
Feb. 28	April 15	June 3	Sept. 3	Nov. 6	Nov. 22	Dec. 2	1990
Feb. 13	March 31	May 19	Sept. 2	Nov. 5	Nov. 28	Dec. 1	1991
March 4	April 19	June 7	Sept. 7	Nov. 3	Nov. 26	Nov. 29	1992
Feb. 24	April 11	May 30	Sept. 6	Nov. 2	Nov. 25	Nov. 28	1993

Jewish

Purim	1st day Passover	1st day Shavuot	1st day Rosh Hashana	Yom Kippur	1st day Sukkot	Simhat Torah	1st day Hanukkah	
March 15	April 14	June 3	Sept. 24	Oct. 3	Oct. 8	Oct. 16	Dec. 16	1987
March 3	April 2	May 22	Sept. 12	Sept. 21	Sept. 26	Oct. 4	Dec. 4	1988
March 21	April 20	June 9	Sept. 30	Oct. 9	Oct. 14	Oct. 22	Dec. 23	1989
March 11	April 10	May 30	Sept. 20	Sept. 29	Oct. 4	Oct. 12	Dec. 12	1990
Feb. 28	March 30	May 19	Sept. 9	Sept. 18	Sept. 23	Oct. 1	Dec. 2	1991
March 14	April 18	June 7	Sept. 28	Oct. 7	Oct. 12	Oct. 20	Dec. 20	1992
March 7	April 6	May 26	Sept. 16	Sept. 25	Sept. 30	Oct. 8	Dec. 9	1993

The Signs of the Zodiac

ARIES
March 21 April 19
TAURUS
April 20 May 20
GEMINI
May 21 June 21
CANCER
June 22 July 22
LEO
July 23 August 22
VIRGO
August 23 September 22
LIBRA
September 23 October 23
SCORPIO
October 24 November 21
SAGITTARIUS
November 22 December 21
CAPRICORNUS
December 22 January 19
AQUARIUS
January 20 February 18
PISCES
February 19 March 20

Traffic Signs

NO TURN ON RED

YIELD

DONT WALK

WALK

DO NOT ENTER

ONLY

ONLY

YIELD

STOP

MERGE

SLOW MOVING VEHICLE
The SMV sign is triangular, reflective red-orange, and visible day or night.

NO PASSING ZONE

R R

Service and Guide Signs

NO U TURN

SCHOOL ZONE
A five-sided sign shaped like an old school house indicates a school crossing or zone.

DO NOT PASS

HILL

CAMPING

CAMPING

HOSPITAL

TRAIL

BIKE ROUTE

NO LEFT TURN

NO RIGHT TURN

KEEP RIGHT

PED XING

CATTLE XING

SIGNAL AHEAD

DIVIDED HIGHWAY ENDS

DIVIDED HIGHWAY

TWO WAY TRAFFIC

SLIPPERY WHEN WET

BIKE XING

DEER XING

Trail and Bike Route signs are green in color. Other Service and Guide signs are in blue.

Table of Weights and Measures

Linear Measure

1 inch	=	2.54 centimeters
1 foot	= 12 inches	= 0.3048 meter
1 yard	= 3 feet	= 0.9144 meter
1 rod (or pole or perch)	= 5½ yards or 16½ feet	= 5.029 meters
1 furlong	= 40 rods	= 201.17 meters
1 (statute) mile	= 8 furlongs or 1,760 yards or 5,280 feet	= 1,609.3 meters
1 (land) league	= 3 miles	= 4.83 kilometers

Square Measure

1 square inch	=	6.452 square centimeters
1 square foot	= 144 square inches	= 929 square centimeters
1 square yard	= 9 square feet	= 0.8361 square meter
1 square rod	= 30¼ square yards	= 25.29 square meters
1 acre	= 160 square rods or 4,840 square yards or 43,560 square feet	= 0.4047 hectare
1 square mile	= 640 acres	= 259 hectares or 2.59 square kilometers

Cubic Measure

1 cubic inch	=	16.387 cubic centimeters
1 cubic foot	= 1,728 cubic inches	= 0.0283 cubic meter
1 cubic yard	= 27 cubic feet	= 0.7646 cubic meter
1 cord foot	= 16 cubic feet	
1 cord	= 8 cord feet	= 3.625 cubic meters

Chain Measure
(Gunter's or surveyor's chain)

1 link	= 7.92 inches	= 20.12 centimeters
1 chain	= 100 links or 66 feet	= 20.12 meters
1 furlong	= 10 chains	= 201.17 meters
1 mile	= 80 chains	= 1,609.3 meters

(Engineer's chain)

1 link	= 1 foot	= 0.3048 meter
1 chain	= 100 feet	= 30.48 meters
1 mile	= 52.8 chains	= 1,609.3 meters

Surveyor's (Square) Measure

1 square pole	= 625 square links	= 25.29 square meters
1 square chain	= 16 square poles	= 404.7 square meters
1 acre	= 10 square chains	= 0.4047 hectare
1 square mile or 1 section	= 640 acres	= 259 hectares or 2.59 square kilometers
1 township	= 36 square miles	= 9,324 hectares or 93.24 square kilometers

Nautical Measure

1 fathom	= 6 feet	= 1.829 meters
1 cable's length (ordinary)	= 100 fathoms	

(In the U.S. Navy 120 fathoms or 720 feet = 1 cable's length; in the British Navy 608 feet = 1 cable's length)

1 nautical mile (6,076.10333 feet, by international agreement in 1954)	= 10 cables' lengths	= 1.852 kilometers
1.1508 statute miles (length of a minute of longitude at the equator)	= 1 nautical mile	
1 marine league (3.45 statute miles)	= 3 nautical miles	= 5.56 kilometers
1 degree of a great circle of the earth	= 60 nautical miles	

Dry Measure

1 pint		= 33.60 cubic inches	= 0.5505 liter
1 quart	= 2 pints	= 67.20 cubic inches	= 1.1012 liters
1 peck	= 8 quarts	= 537.61 cubic inches	= 8.8096 liters
1 bushel	= 4 pecks	= 2,150.42 cubic inches	= 35.2383 liters

Liquid Measure

1 gill		= 7.219 cubic inches	= 0.1183 liter
4 fluid ounces (see next table)	= 1 gill		
1 pint	= 4 gills	= 28.875 cubic inches	= 0.4732 liter
1 quart	= 2 pints	= 57.75 cubic inches	= 0.9463 liter
1 gallon	= 4 quarts	= 231 cubic inches	= 3.7853 liters

Apothecaries' Fluid Measure

1 minim		= 0.0038 cubic inch	= 0.0616 milliliter
1 fluid dram	= 60 minims	= 0.2256 cubic inch	= 3.6966 milliliters
1 fluid ounce	= 8 fluid drams	= 1.8047 cubic inches	= 0.0296 liter
1 pint	= 16 fluid ounces	= 28.875 cubic inches	= 0.4732 liter

Circular (or Angular) Measure

60 seconds (")	= 1 minute (')
60 minutes	= 1 degree (°)
90 degrees	= 1 quadrant or 1 right angle
4 quadrants or 360 degrees	= 1 circle

Avoirdupois Weight
(The grain, equal to 0.0648 gram, is the same in all three tables of weight)

1 dram or 27.34 grains		= 1.772 grams
1 ounce	= 16 drams or 437.5 grains	= 28.3495 grams
1 pound	= 16 ounces or 7,000 grains	= 453.59 grams
1 hundredweight	= 100 pounds	= 45.36 kilograms
1 ton	= 2,000 pounds	= 907.18 kilograms

Troy Weight
(The grain, equal to 0.0648 gram, is the same in all three tables of weight)

1 carat	= 3.086 grains	= 200 milligrams
1 pennyweight	= 24 grains	= 1.5552 grams
1 ounce	= 20 pennyweights or 480 grains	= 31.1035 grams
1 pound	= 12 ounces or 5,760 grains	= 373.24 grams

Apothecaries' Weight
(The grain, equal to 0.0648 gram, is the same in all three tables of weight)

1 scruple	= 20 grains	= 1.296 grams
1 dram	= 3 scruples	= 3.888 grams
1 ounce	= 8 drams or 480 grains	= 31.1035 grams
1 pound	= 12 ounces or 5,760 grains	= 373.24 grams

Miscellaneous

3 inches	= 1 palm
4 inches	= 1 hand
6 inches	= 1 span
18 inches	= 1 cubit
21.8 inches	= 1 Bible cubit
2½ feet	= 1 military pace

The Metric System

Linear Measure

1 centimeter	=	0.3937 inch
1 decimeter	=	3.937 inches
1 meter	=	39.37 inches or 3.28 feet
1 decameter	=	393.7 inches
1 hectometer	=	328 feet 1 inch
1 kilometer	=	0.621 mile
1 myriameter	=	6.21 miles

Square Measure

1 square centimeter	=	0.1549 square inch
1 square decimeter	=	15.499 square inches
1 square meter	=	1,549.9 square inches or 1.196 square yards
1 square decameter	=	119.6 square yards
1 square hectometer	=	2.471 acres
1 square kilometer	=	0.386 square mile

Capacity Measure

1 centiliter	=	.338 fluid ounce
1 deciliter	=	3.38 fluid ounces
1 liter	=	1.0567 liquid quarts or 0.9081 dry quart
1 decaliter	=	2.64 gallons or 0.284 bushel
1 hectoliter	=	26.418 gallons or 2.838 bushels
1 kiloliter	=	264.18 gallons or 35.315 cubic feet

Land Measure

1 centare	=	1 square meter
1 are	=	1,549.9 square inches
1 hectare	=	119.6 square yards
1 square kilometer	=	0.386 square mile

(1 centare = 1 square meter, 1 are = 100 centares = 119.6 square yards, 1 hectare = 100 ares = 2.471 acres, 1 square kilometer = 100 hectares = 0.386 square mile)

Volume Measure

1 cubic centimeter	=	1,000 cubic millimeters = .06102 cubic inch
1 cubic decimeter	=	1,000 cubic centimeters = 61.02 cubic inches
1 cubic meter	=	1,000 cubic decimeters = 35.314 cubic feet

Weights

1 centigram	=	10 milligrams = 0.1543 grain
1 decigram	=	10 centigrams = 1.5432 grains
1 gram	=	10 decigrams = 15.432 grains
1 decagram	=	10 grams = 0.3527 ounce
1 hectogram	=	10 decagrams = 3.5274 ounces
1 kilogram	=	10 hectograms = 2.2046 pounds
1 myriagram	=	10 kilograms = 22.046 pounds
1 quintal	=	10 myriagrams = 220.46 pounds
1 metric ton	=	10 quintals = 2,204.6 pounds

Roman Numerals

I	1	VIII	8	LX	60
II	2	IX	9	LXX	70
III	3	X	10	LXXX	80
IV	4	XX	20	XC	90
V	5	XXX	30	C	100
VI	6	XL	40	D	500
VII	7	L	50	M	1,000

$\overline{V}$	5,000
$\overline{X}$	10,000
$\overline{L}$	50,000
$\overline{C}$	100,000
$\overline{D}$	500,000
$\overline{M}$	1,000,000

Handy Conversion Factors

To change	to	multiply by
acres	hectares	.4047
acres	square feet	43,560
acres	square miles	.001562
Celsius	Fahrenheit	*9/5
	*(then add 32)	
centimeters	inches	.3937
centimeters	feet	.03281
cubic meters	cubic feet	35.3145
cubic meters	cubic yards	1.3079
cubic yards	cubic meters	.7646
degrees	radians	.01745
Fahrenheit	Celsius	*5/9
	*(after subtracting 32)	
feet	meters	.3048
feet	miles (nautical)	.0001645
feet	miles (statute)	.0001894
feet/sec.	miles/hr.	.6818
furlongs	feet	660.0
furlongs	miles	.125
gallons (U.S.)	liters	3.7853
grains	grams	.0648
grams	grains	15.4324
grams	ounces avdp.	.0353
grams	pounds	.002205
hectares	acres	2.4710
horsepower	watts	745.7
hours	days	.04167
inches	millimeters	25.4000
inches	centimeters	2.5400
kilograms	pounds avdp or t	2.2046
kilometers	miles	.6214
kilowatts	horsepower	1.341
knots	nautical miles/hr.	1.0
knots	statute miles/hr.	1.151
liters	gallons (U.S.)	.2642
liters	pecks	.1135
liters	pints (dry)	1.8162
liters	pints (liquid)	2.1134
liters	quarts (dry)	.9081
liters	quarts (liquid)	1.0567
meters	feet	3.2808
meters	miles	.0006214
meters	yards	1.0936
metric tons	tons (long)	.9842
metric tons	tons (short)	1.1023
miles	kilometers	1.6093
miles	feet	5280
miles (nautical)	miles (statute)	1.1516
miles (statute)	miles (nautical)	.8684
miles/hr.	feet/min.	88
millimeters	inches	.0394
ounces avdp.	grams	28.3495
ounces	pounds	.0625
ounces (troy)	ounces (avdp.)	1.09714
pecks	liters	8.8096
pints (dry)	liters	.5506
pints (liquid)	liters	.4732
pounds ap or t	kilograms	.3782
pounds avdp.	kilograms	.4536
pounds	ounces	16
quarts (dry)	liters	1.1012
quarts (liquid)	liters	.9463
rods	meters	5.029
rods	feet	16.5
square feet	square meters	.0929
square kilometers	square miles	.3861
square meters	square feet	10.7639
square meters	square yards	1.1960
square meters	square kilometers	2.5900
square yards	square meters	.8361
tons (long)	metric tons	1.1060
tons (short)	metric tons	.9072
tons (long)	pounds	2240
tons (short)	pounds	2000
watts	BTU/hr.	3.4129
watts	horsepower	.001341
yards	meters	.9144
yards	miles	.0005682

Decimal Equivalents of Common Fractions

1/2	.5000	1/32	.0313	3/11	.2727	6/11	.5455
1/3	.3333	1/64	.0156	4/5	.8000	7/8	.8750
1/4	.2500	2/3	.6667	4/7	.5714	7/9	.7778
1/5	.2000	2/5	.4000	4/9	.4444	7/10	.7000
1/6	.1667	2/7	.2857	4/11	.3636	7/11	.6364
1/7	.1429	2/9	.2222	5/6	.8333	7/12	.5833
1/8	.1250	2/11	.1818	5/7	.7143	8/9	.8889
1/9	.1111	3/4	.7500	5/8	.6250	8/11	.7273
1/10	.1000	3/5	.6000	5/9	.5556	9/10	.9000
1/11	.0909	3/7	.4286	5/11	.4545	9/11	.8182
1/12	.0833	3/8	.3750	5/12	.4167	10/11	.9091
1/16	.0625	3/10	.3000	6/7	.8571	11/12	.9167

Periodic Table of the Elements

Legend:

Atomic Number — 2
Symbol — He
Atomic Weight (or Mass Number of most stable isotope if in parentheses) — 4.0026
Helium

1a	2a	3b	4b	5b	6b	7b	8	8	8	1b	2b	3a	4a	5a	6a	7a	0
1 H Hydrogen 1.00797																	2 He Helium 4.0026
3 Li Lithium 6.939	4 Be Beryllium 9.0122											5 B Boron 10.811	6 C Carbon 12.01115	7 N Nitrogen 14.0067	8 O Oxygen 15.9994	9 F Fluorine 18.9994	10 Ne Neon 20.183
11 Na Sodium 22.9898	12 Mg Magnesium 24.312											13 Al Aluminum 26.9815	14 Si Silicon 28.086	15 P Phosphorus 30.9738	16 S Sulfur 32.064	17 Cl Chlorine 35.453	18 Ar Argon 39.948
19 K Potassium 39.102	20 Ca Calcium 40.08	21 Sc Scandium 44.956	22 Ti Titanium 47.90	23 V Vanadium 50.942	24 Cr Chromium 51.996	25 Mn Manganese 54.9380	26 Fe Iron 55.847	27 Co Cobalt 58.9332	28 Ni Nickel 58.71	29 Cu Copper 63.546	30 Zn Zinc 65.37	31 Ga Gallium 69.72	32 Ge Germanium 72.59	33 As Arsenic 74.9216	34 Se Selenium 78.96	35 Br Bromine 79.909	36 Kr Krypton 83.80
37 Rb Rubidium 85.47	38 Sr Strontium 87.62	39 Y Yttrium 88.905	40 Zr Zirconium 91.22	41 Nb Niobium 92.906	42 Mo Molybdenum 95.94	43 Tc Technetium (97)	44 Ru Ruthenium 101.07	45 Rh Rhodium 102.905	46 Pd Palladium 106.4	47 Ag Silver 107.868	48 Cd Cadmium 112.40	49 In Indium 114.82	50 Sn Tin 118.69	51 Sb Antimony 121.75	52 Te Tellurium 127.60	53 I Iodine 126.9044	54 Xe Xenon 131.30
55 Cs Cesium 132.905	56 Ba Barium 137.34	57-71* Lanthanides	72 Hf Hafnium 178.49	73 Ta Tantalum 180.948	74 W Tungsten 183.85	75 Re Rhenium 186.2	76 Os Osmium 190.2	77 Ir Iridium 192.2	78 Pt Platinum 195.09	79 Au Gold 196.967	80 Hg Mercury 200.59	81 Tl Thallium 204.37	82 Pb Lead 207.19	83 Bi Bismuth 208.980	84 Po Polonium 210.05	85 At Astatine (210)	86 Rn Radon 222.00
87 Fr Francium (223)	88 Ra Radium 226.00	89-103** Actinides (227)	104 Unq† Unnilquadium (261)	105 Unp†† Unnilpentium (262)	106 Unh Unnilhexium (263)	107 Uns Unnilseptium (262)		109 Une Unnilennium (266)									

*Lanthanides

57 La Lanthanum 138.91	58 Ce Cerium 140.12	59 Pr Praseodymium 140.907	60 Nd Neodymium 144.24	61 Pm Promethium (145)	62 Sm Samarium 150.35	63 Eu Europium 151.96	64 Gd Gadolinium 157.25	65 Tb Terbium 158.924	66 Dy Dysprosium 162.50	67 Ho Holmium 164.930	68 Er Erbium 167.28	69 Tm Thulium 168.934	70 Yb Ytterbium 173.04	71 Lu Lutetium 174.97

**Actinides

89 Ac Actinium (227)	90 Th Thorium 232.038	91 Pa Protactinium 231.10	92 U Uranium 238.03	93 Np Neptunium 237.00	94 Pu Plutonium 239.05	95 Am Americium 243.13	96 Cm Curium (247)	97 Bk Berkelium (248)	98 Cf Californium (251)	99 Es Einsteinium (254)	100 Fm Fermium (257)	101 Md Mendelevium (258)	102 No Nobelium (259)	103 Lw Lawrencium (260)

† Other proposed names are kurchatovium (USSR) and hahnium (U.S.)
†† Other proposed names are nielsbohrium (USSR) and rutherfordium (U.S.)

MAPS

Using the World Maps

The following index alphabetically lists the countries that can be located on the handbook maps. Because some of the countries are small and difficult to find, the latitude and longitude specifications for each are also listed. Latitude and longitude refer to imaginary lines that mapmakers use. When used together, these lines will be helpful in locating any point on Earth.

The imaginary lines that go from east to west around the Earth are called lines of **latitude.** Latitude is measured in degrees with the equator being 0 degrees (0°). From the equator, latitude is measured from 0° to 90° North (the North Pole) and from 0° to 90° South (the South Pole). On a map, latitude numbers are printed along the left- and right-hand sides.

Imaginary lines that run from the North Pole to the South Pole are lines of **longitude.** Longitude is also measured in degrees. The prime meridian, which passes through Greenwich, England, is 0° longitude. Lines east of the prime meridian are called *east longitude.* Lines west of the prime meridian are called *west longitude,* and the two meet exactly opposite the prime meridian at 180° longitude. On a map, longitude numbers are printed at the top and bottom.

The latitude and longitude numbers of a place are sometimes called its *coordinates.* In each set of coordinates, latitude is given first, then longitude. To locate a spot on a map using its coordinates, find the spot where the given lines cross. The place will be at or near this point. Take, for example, the country of Australia, which has coordinates 25° S, 135° E. After finding the equator (0°), locate the line 25° south of that. Next, find the line of prime meridian (0°), and then the line 135° to its east. The point at which these two imaginary lines intersect pinpoints Australia.

Index to World Maps

Country	Latitude	Longitude	Country	Latitude	Longitude
Afghanistan	33° N	65° E	Cambodia	13° N	105° E
Albania	41° N	20° E	Cameroon	6° N	12° E
Algeria	28° N	3° E	Canada	60° N	95° W
Andorra	42° N	1° E	Cape Verde	16° N	24° W
Angola	12° S	18° E	Central African Rep.	7° N	21° E
Antigua and Barbuda	17° N	61° W	Chad	15° N	19° E
Argentina	34° S	64° W	Chile	30° S	71° W
Australia	25° S	135° E	China	35° N	105° E
Austria	47° N	13° E	Colombia	4° N	72° W
Bahamas	24° N	76° W	Comoros	12° S	44° E
Bahrain	26° N	50° E	Congo	1° S	15° E
Bangladesh	24° N	90° E	Costa Rica	10° N	84° W
Barbados	13° N	59° W	Cuba	21° N	80° W
Belgium	50° N	4° E	Cyprus	35° N	33° E
Belize	17° N	88° W	Czechoslovakia	49° N	17° E
Benin	9° N	2° E	Denmark	56° N	10° E
Bhutan	27° N	90° E	Djibouti	11° N	43° E
Bolivia	17° S	65° W	Dominica	15° N	61° W
Botswana	22° S	24° E	Dominican Republic	19° N	70° W
Brazil	10° S	55° W	Ecuador	2° S	77° W
Brunei	4° N	114° E	Egypt	27° N	30° E
Bulgaria	43° N	25° E	El Salvador	14° N	89° W
Burkina Faso/U.Volta	13° N	2° W	Equatorial Guinea	2° N	9° E
Burma	22° N	98° E	Ethiopia	8° N	38° E
Burundi	3° S	30° E	Fiji	19° S	174° E

Country	Latitude	Longitude	Country	Latitude	Longitude
Finland	64° N	26° E	Norway	62° N	10° E
France	46° N	2° E	Oman	22° N	58° E
Gabon	1° S	11° E	Pakistan	30° N	70° E
The Gambia	13° N	16° W	Panama	9° N	80° W
Germany	51° N	10° E	Papua New Guinea	6° S	147° E
Ghana	8° N	2° W	Paraguay	23° S	58° W
Greece	39° N	22° E	Peru	10° S	76° W
Greenland	70° N	40° W	Philippines	13° N	122° E
Grenada	12° N	61° W	Poland	52° N	19° E
Guatemala	15° N	90° W	Portugal	39° N	8° W
Guinea	11° N	10° W	Qatar	25° N	51° E
Guinea-Bissau	12° N	15° W	Romania	46° N	25° E
Guyana	5° N	59° W	Rwanda	2° S	30° E
Haiti	19° N	72° W	St. Kitts & Nevis	17° N	62° W
Honduras	15° N	86° W	Saint Lucia	14° N	61° W
Hungary	47° N	20° E	Saint Vincent		
Iceland	65° N	18° W	and the Grenadines	13° N	61° W
India	20° N	77° E	San Marino	44° N	12° E
Indonesia	5° S	120° E	Sao Tome and Principe	1° N	7° E
Iran	32° N	53° E	Saudi Arabia	25° N	45° E
Iraq	33° N	44° E	Scotland	57° N	5° W
Ireland	53° N	8° W	Senegal	14° N	14° W
Israel	31° N	35° E	Seychelles	5° S	55° E
Italy	42° N	12° E	Sierra Leone	8° N	11° W
Ivory Coast	8° N	5° W	Singapore	1° N	103° E
Jamaica	18° N	77° W	Solomon Islands	8° S	159° E
Japan	36° N	138° E	Somalia	10° N	49° E
Jordan	31° N	36° E	South Africa	30° S	26° E
Kenya	1° N	38° E	Spain	40° N	4° W
Kiribati	0° N	175° E	Sri Lanka	7° N	81° E
North Korea	40° N	127° E	Sudan	15° N	30° E
South Korea	36° N	128° E	Suriname	4° N	56° W
Kuwait	29° N	47° E	Swaziland	26° S	31° E
Laos	18° N	105° E	Sweden	62° N	15° E
Lebanon	34° N	36° E	Switzerland	47° N	8° E
Lesotho	29° S	28° E	Syria	35° N	38° E
Liberia	6° N	10° W	Taiwan	23° N	121° E
Libya	27° N	17° E	Tanzania	6° S	35° E
Liechtenstein	47° N	9° E	Thailand	15° N	100° E
Luxembourg	49° N	6° E	Togo	8° N	1° E
Madagascar	19° S	46° E	Tonga	20° S	173° W
Malawi	13° S	34° E	Trinidad/Tobago	11° N	61° W
Malaysia	2° N	112° E	Tunisia	34° N	9° E
Maldives	2° N	70° E	Turkey	39° N	35° E
Mali	17° N	4° W	Tuvala	8° S	179° E
Malta	36° N	14° E	Uganda	1° N	32° E
Mauritania	20° N	12° W	USSR	60° N	80° E
Mauritius	20° S	57° E	United Arab Emirates	24° N	54° E
Mexico	23° N	102° W	United Kingdom	54° N	2° W
Monaco	43° N	7° E	United States	38° N	97° W
Mongolia	46° N	105° E	Uruguay	33° S	56° W
Morocco	32° N	5° W	Vanuatu	17° S	170° E
Mozambique	18° S	35° E	Venezuela	8° N	66° W
Namibia	22° S	17° E	Vietnam	17° N	106° E
Nauru	1° S	166° E	Wales	53° N	3° W
Nepal	28° N	84° E	Western Samoa	10° S	173° W
Netherlands	52° N	5° E	Yemen	15° N	44° E
New Zealand	41° S	174° E	Yugoslavia	44° N	19° E
Nicaragua	13° N	85° W	Zaire	4° S	25° E
Niger	16° N	8° E	Zambia	15° S	30° E
Nigeria	10° N	8° E	Zimbabwe	20° S	30° E
Northern Ireland	55° N	7° W			

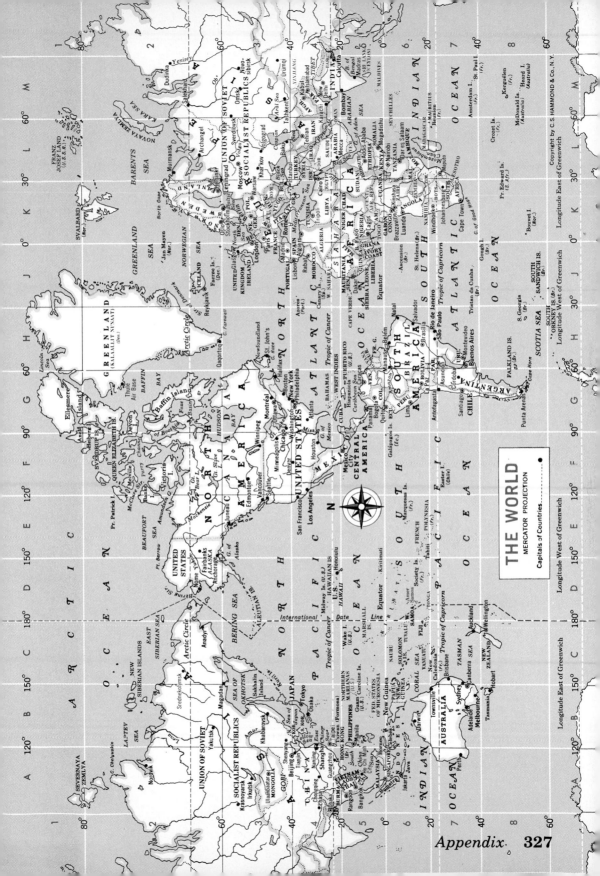

THE WORLD

MERCATOR PROJECTION

Capitals of Countries.............. •

NORTH AMERICA

LAMBERT AZIMUTHAL EQUAL-AREA PROJECTION

SCALE OF MILES

0 200 400 600 800 1000

SCALE OF KILOMETERS

0 200 400 600 800 1000

Capitals of Countries .... ⊙
International Boundaries .... — ∙ —
Canals .... ∙∙∙∙∙∙

© Copyright HAMMOND INCORPORATED, Maplewood, N.J.

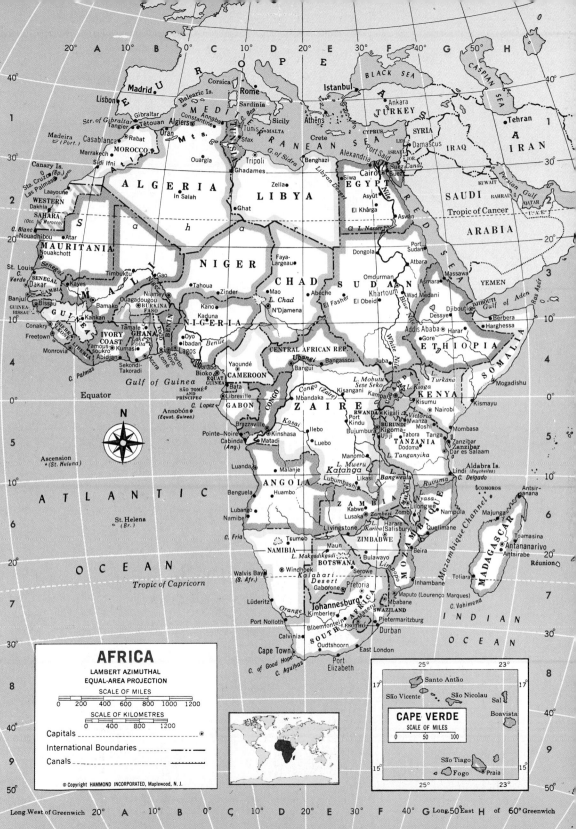

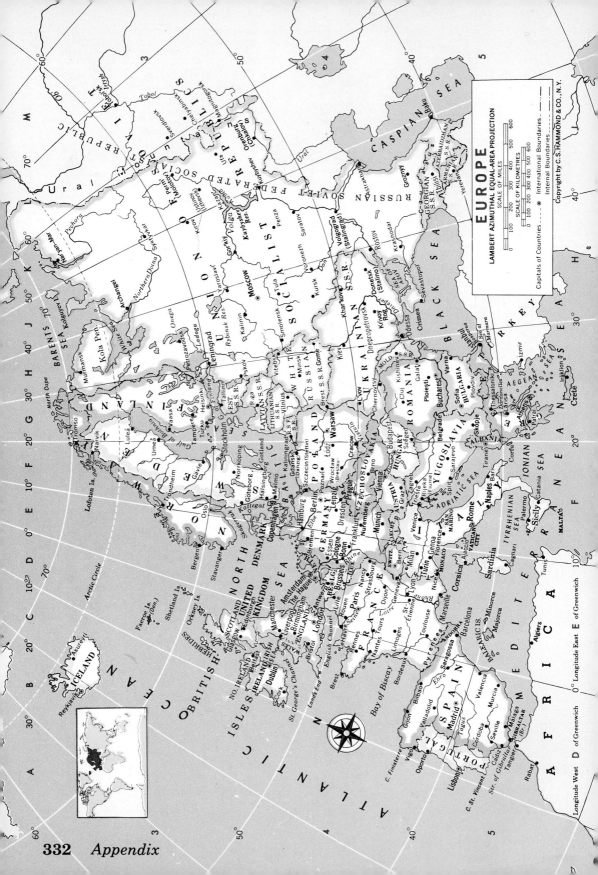

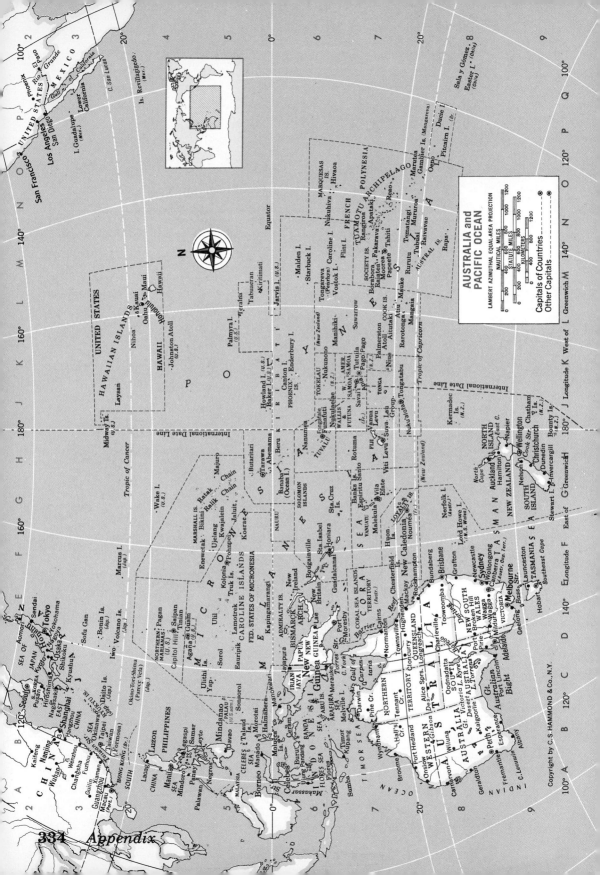

Constitution of the United States of America

Note: The original text of the Constitution has been edited to conform to contemporary American usage. The bracketed words have been added to help you locate information more quickly; they are not part of the Constitution.

The oldest federal constitution in existence was framed by a convention of delegates from twelve of the thirteen original states in Philadelphia in May, 1787, Rhode Island failing to send a delegate. George Washington presided over the session, which lasted until September 17, 1787. The draft (originally a preamble and seven Articles) was submitted to all thirteen states and was to become effective when ratified by nine states. It went into effect on the first Wednesday in March, 1789, having been ratified by New Hampshire, the ninth state to approve, on June 21, 1788. The states ratified the Constitution in the following order:

Delaware	December 7, 1787	South Carolina	May 23, 1788
Pennsylvania	December 12, 1787	New Hampshire	June 21, 1788
New Jersey	December 18, 1787	Virginia	June 25, 1788
Georgia	January 2, 1788	New York	July 26, 1788
Connecticut	January 9, 1788	North Carolina	November 21, 1789
Massachusetts	February 6, 1788	Rhode Island	May 29, 1790
Maryland	April 28, 1788		

[Preamble]

We the people of the United States, in order to form a more perfect Union, establish justice, insure domestic tranquility, provide for the common defense, promote the general welfare, and secure the blessings of liberty to ourselves and our posterity, do ordain and establish this Constitution for the United States of America.

Article I

Section 1

[Legislative powers vested in Congress] All legislative powers herein granted shall be vested in a Congress of the United States, which shall consist of a Senate and House of Representatives.

Section 2

1. **[Make-up of the House of Representatives]** The House of Representatives shall be composed of members chosen every second year by the people of the several States, and the electors in each State shall have the qualifications requisite for electors of the most numerous branch of the State Legislature.

2. **[Qualifications of Representatives]** No person shall be a Representative who shall not have attained to the age of twenty-five years, and been seven years a citizen of the United States, and who shall not, when elected, be an inhabitant of that State in which he shall be chosen.

3. **[Apportionment of Representatives and direct taxes—census]** (Representatives and direct taxes shall be apportioned among the several States which may be included within this Union, according to their respective numbers, which shall be determined by adding to the whole number of free persons, including those bound to service for a term of years, and excluding Indians not taxed, three-fifths of all other persons.—*Amended by the 14th Amendment, section 2.)* The actual enumeration shall be made within three years after the first meeting of the Congress of the United States, and within every subsequent term of ten years, in such manner as they shall by law direct: The number of Representatives shall not exceed one for every thirty thousand, but each State shall have at least one Representative; and until such enumeration shall be made, the State of New Hampshire shall be entitled to choose three; Massachusetts, eight; Rhode Island and Providence Plantations, one; Connecticut, five; New York, six; New Jersey, four; Pennsylvania, eight; Delaware, one; Maryland, six; Virginia, ten; North Carolina, five; South Carolina, five; and Georgia, three.

4. **[Filling of vacancies in representation]** When vacancies happen in the representation from any State, the Executive Authority thereof shall issue writs of election to fill such vacancies.

5. **[Selection of officers; power of impeachment]** The House of Representatives shall choose their Speaker and other officers; and shall have the sole power of impeachment.

Section 3

1. **[The Senate]** (The Senate of the United States shall be composed of two Senators from each State, chosen by the Legislature thereof, for six years; and each Senator shall have one vote.—*Amended by the 17th Amendment, section 1.)*

2. **[Classification of Senators; filling of vacancies]** Immediately after they shall be assembled in consequence of the first election, they shall be divided as equally as may be into three classes. The seats of the Senators of the first class shall be vacated at the expiration of the second year, of the second class at the expiration of the fourth year, and of the third class at the expiration of the sixth year, so that one-third may be chosen every second year; and if vacancies happen by resignation, or otherwise, (during the recess of the Legislature of any State,) the Executive thereof may make temporary appointments (until the next meeting of the Legislature, which shall then fill such vacancies.—*Amended by the 17th Amendment.)*

3. **[Qualification of Senators]** No person shall be a Senator who shall not have attained to the age of thirty years, and been nine years a citizen of the United States, and who shall not, when elected, be an inhabitant of that State for which he shall be chosen.

4. **[Vice President to be President of Senate]** The Vice President of the United States shall be President of the Senate, but shall have no vote, unless they be equally divided.

5. **[Selection of Senate officers; President pro tempore)** The Senate shall choose their other officers, and also a President pro tempore, in the absence of the Vice President, or when he shall exercise the office of President of the United States.

6. **[Senate to try impeachments]** The Senate shall have the sole power to try all impeachments. When sitting for that purpose, they shall be on oath or affirmation. When the President of the United States is tried, the Chief Justice shall preside: and no person shall be convicted without the concurrence of two-thirds of the members present.

7. **[Judgment in cases of impeachment]** Judgment in cases of impeachment shall not extend further than to removal from office, and disqualification to hold and enjoy any office of honor, trust, or profit under the United States; but the party convicted shall nevertheless be liable and subject to indictment, trial, judgment, and punishment, according to Law.

Section 4

1. **[Control of congressional elections]** The times, places, and manner of holding elections for Senators and Representatives shall be prescribed in each State by the Legislature thereof; but the Congress may at any time by law make or alter such regulations, except as to the places of choosing Senators.

2. **[Time for assembling of Congress]** The Congress shall assemble at least once in every year, (and such meeting shall be on the first Monday in December, unless they shall by law appoint a different day.—*Amended by the 20th Amendment, section 2.)*

Section 5

1. **[Each House to be the judge of the election and qualifications of its members; regulations as to quorum]** Each House shall be the judge of the elections, returns, and qualifications of its own members, and a majority of each shall constitute a quorum to do business; but a smaller number may adjourn from day to day, and may be authorized to compel the attendance of absent members, in such manner, and under such penalties as each House may provide.

2. **[Each House to determine its own rules]** Each House may determine the rules of its proceedings, punish its members for disorderly behavior, and, with the concurrence of two-thirds, expel a member.

3. **[Journals and yeas and nays]** Each House shall keep a journal of its proceedings, and from time to time publish the same, excepting such parts as may in their judgment require secrecy; and the yeas and nays of the members of either House on any question shall, at the desire of one-fifth of those present, be entered on the journal.

4. **[Adjournment]** Neither House, during the session of Congress, shall, without the consent of the other, adjourn for more than three days, nor to any other place than that in which the two Houses shall be sitting.

Section 6

1. **[Compensation and privileges of members of Congress]** The Senators and Representatives shall receive a compensation for their services, to be ascertained by law, and paid out of the Treasury of the United States. They shall in all cases, except treason, felony, and breach of the peace, be privileged from arrest during their attendance at the session of their respective Houses, and in going to and returning from the same; and for any speech or debate in either House, they shall not be questioned in any other place.

2. **[Incompatible offices; exclusions]** No Senator or Representative shall, during the time for which he was elected, be appointed to any civil office under the authority of the United States, which shall have been created, or the emoluments whereof shall have been increased during such time; and no person holding any office under the United States shall be a member of either House during his continuance in office.

Section 7

1. **[Revenue bills to originate in House]** All bills for raising revenue shall originate in the House of Representatives; but the Senate may propose or concur with amendments as on other bills.

2. **[Manner of passing bills; veto power of President]** Every bill which shall have passed the House of Representatives and the Senate, shall, before it becomes a law, be presented to the President of the United States; if he approve, he shall sign it, but if not he shall return it, with his objections to that House in which it shall have originated, who shall enter the objections at large on their journal, and proceed to reconsider it. If after such reconsideration two-thirds of that House shall agree to pass the bill, it shall be sent, together with the objections, to the other House, by which it shall likewise be reconsidered, and if approved by two-thirds of that House, it shall become a law. But in all such cases the votes of both Houses shall be determined by yeas and nays, and the names of the persons voting for and against the bill shall be entered on the journal of each House, respectively. If any bill shall not be returned by the President within ten days (Sundays excepted) after it shall have been presented to him, the same shall be a law, in like manner as if he had signed it, unless the Congress by their adjournment prevent its return, in which case it shall not be a law.

3. **[Concurrent orders or resolutions to be passed by President]** Every order, resolution, or vote to which the concurrence of the Senate and House of Representatives may be necessary (except on a question of adjournment) shall be presented to the President of the United States; and before the same shall take effect, shall be approved by him, or being disapproved by him, shall be repassed by two-thirds of the Senate and House of Representatives, according to the rules and limitations prescribed in the case of a bill.

Section 8

[General powers of Congress] The Congress shall have the power:

1. **[Taxes, duties, imposts, and excises]** To lay and collect taxes, duties, imposts, and excises, to pay the debts and provide for the common defense and general welfare of the United States; but all duties, imposts, and excises shall be uniform throughout the United States; *(See the 16th Amendment.)*

2. **[Borrowing of money]** To borrow money on the credit of the United States;

3. **[Regulation of commerce]** To regulate commerce with foreign nations, and among the several States, and with the Indian tribes;

4. **[Naturalization and bankruptcy]** To establish a uniform rule of naturalization, and uniform laws on the subject of bankruptcies throughout the United States;

5. **[Money, weights, and measures]** To coin money, regulate the value thereof, and of foreign coin, and fix the standard of weights and measures;

6. **[Counterfeiting]** To provide for the punishment of counterfeiting the securities and current coin of the United States;

7. **[Post offices]** To establish post offices and post roads;

8. **[Patents and copyrights]** To promote the progress of science and useful arts, by securing for limited times to authors and inventors the exclusive right to their respective writings and discoveries;

9. **[Inferior courts]** To constitute tribunals inferior to the Supreme Court;

10. **[Piracies and felonies]** To define and punish piracies and felonies committed on the high seas, and offenses against the law of nations.

11. **[War; marque and reprisal]** To declare war, grant letters of marque and reprisal, and make rules concerning captures on land and water;

12. **[Armies]** To raise and support armies, but no appropriation of money to that use shall be for a longer term than two years;

13. **[Navy]** To provide and maintain a navy;

14. **[Land and naval forces]** To make rules for the government and regulation of the land and naval forces;

15. **[Calling out militia]** To provide for calling forth the militia to execute the laws of the Union, suppress insurrections, and repel invasions.

16. **[Organizing, arming, and disciplining militia]** To provide for organizing, arming, and disciplining the militia, and for governing such part of them as may be employed in the service of the United States, reserving to the States, respectively, the appointment of the officers, and the authority of training the militia according to the discipline prescribed by Congress;

17. **[Exclusive legislation over District of Columbia]** To exercise exclusive legislation in all cases whatsoever, over such district (not exceeding ten miles square) as may, by cession of particular States, and the acceptance of Congress, become the seat of the Government of the United States, and to exercise like authority over all places purchased by the consent of the Legislature of the State in which the same shall be, for the erection of forts, magazines, arsenals, dock-yards, and other needful buildings;—And

18. **[To enact laws necessary to enforce Constitution]** To make all laws which shall be necessary and proper for carrying into execution the foregoing powers, and all other powers vested by this Constitution in the Government of the United States, or in any department or officer thereof.

Section 9

1. **[Migration or importation of certain persons not to be prohibited before 1808]** The migration or importation of such persons as any of the States now existing shall think proper to admit, shall not be prohibited by the Congress prior to the year one thousand eight hundred and eight, but a tax or duty may be imposed on such importation, not exceeding ten dollars for each person.

2. **[Writ of habeas corpus not to be suspended; exception]** The privilege of the writ of habeas corpus shall not be suspended, unless when in cases of rebellion or invasion the public safety may require it.

3. **[Bills of attainder and ex post facto laws prohibited]** No bill of attainder or ex post facto law shall be passed.

4. **[Capitation and other direct taxes]** No capitation, or other direct, tax shall be laid, unless in proportion to the census or enumeration herein before directed to be taken. *(See the 16th Amendment.)*

5. **[Exports not to be taxed]** No tax or duty shall be laid on articles exported from any State.

6. **[No preference to be given to ports of any State; interstate shipping]** No preference shall be given by any regulation of commerce or revenue to the ports of one State over those of another: nor shall vessels bound to, or from, one State, be obliged to enter, clear, or pay duties in another.

7. **[Money, how drawn from treasury; financial statements to be published]** No money shall be drawn from the Treasury, but in consequence of appropriations made by law; and a regular statement and account of the receipts and expenditures of all public money shall be published from time to time.

8. **[Titles of nobility not to be granted; acceptance by government officers of favors from foreign powers]** No title of nobility shall be granted by the United States: and no person holding any office of profit or trust under them, shall, without the consent of the Congress, accept of any present, emolument, office, or title, of any kind whatever, from any king, prince, or foreign state.

Section 10

1. **[Limitations of the powers of the several States]** No state shall enter into any treaty, alliance, or confederation; grant letters of marque and reprisal; coin money; emit bills of credit; make anything but gold and silver coin a tender in payment of debts; pass any bill of attainder, ex post facto law, or law impairing the obligation of contracts, or grant any title of nobility.

2. **[State imposts and duties]** No State shall, without the consent of the Congress, lay any imposts or duties on imports or exports, except what may be absolutely necessary for executing its inspection laws: and the net produce of all duties and imposts, laid by any State on imports or exports, shall be for the use of the Treasury of the United States; and all such laws shall be subject to the revision and control of the Congress.

3. **[Further restrictions on powers of States]** No State shall, without the consent of Congress, lay any duty of tonnage, keep troops, or ships of war in time of peace, enter into any agreement or compact with another state, or with a foreign power, or engage in war, unless actually invaded, or in such imminent danger as will not admit of delay.

Article II

Section 1

1. **[The President; the executive power]** The executive power shall be vested in a President of the United States of America. He shall hold his office during the term of four years, and together with the Vice President, chosen for the same term, be elected, as follows:

2. **[Appointment and qualifications of presidential electors]** Each State shall appoint, in such manner as the Legislature thereof may direct, a number of electors, equal to the whole number of Senators and Representatives to which the State may be entitled in the Congress: but no Senator or Representative, or person holding an office of trust or profit under the United States, shall be appointed an elector.

3. **[Original method of electing the President and Vice President]** (The electors shall meet in their respective States, and vote by ballot for two persons, of whom one at least shall not be an inhabitant of the same State with themselves. And they shall make a list of all the persons voted for, and of the number of votes for each; which list they shall sign and certify, and transmit sealed to the seat of the Government of the United States, directed to the President of the Senate. The President of the Senate shall, in the presence of the Senate and House of Representatives, open all the certificates, and the votes shall then be counted. The person having the greatest number of votes shall be the President, if such number be a majority of the whole number of electors appointed; and if there be more than one who have such majority, and have an equal number of votes, then the House of Representatives shall immediately choose by ballot one of them for President; and if no person have a majority, then from the five highest on the list the said House shall in like manner choose the President. But in choosing the President, the votes shall be taken by States, the representation from each State having one vote; a quorum for this purpose shall consist of a member or members from two-thirds of the States, and a majority of all the states shall be necessary to a choice. In every case, after the choice of the President, the person having the greatest number of votes of the electors shall be

the Vice President. But if there should remain two or more who have equal votes, the Senate should choose from them by ballot the Vice President.—*Replaced by the 12th Amendment.)*

4. **[Congress may determine time of choosing electors and day for casting their votes]** The Congress may determine the time of choosing the electors, and the day on which they shall give their votes; which day shall be the same throughout the United States.

5. **[Qualifications for the office of President]** No person except a natural born citizen, or a citizen of the United States, at the time of the adoption of this Constitution, shall be eligible to the office of President; neither shall any person be eligible to that office who shall not have attained to the age of thirty-five years, and been fourteen years a resident within the United States. *(For qualifications of the Vice President, see the 12th Amendment.)*

6. **[Filling vacancy in the office of President]** (In case of the removal of the President from office, or of his death, resignation, or inability to discharge the powers and duties of the said office, the same shall devolve on the Vice President, and the Congress may by law provide for the case of removal, death, resignation or inability, both of the President and Vice President, declaring what officer shall then act as President, and such officer shall act accordingly, until the disability be removed, or a President shall be elected.—*Amended by the 20th and 25th Amendments.)*

7. **[Compensation of the President]** The President shall, at stated times, receive for his services, a compensation, which shall neither be increased nor diminished during the period for which he shall have been elected, and he shall not receive within that period any other emolument from the United States, or any of them.

8. **[Oath to be taken by the President]** Before he enter on the execution of his office, he shall take the following oath or affirmation:—"I do solemnly swear (or affirm) that I will faithfully execute the office of President of the United States, and will to the best of my ability, preserve, protect, and defend the Constitution of the United States."

Section 2

1. **[The President to be Commander-in-Chief of army and navy and head of executive departments; may grant reprieves and pardons]** The President shall be Commander-in-Chief of the Army and Navy of the United States, and of the militia of the several States, when called into the actual service of the United States; he may require the opinion, in writing, of the principal officer in each of the executive departments, upon any subject relating to the duties of their respective offices, and he shall have power to grant reprieves and pardons for offenses against the United States, except in cases of impeachment.

2. **[President may, with concurrence of Senate, make treaties, appoint ambassadors, etc.; appointment of inferior officers, authority of Congress over]** He shall have power, by and with the advice and consent of the Senate, to make treaties, provided two-thirds of the Senators present concur; and he shall nominate, and by and with the advice and consent of the Senate, shall appoint ambassadors, other public ministers and consuls, judges of the Supreme Court, and all other officers of the United States, whose appointments are not herein otherwise provided for, and which shall be established by law: but the Congress may by law vest the appointment of such inferior officers, as they think proper, in the President alone, in the courts of law, or in the heads of departments.

3. **[President may fill vacancies in office during recess of Senate]** The President shall have power to fill up all vacancies that may happen during the recess of the Senate, by granting commissions which shall expire at the end of their session.

Section 3

[President to give advice to Congress; may convene or adjourn it on certain occasions; to receive ambassadors, etc.; have laws executed and commission all officers] He shall from time to time give to the Congress information of the state of the Union, and recommend to their consideration such measures as he shall judge necessary and expedient; he may, on extraordinary occasions, convene both Houses, or either of them, and in case of disagreement between them, with respect to the time of adjournment, he may adjourn them to such time as he shall think proper; he shall receive ambassadors and other public ministers: he shall take care that the laws be faithfully executed, and shall commission all the officers of the United States.

Section 4

[All civil officers removable by impeachment] The President, Vice President, and all civil officers of the United States shall be removed from office on impeachment for, and conviction of, treason, bribery, or other high crimes and misdemeanors.

Article III
Section 1

[Judicial powers; how vested; term of office and compensation of judges] The judicial power of the United States, shall be vested in one Supreme Court, and in such inferior courts as the Congress may from time to time ordain and establish. The judges, both of the supreme and inferior courts, shall hold their offices during good behavior, and shall, at stated times, receive for their services, a compensation, which shall not be diminished during their continuance in office.

Section 2

1. **[Jurisdiction of Federal courts]** (The judicial power shall extend to all cases, in law and equity, arising under this Constitution, the laws of the United States, and treaties made, or which shall be made, under their authority; to all cases affecting ambassadors, other public ministers and consuls; to all cases of admiralty and maritime jurisdiction; to controversies to which the United States, shall be a party; to controversies between two or more States; between a State and citizens of another State; between citizens of different States, between citizens of the same State claiming lands under grants of different states, and between a State, or the citizens thereof, and foreign states, citizens, or subjects.—*Amended by the 11th Amendment.)*

2. **[Original and appellate jurisdiction of Supreme Court]** In all cases affecting ambassadors, other public ministers and consuls, and those in which a State shall be party, the Supreme Court shall have original jurisdiction. In all the other cases before mentioned, the Supreme Court shall have appellate jurisdiction, both as to law and fact, with such exceptions, and under such regulations, as the Congress shall make.

3. **[Trial of all crimes, except impeachment, to be by jury]** The trial of all crimes, except in cases of impeachment, shall be by jury; and such trial shall be held in the State where the said crimes shall have been committed; but when not committed within any State, the trial shall be at such place or places as the Congress may by law have directed.

Section 3

1. **[Treason defined; conviction of]** Treason against the United States, shall consist only in levying war against them, or, in adhering to their enemies, giving them aid and comfort. No person shall be convicted of treason unless on the testimony of two witnesses to the same overt act, or on confession in open court.

2. **[Congress to declare punishment for treason; proviso]** The Congress shall have power to declare the punishment of treason, but no attainder of treason shall work corruption of blood, or forfeiture except during the life of the person attainted.

Article IV

Section 1

[Each State to give full faith and credit to the public acts and records of other States] Full faith and credit shall be given in each State to the public acts, records, and judicial proceedings of every other State. And the Congress may by general laws prescribe the manner in which such acts, records, and proceedings shall be proved, and the effect thereof.

Section 2

1. **[Privileges of citizens]** The citizens of each State shall be entitled to all privileges and immunities of citizens in the several States.

2. **[Extradition between the several States]** A person charged in any State with treason, felony, or other crime, who shall flee from justice, and be found in another State, shall on demand of the Executive authority of the State from which he fled, be delivered up, to be removed to the State having jurisdiction of the crime.

3. **[Persons held to labor or service in one State, fleeing to another, to be returned]** (No person held to service or labor in one State, under the laws thereof, escaping into another, shall, in consequence of any law or regulation therein, be discharged from such service or labor, but shall be delivered up on claim of the party to whom such service or labor may be due.—*Eliminated by the 13th Amendment.)*

Section 3

1. **[New States]** New States may be admitted by the Congress into this Union; but no new State shall be formed or erected within the jurisdiction of any other State; nor any State be formed by the junction of two or more States, or parts of States, without the consent of the Legislatures of the States concerned as well as of the Congress.

2. **[Regulations concerning territory]** The Congress shall have power to dispose of and make all needful rules and regulations respecting the territory or other property belonging to the United States; and nothing in this Constitution shall be so construed as to prejudice any claims of the United States, or of any particular State.

Section 4

[Republican form of government and protection guaranteed the several States] The United States shall guarantee to every State in this Union a Republican form of government, and shall protect each of them against invasion; and on application of the Legislature, or of the Executive (when the Legislature cannot be convened) against domestic violence.

Article V

[Ways in which the Constitution can be amended] The Congress, whenever two-thirds of both Houses shall deem it necessary, shall propose amendments to this Constitution, or, on the application of the Legislatures of two-thirds of the several States shall call a convention for proposing amendments, which, in either case, shall be valid to all intents and purposes, as part of this Constitution, when ratified by the Legislatures of three-fourths of the several States, or by conventions in three-fourths thereof, as the one or the other mode of ratification may be proposed by the Congress; provided that no amendment which may be made prior to the year one thousand eight hundred and eight shall in any manner affect the first and fourth clauses in the ninth Section of the first Article; and that no State, without its consent, shall be deprived of its equal suffrage in the Senate.

Article VI

1. **[Debts contracted under the confederation secured]** All debts contracted and engagements entered into, before the adoption of this Constitution, shall be as valid against the United States under this Constitution, as under the Confederation.

2. **[Constitution, laws, and treaties of the United States to be supreme]** This Constitution, and the laws of the United States which shall be made in pursuance thereof; and all treaties made, or which shall be made, under the authority of the United States, shall be the supreme law of the land; and the judges in every State shall be bound thereby, anything in the Constitution or laws of any State to the contrary notwithstanding.

3. **[Who shall take constitutional oath; no religious test as to official qualification]** The Senators and Representatives before mentioned, and the members of the several State Legislatures, and all executive and judicial officers, both of the United States and of the several States, shall be bound by oath or affirmation, to support this Constitution; but no religious test shall ever be required as a qualification to any office or public trust under the United States.

Article VII

[Constitution to be considered adopted when ratified by nine States] The ratification of the conventions of nine States shall be sufficient for the establishment of this Constitution between the States so ratifying the same.

Amendments to the Constitution of the United States

Note: Amendments I to X, popularly known as the Bill of Rights, were proposed and sent to the states by the first session of the First Congress. They were ratified Dec. 15, 1791.

Amendment 1

[Freedom of religion, speech, of the press, and right of petition] Congress shall make no law respecting an establishment of religion, or prohibiting the free exercise thereof; or abridging the freedom of speech, or of the press; or the right of the people peaceably to assemble, and to petition the Government for a redress of grievances.

Amendment 2

[Right of people to bear arms not to be infringed] A well-regulated militia, being necessary to the security of a free State, the right of the people to keep and bear arms, shall not be infringed.

Amendment 3

[Quartering of troops] No soldier shall, in time of peace be quartered in any house, without the consent of the owner, nor in time of war, but in a manner to be prescribed by law.

Amendment 4

[Persons and houses to be secure from unreasonable searches and seizures] The right of the people to be secure in their persons, houses, papers, and effects, against unreasonable searches and seizures, shall not be violated, and no warrants shall issue, but upon probable cause, supported by oath or affirmation, and particularly describing the place to be searched, and the persons or things to be seized.

Amendment 5

[Trials for crimes; just compensation for private property taken for public use] No person shall be held to answer for a capital, or otherwise infamous crime, unless on a presentment or indictment of a Grand Jury, except in cases arising in the land or naval forces, or in the militia, when in actual service in time of war or public danger; nor shall any person be subject for the same offense to be twice put in jeopardy of life or limb; nor shall be compelled in any criminal case to be a witness, against himself, nor be deprived of life, liberty, or property, without due process of law; nor shall private property be taken for public use, without just compensation.

Amendment 6

[Right to speedy trial, witnesses, counsel] In all criminal prosecutions, the accused shall enjoy the right to a speedy and public trial, by an impartial jury of the State and district wherein the crime shall have been committed, which district shall have been previously ascertained by law, and to be informed of the nature and cause of the accusation; to be confronted with the witnesses against him; to have compulsory process for obtaining witnesses in his favor, and to have the assistance of counsel for his defense.

Amendment 7

[Right of trial by jury] In suits at common law, where the value in controversy shall exceed twenty dollars, the right of trial by jury shall be preserved, and no fact tried by a jury, shall be otherwise re-examined in any court of the United States, than according to the rules of the common law.

Amendment 8

[Excessive bail, fines, and punishments prohibited] Excessive bail shall not be required, nor excessive fines imposed, nor cruel and unusual punishments inflicted.

Amendment 9

[Reserved rights of people] The enumeration in the Constitution, of certain rights, shall not be construed to deny or disparage others retained by the people.

Amendment 10

[Rights of States under Constitution] The powers not delegated to the United States by the Constitution, nor prohibited by it to the States, are reserved to the States, respectively, or to the people.

Amendment 11

(The proposed amendment was sent to the states March 5, 1794, by the Third Congress. It was ratified Feb. 7, 1795. It changes Article III, Sect. 2, Para. 1.]

[Judicial power of United States not to extend to suits against a State] The judicial power of the United States shall not be construed to extend to any suit in law or equity, commenced or prosecuted against one of the United States by citizens of another State, or by citizens or subjects of any foreign state.

Amendment 12

(The proposed amendment was sent to the states Dec. 12, 1803, by the Eighth Congress. It was ratified July 27, 1804. It replaces Article II, Sect. 1, Para. 3.)

[Manner of electing President and Vice President by electors] (The electors shall meet in their respective states, and vote by ballot for President and Vice President, one of whom, at least, shall not be an inhabitant of the same state with themselves; they shall name in their ballots the person voted for as President, and in distinct ballots the person voted for as Vice President, and they shall make distinct lists of all persons voted for as President, and of all persons voted for as Vice President, and of the number of votes for each, which lists they shall sign and certify, and transmit sealed to the seat of the government of the United States, directed to the President of the Senate; the President of the Senate shall, in the presence of the Senate and House of Representatives, open all the certificates and the votes shall then be counted; the person having the greatest number of votes for President, shall be the President, if such number be a majority of the whole number of electors appointed; and if no person have such majority, then from the persons having the highest numbers not exceeding three on the list of those voted for as President, the House of Representatives shall choose immediately, by ballot, the President. But in choosing the President, the votes shall be taken by states, the representation from each State having one vote; a quorum for this purpose shall consist of a member or members from two-thirds of the states, and a majority of all the states shall be necessary to a choice. And if the House of Representatives shall not choose a President whenever the right of choice shall devolv e upon them, before the fourth day of March next followin ;, then the Vice President shall act as President, as in tl e case of the death or other constitutional disability of the President. The person having the greatest number of votes as Vice President, shall be the Vice President, if such number be a majority of the whole number of electors appointed, and if no person have a majority, then from the two highest numbers on the list, the Senate shall choose the Vice President; a quorum for the purpose shall consist of two-thirds of the whole number of Senators, and a majority of the whole number shall be necessary to a choice. But no person constitutionally ineligible to the office of President shall be eligible to that of Vice President of the United States.—*Amended by the 20th Amendment, sections 3 and 4.)*

Amendment 13

(The proposed amendment was sent to the states Feb. 1, 1865, by the Thirty-eighth Congress. It was ratified Dec. 6, 1865. It eliminates Article IV, Sect. 2, Para. 3.)

Section 1

[Slavery prohibited] Neither slavery nor involuntary servitude, except as a punishment for crime whereof the party shall have been duly convicted, shall exist within the United States, or any place subject to their jurisdiction.

Section 2

[Congress given power to enforce this article] Congress shall have power to enforce this article by appropriate legislation.

Amendment 14

(The proposed amendment was sent to the states June 16, 1866, by the Thirty-ninth Congress. It was ratified July 9, 1868. It changes Article 1, Sec. 2, Para. 3.)

Section 1

[Citizenship defined; privileges of citizens] All persons born or naturalized in the United States, and subject to the jurisdiction thereof, are citizens of the United States and of the State wherein they reside. No State shall make or enforce any law which shall abridge the privileges or immunities of citizens of the United States; nor shall any State deprive any person of life, liberty, or property, without due process of law; nor deny to any person within its jurisdiction the equal protection of the laws.

Section 2

[Apportionment of Representatives] Representatives shall be apportioned among the several States according to their respective numbers, counting the whole number of persons in each State, excluding Indians not taxed. But when the right to vote at any election for the choice of electors for President and Vice President of the United States, Representatives in Congress, the executive and judicial officers of a State, or the members of the Legislature thereof, is denied to any of the male inhabitants of such State, being twenty-one years of age, and citizens of the United States, or in any way abridged, except for participation in rebellion, or other crime, the basis of representation therein shall be reduced in the proportion which the number of such male citizens shall bear to the whole number of male citizens twenty-one years of age in such State.

Section 3

[Disqualification for office; removal of disability] No person shall be a Senator or Representative in Congress, or elector of President and Vice President, or hold any office, civil or military, under the United States, or under any State, who, having previously taken an oath, as a member of Congress, or as an officer of the United States, or as a member of any State Legislature, or as an executive or judicial officer of any State, to support the Constitution of the United States, shall have engaged in insurrection or rebellion against the same, or given aid or comfort to the enemies thereof. But Congress may by a vote of two-thirds of each House, remove such disability.

Section 4

[Public debt not to be questioned; payment of debts and claims incurred in aid of rebellion forbidden] The validity of the public debt of the United States, authorized by law, including debts incurred for payment of pensions and bounties for services in suppressing insurrection or rebellion, shall not be questioned. But neither the United States nor any State shall assume or pay any debt or obligation incurred in aid of insurrection or rebellion against the United States, or any claim for the loss or emancipation of any slave; but all such debts, obligations, and claims shall be held illegal and void.

Section 5

[Congress given power to enforce this article] The Congress shall have power to enforce, by appropriate legislation, the provisions of this article.

Amendment 15

(The proposed amendment was sent to the states Feb. 27, 1869, by the Fortieth Congress. It was ratified Feb. 3, 1870.)

Section 1

[Right of certain citizens to vote established] The right of citizens of the United States to vote shall not be denied or abridged by the United States or by any State on account of race, color, or previous condition of servitude.

Section 2

[Congress given power to enforce this article] The Congress shall have power to enforce this article by appropriate legislation.

Amendment 16

(The proposed amendment was sent to the states July 12, 1909, by the Sixty-first Congress. It was ratified Feb. 3, 1913.)

[Income taxes authorized] The Congress shall have power to lay and collect taxes on incomes, from whatever source derived, without apportionment among the several States, and without regard to any census or enumeration.

Amendment 17

(The proposed amendment was sent to the states May 16, 1912, by the Sixty-second Congress. It was ratified April 8, 1913. It changes Article 1, Sect. 3, Para. 1 and 2.)

[Election of United States Senators; filling of vacancies; qualifications of electors] The Senate of the United States shall be composed of two Senators from each State, elected by the people thereof, for six years; and each Senator shall have one vote. The electors in each State shall have the qualifications requisite for electors of the most numerous branch of the State Legislatures.

When vacancies happen in the representation of any State in the Senate, the executive authority of such State shall issue writs of election to fill such vacancies: Provided, that the legislature of any State may empower the executive thereof to make temporary appointment until the people fill the vacancies by election as the legislature may direct.

This amendment shall not be so construed as to affect the election or term of any Senator chosen before it becomes valid as part of the Constitution.

Amendment 18

(The proposed amendment was sent to the states Dec. 18, 1917, by the Sixty-fifth Congress. It was ratified by three-quarters of the states by Jan. 16, 1919, and became effective Jan. 16, 1920. It was

repealed by the 21st Amendment.)

Section 1

[Manufacture, sale, or transportation of intoxicating liquors, for beverage purposes, prohibited] After one year from the ratification of this article the manufacture, sale, or transportation of intoxicating liquors within, the importation thereof into, or the exportation thereof from the United States and all territory subject to the jurisdiction thereof for beverage purposes is hereby prohibited.

Section 2

[Congress and the several States given concurrent power to pass appropriate legislation to enforce this article] The Congress and the several States shall have concurrent power to enforce this article by appropriate legislation.

Section 3

[Provisions of article to become operative, when adopted by three-fourths of the States] This article shall be inoperative unless it shall have been ratified as an amendment to the Constitution by the legislatures of the several States, as provided in the Constitution, within seven years from the date of the submission hereof to the States by Congress.

Amendment 19

(The proposed amendment was sent to the states June 4, 1919, by the Sixty-sixth Congress. It was ratified Aug. 18, 1920.)

[The right of citizens to vote shall not be denied because of sex] The right of citizens of the United States to vote shall not be denied or abridged by the United States or by any State on account of sex.

[Congress given power to enforce this article] Congress shall have power to enforce this article by appropriate legislation.

Amendment 20

(The proposed amendment, sometimes called the "Lame Duck Amendment," was sent to the states March 3, 1932, by the Seventy-second Congress. It was ratified Jan. 23, 1933; but, in accordance with Section 5, Sections 1 and 2 did not go into effect until Oct. 15, 1933. It changes Article 1, Sect. 4, Para. 2 and the 12th Amendment.)

Section 1

[Terms of President, Vice President, Senators, and Representatives] The terms of the President and Vice President shall end at noon on the twentieth day of January, and the terms of Senators and Representatives at noon on the third day of January, of the years in which such terms would have ended if this article had not been ratified; and the terms of their successors shall then begin.

Section 2

[Time of assembling Congress] The Congress shall assemble at least once in every year, and such meeting shall begin at noon on the third day of January, unless they shall by law appoint a different day.

Section 3

[Filling vacancy in office of President] If, at the time fixed for the beginning of the term of the President, the President-elect shall have died, the Vice President-elect shall become President. If a President shall not have been chosen before the time fixed for the beginning of his term, or if the President-elect shall have failed to qualify, then the Vice President shall have qualified; and the Congress may by law provide for the case wherein neither a President-elect nor a Vice President-elect shall have qualified, declaring who shall then act as President, or the manner in which one who is to act shall be selected, and such person shall act accordingly until a President or Vice President shall have qualified.

Section 4

[Power of Congress in Presidential succession] The Congress may by law provide for the case of the death of any of the persons from whom the House of Representatives may choose a President whenever the right of choice shall have devolved upon them, and for the case of the death of any of the persons from whom the Senate may choose a Vice President whenever the right of choice shall have devolved upon them.

Section 5

[Time of taking effect] Sections 1 and 2 shall take effect on the 15th day of October following the ratification of this article.

Section 6

[Ratification] This article shall be inoperative unless it shall have been ratified as an amendment to the Constitution by the legislatures of three-fourths of the several States within seven years from the date of its submission.

Amendment 21

(The proposed amendment was sent to the states Feb. 20, 1933, by the Seventy-second Congress. It was ratified Dec. 5, 1933. It repeals the 18th Amendment.)

Section 1

[Repeal of Prohibition Amendment] The eighteenth article of amendment to the Constitution of the United States is hereby repealed.

Section 2

[Transportation of intoxicating liquors] The transportation or importation into any State, territory, or possession of the United States for delivery or use therein of intoxicating liquors, in violation of the laws thereof, is hereby prohibited.

Section 3

[Ratification] This article shall be inoperative unless it shall have been ratified as an amendment to the Constitution by convention in the several States, as provided in the Constitution, within seven years from the date of the submission thereof to the States by the Congress.

Amendment 22

(The proposed amendment was sent to the states March 21, 1947, by the Eightieth Congress. It was ratified Feb. 27, 1951.)

Section 1

[Limit to number of terms a President may serve] No person shall be elected to the office of the President more than twice, and no person who has held the office of President, or acted as President for more than two years of a term to which some other person was elected President shall be elected to the office of the President more than once. But this article shall not apply to any person holding the office of President when this article was proposed by the Congress, and shall not prevent any person who may be holding the office of President, or acting as President, during the term within which this article becomes operative from holding the office of President or acting as President during the remainder of such term.

Section 2

[Ratification] This article shall be inoperative unless it shall have been ratified as an amendment to the Constitution by the legislatures of three-fourths of the several States within seven years from the date of its submission to the States by the Congress.

Amendment 23

(The proposed amendment was sent to the states June 16, 1960, by the Eighty-sixth Congress. It was ratified March 29, 1961.)

Section 1

[Electors for the District of Columbia] The District constituting the seat of Government of the United States shall appoint in such manner as the Congress may direct:

A number of electors of President and Vice President equal to the whole number of Senators and Representatives in Congress to which the District would be entitled if it were a State, but in no event more than the least populous State; they shall be in addition to those appointed by the States, but they shall be considered, for the purposes of the election of President and Vice President, to be electors appointed by a State; and they shall meet in the District and perform such duties as provided by the twelfth article of amendment.

Section 2

[Congress given power to enforce this article] The Congress shall have the power to enforce this article by appropriate legislation.

Amendment 24

(The proposed amendment was sent to the states Aug. 27, 1962, by the Eighty-seventh Congress. It was ratified Jan. 23, 1964.)

Section 1

[Payment of poll tax or other taxes barred in federal elections] The right of citizens of the United States to vote in any primary or other election for President or Vice President, for electors for President or Vice President, or for Senator or Representative in Congress, shall not be denied or abridged by the United States or any State by reasons of failure to pay any poll tax or other tax.

Section 2

[Congress given power to enforce this article] The Congress shall have the power to enforce this article by appropriate legislation.

Amendment 25

(The proposed amendment was sent to the states July 6, 1965, by the Eighty-ninth Congress. It was ratified Feb. 10, 1967.)

Section 1

[Succession of Vice President to Presidency] In case of the removal of the President from office or of his death or resignation, the Vice President shall become President.

Section 2

[Vacancy in office of Vice President] Whenever there is a vacancy in the office of the Vice President, the President shall nominate a Vice President who shall take office upon confirmation by a majority vote of both Houses of Congress.

Section 3

[Vice President as Acting President] Whenever the President transmits to the President pro tempore of the Senate and the Speaker of the House of Representatives his written declaration that he is unable to discharge the powers and duties of his office, and until he transmits to them a written declaration to the contrary, such powers and duties shall be discharged by the Vice President as Acting President.

Section 4

[Vice President as Acting President] Whenever the Vice President and a majority of either the principal officers of the executive departments or of such other body as Congress may by law provide, transmit to the President pro tempore of the Senate and the Speaker of the House of Representatives their written declaration that the President is unable to discharge the powers and duties of his office, the Vice President shall immediately assume the powers and duties of the office as Acting President.

Thereafter, when the President transmits to the President pro tempore of the Senate and the Speaker of the House of Representatives his written declaration that no inability exists, he shall resume the powers and duties of his office unless the Vice President and a majority of either the principal officers of the executive department or of such other body as Congress may by law provide, transmit within four days to the President pro tempore of the Senate and the Speaker of the House of Representatives their written declaration that the President is unable to discharge the powers and duties of his office. Thereupon Congress shall decide the issue, assembling within forty-eight hours for that purpose if not in session. If the Congress, within twenty-one days after receipt of the latter written declaration, or, if Congress is not in session, within twenty-one days after Congress is required to assemble, determines by two-thirds vote of both Houses that the President is unable to discharge the powers and duties of his office, the Vice President shall continue to discharge the same as Acting President; otherwise, the President shall resume the powers and duties of his office.

Amendment 26

(The proposed amendment was sent to the states March 23, 1971, by the Ninety-second Congress. It was ratified July 1, 1971.)

Section 1

[Voting for 18-year-olds] The right of citizens of the United States, who are 18 years of age or older, to vote shall not be denied or abridged by the United States or by any state on account of age.

Section 2

[Congress given power to enforce this article] The Congress shall have power to enforce this article by appropriate legislation.

964

How a Bill Becomes a Law

When a Senator or a Representative introduces a bill, he sends it to the clerk of his house, who gives it a number and title. This is the *first reading,* and the bill is referred to the proper committee.

The committee may decide the bill is unwise or unnecessary and *table* it, thus killing it at once. Or it may decide the bill is worthwhile and hold hearings to listen to facts and opinions presented by experts and other interested persons. After members of the committee have debated the bill and perhaps offered amendments, a vote is taken; and if the vote is favorable, the bill is sent back to the floor of the house.

The clerk reads the bill sentence by sentence to the house; this is known as the *second reading.* Members may then debate the bill and offer amendments. In the House of Representatives, the time for debate is limited by a *cloture rule,* but there is no such restriction in the Senate for cloture. Instead, 60 votes are required to limit debate. This makes possible a *filibuster,* in which one or more opponents hold the floor in an attempt to defeat the bill.

The *third reading* is by title only, and the bill is put to a vote, which may be by voice or roll call, depending on the circumstances and parliamentary rules. Members who must be absent at the time but who wish to record their vote may be paired if each negative vote has a balancing affirmative one.

The bill then goes to the other house of Congress, where it may be defeated or passed with or without amendments. If the bill is defeated, it dies. If it is passed with amendments, a joint Congressional committee must be appointed by both houses to iron out the differences.

After its final passage by both houses, the bill is sent to the President. If he approves, he signs it, and the bill becomes a law. However, if he disapproves, he *vetoes* the bill by refusing to sign it. He then sends the bill back to the house of origin with his reasons for the veto. The objections are read and debated, and a roll-call vote is taken. If the bill receives less than a two-thirds vote, it is defeated and goes no farther. But if it receives a two-thirds vote or greater, it is sent to the other house for a vote. If that house also passes it by a two-thirds vote, the President's veto is *overridden,* and the bill becomes a law.

Should the President desire neither to sign nor to veto the bill, he may retain it for ten days, Sundays excepted, after which time it automatically becomes a law without signature. However, if Congress has adjourned within those ten days, the bill is automatically killed, that process of indirect rejection being known as a *pocket veto.*

Emancipation Proclamation

January 1, 1863

By the President of the United States of America:

A Proclamation

Whereas on the 22d day of September, A.D. 1862, a proclamation was issued by the President of the United States, containing, among other things, the following, to wit:

"That on the 1st day of January, A.D. 1863, all persons held as slaves within any State or designated part of a State the people whereof shall then be in rebellion against the Union States shall be then, thenceforward, and forever free; and the executive government of the United States, including the military and naval authority thereof, will recognize and maintain the freedom of such persons and will do no act or acts to repress such persons, or any of them, in any efforts they may make for their actual freedom.

"That the executive will on the 1st day of January aforesaid, by proclamation, designate the States and parts of States, if any, in which the people thereof, respectively, shall then be in rebellion against the United States; and the fact that any State or the people thereof shall on that day be in good faith represented in the Congress of the United States by members chosen thereto at elections wherein a majority of the qualified voters of such States shall have participated shall, in the absence of strong countervailing testimony, be deemed conclusive evidence that such State and the people thereof are not then in rebellion against the United States."

Now therefore, I, Abraham Lincoln, President of the United States, by virtue of the power in me vested as Commander-in-Chief of the Army and Navy of the United States in time of actual armed rebellion against the authority and government of the United States, and as a fit and necessary war measure for suppressing said rebellion, do, on this 1st day of January, A.D. 1863, and in accordance with my purpose so to do, publicly proclaimed for the full period of one hundred days from the first day above mentioned, order and designate as the States and parts of States wherein the people thereof, respectively, are this day in rebellion against the United States the following, to wit:

Arkansas, Texas, Louisiana (except the parishes of St. Bernard, Plaquemines, Jefferson, St. John, St. Charles, St. James, Ascension, Assumption, Terrebonne, Lafourche, St. Mary, St. Martin, and Orleans, including the city of New Orleans), Mississippi, Alabama, Florida, Georgia, South Carolina, North Carolina, and Virginia (except the forty-eight counties designated as West Virginia, and also the counties of Berkeley, Accomac, Northhampton, Elizabeth City, York, Princess Anne, and Norfolk, including the cities of Norfolk and Portsmouth), and which excepted parts are for the present left precisely as if this proclamation were not issued.

And by virtue of the power and for the purpose aforesaid, I do order and declare that all persons held as slaves within said designated States and parts of States are, and henceforward shall be, free; and that the Executive Government of the United States, including the military and naval authorities thereof, will recognize and maintain the freedom of said persons.

And I hereby enjoin upon the people so declared to be free to abstain from all violence, unless in necessary self-defense; and I recommend to them that, in all cases when allowed, they labor faithfully for reasonable wages.

And I further declare and make known that such persons of suitable condition will be received into the armed service of the United States to garrison forts, positions, stations, and other places, and to man vessels of all sorts in said service.

And upon this act, sincerely believed to be an act of justice, warranted by the Constitution upon military necessity, I invoke the considerate judgment of mankind and the gracious favor of Almighty God.

U.S. Presidents

(* Did not finish term)

1	George Washington	April 30, 1789 - March 3, 1797	. . . . John Adams	1
2	John Adams	March 4, 1797 - March 3, 1801	. . . . Thomas Jefferson	2
3	Thomas Jefferson	March 4, 1801 - March 3, 1805	. . . . Aaron Burr	3
	Thomas Jefferson	March 4, 1805 - March 3, 1809	. . . . George Clinton	4
4	James Madison	March 4, 1809 - March 3, 1813	. . . . George Clinton	
	James Madison	March 4, 1813 - March 3, 1817	. . . . Elbridge Gerry	5
5	James Monroe	March 4, 1817 - March 3, 1825	. . . . Daniel D. Tompkins	6
6	John Quincy Adams	March 4, 1825 - March 3, 1829	. . . . John C. Calhoun	7
7	Andrew Jackson	March 4, 1829 - March 3, 1833	. . . . John C. Calhoun	
	Andrew Jackson	March 4, 1833 - March 3, 1837	. . . . Martin Van Buren	8
8	Martin Van Buren	March 4, 1837 - March 3, 1841	. . . . Richard M. Johnson	9
9	William Henry Harrison* .	March 4, 1841 - April 4, 1841	. . . . John Tyler	10
10	John Tyler	April 6, 1841 - March 3, 1845		
11	James K. Polk	March 4, 1845 - March 3, 1849	. . . . George M. Dallas	11
12	Zachary Taylor*	March 5, 1849 - July 9, 1850	. . . . Millard Fillmore	12
13	Millard Fillmore	July 10, 1850 - March 3, 1853		
14	Franklin Pierce	March 4, 1853 - March 3, 1857	. . . . William R. King	13
15	James Buchanan	March 4, 1857 - March 3, 1861	. . . . John C. Breckinridge	14
16	Abraham Lincoln	March 4, 1861 - March 3, 1865	. . . . Hannibal Hamlin	15
	Abraham Lincoln*	March 4, 1865 - April 15, 1865	. . . . Andrew Johnson	16
17	Andrew Johnson	April 15, 1865 - March 3, 1869		
18	Ulysses S. Grant	March 4, 1869 - March 3, 1873	. . . . Schuyler Colfax	17
	Ulysses S. Grant	March 4, 1873 - March 3, 1877	. . . . Henry Wilson	18
19	Rutherford B. Hayes	March 4, 1877 - March 3, 1881	. . . . William A. Wheeler	19
20	James A. Garfield*	March 4, 1881 - Sept. 19, 1881	. . . . . . Chester A. Arthur	20
21	Chester A. Arthur	Sept. 20, 1881 - March 3, 1885		
22	Grover Cleveland	March 4, 1885 - March 3, 1889	. . . Thomas A. Hendricks	21
23	Benjamin Harrison	March 4, 1889 - March 3, 1893	. . . . Levi P. Morton	22
24	Grover Cleveland	March 4, 1893 - March 3, 1897	. . . . Adlai E. Stevenson	23
25	William McKinley	March 4, 1897 - March 3, 1901	. . . . Garret A. Hobart	24
	William McKinley*	March 4, 1901 - Sept. 14, 1901	. . . . Theodore Roosevelt	25
26	Theodore Roosevelt	Sept. 14, 1901 - March 3, 1905		
	Theodore Roosevelt	March 4, 1905 - March 3, 1909	. . . Charles W. Fairbanks	26
27	William H. Taft	March 4, 1909 - March 3, 1913	. . . . . . James S. Sherman	27
28	Woodrow Wilson	March 4, 1913 - March 3, 1921	. . . . Thomas R. Marshall	28
29	Warren G. Harding*	March 4, 1921 - Aug. 2, 1923	. . . . Calvin Coolidge	29
30	Calvin Coolidge	Aug. 3, 1923 - March 3, 1925		
	Calvin Coolidge	March 4, 1925 - March 3, 1929	. . . . . . Charles G. Dawes	30
31	Herbert C. Hoover	March 4, 1929 - March 3, 1933	. . . . Charles Curtis	31
32	Franklin D. Roosevelt	March 4, 1933 - Jan. 20, 1941	. . . . John N. Garner	32
	Franklin D. Roosevelt	Jan. 20, 1941 - Jan. 20, 1945	. . . . . . Henry A. Wallace	33
	Franklin D. Roosevelt	Jan. 20, 1945 - April 12, 1945	. . . . . . Harry S. Truman	34
33	Harry S. Truman	April 12, 1945 - Jan. 20, 1949		
	Harry S. Truman	Jan. 20, 1949 - Jan. 20, 1953	. . . . . . Alben W. Barkley	35
34	Dwight D. Eisenhower	Jan. 20, 1953 - Jan. 20, 1961	. . . . . . Richard M. Nixon	36
35	John F. Kennedy*	Jan. 20, 1961 - Nov. 22, 1963	. . . . . Lyndon B. Johnson	37
36	Lyndon B. Johnson	Nov. 22, 1963 - Jan. 20, 1965		
	Lyndon B. Johnson	Jan. 20, 1965 - Jan. 20, 1969	. . . . Hubert H. Humphrey	38
37	Richard M. Nixon	Jan. 20, 1969 - Jan. 20, 1973	. . . . Sprio T. Agnew	39
	Richard M. Nixon*	Jan. 20, 1973 - Aug. 9, 1974	. . . . Gerald R. Ford	40
38	Gerald R. Ford	Aug. 9, 1974 - Jan. 20, 1977	. . . Nelson A. Rockefeller	41
39	James E. Carter	Jan. 20, 1977 - Jan. 20, 1981	. . . . Walter Mondale	42
40	Ronald Reagan	Jan. 20, 1981 - Jan. 20, 1985	. . . . George Bush	43
	Ronald Reagan	Jan. 20, 1985 - Jan. 20, 1989	. . . . George Bush	
41	George Bush	Jan. 20, 1989 -	. . . . Dan Quayle	44

Order of Presidential Succession

1. The Vice President
2. Speaker of the House
3. President pro tempore of the Senate
4. Secretary of State
5. Secretary of the Treasury
6. Secretary of Defense
7. Attorney General
8. Secretary of the Interior
9. Secretary of Agriculture
10. Secretary of Commerce
11. Secretary of Labor
12. Secretary of Health and Human Services
13. Secretary of Housing and Urban Development
14. Secretary of Transportation
15. Secretary of Energy
16. Secretary of Education
17. Secretary of Veterans Affairs

Command Statements

Below you will find a list of the most commonly used command statements. Command statements are used when operating a computer. When a command is entered into a computer, the computer will perform a certain action. Each of those actions is described below.

DATA: Allows data to be stored in a computer program. This data can be retrieved during the running of the program by the READ statement.

DIM: Saves space in memory for the size of an array you select.

END: The last statement in a program which stops the program and returns control of the computer to the user.

FOR: Allows the programmer to set up a loop which is to be repeated a specified number of times.

GOSUB: Causes the program to go to a subroutine. When a RETURN statement is made in the subroutine, the program returns to the line following the GOSUB statement.

GOTO: Causes the computer to go to a particular line in the program.

IF: A statement which tells the computer to go to the next line in the program if the argument following the IF statement is false or to go to a given line number if the argument is true.

INPUT: Allows the user to input information from the keyboard for use in a program.

LET: An optional instruction which can be used when a variable in a program is assigned a value. (Example: Let A=25.)

LIST: Displays or prints a copy of the program presently in the computer.

NEXT: Used with the FOR statement. When a NEXT statement is used in a program, the computer branches back to the FOR statement until the loop has been repeated a specific number of times.

PRINT: Instructs the computer to type or display information from a program.

READ: Instructs the computer to read the information in a DATA statement; takes information from a DATA statement and assigns the information to the variable(s) immediately following the READ statement.

REM: Allows the programmer to insert remarks and comments into a program which are used to make the program easier to understand.

RETURN: This command will instruct the computer to go back to the main part of the program. When encountered in a subroutine, this statement will cause the computer to branch to the first statement after the GOSUB command which sent the computer to the subroutine.

RUN: Causes the computer to "run" the program in memory.

THEN: Used with the IF statement. When the argument between the IF and THEN is true, the statements following the THEN statement are performed.

Computer Terms

Address: A number used to identify where a piece of information is located in the computer's memory.

Algorithm: The computer programmer's "plan of attack" showing each step used in the solution of a problem.

Array: A group of variables called by the same name, but having different subscripts.

Back-up: A copy of data or programs used to protect the original copy if it is lost, stolen, or destroyed.

BASIC: *(Beginners All-purpose Symbolic Instruction Code)* A computer language specifically designed to be easy to learn and use. It is commonly used with smaller computers.

Binary: The number system commonly used by computers because the values 0 and 1 can easily be represented electronically in the computer.

Bit: *(BInary digiT)* The smallest piece of information understood by a computer consisting of either a 0 or a 1.

Boot: To start up a computer system by loading a program into the memory.

Bug: An error in a computer program.

Byte: A string of eight bits commonly acting as a single piece of information.

Character: A letter or digit used to display information.

Chip: A small piece of silicon containing thousands of electrical elements. Also referred to as an integrated circuit.

Command: An instruction to a computer to perform a special task.

Compiler: A program which translates an instruction written in a high-level language into machine language so that the instruction can be understood by the computer.

Computer: An electronic device for performing programmed computations quickly and accurately. A computer is made up of five basic blocks: memory, control, the arithmetic logic unit (ALU), input, and output.

Computer program: A list of statements, commands, and instructions written in computer language which, when executed correctly, will perform a task or function.

Control character: A character that is entered by holding down the control key while hitting another key. The control character "controls" or changes information which is printed or displayed.

CPU: *(Central Processing Unit)* The hardware portion of a computer which executes instructions. The "brain" of the computer which controls all other devices.

CRT: *(Cathode Ray Tube)* An electronic vacuum tube, such as that found in a TV, which is used to display information.

Cursor: A symbol on a computer screen which points out where the next character typed from the keyboard will appear.

Data: Information used or produced by a computer program.

Data base: A collection of information which is organized in such a way that a computer can process it efficiently.

Debug: Removing errors from a computer program.

Device: A hardware component of a computer system designed to perform a certain task. A CRT, printer, or disk drive are examples of computer devices.

Digit: A character used to express numbers in a number system. For instance, 0 and 1 are digits in base 2; 0 to 7 are digits in base 8; 0 to 9 are digits in base 10; and 0 to 9, A, B, C, D, E, and F are digits in base 16.

Digital: A class of computers which process information which is in binary form. It is also used to describe information which is in binary form.

Dimension: A statement in a program which tells a computer how large an array is and to set aside memory for that array.

Disk: A magnetic storage device used to record computer information. Each disk appears flat and square on the outside; inside, the disk is circular and rotates so that information can be stored on its many circular tracks.

Disk drive: The device that writes and reads information onto the disk.

Documentation: A practice used by all good programmers in which comments are inserted into a computer program so that someone else can look at the program and understand what a program is supposed to do and how it does it.

DOS: *(Disk Operating System)* A software system that allows a computer to communicate with and control one or more disk drives.

Edit: To change an original document or program by adding, deleting, or replacing parts of it, thus creating a new document or program.

Error: A programming mistake which will cause the program to run incorrectly or not run at all.

Error message: A message, displayed or printed, which tells you an error or problem is in a program.

Execute: To run a computer program.

File: A collection of information stored on a computer device.

Floppy disk: A storage device made of a thin, magnetically coated plastic.

Flowchart: A diagram which shows the steps in a computer program.

Format: To prepare a blank disk for use (also *initialize*).

Graphics: Information which is displayed as pictures or images rather than by characters.

Hardcopy: A printed copy of a program, data, or results.

Hardware: The actual electronic and mechanical components of a computer system. A floppy disk is *hardware,* while a program stored on it is *software*.

Input: Information taken from a disk drive, keyboard, or other device and transported into a computer.

Instruction: Machine language which commands an action to be taken by the CPU *(central processing unit)* of a computer.

Interactive: A computer system in which the operator and computer frequently exchange information.

Interface: The hardware, software, and firmware which is used to link one computer or computer device to another.

K: A term used when describing the capacity of a computer memory or storage device. For example, 16K equals 16x1024 or 16,384 memory addresses.

Keyboard: An input device used to enter information into a computer by striking keys which are labeled much like those on a typewriter.

Letter-quality printer: A printer that produces type quality similar to that of an electric typewriter.

Library: A collection of programs which may be referred to often.

List: A display or printout of a computer program or file.

Load: To take information from an external storage device and *load* it into a computer's memory.

LOGO: A language which combines pictures and words to teach programming to children.

Loop: A series of instructions which is repeated, usually with different data on each pass.

Machine language: The language used to directly instruct computer hardware. The computer uses this language to process data and instructions in binary form.

Mainframe computer: A large computer generally with many operators using it at one time.

Main memory: The memory that is built into a computer.

Memory: The part of the computer which stores information and program instructions until they are needed.

Menu: A detailed list of choices presented in a program from which a user can select.

Microcomputer: A small, inexpensive computer using a microprocessor as its processing unit.

Minicomputer: A computer larger than a microcomputer whose CPU cannot be contained on a single chip; generally used in small business, science, and engineering.

Modem: *(MOdulator DEModulator)* A device which allows computers to communicate over telephone lines.

Monitor: A video screen on which information from a computer can be displayed. By viewing the displayed information, the user can visualize and control the operation of a program.

Output: Information sent from a computer to a disk drive, monitor, printer, or any other external device.

PASCAL: A high-level language designed to teach the principles of structured programming. (Named after Blaise Pascal, a 17th century mathematician.)

Peripheral device: An external device such as a plotter, disk drive, or printer added to a computer system to increase the capabilities of the system.

PILOT: *(Programmed Inquiry, Learning, Or Teaching)* A high-level language used for computer aided instruction.

Printed circuit board: A flat, rigid board commonly made of fiberglass. It is used to hold and electronically connect computer chips and other electrical elements.

Printer: A peripheral device (similar to a typewriter) used to produce printed copies of computer data or programs.

Printout: A copy of computer output produced on paper by a printer.

Processor: The portion of computer hardware that performs machine-language instructions and controls all other parts of the computer.

Program: A step-by-step list of instructions which a computer will follow in order to accomplish a specific task.

Programmer: A person involved in the writing, editing, and production of a computer program.

Programming language: A set of guidelines and rules for writing a program which will perform a task on a computer.

Prompt: A question which asks the user to input information to be processed or to tell the computer which part of a program to branch to.

Resolution: Describes the quality of a video image displayed on a computer monitor or graphics screen.

Save: To take a program or file from main memory and store it on a device (disk, cassette, etc.) for later use.

Sector: A fraction of the recording surface on a disk; a sector is a fraction of a *track*.

Software: Programs which instruct a computer how to perform a desired task.

Spreadsheet: A program used to organize numbers and figures into a worksheet form.

Statement: An instruction in a program which will perform a desired operation.

Storage: Describes the main memory or external devices where information or programs can be stored.

String: A group of consecutive letters, numbers, and characters which are not used for computational purposes.

Subroutine: A group of statements which can be found and used from several different places in a main program.

System: The collection of hardware, software, and firmware that forms a functioning computer.

Telecommunications: Sending and receiving information from one computer to another over long distances via phone lines, satellites, or other forms of communication equipment.

Terminal: A peripheral device which contains a keyboard for putting information into a computer and a monitor to receive output from a computer.

Text: Information in the form of characters which can be read by an individual.

Track: A fraction of the recording surface on a disk. (A track can be compared to the space used by each song on an album.) The number of tracks on a disk varies.

User: A person *using* a computer system.

Variable: A place in the computer's memory which can be assigned a value or have that value read, changed, or deleted from memory by the programmer.

Word: A string of bits treated as a single unit by a computer.

Word processor: A program designed to assist a user in writing letters, memos, and other kinds of text.

Write-enable notch: The small, rectangular cutout in the edge of a disk's jacket used to protect the contents of a disk. If the notch is not present, or is covered by a write-protect tab, information cannot be written on the disk.

Write-protect: To apply a write-protect tab to a disk, making it impossible for new information to be written on the disk. The information on the disk is now protected from being overwritten.

Write-protect tab: A sticker used to cover the write-enable notch on a disk.

APA Research Paper Guidelines
Questions & Answers

Is a separate title page required?	*Yes.* Include a descriptive title, your name, and your instructor (or school if requested) on three separate lines which are centered 2/3 of the way up the page. Place your short title (with page numbers beneath it) flush right at top.
What is an abstract and where does it go?	An abstract is a 75- to 100-word paragraph summarizing your research paper. (See 977.) Place your abstract on a new page after the title page and label it "Abstract" (centered); place your short title and page number (2) flush right at the top.
Are references placed in the text?	*Yes.* Include the author and year; for quotations, add page number.
Do you need a "bibliography" of sources used in the paper?	*Yes.* Full citations for all sources used (books, periodicals, etc.) are placed in an alphabetized list at the end of the paper labeled "References."
Do you need an "appendix"?	*Yes.* Include in an "Appendix" any charts, tables, graphs, etc. when they would otherwise disrupt the paper.
Is the research paper double-spaced?	*Yes.* Do not single-space anywhere.
What about longer quotes?	Type quotations of 40 or more words block style (all lines flush) five spaces in from the lefthand margin. Indent the first line of second and subsequent paragraphs five spaces in multiple-paragraph quotes.
What about margins?	Leave 1-1/2 inch margins on all four sides; do not use right justification if you are using a computer.
What about paging?	Place two or three words of the title (the short title) at top right. Two lines below it (flush right) write the page number. Do not write the author's name.
Do I need to add headings?	If your instructor requests them, headings should be used for major sections and subsections, up to five levels.
Any other special instructions?	Only that you use good quality paper and a printer or typewriter with clear, dark type; also that you avoid hyphenated word breaks at the ends of lines. Other than that, pick a topic you think you might enjoy working with and get started.

APA Documentation Style

Those who write papers in the social sciences—psychology, sociology, anthropology, political science, education, journalism, or public health—usually do not use the Modern Language Association (MLA) documentation style described in "The Research Paper" section (135-172). Instead, they refer to the style guidelines found in the 3rd edition of the *Publication Manual of the American Psychological Association* (APA). The questions and answers at left should give you the necessary guidelines for setting up your research paper.

Parenthetical References ━━━ 971

In APA style, as in the MLA system, you must cite your source in parentheses in the text each time you borrow. Each of these parenthetical citations must be matched to an entry in an alphabetized list called "References" at the end of your paper. Each item in the "References" list should, in turn, refer to one of the citations in the text.

The Form of an Entry

The APA documentation style is sometimes called the "author-date" system because both the author and the date of the publication must be mentioned in the text when you borrow from a source. Both might appear in the flow of the sentence, like this:

> . . . as in a 1988 study by Weissbort, where young aardvarks were found to be . . .

If either name or date does not appear in the text, it must be mentioned in parentheses at the most convenient place, like this:

> According to Simpleton and Doofus (1984), the IQ of American television viewers
>
> averages . . .

or

> In the best available study of couch potatoes (Russet, Spud & Frye, 1990), . . .

One Author: Citing a Complete Work

The correct form for a parenthetical reference to a single source by a single author is **parenthesis, last name, comma, space, year of publication, parenthesis**, like this:

> . . . in which the safety of waterslides has been questioned (Bonzai, 1988).

Note: Final punctuation should be placed after and outside the parentheses.

One Author: More Than One Publication in Same Year

If the same author has published two or more articles in the same year, avoid confusion by placing a small letter *a* after the first work listed in the References list, *b* after the next one, and so on. The order of such works in the References list is determined alphabetically by title.

Parenthetical Citations

> . . . in two populations of teenage acne sufferers (Whytehead & Payne, 1987a, 1987b).

References

Whytehead, Z. T., & Payne, F. L. (1987a). Manifestations of social inhibition in response to sebaceous eruptions in a population of suburban chocolate addicts. Juvenile Hormonal Aberration Quarterly, 9, 26-42.

Whytehead, Z. T., & Payne, F. L. (1987b). Teen acne: Friend or foe? New York: Popular Press.

One Author: Citing Part of a Work

When you quote directly from your source, give the page number, chapter, or section, using the appropriate abbreviations (*p.* or *pp.*, *chap.*, or *sec.*—for other APA-style abbreviations, see 975).

> . . . suggested that eavesdropping on cellular phones "may produce the next big public crisis in civil rights" (Tappin, 1990, p. 37).

Citing a Work with Two to Five Authors

In APA style, all authors—up to as many as five—must be mentioned in the parenthetical citation, like this:

> . . . that as many as 86 percent could not correctly pronounce "Worcestershire sauce" (Lea & Perrin, 1986).

or

> . . . might contribute to cancer in laboratory rats (Sweetner, Weanie, Cafene, Raydonn & Ayer, 1990).

Note: The last two authors' names are always separated by an ampersand (&) without a comma.

For works with more than two but less than six authors, list all the authors the first time; after that, use only the name of the first author plus *et al.* (the Latin abbreviation for *et alii,* meaning "and others"), like this:

> . . . 836 times their body weight per day (Sweetner et al., 1990).

Note: Do not underline *et* or *al.*; place a period after *al.* (but not *et*).

Citing a Work with Six or More Authors

If your source has six or more authors—and that sometimes happens in the social sciences—refer to the work by the first author's name followed by "et al.," both for the first parenthetical reference and all references after it. However, be sure to list all six or more of the authors in your References list.

Corporate Author

A "corporate author" is an organization, association, or agency that claims authorship of a document. Treat the name of the organization as if it were the last name of the author. If the name is long and easily abbreviated, provide the abbreviation in square brackets. Use the abbreviation without brackets in subsequent references, as follows:

First Text Citation:
(National Institute of Mental Health [NIMH], 1990)
Subsequent Citations:
(NIMH, 1990)

No Author

If your source lists no author, treat the first two or three words of the title the same as if they were an author's last name. A title of an article or chapter belongs in quotation marks, whereas the titles of books and other free-standing major works should be underlined:

. . . bats in their belfries ("New England Churches," 1987).

. . . in his scathing satire, <u>War Is Peace</u> (1984), in which the . . .

Indirect (or Secondary) Sources

If you need to cite a source which you have found referred to in another source (i.e., a "secondary" source), mention the original source in your text. Then, in your parenthetical citation, cite the secondary source, using the words "cited in," like this:

. . . study by Guernari (cited in Haber, 1990).

In your References list at the end of the paper, you would write out a full citation for Haber (not Guernari).

Note: Citing secondary sources is taking a shortcut. You may look lazy and unscholarly if you do it often. Use primary sources when you can.

Two or More Works in a Parenthetical Reference

Sometimes it is necessary to lump several citations into one parenthetical reference. In that case, cite the sources as you usually would, separating the citations with semicolons. Place the citations in alphabetical order, just as they would be ordered in the References list:

. . . studies have demonstrated the versatility of Velcro (Klaspe, 1988; Ripp & Stikke, 1988, 1990).

Personal Communications

If you do the kind of personal research recommended elsewhere in *Writers INC*, you may have to cite personal communications which have provided you with some of your knowledge. Personal communications may be personal letters, phone calls, memos, and so forth. Since they are not published in a permanent form, they do not belong among the citations in your References list. Instead, cite them in parentheses, like this:

M. T. Cann (personal communication, April 1, 1990)

or

(M. T. Cann, personal communication, April 1, 1990)

"References" Entries: Books ▬▬▬

The References section (bibliography) lists all of the sources you have cited in your text. It is found at the end of your research paper. Begin your list on a new page (the next page after the text) and number each page, continuing the numbering from the text. The guidelines which follow describe the form of the References section in detail.

The Form of an Entry

An entry generally has three main divisions: author, title, and publication information. Pay attention to the various features of this basic entry:

1. last name first, alphabetized by first letter
2. first (and, if possible, middle) initial followed by a period
3. double space, then date of publication in parentheses, then period and double space
4. complete title and subtitle underlined, with only the first letter of each part capitalized
5. title and subtitle separated by colon and one space
6. period and double space after title
7. place of publication, colon, one space, name of publisher (omit abbreviations "Inc.," "Co.," etc.)
8. period

One Author

Hyde, L. (1983). <u>The gift: Imagination and the erotic life of property</u>. New

York: Vintage Books.

Two or More Authors

Lakoff, G., & Johnson, M. (1980). <u>Metaphors we live by</u>. Chicago: University

of Chicago Press.

Note: Follow the first author's name with a comma; then join the two authors' names with an ampersand (&) rather than the word "and."

No Author

<u>Publication manual of the American Psychological Association</u> (3rd ed.).

(1983). Washington, DC: American Psychological Association.

Note: Here the words "American Psychological Association" are capitalized because they are a proper name. The word "manual" should not be capitalized.

Chapter from a Book, One Author

Geertz, C. (1973). Peep play: Notes on the Balinese cockfight. In C. Geertz,

<u>The interpretation of cultures</u> (pp. 412-453). New York: Basic Books.

Note: When an author's name is given in the middle of the citation, follow the usual order: first initial first. When inclusive page numbers are given (412-453), write out the whole numbers instead of abbreviating them (e.g., **do not** write 412-53).

One Volume of a Multivolume Edited Work

Sternberg, R. J. (Ed.). (1989). <u>Advances in the psychology of human</u>

<u>intelligence</u> (Vol. 5). Hillsdale, NJ: Lawrence Erlbaum Associates.

Single Work from an Edited Collection of Articles

Perkins, D. N. (1983). Why the human perceiver is a bad machine. In J. Beck, B. Hope, & A. Rosenfeld (Eds.), Human and machine vision (pp. 341-364). New York: Academic Press.

Two or More Works by Same Author

Sheehy, G. (1976). Passages: Predictable crises of adult life. New York: Dutton.

Sheehy, G. (1988). Character: America's search for leadership. New York: Morrow.

Note: Here are some rules to follow when arranging the entries in your Reference list.

● Write out the author's full last name for every repeated entry.
● When one author has written two works with **different dates**, the one with the earlier date is placed first.
● If two works by the same author have the **same date**, alphabetize the two entries by the first significant words in the titles. Place a small *a* after the date in the first entry (e.g., 1988a) and a small *b* after the date in the second entry.
● A work by a single author should be placed **before** an entry by the same author with one or more co-authors. If two or more works have the same author but **different co-authors**, alphabetize the entries according to the last names of the co-authors.
● If two different authors have the **same last name**, alphabetize the entries according to the authors' initials.
● Use this list as a reminder:

Simpson, B. (1989).

Simpson, B. (1990a). Cartoon trends in . . .

Simpson, B. (1990b). The dysfunctional family in . . .

Simpson, B., & Groening, M. (1988).

Simpson, B., Groening, M., & Simpson, H. (1987).

Simpson, B., & Simpson, H. (1987).

Simpson, H. (1990).

Corporate (Group) Author

Amnesty International. (1989). When the state kills: The death penalty v. human rights. New York: Author.

Note: The word "author" here means that the group listed as the author (i.e., "Amnesty International") is also the publisher.

An Edited Work, One in a Series

Hunter, S., & Sundel, M. (Eds.). (1989). Midlife myths: Issues, findings, and practice implications. Newbury Park, CA: Sage Publications. (Sage Sourcebooks for the Human Services, Vol. 7)

Note: The descriptive phrase after the citation (Sage . . . Vol. 7) should not be followed by a period.

An "Edition" Other Than the First

Strunk, W., Jr., & White, E. B. (1979). <u>The elements of style</u> (3rd ed.). New York: Macmillan.

A Translation

Piaget, J., & Inhelder, B. (1971). <u>Mental imagery in the child: A study of the development of imaginal representation</u> (P. A. Chilton, Trans.). New York: Basic Books. (Original work published 1965)

Note: This reference is to a source published in English, translated from French. If the original French work was the source you used, give the French title first, followed by the English translation of the title in square brackets, and cite the French publisher.

Article in a Reference Book, Authored

Uslan, M., & Solomon, B. (1981). The Beatles. In <u>Dick Clark's the first 25 years of rock & roll</u> (pp. 156-163). New York: Greenwich House.

Signed Pamphlet

Shaffer, S. M. (1986). <u>Gifted girls: The disappearing act</u> (The Report Card #6). Washington, DC: The NETWORK, Inc., Mid-Atlantic Center for Sex Equity.

Technical or Research Report

Comstock, G. A., & Rubinstein, E. A. (Eds.). (1971). <u>Television and social behavior: Media content and control</u> (Reports and Papers, Vol. 1). Rockville, MD: National Institute of Mental Health.

Government Publication, Corporate Author

National Aeronautics and Space Administration [NASA]. (1989). <u>Human spaceflight: Activities for the intermediate student</u> (NASA Report No. 89-10639). Washington, DC: U.S. Government Printing Office.

Book in a Series

Detweiler, R. (1972). <u>John Updike</u> (Twayne's United States Authors Series, No. 214). Boston: Twayne.

Publisher's Imprint

Leopold, A. (1970). <u>A Sand County almanac, with essays on conservation from Round River</u>. New York: Ballantine Books. (Original work published 1949 and 1953)

Note: This work was originally published in separate parts by Oxford University Press but was repackaged as a single work in paperback. The paperback is cited here.

"References" Entries:
Periodicals

Article in a Scholarly Journal, One Author, Consecutively Paginated

Peder, M. (1987). Rapid eye movement sleep deprivation affects sleep

similarly in castrated and noncastrated rats. Behavioral and Neural Biology,

47, 186-196.

Note: Pay attention to the features of this basic reference to a scholarly journal: **1**) last name and initial(s) as for a book reference, **2**) year of publication, **3**) title of article in lowercase, except for first word; title not underlined or in quotes, **4**) title of journal underlined, **5**) volume number underlined, followed by comma, and **6**) inclusive page numbers.

Journal Article, Paginated by Issue

Sterk, H. (1985). The metamorphosis of Marilyn Monroe. The Central

States Speech Journal, 36 (4), 294-304.

Note: Following the volume number, the issue number (not underlined) is placed in parentheses if the page numbering starts with page 1 at the beginning of the issue. (Some journals number pages consecutively, from issue to issue, through their whole volume year.)

Journal Article, Two Authors

James, P., & Goldstraub, J. (1988). Terrorism and the breakdown of

international order: The corporate dimension. Conflict Quarterly, 8, 69-98.

Journal Article, Two or More Authors, Paginated by Issue

Nelson, M. D., & Jarratt, K. (1987). Spiritual and mental health care of

persons with AIDS. Individual Psychology, 43 (4), 479-489.

Journal Article, More than Six Authors

Schell, B., Sherritt, H., Arthur, J., Beatty, L., Berry, L., Edmonds, L., Kaashoek,

J., & Kempny, D. (1989). Development of a pornography community

standard: Questionnaire results for two Canadian cities. Canadian Journal

of Criminology, 29 (2), 133-152.

Note: In the text, abbreviate the parenthetical citation as follows: (Schell et al., 1989).

Abstract of a Scholarly Article

Anspaugh, L., Catlin, R., & Goldman, M. (1988). The global impact of the

Chernobyl reactor incident. Science, 242 (45), 1513-1518. (From

Abstracts in Anthropology, 1989, 19 (1), Abstract No. 3082)

Review

Ansen, D. (1988, June 27). A hot time in Toontown tonight [Review of Who

Framed Roger Rabbit?]. Newsweek, pp. 56-57.

Signed Article in a Magazine

> Port, O., & Carey, J. (1989, April 10). Fusion in a bottle: Can it be that
>
> easy? Business Week, pp. 86-87.

Note: For popular magazines, immediately after the year, list the date when the issue appeared. Unlike entries for scholarly articles, use the abbreviation "p." or "pp." before the page numbers.

Unsigned Article in a Popular Magazine

> Saving the elephant: Nature's great masterpiece: Banning the ivory trade is
>
> the wrong way to save Africa's vanishing elephants. (1989, July 1).
>
> Economist (London), pp. 15-17.

Signed Newspaper Article

> Trost, C. (1989, July 18). Born to lose: Babies of crack users crowd hospitals,
>
> break everybodies' heart. The Wall Street Journal, p. 1.

Unsigned Newspaper Article

> Angry pilot quits airliner on field as passenger suggests he is drunk. (1990,
>
> April 22). The New York Times, p. 20.

Letter to the Editor

> Burnside, P. (1990, April 17). Against styrofoam packaging [Letter to the
>
> editor]. The Milwaukee Journal, p. 9A.

Note: Here, the "A" indicates that the letter appears in the first section of the newspaper.

Title or Quotation Within an Article's Title

> Prince, S. (1988). Dread, taboo, and "The Thing": Toward a social theory of
>
> the horror film. Wide Angle, 10 (3), 19-29.

"References" Entries: Other Print and Nonprint Sources

Computer Software

> Microsoft Corporation. (1987). Microsoft word: Version 3.0 for the Apple
>
> Macintosh [Computer Word Processing Program]. Redmond, WA: Microsoft
>
> Corporation.

Television and Radio Programs

> Clark, K. (Narrator). (1971). Civilisation: 11. The worship of nature
>
> [Television program]. London: British Broadcasting Corporation (BBC-TV).

Recording

Moon, M. (Compiler). (1980). <u>Movement soul: Sounds of the freedom movement in the South 1963-1964</u> [Sound recording]. New York: Folkways Records.

Audio Cassette

Dobson, J. C. (1989). <u>Love must be tough</u> [Audio cassette]. Waco, TX: Word Books.

Film

John, A. (Director). (1973). <u>Solarflares burn for you</u> [Film]. London: British Film Institute.

Filmstrips, Slide Programs, Videotapes

Chaplin, C. (Director). (1978). <u>Modern times</u> [Video recording]. Farmington Hills, MI: Magnetic Video Corporation. (Original film produced 1936)

Note: For any other medium, including audiotapes, slides, maps, charts, or artwork, follow this same order: name the principal contributor(s) or creator(s); follow with the contributor's role in parentheses; following the title, identify the medium in square brackets.

Published or Recorded Interview, No Author

Dialogue on film: Steven Spielberg. (1988, June). [Interview with Steven Spielberg]. <u>American Film</u>, <u>13</u>, 12-16.

Published Interview, Titled, Single Author

Sweet, L. (1988, April). An actor's story. [Interview with Robert Townsend, director of <u>Hollywood Shuffle</u>]. <u>Monthly Film Bulletin</u>, <u>55</u>, 100.

Abbreviations in APA Style ——————— 975

chap.	chapter
ed.	edition
rev. ed.	revised edition
2nd ed.	second edition
Ed. (Eds.)	Editor (Editors)
Trans.	Translator(s)
p. (pp.)	page (pages)
Vol.	Volume (as in Vol. 4)
vols.	volumes (as in 4 vols.)
No.	Number
Pt.	Part
Tech. Rep.	Technical Report
Suppl.	Supplement

Note: For additional abbreviations, see 168; to abbreviate states, use the official two-letter U.S. Post Office abbreviations (706).

976

Short title.
Page number.

Chilean Grape Scare

1

Title
By-line
School
**(all centered,
2/3 from
bottom,
double-
spaced.)**

The Chilean Grape Scare: Did It Go Too Far?

Susie Gruber

Iowa State University

Chilean Grape Scare

2

Abstract

The U.S. ban on fruit imported from Chile in response to the discovery of two cyanide-tainted grapes on March 2, 1989, was unnecessarily broad, overly cautious, and ineffective. The ban cost Chile $240 million and 17,000 jobs and hurt its improving worldwide reputation at a time when Chile was struggling to repay a $16 billion foreign debt. The random sampling of 5% of 13,000 crates failed to lay consumer fears to rest yet turned up no further contamination. The biggest task now is not to screen produce but to restore consumer confidence in the produce industry. Careful inspection and selection by shoppers is the most powerful deterrent to further tampering.

Center
"Abstract."

Short title and page number double-spaced.

75-150 word abstract (double-spaced)

Place abstract on page by itself.

The Chilean Grape Scare: Did It Go Too Far?

The 1989 government detention and ban on Chilean fruit
imports to the United States was excessive and exaggerated
for the circumstances. Because of the warning put out by
the Food and Drug Administration (FDA), many consumers were
permanently scared away from Chilean or other imported
produce. Their fears, along with millions of tons of fruit
that had either to be returned to distributors, pulled off
the shelf, or allowed to spoil because there was not enough
cold storage space available for a crisis of this kind, cost
American as well as Chilean distributors, wholesalers, and
retailers millions of dollars that will not all be repaid to
them.

On March 2, 1989, the U.S. Embassy in Santiago, Chile,
received an anonymous phone call claiming that fruit on its
way to the United States had been poisoned. No details were
given. No other countries were threatened. Officials in
Washington, D.C., were first notified of the threat on March 3,
and the FDA started detaining fruit the day after that.
The FDA decided on March 6 to release the fruit they had
been holding after the State Department stated it thought
the phoned-in threat was most likely a hoax. A second call
came to the embassy on March 10. The State Department went
on with its original thinking that this was a hoax while
the FDA increased its usual inspections (Ingersoll, 1989,
March 14).

On March 12 two suspect red seedless grapes were found
to have small rings of a crystalline substance surrounding
apparent punctures. Subsequent tests proved they had been
injected with cyanide. The original amount injected into the
grapes was not known, since cyanide reacts with the acid in
grapes to become a gas which then would have dissipated during

the 10-14 day journey from Chile. The amount left in the
two grapes, three-tenths of a milligram, was not enough to make
a child sick (Ingersoll, 1989, March 14). It takes between
200 and 300 milligrams to kill an adult, an amount which at
the concentration found in the two tainted grapes would
require an adult to eat almost seven hundred grapes.
Officials at Canada's Health and Welfare Department were
notified of the findings on March 13.

It has not been ascertained whether the tampering took
place in Chile or in the United States. The doctored grapes
were located in a crate that was already off the ship and
sitting on the dock in Philadelphia. The caller who phoned
in the first threat claimed that the tampering was a protest
against the military dictatorship of Chile's ruler Augusto
Pinochet (Underwood, 1989, March 27). The government in
turn blamed the outlawed Communist party. A spokesman for
the Communists denied their involvement. Jose Marino,
commander of the Chilean Navy, blamed both the United States
and the Communists. U.S. officials could not quite make
the connection between the tampering and the political
protest, as the fruit leaving Chile was bound for other
destinations including Germany, Japan, and Canada.

After the detection of the poisoned grapes, a full ban
was immediately put on all Chilean fruit imports so that the
shipments could be inspected. The ban included grapes, plums,
nectarines, peaches, pears, raspberries, honeydew melons,
blueberries, cantaloupes, seedless watermelons, Juan Canary
melons, cactus pears, quince, and Granny Smith apples. The
first task facing the FDA was finding a feasible method
for inspecting the incoming fruit. Three days after finding
the tainted grapes, an FDA spokesman was quoted as saying
that his agency was "trying to find a way of checking enough

Citation: last name and year with date because source is a newspaper.

of the stuff and release the product so there's reasonable

For two co-
authors, use
last names
with amper-
sand (&). For
direct
quotation,
cite page
number.
"A" refers to
newspaper
section.

assurance of the safety of food" (Gibson & Ingersoll, 1989,
March 16, p. A18).

    The inspection was different than any other routine
checks that may have taken place in the past because of the
scale of the search, the involvement of another country, and
the large amount of fruit that had already been distributed
that was potentially tainted (Sun, 1989, March 18). After
inspection of more than 13,000 crates of fruit during the next
five days, no more adulterations were found. One suspect
nectarine was found and the whole crate confiscated for
testing. No reports of cyanide were made. The ban was
subsequently lifted on grapes, berries, and vegetables. Other
fruits were not immediately released for sale even though
grapes were the only fruit found to have been contaminated.

**End of
narrative;
beginning of
logical
argument.**

Another anonymous threatening call was received 15 minutes
before the ban was to be lifted on March 15, but it did not
affect the FDA's decision to release the quarantined fruit.

    The U.S. government could be excused for skittishness
because the grape crisis occurred not long after a major
public uproar over the use of the pesticide Alar in apples.
However, in the Chilean grape scare, the government was
guilty of overreaction, considering the excessive costs to
Chile, the ineffectiveness of its own inspection program,
and, above all, the damage to consumer trust in the produce
industry.

**Restatement
of thesis;
prediction of
three main
subargu-
ments
to come.**

    The grape scare could not have come at a more inopportune

**Considera-
tion of 1st
subargu-
ment: exces-
sive costs to
Chile.**

time for the Chilean fruit industry. The grape season was
in full swing and the apple season was just beginning. Moreover,
Chile's economy was undergoing a boom created by fruit
exportation, its second-largest export industry after copper.
Chile is a major provider of soft-skinned fruits to the U.S.

and other countries. Its growing season runs from January
to late April, during which time two-thirds of its exports
go to the United States until the California and Arizona
growing seasons start and domestic fruit competes with Chile's
supply. The U.S. ban, however, dampened the Chilean boom by
cutting off the $75 to $100 million that Americans provide in
fruit sales each week and caused a temporary shortage of
most fruits until the American seasons started.

There are many estimates about the actual loss as a direct
result of the ban. To date, it is estimated that Chile lost
at least $240 million, including approximately 3.5 million
cases of fruit that had to be destroyed because they rotted
on the docks before they could be inspected (Cimons, 1989, [Source of data cited.]
March 24). In addition to fruit and money lost, as many as
17,000 people lost their jobs, and several farms, especially in
the apple regions, were placed in danger of bankruptcy. There
are many losses which can not be recovered. The World Bank
and the government of Chile will only compensate for disposing
of the already imported fruit that had to be destroyed.
Inspection costs will have to be paid by the importers.

This crisis could cause a major setback in the progress
that Chile has made in recent years toward paying off its
$16 billion dollar foreign debt (Cohen, 1989, March 15).
Ironically, the U.S. has unnecessarily punished the country
that it had been holding up as an example for other struggling
countries. Besides hurting Chile's recovering economy, the
[Final point (consumer trust) forecasted.] ban has also hurt its reputation. Although Chile may recoup
the economic losses (or rather make up for them) in two years,
the trust of foreign consumers may never be fully regained.

Even if the costs to Chile had been justified, there
was no way, practically speaking, for a significant enough [Transition to 2nd major subargument: inadequate inspection.]
amount of fruit to be inspected to guarantee that bad fruit

would not be passed on to the customers. The inspection used
a sampling of 5% of each shipload (or a minimum of 15,000
crates). The Wall Street Journal quoted Richard Davis,
Philadelphia regional spokesman for the FDA, as saying, "We
had no information at all about what product or what crate
or anything to inspect" ("Finding of Tainted Grapes," 1989,
March 16, p. A18). It was rather amazing, then, that any
contaminated produce at all was found. The detection of
the poisoned grapes, according to FDA Commissioner Frank
Young, was "a significant incidence" ("Finding of Tainted
Grapes," 1989, March 16, p. A18). However, the failure to
replicate the finding left the significance of the first
finding in question.

     There are questions, as well, about the U.S. government's
purposes in taking such severe initial steps. If the
government was taking the phoned-in threats seriously, why
was the ban called off (as planned) fifteen minutes after
a third threat was received? FDA Commissioner Young said in
reaction to the third threat, "If you are prepared to release
the fruit after two threats, another threat doesn't change
that. We expect further threats as this person gets more
frustrated" (Ingersoll, 1989, March 20, p. B6). Young's
manner seemed rather nonchalant, as if he was implying that
he expected the perpetrator to continue to cry wolf and the
FDA to let the fruit go through. This does not sound like
the voice of a government agency critically concerned about
the welfare of the people of the United States.

     The FDA knew this was not a hoax after they found two
tainted grapes. The crisis did not turn out to be the great
disaster that was probably expected, but if it was bad enough
to merit the initial quarantine and subsequent ban after the
discovery of the grapes, why was this third threat not taken

Source cited in sentence.

Reference to article written by staff reporter; pages cited by exact quotation; writer uses shortened title in quotation marks.

Deepening of 2nd subargument: questioning of government's motives.

as seriously as the first two? Also, if the FDA was so
concerned about contaminated fruit getting into the markets,
why were the percentages of fruit actually being checked
"quietly lowered" by March 27 from 5% to 4% of the crates per
ship and by April 6 down to 1% of the crates per ship? Why
did the FDA not want the public to know it was not going to
be inspecting as much fruit as it had started out inspecting?
It was speculated that the FDA lifted the ban sooner than it
had planned in order to avoid numerous lawsuits for damages
incurred by distributors, retailers, wholesalers, and
Chilean agencies (Ingersoll, 1989, April 14). Apparently,
then, a leading factor in the government's thinking was
to prevent a public outcry while it protected itself from
legal damage.

 FDA and other government officials involved in making
the decisions affecting the outcome of the fruit scare
needed to realize that there was no way for the entire stock
of fruit to be checked and that they could not promise, based
on a partial inspection of the imported fruit, that no one
would fall ill or ingest a fatal contaminant. Considering
that such a large majority of the fruit was released to the
distributors without being inspected, the comprehensive ban
on all fruit imported from Chile must be viewed as overly
cautious. An editoralist in The Wall Street Journal joked
that by the FDA's logic, cars should be banned from the
streets, since they represent an even greater threat of death
("Fruit Frights," 1989, March 17).

 The net result of the U.S. government's actions was an
unnecessarily large decline, worldwide, in consumer trust in
imported produce. Canada put the same sanctions on Chilean
fruit as did the U.S., even though it received no threats of
tampering and no tainted fruit was ever found there. The

Writer continues to present information, but now in the context of critical questioning in building of a case.

Third restatement of general thesis.

Citation of editorial with no author; title in quotes.

Transition to 3rd subargument: loss of consumer trust.

Reference to Canadian embargo reinforces comments on loss of trust.

Prime Minister's office commented that they were not taking any chances this time in light of a situation two years before when tuna known to be spoiled was allowed into the markets. Officials also did not want to chance any deaths as they had when toxic Prince Edward Island mussels had been sold a couple of years before, resulting in two deaths and several other illnesses. Consumer's Association of Canada President Ruth Robinson spoke up for her side: "The safety of Canadians has to come first. Consumers have to have confidence that what is out there is safe" (Underwood, 1989, March 27, p. 11). She was satisfied with the way the Canadian government reacted.

The ban, nevertheless, seemed to have a far-reaching negative effect on many people. Carrie Sirota of Cote-St. Luc said, "As a consumer it's pretty upsetting. You can't trust anything anymore." Schoolteacher Carol Thornton of Vancouver added, "It can take one thing like this and I lose my confidence" (Underwood, 1989, March 27, p. 12). She said that she would never buy Chilean produce again.

Ms. Robinson brought up a key point in the argument when she said that consumers need to have confidence in the products they buy. Confidence is an individual feeling of trust that cannot be formed for a person by anyone else. A consumer should be able to go to the supermarket and pick out a bunch of grapes or the nicest looking apples he can find. He should feel comfortable with the choice that he made for himself when he gets his purchases home.

Reference to article in weekly news-magazine, includes date.

The FDA has regulations for keeping fruit safe for the public, but it does not examine produce for much other than pesticide residues unless there is a reason to believe there is another problem (Silberner, 1989, March 27). Thus, if embargoes and random sampling cannot guarantee safety, some of the responsibility has to rest with the consumer. The

buyer should know what is suspect and what is not.   FDA
Commissioner Frank Young recommended that any produce that
was discolored or punctured be avoided ("More Chilean
Fruit," 1989, March 22).   It doesn't take a college degree to
know that it is not a good idea to eat fruit that has
changed colors or that has holes in it.

  Restoring consumer confidence in Chilean produce may be
the biggest task at hand. If there is something wrong with
the produce (or if someone claims to have tampered with a
product), there is a reason to inspect it.   But if inspection
is just a matter of policy, who is to say the government
is not shirking its day-to-day obligation of making sure the
fruit is safe to consume?

  In whatever way the United States government responds,
consumers still have to take some responsibility. There are
no warranties on life. No marketing system can be made
entirely foolproof. Regardless of the actions of governments,
the public needs to keep their eyes open to what they feed
their families. If something looks wrong in the store, leave
it there and report it. Don't buy it. As Americans, we can't
stop our daily routines every time someone threatens us. We
as a powerful nation will continue to be threatened. We don't
need to run scared but rather to walk forward with eyes open.
We need to be careful, not paranoid.

  "Is the American public going to stop eating every time
someone makes a threatening phone call?" asked Darrel
Fulness, a large California food importer (Stevenson, 1989,
March 16, p. B10). "Is our food supply so tainted that candy
is safer than salad?" asks consumer affairs analyst Joanne
Silberner. Her sensible answer--no--is one which the whole
nation should accept. "Food-related horror stories . . . make
gripping news, but their threat to health is vastly

Transition to summarizing point: consumers have responsibility.

Exaggerated questions supply contrast to sensible conclusion.

exaggerated. . . . The easiest way to limit produce hazards is to select from fruits and vegetables more carefully, not give them up" (1989, March 27, p. 59).

References

Cimons, M. (1989, March 24). Chile, World Bank to compensate for fruit ban losses. Los Angeles Times, pp. IV1, 11.

Cohen, R. (1989, March 15). U.S. warning on fruit threatens boom fueling Chile's economic turnaround. The Wall Street Journal, p. A4.

Finding of tainted grapes seen as remarkable feat. (1989, March 16). The Wall Street Journal, p. A18.

Fruit frights. (1989, March 17). The Wall Street Journal, p. A14.

Gibson, R., & Ingersoll, B. (1989, March 16). FDA seeks safe way to release for sale tons of quarantined fruit from Chile. The Wall Street Journal, p. A18.

Ingersoll, B. (1989, March 14). Cyanide found in grapes sent from Chile. The Wall Street Journal, pp. A3, 17.

Ingersoll, B. (1989, March 20). Quarantined Chile fruit to be destroyed: FDA plans unprecedented inspections. The Wall Street Journal, p. B6.

Ingersoll, B. (1989, April 14). FDA calls off its inspection of Chilean fruit. The Wall Street Journal, p. A5.

More Chilean fruit allowed back in U.S. if 5% pass inspection. (1989, March 22). The Wall Street Journal, p. C14.

Silberner, J. (1989, March 27). Protecting against one bad apple: Buyer awareness is the best defense. U.S. News and World Report, pp. 56-59.

The letter (or Roman numeral) before the page number refers to the section of the newspaper.

Two authors joined by "&." Both last names followed by initial.

"References" centered 1-1/2" from top.

List of sources alphabetized by last name.

Year (in parentheses) follows author's name.

First and middle names written as initials.

Titles lowercase except for first word.

Reference to newspaper article on discontinuous pages.

Three sources by same author; place in order of date.

Article without byline alphabetized by first significant word of title.

Stevenson, R.W. (1989, March 16). Scare on grapes prompts worries of major losses. The New York Times, pp. A1, B10.

Sun, L.H. (1989, March 18). Ban's bitter fruit: How much lost and who pays? The Washington Post, p. A22.

Underwood, Nora. (1989, March 27). Forbidden Fruit: Tons of grapes were destroyed after traces of cyanide led to bans on Chilean fruit. Maclean's, pp. 10-12.

Reference to newspaper article continued in separate section.

The INDEX

(*Please note:* The index which follows contains topic numbers, not page numbers. For more information on using the index, see Handbook *iii*.)